Teaching English Abroad

Talk your way around the world!

Susan Griffith
with Victoria Pybus

Distributed in the U.S.A. by Peterson's
2000 Lenox Drive, Lawrenceville, N.J. 08648-4764
www.petersons.com
800-338-3282

Published by Vacation Work, 9 Park End Street, Oxford
www.vacationwork.co.uk

First published 1991
Fifth edition 2001

TEACHING ENGLISH ABROAD

by Susan Griffith

Revised by Victoria Pybus and Susan Griffith

Copyright © 2001

ISBN 1-85458-250-X

Cover Design: Miller Craig & Cocking Design Partnership

Typesetting by WorldView Publishing Services

Illustrations by John Taylor

Map by Andrea Pullen and Richard Guellala

Publicity: Roger Musker

Printed by William Clowes Ltd., Beccles, Suffolk, England

CONTENTS

PART I INTRODUCTION

PART II COUNTRY BY COUNTRY GUIDE

PART III APPENDICES

Acknowledgments

The new revised edition of *Teaching English Abroad* would not have been possible without the help of scores of ELT teachers and the people who employ them. They have generously shared their wealth of information, insights and anecdotes. As well as all the people who helped with the four previous editions, I would like to thank the following for their contributions, some of them substantial, to the research and writing of this updated edition.

I owe a special debt of thanks to Victoria Pybus who uncomplainingly bore the brunt of updating the infinite details in this book. I am also grateful to Mary Ann Lund, assistant and tireless researcher, who brought a fresh and eagle eye to the text.

Turkey	John Boylan & Olivene Aldridge-Tucker
Egypt	Daniel Boothby
Australia	Simon Brooks
Austria	Rebecca Chapman
Greece	Jain Cook
Russia	Robert Jensky
Thailand	Annette Kunigagon
Indonesia	Tim Leffel
Oman	Sandeha Lynch
Spain	Michelle Manion
Slovakia	Stephen Mills
Mongolia	Rabindra Roy
Baltics	Rhys Sage
Taiwan	Amanda Searle
Poland	Wayne Stimson
Argentina	Elizabeth Tenney
Bolivia	Ben Yeomans
Japan	Mark Zeid
Miscellaneous	Stephen D. Curry

Preface

The year 2001 has been declared the European Year of Languages. Although the intention is to celebrate diversity, we all know which language the vast majority of citizens are eager to master. On the day that this is being written, the authorities in some Swiss cantons will decide whether to elevate the status of English to that of a second language. Supporters argue that the French, German and Italian communities of Switzerland barely speak to each other and that English might provide a neutral means of communication. If even the nationalistic Swiss are prepared to advance the cause of English, how much more enthusiastically have other nations embraced it, all eager to participate in the global culture we seem to have created for the 21st century.

An ability to teach the English language is surely the most globally mobile skill there is. The teaching industry which services the world demand continues to mushroom: private language institutes have opened in areas of the world once closed to EFL teachers from Riga to Rangoon, Taipei to San José.

There is no average profile of the travelling teacher. For this fifth edition of *Teaching English Abroad*, I have received enthusiastic feedback from, among others, a young woman from Cardiff who taught school children in Zanzibar, a computer scientist from Manchester who fell in love with a Bolivian woman while teaching in La Paz, a politics graduate who spent the summer teaching at a summer camp in Poland, an experienced English teacher who achieved his ambition to teach in Mongolia, a young American woman who overcame the work permit problem in Spain by fixing up a live-in language exchange through an agency in Castile, a man who sold his printing business after 14 years to teach in Brazil and a gap year student whose contact with Burmese refugees during her year out teaching so galvanised her that she returned home to study Southeast Asian languages at university. A friend of mine, mother of four, is heading off from Cambridge to Barcelona soon to do the four-week TEFL course in order to fund a year or two in that city. The beauty of English teaching is that it is accessible to so many.

Interwoven with the actual experiences of people who have taught English abroad, is specific job vacancy information. Six hundred and eighty-one language schools and teaching organisations around the world submitted details of their teaching vacancies for this edition, and in addition the addresses of hundreds of other schools and agencies are provided. My aim has been to make the information in this book as concrete as possible, to cut the waffle. Unlike other books in the field, this one does not rely exclusively on information supplied by the ELT establishment. What is just as valuable for the potential job-seeker is the unofficial word-of-mouth information, for example the likelihood of an employer in Korea breaking a contract, whether a certain organisation might sometimes hire people without paper qualifications, or how hard it is to get a working visa in Moscow.

Teaching English Abroad tries to maintain a fine balance. On the one hand, it is not aimed primarily at the career EFL teacher who already has access to a wide range of information on working abroad. Neither is it intended to encourage layabouts and illiterates to masquerade as teachers, nor to bluster their way into jobs abroad on the insufficient grounds that they are native speakers of the language. But between these two extremes, countless people have the appropriate background and personality to become successful teachers of their native language. It remains the case that the majority of TEFL teachers leave the profession after a couple of years, poised to succeed in any workplace where thinking on your feet is required.

Like every enterprise, teaching English in foreign cultures has its specific rewards and risks which I have tried to identify throughout, in the hope of easing the path for those who are tempted but remain hesitant. This book can be the stepping stone to a brilliant and memorable year or two abroad.

Susan Griffith
Cambridge, November 2000

PART I

Introduction

Training
Finding a Job
Preparation
Problems

Introduction

One billion people speak or are trying to speak English, according to an estimate published by the British Council. It is not clear who has counted them all, but it has been said that 300 million people are learning English at the present time. Nine-tenths of the world's electronically stored information is in English and a majority of the 50 million Internet users communicate in the language you are reading at this moment. Mind-boggling statistics aside, the demand for instruction at all levels by people who happen to speak English as their mother tongue is enormous and set to continue increasing for the foreseeable future.

For whatever historical and economic reasons, English has come to dominate the world, the twenty-first century sequel of colonialism. When the newly liberated nations of Eastern Europe sloughed off Russian, they turned in very large measure to English rather than to the other main European languages. Countries as far-flung as Cambodia, Namibia and Turkmenistan are busy making English one of the keystones of their educational systems. In German-speaking Switzerland, there are signs that English is replacing French as the preferred second language at school. English is the international language of science, of air traffic control and to a very large extent of trade and export. This is bad news for all those Germans, Swedes and French Canadians who would like to market their language skills in order to fund a short or long stay abroad. But it is English speakers, mainly from Britain, Ireland, North America and Australia/New Zealand who accidentally find themselves in possession of such a sought-after commodity.

Some Definitions

The commonly used acronyms ELT, TEFL, TESL and TESOL can be confusing, especially since they are often used interchangeably. ELT, which stands for English

Language Teaching, has come to be the mainstream expression in the UK (preferred by such august bodies as the University of Cambridge and by the publishers of the main journal in the field). But most people still refer to TEFL (pronounced 'teffle'), Teaching English as a Foreign Language. TESL stands for Teaching English as a Second Language, and TESOL means Teaching English to Speakers of Other Languages. English is learned as a *foreign* language by people who may need the language for certain purposes such as business or tourism but who live in countries where English has no official status. English is learned as a *second* language when it will have to be used for day to day life, for example by emigrants to the UK and the USA or by inhabitants of ex-colonies where English retains official status and may well be the medium of instruction in schools. (English is the official or joint-official language in 75 countries.)

Because this book is for people who want to travel abroad to teach, the term TEFL is mainly used as well as ELT. Teachers of ESL are normally involved with multicultural education. In the USA, the vast majority of English language teaching is of ESL because of the huge demand for English among foreigners who have emigrated to the USA. Therefore the term ESL dominates in American contexts, even when (technically) EFL is meant.

The acronym TESOL covers both situations, yet it is not widely used apart from in institutions which favour the Trinity College *London* qualifications known as the Certificate and Licentiate Diploma in TESOL (see Training section later) and also in the context of the American organisation TESOL Inc., which is the largest English teachers' organisation in the world claiming more than 15,000 members.

There is no shortage of other acronyms in the world of TEFL. One of the main ones is ESP which means English for Specific Purposes. ESP aims to match language teaching with the needs of various professions such as business, banking, tourism, medicine, science and technology, secretaries, etc. Business English is probably the most important in this category (and 'English for Shopping' as sometimes offered in Japan is the least important). Because a great many learners are motivated by a desire to use English at work, they want their teachers to adopt a functional rather than a structural approach. In other words they want to have lessons in which they can pretend to be telephoning a client, recommending, advising, agreeing, complaining and so on. They are certainly not interested in the subjunctive.

EAP stands for English for Academic Purposes, i.e. English at an advanced level taught to students who are normally planning to study at foreign universities. EAP is largely in the hands of government-funded programmes, such as those run by the British Council.

Note that the acronym TOEFL can cause confusion. The Test of English as a Foreign Language is a US-based standardised test administered to language learners. Passing a TOEFL exam is widely held to be a reliable indicator of how well an individual can communicate in English. The focus of many language schools abroad is to prepare candidates for the exam, and so may advertise for teachers with 'TOEFL' experience.

SCOPE OF OPPORTUNITIES

The range of locations and situations in which English is in demand covers an enormous spectrum. If TEFL is booming in Myanmar and Kazakhstan, there can be few corners of the world to which English has not penetrated. English has been called a 'barometer of Western influence' and there is only a handful of countries in the world which have rejected Western influence outright (like Bhutan and Iraq) and which therefore have no call for EFL teachers. More important nations with their own native English-speaking population (like India) are also not promising destinations for the aspiring teacher.

Nearly a decade has passed since the arrival of the single European market which precipitated the greatest expansion of the English language in Europe's history. There has been an enormous increase in demand especially from companies and professionals eager to participate in an integrated Europe. The field of teaching English to young children is especially flourishing in Mediterranean countries. The attraction of European Union countries for British and Irish teachers is enhanced by the fact that they have the legal right to work.

The kinds of people who want to learn English are as numerous as the places in which they live. The Asian economic crisis a few years ago prompted a decline in the number of 'leisure students', people attending English classes simply for pleasure; yet the market has recovered amazingly quickly. The area of the industry which seems to be booming almost everywhere is the teaching of children (known as Young Learners in the trade). Kids as young as three are being sent to private English classes to improve their career prospects.

People around the world can think of a dozen reasons why they need to sign up for private English lessons. A Taiwanese student dreams of studying at UCLA. The wife of the Peruvian ambassador in Islamabad wants to be able to speak English at official functions. A Greek secondary school student has to pass her English exams in order to proceed to the next year and, like most of her classmates, attends a private tutorial college for English lessons. A Siberian worker associates English with the language of freedom and liberalism. A Turkish youth wants to be able to flirt with tourists from northern Europe. A Mexican waiter wants to get a job in the Acapulco Hilton. A Saudi engineer has to be able to read reports and manuals in English for his job. The list is open-ended, and prospects for hopeful teachers are therefore excellent. There are also hundreds of international schools throughout the world where English is the medium of instruction for all subjects and there may be specific EFL vacancies. These will be of most interest to certified teachers who wish to work abroad.

But the situation is not all rosy for the prospective teacher. As the profile of the English language has risen, so has the profile of the profession which teaches it, and the number of qualified and experienced English teachers has increased along with the rise in demand. The phenomenal explosion in the availability of training courses means that a much higher proportion of job-seekers has a TEFL certificate than was the case a decade ago, and (quite rightly) foreign language schools are becoming more selective when hiring staff.

People who cruise into a country expecting to be hired as an EFL teacher simply on the basis of being a native speaker are in most cases (though not quite all) in for a nasty shock. Employers at all levels will ask for evidence of the ability to teach their language or at least a university degree as proof of a sound educational background. Certainly without a degree, a TEFL qualification or any relevant experience, the scope of opportunities shrinks drastically.

Who is eligible to teach?

Anyone who can speak English fluently and has a lively positive personality has a fighting chance of finding an opening as a teacher somewhere. Geordies, Tasmanians and Alabamans have all been known to be hired as English teachers (not to mention Norwegians and North Africans), though most employers favour native speakers of English without a heavy regional accent. Depending on the economic and cultural orientation of a country, schools will prefer British English (what the Director-General of the British Council likes to call 'standard English') or North American English. For obvious geopolitical reasons Europe and Africa incline towards Britain while Latin America and the Far East incline towards the USA. Many countries have no decided preference, for example Indonesia and Turkey. Clear diction is usually more important than accent.

English language teaching is an industry which is seldom regulated, giving rise to a host of cowboy schools, which are mentioned (usually disparagingly) throughout this book. The other side of the coin is the proliferation of cowboy *teachers*, who have no feel for language, no interest in their pupils and no qualms about ripping them off. The issue of qualifications must be considered carefully. It is obviously unwise to assume that fluency in English is a sufficient qualification to turn someone into an EFL teacher. Many experienced teachers of English come to feel very strongly that untrained teachers do a disservice both to their pupils and to their language. Certainly anyone who is serious about going abroad to teach English should turn to the relevant chapter to consider the training options.

Among the army of teachers-cum-travellers, there are undoubtedly some lazy, spiritless and ungrammatical native speakers of English who have bluffed their way into a teaching job. Most books and journals about language teaching are unanimous in their condemnation of such amateurs. Yet there are some excellent teachers who have learned how to teach by practising rather than by studying. For certain kinds of teaching jobs, a background in business and commerce might be far more useful than any paper qualifications in teaching. Therefore we have not excluded the unqualified teacher-traveller from our account. As long as they take their responsibilities seriously and bear in mind that their pupils have entrusted them with significant quantities of time and money to help them learn, they need not bring the EFL profession into disrepute. Some untrained teachers we talked to during the research for this book found the responsibility so unnerving that they promptly enrolled in a TEFL course before unleashing themselves on an unsuspecting language-learning public.

Non-native speakers should not assume that their services will not be in demand outside their home countries. Richard Ridha Guellala was born in Holland, raised in Tunisia and partly educated in England, and now has one of the most highly respected qualifications in TEFL, the Cambridge Diploma. While teaching in Thailand he wrote:

> *Most non-native speakers think that a position as an EFL teacher is impossible for them. However I came to the conclusion that even unqualified non-native speakers are often hired by Asian schools, as long as they project a professional image during the interview, speak clearly, are well-groomed, know the basics of English grammar and are fluent in the language. Scandinavians and Dutch are sometimes even more successful in finding teaching jobs at top schools than native speakers. True, we non-native speakers possess a rather 'heavy' or 'funny' accent but, believe it or not, some Asian employers favour our accents to the native speaker's because we speak more slowly and use very simple basic vocabulary.*

At an extreme opposite from the casual teacher-traveller is the teacher who makes ELT a career. Only a minority of people teaching English abroad are professional teachers. Career prospects in ELT are in fact not very bright. After teachers have achieved a certain level of training and experience, they can aspire to work for International House and then for the British Council. From there, they might become a director of studies at a private language institute, though are unlikely to become a director unless their primary interest is business and administration or unless they have some capital to invest in order to buy and run their own school.

An increasing number of early-retired and other mature people is becoming interested in teaching English abroad for a year or two. Although it may be true that in certain contexts, language institutes are more inclined to employ a bright young graduate, if only for reasons of image, there are plenty of others who will value maturity, especially the growing number of establishments which specialise in teaching young children. Recently there has been a noticeable shift in the market of English learners to the younger age groups, with whom hopeful teachers fresh from university are often poorly equipped to cope.

What employers are looking for

Between the dodgy operators and the British Council is a vast middle ground of respectable English teaching establishments. Many would prefer to hire only qualified staff, yet they are not always available. On the whole these schools are looking for teachers with a good educational background, clear correct speech, familiarity with the main issues and approaches to TEFL and an outgoing personality. A BA and/or TEFL certificate is no guarantee of ability as Marta Eleniak observed in Spain where she taught during her gap year (after doing a one-week introductory TEFL course):

> *I've seen graduate teachers make such a mockery of the enterprise that it's almost criminal. TEFL is creative teaching. Forget about your educational experiences. In TEFL you have got to be able to do an impression of a chicken, you've got to be a performer. And you have to be flexible. If the pupils are falling asleep, conduct a short aerobics class and change tack to something more interesting. A good teacher builds a rapport with the class, and is enthusiastic, patient, imaginative and genuinely interested in the welfare of the pupils.*

A sophisticated knowledge of English grammar is not needed, since in most cases, native speakers are hired to encourage conversation and practise pronunciation, leaving the grammar lessons to local teachers. On the other hand, a basic grasp is necessary if only to keep up with your pupils.

MOTIVES FOR TEACHING ENGLISH

There are perhaps five main types of individual to be found teaching English from Tarragona to Taipei: the serious career teacher, the student of the prevailing language and culture who teaches in order to fund a longer stay, the long-term traveller who wants to prolong and fund his or her travels, the philanthropic or religious person sponsored by an aid organisation, charity or mission society, and finally the misfit or oddball, perhaps fleeing unhappiness at home.

In many countries, English teaching is the most easily attainable employment, in fact the *only* available employment for foreigners. Anyone who wants to transcend the status of mere tourist in a country like Thailand, Peru or Japan will probably be attracted to the idea of teaching English. The assumption behind some thinking at the snobbish end of the EFL spectrum is that people who do it for only a year or two as a means to an end (e.g. learning Chinese, studying Italian art, eating French food) are necessarily inadequate teachers.

There are small pockets of people (mainly in the Far East) whose sole ambition is to earn as much money as possible to pay off debts or fund further world travels. These are seldom good teachers if only because they take on so many hours of teaching that they can't possibly prepare properly for their lessons. But for most teachers, making a lot of money is not a priority or, if it was at the outset, they are soon disillusioned.

Salaries in popular tourist destinations (like Paris, Barcelona, Chiang Mai) may actually be lower than in less appealing neighbouring towns, even though the cost of living is higher. Pay scales are relatively meaningless out of context. For example the high salaries paid in Japan are usually eaten up (at least in the first year) by high rents and other expenses. When converted into sterling a salary in Brazil or Turkey might sound reasonable, but chronic inflation and currency devaluations could soon alter the picture. In some countries like the Ukraine and Kenya, a TEFL salary may not be enough to fund anything beyond a very spartan lifestyle, and savings from home are essential to fund any travelling. Yet the majority of people who spend time abroad teaching English are able to afford to live comfortably and have an enjoyable time without feeling pinched, but end up saving little.

RED TAPE

The European Union consists of the UK, Ireland, Netherlands, Belgium, Luxembourg, Denmark, Sweden, Finland, Austria, France, Germany, Italy, Greece, Spain and Portugal, the latter six of which have enormous EFL markets. Within the EU the red tape should be minimal for all nationals of member states who wish to work in any capacity (though the relevant sections of the country chapters make it clear that this is not always the case). Anyone who intends to stay for more than three months requires a residence permit, which may be a bureaucratic hassle to obtain but should not be cause for anxiety, once you have a teaching job.

 · Outside the EU, legislation varies from country to country. In theory there is also 'free reciprocity of labour' within the European Economic Area. The EEA takes in those Western European countries that have decided to stay outside the Union, viz. Iceland, Liechtenstein, Norway and Switzerland.

All of this means that British and Irish nationals have a significant advantage over Americans, Canadians, Australians and New Zealanders when job-hunting in Europe. Although not impossible for other nationalities, it is very difficult for them to find an employer willing to undertake the task of proving to the authorities that no EU national is available or able to do the job. Brian Komyathy from Long Island New York was pleasantly surprised at how easy it was to arrange a job in Hungary, but then correspondingly disappointed when he made enquiries about moving to an EU country the following year:

> *European walls of regulations do not exactly bespeak, 'Americans welcome aboard'. I'm technically eligible to acquire Irish and hence EU citizenship through my grandparents, so as soon as various documentary records are located and processed I'll not have the problems I do now. A slew of phone calls convinced me of the necessity of taking this course. Greece will be my last resort since it was the only place which didn't (figuratively) hang up on me when they recognised the origin of my accent.*

International exchange organisations may be able to assist. For example the Council on International Educational Exchange (633 Third Avenue, 20th Floor, New York, NY 10017-6706) runs work abroad programmes for students in a number of countries and arranges for temporary work permits to be issued. With offices in France, Germany, Italy and Spain, Council might seem an obvious contact for Americans seeking to teach English in Europe, however the time limits of the programme (three to six months) make participants unattractive to employers who normally want teachers to stay for the nine or ten months of the academic year.

Other US-based organisations (InterExchange for instance) cooperate with partner organisations in various countries like the Czech Republic, Jamaica, China and many others, to place native speaker teachers in schools or institutes, often as volunteers. For particulars, see the chapter *Finding a Job: Opportunities for North Americans*.

The immigration authorities of many countries accord English teachers special status, recognising that their own nationals cannot compete as they can for other jobs. Other countries may lack the mechanism for granting work visas to English teachers and so will often turn a blind eye to those who teach on tourist visas, since everyone knows that locals are not being deprived of jobs, rather they're being given an advantage by having the chance to learn English.

The President of a major language school group Bénédict makes a useful suggestion in his standard reply to enquiries from job-seekers:

> *If you are looking for a teaching job you must remember that the present crisis makes it often difficult for foreigners to obtain the necessary authorisations. In such cases it may be useful to seek a study-and-teach solution. Such an exchange is frequently possible for short-term or long-term periods.*

Teachers who fix up a job before leaving home can usually sort out their visas or at least set the wheels in motion before arrival, which greatly simplifies matters. The majority of countries will process visas only when they are applied for from outside the country. Otherwise it may be necessary to go to your chosen country on a tourist visa, find a job, then leave the country to apply for the work visa. The restrictions and procedures for obtaining the appropriate documentation to teach legally are set out in *Part II* of this book country by country. Prospective teachers should contact the relevant Consulate for the official line (addresses in *Appendix 2*). If there is any doubt, ring the embassy a second time to confirm the original information. It is amazing how inconsistent such sources of information can be. Always enlist the help of your employer who should be familiar with procedures (assuming he or she has hired foreign teachers before) and who should be willing to help defray the often considerable costs.

If you do get tangled up in red tape, always remain patient with consular officials. If things seem to be grinding to a halt, it may be helpful to pester them, provided this is done with unfailing politeness.

REWARDS AND RISKS

The rewards of teaching abroad are mostly self-evident: the chance to become integrated in a foreign culture, the pleasure of making communication possible for your students, the interesting characters and lifestyles you will encounter, a feeling of increased self-reliance, a better perspective on your own culture and your own habits, a base for foreign travel, a good suntan ... and so on. Good teachers (e.g. those who enjoy doing impressions of chickens?) often find their classes positively fun and place a high value on the relationships they form with their students. Teaching is a lot of fun when it's done right. One-to-one teaching can also be enjoyable since you have a better chance to get to know your students or clients. (By the same token, it can be a miserable experience if you don't get on, since there is no escape from the intimacy of the arrangement.) Off-site teaching provides glimpses into a variety of workplaces and private homes, perhaps even resulting in hospitality and friendship with your students.

As competition for jobs has increased, working conditions have not improved. There is a growing tendency for EFL teachers to be offered non-contract freelance work, with no guarantee of hours, making it necessary for them to work for more than one employer in order to make a living. Job security is a scarce commodity. Part-time workers of course miss out on all the benefits of full-time work such as bonuses, holiday pay, help with accommodation in some cases and so on.

Uninitiated teachers run the risk of finding themselves working for a shark or a cowboy who doesn't care a fig about the quality of teaching or the satisfaction of the teachers, as long as pupils keep signing up and paying their fees. 'Client satisfaction' is their only criterion of success; business takes complete precedence over education. Exploitation of teachers is not uncommon since the profession is hampered by a lack of both regulation and unionisation.

The job of teaching English is demanding; it demands energy, enthusiasm and imagination, which are not always easy to produce when confronted with a room full of stonily silent faces. Instead of the thrill of communication, the drudgery of language drills begins to dominate. Instead of the pleasure of exchanging views with people of a different culture, teachers become weighed down by sheaves of photocopies and visual aids. Like most jobs when done right, teaching English is no piece of cake and is at times discouraging, but invariably it has its golden moments. It offers opportunities for creativity, learning about other cultures and attitudes, making friends and of course travelling. Not a bad job in many ways.

Roberta Wedge writes amusingly on a possible spin-off from a teaching contract abroad:

> *TEFL is one of the most sex-balanced job fields I know (though the Director of Studies is usually a man) and, for those who are interested, the possibilities of finding your one true love appear to be high. 'Thrown together in an isolated Spanish village, eating tapas in the bar, hammering out lesson plans together – we found we have so much in common.' And a year later they were married. (A true story.)*

TEACHING
PROFICIENCY
TEST

...~~~~~...

PASS WITH
CREDIT

Training

THE VALUE OF ELT QUALIFICATIONS

Training in teaching English as a foreign language is not absolutely essential for successful job-hunting; but it makes the task easier by an order of magnitude. Anyone with the Cambridge Certificate (CELTA) or the Trinity Certificate in TESOL (both discussed in detail below) is in a much stronger position to get a job in any country where English is widely taught. These Certificate courses provide a rigorous introduction to teaching English in just one month full-time (admittedly at considerable expense), and so anyone interested in spending some time teaching abroad should seriously consider enrolling in a Certificate course. There are numerous other kinds of qualifications available, some obtainable after a weekend course and others after years of university study; many are described briefly in the *Directory of Training Courses* below.

However, the Cambridge and Trinity Certificates should not be thought of as a magical passport to work. Increasingly, even Certificate-holders are having to struggle to find a decent job, mainly because so many more people now have the qualification than five or ten years ago. Many language schools, especially in France and Germany, will not want to hire a novice teacher and are unlikely to be tempted to take on anyone who does not present a dynamic and energetic image. Still, the four-week Certificate training continues to give applicants an important edge over the competition.

Increasing your marketability is not the only reason to get some training. The assumption that just because you can speak a language you can teach is simply false. There may be plenty of people who have a natural flair for teaching and who can do an excellent job without the benefit of a Certificate or any other English Language Teaching (ELT) qualification. (As mentioned earlier, the term ELT has come to be preferred to TEFL in many contexts.) There are, however, many other people who, when faced with a class full of eager adolescents, would not have a clue where to begin. Doing a TEFL course cannot fail to increase your confidence and provide you with a range of ideas on how to teach and (just as important) how not to teach. Even a short introductory course can usually illustrate methods of making lessons interesting and of introducing the range of teaching materials and approaches available to the novice teacher. What is needed more than theory or academic attainment, is an ability to entertain and to dramatise, but not without a framework into which your classroom efforts can be placed.

A perpetual problem which a TEFL course solves is the general level of ignorance of grammar among native speakers. Native-speaker teachers often find that their pupils, who are much better informed on English grammar than they are, can easily catch them out with questions about verb tenses and subjunctives, causing embarrassment all round. Some training courses can also introduce you to the cultural barriers you can expect to encounter and the specific language-learning difficulties experienced by various nationalities (many of which will be touched on in the country chapters).

Some go so far as to see training almost as a moral obligation. Completely untrained teachers may end up being responsible for teaching people who have paid a great deal of money for expert instruction. This is of special concern in countries which have been inundated with 'tourist-teachers', while the Ministries of Education may be struggling to create all-graduate teaching professions. If you happen not to be a natural in the classroom, you may well fail to teach anything much to your pupils, whether they be young children in Hong Kong or businessmen in Portugal.

Not satisfied that a one-week course was enough to qualify him as a teacher, Ian Abbott went on to do the Cambridge Certificate at International House in Rome and summarises his view of TEFL training:

I wouldn't recommend teaching English as a foreign language without investing in a course first. You've got to remember that the people coming along to your lessons are desperate to learn your language and it is costing them a small fortune. It is only fair that you know what you are doing and can in the end take that money without guilt, knowing you haven't ripped them off to increase your travel funds.

One of the practical advantages of joining a TEFL course is that many training centres have contacts with recruitment agencies or language schools abroad and can advise on, if not fix up, a job abroad for you at the end of the course. Training centres differ enormously on how much help they can offer. If the 'after-sales service' is important to you, shop around before choosing which training course to patronise.

Even in countries where it may be commonplace to work without a formal TEFL qualification (for example Thailand and Japan), teachers who lack a specific grounding in TEFL will often be at a disadvantage, since the jobs they are likely to get will be with schools at the cowboy end of the market who may in turn be more likely to offer exploitative conditions. In some countries (such as Turkey) a TEFL certificate is a prerequisite for a work visa, which is yet another justification for doing some formal training before setting off.

RANGE OF COURSES

There is a bewildering array of courses available, at vastly different levels and costs, so it is wise to carry out some careful research before choosing. A comprehensive guide to the courses on offer both in the UK and abroad is contained in the annual *ELT International Careers Guide* which includes tables comparing duration, cost, location and starting dates of training courses at all levels. It explains the differences among the various certificates, diplomas and MAs on offer as well as introductory and correspondence courses in more detail than the scope of this book allows. It is available from large bookshops or directly from the same address as that of the monthly journal *EL Gazette*, Dilke House, 1 Malet St, Bloomsbury, London WC1E 7AJ (020-7255 1969). It is revised regularly and now in the tenth edition (2000/01) and costs £12.95/US$24.95. The UK distributors are Book Systems Plus (BSP House, Station Road, Linton, Cambs. CB1 6NW; tel 01223-894870; fax 01223-894871); add £2 for postage.

The British Council Information Centre (Bridgewater House, 58 Whitworth St, Manchester M1 6BB; 0161-957 7755) publishes a free information leaflet *How to Become a Teacher of English as a Foreign Language* and distributes lists of Academic Courses in TEFL, Cambridge Certificate and Diploma courses and Trinity College Certificate and Licentiate Diploma courses, all described below.

If you need help funding a training course, you may be eligible for a Career Development Loan. CDLs are bank loans covering up to 80% of the cost of a vocational course lasting less than two years. Payment can be deferred until three months after the course finishes, whereupon repayments have to be made. The participating banks are Barclays, the Cooperative, Royal Bank of Scotland and the Clydesdale. Write for details to Freepost, Career Development Loans (tel. 0800 585505). Note that long term unemployed may be eligible for a 100% loan. Ask your prospective course provider for details.

When choosing a course, it is worth asking certain questions which will indicate how useful the qualification will be at the end of it, such as, is there any external validation of the course and how much opportunity is there for teaching practice? Also find out what size a class you will be in (10-12 is much better than 15-20) and what qualifications and experience the tutors have.

The *Directory of Training Courses* in this chapter organises the courses available under various headings. The 100+ hour Certificate courses externally validated by the University of Cambridge and Trinity College *London*, 'Academic and Other Recognised Courses' which are primarily full academic courses offered at universities (this list is far from comprehensive), a few 'Distance Learning' courses, 'Short Introductory Courses in the UK' and, finally, a selection of courses offered worldwide 'Training Courses Abroad'.

CERTIFICATE COURSES

The most useful qualification for anyone intending to spend a year or more abroad as an English teacher is a Certificate in English Language Teaching validated by one of the two examination bodies active in the field of ELT, the University of Cambridge Local Examinations Syndicate (UCLES) and Trinity College *London*. The Certificate qualification is acquired after an intensive 100-120 hour course offered full-time over one month or (increasingly) part-time over several months.

Most centres expect applicants to have the equivalent of university entrance qualifications, i.e. three GCSEs and two A levels and some require a degree. Admission to the course is at the discretion of the course organiser after a sometimes lengthy selection process. Places on courses at the well-established centres may be difficult to get because of high demand, especially in summer, so early application is advised.

Applicants must be able to demonstrate a suitable level of language awareness and convince the interviewer that they have potential to develop as a teacher. Past academic achievement is less important than aptitude; even a PhD does not guarantee acceptance. Most schools will send you a task sheet or grammar quiz as part of the application. Sample questions might be 'how would you convey the idea of regret to a language learner?' or 'describe the difference in meaning between *I don't really like beetroot* and *I really don't like beetroot*?

Courses are not cheap but should be viewed as an investment and a potential passport to a worthwhile profession in many different countries. In fact, prices have not risen much over the past two years, with many centres trying to survive amidst keen competition. The range is about £700 to £1,000 for a full-time course with an average halfway between those two figures. Most centres include the validation body's fee, variously called assessment, moderation or examination fee, which is roughly £75. Many colleges of further education offer the Trinity or Cambridge Certificate part-time and these are normally less expensive, as low as £350-£400. If the Further Education Funding Council acts on recent recommendations, prices in the FE sector could fall even further.

Timetables for part-time courses vary, but the norm is to attend classes one or two evenings a week for one or two terms of the academic year plus occasional full days for teaching observation and practice. Some universities and colleges have language institutes which run intensive TEFL courses at various levels on a commercial basis, and fees at these institutions are often equivalent to private training courses.

Once accepted onto a Certificate course, you will normally be given a pre-course task to familiarise yourself with some key concepts and issues before the course begins. Full-time courses are very intensive and 100% attendance is required, so you need to be in a position to dedicate yourself completely to the task in hand for four weeks. The standard of teaching is high, the course rigorous and demanding and the emphasis is on the practice of any theory taught. One of the requirements is that participants teach a minimum of six hours of observed lessons to real live English language students.

Cambridge

The Cambridge CELTA (Certificate in English Language Teaching to Adults) was previously known as the Cambridge/RSA CELTA, before that the CTEFLA, and before that as the Prep.Cert. The syllabus and assessment were thoroughly revised after a lengthy period of piloting and consultation with course providers and professionals in the field. The course is administered and regulated by the University of Cambridge Local Examinations Syndicate or UCLES (Syndicate Buildings, 1 Hills Road, Cambridge CB1 2EU; tel 01223 553355/efl@ucles.org.uk/ www.cambridge-efl.org.uk). The RSA part of the name and logo stood for Royal Society of Arts and has just been dropped from the certificate which is now just known as the Cambridge Certificate.

Pass certificates are awarded by the University of Cambridge to successful candidates. The grades are Pass, Pass 'B' and Pass 'A'. The pass rate is normally an encouraging 90% or over, simply because Cambridge requires that course providers take a great deal of care in selecting candidates in the first place.

The CELTA is very widely recognised in the international field of English language teaching. A summary of the CELTA course content includes language awareness and knowledge; understanding adult learners; the roles of teachers and learners; the principles and practice of effective teaching (including classroom management, lesson planning approaches and techniques for teaching language and skills in the classroom); using materials and resources; and professional development. A new course offered by Cambridge is the CELTYL (Certificate in English Language Teaching to Young Learners). Further information about the content of the courses and methods of assessment are available from UCLES, together with a list of the more than 300 centres both in Britain and abroad where the courses are offered.

A free job placement service has been introduced. This allows candidates who have been accepted onto a CELTA course to register with specified institutions who will attempt to match candidates with jobs worldwide.

Cambridge courses are offered in a surprising number of locations from San Francisco to Sydney. In fact there are 96 overseas centres. The British Council run a few Certificate courses, for example in Milan, Naples, Istanbul, Cairo, Oman, Hong Kong and Kuala Lumpur, while International House offer Cambridge Certificate courses in a number of overseas centres such as Barcelona, Lisbon,

Kraków, Rome and Cairo. Other foreign venues are listed in the information from UCLES including 16 centres in Australia and six in New Zealand. The CELTA is going from strength to strength in North America where US-based employers are steadily becoming more aware of it. There are now 13 Cambridge-recognised centres in North America.

Possible advantages of doing a Cambridge Certificate abroad are that you may already be teaching or living in that country and want to upgrade your qualifications locally; the course and cost of living may be cheaper than in England (Istanbul, Cairo and Bangkok are especially favoured for this reason); and course participants would almost certainly be put in touch with local employers, making it much easier to land a job than if applying from home. A further advantage is that when you are living in a non-English speaking environment, you might become more sensitive to the difficulties faced by language learners and more attuned to the importance of cultural differences.

Trinity College London

The other principal initial Certificate in TESOL is awarded by Trinity College *London,* 89 Albert Embankment, London SE1 7TP. Tel: 020-7820 6100. Fax: 020-7820 6161. E-mail: tesol@trinitycollege.co.uk. Website: www.trinitycollege.co.uk. When job details in this book and elsewhere say 'Cambridge or equivalent', they are referring primarily to the Trinity College qualifications which are regarded as having equal academic standing. The Trinity College Certificate (CertTESOL) has continued to enjoy tremendous success with a constantly increasing list of centres (currently 100+) which offer the courses mostly in Britain but also abroad (including South America).

Trinity College *London* stipulates a minimum of 130 hours offered intensively over a minimum of four weeks or part-time over a longer period. Some have a distance-learning component but this cannot count towards the minimum hours. A summary of the course content includes grammar and phonology, a range of teaching approaches and methodologies, classroom management and motivation, hands-on experience of teaching aids (from blackboards to computers), introduction to the learning of an unknown language (in which trainees receive some instruction in Arabic or whatever), lesson planning and a minimum of six hours of observed and assessed teaching practice and at least four further hours observing experienced teachers. Trinity works closely with BATQI (the British Association of TESOL Qualifying Institutions) to ensure that its Certificate and Diploma qualifications meet their national guidelines for TESOL training in the UK.

Trinity have also introduced a Certificate in Teaching English to Young Learners (TEYL) which is aimed primarily at practising primary teachers. They are also planning to introduce special short add-on-courses for those wishing to teach one-to-one.

Every year, thousands choose Trinity to kick-start their career

TESOL TESOL

Trinity's CertTESOL is the natural first choice

- a qualification with international recognition
- course providers who have successfully undergone a rigorous process leading to validation
- more than 100 course providers in the UK and overseas
- accepted by The British Council in accredited UK institutions and by employers worldwide

Two years' teaching experience ...
take the Trinity LTCL TESOL diploma

- a qualification reflecting substantial teaching experience and theoretical knowledge
- accepted by The British Council in accredited UK institutions and by employers worldwide

As part of Trinity's continuous process of revision and renewal, a new diploma syllabus is being developed for 2001—in co-operation with BATQI and BIELT—to include a wider range of assessment formats.

Become a Trinity CertTESOL course provider

- benefit from continuing support from Trinity's head office team

To find out more, contact:
TESOL Information
Trinity College *London*
89 Albert Embankment, London SE1 7TP, UK
Tel: +44 (0)20 7820 6100   *Fax:* +44 (0)20 7820 6161
e-mail: tesol@trinitycollege.co.uk   *Website:* www.trinitycollege.co.uk

Trinity
The International Examinations Board

The Trinity course is just as strenuous as its competitor, as Jayne Nash describes:

My TESOL course in Coventry was certainly very intensive, with a wide variety of tasks, tutoring sessions, projects and seminars. We covered English grammar, language teaching, the use of teaching aids, classroom management... We were marked on a student profile (four one-to-one sessions with a designated English language learner), a language learning diary (10 hours of Mandarin Chinese lessons, giving us the idea of how it feels to be a learner), 4 live teaching practices, 3 with foreigners at the College and the other in a local primary school teaching Asian children, and 7 observations (4 video and 3 live). We also had a grammar/phonetics/ linguistics exam and a short project presentation (I put together a teaching pack with visual aids for teaching in Africa).

Even after such a wide-ranging practical course, Jayne goes on to say that 'no amount of training can prepare you for the real thing,' though it did make her realise what a challenging occupation TEFL is.

Choosing a Certificate Course

It is up to prospective trainees to weigh up the pros and cons of the courses available to them and to establish how rigorously the course he or she is considering is monitored. One reservation that a few employers abroad have expressed is that the proliferation of Certificate courses has made it more difficult to maintain a uniform standard, especially since so much of the assessment of candidates is subjective. The general decline in standards of literacy in Britain and North America has also prompted some to complain of a decline.

When it comes to work load, trainees in both Certificate courses complain of a punishing schedule. But most come away claiming that the course elements are superb. At the time, participants sometimes feel as though they are drowning in information, but realise that the course has to pack a great deal of material into four brief weeks. The majority who go on to teach abroad are very grateful for the training it gave them, as in the case of Andrew Sykes teaching in Bordeaux:

As for the Certificate course that I did at Leeds Metropolitan University, it was certainly one of the most stimulating, challenging and interesting things I have ever studied for. Initially I felt a bit out of place – I had a background of science A levels, a maths degree and 2^1/2 years as a (failed) accountant. The course was professionally run and there were good teacher-student relations. Most people had never taught anybody anything before in their life, but we were gradually eased into teaching by the supportive teaching staff who were refreshingly (and diplomatically) critical when required to be. A criticism which some students had was that there wasn't enough feedback about what was expected to gain a pass, let alone achieve an A or B. The best recommendation for the course is perhaps that I would never have felt comfortable teaching without it.

So even if your social life disappears for a month and all you can talk about at weekends is gerunds and infinitives, the consensus is that it is worthwhile.

The University of London Institute of Education offers a Certificate in English Teaching for practising teachers outside the UK. It can be studied in modular form and is taught locally by approved course directors. Certification counts towards the Institute of Education's Diploma in TESOL. For further details contact Teresa Jacobs (ULCET), Edexcel International, 32 Russell Square, London WC1B 5DN (020-7393 4182; fax 020-7331 4022).

Other Recognised Qualifications

Beyond the Certificate is the Diploma. Whereas the Certificate is considered a pre-service qualification, the Diploma (as distinct from any old diploma with a lower case) is an in-service course which is followed by practising EFL teachers. The Cambridge Diploma in English Language Teaching to Adults (DELTA) and the Trinity Licentiate Diploma (LTCT TESOL) are high-level qualifications normally open to graduates who have at least two years of recent ELT classroom experience. The Diploma course is offered intensively over 12 weeks but more usually part-time over several months or a year. The fees of over £1,000 are sometimes subsidised by employers.

Increasingly, universities (especially the former polytechnics) from Brighton to Belfast offer their own Certificate or Diploma in TEFL. Most are one or two year courses, full or part-time, and are more academic than Cambridge and Trinity courses. It is important to do some research before committing yourself to a course so that you are sure that the qualification you obtain will be recognised by employers both in the UK and overseas. Once again find out if there is some form of external assessment and whether the course includes a reasonable amount of teaching practice. Stephen Curry felt let down by the course he chose:

I called my local university to see what courses were available and was advised that they could provide a course consisting of two modules, one from the PGCE and one from the MEd programme which would be equivalent in status to a one-month Certificate and would be 'recognised'. The course of study took from May to February to complete. It was a lot of hard work, research based and absolutely no fun whatsoever. I did the course on the understanding that it would lead to a stand-alone TEFL certificate. I have since tried to get the university to confirm in writing that this module carries the recognition they claimed it would but they now say that they cannot do this. Unfortunately it was not until the latter stages of the course that I (and others) began to see that the eventual outcome would be a qualification that was unlikely to be recognised in the eyes of anyone outside the university, let alone as being equivalent to the Cambridge/Trinity certificate.

The British Association of TESOL Qualifying Institutions (BATQI Secretariat, University of Bristol, Graduate School of Education, 35 Berkeley Square, Bristol BS8 1JA; www.globalnet.co.uk/~webling/BATQI/ index.htm; e-mail: g.m.clibbon@bristol.ac.uk) is the relevant regulatory body for state providers of TEFL training courses.

A number of undergraduate institutions offer TESL as part of an undergraduate course; the weighty *UCAS Handbook* lists all university courses in the UK and can be consulted in any careers or general library. The highly respected PGCE (Post Graduate Certificate in Education) in TESOL was abolished in the early 1990s and trainee teachers are now able to study TESOL only as a subsidiary subject. The Graduate Teacher Training Registry (Fulton House, Jessop Avenue, Cheltenham, Gloucestershire GL50 3SH; tel: 01242 225868; www.gttr.ac.uk) should be able to provide information on relevant options, though their website does not list TEFL as an option. The Teaching Information Line (01245 454454) might also offer advice.

MA courses in ELT and Applied Linguistics are offered at dozens of universities and colleges. Some (like Aston University) offer a Master's by distance learning in collaboration with the British Council. Arguably, there is a world oversupply of MAs, since there is a relative scarcity of high level posts which require an MA; for example the British Council has only ten or so positions a year. On the other hand, an MA is a pre-requisite in some countries (see section on Oman).

Introductory Courses

Although the Cambridge and Trinity Certificates are sometimes referred to as 'introductory courses', there are many cheaper, shorter and less rigorous introductions to the subject. With the dramatic rise in the popularity of Certificate courses there has been a decline in what might be considered as more amateurish courses, though these do have a role to play, for example for school leavers who would not be accepted onto a Certificate course or for the curious who do not want to commit themselves to a month-long course nor pay £700 or £800.

Because there are so many commercial enterprises and 'cowboy' operators cashing in on the present EFL boom, standards vary and course literature should be studied carefully before choosing. Most people who have done a TEFL training course claim that the most worthwhile part is the actual teaching practice, preferably to living breathing foreigners rather than in mock lessons to fellow participants. The fact is that most short introductory courses do not allow for much chance to do teaching practice. Many schools looking for teachers have expressed the view that peer-teaching is of little value.

The more upmarket introductory courses often present themselves as an opportunity to sample the field to see whether you want to go on to do a Certificate at a later stage. Others make their course sound as if it alone will be sufficient to open doors worldwide. It would be unreasonable to expect a weekend or five-day course to equip anyone to teach, but most participants do find them helpful. The majority of residential courses last one week (i.e. five days) and cost between £125 and £190, not counting accommodation. Almost all will issue some kind of certificate which can sometimes be used to impress prospective employers. Anyone who wants a job after doing a short course should aim to do it in the spring when the majority of jobs are advertised for the following academic year. Many people who complete an introductory or 'taster' course go on to do an intensive certificate, often at the same centre.

A number of private language centres offer their own short courses in TEFL which may focus on their own method, developed specifically with the chain of schools in mind (for example Berlitz), or may offer a more general introduction. Anyone who wishes to specialise in the highly marketable field of business English should enquire about specialist courses such as those offered by the London Chamber of Commerce & Industry (LCCI) which validates a certificate in teaching English for business.

Distance Learning

Some practising teachers of English who want to obtain a qualification are attracted to the idea of self-study by distance learning, partly because it will be cheaper than a conventional course and because it can be done in the candidate's own time and/or in any part of the world. Course providers are making increased use of electronic communications, doing away not only with the necessity of having physical access to a training course but of being dependent on the post, often unreliable in distant parts of the world. Some companies are delivering complete courses on-line for example *i-to-i* which for some years has been offering intensive weekend courses around the UK (www.onlinetefl.com). *Open Learning International* based in Wales and *TEFL International* with a mailing address in Hong Kong promise an affordable TESOL education via the internet to people (preferably those with some ESL teaching experience behind them) anywhere in the world.

As a part of the general move within the profession to monitor standards and offer assurances of quality, the College of Teachers (Coppice Row, Theydon Bois, Epping, Essex CM16 7DN; 01992 812727/fax 01992 814690/ www. collegeofteachers. ac.uk) is the main awarding body. It has accorded recognition to a few distance learning course providers. The Accreditation Council for TESOL Distance Education Courses (ACTDEC) to which a handful of course providers belongs was set up in the mid-1990s. A copy of their code of practice can be requested from the Secretary, 21 Wessex Gardens, Dore, Sheffield S17 3PQ (fax 0114 236 0774; t-link@vip.solis.co.uk). Typically, distance courses at the professional end of the spectrum involve at least 150 hours of home study. Some offer distance learning in combination with a residential element sometimes referred to as a hybrid course.

People considering this route to TEFL training should be cautious. The most obvious disadvantage is the lack of face-to-face teaching practice, though some do provide opportunities for blocks of teaching practice and others provide plenty of tutor feedback. If you are not satisfied with the course but have paid your money (typically £400+ for a certificate course), you have little recourse. One way of ascertaining the worth of a distance learning course you may be considering is to ask to be put in touch with past students. For example *Global English* asks its students to complete appraisal forms, many of which are very positive, for example one filled out by Glyn Askey from Yorkshire:

> *Having had an interest in TEFL for some time, I required a course which would give me an insight into TEFL at an affordable cost. I found that the Global English course made you think from the outset about your students, your lesson planning and the methods of teaching... A well put together course and positive friendly feedback.*

Of the range of distance courses and qualifications on offer, most offer professional courses of quality. One or two are sound but provide relatively short basic programmes, yet frequently lead to a so-called Diploma. A few however have a definite credibility gap; even their course information and covering letters are riddled with spelling and grammatical mistakes. Be especially cautious if the organisation operates from a PO Box and/or provides no telephone number.

Details of introductory, internet and distance training courses both in Britain and abroad are provided in the *Directory of Training Courses* which follows.

Training in the US

Most TESL training in the US is integrated into university degree courses in Applied Linguistics at both the undergraduate and graduate levels. Until the beginning of the decade, there were virtually no short intensive courses in TEFL available in North America. That has now changed. In addition to the eight Cambridge centres in the US, there are a number of independent TEFL training organisations offering four-week intensive courses (see *Directory of Training Courses* below). The major providers like ITC, New World Teachers, Transworld and Worldwide Teachers are well connected with language schools abroad (particularly in Latin America and the Far East). Their publicity and newsletters contain lots of quotations from ex-trainees who have found work all around the world, so their emphasis is on assisting with job placement. Competition is keen, and prices fairly consistent at about $2,000 for a four-week course.

There are a few one-semester courses in TESL offered at American colleges and universities. Increasingly American universities are offering intensive TESL training. If you cannot afford to do a course but want to learn about TEFL, it may be possible to audit such a course. One resource for finding a programme of study in the field of TESOL within North America is the *Directory of Professional Preparation Programs in TESOL in the United States and Canada*. This is the most comprehensive listing available, containing information about graduate, PhD and certificate programmes. Each entry lists contact information, course descriptions, faculty information and tuition costs. The 1999-2001 edition costs US$44.95 plus 12% postage (or $29.95 plus postage for TESOL members; see *Finding a Job*). A useful companion is *The Handbook of Funding Opportunities in the Field of TESOL* for US$18.95 plus $4.50. The *Career Counsel* is a free newsletter that gives basic information about the profession. All of these publications are available from TESOL (Teachers of English to Speakers of Other Languages, Inc.), 700 South Washington Street, Suite 200, Alexandria, Virginia 22314-4287 (703-836 0774/fax 703-836-6447; e-mail careers@tesol.org/ www.tesol.org or www.careers.tesol.org).

It is easier to get practical experience of teaching English (without a qualification) by joining one of the many voluntary ESL programmes found in almost every American city, run by community colleges, civic organisations and literacy groups. Literacy Volunteers of America operate in most states and offer volunteer tutors a free 18-hour pre-service training programme but you have to buy the materials (about $35). Their headquarters are at 635 James Street, Syracuse, NY 13203-2214; 800-LVA-8812; www.literacyvolunteers.org. Laubach Literacy (1320 Jamesville Avenue, Syracuse, NY; www.laubach.org) offers a 12-hour tutor training workshop for their volunteers; they also oversee literacy projects in dozens of countries overseas.

The Australasian equivalent of the US directory mentioned above is *Teacher Training in TESOL: A Directory of Courses in Australia and New Zealand* which costs A$30 within Australia and A$35 to overseas addresses (surface post). Unfortunately, the most recent edition is 1996; order details are available from the ELICOS Association (www.elicos.edu.au).

DIRECTORY OF TRAINING COURSES

Cambridge Certificate (CELTA) Courses in the UK

All courses last four weeks full-time unless otherwise stated. The fees quoted (which should be taken merely as a guide) include the CELTA examination fee of £74.70 unless otherwise stated.

ANGLIA POLYTECHNIC UNIVERSITY, East Road, Cambridge CB1 1PT. Tel: 01223 363271. Fax: 01223 352933. E-mail: m.l.baker@anglia.ac.uk. Full-time in July and August only. 9.30am-5pm. Includes 6 hours of teaching practice and 8 hours of observation of experienced teachers. £970 (including examination fee). Accommodation can be arranged in APU halls of residence. Information is supplied about jobs.

ANGLO-CONTINENTAL TEACHER TRAINING CENTRE, 29-35 Wimborne Road, Bournemouth BH2 6NA. Tel: 01202 557414, ext 282. Fax: 01202 556156. E-mail: english@anglo-continental.com. Website: www.anglo-continental.com. Full-time (125 hours) 3 courses per year. £900. Part-time courses over 6 months proposed. Accommodation can be arranged.

ANGLOSCHOOL, 146 Church Road, Upper Norwood, London SE19 2NT. Tel: 020-8653 7285. Fax: 020-8653 9667. E-mail: english@angloschool.co.uk. 4-week courses 4 times a year. £900. Video and booklet on basic teaching techniques available. 8 trainees maximum on course.

BARNET COLLEGE, Wood Street, Barnet EN5 4AZ. Tel: 020-8275 2828. Fax: 020-8441 5236. E-mail: s.alderton@barnet.ac.uk. Website: www.barnet.ac.uk. Intensive courses January-February, April-May, June-July, September-October and November. Part-time evening course September-June. £750. Possibility of short-term accommodation.

BASIL PATERSON EDINBURGH LANGUAGE FOUNDATION, Dugdale McAdam House, 22-23 Abercromby Place, Edinburgh EH3 6QE. Tel: 0131-556 7695. Fax: 0131-557 8503. E-mail: courses@bp-coll.demon.co.uk. Website: www.basilpaterson. co.uk. 8 courses per year. £999. Accommodation service available. Early application advised. Information from Helen Anderson CELTA course director.

BEDFORD COLLEGE, Enterprise House, Old Ford End Road, Bedford MK40 4PF. Tel: 01234 271492. Fax: 01234 364272. E-mail: gp67@dial.pipex.com. Website www.bedford.ac.uk. Part-time introductory course; also CELTA.

BELL TEACHER TRAINING INSTITUTE, Hillscross, Red Cross Lane, Cambridge CB2 2QX. Tel: 01223 212333. Fax: 01223 410282. E-mail: info@bell-schools.ac.uk. Website: www.bell-schools.ac.uk. Full-time and part-time courses all year round. Part-time DELTA course also offered.

BELL LANGUAGE SCHOOL, NORWICH, Bowthorpe Hall, Norwich NR5 9AA. Tel: 01603 745615. Fax: 01603 747669. E-mail: Sarah.knights@bell-schools.ac.uk. Website: www.bell-schools.ac.uk. Full-time courses offered 5 times per year. £890. 8-week full-time DELTA course also offered. £1,250.

BELL LANGUAGE SCHOOL, SAFFRON WALDEN, South Road, Saffron Walden, Essex CB11 3DP. Tel: 01799 522918. Fax: 01799 526949. E-mail: info@bell-schools.ac.uk. Full-time DELTA course.

BLACKBURN COLLEGE, Gateway Centre, Feilden St, Blackburn BB2 1LH. Tel: 01254-292929 (student services enquiries). E-mail: m.osmaston@blackburn.ac.uk. Part-time course over academic year (September-June); one day per week. £320. Covers EFL and ESOL with particular focus on teaching adults in Britain. Advice and guidance on job-finding.

THE BOURNEMOUTH AND POOLE COLLEGE, The Lansdowne, Bournemouth, Dorset BH1 3JJ. Tel: 01202-205357. Fax: 01202-205462. Website: www. thecollege.co.uk. Part-time, 16-week courses twice a year. £750. Also introduction to TEFL (part-time, 5 weeks, £75) and Trinity Diploma course (part-time, 12 weeks, £975). Accommodation can be found if required. General advice about jobs given. Use of Learning Resource Centre and computer facilities,including free access to internet.

BRASSHOUSE CENTRE, 50 Sheepcote Street, Birmingham B16 8AJ. Tel. 0121-303 0114. Part-time once a year (October-March).

BROMLEY SCHOOL OF ENGLISH, 2 Park Road, Bromley, Kent BR1 3HP. Tel: 020-8313 0308. Fax: 020-8313 3957. E-mail: info@bromleyschool.com. Website: www.bromleyschool.com. Full-time, 4-week course offered monthly. £795 reducing to £495 with funding. Accommodation with host family £11 per night half board. Information, advice and references given for jobs.

BROOKLANDS COLLEGE, Heath Road, Weybridge, Surrey KT13 8TT. Tel: 01932 797741. Fax: 01932 797800. E-mail: courses@brooklands.ac.uk. Full-time course 25th June to 20th July only. Part-time daytime courses 16 weeks September-January and February-July. £750. Courses include sessions on finding work. College accommodation office can advise.

CANTERBURY CHRIST CHURCH UNIVERSITY COLLEGE, North Holmes Road, Canterbury CT1 1QU. Tel: 01227 458459. Fax: 01227 781558. E-mail: ipo@cant.ac.uk. Website: www.cant.ac.uk. Courses offered full-time (5 weeks) and part-time (16 weeks), both once a year. £1050. Diploma/MA in TESOL also offered, plus short summer courses (£573). Homestay or college residence accommodation can be arranged. No help given with job placements.

CILC (Cheltenham International Language Centre), Cheltenham & Gloucester College of Higher Education, Francis Close Hall, Swindon Road, Cheltenham, Glos. GL50 4AZ. Tel: 01242 532925. Fax: 01242 532926. E-mail: cilc@chelt.ac.uk. Website: www.chelt.ac.uk/msm/cilc. Cambridge centre offering full-time (5 weeks) courses throughout the year. One-day taster courses also offered. Homestay or self-catering accommodation.

CITY OF BATH COLLEGE, Avon Street, Bath BA1 1UP. Tel: 01225 312191. Fax: 01225 444213. E-mail: bulld@citybathcoll.ac.uk. Full-time and part-time CELTA courses and DELTA courses. Accommodation can be arranged with local families.

CITY OF BRISTOL COLLEGE, Languages Dept., Brunel Centre, Ashley Down, Bristol BS7 9BU. Tel: 0117 904 5178. Fax: 0117 904 5180. E-mail: alicoris@sbristol.tcom.uk. Part-time courses (2 days per week for 10 or 12 weeks) starting September, January and April. £950. Accommodation can be arranged. Help also given with job placement.

COLLEGE OF NORTH WEST LONDON, EFL Section, Kilburn Centre, Priory Park Road, London NW6 7UJ. Tel: 020-8208 5328. Fax: 020-8208 5151. E-mail: Krystyna.vargas@cnwl.ac.uk. Website: www.cnwl.ac.uk. Once a year. 23 weeks. £550. No accommodation.

CONCORDE INTERNATIONAL STUDY CENTRE, Arnett House, Hawks Lane, Canterbury, Kent CT1 2NU. Tel: 01227 451035. Fax: 01227 762760. E-mail: info@concorde.ltd.uk. Website: www.concorde.ltd.uk. Full-time courses twice a year. £798 plus validation fee. Accommodation can be arranged (guest houses/hotels or host families). Offer employment on Easter and Summer schools, and display adverts of job vacancies at home and abroad. Also offers distance learning course.

CROYDON CONTINUING EDUCATION & TRAINING SERVICE (CETS), English and Bilingual Skills, South Norwood Centre, Sandown Road, South Norwood, London SE25 4XE. Tel: 020-8656 6620. Fax: 020-8662 1828. Part-time course over 25 weeks from September to May. 2 half-day sessions a week. £700 with concessions. Also offer an ESOL component for teaching minority groups in this country. Annual vacancies in large ESOL department at CETS.

DEVON SCHOOL OF ENGLISH, The Old Vicarage, 1 Lower Polsham Road, Paignton, Devon TQ3 2AF. Tel: 01803 559718. Fax: 01803 551407. E-mail: english@devonschool.co.uk. Website: www.devonschool.co.uk. Full-time once or twice a year. Accommodation with host families or self-catering.

DUNDEE COLLEGE, Melrose Terrace, Dundee DD3 7QX. Tel: 01382 834898. Fax: 01382 322286. E-mail: dic@dundeecoll.ac.uk. Full-time courses 2/3 times a year (dependent on demand) starting July/August, September and possibly November. £795. Accommodation can be arranged. No help with job placement.

EASTBOURNE COLLEGE OF ARTS AND TECHNOLOGY, Cross Levels Way, Eastbourne BN21 2UF. Tel: 01323 644711. Fax: 01323 412239. Offer intensive one-month and part-time 6-month courses. 5 various courses per year. £390 plus £90 registration fee. Accommodation can be provided, and job information is passed on to students.

EMBASSY CES HASTINGS, Palace Court, White Rock, Hastings, East Sussex TN34 1JY. Tel: 01424 720100. Fax: 01424 720323. E-mail: training@embassyces.com. Monthly £850. Self-catering accommodation approximately £50 a week. Also offers Cambridge Diploma (DELTA), 2-week course on teaching young learners, Business English, and a wide range of other 2-week specialist courses. Helps with recruitment in their 35 summer schools in the UK and Ireland. CELTA Centres also in New York (e-mail: infousa@embassyces.com) and Prague (e-mail: ilcprague@studygroupintl.com).

EMBASSY CES NEWNHAM, International Teacher Training Institute, 8 Grange Road, Cambridge, CB3 7DU. Tel: 01223-311344. Fax: 01223 461411. E-mail: slaslett@bcmanor.bsg.ac.uk. February, May, August, October/November. £940. Accommodation in various self-catering approximately £60 per week. Helps with recruitment in their 35 summer schools in the UK and Ireland.

FARNBOROUGH COLLEGE OF TECHNOLOGY: Manor Walk, Aldershot, GU12 4JW. Tel: 01252-407300. part-time, 32 weeks. Held every year. £700.

FILTON COLLEGE, Filton Avenue, Bristol BS34 7AT. Tel: 0117-931 2121. Fax: 0117-909 2233. Part-time September to May/June.

FRANCES KING TEACHER TRAINING, 5 Grosvenor Gardens, Victoria, London SW1W 0BD. Tel: 020-7630 8055. Fax: 020-7630 8077. E-mail: gerald@francesking.co.uk. Website: www.francesking.co.uk/teachertraining. Four-week intensive courses throughout the year. Price at time of press: £799. Help with accommodation. Jobs noticeboard and contact with a range of employers/agencies.

GEOS ENGLISH ACADEMY, 55-61 Portland Road, Hove, East Sussex BN3 5DQ. Tel: 01273 735975. Fax: 01273 732884. E-mail: info@geos-brighton.com. Website: www.geos-brighton.com. Intensive courses throughout the year. £870. Accommodation can be arranged. Help given with job placements. Highly practical course with maximum 12 trainees.

GLOSCAT (Gloucester College of Arts & Technology), Park Campus, 73 The Park, Cheltenham, Glos. GL50 2RR. Tel: 01242 532129. E-mail: Burdep@Gloscat.ac.uk. Full-time (6 weeks) three times a year. Part-time (6 months) January-June.

HAMMERSMITH & WEST LONDON COLLEGE, Gliddon Road, London W14 9BL. Tel: 020-8563 0063. Fax: 020-8748 5053. E-mail: college@hwlc.ac.uk. Website: www.hwlc.ac.uk. Full-time starting September, November, January, March, May, July and August; or part-time January-June and September-March (evenings). £695. Also offer Cambridge DELTA (£850).

HANDSWORTH COLLEGE, Soho Road, Birmingham B21 9DP. Tel: 0121-551 6031. E-mail: l.webster@handsworth.ac.uk. Part-time once a year (36 weeks, 1 day per week; either Mondays 9.30am-4.30pm or Wednesdays 9.30am-4.30pm). Approximately £400 or possibility of no-fees-policy if funding available. Emphasis on ESL as well as EFL.

HARROW COLLEGE, Temple House Campus, 221-225 Station Road, Harrow, Middlesex HA1 2XL. Tel: 020-8909 6594. Fax: 020-8909 6061. E-mail: lkoten@harrow.ac.uk. Part-time courses lasting 2-3 terms. Tuesdays 9.30am-5pm. £564. No accommodation or job placement help available. Extra hours of assisting in classrooms to give more hands-on experience.

HARROW HOUSE INTERNATIONAL COLLEGE, Harrow Drive, Swanage, Dorset BH19 1PE. Tel: 01929 424421/422852. Fax: 01929 427175. E-mail: harrowhouse@mailhost.lds.co.uk. 6 courses per year. £875 inclusive. Alternatives include course plus host family full-board accommodation for £1,195 or course plus on-site full-board accommodation in single study bedroom for £980. Extensive sporting facilities available to trainees. Trainees have 24 hour access to multi-media self-access centre which has computers, videos, audio equipment and library facilities. Maximum 10 trainees per course.

HILDERSTONE COLLEGE, Broadstairs, Kent CT10 2AQ. Tel: 01843 869171. Fax: 01843 603877. E-mail: info@hilderstone.ac.uk. Website: www. hilderstone.ac.uk. UCLES CELTA and Introductory Courses in ELT at various times throughout the year with trainers of international standing. Successful candidates are given advice and contact addresses for finding work abroad. Accommodation can be arranged with local families.

HUDDERSFIELD TECHNICAL COLLEGE, New North Road, Huddersfield, West Yorkshire HD1 5NN. Tel: 01484 536521. Fax: 01484 511885. Full-time and part-time (16 weeks). £750; remission of fees arranged if in receipt of benefit. Accommodation can be arranged if necessary. Guidance offered with jobs.

Intensive School of English & Business Communication

34 Duke Street, Brighton, BN1 1BS
tel: 01273 384800 / 700666 fax: 01273 236872
email: info@ise.uk.com   web: www.ise.uk.com

Study English for IELTS, FCE, CPE, CAE, PETor Business Exams only £5 / hour.
Teach EFL? We offer Cambridge CELTA teaching qualification part time (20 weeks) or full time (4 weeks) for £850.00 inclusive. Applicants must be 20+.
Also LCCI FTBE Business Teaching Qualification FT& PT£400. Ideal for executives.
Start dates throughout the year. Locations worldwide. Contact Chris Edge at ISE.

High quality, Low price study - High quality, Low price study

INTENSIVE SCHOOL OF ENGLISH & BUSINESS COMMUNICATION, 34 Duke St, Brighton BN1 1BS. Tel: 01273 384800/700666. Fax: 01273 236872. E-mail: info@ise.uk.com. Website: www.ise.uk.com. Full-time or part-time over 20 weeks. £850 inclusive. Applicants must be 20+. Also LCCI FTBE Business Teaching qualification. Full-time and part-time. £400. Starting dates throughout the year.

INTERNATIONAL HOUSE LONDON, 106 Piccadilly, London W1J 7NL. Tel: 020-7518 6999. Fax: 020-7518 6998. E-mail: info@ihlondon.co.uk. Website: www.ihlondon.com. Full-time 4-week courses offered monthly, as well as 6 part-time courses per year. Part-time courses are for 11 weeks (Tuesday and Thursday evenings and 5 Saturdays). International House London is an educational trust and a pioneering organisation in the field of EFL. The IH World Organisation consists of 120 affiliate schools in over 30 countries around the world. Many of the affiliate schools also offer teacher training programmes (CELTA and DELTA). IH London offers a full-time 3-month DELTA and a distance training programme for the Diploma in Educational Management (ELT) in conjunction with Aston University. One-week courses TEFL Update and Discover TEFL both run four times a year. Teacher training courses for native speakers of Spanish, French, German, Italian and Japanese run 3 times a year for full-time 4-week courses and once a year for the 11-week part-time option.

INTERNATIONAL HOUSE NEWCASTLE UPON TYNE, 14-18 Stowell St, Newcastle upon Tyne NE1 4XQ. Tel: 0191-232 9551. Fax: 0191-232 1126. E-mail: ihnew@compuserve.com. Website: www.ihnew.co.uk. Full-time CELTA courses offered all year round and DELTA courses in July/August and January/February with a free 2-week extension at the end. Apply early. Accommodation can be arranged for £55 per week. Help with job hunting given.

INTERNATIONAL TEACHING AND TRAINING CENTRE (ITTC), 674 Wimborne Road, Winton, Bournemouth BH9 2EG. Tel: 01202 531355. Fax: 01202 538838. E-mail: celta-dtefla@ittc.co.uk. Website: www.ittc.co.uk. 4-weeks. Offered every month. £1069-£1,109.70 (inc. UCLES fee and VAT). Also DELTA 8-9 weeks. Three times a year. £1742.75-£1,804.75 (incl. UCLES fee and VAT). Accommodation can be arranged with a local host family at £70 per week (£76 in summer), comprising single room, half board Monday to Friday and full board at the weekend. Help with job finding through Centre website.

LANGUAGE CENTRE, York College of Further & Higher Education, Tadcaster Road, York YO2 1UA. Tel: 01904 770366. E-mail: pdupont@yorkcollege.ac.uk. Part-time evening CELTA course over 22 weeks from October. Approx. £770 including exam fees. Contact with schools abroad for posts. VSO sponsored.

LANGUAGE LINK TRAINING, 181 Earl's Court Road, London SW5 9RB. Tel: 020-7370 4755. Fax: 020-7370 1123. E-mail: languagelink@compuserve.com. Website: www.languagelink.co.uk. Monthly courses. Inclusive cost £695. Teaching practice in small groups. Can help place successful candidates in posts in Central and Eastern Europe (see *Recruitment Organisations* entry). Also offers part-time CELTA (£850) and DELTA courses.

LEEDS METROPOLITAN UNIVERSITY, Centre for Language Study, Beckett Park Campus, Leeds LS6 3QS. Tel: 0113 283 7440. Fax: 0113 274 5966. E-mail: cls@lmu.ac.uk. Website: www.lmu.ac.uk/cls. 4-week course offered 9 times per year. £615-£900. Pre-course preparation task (distance learning) and post course contact/support available including regular trainee newsletter. Informal help with placements.

University Certificate in TEFL also available. Accommodation possible by arrangement (host family). Also offer Trinity Certificate and MA Language Teaching (see listings).

MID-KENT COLLEGE, Oakwood Park, Tonbridge Road, Maidstone ME16 8AQ. Tel: 01622 691555. Fax: 01622 695049. Part-time over 2 semesters; evenings twice a week and daytimes once a week. £600.

MORAY HOUSE ENGLISH LANGUAGE CENTRE, Holyrood Road, Edinburgh EH8 8AQ. Tel: 0131-651 6332. Fax: 0131-557 5138. E-mail: ELC@mhie.ac.uk. Full-time courses.

MULTI LINGUA, Administration Centre, Abbot House, Sydenham Road, Guildford, Surrey GU1 3RL. Tel: 01483 535118. Fax: 01483 534777. E-mail: mail@multi-lingua.co.uk. Full-time 4-week certificate course held monthly. £745. Also offer full-time and part-time Multi Lingua (ML) TEFL Certificate and one-week Prep. courses(see *Academic & Other Recognised Courses* below). Successful learners are registered with Futures Recruitment. ILA vouchers accepted.

NEWCASTLE COLLEGE, ESOL Section, School of Access, Parson's Building, Rye Hill Campus, Scotswood Road, Newcastle-upon-Tyne NE4 7SA. Tel: 0191-200 4467. Fax: 0191-273 3155. E-mail: sjohnson@ncl-col.ac.uk. Part-time twice a year (1 afternoon and two evenings a week for 15 weeks starting in September or January) £795. Help may be given to find suitable college or private accommodation. Database of potential employers.

NEW COLLEGE NOTTINGHAM, Clarendon City College, The Adams Building, Stoney Street, The Lace Market, Nottingham NG1 ILJ. Tel: 0115 9104677 /9104658. Fax: 0115 9104722. E-mail: enquiries@ncn.ac.uk. Website: www.

ncn.ac.uk. Part-time 15-week, day and evening courses starting in February and September each year. £790. Full-time intensive 5-week course July and August.

NORTH TRAFFORD COLLEGE, Talbot Road, Stretford, Manchester M32 0XH. Tel: 0161-872 3731. Fax: 0161-872 7921. E-mail: admissions@northtrafford.ac.uk. 24 weeks part-time from October. £675 including exam fee.

NOTTINGHAM LANGUAGE CENTRE, Nottingham Trent University, Burton Street, Nottingham, NG1 4BU. Tel: 0115 848 6156. Fax: 0115 848 6513. E-mail: nlc.@ntu.ac.uk. Website: http://nlc.ntu.ac.uk. Full-time 4-week course twice yearly in January and July. £800. Hall of residence accommodation in July only otherwise homestay can be arranged on request. Also part-time course lasting one academic year. £500. Also offers DELTA and MA in ELT.

OXFORD BROOKES UNIVERSITY, International Centre for English Language Studies, Gipsy Lane Campus, Headington, Oxford OX3 0BP. Tel: 01865 483874. Fax: 01865 484377. E-mail: icels@sol.brookes.ac.uk. Website: www.brookes.ac. uk/sol/home/icels.html. 1 full-time course in July and 2 part-time courses during the year (2 full days and 1 evening per week). 10 weeks (end of September to early December) or 8 weeks (mid-April to mid-June). £1,115 plus £74.70 exam fee. Access to all university facilities including libraries, computers, sports centre, cafés, etc. CELTA noticeboard for jobs which is regularly updated. Lodgings list available.

OXFORD COLLEGE OF FURTHER EDUCATION, Oxpens Road, Oxford OX1 1SA. Tel: 01865 269268. Fax: 01865 240574. E-mail: Steven_Haysham@ oxfe.ac.uk. Intensive course in July. Part-time over 12 weeks: 3 mornings a week starting September, January and April. Also 2 evenings a week January to June. Both part-time and intensive course costs £775. Also offers DELTA.

PILGRIMS, Pilgrims House, Orchard Street, Canterbury, Kent CT2 2BF. Tel: 01227 762111. Fax: 01227 459027. E-mail: clientservices@pilgrims.co.uk. Courses held on University campus, 5 times a year. Self-catering accommodation in 5-bedroom on-campus house. Private room in college residence with full board also available. Pilgrims invite groups of students from abroad specifically for Cambridge teaching practice. Offer more teaching practice time than prescribed minimum. Steady stream of job offers from Europe, Asia, etc.

RANDOLPH SCHOOL OF ENGLISH, 13 Randolph Crescent, Edinburgh EH3 7TT. Tel/fax: 0131-662 8493. E-mail: randolphse@aol.com. Website: http://members. aol.com/randolphse. Full-time courses 6 times a year. £870. Accommodation can be arranged. As much assistance as possible given in finding a job.

REGENT LONDON, 12 Buckingham Street, London WC2N 6DF. Tel: 020-7872 6620. Fax: 020-7872 6630. E-mail: london@regent.org.uk. Website: www. regent.org.uk. 7 times a year. £750. Accommodation can be arranged in host families or hostels starting at £95 for a week bed and breakfast. Possibly also part-time course running for 20 weeks (2 evenings a week) from September.

REGENT OXFORD, Teacher Training, 90 Banbury Road, Oxford OX2 6JT. Tel: 01865 515566. Fax: 01865 512538. E-mail: oxford@regent.org.uk. Website: www.regent.org.uk. 12 courses a year. £750 plus VAT and registration fee. Offers more hours of input (mornings and afternoons) than many centres. Help given with job-finding, based on files of reports from ex-trainees and teachers. Opportunities for unobserved teaching at 4 levels.

ST GILES COLLEGE HIGHGATE, 51 Shepherd's Hill, Highgate, London N6 5QP. Tel: 020-8340 0828. E-mail: edtrust@stgiles1.demon.co.uk. Website: www.tefl-stgiles.com. 4-week full-time courses held monthly. Maximum 12 participants. Fees £895. Accommodation can be arranged (homestay, residence, hotel). Job counselling service. Also offers courses for Overseas Teachers of English (British Council accredited). Over 40 years' experience.

ST GILES COLLEGE BRIGHTON, 3 Marlborough Place, Brighton, Sussex BN1 1UB. Tel: 01273-682747. Fax: 01273-689808. E-mail: stgiles@pavilion.co.uk. Website: www.tefl-stgiles.com. 4-week full-time course offered 10 times a year (between September and June). Fees £895. Accommodation can be arranged with local families for £78 a week. Job counselling service. Also offers courses for Overseas Teachers of English (British Council accredited).

SAXONCOURT TEACHER TRAINING, 59 South Molton Street, London W1Y 1HH. Tel: 020-7499 8533. Fax: 020-7499 9374. E-mail: tt@saxoncourt.com. Website: www.saxoncourt.com. CELTA courses run monthly (£719). Also offer introductory TEFL course and Trinity Diploma by distance learning for Saxoncourt-contracted teachers working overseas. Saxoncourt TT is based within Shane English School in London. Shane is recognised by the British Council and is a member of ARELS. Many jobs available around the world through Saxoncourt & English Worldwide Recruitment (see *Finding a Job).*

SKOLA TEACHER TRAINING, 21 Star St, London W2 1QB. Tel: 020-7706 7676. Fax: 020-7724 2219. E-mail: skola@easynet.co.uk. Website: www.skola.co.uk. Full-time £725 and part-time £850. Course dates on website. Also offer the Cambridge CELTA Extension course in Teaching Young Learners and the DELTA. Help with recruitment occasionally available.

SOAS (School of Oriental and African Studies), University of London, English Language Unit, Thornhaugh St, Russell Square, London WC1H 0XG. Tel: 020-7898 4828. Fax: 020-7898 4829. E-mail: english@soas.ac.uk. Website: www.soas.ac.uk/elu. Full-time in summer. £880. University accommodation service can advise.

SOLIHULL COLLEGE, The Language Exchange, Solihull College, Blossomfield Road, Solihull B91 1SB. Tel: 0121-678 7172. Fax: 0121-678 7276. E-mail: pat.morris@solihull. 4-week intensive; 8-week (2½ days a week); and eleven weeks (two evenings and Saturdays). Four courses per year. £750. Accommodation can be arranged. Also offers 9-10 weeks DELTA once a year. £950.

SOUTH THAMES COLLEGE, 50 Putney Hill, London SW15 6QX. Tel: 020-8918 7354. Fax: 020-8918 7347. E-mail: denises@south-thames.ac.uk. 8-week course (daytime classes) offered in May/June, part-time evening course (20 weeks September-March) and full-time course in summer. £690 including exam fee. Bed & breakfast list may be available. Trainees receive some tuition in a foreign language. May be able to match students to individual job vacancies.

SOUTH TRAFFORD COLLEGE, Manchester Road, West Timperley, Altrincham, Cheshire WA14 5PQ. Tel: 0161-952 4720. Fax: 0161-952 4672. E-mail: language@stcoll.ac.uk. Part-time, 30-week course beginning in September. £625. Also offer 15-week CENTRA Foundation Certificate in TEFL twice a year, beginning September and January (£95). Good contacts for job placement.

SOUTHWARK COLLEGE, EFL Section, Waterloo Centre, The Cut, London SE1 8LE. Tel: 020-7815 1600. Fax: 020-7261 1301. 5-week CELTA course. £695 including moderation fee and pre-course distance learning component. Also offer Trinity CTESOL (20 weeks part-time, £685) and CEELT (10 weeks part-time, £345).

STANTON TEACHER TRAINING, Stanton House, 167 Queensway, London W2 4SB. Tel: 020-7221 7259. Fax: 020-7792 9047. E-mail: study@stanton-school.co.uk. Website: www.stanton-school.co.uk. 4-week courses every month, £682 including UCLES fee. Homestay accommodation or in nearby hostels. Fully equipped staff room for trainees. High proportion of guided lesson preparation. One jobs presentation during the course. Noticeboards of vacancies in the trainee staffroom. Bed and breakfast in local homes or hostels can be arranged.

STEVENSON COLLEGE, Bankhead Avenue, Sighthill, Edinburgh EH6 4PL. Tel: 0131-535 4700. Fax: 0131-535 4666. E-mail: info@stevenson.ac.uk. Part-time evening course September-December. Full-time course also offered.

Accommodation can be arranged with host families.

STOKE-ON-TRENT COLLEGE, Cauldon Campus, Stoke Road, Shelton, Stoke-on-Trent ST4 2DG. Tel: 01782 208208. Fax: 01782 603504. E-mail: dston@stokecoll.ac.uk. Part-time (2 afternoons and 2 evenings per week for one term) offered three times a year (starting September, February and July). £860.

STUDIO SCHOOL, 6 Salisbury Villas, Station Road, Cambridge CB1 2JF. Tel: 01223 369701. Fax: 01223 314944. E-mail: marketing@studiocambridge.co.uk. CELTA courses in March, May and September. £880. Accommodation can be arranged. Successful candidates may be offered temporary contracts.

TORBAY LANGUAGE CENTRE, Conway Road, Paignton, Devon TQ4 5LH. Tel: 01803 558555. Fax: 01803 559606. E-mail: val@teachers.freeuk.com. Full-time twice a year. £830 plus exam fee. Accommodation available in school-owned hotel or host families. Guarantee summer employment for all successful candidates.

UNIVERSITY OF DURHAM LANGUAGE CENTRE, Elvet Riverside, New Elvet, Durham, DH1 3JT. Tel: 0191-374 3716. Fax: 0191-374 7790. Intensive courses offered at Easter, in July, August and September. £890 approximately. Accommodation can be arranged from £40 p.w. for self-catering.

UNIVERSITY OF GLASGOW EFL UNIT, Hetherington Building, Bute Gardens, Glasgow G12 8RS. Tel: 0141-330 4220. Fax: 0141-339 1119. E-mail: E.Dunbar@efl.arts.gla.ac.uk. Website: www.efl.arts.gla.ac.uk. Part-time once a year (4 months) and full time once a year in July.

UNIVERSITY OF STRATHCLYDE, English Language Teaching Division, Jordanhill Campus, 76 Southbrae Drive, Glasgow G13 1PP. Tel: 0141-950 3620. Fax: 0141-950 3219. E-mail: jackie.holloway@strath.ac.uk. Full-time: February, May and June/July. Part-time: spring and summer. Cost approx £995.

UNIVERSITY OF WALES COLLEGE, NEWPORT, Allt-yr-yn Campus, P.O. Box

180, Newport NP20 5XR. Tel: 01633 432579. E-mail: jennifer.cann@ newport.ac.uk. 4 weeks at Easter, July and August. £900 approximately. Accommodation available in halls of residence (en suite and self-catering). Help with placements as far as possible.

WALTHAM FOREST COLLEGE, Forest Road, London E17 4JB. Tel: 020-8501 8091/8198. Fax: 020-8501 8001. E-mail: efl@waltham.ac.uk. Website: www.waltham.ac.uk. 1 intensive course per year (June/July) and part-time from September to March (2 evenings per week). £450 plus £200 for moderation, materials and Centre expenses. Also offer part-time DELTA from January to December.

WEST HERTS COLLEGE, Cassio Campus, Langley Road, Watford WD1 3RH. Tel: 01923 812049/812055. Fax: 01923 812053. Cambridge Cert. runs in September each year. Part-time. 23 weeks. From £700.

WESTMINSTER COLLEGE, Castle Lane, London, London SW1E 6DR. Tel: 0207-828 3771. E-mail: martin_brindle@westminster.cfe.ac.uk. 4 weeks, 7 courses per year including July. £595. Links with largest agencies for job placement. Also part-time DELTA (1 year) Jan-Dec.

WIGAN & LEIGH COLLEGE, PO Box 53, Parsons Walk, Wigan, Lancashire WN1 1RS. Tel: 01942 761563. Fax: 01942 501572. 12 week course offered twice a year. £600 plus UCLES registration. Fee remission for unemployed in receipt of benefit. Also offer Cambridge Diploma and 4 week Introduction to TESOL.

WOOLWICH COLLEGE, Villas Road, Plumstead, London SE18 7PN. Tel: 020-8488 4800 and 020-8488 4815 (direct line to course tutor). Full-time 4 times a year. 3 part-time courses per year. Course fee is £578. No accommodation provided but assistance given in finding some. Candidates get 23% tax relief if they are aged 30 plus. College Access Fund may help with part of the fee and for books and travel. At the end of each course, 2 trainees are selected to teach ESOL/EFL classes at the payment rate of £17.55 per hour. Applications to Ms Manju Dhanda, CELTA tutor and organiser.

Cambridge Certificate (CELTA) Courses Abroad

The following centres, listed alphabetically by country, offer the Cambridge Certificate course.

Australia

AUSTRALIAN TESOL TRAINING CENTRE, Level 6, 530 Oxford Street (PO Box 82), Bondi Junction, NSW 2022. Tel: 2-9389 0249. Fax: 2-9389 7788. E-mail: lynnev@ace.edu.au. Full-time (4 weeks) and part-time (12 weeks). A$2,150. Longest established and largest Cambridge Centre in Australia. Also offers 1-week introductory courses.

BUCKINGHAM COLLEGE OF ENGLISH, 21 Hindmarsh Square, 5000 Adelaide, South Australia. Tel: +61 8 83593535. Fax: +61 8 83593550. E-mail: buckingham@ice.com.au Full-time (4 weeks) and part-time (12 weeks). 6 times per year. Both full and part-time; both cost A$2,000. Accommodation provided. Recruits for overseas schools.

HOLMESGLEN LANGUAGE CENTRE, Holmesglen Institute of TAFE, PO Box 42, Chadstone, Victoria 3148. Tel: 3-9564 1820. Fax: 3-9564 1712. E-mail: lfoster@holmesglen.vic.edu.au. Full-time courses offered 6 times a year and part-time (18 weeks) 4 times a year. DELTA offered once a year over 8 months. Also offers 1-week introductory and refresher TEFL courses on demand. Accommodation can be organised with homestay families or help can be given to find short-term rental accommodation. Help is given with job placement.

HOLMES INSTITUTE TEACHER TRAINING, 185 Spring Street, Melbourne, Victoria 3000. Tel: 3-9662 2055. Fax: 3-9662 2083. E-mail: holmes@ holmescolleges.com. Website: www.holmescolleges.com. 9 full-time CELTA courses a year. A$2,150. City centre location. Accommodation available.

INSEARCH UNIVERSITY OF TECHNOLOGY, SYDNEY (UTS) Ground Floor, 10 Quay Street, PO Box K1085, Haymarket, Sydney, NSW 2000. Tel: (02) 9218 8600. Fax: (02) 9211 4334. E-mail:enquiries@insearch.edu.au. Website: www.insearch.edu.au. Full-time 8 times a year and 10-week part-time courses 4 times. A$2,370 (+GST at 10%). Homestays can be arranged. Insearch, UTS has centres in Chiang Mai, Medan, Shanghai, Shenyang, Kitakyusha, Oman and Fujairah. Preference for employment at all centres is given to Insearch, UTS CELTA graduates.
INSTITUTE OF CONTINUING & TESOL EDUCATION (ICTE), The University of Queensland, Brisbane 4072. Tel: 7-3365 6565. Fax: 7-3365 6599. E-mail: tesol.enrol@mailbox.uq.edu.au. CELTA course given 4 times a year (Jan/Feb, May/June, October/Nov) over 4 weeks. A$2,500 per course (including assessment fee). Accommodation can be arranged on request. Information given on where to obtain assistance with job placement.
INTERNATIONAL HOUSE QUEENSLAND, English Language College (Cairns), Box 7368, 130 McLeod St, Cairns, Queensland 4870. Tel: 07-40313466. Fax: 07 40313464. E-mail: admin@ihqld.com. Website: www.webcom.com/ihq. Full-time course every 4 months. AS$2,300 if booked more than a month in advance, otherwise AS$2,300. Homestays from $160 per week.
INTERNATIONAL HOUSE SYDNEY, Level 6, 58 York Street, Sydney NSW 2000. Tel: 2-9262 2886. Fax: 2-9262 2872. E-mail: nrendall@campusgroup.com.au. Website: www.ihsydney.com. Full-time in January, March, May, June, July and November. Part-time (12 weeks) starting February and August. $A2,350. Homestay accommodation can be arranged. A job club helps with CVs, contacting schools and giving advice.
LA TROBE UNIVERSITY LANGUAGE CENTRE, Bundoora, Melbourne, VIC 3083. Tel: 3-9479 1722. Fax: 3-9479 3676. E-mail: languagecentre@latrobe.edu.au. Website: www.latrobe.edu.au. Full-time 4-5 times a year. A$2,150.
MILNER INTERNATIONAL COLLEGE OF ENGLISH, 379 Hay St, Perth, Western Australia 6000. Tel: 8-9325 5444. Fax: 8-9221 2392. E-mail: milner@ wantree.com.au. Full-time courses 5 times a year. A$2,350. Flats available for A$160-200 a week, homestays for A$150 a week.
PHOENIX ENGLISH LANGUAGE ACADEMY, P.O. Box 256, Leederville, Western Australia 6903. Tel: +61 8 9227 5538. Fax: +61 8 9227 5540. E-mail: info@phoenixela.com.au Website: www.phoenixela.com.au Intensive, 4-week course, 4 times a year. AU$2,200. Homestay, hostel, apartment can be arranged on request. Session on finding work. Strong candidates will be offered work at the Phoenix depending on student numbers.
RMIT UNIVERSITY, Centre for English Language Learning, 480 Elizabeth St, Melbourne, Victoria 3000. Tel: 3-9639 0300. Fax: 3-9639 0300. E-mail: cell@rmit.edu.au. Web-site: www.training.rmit.edu.au. Full-time 4 times a year, part-time (16 weeks) twice a year. A$2,195. Homestays can be arranged.
ST. MARK'S INTERNATIONAL COLLEGE, 375 Stirling St, Perth, WA 6000. Tel: 8-9227 9888. Fax: 8-9227 9880. E-mail: academic@geosperth.com.au. Part-time (12 weeks) 4 times a year. A$2,350.
SOUTH AUSTRALIAN COLLEGE OF ENGLISH (SACE), 254 North Terrace, Adelaide, SA 5000. Tel: 8-8232 0335. Fax: 8-8223 7206. E-mail: sacecoll@camtech.net.au. Full-time and part-time courses. A$2,050.
TASMANIAN COLLEGE OF ENGLISH (SACE Hobart), 322 Liverpool Street, Hobart, Tasmania 7000, Australia. Tel: 3-6231 9911. Fax: 3-6231 9912. E-mail: sacetas@tassie.net.au. Website: www.sacecoll.sa.edu.au. Full-time 3 times a year. $A2,000 all inclusive. Accommodation must be arranged independently. Small classes. College housed in heritage mansion.

Austria

bfi VIENNA, Vocational Training Institute Vienna, Kinderspitalgasse 5, A-1090 Vienna. Tel: 1-404 35 114. Fax: 1-404 35 130. E-mail: bfi.dion@bfi-wien.or.at.

Website: www.bfi-wien.or.at. Full-time (July; 4 weeks) and part-time (February-April; 2 evenings and Saturday for 8 weeks). AS 20,000. Accommodation available at AS 4,000 per month. No help with graduate placement.

Bahrain

THE BRITISH COUNCIL, BAHRAIN, P.O. Box 452, Manama, Bahrain. Tel: 261 555. Fax: 258 689. E-mail: amanda.burrell@britishcouncil.org.bh. Part-time CELTA courses offered 2/3 times a year for 645 dinars. Contact Nick.Baguley@britishcouncil.org.bh

Canada

COLUMBIA COLLEGE, 500-555 Seymour Street, Vancouver, British Columbia V6B 6J9. Tel: 604-683-8360. Fax: 604-682-7191. E-mail: jrjanz@columbiacollege.bc.ca. Website: www.columbiacollege.bc.ca. Intensive (4 weeks) 6 times a year. C$2,500.
INTERNATIONAL LANGUAGE INSTITUTE (ILI), 5151 Terminal Rd. 8th Fl, Halifax, Nova Scotia B3J 1A1. Tel: 902-429-3636. Fax: 902-429-2900. E-mail: study@ili-halifax.com. Website: www.ili-halifax.com/celta/. Full-time, five times a year in May, June, July, August and September. US$1,500 or US$2,099 with homestay package.
KWANTLEN UNIVERSITY COLLEGE, 1266 72nd Ave. Surrey, British Columbia V3W 2M8. Tel: 604-599-2693. Fax: 604-599-2716. E-mail: celta@kwantlen.bc.ca. Website: www.kwantlen.bc.ca/esl/CELTA.htm. Kwantlen runs 4 CELTA courses (150 hours) per year, both full-time (4 weeks) and part-time (12 weeks). Help given with job placement. Courses held at the Richmond Campus, 5 minutes from the airport and a 25-minute drive from downtown Vancouver. Homestay accommodation can be arranged.
LANGUAGE STUDIES CANADA, 124 Eglinton Avenue West, Suite 400, Toronto, Ontario M4R 2G8. Tel: 416-488-2200. Fax: 416-488-2225. E-mail: celta@tor.lsc-canada.com. Website: www.lsc-canada.com. 8 intensive courses offered a year. C$2,150 plus texts. Accommodation co-ordinator assists with homestay or accommodation in residences or apartment hotels. Notice boards, addresses and contacts provided. Wheelchair accessible. Most LSC graduates gain immediate employment.

Czech Republic

INTERNATIONAL LANGUAGE CENTRES, Lupácova 1, 130 00 Prague 3. Tel: (2) 9000 2685. Fax: (2) 231 8584. E-mail: ilcprague@studygroupintl.com. Full time courses. Prices on application. Accommodation can be arranged.

Egypt

AMERICAN UNIVERSITY IN CAIRO, Centre for Adult and Continuing Education, PO Box 2511, Cairo. Tel: 2-02357 6870. Fax: 2-355 7565. www.aucegypt.edu. US enquiries to 420 Fifth Avenue, 3rd Floor, New York, NY 10018-2729 (212-730-8800/fax 212-730-1600/e-mail: aucegypt@aucnyo.edu). Full-time CELTA course. Also offer MA in Teaching English as a Foreign Language (MA/TEFL).
INTERNATIONAL HOUSE ILI, Teacher Training Department, Mohamed Bayoumi Street, off Merghany Street, Heliopolis, Cairo. Tel: (2) 291 9295 & 418 9212. Fax: (2) 415 1082. E-mail: ili@ritsec3.com.eg. Full-time courses five times a year from the beginning of February to mid-December. Also part-time (12 weeks) from mid-March to June. £575 (excluding Cambridge registration fee). Young Learners extension course offered in February and September. £295 excluding registration fee. Accommodation can be arranged in a shared flat for between £120 and £150. Trainees can be met at the airport and taken to their accommodation. For more details contact the above or International House in London (020-7518 6999).

France

STUDY GROUP INTERNATIONAL/ILC FRANCE, 13 Passage Dauphine, 75006 Paris. Tel: 1-44 41 80 20. Fax: 1-44 41 80 21. E-mail: ilcfrance@studygroupintl. com. Website: www.studygroupintl.com or www.ilcfrance.com. 4-week intensive (140 hours) courses held 9 times a year. Prices on application.

Germany

MUNCHNER VOLKSHOCHSCHULE, Fachgebiet Englisch, Postfach 80 11 64, 81611 München. Fax: 89-480 06 253. 5 week intensive course offered once a year in July/August. DM2,600. Accommodation not available. Small groups. General advice given on jobs. Opportunity for some successful trainees to work in Munich on a freelance basis. Information sent out from October preceding the course. Also offer one-week introductory Preliminary Certificate course.

Greece

MENTOR T.T., Maizonos 132, Patras. Tel: 61-335 314. Fax: 222 447. Full-time courses 3 times a year, one part-time course (one year). Some arrangements for accommodation are possible. Help given with job placements.

Hong Kong

THE BRITISH COUNCIL, HONG KONG, 3 Supreme Court Road, Admiralty, Hong Kong. Tel: 2913 5581 (Rebecca Ho). Fax: 2913 5588. E-mail: rebecca.ho@ britishcouncil.org.uk. Semi-intensive course: intensive first week followed by 8 weeks part-time (Monday evenings and Saturday mornings). 4 courses a year starting August, November, February and May. HK$19,600. Also offer Certificate in English Language Teaching to Young Learners (CELTYL). Three courses a year from September, November and May. 3 days intensive followed by 8/9 weeks part-time. HK$19,600.

Hungary

INTERNATIONAL HOUSE, Teacher Training Institute, Bimbó út 7, 1022 Budapest. Tel: +36-1-212 4010. Fax: +36-1-316 2491. E-mail: ttraining@ih.hu. Website: www.ih.hu. Full-time courses in January, February, March, May, June, July and August; part-time courses (3 evenings per week) from end of September and beginning of March. £799 includes course fee and self-catering accommodation; £999 includes the above plus return airfare from London. Also offer DELTA as well as training in teaching business English and younger learners. Assistance given with finding employment locally and abroad.

Indonesia

THE BRITISH INSTITUTE (TBI), Jl. H.R. Rasuna Said, Setiabudi Plaza, 2nd Floor, Jakarta 12920. Tel: 21-525 6750. Fax: 21-520 7574. E-mail: tchtrain@unisad.co.id Website: www.tbi Intensive 4-week courses a year. US$1,750. Also ITE (introductory course) 1 week three times a year.assistance can be provided to find local guest house accommodation.

Ireland

LANGUAGE CENTRE OF IRELAND, 45 Kildare St, Dublin 2. Tel: 1-671 6266. Fax: 1-671 6430. E-mail: info@lci.ie. Full-time and part-time (9 weeks) 3 times a year.
LANGUAGE CENTRE, UCC, The National University of Ireland, Cork. Tel: 21-902043/903225. Fax: 21-903223. 4-week intensive and 10-12 week part-time courses. IR£900. Homestay/residence available during summer intensive course, accommodation lists and advice in other cases. Noticeboard of vacancies. Part-time DELTA also available, IR £1,600.

Italy

THE CAMBRIDGE SCHOOL, Via San Rocchetto 3, 37121 Verona. Tel: 45-800 3154. Fax: 45-8014900. E-mail: info@cambridgeschool.it. 2 full-time courses in June/July and September. Part-time course January to June. Cost is 2,500,000 Lire. Help can be given with accommodation (hotel, hostel, family, apartments). Help given with finding placements for graduates.
INTERNATIONAL HOUSE – PALERMO, Via Gaetano Daita 29, 90139 Palermo. Tel: (091) 584954. Fax: (091) 323965. E-mail: ihpa1@gestelnet.it. Full-time CELTA course offered in June. £1,000. Small flats available for £200 per month. Applications early Jan-Feb. 1-year in-service DELTA course also offered. Contact P. Durden.
INTERNATIONAL HOUSE – ROME, Viale Manzoni 22, 00185 Rome. Tel: 06-704 76 894. Fax: 06-704 97 842. E-mail: ihroma.mz@ihromamz.it. Website: www.ihromamz.it. Full-time (June, July, September, February) and semi-intensive

twice a week for 3 months (October to December and March to May). 2,500,000 Lire plus exam fees. Accommodation provided if necessary for 700,000 Lire per month. Also run CELTYL and DELTA courses.

Kuwait

THE BRITISH COUNCIL, KUWAIT, PO Box 345, 13104 Safat. Tel: +965 252 0067/8. Fax: 252 0069. E-mail: annie.stewart@kwt.britishcouncil.org. Offers part-time (15 weeks) CELTA; part-time (15 weeks) CELTYL and part-time DELTA (9 months). Twice a year CELTA & CELTYL and DELTA depending on demand. Cost £1,100 (CELTA/YL) and £1,500 DELTA. Places are offered to people already resident in Kuwait because of strict visa regulations.

Lebanon

American Lebanese Language Center (ALLCS), Confidence Center, 1, Horch Tabet, Sin-el-Fil, Beirut, Lebanon. Tel: +961 1 500 978. Fax: +961 1 510 485. E-mail: allcs@inco.com.lb Website: www.allcs.edu.lb Full-time, 4-weeks course about 3 times a year. Cost US$1000. Accommodation can be arranged. The only Cambridge centre in Lebanon at time of press.

Malaysia

THE BRITISH COUNCIL, KUALA LUMPUR, The Teaching Centre, 3rd & 4th Floors, Wisma Hangsam, 1 Jalan Hang Lekir, 50000 Kuala Lumpur. Tel: 603-230 6304. Fax: 603-232 9448. E-mail: kualalumpur.tc.@britishcouncil.org.my Website: www.britishcouncil.org.my. Full-time courses (5 weeks) start in July and August. Part-time courses (10 weeks) start in January, April and September/October. Course fee each session: 4,300 ringgit.

Malta

NSTS ENGLISH LANGUAGE INSTITUTE, International Teacher Training Centre, 220 St. Paul Street, Valletta VLT07. Tel: 246628 ext. 226; fax: 230330; amarsh@nsts.org/ www.nsts.org). CELTA offered intensively in August and November and semi-intensively over 14 weeks from January. About 1400 Euros for tuition only (120 hours). Low cost self-catering accommodation available.

Netherlands

BRITISH LANGUAGE TRAINING CENTRE, Oxford House, N.Z. Voorburgwal 328E, 1012 RW Amsterdam. Tel: (20) 622 36 34. Fax: (20) 626 49 62. E-mail: bltc@bltc.nl. Website: www.bltc.nl. 4-week full-time course offered once a year, and 12-week part-time course twice a year. 3,700 guilders. Wide mix of approaches, including business and one-to-one sessions. Advice on job-finding.

New Zealand

AUCKLAND LANGUAGE CENTRE, PO Box 105035, Auckland. Tel: 9-303 1962. Fax: 9-307 9219. E-mail: akldlang@ihug.co.nz. 4 full-time courses per year. Courses didn't run 2000/1.

CAPITAL LANGUAGE ACADEMY, PO Box 1100, Wellington (Street address: 49-51 Courtenay Place, Wellington). Tel +64-4-801 6010. Fax: 4-385 6655. E-mail: 100245.13@compuserve.com. 4 times a year. NZ$2,700. Homestay accommodation can be arranged.

ILA SOUTH PACIFIC LTD., PO Box 25-170, 21 Kilmore Street, Christchurch. Tel: 3-379 5452. Fax: 3-379 5373. E-mail: Julie van Dyk on staffch@ila.co.nz. Website: www.ila.co.nz. 5 CELTA courses a year (January, February, June, October, November). Homestay or bed and breakfast accommodation can be arranged.

LANGUAGES INTERNATIONAL, 27 Princes St (PO Box 5293), Auckland 1. Tel: 9-309 0615. Fax: 9-377 2806. E-mail: success@langsint.co.nz. Website: www. langsint.co.nz. 5 times a year. NZ$2,850. Also offers DELTA course part-time.

UNIVERSITY OF WAIKATO LANGUAGE INSTITUTE, PO Box 1317, Waikato Mail Centre, Hamilton. Tel: 7-838 4193. Fax: 7-838 4194. E-mail: language@ waikato.ac.nz. Full-time 2-3 times a year (mid-June to mid-July and mid-November to mid-December). NZ$2,850. Hostel accommodation available on campus (though course is run off-campus). Employment session at end of course. University also offers postgraduate MA and Diploma of Second Language Teaching.

Oman

BRITISH COUNCIL, PO Box 73, Postal Code 115, Medinat Sultan Qaboos. Tel: 600548 ext 221. Fax: 698018. E-mail: frances.hughes@om.britishcouncil.org. Intensive course (4 weeks) and part-time course (3 days a week for 10 weeks), both 4 times a year. Also Young Learners course and DELTA (one a year).
POLYGLOT INSTITUTE, PO Box 221 (Postal Code 112), Ruwi. Tel: 701261. Fax: 794602. Part-time (10 weeks) twice a year. Accommodation can be arranged.

Poland

ELS-BELL SCHOOL OF ENGLISH, ul. Polanki 110, 80-308 Gdansk, Poland. Tel/fax: 48 58-554 83 82. Fax: 58 554 83 88. E-mail: elsbell@poczta.onet.pl. CELTA 4 weeks in June/July. Approx. £700. Part-time DELTA available October-May. £1,090. Accommodation can be arranged on request. Help given with job placement.
INTERNATIONAL HOUSE KATOWICE, Part of IH Teacher Training Centre in Wroclaw. All correspondence to: Teacher Training Centre, International House, Lesczy skiego 3, 50-078 Wroclaw. Tel/fax: +48 (71) 78 17 293 or 372 36 98. E-mail: ttcentre@id.pl. Website: www.ih.com.pl.

INTERNATIONAL HOUSE KRAKOW, ul. Pilsudskiego 6, 31-109 Kraków. Tel: +48 (12) 421 94 40/422 64 82. Fax: +48 (12) 430 10 00. E-mail: admin@ih.pl. Website: www.ih.pl. Longest-established Cambridge training centre in Poland offering intensive CELTA courses all year round. £640 plus UCLES registration fee of £75. Accommodation available for £120 per month. Pass rate in 2000 was 96%. Successful graduates are often offered posts with the school. Also offer DELTA full-time (8 weeks March to May) and part-time (22 weeks); cost is £890 plus UCLES examination fee of £190.
INTERNATIONAL HOUSE/CJO WROCLAW, Teacher Training Centre, ul. Leszczy skiego 3, 50-078 Wroclaw. Tel/fax: +48 (0)71 78 17 293 or 372 3698. E-mail: ttcentre@id.pl. Website: www.ih.com.pl. 4-week intensive CELTA course in August. Cambridge YL extension course (2 weeks intensive) Jan/Feb, June and September. Teaching English for Business (TEB) Jan/Feb, June and September. Cambridge DELTA (9 week intensive) March-May, July-August. For CELTA candidates, flight allowance paid if subsequently employed by IH/CJO schools in Wroclaw, Katowice, Opole or Bielsko-Biala.

Teacher Training in Wroclaw, Poland

Camb/RSA: CELTA (4 wk), **DELTA** (9 wk). **YL** young learners extension (2 wk).
Other courses: Teaching English for Business (1 wk). **DoS Skills** (1 wk).
Discounts for candidates working at IH Wroclaw, Katowice, Opole, Bielsko-Biala.
Accommodation provided.

TT Centre, International House, ul. Leszczynskiego 3, 50-078 Wroclaw, Poland.
☎ Phone/Fax: +48 71 372 3698.   **E-mail:** ttcentre@id.pl
Website: http://www.ih.com.pl

Portugal

INTERNATIONAL HOUSE LISBON, Rua Marquês Sá da Bandeira 16, 1050-148
Lisbon. Tel: (21) 315 1496. Fax: (21) 353 0081. E-mail: ihlisbon@mail.telepac.pt.
CELTA and CELTYL courses 8 times a year. 210,000 escudos. Also part-time
DELTA course (300,000 escudos) and TEFL introduction courses (see listing).

TEACHER TRAINING
IN LISBON

RSA/CAMBRIDGE CELTA
RSA/CAMBRIDGE CELTYL
RSA/CAMBRIDGE DELTA

 **International House
Teacher Training**

International House Lisbon has been training teachers since
1972 and has acquired a well-deserved reputation for the
professionalism of its trainers, the friendliness of its staff and
the excellence of its results.

Enquiries: International House Teacher Training
International House
Rua Marqês Sa da Bandeira 16 - 1050 Lisbon
Tel: (35121) 3151496   Fax: (35121) 3530081
E-mail: ihlisbon@mail.telepac.pt   Website: www.international-house.com

Russia

BKC-INTERNATIONAL HOUSE MOSCOW, Teacher Training Centre, Tverskaya
str. 9, building 4, Moscow 103009. Tel: (95) 234 03 14. Fax: (95) 234 03 16. E-mail:
t-training@bkc.ru. Website: www.bkc.ru. Full-time CELTA courses (4 weeks) 3-4
times a year. DELTA also available. Accommodation can be arranged on request.
Job opportunities for successful trainees.

Singapore

THE BRITISH COUNCIL SINGAPORE, Holland Village, 362 Holland Road, Singapore 278696. Tel: 463 5525. Fax: 463 2970. E-mail: pctcr.andrews@britishcouncil.org.sg. Website: www.britishcouncil.org.sg. Part-time: 2 full days per week for 10 weeks. £1,000. Not open to people on a Social Visit Pass and not possible to get a Student Pass for teacher training courses. 20-hour Introductory courses also offered.

South Africa

THE ENGLISH CENTRE, DURBAN, 21 Nunhead Road, Manor Gardens, Durban (Postal Address: Box 50800, Musgrave, Durban 4062). Tel: 31-261 9445. Fax: 31-261 9474. E-mail: info@englishcentre.co.za. Website: www.englishcentre.co.za. Full-time courses 3 times a year. Also introductory TEFL course run on demand. Accommodation organised as required. Centre will suggest places to look for employment.
LANGUAGE LAB INTERNATIONAL HOUSE, 54 De Korte Street, Braamfontein, Johannesburg 2001. Tel: 11-339 1051. Fax: 11-403 1759. E-mail: langlab@icon.co.za. Full-time 3 times a year in February, June and November. R7,200 (increases expected as rand loses value). Accommodation can be provided.
SHANE ENGLISH SCHOOL/INTERNATIONAL HOUSE, Windermere, Portswood Business Park V & A Waterfront, P.O. Box 52199, 8002 Cape Town. Tel: 27 21 4198524. Fax: 27 21 4198527. E-mail: info@ihcapetown.co.sa. Website: www. ihcapetown.co.sa. 4-weeks intensive. Offered three times a year (March/April, June/July, Oct./Nov.). 7,200 rand. Accommodation can be arranged. Help with placement.

Spain

TEFLA in MADRID

THE BRITISH LANGUAGE CENTRE, MADRID, SPAIN

A friendly, supportive and professional environment in which to follow an English language teacher training course. We have trained over 1500 teachers on a variety of courses.

We offer the RSA/Cambridge Certificate & Diploma in ELT, both full and part time, all the year round.

There are also a variety of other specialised training courses for teachers of English as well as Spanish language courses.

Advice and help are given if looking for a teaching post and accommodation is provided.

Enquiries to: The Director, Teacher Education,
The British Language Centre,
Calle Bravo Murlito, 377, 2,
28020 Madrid, Spain

Tel: (00 34) 91 733 0739   Fax: (00 34) 91 314 5009
E-mail: ted.blc@cospa.es   www.cospa.es/blc/

THE BRITISH LANGUAGE CENTRE, Calle Bravo Murillo 377-2°, 28020 Madrid. Tel: 91-733 07 39. Fax: 91-314 50 09. E-mail: ted.blc@cospa.es. Website: www.cospa.es/blc. Full-time 4 weeks and part-time (12 weeks) CELTA and DELTA all year round. 160,000 pesetas. Help given with accommodation (approximately 40,000 pesetas a month). Also offer Cambridge Diploma course and intro courses (see listings) plus LCCI Business English Teaching Course.

CAMPBELL COLLEGE, Teacher Training Centre, Calle Pascual y Genis, 14-4a, 46002 Valencia. Tel/fax: 96-352 4217. E-mail: campbell@cpsl.com. Website: www.cpsl.com/campbell. Cambridge CELTA 4-week courses in February, May, July and November. Also Diploma Courses. Accommodation and job placement services.

CLIC INTERNATIONAL HOUSE SEVILLE, Teacher Training Department, Méndez Núñez 7, 41001 Seville. Tel: (95) 450 0316. Fax: (95) 450 0836. E-mail: clic@clic.es. Website: www.clic.es. 4-week intensive Cambridge CELTA courses all year round. Price 180,000 pesetas. Accommodation service available. Lectures and personal help on job placement. Also offer Cambridge DELTA and CELTYL courses.

INTERNATIONAL HOUSE BARCELONA, Calle Trafalgar 14, 08010 Barcelona. Tel: 93-268 4511. Fax: 93-268 0239. E-mail: training@bcn.ihes.com. Website: www.ihes.com/bcn. Full-time throughout the year and one part-time course. 189,000 pesetas. Help given with accommodation.

INTERNATIONAL HOUSE MADRID, C/ Zurbano 8, 28010 Madrid. Tel: (91) 310 1314. Fax: (91) 308 5321. E-mail: ttraining@ihmadrid.es Website: www.ihmadrid.es/ Full-time CELTA courses offered May, June, July, and September; part-time (3 months) courses January to March, April to June and October to December. 180,000 pesetas. Also offers CELTYL and DELTA full-time

(2 months) and part-time (6 months) costing 235,000 pesetas plus exam fee. Post course employment service offered.

Switzerland

THE BELL SCHOOL, GENEVA, 12 Chemin des Colombettes, 1202 Geneva. Tel: +41 22-740 20 22. Fax: +41 22-740 20 44. Full-time in Geneva and Zurich. Part-time courses also offered.

UNIVERSITY OF BERN Department of Applied Linguistics (AAL), Unitobler, 3000 Bern 9. Tel +41 31 631 83 91. Fax: +41 31 631 36 03. E-mail: murray@aal.unibe.ch Website: www.aal.unibe.ch/englisch/CELTA.html.
One-month full-time (July) and 6 months part-time (January to June). SFr 3,700. No accommodation. Placement assistance for those with a Swiss work permit.

VOLKSHOCHSCHULE, ZURICH, Splügenstrasse 10, 8002 Zurich. Tel: 1-205 84 94. Fax: 1-205 84 85. E-mail: vhszh@access.ch. Website: www.vhszh.ch. 16-week part-time courses twice a year. No assistance is possible with gaining residence or working permission, nor can accommodation be provided. Contact John Potts (CELTA Course Director).

Thailand

ECC (THAILAND), 430/17-24 Chula Soi 64, Siam Square, Bangkok 10330. Tel: 2-253 3312. Fax: 2-254 2243. E-mail: academic@eccthai.com. Website: www.eccthai.com. 5 full-time courses per year. US$1,200. Central Bangkok guest houses cost 400-700 Baht per night. CELTA graduates are offered full-time teaching contracts with ECC at one of their 50 branches in Bangkok and throughout the country. ECC offers other short courses: Teaching English to Young Learners and Teaching Business English.

Turkey

THE BRITISH COUNCIL, IZMIR, Teachers' Centre, 1374 Sokak No. 18, Selvili Is Merkezi K3, 35210 Cankaya-Izmir. Tel: 23-2446 0131. Fax: 23-2446 0130. E-mail: steve.darn@britcoun.org.tr. Four week full-time course from mid-June, £900 including exam fee.
THE ENGLISH PREPARATORY SCHOOL, Eastern Mediterranean University, PO Box 95, Gazi Magusa, Mersin 10. Tel: 392-630 1426/1330. Fax: 392-365 1634. E-mail: john.eldridge@emu.edu.tr. Website: www.eps.emu.edu.tr Part-time course (October to June) run annually. £750. Also offer DELTA course (£1,250). Accommodation not provided, but available. Help with job placement, and possibility of work within school for best candidates. Jobs may be offered to the best candidates. Also hold annual ELT conference in February.
INTERNATIONAL TRAINING INSTITUTE, Istiklal Cad., Kallavi Sokak 7-9, Kat. 4, Galatasaray, Istanbul, Turkey. Tel: 212-243 2888. Fax: 212-245 3163. E-mail: iti_ist@yahoo.com. 4-week intensive course in July. 2 part-time courses per year (10 weeks). £900. Job placement service. Other courses CELTYL, DELTA, ELT Management, Drama in ELT.

United Arab Emirates

THE BRITISH COUNCIL, ABU DHABI, PO Box 46523, Abu Dhabi. Tel: 2-659300. Fax: 2-6664340. E-mail: iain.mackie@britishcouncil.org.ae. Intensive (4 weeks) once or twice a year. No accommodation.

Uruguay

QUEEN VICTORIA INSTITUTE, Libertad 2791, Montevideo, CP 11300, Uruguay. Tel: +598 2 7082577. Fax: +598 2 7080943. E-mail: qvi@adinet.com.uy Website: www.queenvictoria.com.uy CELTYL (Certificate in English Language Teaching to Young Learners). Full-time course (4 weeks February and July)); part-time course (8 months from the end of April to the end of November). Cost US$1750. Hotel or hostel accommodation or with a host family. Can help place graduates.

USA

ELC@Language Exchange, 1 East Broward Blvd, Suite 303W, Fort Lauderdale, FL 33301. Tel: 954-525-9100. Fax: 954-525-9188. E-mail: tefltraining@hotmail.com. Website: www.tefltraining.com. 7 intensive courses per year in groups of 10. $2,100.
EMBASSY CES, The Center for English Studies, 330 Seventh Avenue, New York, NY 10001. Tel: 212-629-7300. Fax: 212-736-7950. E-mail: ahaber@studygroupintl.com. Website: www.studygroupintl.com. Seven full-time courses per year. $2,325. Accommodation in student residences and bed and breakfasts. Job counselling given.
INTERNATIONAL HOUSE SAN FRANCISCO, 49 Powell Street, 2nd Floor, San Francisco CA 94102. Tel: 415-989-4473. Fax: 415-989-4440. E-mail: teachertraining@ih-portland.com. Website: www.ih-usa.com. Full-time 4-week course. Half board homestay accommodation $195 per week. Application through Portland IH (see next page).
INTERNATIONAL HOUSE – TEACHER TRAINING USA, 200 SW Market Street, Suite 111, Portland, OR 97201. Tel: 503-224-1960. Fax: 503-224-2041. E-mail: teachertraining@ih-portland.com. Website: www.ih-usa.com. Also IH Teacher Training USA, 320 Wilshire Blvd, Third Floor, Santa Monica, CA 90401. Tel: 310-394-8618. Fax: 310-394-2708. Also at 2725 Congress Street, Suite 2M, San Diego, CA 92110. Tel: 619-299-2339. Fax: 619-299-0235. Full-time 4-week CELTA courses run 6-8 times a year. $2,150. Half-board homestay accommodation arranged for $150-$185 per week, or apartments available in Portland or Santa Monica. Help with job placement worldwide given. Applications for all IH locations should be sent to the Portland centre. Portland centre also offers the

DELTA (12 weeks full-time US$4,145) and methodology and language courses for non-native teachers.

ST GILES LANGUAGE TEACHING CENTER, One Hallidie Plaza, Suite 350, San Francisco, CA 94102. Tel: 415-788-3552. Fax: 415-788-1923. E-mail: sfstgiles@slip.net. Website: www.stgiles-usa.com. Full-time, four-week courses, ten times a year. Twelve-week, part-time courses twice yearly. $2,695. Trainees are eligible for a graduate credit recommendation of six hours (MA TESOL) and lifelong job assistance. Contact the Director of Teacher Training.

Trinity College London Certificate (TESOL) Courses

All courses last four weeks full-time unless otherwise stated. The Trinity College moderation fee is fixed by individual course providers, though is usually £80.

ABERDEEN COLLEGE, Gallowgate, Aberdeen AB25 1BN. Tel: 01224 612000. Fax: 01224 612001. Part-time September-March; 6-9 hours per week.
BASINGSTOKE COLLEGE OF TECHNOLOGY, Worting Road, Basingstoke, Hants. RG21 8TN. Tel: 01256 354141. Direct line to Languages Dept: 01256-306350. Fax: 01256 306444. E-mail: annabel.stowe@bcot.ac.uk. Website: www.bcot.ac.uk/content/businessservices/languageservices.htm. Intensive course once a year in July. Part-time from September/October for 6 months, either one day a week or two evenings a week. £675. Accommodation with host families if necessary. Links with local firms requiring ESP and local summer schools for EFL.
BLACKPOOL & THE FYLDE COLLEGE, Ashfield Road, Bispham, Blackpool, Lancashire FY2 0HB. Tel: 01253 352352. Fax: 01253 356127. E-mail: visitors@blackpool.ac.uk. Part-time once a year: 3 hours a week for 30 weeks. £550. Access to job offers received in School.
BOLTON COLLEGE, Manchester Road, Bolton BL2 1ER. Tel: 01204 531411. Fax: 01204 380774. Part-time, one evening a week from September to June with teaching practice (using 4 levels of language classes) during the day. £500 plus moderation fee of £80.
BRACKNELL & WOKINGHAM COLLEGE, Montague House, Broad Street, Wokingham, Berks. RG40 1AU. Tel: 0118 978 2728. Fax: 0118 989 4315. E-mail: colette.galloway@bracknell.ac.uk. Part-time (32 weeks, over a third of which is observation and practice teaching of EFL students on-site). £650 (including exam fee). Also, part-time Trinity College Diploma course over 22 weeks; £400 (excluding exam fee).
BRADFORD COLLEGE, English Language Centre, Old Building, Great Horton Road, Bradford BD7 1AY. Tel: 01274 753207. Fax: 01274 741553. E-mail: elc@bilk.ac.uk. Website: www.bilk.ac.uk. Full-time courses offered 4 times a year, part-time courses (30 weeks) once a year. £700. Accommodation available in host

family (half-board or self catering) and in halls of residence. Voluntary placements before going abroad, and jobs notice-board with regular bulletins.

BURY COLLEGE, Peel Centre, Market Street, Bury, Lancs. BL9 OEE. Tel: 0161-280 8280. Fax: 0161-280 8228. E-mail: information@burycollege.ac.uk or david.marrs@burycollege.ac.uk. Website: www.burycollege.ac.uk. Part-time evening course (Thursdays 6-9pm) September to Easter or January to June. Approx. £625 plus moderation fee of £75.

CICERO LANGUAGES INTERNATIONAL, 42 Upper Grosvenor Road, Tunbridge Wells, Kent TN1 2ET. Tel: 01892 547077. Fax: 01892 522749. E-mail: enrolments@cicero.co.uk. 4-week courses in January, February, March, May, September, October and November. Half-board accommodation with local families. Links with language schools abroad.

CITY COLLEGE MANCHESTER, Fielden Centre, 141 Barlow Moor Road, West Didsbury, Manchester M20 2PQ. Tel: 0161-957 1660. Fax: 0161-434 0443. E-mail: aspencer@ccm.ac.uk. Part-time course over 12, 16 or 30 weeks. Full-time: 4 weeks in Manchester, or 2-3 weeks in Manchester followed by 2 weeks in Spain or Greece.

COLCHESTER INSTITUTE, Sheepen Road, Colchester, Essex CO3 3LL. Tel: 01206 518765/518187/518713. Fax: 01206 763041 (Attn. TEFL Admissions) /518187/518186. E-mail: efl@colch-inst.ac.uk. 3 Certificate courses per year, 9 weeks intensive F/T attendance plus 4 weeks of distance learning. Accommodation in Colchester can be arranged.

COVENTRY TESOL CENTRE, Coventry Technical College, Butts, Coventry CV1 3QD. Tel: 01203 526742. Fax: 01203-526743. E-mail: language@covcollege.ac.uk Full-time 8 times a year; part-time over the academic year. £695 including moderation fee. Accommodation can be arranged through college accommodation office. Also offer Trinity Cert. courses in Czech Republic, Hungary, Spain, Poland and Turkey. Same fee plus £300 for accommodation overseas. Also, flexible distance learning Diploma course.

DARLINGTON COLLEGE OF TECHNOLOGY, Cleveland Avenue, Darlington, Co. Durham DL3 7BB. Tel: 01325 503050. Fax: 01325 503000. E-mail: intoffice@darlington.ac.uk. Website: www.darlington.ac.uk. Part-time (36 weeks starting in January). £211 plus moderation fee. List of local homestays/flats available. Foreign language offered as part of course.

EF ENGLISH FIRST TEACHER TRAINING, 1-3 Farman Street, Hove, East Sussex BN1 3AL. Tel: 01273 747308. Fax: 01273 746742. E-mail: e1recruitment@ef.com. Website: www.ef.com. 4-week course offered monthly. Optional fifth week focusing on teaching abroad, business English and teaching young learners, together with additional teaching practice if desired. Cost £850. EF aims to recruit successful trainees from the course to work for EF schools worldwide (see *Recruitment Organisations*).

GATESHEAD COLLEGE, Durham Road, Gateshead NE9 5BN. Tel: 0191-490 0300. Fax: 0191-490 2313. E-mail: cynthia.hall@gateshead.ac.uk (administrator). Website: www.gateshead.ac.uk. Part-time September to May (evenings).

GOLDERS GREEN TEACHER TRAINING CENTRE, 11 Golders Green Road, London NW11 8DE. Tel: 020-8731 0963. Fax: 020-8455 6528. E-mail: ggcol@easynet.co.uk. Website: www.goldersgreen-college.co.uk. Courses offered: five-week full-time courses of 175 hours. Courses run in Oxford Street and Golders Green centres every six weeks throughout the year. Part-time thirteen-week evening courses March and September. Price £645 plus moderation fee of £77.50. Accommodation available: £70-80 per week. Excellent job placement service for all graduates. Contact: Dig Hadoke, Course Director.

GROVE HOUSE LANGUAGE CENTRE, Carlton Avenue, Greenhithe, Kent DA9 9DR. Tel: 01322 386826. Fax: 01322 386347; E-mail: Grovehouse@btinternet.com. 4 weeks. Three to four courses offered per year. Cost £875. Accommodation can be arranged with host family, hotel or guest house. Accommodation arranged.

GUILDFORD COLLEGE, Stoke Park, Guildford GU1 1EZ. Tel: 01483 448500. Fax: 01483-448600. E-mail: info@guildford.ac.uk. Website: www.guildford.ac.uk.

Part-time: one evening per week over one year, or one day a week over six months. Cost £450 plus £30 for books and photocopying. No accommodation, nor graduate placement.
HOPWOOD HALL COLLEGE, Rochdale Campus, St. Mary's Gate, Rochdale OL12 6RY. Tel: 01706 345346/freephone 0800 834297. Fax: 01706 641426. E-mail: enquiries@hopwood.ac.uk. Web-site: www.hopwood.ac.uk. Part-time (30 weeks) once a year. Starts September.
HULL COLLEGE, School of Humanities, Languages & EFL, Park Street Centre, Hull HU2 8RR. Tel: 01482 329943. Fax: 01482 598989. E-mail: wchan@hull-college.ac.uk. 15 hours a week for 10 weeks plus 1 reading week offered termly. £250.
INLINGUA TEACHER TRAINING & RECRUITMENT, Rodney Lodge, Rodney Road, Cheltenham, Glos. GL50 1JF. Tel: 01242 253171. Fax: 01242 253181. E-mail: recruitment@inlingua-cheltenham.co.uk. Website: www.inlingua-cheltenham.co.uk. Full-time 5 week courses offered year round, and part-time course over 33 weeks. Each costs £895 plus £77.50 moderation fee. Applicants are interviewed in person. Most successful applicants find work through inlingua's recruitment service which places teachers in schools worldwide (see *Finding a Job*).

INTERNATIONAL LANGUAGE INSTITUTE/ILI, County House, Vicar Lane, Leeds LS1 7JH. Tel: 0113 242 8893. Fax: 0113 234 7543. E-mail: 101322.1376@compuserve.com. 5-week full-time course offered once a year from November. £874. Half-board accommodation available. More than half of 130 hour course consists of teaching practice.
INTERNATIONAL TRAINING NETWORK, Exchange Buildings, Upper Hinton Road, Bournemouth, Dorset BH1 2HH. Tel/fax: 01202 789689. E-mail: itnet@globulnet.co.uk. Website: www.users.globalnet.co.uk/~itnet. Intensive 5-week course offered 7 times a year. Family accommodation with half-board can be arranged. Specifically train Christians who want to go into the mission field as TEFL teachers. Assistance with job placement given. Also one-week introductory courses. Courses also in Poland and Australia.
ITS ENGLISH SCHOOL, HASTINGS, 43-45 Cambridge Gardens, Hastings, East Sussex TN34 1EN. Tel: 01424 438025. Fax: 01424 438050. E-mail: itsbest@its-hastings.co.uk. Intensive 5-week courses offered with family accommodation. Also offer Trinity Diploma, part distance learning, part attendance and courses for foreign teachers of English.
JOSEPH PRIESTLEY COLLEGE, Alec Beevers Centre, Burton Avenue, Leeds, W. Yorks. LS11 5ER. Tel: 0113 307 6002 1994. Fax: 0113 271 3456. E-mail: hhartmann@joseph-priestley.ac.uk Courses vary but usually there is an intensive 5-week course in summer and a semi-intensive (13-week) course twice a year starting at the end of October and the end of February. £565.

KENT SCHOOL OF ENGLISH, 3 Granville Road, Broadstairs, Kent CT10 1QD. Tel: 01843 874870. Fax: 01843 860418. E-mail: enquiries@kentschool.co.uk. Intensive twice a year. £690. Host family or guest house accommodation can be arranged.
LANGSIDE COLLEGE GLASGOW, 50 Prospecthill Road, Glasgow G42 9LB. Tel: 0141-649 4991/2256. Fax: 0141-632 5252. E-mail: tfoster@perseus.langside.ac.uk. Part-time over academic year. £500 plus moderation fee. Also offer part-time Trinity Diploma. Help with job placement. Also offer part-time introduction to TESOL. Non-graduates accepted onto course, provided they show good language awareness and well-developed interpersonal skills.
LANGUAGE LINK TRAINING, 181 Earl's Court Road, London SW5 9RB. Tel 020-7370 4755. Fax 020-7370 1123. E-mail: languagelink@compuserve.com. Website: www.languagelink.co.uk. Intensive courses held monthly. £723 plus moderation fee. Teaching practice in small groups. Can help place successful candidates in posts in Central and Eastern Europe (see Recruitment Organisation entry). Also offers CELTA, 1-week Introduction to TEFL and 1 or 2-week booster course for non-native English teachers 3 times a year.
THE LANGUAGE PROJECT, 78-80 Colston Street, Bristol BS1 5BB. Fax: 0117-907 7181. Tel: 0117 927 3993. E-mail: administration@langproj.demon.co.uk. Website: www.languagewise.com. 5-week, full-time intensive course 4/5 times a year beginning January, March, June, September and October. £900 including moderation. Also Diploma course £900 plus exam fee full-time (10 weeks) or £550 plus exam fee part-time (20 weeks). Help with placement worldwide. Also offer introduction to TEFL/TESL

LANGUAGES TRAINING & DEVELOPMENT – see West Oxon. Training Services
LEEDS METROPOLITAN UNIVERSITY, Centre for Language Study, Beckett Park Campus, Leeds LS6 3QS. Tel: 0113 283 7440. Fax: 0113 274 5966. E-mail: cls@lmu.ac.uk. Website: www.lmu.ac.uk/cls. Part-time, 1 academic year (i.e. once

a year) £400-£500. University Certificate in TEFL also available. Also offer CELTA and MA Language Teaching (see listings).

LEWES TERTIARY COLLEGE, Mountfield Road, Lewes, East Sussex BN7 2XH. Tel: 01273 483188. Fax: 01273 477692. E-mail: info@lewescollege.ac.uk. Website: www.lewescollege.ac.uk. 26-week part-time course (Tuesday evenings plus 6 Saturday sessions), held once a year. £590, with 20% discount for students in receipt of benefits. No accommodation.

LONDON STUDY CENTRE, Munster House, 676 Fulham Road, London SW6 5SA. Tel: 0207-731 3549/731 1200. Fax: 0207-731 6060/731. E-mail: english_language@compuserve.com. Website: www.londonstudycentre.com. Full-time (5 weeks) throughout the year and part-time (15 weeks) starting January, May and September. £800. Course and career counselling. Accommodation advice available.

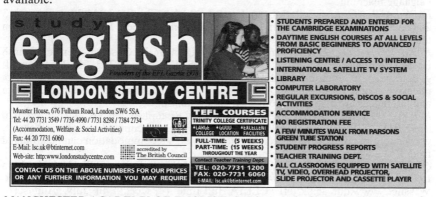

MANCHESTER ACADEMY OF ENGLISH, St Margaret's Chambers, 5 Newton St, Manchester M1 1HL. Tel: 0161-237 5619. Fax: 0161-237 9016. E-mail: english@manacad.co.uk. Website: www.manacad.co.uk. City centre English language school accredited by the British Council. Four and a half week intensive courses leading to Trinity Certificate in TESOL ofered six times a year; cost £799 plus moderation fee. Accommodation can be provided: homestay (with full board) £87.50 per week, half board £80, or (July and August only) city centre self-catering in student hall £65 per week.

MANCHESTER COLLEGE OF ARTS AND TECHNOLOGY, Department of Language Studies, Lower Hardman St. Manchester M3 3ER. Tel: 0161-953 2266. Fax: 0161-953 2259. E-mail: sheila_greenhalgh@mancat.ac.uk. Part-time September to May (Tuesday and Thursday evenings 6-8pm). £615. Course run in established FE college with many foreign students. Help given with job placement.

MIDDLESBROUGH COLLEGE, Kirby Campus, Roman Road, Linthorpe, Middlesbrough, TS5 5PJ. Tel: 01642 333333. Fax: 01642 333310. E-mail: r.smith@mbro.ac.uk. Website: www.mbro.ac.uk. Part-time course once a year (3 hours a week).

NORTHAMPTON COLLEGE, Military Road, Northampton NN1 3ET. Tel: 01604 734170/2. Fax: 01604 734183. Part-time once a year September to June (Tuesday evenings 6pm-9pm plus 4 Saturdays). £468 plus moderation fee (approx. £75).

NORTHBROOK COLLEGE SUSSEX, Modern Languages Department, Littlehampton Road, Goring-by-Sea, West Sussex BN12 6NU. Tel: 01903 606243. Fax: 01903 606207. E-mail: s.sscowen@nbcol.ac.uk. Website: www.northbrook.ac.uk. Full-time starting January, March, June, July September and October; part-time (Thursday evenings 6-9pm) starting January, April and September. TESOL cost £532. College also offers Preparatory courses (see listing in *Introductory Courses*).

OAKLANDS COLLEGE, St Albans City Campus, St Peters Road, St Albans, Herts. AL1 3RX. Tel: 01727 737000. Fax: 01727 737273. E-mail: helen.day@

oaklands.ac.uk. Intensive courses (5 weeks), semi-intensive (12 weeks) and part-time evening courses (36 weeks). Also offer Licentiate Diploma. Accommodation service available.

OXFORD HOUSE COLLEGE, 28 Market Place, Oxford Circus, London W1W 8AW. Tel: 020-7580 9785. Fax: 020-7323 4582. E-mail: tesol@oxfordhouse.co.uk. Website: www.oxford-house-college.ac.uk. Large Trinity college validated centre offering TESOL courses full-time (4 weeks) or part-time (13 weeks). 4-week course offered in London, and locations abroad, currently Barcelona and Tuscany. The Trinity Diploma course (for experienced teachers only) is also offered, by distance learning or part-time in London (13 weeks). Jobs board shows job vacancies. Graduates of the college are given discounts on further courses and free membership of the Oxford House Club, which organises monthly seminars in London on English language teaching.

PARK LANE COLLEGE, Park Lane, Leeds LS3 1AA. Tel: 0113 244 3011. Fax: 0113 244 6372. Part-time (September-June); 1 afternoon per week. £380 plus moderation fee.

PLYMOUTH COLLEGE OF FURTHER EDUCATION, Goschen Centre, Saltash Rosas, Plymouth PL1 2BD. Tel: 01752 305277. Fax: 01752 305065. E-mail: ggodfrey@pcfe.plymouth.ac.uk. Part-time September to June. £998.75. Also, intensive course in June £950. Accommodation can be arranged if required. Advice and references are also given to help with job hunting.

POLYGLOT LANGUAGE CENTRE, 214 Trinity Road, London SW17 7HP. Tel: 020 8767 9113. Fax: 020 8767 9104. E-mail: polyglot@compuserve.com. Website: www.polyglot.co.uk. Courses run 6-7 times a year. Accommodation can be arranged from £70 a week.

QUEEN'S UNIVERSITY OF BELFAST TEFL CENTRE, Belfast BT7 1NN, Northern Ireland. Tel: 028 9033 5373/4. Fax : 028-9033 5379. E-mail: tefl@qub.ac.uk. Website: www.qub.ac.uk/tefl. CELTA full-time (4 weeks) in July, August or September and part-time (4 months) September to January or February to June. Also offer DELTA (12 weeks full-time or 9 months part-time), £1,300 and MA (see *Academic Courses*). Accommodation can be arranged from £50 per week. Help is given with job placement.

THE REGENCY SCHOOL OF ENGLISH, Royal Crescent, Ramsgate, Kent CT11 9PE. Tel: 01843 591212. Fax: 01843 850035. E-mail: regency school@bt.internet.com. Website: www.regencyschool.co.uk. Twice a year (April and November). £750. Accommodation can be arranged for £90 per week half-board. Also offer 5-day introductory course.

REGENT EDINBURGH, 29 Chester Street, Edinburgh EH3 7EN. Tel: 0131-225 9888. Fax: 0131-225 2133. E-mail: edinburgh@regent.org.uk. 4-week intensive offered 10 times a year. £800. Accommodation can be arranged on request. Centre often contacted by schools and agencies looking for newly-qualified teachers. Extra unassessed teaching practice between courses, to boost confidence.

RICHMOND ADULT & COMMUNITY COLLEGE, Clifden Centre, Clifden Road, Twickenham, Middlesex TW1 4LT. Tel: 020-8891 5907. Fax: 020-8332 6560. E-mail: lisa@racc.org.uk. Website: www.racc.org.uk. Part-time over 35 weeks January to December (one afternoon per week). Teaching observation and practice all done on premises. £843 plus moderation fee. Mature students welcome.

ST BRELADE'S COLLEGE, Mont Les Vaux, St. Aubin, Jersey JE3 8AF. Tel: 01534 741305. Fax: 01534 741159. Twice a year (March and September). £750 plus exam fee. Bed & breakfast accommodation for £70 per week. 2-month distance learning and 4 weeks residential course.

ST GEORGE'S SCHOOL OF ENGLISH, 76 Mortimer St, London W1N 7DE. Tel: 020-7299 1700. Fax: 020-7299 1711. E-mail: teflenq@stgeorges.co.uk & info@stgeorges.co.uk & canderson@stgeorges.co.uk. Website: www.stgeorges.co.uk. Courses: TESOL Cert. 4-week intensive £495 (plus £77.50 Trinity fee due in week

1). 13-week part-time £545 (plus Trinity fee). Monday, Wednesday and Thursday evenings, plus 5 Saturday mornings.

TESOL Diploma via distance learning with flexible length of course costs £895 (plus £240 for Trinity exams, due as exam dates near). Includes a 2-week practical teaching block at SGI. Payment by installments allowed but works out costing more.

Job Prospects: there is a system for giving trainees work contacts and finding them jobs with agencies and a variety of schools worldwide.

ST GILES COLLEGE LONDON CENTRAL, 154 Southampton Row, London WC1B 5AX. Tel: 020-7837 0404. Fax: 020-7837 4099. E-mail: londonc@stgiles.u-net.com Website: www.tcfl-stgiles.com 4-week full-time course. Maximum 12 participants. £650 plus moderator's fee of £77.50. Accommodation can be arranged (homestay, residence, hotel). Also offers courses for Overseas Teachers of English (British Council accredited).

ST. MARY'S COLLEGE, Waldegrave Road, Twickenham, TW1 4SX. Tel: 020-8240 4346. Fax: 0208 240 4365. E-mail: grantk@smuc.ac.uk. Website: www.smuc.ac.uk. Four-week intensive courses throughout the year. £720. Help with finding local accommodation given. Also offer MA in applied linguistics and ELT. Assist graduates with job placement.

SANDWELL COLLEGE, Crocketts Lane, Smethwick, West Midlands B66 3BU. Tel: 0121-556 6000 (ext. 6306). Fax: 0121-253 6322. E-mail: gill.clarke@sandwell.ac.uk. One part-time course per year. £700 (concessions if unwaged).

SHEFFIELD HALLAM UNIVERSITY TESOL CENTRE, School of Education, Collegiate Crescent Campus, Sheffield S10 2BP. Tel: 0114 225 2240. Fax: 0114 225 2280. E-mail: tesol@shu.ac.uk. 12 weeks distance learning plus 4 weeks intensive full-time study block. 2-3 times a year. £900.

SIDMOUTH INTERNATIONAL SCHOOL, May Cottage, Sidmouth, Devon EX10 8EN. Tel: 01395 516754. Fax: 01395 579270. E-mail: efl@sidmouth-int.co.uk. Website: www.sidmouth-int.co.uk. Full-time three times a year. £895. Accommodation can be arranged. Teaching practice includes 6 hours group teaching and 4 hours one-to-one. Also Dip one year distance learning with in-house beginning and end. £1,200.

SOUTH EAST ESSEX COLLEGE, Carnarvon Road, Southend-on-Sea, Essex SS2 6LS. Tel: 01702 220400. Fax: 01702 432320. E-mail: learning@se-cssex-college.ac.uk. Part-time Trinity Cert. TESOL over one academic year. £550.

SOUTHWARK COLLEGE, EFL Section, Waterloo Centre, The Cut, London SE1 8LE. Tel: 020-7815 1682. Fax: 020-7261 1301. CTESOL courses offered part-time over 20 weeks between January and June. £695.

STOCKPORT COLLEGE OF FURTHER & HIGHER EDUCATION, Wellington Road South, Stockport, SKI 3UQ. Tel: 0161 958 3115/3118. Fax: 0161 480 6636. E-mail: jill.cregeen@stockport.ac.uk. 1 course per year part-time September to March. 2 evenings a week plus 6 hours' daytime teaching practice. £799. Guidance given in finding jobs with various organisations.

STRANMILLIS COLLEGE, Stranmillis Road, Belfast BT9 5DY, Northern Ireland. Tel: 01232 381271. Fax: 01232 664423. Full-time course each September. £795. Accommodation available in halls of residence, if required. Central location. Informal advice given with job placement.

STUDENTS INTERNATIONAL LTD., 158 Dalby Road, Melton Mowbray, Leicestershire LE13 OBJ. Tel: 01664 481997. Fax: 01664 563332. E-mail: studentsint@compuserve.com. 6 full-time courses. £795. Host family accommodation for £90 a week half board. Unknown language is Arabic.

SURREY ADULT EDUCATION in conjunction with Brooklands College, Churchfield Centre, Churchfield Road, Weybridge KT13 8DB. Tel: 01932-847029. Fax:01932-844602. Part time (22 weeks from October to May), Wednesday, 9.15am-3.15pm. Teaching practice on established classes. Job placement bulletin available. Also offer Licentiate Diploma at Brooklands College, Esher Green

Centre, 19 Esher Green, Esher, Surrey KT10 8AA. Tel 01372-465374. Fax 01372-463696. Part-time (Wednesday evenings for 3 terms October to July).
SURREY LANGUAGE CENTRE, 39 West Street, Farnham, Surrey GU9 7DR. Tel: 01252 723494. Fax: 01252 717692. E-mail: slc@surreylanguage.co.uk. Website: www.surreylanguage.co.uk. Full-time offered monthly. £720 including moderation fee. Local accommodation can be arranged.
SUSSEX LANGUAGE INSTITUTE, University of Sussex, Falmer, Brighton, E. Sussex, BN1 9QN. Tel: 01273 678006. Fax: 01273 678476. E-mail: R.De-Witt@sussex.ac.uk. Website: www.sussex.ac.uk/langc. Certificate courses several times a year in July/August (4 weeks) and September (5 weeks). £810. Also Short Introduction to TEFL course (1 week) £140. Assistance in finding accommodation given if necessary.

UNIVERSITY OF

SUSSEX
AT BRIGHTON

Promoting
excellence in
teaching and
research

Sussex Language Institute

★ **Highly qualified and experienced trainers**

★ **Facilities of a Major University Campus**

★ **Beautiful South Downs and Seaside Location**

1-week Introduction to TEFL Courses
4-week Trinity College Certificate Courses in TESOL

Contact Linda Gunn, tel: 01273 678006, fax: 01273 678476

http://www.sussex.ac.uk.langc/

SUTTON COLLEGE OF LIBERAL ARTS, St. Nicholas Way, Sutton, Surrey SM1 1EA. Tel: 020-8770 6902. Fax: 020-8770 6933. Part-time (32 weeks) September to July.
UNIVERSAL LANGUAGE TRAINING (ULT), Woking College, Rydens Way, Woking, Surrey GU22 9DL. Tel: 01483 770911. Tel/fax: 01483 770848. E-mail: enquiry@universal-language.co.uk. Website: www.universal-language.co.uk. 4-week intensive courses offered year round and part-time courses over 16 weeks. Free introductory seminars. £695 plus Trinity moderation fee of £80. Host families available. Job contacts. 4-week course also held in Zamora, Spain in August.
UNIVERSITY COLLEGE CHICHESTER, Centre for International Education and Management, Bognor Regis Campus, Upper Bognor Road, Bognor Regis, W.Sussex PO21 1HR. Tel: 01243 816216. Fax: 01243 816272. E-mail: ciem@ucc.ac.uk. Website: www.chihe.ac.uk. Part-time courses lasting 2 semesters, once a year. £450. Campus accomodation and housing placement service available. Careers advice given. Also offer joint honours degree in English Language Teaching.
UNIVERSITY OF LUTON, Department of Linguistics, Castle Street, Luton, Bedfordshire LU1 3JU. Tel: 01582 489022. Fax: 01582 489014. E-mail: edward.hounslow@luton.ac.uk. 4-week full-time Certificate programme in July. Also part-time once a year.
UNIVERSITY OF ST. ANDREWS, English Language Teaching, Butts Wynd, St. Andrews, Fife KY16 9AL. Tel: 01334 462255. Fax: 01334 462270. E-mail: amm3@st-and.ac.uk. Website: www.st-and.ac.uk/services/elt/tesol.html. Trinity College Cert. (cost about £850) and Licentiate Diploma. Also offer 30-hour introductory course 3 times a year.
UNIVERSITY OF THE WEST OF ENGLAND, Faculty of Languages, Coldharbour Lane, Frenchay, Bristol BS16 1QY. Tel: 0117 9656261. Fax: 0117 3442820. E-mail: george.mann@uwe.ac.uk. 5-week courses once a year. £975. Accommodation can be arranged, if available, through student accommodation service. Placement advice given during course. Certificate also available as a final-year degree option.

UNIVERSITY OF WALES, CARDIFF (ELSIS), 53 Park Place, Cardiff CF10 3AT.
Tel: 029-2087 6587. Fax: 029-2023 1968. E-mail: dalymc@cardiff.ac.uk. 4-week
courses 4 times a year. £975. Accommodation can be arranged. ELSIS advise on, but
do not find, jobs.
UNIVERSITY OF WOLVERHAMPTON, School of Humanities, Languages and
Social Sciences, Stafford Street, Wolverhampton WV1 1SB. Tel: 01902 322484.
Fax: 01902 322739. E-mail: efl@wlv.ac.uk. Part-time (one evening a week). £850
plus moderation fee.
WALTHAM FOREST COLLEGE, Forest Road, London E17 4JB. Tel: 020-8501
8091/8198. Fax: 020-8501 8001. E-mail: efl@waltham.ac.uk. Website:
www.waltham.ac.uk. One intensive course (5 weeks) in June/July and one part-time
course September to March (2 evenings a week and weekend).
WEST OXON TRAINING SERVICES, Languages Training and Development Ltd.,
116 Corn Street, Witney, Oxfordshire OX8 7BU. Tel: 01993 894710. Fax: 01993
706066. E-mail: ltd@westoxon-ts.co.uk. Intensive 8-week course starting monthly.
Free to non-graduates under 25 or anyone already unemployed for 6 months or
disabled. Undergraduates and gap year students may also be eligible. Eligibility is
complicated so interested candidates should contact LTD for advice. Placement
assistance available especially in Spain through LTD office in Barcelona. LTD also
offers London Chamber of Commerce Certificate in Teaching English for Business.
WINDSOR SCHOOLS, 21 Osborne Road, Windsor, Berkshire SL4 3EG. Tel: 01753
858995. Fax: 01753 831726. E-mail: info@windsorschools.co.uk. Website:
www.windsor.schools.btinternet.co. Full-time offered monthly and part-time (4
months or 1 academic year). £799 (incl. VAT). Also offer Trinity Diploma course
(£799 plus exam fees). Accommodation can be arranged for £70-£95 per week.
Associated English schools for teaching practice in UK and placement in schools in
Europe (especially Spain, Italy, South America and Asia). Cert TESOL also offered
in Barcelona.
WIRRAL METROPOLITAN COLLEGE, The English Language Unit, IBMC, Europa
Boulevard, Conway Park, Birkenhead, Wirral CH41 4NT. Tel: 0151-551 7088/7114.
Fax: 0151-551 7001/7062. E-mail: harriet.parker@wmc.ac.uk. Website:
www.wmc.ac.uk/esol/. Part-time over 30 weeks (January-June). £640. In-house
teaching practice. Local accommodation can be found if required. Bilingual trainees
welcome with proficiency level of English. Comprehensive student support
available.

Argentina

CENTUM, SERVICIOS DE IDIOMAS, Bartlomé Mitre 811, 4th floor, 1036 AAO
Buenos Aires. Tel: 1-14 328-5150. Fax:1-14 328-2385. Part-time over 32 weeks
(academic year). 140 hours total. Emphasis on teaching Business English. Specialist
50-hour course in Teaching English for Business offered. Also offer Licentiate
Diploma course. Accommodation not provided.

Australia

EAST COAST COLLEGE OF ENGLISH, Level 1, 295 Ann Street, Brisbane,
Queensland, Australia 4000. Tel: +61 7 3229 0350. Fax: +61 7 3229 0850. E-mail:
ecce@bit.net.au Website: www.ecce.bit.net.au/ 4-week full-time (AU$2695) or 14-
week part-time (AU$2895). 4/5 times yearly. Host family and other accommodation
options can be arranged. Also offered are development courses combining language
enrichment with current ESL teaching methodology for overseas teachers.

Cyprus

FORUM LANGUAGE CENTRE, P.O. Box 25567, Nicosia 1310, Cyprus. Tel: +(2)
319166. Fax: (2) 497766. E-mail: forum1@cytanet.com.cy. Website: www
.geocities.com/forumlc. Part-time course: 2 mornings per week for 20 weeks; part-
time course: 1 evening a week for 40 weeks. £795 Cypriot pounds.

Hong Kong

ENGLISH FOR ASIA LTD, 303, Workingbond Commercial Centre, 162, Prince Edward Road West, Kowloon. Tel: 2366 3792. Fax: 2392 2424. E-mail: info@englishforasia.com. Website: www.englishforasia.com. Full-time courses 3 times a year. HK$15,900. Help with accommodation costing from HK$4,000 for a simple bed sit to HK$8,000 for a good hotel room. Session at the end of the course outlining the best places to find work in Hong Kong and China. Local schools and EFL institutions frequently contact English for Asia when they are recruiting. Course also features Young Learner component, and distance learning module covering methodology, phonetics and language awareness.

Cert. TESOL in Hong Kong

♦ 4 week intensive courses
♦ Pre-course starter pack
♦ ELT self-access centre
♦ Computer facilities

Trinity
Registered Examination Centre

Contact...

Tel: (+852) 2366 3792
Fax: (+852) 2392 2424
info@englishforasia.com
www.englishforasia.com
...for a free
information pack

Indonesia

IALF BALI, Jalan Kapten Agung 17, Denpasar 80232, Bali. Tel: 62-361 221783. Fax: 62-361 263509. E-mail: ehunt@ialfbali.co.id. Website: www.ialf.edu. 4-weeks. 3 times per year. US$1,500. Wide range of accommodation available. Help with looking for jobs worldwide.

New Zealand

EDENZ COLLEGES, (formerly International Academy of Languages), P.O. Box 10-222, Dominion Road, Auckland, New Zealand. Tel: 9-522 1211. Fax: 9-522 1511. E-mail: tim@edenz.com. Website: www.edenz.com. Intensive (4 weeks) and part-time (14 weeks) Trinity TESOL Certificate courses. Cost US$1500. Placement not guaranteed but big demand for graduates to work in NZ and Asian Language schools. INTERNATIONAL PACIFIC COLLEGE, Institute of TESOL, Private Bag 11 021, Palmerston North, New Zealand. Tel: 6-354 0922. Fax: 6-354 0935. 4-weeks full-time plus pre-course distance learning component. Offered 4 times a year. NZ$2,800. Help can be given in finding accommodation. Emphasis on intercultural awareness. SEAFIELD SCHOOL OF ENGLISH, 99 Seaview Road, (PO Box 18516), New Brighton, Christchurch, New Zealand. Tel: 3-388 3850. Fax: 3-388 4970. E-mail: succeed@seafield.co.nz. 3 months of distance learning followed by a 4-week intensive certificate course, offered 4 times a year. NZ$2,850. Also Trinity LTCL (TESOL) Diploma, 9 months distance learning in conjunction with Sheffield Hallam University, followed by a 2-week intensive course. NZ$4,550.

Spain

NEXT TRAINING ESPANA, Rocafort 241-243, 6°-5a, E-08029 Barcelona, Spain. Tel: +34 93 322 02 00. Fax: +34 93 322 34 95. E-mail: tesol@next-training.es. Website: www.tefltraining.com. Trinity College Cert TESOL offered full-time and part-time in Barcelona and Rome. London Chamber of Commerce and Industry Teaching Business English (Cert TEBESOL); two weeks full-time in Barcelona.

time in Barcelona or Rome. Accommodation provided. If qualified and looking for a job, check website www.next-training.es.

UNIVERSAL LANGUAGE TRAINING (ULT), Woking College, Rydens Way, Woking, Surrey GU22 9DL. Tel: 01483 770911. Tel/fax: 01483 770848. E-mail: enquiry@universal-language.co.uk. Website: www.universal-language.co.uk. 4-week course held in Zamora, Spain in August.

Uruguay

DICKENS INSTITUTE, 21 De Setiembre 2744, Montevideo 11300, Uruguay. Tel: 2-711 2103. Fax: 2-711 3487. E-mail: dickens@adinet.com.uy. Part-time over 2 years and aimed primarily at Uruguayan teachers.

Academic and Other Recognised Courses

This represents a small selection of university courses in TEFL/TESL in the UK.

ASTON UNIVERSITY, Language Studies Unit, Department of Languages and European Studies, Aston Triangle, Birmingham B4 7ET. Tel: 0121-359 3611 ext. 4236. Fax: 0121-359 2725. E-mail: lsu@aston.ac.uk. 4-week Certificate in TEFL aimed at recent graduates. Held in August. £760. Self-catering accommodation in halls of residence available for £60 per week. Also Advanced Certificate in TEFL for experienced teachers of any discipline: 6 months by distance learning start any time. Also Master's in TESOL/TESP for experienced graduates by distance learning over 2-5 years. Local resource centres in Spain, Greece, Turkey, Hungary, Japan, etc. Assessment by assignment with exams optional.

CANTERBURY CHRIST CHURCH UNIVERSITY COLLEGE, North Holmes Road, Canterbury CT1 1QU. Tel: 01227 458459. Fax: 01227 781558. E-mail: ipo@cant.ac.uk. Website: www.cant.ac.uk. Offer Diploma/MA in TESOL. Diploma only, £1240 (10 months full-time); diploma plus MA, £2,720 (12 months full-time). Homestay or college residence available.

KING'S COLLEGE, LONDON, English Language Centre, Strand, London WC2R 2LS. Tel 020-7848 1600. Fax: 020-7848 1601. E-mail: elc@kcl.ac.uk. Website: www.kcl.ac.uk/elc. 1 year MA in ELT and Applied Linguistics. Approx. £1,340 per year; (part-time home students), £4,005 per year (part time overseas students), £2,675 (full time home students), £8,100 (full time overseas students). Candidates with UCLES DELTA can enter MA on a fast-track basis, by-passing one module. Also offer UCLES DELTA part-time (one eveing a week for a year). Approximately £850 plus UCLES examination fee.

LEEDS METROPOLITAN UNIVERSITY, Centre for Language Study, Beckett Park Campus, Leeds LS6 3QS. Tel: 0113 283 7440 (+44 113 283 7440 from outside the UK). Fax: 0113 274 5966 (+44 113 274 5966 from outside the UK). E-mail: cls@lmu.ac.uk. Website: www.lmu.ac.uk/cls. 1 year full-time or part-time. Weekend or block study periods enable distance learning. Focus on reflective practitioner and research applied to teaching/learning context. Also offer CELTA and Trinity Cert TESOL (see listings).

LONDON GUILDHALL UNIVERSITY, The English Language Centre, Old Castle Street, London E1 7NT. Tel: 020-7320 1251. Fax: 020-7320 1253. E-mail: elc@lgu.ac.uk. London Guildhall University Certificate in Teaching International Business English offered twice a year in January and July (and on demand for groups). Course lasts 2 weeks (£570). Accommodation available in halls of residence.

MIDDLESEX UNIVERSITY, Admissions Office, School of Humanities and Cultural Studies, Middlesex University, White Hart Lane, London N17 8HR. Tel: 020-8362 5404. Fax: 020-8362 5965. E-mail: p.fanning@mdx.ac.uk. Website: www.ilrs.mdx.ac.uk/lang/eng_non.htm. TEFL forms half of a three-year undergraduate joint degree. Provides BATQI-recognised level 1 qualification, plus additional academic content. The BATQI-relevant modules are also open to existing university graduates on a one-year, part-time basis (Sept-June, £750). Other level 1 qualifications can be accredited as part of the degree. Also offer an MA in TEFL and Applied Linguistics: one year full-time, for practitioners with at least two years' classroom experience.

MULTI LINGUA, Administration Centre, Abbot House, Sydenham Road, Guildford, Surrey GU1 3RL. Tel: 01483 535118. Fax: 01483 534777. E-mail: mail@multi-lingua.co.uk. 4-week Multi Lingua (ML) TEFL Certificate course and part-time ML TEFL Certificate course as well as 4-week Cambridge CELTA course; all cost £745. One week full-time ML TEFL Prep. course and Teaching English for Business course. Successful learners are registered with Futures Recruitment. ILA vouchers accepted.

QUEEN'S UNIVERSITY OF BELFAST, TEFL Centre, Belfast, Northern Ireland BT7 1NN. Tel: 01232 335373. Fax: 01232 335379. E-mail: tefl@qub.ac.uk. MA in English Language Teaching. 1 year full-time. £2,400 for EU students, £6,730 non-EU. Accommodation available in university residences for £49 per week. Also offer

the Trinity Certificate (TESOL) and Cambridge DELTA.
UNIVERSITY OF BRIGHTON, The School of Languages, Falmer, Brighton, East Sussex BN1 9PH. Tel: 01273 643337. Fax: 01273 690710. E-mail: slweb@bton.ac.uk. Offers Diploma and MA in TESOL; full-time September-June or 2 years part-time. These are both postgraduate courses; applicants must have some English teaching experience for the Diploma, and 2-3 years for the MA.
UNIVERSITY OF EDINBURGH, Institute for Applied Language Studies, 21 Hill Place, Edinburgh EH8 9DP. Tel: 0131-650 6200. Fax: 0131-667 5927. E-mail: ials.enquiries@ed.ac.uk. Website: www.ials.ed.ac.uk. Runs 13 specialist summer courses for teachers, mostly in July and August. 3-week courses cost £670. 2-week courses cost £466. *Teaching & Learning English* – 3 weeks with choice of start dates in July and August or 2 weeks in September; *Teaching Languages for Specific Purposes* – 3 weeks; *Teaching English for Medical Purposes, for Business Purposes* and for *Legal Purposes* – 2 weeks; *Teaching Literature in EFL* – 3 weeks; *Drama for TEFL* – 3 weeks; *Grammar and Communicative Teaching* – 3 weeks; *Teaching Young Learners* – 3 weeks; *Pronunciation for Language Teachers* – 2 weeks; *Training to Train* – 3 weeks. *Computer Assisted Language Learning* – 1 week in July (£258) and *Introduction to TEFL* – 1 week June and possibly others (£150). Also offers University of Edinburgh Certificates: *Advanced Certificate in Teaching English for Specific Purposes* – (10 weeks) £1,550; *Certificate in the Description of Contemporary English.* Also offer *English for TEFL/Applied Linguistics* in EAP programme – 4 weeks (£760); *Cambridge DELTA* (10 weeks) £1,595 including exam fee, and *MSc in Applied Linguistics.*

UNIVERSITY OF CENTRAL LANCASHIRE, Department of Languages, Preston, Lancashire PR1 2HF. Tel: 01772 893136. Certificate in TEFL. Full-time for 4 weeks in July/August. About £600 plus £50 per week if accommodation is required. Accommodation is available in halls of residence or host family.
UNIVERSITY OF ESSEX, EFL Unit, Department of Language & Linguistics, Wivenhoe Park Campus, Colchester, Essex CO4 3SQ. Tel: 01206 872217. Fax: 01206 873107. E-mail: dilly@essex.ac.uk. Website: www.essex.ac.uk. Diploma in TEFL (3 terms), Certificate in Teaching English as a Foreign Language/CTEFL (1 term), Certificate in English for Language Teaching/CEFLT (1 term) and CEELT Preparation Course (3 weeks).
UNIVERSITY OF EXETER, Graduate Studies Office, School of Education, Heavitree Road, Exeter EX1 2LU. Tel: 01392 264838/4815/4728. Fax 01392-264810/4902. E-mail: ed-cpd@exeter.ac.uk/ ed-rsu@exeter.ac.uk. B.Phil.(Ed) and M.Ed. (one year); and Certificate in Advanced Professional Studies in ELT (one term); Ed.D in TEFL (taught doctorate), 2 years full-time or 4 years part-time. Please see www.ex.ac.uk/education/subjects/tefl.htm. Majority of students are teachers from overseas.

UNIVERSITY OF MANCHESTER, Postgraduate Admissions Office, School of Education, Oxford Road, Manchester M13 9PL. Tel: 0161-275 3463. Fax: 0161-275 3528. E-mail: education.enquiries@man.ac.uk. Website: www.man.ac.uk/langlit. Offers MEd TESOL and MEd Educational Technology TESOL both 1 year, full-time or 2-3 years part-time. Full-time courses start every September and part-time courses in September and January. Also offers similar weight courses as distance learning (see *Distance Learning*). Costs from £2,740.

THE UNIVERSITY
of MANCHESTER

MEds at Manchester

Choose from the following programmes:

Distance

MEd ELT   A distance/summer or fully distance modular programme offering a wide choice of course components and flexible start dates. New fully distance programme commences each January.

MEd in Educational Technology and ELT   As the MEd ELT, but with an emphasis on the role of educational technology in ELT. Also available world wide fully distance if you have internet access.

On-site

MEd TESOL   The full-time (also available locally part-time) version of the MEd ELT.

MEd in Educational Technology and TESOL   The full-time (also available locally part-time) version of the MEd in Ed Tech and ELT.

For further details please contact:
Postgraduate Admissions Office, School of Education, University of Manchester, Oxford Road, Manchester M13 9PL, UK   Tel: + 44 161-275 3617/3463   Fax: + 44 161-275 3528
Email: education.enquiries@man.ac.uk   URL: http://www.man.ac.uk/langlit/

UNIVERSITY OF READING, School of Linguistics and Applied Language Studies, Whiteknights, PO Box 241, Reading RG6 6WB. Tel: 0118-931 8511. Fax: 0118-975 6506. E-mail: CALS@reading.ac.uk. MA Master's in the Teaching of English as a Foreign Language and MA in Applied Linguistics. On campus: full-time (October to June/September) or part-time/modular (typically 2-3 years); or by distance study starting May and November and lasting between 2 and 5 years. Tuition fees for campus-based course are £2,810-£3,230 (EU) or £6,860-£7,940 (non-EU). Distance study fees are £4,695 payable in instalments. Campus accommodation available. Flexible programme of study available combining different modes.
UNIVERSITY OF STIRLING, Centre for English Language Teaching, Stirling FK9 4LA. Tel: 01786 467934. Fax: 01786 466131. E-mail: st1@stir.ac.uk. Website: www.stir.ac.uk. Undergraduate degrees in ELT and Postgraduate degrees in TESOL with options in CALL (among others).
UNIVERSITY OF WARWICK, Centre for English Language Teacher Education, Coventry CV4 7AL. Tel: 02476 523200. Fax: 02476 524318. E-mail: CELTE@warwick.ac.uk. Website: www.warwick.ac.uk/EAP. MA in ELT/ESP/ELTYL/ELSM. Also offers 10-week course in ELT, ESP and Teaching Young Learners (January to March).

Distance Learning Courses

BLUEFEATHER SCHOOL OF LANGUAGES, 35 Montpelier Parade, Monkstown, Dublin, Ireland. Tel: 1-280 6288. Fax: 1-280 6035. E-mail: TEFL@bluefeather.ie. Website: www.bluefeather.ie. Distance learning course validated by ATT (Association for TEFL Training in Ireland). Also offer range of residential courses.

EUROLINK, Teacher Training, 3 Abbeydale Road South, Sheffield S7 2QL. Tel: 0114-262 1522. Fax: 0114-236 0774. E-mail: eurolink@vip.solis.co.uk. TEFL/TESOL Certificates, Diplomas and Masters by distance learning only. Ask for a prospectus.

GLOBAL ENGLISH, 71 Parkway, Exeter, Devon EX2 9NB. Tel/fax: 01392 664378. E-mail: info@global-english.co.uk. Website: www.global-english.co.uk. Offers TEFL Certificate Course (approximately 150 study hours) and Introduction to TEFL (40 hours). Also TEFL with Business Certificate course. In-house assessment. All students assigned a personal tutor. Students of the certificate course are given written course assessment on completion, which acts as a reference, and have 14-day money back guarantee. Advice given on how to get started, and individual job help available from tutor.

TRAIN TO TEACH EFL
by distance learning

- Introduction to TEFL course
- TEFL Certificate course
- TEFL Certificate course with business

Full tutorial support and career advice

GLOBAL ENGLISH
71 Parkway, Exeter EX2 9NB, UK. Phone/fax 44 (0)1392 664378
email: info@global-english.co.uk   website: www.global-english.co.uk

INTESOL, 19 Lower Oakfield, Pitlochry, Perthshire PH16 5DS, Scotland. Tel/fax: 01796 474199. E-mail: Lynda@INTESOL.freeserve.co.uk. Website: www.intesoltraining.com. Distance Learning Preliminary Certificate in TESOL - £195 UK, £210-£230 overseas. Certificate of Educational Studies in TESOL (accredited by the Accreditation Council for TESOL Distance Education Courses) £345 UK, £365-£385 overseas. Teaching practice available on completion of the course. Also offer hybrid distance learning/residential courses in Scotland and London. Close contact with recruitment agency and schools overseas to place trainees.

i-to-i, One Cottage Road, Headingley, Leeds LS6 4DD. Tel: 0870-333 2332. Fax: 0113 274 6923. E-mail: info@i-to-i.com. Website: www.i-to-i.com. Independent TEFL training organisation. Online short TEFL course that you can log on to from anywhere in the world. Aimed at travellers, it is a practical web-based course with support from trained 'virtual tutors.' Go to www.onlinetefl.com. Cost £270 or $400.

LANGUAGE 2 ASSOCIATES, 25 Woodway Crescent, Harrow, Middlesex HA1 2NH. Tel: 020-8907 2618. Fax: 020-8909 1885. E-mail: langtwo@beeb.net. Distance learning courses for teachers – Introductory, Certificate and Diploma TESOL courses, also EYL (English for Young Learners), Grammar and Phonology courses. Established since 1988.

LONDON TEFL BUREAU, Suite 401, 302 Regent St, London W1R 6HH. Tel: 020-7580 4242. 4 weeks intensive TEFL Certificate and 8 weeks standard courses. Introductory to advanced levels offered, also English for Young Learners, Business English and Linguistic courses.

*NET LEARN LANGUAGES,*Roman House, 9/10 College Terrace, London E3 5AN. Tel: 020-8981 1333. Fax: 020-8981 7333. E-mail: Eric@nll.co.uk. Website: www.nll.co.uk or www.colte.com. Certificate in On-Line Teaching of English for experienced and qualified TEFL teachers (CELTA, CertTESOL or equivalent) who want to learn how to use the internet as a teaching medium. On-line study (45 hours) can be combined with live internet meetings mid-week or at weekends (30 hours). £295. 5 or more starting dates a year. Tutor support available by e-mail and NetMeeting. Course is also offered in London (6 days; £345).

OPEN LEARNING INTERNATIONAL (OLI), 72 Pentyla Baglan Road, Port Talbot, Wales SA12 8AD. Tel: 780 862 1283. E-mail: train@olionline.com. Website: http://olionline.com. OCR Certificate and Diploma by distance learning via the internet. $920-$1,320. OLI will put enquirers in e-mail touch with past students.

ROBACO, 8 Nesburn Road, Barnes, Wearside SR4 7LR. Tel: 07712 579 775. E-mail: rb@robaco.net or admin@robaco.net. Website: www.robaco.net. Certificate (£695), diploma (£879), MTefl (£2,055) courses by distance and/or internet learning plus moderation, certification, teaching practice at Bournemouth school. Recruitment for posts abroad.

SAXONCOURT & ENGLISH WORLDWIDE 124 New Bond Street, London W1Y 9AE; tel 0207-491 1911; fax 0207-493 3657. E-mail: recruit@saxoncourt.com. Website: www.saxoncourt.com. Trinity Diploma. Candidates are mainly EFL teachers currently working abroad. Saxoncourt & EWW is primarily a recruitment agency and so can help graduates find jobs (see chapter *Finding a Job*).

TEFL INTERNATIONAL, PO Box 34968, King's Road Post Office, Hong Kong (or 1 Braemar Hill Road, Palisades Club, Hong Kong). Tel: 2491 4938. E-mail: info@teflintl.com. Website: www.teflintl.com. TESOL Online Certificate course, recommended for participants who have had some ESL teaching experience. Prices from US$1,350 to US$1,850. Also offer an Advanced credential (Diploma level) for teachers with a minimum of 2 years experience. Also offer on-site certificate course in Hong Kong.

TRAVEL-TEACH ENGLISH, 1-888-270-2941 in US. Tesol teacher certification by correspondence. US$450 FOR 60-hour course.

UNIVERSITY OF MANCHESTER, Postgraduate Admissions Office, School of Education, Oxford Road, Manchester M13 9PL. Tel: 0161-275 3463. Fax: 0161-275 3528. E-mail: education.enquiries@man.ac.uk. Website: www.man.ac.uk/langlit. MEd ELT or MEd in Educational Technology and ELT. Both degrees are 3-5 years part-time (completely by distance training and/or summer attendance). Courses start every October and April. £3,850. For on-site courses see *Academic and Other Recognised Courses*.

Short Introductory Courses

BEDFORD COLLEGE, Enterprise House, Old Ford End Road, Bedford MK40 4PF. Tel: 01234 271492. Fax: 01234 364272. E-mail: gp67@dial.pipex.com. Part-time introductory course. Also offer CELTA.

BENEDICT INTERNATIONAL LTD, 74 Baxter Court, Norwich, Norfolk, NR3 2ST. Tel/fax: 01603-301522. E-mail: emma@griffin.fsbusiness.co.uk. Intensive weekend introductory TEFL courses. 24 hours and 36 hours of guided self-study. £195 includes a self-study guide that compliments the course. Job placements available.

BERLITZ (UK) LTD., 9-13 Grosvenor St, London W1A 3BZ. Tel: 020-7915 0909. Fax: 020-7915 0222. E-mail: rosalie.gowland@berlitz.co.uk. Website: www.berlitz.com. Do not run open TEFL training courses. Compulsory method training course for all employees, lasting 1-2 weeks. Normally course is taken at hiring centre.

CILC (Cheltenham International Language Centre), Cheltenham & Gloucester College of Higher Education, Francis Close Hall, Swindon Road, Cheltenham, Glos. GL50 4AZ. Tel: 01242 532925. Fax: 01242 532926. E-mail: cilc@chelt.ac.uk. Website: www.chelt.ac.uk/msm/cilc. CELTA centre which offers one-day taster courses.

DUNDEE COLLEGE, Blackness Road, Dundee DD1 5UA. Tel: 01362 834 898. Fax: 01362 322 286. E-mail: dic@dundeecoll.ac.uk. 2-day introductory courses in TEFL 3 times a year (October 28/29, February 24/25 and May 19/20). Accommodation can be arranged.

GREENHILL COLLEGE, Temple House Site, 221-225 Station Road, Harrow, Middlesex HA1 2XL. Tel: 0181-869 8805. Fax: 0181-427 9201. E-mail: enquiries@harrow.ac.uk. CELTA centre which offers 1-week TEFL Introductory course in July, £170. 1 or 2 day taster days and refresher courses also given, £30 a day. Help with accommodation can be given.

INTERNATIONAL HOUSE HASTINGS, White Rock, Hastings, East Sussex TN34 1JY. Tel: 01424 720100/720104. Fax: 01424 720323. E-mail: training@ ilcgroup.com. Various 2-week specialist courses for TEFL teachers. Self-catering accommodation approx. £45 a week. Also offers CELTA and DELTA.

INTERNATIONAL HOUSE LONDON, 106 Piccadilly, London W1J 7NL. Tel: 020-7518 6999. Fax: 020-7518 6998. E-mail: info@ihlondon.co.uk. Website: www.ihlondon.com. One-week courses TEFL Update and Discover TEFL 4 times a year. For other courses offered, see CELTA entry.

INTERNATIONAL LANGUAGE INSTITUTE/ILI, County House, Vicar Lane, Leeds LS1 7JH. Tel: 0113 242 8893. Fax: 0113 234 7543. E-mail: 101322.1376@ compuserve.com. Trinity centre which offers one-week (25 hours) intro course, £135. Accommodation with a family can be arranged. Suitable for anyone considering taking up TEFL at UK summer schools or overseas. Practice teaching in peer groups.

INTESOL, 19 Lower Oakfield, Pitlochry, Perthshire PH16 5DS. Tel/fax: 01796 474199. E-mail: Lynda@intesol.freeserve.co.uk. Website: www.intesoltesoltraining. com. 4-week courses in TESOL – 2 weeks homestudy combined with 2 weeks residential in Scotland. 2 courses per year. £795 includes accommodation and meals. London £495 does not include accommodation or meals. Close contact with recruitment agency and schools overseas to place trainees.

i-to-i, One Cottage Road, Headingley, Leeds LS6 4DD. Tel: 0870-333 2332. Fax: 0113 274 6923. E-mail: info@i-to-i.com. Website: www.i-to-i.com. Intensive TEFL courses. 20 hour weekend courses at venues in 13 UK cities. Extensive guidance on work opportunities abroad. Also an optional 20-hour home-study Grammar module. Fees are £195 for waged applicants, £175 for unwaged and students. On-line TEFL course also available from any location worldwide. Courses include on-line tutor back-up and CD Rom. Price £270/US$400. Internet address: www.onlinetefl.com.

ITS ENGLISH SCHOOL, HASTINGS, 43-45 Cambridge Gardens, Hastings, Sussex TN34 1EN. Tel: 01424 438025. Fax: 01424 438050. E-mail: itsbest@its-hastings.co.uk. Website: www.its-hastings.co.uk. Trinity centre which offers 5-day short Certificate in Teaching Practice. Times by arrangement. £185. Accommodation with local families from £60 per week half board.

LANGSIDE COLLEGE GLASGOW, 50 Prospecthill Road, Glasgow G42 9LB. Tel: 0141-649 4991/2256. Fax: 0141-632 5252. E-mail: tfoster@perseus.langside.ac.uk. Introduction to TESOL one evening per week for 10 weeks, given 3 times a year. £80 including materials. Also offer Trinity Certificate and Diploma.

LANGUAGE LINK TRAINING, 181 Earl's Court Road, London SW5 9RB. Tel: 020-7370 4755. Fax: 020-7370 1123. E-mail: languagelink@compuserve.com. Website: www.languagelink.co.uk. One-week pre-TESOL introductory courses according to demand. Includes observation in Language Link schools. Also offer Trinity TESOL Cert. and CELTA (see listings).

THE LANGUAGE PROJECT, 78-80 Colston Street, Bristol BS1 5BB. Tel 0117-9077181; Fax: 0117 9273993. E-mail: administration@langproj.demon.co.uk. Website: www.languagewise.co.uk. Introduction to TEFL/TESL. One-week intensive course offered monthly. Introduction to every aspect of practical classroom teaching. £150. Also offer Trinity TESOL five times a year and Trinity Diploma in TESOL twice a year. Assistance in finding accommodation provided.

MAINSTREAM ENGLISH LANGUAGE SKILLS COURSES LTD., 29 Royal Crescent, London W11 4SN. Tel/fax: 020-7602 6683. E-mail: englishgrammar@mainstreamenglish.fsnet.co.uk. Pre-CELTA/TESOL pre-teaching course in Clarification and Consolidation of Grammar with emphasis on how to teach English grammar to overseas students. 40 hours tuition spread over 1 or 2 weeks, offered year round £250. Reasonably priced accommodation within easy access. Possibility of doing course by distance learning.

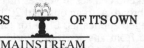
MULTI LINGUA, Administration Centre, Abbot House, Sydenham Road, Guildford, Surrey GU1 3RL. Tel: 01483 535118. Fax: 01483 534777. E-mail: mail@multi-lingua.co.uk. 5-day TEFL Preparatory course (or 5 consecutive Saturdays) held monthly. £215. Also one-week Teaching English for Business course 6 times a year. £390. Family accommodation arranged for £100. Also offer 4-week ML Certificate course (see listing under 'Academic and Other Recognised Courses').

NEWHAM COLLEGE OF FURTHER EDUCATION, East Ham Campus, High Street South, East Ham, London E6 3AB. Tel: 0181-257 4000. Fax: 0181-257 4307. Initial Teacher Cert. ESOL & Basic Skills (City & Guilds 9281). 5 hours p.w. for 14 weeks. Twice a year in autumn and spring terms. Also offers part-time CELTA.

NORTHAMPTON COLLEGE, Military Road, Northampton NN1 3ET. Tel: 01604 734170/2. Fax: 01604 734183. Introduction to TEFL. Part-time over 10 weeks (daytimes) plus 1 Saturday. Once a year April to June. Approx. £45. Basic introduction offering a taste of TEFL. Also offers the Trinity Cert. TESOL.

NORTHBROOK COLLEGE SUSSEX, Modern Languages Department, Littlehampton Road, Goring-by-Sea, West Sussex BN12 6NU. Tel: 01903 606243. Fax: 01903 606207. E-mail: s.sscowen@nbcol.ac.uk. Website: www.northbrook. ac.uk. Pre-TESOL Preparatory course. 4 weeks (full-time) in July, October, December, February/March and May. Part-time evening class offered three times a

year. £126 full-time (£68 concessions), £65 part-time (£35 concessions). Accommodation can be arranged for £70-£75 per week. Also offer Trinity Cert.
NOTTINGHAM LANGUAGE CENTRE, Nottingham Trent University, Burton Street, Nottingham, NG1 4BU. Tel: 0115 848 6156. Fax: 0115 848 6513. E-mail: nlc.@ntu.ac.uk. Website: http://nlc.ntu.ac.uk. One week full-time course 3 times per year (spring, autumn, winter) £125. Homestay is available on request all year round. Course is aimed at experienced EFL teachers wanting to brush up their skills.
SAXONCOURT TEACHER TRAINING, 59 South Molton Street, London W1Y 1HH. Tel: 020-7499 8533. Fax: 020-7499 9374. E-mail: tt@saxoncourt.com. Website: www.saxoncourt.com. Introductory TEFL course throughout the year. Also offer CELTA and Trinity Diploma by distance learning.
SHEFFIELD HALLAM UNIVERSITY, TESOL Centre, School of Education, 36 Collegiate Campus, Sheffield S10 2BP. Tel: 0114 225 2240. Fax: 0114 255 2280. E-mail: tesol@shu.ac.uk. Trinity centre which offers intro courses.
SUSSEX LANGUAGE INSTITUTE, University of Sussex, Falmer, Brighton, E. Sussex, BN1 9QN. Tel: 01273 877715. Fax: 01273 678476. E-mail: R.De-Witt@sussex.ac.uk. Website: www.sussex.ac.uk/langc. 1-week Introduction to TEFL course held several times a year. £140. Also offers the Trinity CertTESOL course.
TEFL TRAINING, Freepost, Stonesfield, Witney, Oxon. OX8 8BR. Tel: 01993 891121. Fax: 01993 891996. 20-hour weekend seminar plus 80 hours of self-study. Monthly in London and other centres nationwide. £235 (concessions for students and unemployed).

Teach English Abroad?

The most comprehensive and economic package on the market

"I learned more on this weekend than on an entire one-year PGCE" – **past student**

TEFL training's mix of intensive practical weekend seminar, guided self-study and careers advice costs less than a quarter of the fee for 4-week courses, and equips you to start teaching effectively at once.

For more information write to:
TEFL training (TA)
FREEPOST Stonefield, WITNEY OX8 8BR
or phone 01993 891121

TEACHER TRAINING INTERNATIONAL (TTI), 3 Queensberry Place, South Kensington, London SW7 2DL. Freephone 0800 174031. Fax: 01491 411383. One day introductory workshop/taster day (one Saturday every month or so), £35. Grammar Awareness for TEFL (4 Friday evenings, 8 courses a year) and 6-week evening TEFL certificate in Camden (Monday and Wednesday evenings or Tuesday and Thursday evenings). £580.

TEACHING ABROAD, Gerrard House, Rustington, West Sussex BN16 1AW. Tel: (01903) 859911. Fax: (01903) 785778. E-mail: info@teaching-abroad.co.uk. Website: www.teaching-abroad.co.uk. Placement agency (see *Finding a Job*) which sends paying volunteers to many countries now runs optional weekend TEFL courses in Arundel (West Sussex) and London. £215. Various dates.

UNIVERSITY OF EDINBURGH, Institute for Applied Language Studies, 21 Hill Place, Edinburgh EH8 9DP. Tel: 0131-650 6200. Fax: 0131-667 5927. E-mail: ials.enquiries@ed.ac.uk. Website: www.ials.ed.ac.uk. Introduction to TEFL. 1 week in June. £150. Accommodation can be arranged. Also offer many specialist summer courses (see *Academic & Other Recognised Courses*).

UNIVERSITY OF ST. ANDREWS, English Language Teaching, Butts Wynd, St. Andrews, Fife KY16 9AL. Tel: 01334 462255. Fax: 01334 462270. E-mail: amm3@st-and.ac.uk. 30-hour introductory course 3 times a year. Also offer Trinity College Certificate.

WEST HERTS COLLEGE, Cassio Campus, Langley Road, Watford, Herts. WD1 3RH. Tel: (01923) 812 049/812 055. Fax: (01923) 812 480. Introduction to Teaching English as a Foreign or Second Language runs in June each year. 4 evenings (7-9pm). From £50. College facilities.

WIGAN & LEIGH COLLEGE, PO Box 53, Parsons Walk, Wigan, Lancs. WN1 1RS. Tel: 01942 761563. Fax: 01942 761572. Introduction to TESOL over 4 weeks. Variable dates, £100. Also offer CELTA and DELTA £600 plus UCLES registration.

Training Courses Abroad (Non-Cambridge/Non-Trinity)

Australia

AUSTRALIAN TESOL TRAINING CENTRE, Level 6, 530 Oxford Street (PO Box 82), Bondi Junction, NSW 2022. Tel: 2-9389 0249. Fax: 2-9389 7788. E-mail: lynnev@ace.edu.au. CELTA centre which offers several one-week intro courses throughout the year. A$395. Homestay accommodation can be arranged.

ENGLISH LANGUAGE AND LITERACY SERVICES (ELLS), Adelaide Institute of Technical and Further Education (part of the Government Department of Education, Training and Employment), 5th Floor, Renaissance Centre, 127 Rundle Mall, Adelaide, South Australia 5000. Tel: 8-8226 6555. Fax: 8-8226 6882. E-mail: kwatson@adel.tafe.sa.edu.au. Website: www.tafe.sa.edu.au/institutes/adelaide/ells/tesol.shtml. Certificate in TESOL : 220 hour accredited course offered as a 4-week intensive and 11-week and 13-week part-time day and evening courses.

HOLMESGLEN LANGUAGE CENTRE, Holmesglen Institute of TAFE, PO Box 42, Chadstone, Victoria 3148. Tel: 3-9564 1820. Fax: 3-9564 1712. E-mail: larryf@holmesglen.vic.edu.au. 1-week Introductory Course in English Language Teaching offered and 1-week Refresher Course in English Language Teaching (on demand). One-day Professional Development Workshops for ESL Teachers (on demand). Highly trained and experienced staff with strong overseas knowledge. Modern facilities.

Austria

BUSINESS LANGUAGE CENTRE, Charles La Fond & Co. KEG, Trattnerhof 2, 1010 Vienna. Tel: (0)1 533 70 010. Fax: (0)1 532 85 21. E-mail: blc@blc.co.at. Website: www.blc.co.at. London Chamber of Commerce (LCCI) Certificate for Teaching English for Business.

Canada

ATLANTIC OVERSEAS TEACHING INSTITUTE, 1106 Barrington St, Halifax, Nova Scotia B3H 2R2. Tel: 902-423-4767. Fax: 902-422-4724. E-mail: aoti@istar.ca. Website: http://home.istar.ca/~aoti. TEFL Certificate Programme includes placement assistance and ongoing follow-up. 3 formats available each month except December. 10 evenings over 3 weeks, one-week intensive (full-day sessions) or 5 consecutive Saturdays. C$555. Accommodation list and rates provided.

CANADIAN GLOBAL TESOL TRAINING INSTITUTE, PO Box 41081, Edmonton, Alberta, Canada T6J 6M7. Tel: (780) 438-5704. Fax: (780) 435-0918. E-mail: tesol@cdnglobalinst.com. Website: www.cdnglobalinst.com. 5 day, 45 hour intensive TESOL Certification course, in class or by correspondence worldwide. Inclusive prices are C$450 in Canada, US$450 in other countries. Other courses offered by correspondence include Teaching Business English (US$250), Teaching TOEFL Preparation (US$250) and Teaching Comprehensive Grammar (US$250). 50 courses per year in 20 cities across Canada. Accommodation can be arranged. Contacts with recruiters and language schools for employment.

LANGUAGES INTERNATIONAL (TORONTO) INC., 330 Bay Street, Suite 910, Toronto, Ontario M5H 2S8. Tel: (416) 361-2411. Fax: (416) 361-2403. E-mail: litoront@istar.ca. Website: www.litoronto.com. 4-week Introductory TESL Certificate course several times a year at C$625. Also offers 8-week 100 hour course. Homestay and reasonably priced accommodation arranged near school. Refers graduates to recruiters and potential employers and maintains current job listings. Valuable practice teaching period included in programme.

Has partner colleges in Vancouver (VanWest College; website: www.vanwest.com) and Montreal (A.L.I. contact Gregory Mattei; info@alint.com or Website: www.alint.com).

UNIVERSITY OF SASKATCHEWAN, CERTESL Program, Extension Credit Studies, 326 Kirk Hall, 117 Science Place, Saskatoon, Saskatchewan S7N 5C8. Tel:

(306) 966-5563. Fax: (306) 966-5590. E-mail: extcred@usask.ca. www. extension.usask.ca/go/certesl. Certificate Program in Teaching English as a Second Language (CERTESL). Part-time distance study plus optional on-campus practicum. Total of 6 courses cost C$335 each for Canadian students, $502.50 for international students.

WINFIELD COLLEGE, Main Floor, 788 Beatty St, Vancouver, BC V6B 2M1. Tel: (604) 608-0538/ 1-800-821-TESL. Fax: (604) 608-0539. E-mail: Study@WinfieldCollege.com. Website: www.WinfieldCollege.com. 100-hour courses offered full-time for 1 month, part-time over 3 months or by distance education. Also one-week 40-hour intensive course. All courses include practicum and are offered year-round. Price from C$900 (US$600) for full course; C$485 for short course. Recommendations given on local accommodation (approx C$75 per night). College is recognised by federal Human Resources Canada and registered with the provincial Private Post-Secondary Education Commission.

Czech Republic

ITC INTERNATIONAL TEFL CERTIFICATE, PRAGUE, Main Office: Kaprova 14, 110 00 Prague 1. Tel/fax: (2) 2481-7530/(2) 2481-4791. US Voice-mail: 1-800-915-5540. US Fax: (815) 550-0086. Australian Voice mail: 1-300-368-189. E-mail: info@itc-training.com. Website: www.itc-training.com. Offers internationally-recognised 4-week TEFL Certificate courses in Prague and Barcelona. More than 1,500 have graduated from ITC's course. Sessions held year-round on a monthly basis. Course is designed for individuals with little or no teaching experience. Trainees receive extensive supervised teaching practice with foreign students. US$1,500 includes registration, course manual, immediate job guarantee in Eastern Europe, lifetime job assistance and employment contacts worldwide. City tour, survival Czech lessons, cultural orientation and welcome dinner also included. Job

workshop and career counselling during and after course. On-site EFL school with job opportunities for graduates. Housing and work visa assistance available. ITC is a member of the American Chamber of Commerce in Prague. (See also Spain below).

VIA LINGUA, Thamova 7, 186 00 Prague. Tel/fax: (2) 217 02 101; fax: (2) 217 02 102. E-mail: vialingua@mbox.vol.cz. Website: via-lingua.cz. 4-week intensive (120 hours) throughout the year. US$1,500 with accommodation; US$1,200 without. 10 hours practice teaching of local Czech students. Help with graduate job placements and guaranteed employment.

Egypt

AMERICAN UNIVERSITY IN CAIRO, PO Box 2511, Cairo. Tel: 2-357 6840. Fax: 2-355 7565. US enquiries to 420 Fifth Avenue, 3rd Floor, New York, NY 10018-2729 (212-730-8800/fax 212-730-1600/e-mail: aucegypt@aucnyo.edu). MA in Teaching English as a Foreign Language (MA/TEFL). Full-time students can complete the course in two years (fall and spring semester, plus optional summer). Tuition $5,150 per semester. Shared room is $1,320, and single room is $2,140. Programme tries to balance theory and practice. American-style education in an overseas setting. Informal help given with job search.

France

THE AMERICAN UNIVERSITY OF PARIS, Division of Continuing Education, 102 rue Saint Dominique, 75007 Paris. Tel: 1-40 62 07 20. Fax: 1-40 62 07 17. E-mail: ce@aup.fr. Website: www.aup.fr. TEFL Certificate over 8 weeks: October, January,

April, June (daytime Monday-Friday). Practice teaching Tuesday and Thursday evenings or Saturday mornings. F17,000. Career counselling and job assistance included.

WICE, 20 boulevard du Montparnasse, 75015 Paris. Tel: 1-45 66 75 50. Fax: 1-40 65 96 53. E-mail: wice@club-internet.fr. Website: www.wice.org. TEFL Certificate in conjunction with Rutgers State University, Newark Campus, New Jersey, USA. One month accelerated (full-time) courses in June and September. Part-time courses (October-May) with choice of morning, afternoon or evening sessions on Tuesdays and Thursdays. F9,300 accelerated and F9,800 year-long; F350 membership fee for WICE is included in the price. No accommodation.

Germany

MUNCHNER VOLKSHOCHSCHULE, Fachgebiet Englisch, Postfach 80 11 64, 81611 München. Fax: 0049 89 48006 2 52. 1-week Preliminary Certificate in TEFL. Once a year in September. DM270. Information can be sent from May preceding the course. Also offers CELTA.

Greece

CELT ATHENS, 77 Academias Street, 106 78 Athens. Tel: (1) 330 2406. Tel/fax: (1) 33 1455. E-mail: celt@celt.gr. Website: www.celt.gr. Introductory Methods Course in TEFL 100-hrs full-time or part-time; cost approx. $1,000. Cambridge DELTA part-time 8 months or 16 months, approx. $3,500. Short 20 hour refresher workshops: teaching English to young learners, teaching adults, teaching English through drama, teaching exam preparation classes, approx. $200 per course. LoL Diploma in translation (English to Greek); modern Greek and English as a Foreign Language courses for adults.

Hong Kong

THE BRITISH COUNCIL, 3 Supreme Court Road, Admiralty, Hong Kong. Tel: (852) 2913 5581. Fax: (852) 2913 5588. E-mail: rebecca.ho@britishcouncil.org.hk. Certificate in Teaching English to Young Learners (CELTYL). Three courses a year starting September, November and May. 3-days intensive followed by 8 or 9 weeks part-time. HK$19,600.

TEFL INTERNATIONAL, PO Box 34968, King's Road Post Office, Hong Kong (or 1 Braemar Hill Road, Palisades Club, Hong Kong). Tel: 2491 4938. E-mail: info@teflintl.com. Website: www.teflintl.com. Contact information available in Thailand from 38/53-55 Moo 1, Klaeng, Muang Rayong 21160 (38-652 280). 4-week certificate course. TESOL Online Certificate course. US$1,350 to US$1,850. Private accommodation included in course fee. Assistance with job placement (TEFL vacancies are posted on website). Also offer certificate and other courses by distance learning.

Hungary

NEW WORLD TEACHERS, 605 Market Street, Suite 800, San Francisco, CA 94105, USA. San Francisco training centre (see contact details and listing below in USA) which offers 4-week TEFL Certificate course in Budapest for $2,950 plus $400 accommodation. Courses also available in the US, Mexico and Thailand.

Ireland

The Recognised English Language Schools Association (RELSA) of Ireland promotes its own Association for Teaching Training in TEFL (ATT) Certificate, which involves a practical course of 100-120 hours duration costing between IR£600 and IR£1,000. Shorter ATT courses are the Preliminary (40 hours for approx. £190) and the Foundation (varying lengths). A list of member schools may be requested from RELSA at 17 Camden St Lower, Dublin 2 (1-475 3122/fax 1-475 3088).

BLUEFEATHER SCHOOL OF LANGUAGES, 35 Montpelier Parade, Monkstown, Dublin, Ireland. Tel: 1-280 6288. Fax: 1-280 6035. E-mail: TEFL@bluefeather.ie. Website: www.bluefeather.ie. Range of courses: 40-hour Preliminary, 70-hour Foundation, 100-hour Advanced and 125-hour Diploma courses as well as by distance learning. College-based courses once a month; Diploma once a year. Cost from IR£200 to IR£500. Accommodation can be provided with host families, in hostel or B & B. Many opportunities for practice with EFL students in small groups. Assistance with job placement.

CENTRE OF ENGLISH STUDIES, 31 Dame Street, Dublin 2. Tel: 1-671 4233. Fax: 1-671 4425. E-mail: info@ces.ireland.ie. Website: www.ces.ireland.ie. ESP Teacher Training validated by ACELS. Accommodation can be arranged.

EXCEL INTERNATIONAL LANGUAGE & BUSINESS, University College Cork Enterprise Centre, North Mall, Cork, Ireland. Tel: 21-304770. Fax: 21-304772. E-mail: enquiry@excel.ie. 40-hour Preliminary course from Monday to Friday plus exam the following Tuesday afternoon, offered twice a month; £190. Also 30-hour Foundation course Monday to Friday offered every 3 months (subject to demand); £130. Courses validated by ATT. Host family or B & B accommodation arranged. Contact Mary McCarthy, Administrator.

INTERNATIONAL TEFL COLLEGE OF IRELAND, 6 Merrion Square North, Dublin, 2. Tel/fax: 1-280 7001. 100 or 120 hour TEFL training courses. 4-6 weeks tuition (daytime and evenings). Offered monthly throughout the year. £200-£300. Accommodation available on request. Teaching practice and placement. Contact Maria Hayes.

TEFL TRAINING INSTITUTE OF IRELAND, 38 Harrington St, Dublin 8. Tel: 1-4784035; Fax: 1-4784038; E-mail: dublang@iol.ie. Website: www.dublinlanguage. com. Certificate and Diploma in TEFL validated by ATT. Offered monthly. Host family accommodation available.

UNIVERSITY OF LIMERICK, Plassey Technological Park, Limerick. Tel: 61-202700. Fax: 61-202556. E-mail: Admissions@ul.ie. Website: www.ul.ie/~lcs/ TEFL. MA in TEFL. One year from September.

Italy

A.C.L.E. (ASSOCIAZIONE CULTURALE LINGUISTICA EDUCATIONAL), Via Roma, 54, 18038 Sanremo. Tel/fax: 0039 0184 506070. E-mail: info@acle.org. Website: www.acle.org. Distance plus 3-day intensive TEFL introductory course with accommodation included. Registration £30 plus £120 course fee is deducted from final wages. Successful students (96% in 2000) work as paid counsellors teaching English at camps throughout Italy (see *Italy* chapter). This project offers a combination of theory plus invaluable practical experience with emphasis on drama and child-centred learning activities. TEFL Certificate issued at the end of the working period at Summer and City Camps.

Japan
PROMETHEUM SCHOOL OF LANGUAGES, San Francisco. Tel: 415-543-2992/415-409-1400. E-mail: psl@teflpro.com/ Website: www.teflpro.com. TEFL certificate programmes: 4 week intensive courses in Tokyo (also San Francisco) and distance courses. $2,800 includes course tuition in Japan, airfare from California, furnished apartment and airport pick-up. Job placement assistance given in perpetuity. Also arranges paid internships at Japanese universities (see chapter).

Mexico
NEW WORLD TEACHERS, 605 Market Street, Suite 800, San Francisco, CA 94105 (800-644-5242). San Francisco training centre (see contact details and listing below) which offers 4-week TEFL Certificate course at the University of Guadalajara in Puerto Vallarta for $2,750 plus $400 accommodation. Courses also available in the US, Hungary and Thailand.

WORLDWIDE TEACHERS DEVELOPMENT INSTITUTE, 264 Beacon Street, 3rd Floor, Boston, MA 02116. Tel: 800-875-5564. Fax: (617) 262-0308. E-mail: bostontefl@aol.com. Website: www.BostonTEFL.com. Intensive TEFL and Cert.TBE (Business English) certificate programs offered in Guadalajara, Mexico, or via Distance Learning. Courses also offered in Boston (see USA).

Portugal
INTERNATIONAL HOUSE LISBON, Rua Marquês Sá da Bandeira 16, 1050-148 Lisbon. Tel: 21-315 14 96. Fax: 21-353 00 81. E-mail: ihlisbon@mail.telepac.pt. Cambridge CELTA centre which offers 2-week introductory course to EFL (10,000 escudos) and 2-week Young Learners Extension Course (120,000 escudos).

Russia
BENEDICT SCHOOL, St Petersburg, Ul Pskovskaya 23, 1900008 St Petersburg, Russia. Tel: (812) 113 85 68. Fax: (812) 114 10 90. E-mail: benedict@infoprol.spb.su. Work-study programme, a two-part programme combining theoretical and practical aspects of TEFL. On completion of the teaching practice, candidates will receive the internationally recognised Benedict School TEFL Certificate and a reference. 36 hours plus 36 hours self-study. Courses run throughout the year. £165 including guide.

Singapore
THE BRITISH COUNCIL, 236A Holland Road, Singapore. Tel: 463 5525. Fax: 463 2970. Specific introductory Courses for teaching adults, young learners and home tuition. Intro courses are part-time (2 2-hour sessions per week for 5 weeks, 4 times a year). £200 approx. Also offer part-time CELTA.

South Africa
ONE WORLD LANGUAGE SCHOOL CAPE TOWN, 37 Strand Street, Cape Town 8001. Tel/Fax: (21) 423-1833. E-mail: owlstudy@iafrica.com. Website: www.owls.co.za. Short, introductory, entry-level TEFL courses for one week, once a month. £80. Accommodation offered on request, and help with graduate placement. School recognised by South African Council of Educators.

Spain
THE BRITISH LANGUAGE CENTRE, Calle Bravo Murillo 377-2°, 28020 Madrid. Tel: 91-733 07 39/733 04 08. Fax: 91-314 50 09. Cambridge/RSA centre which offers Pre-Diploma course (32 hours over 8 weeks) in the autumn. 40,000 pesetas. *INTERNATIONAL CAREER CENTER (ICC),* Calle Balmes 184, 4°-2°, 08006 Barcelona. Tel: (93) 415 3846/fax (93) 415 3049. In the US: PO Box 94, Winthrop, WA 98862; tel/fax: 888-256-2519; info@teflbarcelona.com/ www.teflbarcelona.com). 100-hour TEFL Certificate course offered monthly. $1,200 including course

manual and job workshop. Lifetime job assistance. Work visa assistance and support. Housing option with Spanish family or shared apartment from $600.
INTERNATIONAL HOUSE BARCELONA, Calle Trafalgar 14, 08010 Barcelona. Tel: (93) 268 4511. Fax: (93) 268 0239. E-mail: training@bcn.ihes.com. Website: www.ihes.com/bcn. Business English Teachers course. 36 hours over 2 weeks. July and September. Cost 48,000 pesetas. Also, Director of Studies Training Course (International House Barcelona). 1 week. July. Cost 48,000 pesetas. Help given with finding accommodation.
ITC INTERNATIONAL TEFL CERTIFICATE BARCELONA, Mediterrani, Estudis Superiors de Turisme, Edifici Mediterrani, Rocafort, 104, 08015 Barcelona. US Voice mail: 1-800-915-5540. US Fax: (815) 550-0086. Australian Voice mail: 1-300-368-189. E-mail: info@itc-training.com. Website: www.itc-training.com. Offers internationally-recognised 4-week TEFL Certificate course in Prague and Barcelona. More than 1,500 have graduated from ITC's course. Sessions held year-round on a monthly basis. Course is designed for individuals with little or no teaching experience. Trainees receive extensive supervised teaching practice with foreign students. US$1,500 includes registration, course manual, lifetime job assistance and employment contacts worldwide. City tour, cultural orientation and welcome dinner also included. Job workshop and career counselling during and after course. On-site EFL school with job opportunities for graduates. Housing and work visa assistance available. ITC is registered by the Ministry of Education in Spain. (See listings for Czech Republic above for information on Prague programme.)

Thailand

NEW WORLD TEACHERS, 605 Market Street, Suite 800, San Francisco, CA 94105, USA. San Francisco training centre (see contact details and listing below) which offers 4-week TEFL Certificate course in Phuket ($3,200 plus $400 accommodation). Courses also available in the US, Mexico and Hungary.
TEFL INTERNATIONAL, 38/53-55 Moo 1, Klaeng, Muang Rayong 21160 (38-652 280). E-mail: info@teflint.com. Website: http://teflint.com. 130-hour+ certificate course. US$1,500 but $1,000 paid by Nava Education if participants teach for them for 6 months (navaoperations@nls.ac.th). Also offer certificate and other courses by distance learning.

Turkey

INTERNATIONAL TRAINING INSTITUTE, Istiklal Cad., Kallavi Sokak 7-9, Galatasaray, Istanbul. Tel: 212-243 2888. Fax: 212-245 3163. E-mail: tomitithom@arti.net.tr. CELTA centre which runs Introduction to TEFL and CELTYL courses. Accommodation can be arranged in shared flat.

USA

BOSTON LANGUAGE INSTITUTE, 648 Beacon Street, Boston, MA 02215. Tel: (617) 262-3500. Fax: (617) 262-3595. E-mail: tefl@boslang.com. Website: www.teflcertificate.com. Intensive 4-week TEFL Certificate courses (120 hours) offered monthly. Also available part-time. Optional 1 week add-on certificate in Teaching Business English. Tuition $2,195 includes texts and lifetime job assistance. Homestay accommodation available from $160 per week.
HAMLINE UNIVERSITY, TEFL Certificate Program, Graduate School of Education, 1536 Hewitt Avenue, St. Paul, MN 55104, USA. Tel: (651) 523-2853/800-888-2182. Fax: (651) 523-2489. E-mail: bparrish@gw.hamline.edu. Three intensive one-month courses per year (July, August and April). One 10-week semi-intensive (January-March) and 1 evening extensive (September-March). Prices $1,970-$2,295. On-campus housing available except in August (approximately $600 per month including meals). Focus is on hands-on learning. Ongoing career counselling provided. Graduate credit granted.
LADO INTERNATIONAL COLLEGE, 2233 Wisconsin Avenue NW, Washington, DC 20007, USA. Fax: (202) 337-1118. E-mail: TeacherTraining@ladoent.com.

Web-site: www.LADO.com/Teacher/Home_T.htm. Lado Teaching Certificate Program based on Dr. Robert Lado's own Total Approach Method for teaching English communication skills. Full-time (8 hours per day) for 4 weeks, offered monthly. $1,750. Compulsory 20 hours of teaching practice on-site. Shared accommodation can be arranged. Has links with schools operating in Japan and recruitment companies in Korea.

MIDWEST TEACHER TRAINING PROGRAM, 19 Pinckney Street, Madison, WI 53703. Tel: 800-765-8577. Fax: 608/257-4346. E-mail: info@mttp.com. Website: www.mttp.com. TEFL Certificate Course lasting 5 weeks (130 hours including ten hours of teaching practice). 6 times a year. Can arrange homestays for trainees year-round and dormitory rooms in the summer. Part of a larger ESL school. Job

placement service including resource library, résumé writing/interviewing workshop and personal résumé editing.

NEW WORLD TEACHERS, 605 Market Street, Suite 800, San Francisco, CA 94105. Tel (within the USA): 800-644-5424. Tel (from overseas): 415-546-5200. Fax: 415-546-4196. E-mail: teachersSF@aol.com. Website: www.goteach.com. Intensive TEFL Certificate courses (4 weeks, $2,000-$2,100) or part-time (10 weeks, $1,950) offered year-round. Courses emphasise teaching American English. Specialised workshops on teaching EFL to young learners also available. Accommodation in the school's own guest house in San Francisco. Courses also available in Mexico, Hungary and Thailand. Extensive job placement assistance including personal counselling, database of international employers and internet access to network of TEFL graduates around the world.

PROMETHEUM SCHOOL OF LANGUAGES, San Francisco. Tel: 415-543-2992/415-409-1400. E-mail: psl@teflpro.com/ Website: www.teflpro.com. TEFL certificate programmes: 4 week intensive courses in US (also Japan) or distance courses. Job placement assistance. Also arrange paid internships at Japanese universities (see chapter).

SCHOOL OF TEACHING ENGLISH AS A SECOND LANGUAGE, Seattle University School of Education, 2601 NW 56th Street, Seattle, WA 98107. Tel: 206-781-8607. Fax: 206-781-8922. E-mail: tulare@seattleu.edu. Website: www.seattleu.edu/soe/stesl. 12-credit, 4-week intensive courses (monthly), non-intensive evening courses (quarterly), and new on-line courses (quarterly). $195 per credit. Studio apartments onsite or rooms in the area available. Course carries college credit. Counselling, employment information room and monthly employment seminars.

SCHOOL FOR INTERNATIONAL TRAINING, Center for Teacher Education, Training and Research, Kipling Road, PO Box 676, Brattleboro, VT 05302-0676. Tel: 802-258-3350. Fax: 802-258-3316. E-mail: tesolcert@sit.edu. Website: www.sit.edu/tesolcert. 130-hour TESOL Certificate. 4-5 times a year. Course also offered occasionally in Recife (Brazil), Kyoto (Japan) and Brisbane (Australia). From Training Directory: Courses Abroad

TRANSWORLD SCHOOLS, CTEFL Training at Transworld Schools, 701 Sutter Street, 2nd Floor, San Francisco, CA 94109. Tel: 1-888-588-8335/415-928-2835. Fax: 415-928-0261. E-mail: transwd@aol.com. Website: www.transworldschools.com. Comprehensive Certificate in Teaching English as a Foreign Language (4 weeks full-time, 12 weeks part-time $1,800); Certificate in Teaching English as a Foreign Language (3 weeks full-time, 9 weeks part-time $1,600): Intensive CTEFL (for working teachers – 2 weeks full-time; 6 weeks part-time $1,500); Advanced CTEFL (for certified teachers – 1 week full-time; 3 weeks part-time $800). All courses Approved by State of California, BPPVE. High quality training at low tuition. Accommodation within 5 minutes walk in downtown San Francisco; ranges $150-$250 per week. Job placement worldwide and lifetime job assistance. CTEFL courses include evaluated Teaching Practice with foreign students, Grammar, Language Skills, Business English and ESP, Teaching Children, Computer Assisted Language Learning, TOEFL and Syllabus design. Facilities include multi-media computer lab, video and Internet access.

UNIVERSITY OF CALIFORNIA IRVINE EXTENSION, PO Box 6050, Irvine, CA 92716-6050. Tel: 714-824-8196. Fax: 714-824-8065. English and Certificate Programs for Internationals, Post Box 6050, Irvine, CA 92616-6050. Tel: 949-824 5991. Fax: 949-824-8065. TEFL Certificate is 6 months. $4,495.

WASHINGTON ACADEMY OF LANGUAGES, TESL Program, 98 Yesler Way, Seattle, WA 98104. Tel: 206-682-4463 or toll-free 888-682-4463. Fax: 206-224-7927. Website: www.wal.org. Graduate TESL/TEFL Certificate offered in conjunction with Seattle Pacific University. 8 courses for total of 24 quarter credits. Offered intensively as 8-week summer course or in evening classes over academic year. $3,902 total cost for non-US residents, $3,040 for US citizens including credit fees. Campus or homestay accommodation can be arranged during summer school.

WORLDWIDE TEACHERS DEVELOPMENT INSTITUTE OF GUADALAJARA, 264 Beacon Street, 3rd Floor, Boston, MA 02116. Tel: 800-875-5564; 617-262 5722. Fax: 617-262-0308. E-mail: bostontefl@aol.com. Website: www.BostonTEFL.com. Intensive TEFL and Cert. TBE (Business English) certificate programs offered in Boston or via Distance Learning. Harvard University Club or other accommodation. (PDP) Mass. Dept. of Education. Course also offered in Guadalajara (see Mexico).

Finding a job

Teaching jobs are either fixed up from home or sought out on location. Having a job arranged before departure obviously removes much of the uncertainty and anxiety of leaving home for an extended period. It also allows the possibility of preparing in appropriate ways, sorting out the right visa, researching the course books in use, etc. Others prefer to meet their employer and inspect the school before signing a contract. It is always an advantage to meet other teachers and learn about the TEFL scene in that particular place firsthand before committing yourself, rather than accepting a job in complete ignorance of the prevailing conditions. But of course this is not always feasible.

Employers normally choose their staff several months before they are needed, so most schools advertise between April and July for jobs starting in September. If you want to fix up a job in person, you will either have to go on a reconnaissance mission well in advance of your proposed starting date or take your chances of finding a last-minute vacancy.

There are three ways of fixing up a teaching job in advance: by answering an advertisement, using a recruitment agency (which includes the large international English teaching organisations like International House) or conducting a speculative job search, i.e. making contact by e-mail or letter with all the schools whose addresses you can find in books, lists or on the internet.

ADVERTISEMENTS

Luckily for the job-seeking teacher in the UK, two publications have a virtual monopoly on TEFL adverts. The two places to look are the Classified Adverts of the *Education Guardian* every Tuesday and the *Times Educational Supplement* published on Fridays but available in newsagents throughout the week. Outside the peak recruiting time (Easter to August), advertisements for TEFL training courses outnumber actual job vacancies but it is always worth having a look.

The monthly *EL Gazette* is a good source of news and developments in the ELT industry for all interested individuals, though it is pitched at the professional end of the market. Single issues of the journal cost £2.90/$5.50 while an annual subscription costs £32.50 (UK & Europe), £42 worldwide. Contact *EL Gazette*, Dilke House, 1 Malet St. Bloomsbury, London WC1E 7JN (020-7255 1969) or in the US: PO Box 61202, Oklahoma City, OK 73146 (fax 405-557-2538).

EL Prospects is the monthly employment supplement which comes free with the *EL Gazette*. It can also be subscribed to separately; the current rate is £9.95 for six issues within Europe or for four issues outside Europe. Each issue lists vacancies according to region e.g. Pacific Rim, Central Asia, etc. Quite a high percentage of the listings provide only an e-mail address.

Relevant adverts occasionally appear in other places such as *Overseas Jobs Express,* the *Guardian Weekly, The Times* (on Wednesdays), the *Graduate Post,* etc. but these are insignificant in comparison.

One of the best sources of job ads for qualified TEFL teachers is TESOL Inc's *Placement Bulletin.* The electronic newsletter includes ESL/EFL job listings and articles about employment in ESOL. An e-mail subscription is free with membership in TESOL (Teachers of English to Speakers of Other Languages, Inc.), 700 S Washington St, Suite 200, Alexandria, VA 22314 (703-836 0774/fax 703-836-6447; careers@tesol.org/ www.tesol.org).

Another American publication in the field of overseas education is *The International Educator* (PO Box 513, Cummaquid, MA 02637, USA; and 102A Pope's Lane, London W5 4NS; fax 020-8840 2587/e-mail: tie@capecod.net/ www.tieonline.com). It concentrates on jobs in international English-medium schools, most of which follow an American curriculum, British curriculum or the International Baccalaureate (IB). The schools which advertise in *TIE* mainly employ qualified primary and secondary teachers of all subjects. The EFL/ESL jobs that are advertised are normally open to EFL teachers with experience of teaching children and not just adults. The journal is published four times a year (October, December, February and April) plus a Jobs Only Supplement is produced in June. An annual subscription costs £28 ($45 for residents of the US & Canada), while membership which includes various extras (discounts, travel insurance, etc.) costs £40/$65. This also enables readers to see the jobs online and put their own CVs online.

Job-seekers without a computer can still turn to print. *ESL Magazine* (220 McKendree Ave, Annapolis, MD 21401; 410-570-0746; www.eslmag.com) lists TEFL job vacancies and includes articles not posted on the internet. An annual subscription of six issues costs $16.95 in the US or $34.95 worldwide.

Yet another publication of interest to international job seekers is the *International Employment Gazette* (423 Townes Street, Greenville, SC 29601, tel USA; 864-235 4444; fax 864-235 3369; e-mail: intljobs@aol.com; website: www.interemployment.com). IEG is published every two weeks and contains details of ELT vacancies and recruitment organisations in North America. A three-month subscription costs $35 in the US ($45 foreign).

Various newsletters and publications contain lists of international schools which normally do not relate to actual vacancies. Given that any good library (public or careers) should have a copy of one of the Directories of International Schools (like the ones available from ECIS in the UK or ISIS in Princeton), it may be superfluous to purchase separate lists.

Education Information Services (EIS) (PO Box 620662, Newton, MA 02162-0662; 781-433-0125/fax: 781-237-2842) publishes every six weeks a list of about 150 openings in international and American schools of interest primarily to US-certified teachers. They publish lists with names and addresses of American overseas and international schools in all countries of the world. They are also building up lists of the leading language schools in many countries which hire EFL teachers.

OPENING ENGLISH SCHOOL

ENGLISH TEACHERS REQUIRED

We are a multinational company and leader in the field of English teaching. Our method is based on advanced multimedia technology, which allows us to provide a personalised study plan for every student.

Opening English School was founded in 1996 and is expanding internationally. We have a team of more than 2,500 people, including more than 1,000 teachers, serving the needs of over 60,000 students.

We are looking for enthusiastic teaching professionals to work in our schools in Spain, Italy, Portugal, France, Greece, Poland and Brazil. We offer a stimulating work environment and the chance to be a part of a fantastic team. What's more, we are committed to developing the full professional potential of all our team members with in house training and our unique system of internal promotion.

IF YOU ARE INTERESTED IN MAXIMISING YOUR POTENTIAL AS PART OF A GREAT TEAM, WHY NOT JOIN US?

For further details send your CV to:
The Human Resources Department,
Opening English School,
Plaça Francesc Macia 7,
08029 Barcelona,
Spain.
Fax (93) 366 7905;
E-mail: amolpeceres@openingschool.com

Other sources of addresses of mainstream schools abroad (as opposed to language schools) include the *Bulletin of Overseas Teaching Opportunities* which costs $42 per year (Overseas Academic Opportunities, 72 Franklin Ave, Ocean Grove, NJ 07756; tel/fax 732-774-1040). It lists about 50 vacancies each month, a few of which hire EFL teachers.

The internet offers an increasingly useful medium for EFL recruiters and teachers alike. For schools, a web-site offers a means of publicity and also an international advertising medium for reaching potential teaching staff. It is far quicker and cheaper for schools in, say, Thailand, Ecuador or Russia to post vacancy notices on the internet than it would be to place an advert in a foreign newspaper. Teachers looking for employment can use search engines to look for all pages with references to EFL, English language schools and recruitment. CVs can be e-mailed quickly and cheaply to advertising schools, who can then use e-mail themselves to chase up references. This presupposes a degree of IT awareness and access but it is certainly a useful supplement to traditional jobsearch methods. Already there are some schools which advertise solely on the internet. See the list of TEFL websites at end of chapter *Finding a Job*.

Interpreting Adverts

Jobs are listed year round, though schools which advertise in February or October are often advertising a very urgent vacancy, e.g. 'to start immediately, good salary, air fares, accommodation' – but these are exceptional.

Almost all adverts specify TEFL training/experience as a minimum requirement. But there is always a chance that this is merely rhetorical. Those who lack such a background should not feel defeated before they begin, since a TEFL background may turn out not to be essential. A carefully crafted CV and enthusiastic personality (not to mention a shortage of suitable applicants) could well persuade a school that they don't really have to insist on a Cambridge or Trinity Certificate with two years experience after all.

The *Times Educational Supplement* (or *TES*) includes two relevant headings. 'Overseas Appointments' primarily (but not exclusively) lists jobs in English-medium schools, while 'English as a Foreign Language' is for TEFL jobs outside Britain. Although there is no guarantee that schools which use the hallowed pages of the British educational press for their siren songs of employment will be reasonable employers, most are established schools which go to the trouble and expense of recruiting abroad.

Advertisements will often include a contact name or company in the UK to which enquiries should be addressed for posts abroad. This may be a TEFL training centre or a language school in the UK which is in contact with language schools abroad or it may just be an ex-employee who has agreed to do some recruitment for a commission fee. When discussing terms and conditions with an agent, bear in mind that the agent may be more interested in collecting his commission for finding someone to fill the vacancy than he is in conveying all the facts.

Occasionally cases crop up of misleading or even fraudulent ads. A case a few years ago resulted in a headline in the *Times Educational Supplement:* 'Thousands conned by Botswana job hoax.' A conman placed adverts for teaching jobs in a fictitious school in Botswana, sent a letter of acceptance to all who applied and a request for $100 as a visa processing fee. Even if this sort of bare-faced fraud is rare, it is best to be sceptical when interpreting ads, including on the internet where promises of earning huge salaries are usually pie-in-the-sky.

Based on his experience of answering advertisements placed by Turkish language schools, John Boylan has drawn up a glossary of terms, helping new applicants to 'read between the lines':

'Dollar Linked Salary' – Paid in the local currency and only linked to the dollar
    every three or six months
'Free Accommodation' – no way can you afford to rent a place of your own. You

have no say in who your flatmates are.
'Paid Flight' – this is usually for a one-way flight
'Leading School' – all the schools say this about themselves
'Provides In-Service Training' – weekly, monthly or annually
'Degree and Cert essential' – that's what the Ministry of Education wants. Will
   recruit anybody if desperate (good schools) or anybody at all (cowboys)
'Central Location' – near all the good pubs
'Young and Dynamic Team' – be like a student again
'Teachers are encouraged to use their own materials and be creative' – there isn't
   much in the way of resources.

Apart from newspapers, there are a few other places where vacancies abroad
might be mentioned. ELT training centres often have numerous links with foreign
schools and may have a notice board with posted vacancies (as in the case of
International House in Piccadilly). Unless you are a trainee at the relevant centre,
it will probably be tricky consulting such a notice board, but a co-operative
secretary might not mind a *potential* trainee consulting the board. University
careers offices may also have contacts with schools abroad to which their
graduates have gone in the past, so if you have a university connection, it is worth
making enquiries.

THE BRITISH COUNCIL

The British Council is the largest ELT (English language teaching) employer in the
world. The Council represents the elite end of the English language teaching
industry. At its own Teaching Centres in 60 countries, it offers the highest quality
language teaching available in those countries and employs the best qualified
teachers, so it is important to understand that the British Council will not welcome
applications from very inexperienced or unqualified teachers. The British Council is
a very professional organisation and jobs with them tend to come with attractive
terms and conditions.

Council offices abroad are normally well-informed about opportunities for
English language teaching locally. Most maintain a list of private language schools
(while making it clear that inclusion does not confer recognition), which is often a
useful starting point for a job search. Whether they will send it in advance or give a
copy to enquirers is at the discretion of staff. Some British Council offices even
publish informal leaflets about teaching possibilities.

The Council publishes an *Address Book* of its offices worldwide which is
updated quarterly. A copy can be requested from the Council's Information Centre
(Bridgewater House, 58 Whitworth St, Manchester M1 6BB; 0161-957 7755) or
checked on the web at www.britishcouncil.org/where/addressbook.doc. While
researching the current edition of this book, most of these offices were written to and
any relevant responses have been included in the country chapters.

The charter of the British Council defines its aims as 'to promote Britain abroad,
providing access to British ideas, talents and experience in education and training,
books and periodicals, the English language, the arts, the sciences and technology.'
It is non-profit-making and works non-politically in more than 100 countries. It
employs about 7,500 staff in all, divided between Britain and abroad, a good
percentage of whom are involved with the teaching of the English language in some
capacity. Other work which the Council carries out includes the running of libraries,
the organisation of cultural tours and exchanges, etc. But language teaching and
teacher recruitment remain one of its central concerns.

A useful starting place for qualified teachers is to request their recruitment
literature which is available free of charge from the Teaching Centre Recruitment
Unit, (10 Spring Gardens, London SW1A 2BN; 020-7389 4931.
www.britcoun.org/english).

Structure of the British Council

The British Council is a large and complex institution with two headquarters: one at 10 Spring Gardens London SW1A 2BN (020-7930 8466) and the other at Bridgewater House, 58 Whitworth St, Manchester M1 6BB (0161-957 7000). Telephone callers who do not know exactly which department they need should contact the Council's Information Unit in Manchester (0161-957 7755).

Here is a layman's guide to the sections and departments of possible interest to prospective teachers:

Educational Enterprises, 10 Spring Gardens, London SW1A 2BN. Tel: 020-7389 4931. Fax: 020-7389 4140. E-mail: teacher.vacancies@britishcouncil.org.
Educational Enterprises is the name for the department which oversees the Council's 120 or so teaching outlets around the world. The recruitment unit is responsible for the bulk of the hiring of contract teachers. Each Teaching Centre employs between 3 and 200 teachers, many of whom are qualified to Diploma level, though some centres will consider applications from people with a certificate level qualification and experience.

Teaching Centres recruit both through London and locally. Qualified teachers who are planning to move to a location where there is a British Council Teaching Centre would be welcome to apply direct to the Teaching Centre Manager for information on opportunities for local contracts. At the time of writing, the Teaching Centre Recruitment Unit anticipated hiring about 300 teachers in the coming year, as well as 25 middle managers and the same number of managers, many of whose posts are filled through internal transfer. The British Council regularly advertises in the national press. It also has its own web-site with a vacancy list www.britcoun.org/english/engvacs.htm. They especially welcome applications from teachers with experience or an interest in specialist areas such as Young Learners, Business English, skills through English, IT/CALL, etc.

Contracts are normally for two years and renewable. Recruitment goes on year round though the majority of vacancies are still for September/October starts. Interviews for these posts are held in London between April and August. Although terms and conditions vary from centre to centre, the terms of employment with the British Council are very favourable. Teachers recruited through Educational Enterprises usually have their airfares paid, an allowance for shipping their belongings and an attractive salary package. Many teachers value all the intangible benefits such as the security of working for an established institution, and encouragement of professional development with possible perks such as receiving a subsidy to study for a Diploma qualification or other training grants. Once you have secured one job with the Council, it is possible to move to other jobs in other places, since the Council regularly notifies its network of all vacancies.

Overseas Appointments Service/OAS, Bridgewater House, 58 Whitworth St, Manchester M1 6BB; 0161-957 7384.
The Overseas Appointments Service recruits personnel for posts abroad in universities, teacher training colleges, ministries of education, etc. The majority of educational vacancies are related to ELT but by no means all, since the Council is often asked to provide technical experts for educational establishments abroad.

A substantial part of OAS's work is on behalf of the UK government's Department for International Development (Abercrombie House, Eaglesham Road, East Kilbride, Glasgow G75 8EA; www.dfid.gov.uk) formerly the Overseas Development Administration (ODA). Large display adverts bearing both logos can occasionally be seen in the *Times Educational Supplement* and the *Guardian*. Anyone who is sufficiently qualified to be eligible for these positions can submit an application which will be kept active for a calendar year.

Information Centre, Bridgewater House, 58 Whitworth St, Manchester M1 6BB; 0161-957 7755/fax 0161-957 7762.

The Information Centre distributes two information packs to members of the public: *How to Become a Teacher of English as a Foreign Language* which includes lists of TEFL courses, and *British Council Accredited English Language Schools in the UK.*

RECRUITMENT ORGANISATIONS

Major providers of ELT and teacher placement organisations of various kinds may be able to assist prospective teachers in English-speaking countries to find teaching jobs. Some are international educational foundations; some are voluntary organisations like VSO or charities; some are major chains of commercial language schools; and others are small agencies which serve as intermediaries between independent language schools abroad and prospective teachers. The companies and organisations listed in this chapter have been assigned to the following categories (though there is some blurring of distinctions): International ELT Organisations (including the major language school chains); Commercial Recruitment Agencies; Voluntary, Gap Year and Religious Organisations; North American Organisations which cater primarily (though not exclusively) to citizens of the US and Canada; and, finally, Placement Services for British and American state-qualified teachers. Note that agencies and organisations which operate only in one country or one region are described in the country chapters in the second part of this book.

It is hardly worthwhile for a family-run language school in northern Greece or southern Brazil to pay the high costs which most agencies charge schools just to obtain one or two native speaker teachers. Vacancies that are filled with the help of agencies and recruitment consultants tend to be at the elite end of the ELT market. Jobs advertised by agencies are usually for specialised or high level positions, for example in corporations with in-house EFL programmes or foreign governments.

Agencies make their money by charging client employers; the service to teachers is normally free of charge. By law in the UK, no fee can be charged to job-seekers either before or after placement, except if a package of services is sold alongside (e.g. insurance, visas, travel, etc.) Note that different rules apply in other countries, so that placement fees are the norm in the US. Some of the best recruitment organisations to deal with are ones which specialise in a single country in situ, such as English Educational Services in Madrid or Cambridge Teachers Recruitment in Athens (see Spain and Greece chapters). They tend to have more first-hand knowledge of their client schools.

On the other hand, the use of an intermediary by foreign language institutes is no guarantee of anything. Particularly in the American context, small independent recruiters are sometimes trying to fill vacancies that no one in the country who is familiar with the employer would deign to fill. As the American Rusty Holmes said of his employer in Taiwan, 'The school was so bad it had to recruit from America.' If you are in any doubt about the reliability of an agency or the client he/she represents, it is a sensible precaution to ask for the name of one or more previous teachers whom you can ask for a first-hand account. It is a bad sign if the agency is unable or reluctant to oblige.

The hiring of teachers for chain schools abroad is done either at a local level (so direct applications are always worthwhile) or centrally, especially if the affiliated school has trouble filling vacancies on its own.

One way in which recruitment agencies work is to create a database of teachers' CVs and to try to match these with suitable vacancies as they occur. In order to be registered with such an agency it is normally essential to have a relevant qualification, often at least the Cambridge or Trinity Certificate. When applicants outnumber vacancies, it is not surprising to hear that most agencies are unwilling to register non-nationals without superior qualifications. Recruitment agencies in the UK may find it difficult to cope with applications from the US since it is difficult to translate qualifications; one mentioned that because of anti-discrimination legislation, American applicants do not always mention their age or sex, which most language school directors want to know.

Smaller agencies may have fewer vacancies on their books but they can often offer a more personal service. It is a legal requirement for agencies to obtain references from any client to which it wants to send teachers. A good agency will provide a full briefing and information pack on the school in particular and the country in general, and will make sure that the contract offered is a reasonable one. If a job doesn't work out, the agency should provide a back-up service and make itself available to sort out misunderstandings and (if appropriate) offer an alternative placement. Marisa Wharton describes the support an agency should provide when things go wrong:

When our employers in the Czech Republic broke the contract and behaved like mafiosi, our agency was very helpful. They found my husband a different job in Poland, so at least one of us has been placed. At the moment they are trying to sort out some sort of compensation for us.

International ELT Organisations

The Bell Educational Trust, Overseas Department, Hillscross, Red Cross Lane, Cambridge CB2 2QX. Tel: 01223-246644. Fax: 01223-414080. E-mail: info.overseas@bell-schools.ac.uk. Website: www.bell-schools.ac.uk Bell recruits teachers for ELT posts in its associated schools in Thailand, and for any current overseas projects. Bell's subsidiaries and associates in Hungary, the Czech Republic, Switzerland, Poland, Italy, Spain and Romania conduct their own recruitment, but a list of contact addresses can be obtained from the Overseas Department. Candidates are usually required to have a degree and a recognised TEFL qualification.

Bénédict Schools, 3 Place Chauderon, P.O. Box 270, 1000 Lausanne 9, Switzerland. Tel: (21) 323 66 55. Fax: (21) 323 67 77. E-mail: benedict@ worldcom.ch. Website: www.benedict-schools.com. Have over 80 business and language schools in Europe, Africa, South and North America on a franchise basis. Each school hires its own TEFL-qualified teachers, but some also run in-house training courses. A list of addresses is available from the Swiss headquarters or from their website. Bénédict Schools work in association with International Language Academies and Nord Anglia (entry below). There are ILAs in the UK, US, New Zealand, Australia, Russia, the Ukraine and Vietnam (www.language-academies.com).

Benedict International Ltd., 74 Baxter Court, Norwich, NR3 2ST. Tel/fax: 01603 301522. E-mail: emma@griffin.fsbusiness.co.uk. Job placements in various locations around the world. The main destinations are Eastern Europe and Russia. Graduates with TEFL certificate and teaching experience welcome to apply.

Berlitz UK, 9-13 Grosvenor Street, London W1A 3BZ. Tel: 020-7915 0909. Fax: 020-7915 0222. Berlitz Inc., 400 Alexander Park, Princeton, NJ 08540-6306, USA. Tel: (609) 514-9650. Fax: (609) 514-9672. Website: www.berlitz.com Berlitz is one of the largest language training organisations in the world with about 400 centres in 40 countries. It is also one of the oldest; Berlitz celebrated its 122nd anniversary in 2000. The company's core business is language and cultural training, and teacher vacancies occur most often in Latin America, Spain, Italy, Germany, France and Korea. All Berlitz teachers are native-fluent speakers and university graduates who are trained in the 'Berlitz Method,' a direct 'see-hear-speak' teaching approach that does not rely on translation. Berlitz is known for supervising their teachers' techniques very closely, and deviation from the method is not permitted. When Berlitz has urgent vacancies to fill, usually in Spain and Italy, it places an advertisement in British newspapers inviting any interested university graduates to attend interviews in London, Manchester, Edinburgh or Dublin. Normally, however, Berlitz schools abroad employ teachers directly, usually on a part-time basis initially, after they have completed a two-week training course.

BIELT Job Centre, British Institute of English Language Teaching, PO Box 1109, Headington, D.O. Oxford OX3 8XR. Tel/fax: 01865 742086. E-mail: enquiries@bielt.org. This professional body, set up in the past couple of years to act as the voice of the ELT profession, is in the process of setting up a job-finding service for members in association with major and smaller independent ELT recruiters. Membership is open to anyone with a recognised teaching or academic TEFL qualification. They anticipate posting 1,000-2,000 jobs on-line per year.

British Council – see section above.

C*f*BT The Teaching Agency, 6 Lampton Road, Hounslow, Middlesex TW3 1JL. Tel: 020-8814 8200. Fax: 020-8814 8209. E-mail: teachingagency@cfbt-hq.org.uk. Website: www.cfbt.com. Recruits and manages EFL/EAP/ESP/Primary/Secondary teachers and instructors for its own projects and a diverse range of public and private sector clients overseas. C*f*BT International Department, 4 The Chambers, East Street, Reading RG1 4JF. Tel: 0118-952 3900. Fax: 0118-952 3924. E-mail: intrecruit@cfbt-hq.org.uk/ Website: www.cfbt.com. Recruit educational consultants for aid work in developing countries with regional bases in Africa, South East Asia, Eastern Europe, the Gulf and the Caribbean.

Central Bureau for International Education & Training, 10 Spring Gardens, London SW1A 2BN. Tel: 020-7389 4004. Fax: 020-7389 4426. E-mail: centralbureau@britishcouncil.org. Website: www.centralbureau.org.uk. Also offices in Scotland (3 Bruntsfield Crescent, Edinburgh EH10 4HD), Northern Ireland (7 Fountain Street, Belfast BT1 5EG; 028-9024 8220) and Wales (28 Park Place, Cardiff CF1 3QE; 029-2039 7346). The Central Bureau administers various exchange programmes for certified teachers and language assistant placements to help local teachers of English in many countries from France to Venezuela.

Applicants for assistant posts must be aged 20-30, native English speakers, with at least two years of university-level education, normally in the language of the destination country. In some countries (especially in Latin America and Eastern Europe) posts are of particular interest to graduates interested in a career in TEFL. Application forms are available from October; the deadline is December of the preceding academic year.

Council Exchanges: Council UK, 52 Poland St, London W1V 4JQ, UK. Tel: 020-7478 2000. Fax: 020-7734 7322. In Australia: P O Box Q577, QVB Post Office, 1230 Sydney, NSW. Tel: (2) 9373 2730. Fax: (2) 9373 2731. E-mail: TiC@councilexchanges.org. Website: www.councilexchanges.org/work/ticfacts.htm. Council administers the Japan Exchange & Teaching (JET) and Teach in China Programmes (see respective chapters). The US headquarters are listed under *Opportunities for North Americans* below.

EF English First, Teacher Recruitment Centre, EF House, 1-3 Farman Street, Hove East Sussex BN3 1AL. Tel: 01273 747308. Fax: 01273 746742. E-mail: e1recruitment@ef.com/ kate.guy@ef.com. Website: www.ef.com. EF has schools in Indonesia, Russia, Poland, China, Mexico, Morocco, Ecuador, Lithuania, Azerbaijan, Kazakhstan, Slovenia, Singapore and Thailand. Recruitment of up to 400 EFL qualified teachers takes place all year round and senior posts are available too. In the US contact: EF Education (Human Resources, EF Education, One Education Street, Cambridge, MA 02141; 617-619-1955/fax 617-619-1001; Careers@ef.com).

ELS Language Centers, International Division, 400 Alexander Park, Princeton NJ 08540. Tel: 609-750-3512. Fax: 609-750-3596. E-mail: smatson@els.com. Website: www.els.com. ELS Language Centers have recently become linked to Berlitz (hence the sharing of an address) but their 50 franchised English language schools overseas remain separate. The most efficient way to apply for a job is direct to the individual centres in countries including Brazil, China, Colombia, Egypt, Indonesia, Japan, Kuwait, the Lebanon, Malaysia, Oman, Panama, Qatar, Saudi Arabia, South Korea, Taiwan and the United Arab Emirates. All addresses are listed on their admirably clear website. The International Division is a clearinghouse of recruitment for ELS's overseas franchises in a range of countries in Latin America, Asia and the Middle East (but not Europe). The minimum requirements to recommend an applicant for overseas placement are a bachelor's degree in any subject and completion of a 130-hour TEFL or TESL certificate programme. Applicants should submit a résumé, cover letter and copies of two letters of recommendation to the above address, marked for the attention of Overseas Recruitment. The largest franchise is in Taiwan where there are 18 ELSI schools. For the Taiwan contact address see *Taiwan* chapter or e-mail elsjobs@ms54.hinet.net.

Note that ELS is represented in London at 3 Charing Cross Road, London WC2H 0HA. The UK Recruitment Officer is particularly active in recruiting teachers for ELS-affiliated schools in Korea (see chapter). ELS Language Centers are expanding in the Middle East too (see chapter).

ELT Banbury, 49 Oxford Road, Banbury, Oxon. OX16 9AH. Tel: (01295) 263480/263502. Fax: (01295) 271658. Website: www.elt-banbury.com. Maintains Teacher Directory for worldwide recruitment. CELTA or Trinity Certificate is minimum requirement. Recruits for its own centres in 14 countries (Europe, Far East and Middle East) and on behalf of other institutions.

inlingua Teacher Training & Recruitment, Rodney Lodge, Rodney Road, Cheltenham, Glos. GL50 1HX. Tel: 01242 253171. Fax: 01242 253181. E-mail: recruitment@inlingua-cheltenham.co.uk. Website: www.inlingua-cheltenham.co.uk. Has more than 300 centres worldwide (operating as separate businesses) for which it recruits over 200 teachers annually. The majority are for schools in Spain, Italy, Germany, Russia, Poland, Turkey and Singapore. Opportunities also exist in France,

⟨⟩ **inlingua** Teacher Training & Recruitment

Specialists in **TEFL** Recruitment Worldwide
100s of posts for qualified teachers in -

Spain, Italy, Germany, Poland, Russia, Turkey
Singapore, Venezuela, The Far East & other locations

Min. Cert. TESOL/CELTA   See entry in Training Chapter

Rodney Lodge, Rodney Road, Cheltenham GL50 1HX - Tel: (01242) 253171

Korea, Thailand, Indonesia, Venezuela and other destinations. The minimum requirement is a Trinity Certificate in TESOL or a CELTA. Interested applicants should send in a CV. (Note that inlingua Teacher Training and Recruitment in Cheltenham offer the Trinity Certificate course; see *Training*). Every effort is made to find posts for American citizens in Europe.

International Certificate Conference (ICC), Secretariat, Hansaallee 150, D-60320 Frankfurt, Germany. Tel: (69) 56 02 01 66. Fax: (69) 56 02 01 68. E-mail: icc_europe@compuserve.com   Website: www.icc-europe.com.   Umbrella organisation for adult education associations (e.g. *Volkshochschulen* or folk high schools) in 13 European countries co-operating on the learning and teaching of foreign languages in Europe. Can provide enquirers with a list of member organisations and contact names. Have recently begun running specialist training courses for TEFL teachers in adult education.

International House, 106 Piccadilly, London W1V 7NL. Tel: 020-7518 6970. Fax: 020-7518 6971. E-mail: hr@ihlondon.co.uk. Website: www.ihlondon.com or www.ihworld.com. International House London is an educational trust which was established in 1953. Since then it has been providing teacher training and language programmes to people from all over the world. The affiliate network consists of 120 schools in more than 30 countries who work together to help raise the standards of language teaching worldwide.

The Human Resources department at IH London helps to recruit both teachers and senior staff for the affiliate schools overseas. The minimum requirement for teaching posts is the Cambridge CELTA or the Trinity TESOL Certificate. All schools provide educational support and are well resourced. A transfer system is operated whereby teachers can move from country to country, and solid career routes exist with opportunities to move up within the organisation. For further information on teaching and senior posts abroad please contact the Human Resources department on 020-7518 6970.

Language Link, 21 Harrington Road, London SW7 3EU. Tel: 020-7225 1065. Fax: 020-7584 3518. E-mail: languagelink@compuserve.com. Website: www.languagelink.co.uk; also www.jobs.ru. Training and recruitment agency which places about 200 qualified (including newly qualified) teachers in its network of affiliated schools in Slovakia, Poland, Russia, Czech Republic, Germany, the Ukraine, Vietnam, China, etc. Minimum qualifications are TEFL Cert. or PGCE or experience. Employment contracts are from 36 weeks to 2 years. 24 contact hours per week. Local pay rates. Shared apartment accommodation is usually provided at no additional cost or deduction from the salary. Interested teachers should ring to arrange an interview (in the UK or in Russia etc.), and then send CV and photo. (See Training chapter for details of Language Link's regular Trinity Certificate courses.)

Linguarama, Group Personnel Department, Oceanic House, 89 High St, Alton, Hampshire GU34 1LG. Tel: 01420 80899. Fax: 01420 80856. E-mail:

🌐 Linguarama
Language training for business

Linguarama is the largest UK based organisation specialising in language training for business with some thirty centres across Europe. For TEFL qualified graduates with the ability and ambition to develop we offer:

* Flight, initial accommodation and good terms
* Materials, training and teaching support
* Structured career development

Please contact: Personnel, Linguarama, Oceanic House, 89 High Street, Alton, GU34 1LG.
Tel: (01420) 80899   Fax: (01420) 80856   E-mail: personnel@linguarama.com
See our web site for more vacancies: http://www.linguarama.com/jobs

---

personnel@linguarama.com. Website: www.linguarama.com. Linguarama specialises in providing language training for professionals. Applicants for jobs in Linguarama language schools abroad must have at least a degree and a Cambridge/Trinity Certificate (or equivalent). Linguarama finds placements for 700-800 teachers and has two offices in London (for teacher interviews, visa services, etc.) as well as the above address which deals with vacancies at over 30 European centres in Germany, France, Spain, Italy, Finland and Central Europe.

Nord Anglia International Language Academies: 10 Eden Place, Cheadle, Cheshire SK8 1AT. Tel: 0161-491 4191. Fax: 0161-491 4409/4410. Website: www.language-academies.com. Nord Anglia is an international EFL organisation that operates over 80 summer schools in the UK and has various outlets abroad including Ukraine, Spain, Poland, Portugal and Taiwan. Anyone interested in working for an ILA abroad should contact the head office in Cheadle for the addresses. Alternatively, teachers are invited to send their CVs to: International Recruitment, Nord Anglia Education Personnel, No 9, Swinsens Yard, Stony Stratford, Milton Keynes MK11 1SY.

Opening English School, Via Augusta 238, 08021 Barcelona, Spain. Tel: (93) 241 89 00. Fax: (93) 241 89 10. E-mail: awesterman@openingschool.com. Recruits 450 teachers for Spain and also recruits for schools in France, Greece, Brazil and Portugal. The selection process takes place in the Barcelona office where CVs should be sent in the first instance. From there the CVs will be sent to a representative in each country. Eventually there will be an address for applications in each country.

Overseas Placing Unit – part of the European Employment Service Network (EURES). Occasionally language school vacancies are registered with the OPU. Access to this vacancy information is available through local Jobcentres only.

Saxoncourt and English Worldwide 124 New Bond Street, London W1Y 9AE. Tel: 0207-491 1911. Fax: 0207-493 3657. E-mail: recruit@saxoncourt.com. Website: www.saxoncourt.com. One of the largest UK-based recruiters of EFL teachers, Saxoncourt places over 600 teachers per year in schools in 30 countries. Currently, clients are based in Japan, Taiwan, Poland, China, Italy, Spain, Russia, Thailand, France, Peru, Brazil and elsewhere. Applications are welcome, particularly from candidates with CELTA, Trinity or TESOL or equivalent qualifications. Interviews are held in London, New Zealand, Canada and South Africa. Interested candidates should send a covering letter and CV. In London there is also a Teacher Information centre for candidates to drop in and gather information and advice about teaching English overseas.

Soros Professional English Language Teaching (SPELT) Program: Open Society Institute, 400 W. 59th Street, 4th Floor, NY, NY 10019. Tel: (212) 548-0136. Fax: (212) 548-4650. E-mail: spelt@sorosny.org. Open Society Institute's English

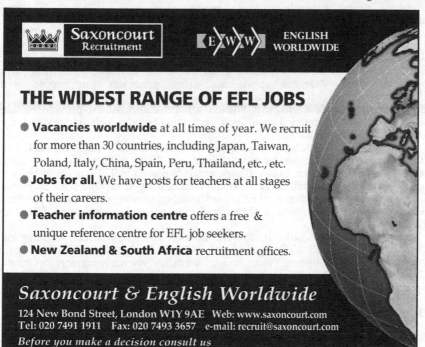

Language Program places instructors at universities and teacher training colleges in Azerbaijan, Bosnia and Herzegovina, Croatia, Georgia, Haiti, Kyrgyzstan, Mongolia, Russia, Tajikistan, Uzbekistan and Yugoslavia. An MA in Linguistics or TESOL is required in most cases, although EFL Certification will be considered. Prior teaching experience is required. US nationality is not necessary

University of Cambridge Local Examinations Syndicate (UCLES), Syndicate Buildings, 1 Hills Road, Cambridge CB1 2EU. An established feature of the course Certificate in English Language Teaching to Adults (CELTA) administered by UCLES is a free job placement service for candidates in the UK (see description of Cambridge Certificate Courses in the *Training* chapter).

Wall Street Institute International, Rambla de Catalunya 2-4, Planta Baixa, 08007 Barcelona, Spain. Tel: (93) 412 00 14/301 00 29. Fax: (93) 412 38 03. Website: www.wsi.com or www.wallstreetinstitute.com. Expanding chain of 250 commercial language institutes for adults, which employ approximately 750 full-time EFL teachers in Europe (Spain, Switzerland, Portugal, Italy, France and Germany) and Latin America (Mexico, Chile, Venezuela). For details about employment in a specific centre or country, contact individual centres or the country's 'Master Center' which in some cases acts as a clearinghouse for vacancies. The minimum requirements for teachers are: native speaking, university degree, professional attitude and appearance, and ability to work within the framework of a well-defined method and system, developed by WSI and using a combination of interactive multimedia laboratory study and classes with native speakers. WSI is part of Sylvan Learning Systems Inc.

Commercial Agencies

Anyone with a TEFL background should email or write to relevant agencies with a CV and covering letter, preferably enclosing a self-addressed envelope or (if overseas) international reply coupons. Agencies which specialise in a single country are not included in this chapter, but are mentioned in the country chapters.

Anglo-Pacific (Asia) Consultancy, Suite 32, Nevilles Court, Dollis Hill Lane, London NW2 6HG. Tel: 020-8452 7836/020-8452 2826. Educational consultancy which specialises in recruitment in Thailand, Taiwan, China and the rest of Southeast Asia. Also offers careers guidance to TEFL teachers returning from overseas. They welcome approaches from graduates (or people with HND/equivalent higher qualifications) who have a recognised TEFL Certificate. Place teachers at all levels in the public and private sectors. Aim to provide teachers with background information about their destination country including teaching tips and cultural information.

Avalon House, 8 Denmark St, London WC2H 8LS. Tel: 020-7916 5524. Fax: 020-7916 5261. E-mail: dos@avalonschool.co.uk. 35-40 teacher placements made per year in Brazil, France, Spain, China, etc. Ads placed in TEFL press in UK and on internet. Interviews held in London and occasionally at satellite schools abroad. Candidates must have degree, TEFL certificate or similar and some experience. Salaries negotiable according to local conditions, normally starting at £10,000 for 12-month contract.

Euronet (Group) Ltd., Bridgefoot House, 159 High Street, Huntingdon, Cambridgeshire, PE18 6TF. Tel: 01480 377000. Fax: 01480 377003. E-mail: vacancymanager@euronetservices.co.uk. Website: www.euronetservices.co.uk. General recruitment agency that has a TEFL section (contact Jenny MacLeod). Specialises mainly in TEFL jobs in the Gulf countries and Europe.

Langstar Educational Services, 105 Hundred Acres Lane, Amersham, Bucks. HP7 9BN. Tel: (01494) 727590. Fax: (01494) 724454. E-mail: langstar@ oles.net. Recruit teachers mainly for Poland, Turkey, Italy and occasionally elsewhere in Europe. Keep teachers' CVs on file. As a rule, minimum requirement is a recognised TEFL Certificate. Also recruit teachers for Langstar Summer School for which a TEFL Certificate is not essential.

TEFLNet Recruitment, Yapham Grange, Yapham Mill, York YO42 1PB. Tel/fax: 01759-305586. E-mail: teflnet@langwork.demon.co.uk. TEFLNet is an independent recruitment service which matches the requirements of EFL schools, colleges and training organisations with the qualifications, experience and preferences of EFL teachers and trainers. Placements are available for newly qualified teachers through to specialists. About two-thirds of positions require a degree and most require a Trinity or Cambridge TEFL Certificate. Main destinations are Asia (especially Thailand) and Eastern Europe (especially Poland).

Teacher Recruitment International (Aust), PO Box 1317, Sydney South, NSW 1235, Australia. Tel/fax: 2-9328 3930. E-mail: triaust@ozemail.com.au. Places mostly Australian and New Zealand teachers of ESL/EFL in language institutes and colleges in Asia and the Middle East. Candidates must have a CELTA and in most cases an Honours degree in English or Applied Linguistics.

Voluntary, Gap Year and Religious Organisations

Christians Abroad, Room 233 Bon Marché Centre, 241-251 Ferndale Road, London SW9 8BJ. Tel: 020-7346 5951. Fax: 020-7346 5955. E-mail: projects@cabroad.org.uk. Web-site: www.cabroad.org.uk. Ecumenical charity which provides information and advice to people of any faith or none who are thinking of working overseas, whatever their circumstances, whether short or long term, voluntary or paid. A free information booklet lists a variety of voluntary organisations in the UK and overseas, some of which are looking for EFL teachers. For qualified people, *Opportunities Abroad,* a monthly listing of vacancies is available on subscription and a database of skilled personnel is kept and searched on behalf of agencies looking for staff. Christian professional EFL and English teachers are often sought by organisations and agencies working in Africa and the Far East. At the time of writing, Christians Abroad itself was recruiting EFL teachers for

Japan, China, Hong Kong and Tanzania.

The most important voluntary agency in the UK recruits EFL teachers as well as many other kinds of volunteer.

VSO Voluntary Service Overseas, 317 Putney Bridge Road, London SW15 2PN. Tel: 020-8780 7500. Fax: 020-8780 7300. E-mail: enquiry@vso.org.uk. Website: www.vso.org.uk. VSO works in more than 74 countries in Africa, Asia and the Pacific. The largest programmes are in China, Vietnam, Rwanda, Indonesia, Ethiopia and Malawi. There are a growing number of placements in Eastern Europe.

Volunteer requirements vary. Most placements are for Britons aged 20 to 68. The minimum qualification is a degree (or two years' teaching experience *and* a teaching qualification). There are also positions for teachers with extensive experience.

The VSO package for its volunteers includes airfares, medical cover, National Insurance contributions, rent-free accommodation and a modest salary in line with local pay rates. In addition there are three grants: a start-up grant (to be applied for), a mid-tour travel grant and a resettlement grant. VSO also provides full in-country support including pre-departure training and briefing, basic language and cultural orientation on arrival prior to starting placement. Graduates can apply for an advance on their grants to help pay for a TEFL qualification if needed.

VSO holds regular VSO information evenings and open days, which are advertised through the local press and on the internet. EFL training days are held in September and February at Shakespeare's Globe Theatre in London. Returned volunteers attend these events to allow potential volunteers to get a fuller picture of VSO work in action. Alternatively, it is possible to talk to a returned volunteer about their experiences overseas by calling 0845-603 0027 (local call rates apply).

A number of UK organisations make it possible for school-leavers in their gap year to work for six months abroad, and many of these placements are in schools where volunteers teach English. Most of the organisations listed here are founder members of the Year Out Group (PO Box 29925, London SW6 6FQ; 07980 395789/ www.yearoutgroup.org) formed to promote well-structured gap year programmes:

GAP Activity Projects, 44 Queen's Road, Reading, Berks. RG1 4BB. Tel: (0118) 959 4914. Fax: (0118) 957 6634. E-mail: volunteer@gap.org.uk. Website: www.gap.org.uk. Positions for school leavers and very occasionally college leavers, including many as teaching assistants, in Latin America (Argentina, Brazil, Chile, Ecuador, Mexico and Paraguay), Asia (China including Hong Kong and Macau, India including working with Tibetan refugees, Japan, Malaysia, Nepal, Thailand and Vietnam), the Middle East, Africa (Lesotho, Swaziland, South Africa, Tanzania, Zambia) and Central Europe (Czech Republic, Hungary, Poland, Romania, Russia and the Slovak Republic). Posts are for between four and eleven months (six is average) and cost the volunteer £685 plus air fares and insurance, while board, lodging and (sometimes) pocket money are provided. A one or two week Teaching Skills course costing £120-£190 is mandatory for those undertaking to teach English.

Gap Challenge, Black Arrow House, 2 Chandos Road, London NW10 6NF. Tel: 020-8537 7980. Fax: 020-8961 1551. E-mail: welcome@world-challenge.co.uk. Web-site: www.world-challenge.co.uk. Provides gap year students and graduates aged 18-25 with 3 and 6 month voluntary work placements in a range of countries. Departures are in September and January each year. Teaching positions available in India (Manali and Goa), Nepal (Kathmandu and Pokhara), Tanzania (Zanzibar), Malawi, Malaysia, Belize and Peru. Inclusive placement fees £1,600-£2,700 including airfares.

Involvement Volunteers, PO Box 218, Port Melbourne, Victoria 3207, Australia. Tel: (3) 9646 9392. Fax: (3) 9646 5504. E-mail: ivimel@iaccess.com.au. Website: iaccess.com.au/ivimel/index.html. UK office: 7 Bushmead Ave, Kingskerswell, Newton Abbot, Devon TQ12 5EN. Tel: 01803 872594. E-mail: ivuk@hotmail.com. European office: IV Deutschland, Naturbadstr. 50, 91056 Erlangen (tel/fax 91-358075; ivde2@t-online.de). A few of their many projects for

paying volunteers worldwide involve teaching spoken English at village schools.
i-to-i, One Cottage Road, Headingley, Leeds LS6 4DD. Tel: 0870-333 2332.
Fax: 0113 274 6923. E-mail: info@i-to-i.com. Website: www.i-to-i.com. A TEFL
training and voluntary placements organisation specialising in voluntary English
teaching in Latin America, Africa, Russia and Asia. Each year they train over 1,000
teachers and place them in a variety of establishments worldwide. Departure dates
are flexible and placements can last from one to six months. For teaching placements
TEFL training is provided (see *Training: Short Introductory Courses*). Placements
include a comprehensive country briefing before UK departure and full back up
from on-the-ground i-to-i co-ordinators overseas. Board and lodging are normally
included as well as an airport 'meet-and-greet' service.

The Project Trust, The Hebridean Centre, Ballyhough, Isle of Coll, Argyll
PA78 6TE. Tel: (01879) 230444. Fax: (01879) 230357. E-mail:
projecttrust@compuserve.com. Satellite office in London: 020-7796 1170. An
educational charity which sends British school-leavers aged 17-19 overseas for a
year starting between July and September. About two-thirds of all 200+ placements
are made to English-teaching projects in schools in a great many countries:
Botswana, Brazil, Chile, China, Cuba, Egypt, Guyana, Honduras, Hong Kong,
Indonesia, Japan, Jordan, Malaysia, Namibia, Pakistan, Peru, Sri Lanka, Thailand,
Uganda, Vietnam and Zimbabwe. Volunteers are required to fund-raise a proportion
of the cost of their year abroad, which in 2000/2001 is £3,250. Applications can be
processed between 8 and 17 months prior to departure to allow time for pre-service
training to take place.

Students Partnership Worldwide (SPW), 17 Dean's Yard, London SW1P 3PB.
Tel: 020-7222 0138. Fax: 020-7233 0008. E-mail: spwuk@gn.apc.org. Website:
www.spw.org. Educational and environmental programmes lasting 4-10 months in
Africa and Asia for 18-28 year olds. Emphasis upon non-formal participatory
learning and youth development projects. Programme costs include travel,
insurance, living expenses, administration and in-country support by SPW staff. Pre-
departure briefings in London are advisable; in-country training (3-6 weeks) is
obligatory. Basic language and TEFL training is given.

Teaching & Projects Abroad, Gerrard House, Rustington, West Sussex BN16
1AW. Tel: (01903) 859911. Fax: (01903) 785779. E-mail: info@teaching-
abroad.co.uk. Website: www.teaching-abroad.co.uk. About 1,000 people are
recruited annually. The majority are taken on as English language teaching assistants.
Volunteers work in Ukraine, Russia, (Moscow, St. Petersburg and Siberia), India,
Ghana, Mexico and China. Most recently, there are projects teaching in Peru, Togo,
Thailand and South Africa. Volunteers are provided with board and accommodation,
placement and working arrangements, travel from the local HQ to the placement and
insurance. Classes are small groups of children aged five to sixteen (mainly 13-19
year-olds in China). In Mexico some work is in universities and in Moscow adults in
continuing education. No TEFL background required but good spoken English and
university entrance qualification. Age limits 17 to 70 years. Average volunteer joins
for 3 or 4 months at his or her choice of dates. 18 hours weekly contact time. Self-
funded packages cost from £795-£1,595 (excluding airfares). Local resident staff
help arrange accommodation and placements. Have introduced their own weekend
TEFL courses (see entry in *Introductory Training Courses*). Contact J. Locke, Deputy
Director at the above address or call in to the Sussex office. Also recruits through the
internet, directories, fairs, open days and word-of-mouth.

Travellers, 7 Mulberry Close, Ferring, West Sussex BN12 5HY. Tel/fax: 01903
502595. E-mail: info@travellersworldwide.com. Website: www.travellersworldwide.
com. Volunteers can teach conversational English (and/or other subjects like music,
maths and sport) in a growing range of less advantaged countries including India,
Nepal, Sri Lanka, Russia, Cuba, South Africa, Ukraine and Malaysia. No formal
teaching qualifications are required. Programmes are available throughout the year,
lasting from two weeks to a year. Sample charges for 2-3 months are India/Sri Lanka

£925 and Ukraine £775. Prices include food and accommodation plus transport from airport to school but do not include international travel which can also be arranged.

Charities and mission societies which occasionally require EFL teachers include:

Concern Worldwide, 52-55 Lower Camden St, Dublin 2, Ireland. Tel: +353 1-4177799. E-mail: hrenquiries@concern.ie. Website: www.concern.ie. UK office: 248-250 Lavender Hill, London SW11 1LJ. Tel 020-7738 1033. Fax: 020-7738 1032. Recruits mainly primary school certified teachers (B.Ed, Cert.Ed or PGCE) for many countries including Bangladesh, Cambodia, Ethiopia, Mozambique, Rwanda, Tanzania and Uganda. Focus is on curriculum development and teacher training rather than classroom teaching.

Interserve, 325 Kennington Road, London SE11 4QH. Tel: 020-7735 8227. Fax: 020-7587 5362. E-mail: enquiries@isewi.org. Website: www.interserve.org. Teaching posts in India, Pakistan, Nepal, Mongolia, East Asia, Central Asian Republics and North Africa. Teachers raise their funding within the UK. Also short-term placements (4-9 months) for church-going school leavers. Programme costs about £1,500.

OMS International, 1 Sandileigh Avenue, Manchester M20 3LN. Tel: 0161-283 7992. Fax: 0161-283 8981. E-mail: OMSUK@compuserve.com and website: www.omsinternational.org/uk
US Headquarters: PO Box A, Greenwood, IN 46142-6599). An evangelical, independent, Christian mission organisation which provides English lessons through OMS affiliated national churches in 17 countries worldwide. Some of the opportunities for self-funded Christian volunteers include; 3 weeks in Korea, 10 weeks in Mexico, 3 months in Ecuador, up to one year in Hungary and up to 5 years elsewhere.

United Nations Volunteers, Palais de Nations, CH-11211 Geneva 10, Switzerland. Some of their 2-year professional postings are for voluntary English teachers.

World Exchange, St Colm's International House, 23 Inverleith Terrace, Edinburgh EH3 5NS. Tel: 0131-315 4444. Fax: 0131-315 2222. E-mail: we@stcolms.org. Website: www.world-exchange.org. 10-12 month placements in Africa, Asia, Latin America, the Middle East, the Caribbean with community organisations and projects linked to churches. Volunteers live and work as part of the community. Flexibility, respect for a host country's culture, and willingness to adapt are considered to be as valuable as skills and experience. Training and support are provided prior to departure, including fundraising advice. Volunteers are expected to fund their own placement by raising about £2,350 which includes travel and training expenses.

Opportunities for North Americans

Although the companies, agencies and charities listed here are based in the US and cater primarily to North Americans, some may be in a position to help overseas applicants. Recruitment agencies in the United States have stronger links with Latin America and the Far East than with Europe. As in Britain, some organisations are involved primarily with English-medium international schools following an American curriculum and are looking to recruit state-certified teachers; these are listed separately at the end of this section. It should be noted that unlike in Britain, recruitment agencies are permitted to charge the candidate a substantial fee for successful placement.

The most important organisations for Americans looking for employment opportunities in the field of TEFL are:

TESOL (Teachers of English to Speakers of Other Languages, Inc.), 700 S Washington St, Suite 200, Alexandria, VA 22314 (703-836-0774/fax 703-836-6447; tesol@tesol.org/ www.tesol.org). A key organisation for English language teachers in the US and worldwide, TESOL is a non-profit, professional association which offers various publications and services to members (who number around 15,000). Basic membership is $50 ($36 for students). Members can receive a listing of job

vacancies worldwide, or search jobs online. TESOL also organises an Employment Clearing House (ESL/EFL job fair) at TESOL's annual convention held every March. Hundreds of jobs are posted, and interviews and hiring are conducted on-site.

Peace Corps, Room 803E, 1111 20th Street NW, Washington, DC 20526. Tel: 1-800-424-8580. Web-site: www.peacecorps.gov/volunteer/education/assignments. html. TEFL has historically been one of the major programme areas of the Peace Corps which has English teaching programmes in over 70 countries. Volunteers, who must be US citizens, over age 18 and in good health, are sent on two-year assignments. Peace Corps volunteers teach at both secondary and university level while some become involved with teacher training and curriculum development. It can take up to a year between application and departure. Volunteers must have a minimum of 3 months experience of ESL tutoring one-to-one or classroom teaching.

Office of English Language Programs, US State Department, SA 44, Room 304, 301 4th Street, SW, Washington DC 20547. Tel: 202-619-5892. Fax 202-401-1250 Website: http://exchanges.state.gov/education/engteaching. Formerly known as the US Information Agency and now part of the US Department of State, this office runs a network of overseas field offices based in United States Embassies and known as the Public Affairs Department of American Embassies. They promote US culture and are therefore (broadly speaking) the counterpart of the British Council. Many Public Affairs Departments provide English language instruction as do binational centres (which are locally run) located in about 100 countries, mainly in the developing world. Addresses are listed on http://e.usia.gov/education/engteaching/eal-elp1.htm. Most teachers for binational centers are hired directly by the centre in question. The English Teaching Fellow Program places TESL/TEFL graduates in language centres abroad including binational centres. Qualified candidates who want to teach in US Department of State Cultural Centers should obtain the official federal application form (171) and submit it to the English Teaching Specialists Department, Room 523, at the above address.

The **Fulbright Scholar Program** administered by the US Department of State, provides grants for teaching English in over 30 countries. A doctorate is usually required, although a Master's degree is sufficient in some countries. Applicants must be US citizens. Application information is available from the Council for International Exchange of Scholars (3007 Tilden St NW, Suite 5L, Washington, DC 20008-3009; 202-686-7877/e-mail: apprequest@cies.iie.org/ www.cies.org).

WorldTeach Inc., Center for International Development, Harvard University, 79 John F Kennedy Street, Cambridge, MA 02138. Tel: 617-495-5527/800-4-TEACH-0. Fax: 617-495-1599. E-mail: info@worldteach.org. Website: www.worldteach.org. Private, non-profit organisation founded in 1986 which places several hundred volunteers as teachers of EFL or ESL in countries which request assistance. Currently, WorldTeach provides college graduates with one-year contracts to Costa Rica, Ecuador and Namibia. 6-month opportunities available in China (Yantai) where volunteers teach adults, and in Mexico, South Africa and Honduras where volunteers teach English to nature guides. Also Summer Teaching Programme at a language camp for Chinese high school students in Yantai. All participants pay a programme fee (from $3,800) which covers training, airfares, orientation and insurance. Housing is provided locally and volunteers are given a stipend based on local rates of pay (roughly US$200 per month). Applicants accepted year round. Participants do not have to be US citizens, but must have a BA (except for the summer programmes). Contact: Robin Teater, Executive Director.

World University Service of Canada, 1404 Scott St, PO Box 3000, Ottawa, Ontario, Canada J8J 6H8. Tel: (613) 798-7477. Fax: (613) 798 0990. E-mail: recruit@wusc.ca or mgeoffroy@wusc.ca. Canadian ESL teachers to range of countries including Vietnam.

Amity Volunteer Teachers Abroad (AVTA), Amity Institute, 10671 Roselle St, Suite 101, San Diego, CA 92121-1525 (858-455-6364/fax 858-455-6597; mail@amity.org/ www.amity.org). Provides voluntary teaching opportunities in Latin America (Argentina, Peru, Mexico, the Dominican Republic), Africa (Senegal and Ghana) and France. ATVA volunteers are given full room and board with a host family as well as pocket money amounting to about $15-$25 a week. Participants must be at least 21, stay for eight or nine months from January/February or August/September and have a knowledge of Spanish (for Latin America).

ELTAP (English Language Teaching Assistant Program), University of Minnesota-Morris, Minnesota 56267 (320-589-6464; jkuechle@mrs.umn.edu;

www.mrs.umn.edu/cerp/eltap. Placement of university students for a minimum of 11 weeks at various times of year in huge range of countries from Belarus to Cameroon. $300 placement fee plus travel and living expenses.

The following commercial language providers and volunteer recruitment agencies may be able to assist EFL job-seekers:

EF Center Boston, Teacher Recruitment, One Education Street, Cambridge, MA 02141. Web-site: www.ef.com/EFWeb/EF1/English_First.htm. Largest number of vacancies in Russia, Indonesia, China, Poland and Morocco. Recruitment takes place year-round.

English for Everybody, ITC, Kaprova 14, 110 00 Prague 1. Tel: 2-2481 4791. Fax: 2-2481 7530; E-mail: EFE@itc-training.com (Subject EFE). Agency, affiliated to training organisation ITC, matches clients with suitable posts in the Czech Republic and elsewhere in Eastern Europe. Candidates must have a university degree and either a TEFL Certificate or relevant experience. Assistance fee US$450.

Friends of World Teaching, P.O. Box 84480, San Diego, California 92138-4480. Tel: 1-800-503 7436. E-mail: director@fowt.com. Places graduating seniors in posts in many different countries. Vacancies occur throughout the year for teachers, counsellors and school administrators. Qualification requirements for the most part are similar to those in the United States. However, many English-speaking schools abroad do not require state certification. Salaries vary, but in most cases compare favourably with those in the US.

Global Routes, 1814 Seventh Street, Suite A, Berkeley, CA 94710. Tel: (510) 848-4800. Fax: (510) 848-4801. E-mail: mail@globalroutes.org. Website: www.globalroutes.org/college.html. Offer 12-week voluntary internships to students who teach English and other subjects in village schools in Kenya, Ecuador, Costa Rica, Thailand and most recently India (Dharmsala), as well as on a Navajo reservation in the US. There are no specific requirements apart from a knowledge of Spanish for Ecuador and Costa Rica. The programme fee is $3,950 for the summer and $4,250 at other times (excluding airfares). Academic credit is available.

Global Volunteers, 375 East Little Canada Road, St. Paul, MN 55117-1628. Tel: 800-487-1074. E-mail: email@globalvolunteers.org. Website: www.globalvolunteers.org. One, two or three week placements as English conversation assistants in southern Spain, southern Italy, eastern Poland, Romania and Greece, as well as a range of developing countries. Fees from $1,795 plus travel. Monthly e-mail newsletter can be obtained by signing up on the website.

The following consultancies and exchange organisations may be able to guide students towards a range of overseas options including teaching English:

Council Exchanges,: 633 3rd Avenue, 20th Floor, New York, NY10017, USA. Tel: 1-888-268 6245. Fax: (212) 822-2689. E-mail: info@councilexchanges.org. Website: www.councilexchanges.org/work/ticfacts.htm. Administers Teach China programme in the US (see China chapter). Also, runs work abroad programmes for students in France, Germany, Costa Rica and other countries. Participants are given visas which allow them to work at any job for the time allowed. Council has offices in London, Paris and Sydney and other cities that advise participants on English teaching opportunities.

InterExchange, 161 Sixth Avenue, New York, NY 10013. Tel: (212) 924-0446 ext. 109. Fax: (212) 924-0575. E-mail: info@interexchange.org. Website: www.interexchange.org. Arranges teaching assistantships in Bulgaria, Poland, Russia and Ukraine. Placement fee of $400-$600.

Alliances Abroad, 702 West Avenue, Austin, Texas 78701. Tel 1-888-6-Abroad/1-888-622-7623. E-mail: info@alliancesabroad.com. Website: www.alliancesabroad.com. Run a teaching placement programme in Latin America and Asia. Volunteers get a monthly stipend or free board and lodging. Placement fees from US$750 to US$1,400 which includes emergency insurance, placement and accommodation. Participants can choose to live with host families or in apartments, depending on location.

Certified Teachers

Certified primary and secondary teachers who want to work in mainstream international schools abroad should be aware of the following agencies and organisations which match up qualified candidates with vacancies. Most of the hiring for primary and secondary schools abroad (often referred to in the American context as K-12 – kindergarten to grade 12) is done at recruitment fairs included on the list below. The files of job-seekers are added to a database which can be consulted by recruiters who then choose whom they want to interview. Candidates who successfully land a job abroad with the help of a US agency may have to pay a placement fee of $300-$600, though in some cases the employer underwrites this expense.

ECIS (European Council of International Schools), 21 Lavant St, Petersfield, Hants. GU32 3EL. Tel: 01730 268244. E-mail: staffingservices@ecis.org. Assists only teachers who have a B.Ed. or PGCE with at least two years' teaching experience. They publish a new edition of the *International Schools Directory* every year; the most recent edition costs £35/$57.

Gabbitas Educational Consultants, 126-130 Regent Street, London W1R 6EE. Fax: 20-7437 1764. E-mail: admin@gabbitas.co.uk. Website: www.teacher-recruitment.co.uk. Venerable institution which maintains a register of qualified and experienced teachers available for teaching posts in South America, the Middle East, Africa and many other parts of the world. Current vacancies may be found on the Gabbitas website.

WES Worldwide Education Service, Canada House, 272 Field End Road, Eastcote, Middlesex, HA4 9NA. Tel 020-8582 0317. Fax 020-8429 4838. E-mail wes@wesworldwide.com. Educational consultancy which recruits mostly fully-qualified teachers for full-time posts with British and international schools worldwide. WES maintains a register of qualified teachers.

Central Bureau for International Education & Training – Teachers Team, British Council, 10 Spring Gardens, London SW1A 2BN. Tel: 020-7389 4846; fax 020-7389 4426. Opportunities exist for UK teachers of modern foreign languages to swap their job with a partner from Austria, France, Germany, Spain or Switzerland, for a period of three weeks to a year.

League for the Exchange of Commonwealth Teachers, Commonwealth House, 7 Lion Yard, Tremadoc Road, Clapham, London SW4 7NQ. Placements abroad for experienced teachers in Commonwealth countries, Barbados to South Africa.

Q.T.S. Quality Services for Teachers and Schools, Churchill House, 27 Otley Old Road, Leeds LS16 6HB. Tel 0113-230 1141; Fax 0870 056 1164. E-mail: director@qts-worldwide.com. Website: www.qts-worldwide.com. Teacher recruitment worldwide. Qualifield teachers (all key stages) with UK experience should send a CV and full details to register on the QTS database.

International Schools Services, PO Box 5910, Princeton, NJ 08543, USA. Tel: (609) 452-0990. Fax: (609) 452-2690. E-mail: edustaffing@iss.edu. Web-site: www.iss.edu. Teaching opportunities for educators and certified teachers in private American and international schools around the world. ISS candidates attend annual US-based International Recruitment Centers (IRCs) where headteachers of overseas schools interview potential staff. Applicants must have a bachelor's degree and two years of current relevant experience. IRC registration materials are provided upon approval of application.

Queen's University, Placement's Office, Faculty of Education, Kingston, Ontario K7L 3N6, Canada. Tel: (613) 533-6222. Fax: (613) 533-6691. E-mail: traversa@educ.queensu.ca. Website: http://educ.queensu.ca/~placement. Host an annual recruiting fair in February for international schools. Registration costs

C$100. Teacher certification required plus at least two years' K-12 teaching experience.

Search Associates, PO Box 168, Chiang Mai 50000, Thailand. Tel: +66 53 244322. Fax: +66 (53) 260118. E-mail: deelman@loxinfo.co.th. Website: www.search-associates.com. US address: PO Box 636, Dallas, PA 18612. Not for TEFL teachers but offers information about international schools and placement assistance for teachers with mainstream school experience (with pupils aged 3-18). Long-term positions (1-3 year contracts) only. Teacher fee is about £75. Teacher/recruiter job fairs annually in England, Germany, Dubai, Kuala Lumpur, Australia and New Zealand and various North American locations.

Teacher Recruitment International (Aust), PO Box A1317, Sydney South, NSW 1235 Australia. Tel: +61 2 9328 3930. Fax +61 2 9328 3930. E-mail: triaust@ozemail.com.au. Place teachers in secondary school (English curriculum) posts in international schools in Asia and the Middle East. Prefer Australian and New Zealand candidates.

University of Northern Iowa, Overseas Placement Service for Educators, UNI, Cedar Falls, Iowa 50614-0390. Tel: (319) 273-2083. Fax: (319) 273-6998. E-mail: overseas.placement@uni.edu. Web-site: www.uni.edu/placement/overseas. Educators must hold current certification in elementary or secondary education. A comprehensive service includes the annual UNI Overseas Recruiting Fair in February/March.

SPECULATIVE JOB HUNT

Only a small percentage of language schools advertise in the foreign press or use an agency. The vast majority depend on local adverts, word of mouth, personal contacts, the internet and direct approaches. Therefore a speculative job search probably has a better chance with TEFL jobs than in many other fields of employment. For a successful campaign, only two things are needed: a reasonable CV and a list of addresses of potential employers.

Applying in Advance

Entire books and consultancy companies are devoted to showing people how to draw up an impressive curriculum vitae (or résumé as it is called in the USA). But it is really just a matter of common sense. Obviously employers will be more inclined to take seriously a well-presented document than something scribbled on the back of a dog-eared envelope. Obviously any relevant training or experience should be highlighted rather than submerged in the trivia about your schooling and hobbies. If you lack any TEFL experience, try to bring out anything in your past which demonstrates your 'people skills', such as voluntary work, group counselling, one-to-one remedial tutoring, etc. and your interest in (and ability to adapt to) foreign countries. If you are targeting one country, it would be worth drawing up a CV in the local language; Judith Twycross was convinced that her CV in Spanish was a great asset when looking for teaching work in Colombia. If you get the job, however, be prepared for your new employer to expect you to be able to speak the vernacular.

Attitudes and personality are probably just as important as educational achievements in TEFL, so anything which proves an aptitude for teaching and an extrovert personality will be relevant. Because this is difficult to do on paper, some eager job-hunters have gone so far as to send off a video of themselves, preferably a snippet of teaching. This is not worth doing unless (a) a school has expressed some interest and (b) you can make a good impression on an amateur video. A cheaper alternative might be to send a photo and a cassette of your speaking voice, again assuming this will be a help rather than a hindrance.

The other essential ingredient is a list of addresses. Each of the country chapters in this book provides such a list and recommends ways of obtaining other addresses, for example by contacting a federation of language schools (if there is one) or the British Council in your destination country. It is always worth writing to or even phoning the local British Council office, since they may be prepared to offer a general assessment of the local TEFL scene as well as provide a list of selected language schools in their region (for the benefit of enquiries from local language learners). The degree of their helpfulness will be at the discretion of the English Language Adviser or her/his secretary.

The book in your hand provides a good starting place for gathering a list of addresses, by including entries for about 500 institutes and organisations. Their teacher requirements were all checked and updated in 2000. At the end of each country chapter are lists of other school addresses (more than 1,000 in total). Although they did not confirm their requirements, possibly because they did not want a small number of vacancies to be widely publicised, it is still possible that they will be looking for qualified candidates when you are looking for work.

Note that international telephone access codes are 00 from Britain, 011 from the US. Individual country's codes can be found listed at the front or back of telephone directories. The numbers quoted throughout this book give the area codes minus the prefix 0 which should be used only when dialling within the country rather than from abroad.

The most comprehensive source of addresses of language schools is usually the Yellow Pages which in many cases can now be consulted on-line. Just type Yellow Pages and your destination country into a search engine and then search for *Scuoli di Lingue* in Italy, *Jazykova Skola* in the Czech Republic and so on. If you have a contact in your proposed destination city you could impose on them to photocopy the relevant pages.

Of course it has to be stressed that it is difficult, and increasingly so, to set up a firm job offer simply by correspondence. A language school would have to be fairly desperate to hire a teacher they had never met for a vacancy that had never been advertised. It is a good idea to follow up any hint of interest with a phone call. The best time to phone language school directors is six or seven weeks before the beginning of term. Perhaps the school has a contact in your country who would be willing to conduct an informal interview on their behalf. Perhaps the school will be content with a telephone interview.

If your credentials are not the kind to wow school directors, it might still be worth sending off a batch of warm-up letters, stating your intention to present yourself in person a couple of weeks or months hence. Even if you don't receive a reply, such a strategy may stick in the mind of employers, as an illustration of how organised and determined you are.

Interviews

Schools which advertise in foreign journals often arrange for candidates to be interviewed either by their own representative or by a proxy, such as a previous teacher or an appointed agent. Interviews can take place in strange and unlikely places including private homes. As a woman Roberta Wedge felt that she had to be cautious. Once she was stuck in a seedy pub at the end of a tube line at 9pm looking eagerly at every man who came through the door, and then the Director of Studies stood her up. Take along a friend if you are nervous.

Sometimes large organisations like Berlitz arrange open days and invite anyone who wants to be interviewed to come along. Chances are that British job-seekers will have to travel to London for an interview. Whether you are interviewed at home or abroad, slightly different rules apply. For example smart casual dress, neither flashy nor scruffy, is appropriate in Britain, while something a little more formal might be called for in certain cultures. Even if all your friends laugh when you pack a suit before going abroad, you may find it a genuine asset when trying to outdo the competition. As Steven Hendry, who has taught English both in Japan and Thailand with none of the usual advantages apart from traveller's canniness, says: you may not need a tailor-made suit but you definitely need to be able to present a conservative and respectable image.

As with the CV, so at interview. Highlight anything that is remotely connected with teaching even if it has nothing to do with the English language, and do it energetically and enthusiastically. Yet keenness will seldom be sufficient in itself. You do not have to be an intellectual to teach English; in fact the quiet bookish type is probably at a disadvantage. An amusing illustration of this is provided by Robert Mizzi's description of his interview for the JET Programme in the Japan chapter.

Without a TEFL background you should do a certain amount of research, e.g. acquaint yourself with some of the jargon such as 'notional', 'communicative-based', etc. It is not uncommon for an interviewer to ask a few basic grammar questions. To help you deal with this eventuality you might turn to the list of recommended reading in the chapter on *Preparation*. By visiting the ELT section of a bookshop, you can begin to familiarise yourself with the range of materials on offer. Always have some questions ready to ask the interviewer, such as 'Do you use Cambridge or Streamline?', 'What audio materials do you have?' 'Do you encourage the use of songs?' or 'Do you teach formal grammar structures?' If you are looking for an opening in a business context, you might pick up a few tips from the section on Interviews in the chapter on Germany.

You will certainly be asked how long you intend to stay and (depending on the time of year) nothing less than nine months will be considered. They will also want to know whether you have had any experience. With luck you will be able to say truthfully that you have (at least) taught at a summer school in Britain (again, see chapter on *Preparation*). Some applicants who are convinced that they can do a good job make a similar claim, untruthfully, knowing that at the lower end of the TEFL spectrum this will never be checked. Similarly some candidates claim to have done a TEFL course and pretend to have left the certificate at home. A certain amount of bluffing goes on in all interviews, so you'll just have to decide how far you are prepared to go. Bear in mind that the true depths of your ignorance could easily be plumbed ('Ah, so you've used Cambridge. Why do you prefer it to Streamline?').

Another of your skills you may be tempted to exaggerate is your knowledge of the local language. Philip Dodd was hired by a language teaching agency in Madrid on the understanding that he could speak fluent Spanish and was sent out on his first assignment, to give English lessons to a young child living in a wealthy suburb. He was greeted at the door by the mother who wished to make sure of a few things before she entrusted her precious offspring to this stranger. Not able to follow her voluble stream, Philip nodded affably and said 'si' whenever he guessed it was appropriate. After one of his affable 'si's', the woman's face turned grey and she ordered him out of her house. He still doesn't know what he said that was so shocking. On the other hand, a certain inflation of your abilities may be expected, and will be met with distortions of the truth from the employer as you both decide whether you are going to hit it off.

Of course many applicants will be able to avoid potential embarrassment at interview by having prepared themselves for a stint as a teacher. If you have done a TEFL course of any description, be sure to take along the certificate, however humble the qualification. Even schools in farflung places are becoming increasingly familiar with the distinctions between various qualifications and are unlikely to confuse a Cambridge Certificate with an anonymous correspondence 'certificate'. In Asia especially, nothing short of the original will do, since there are so many counterfeit copies around.

If you have a university degree, be sure to take the certificate along. Even if the interviewer is prepared to take your word for it, the school administration may need the document at a later stage either to give you a salary increment or to obtain a work permit. Adam Hartley, who taught English in China, hadn't realised that his MA would have earned him a higher salary; although he arranged for two separate copies to be sent from Britain, neither arrived and he had to be content with the basic salary. Americans should take along their university transcripts; any school accustomed to

Pretending to speak the language can get you into hot water

hiring Americans will be familiar with these. Also take along any references; something written on headed paper will always impress, even if your previous jobs were not in teaching.

Once the interviewer indicates that you are a strong contender, it is your turn to ask questions. Ask about the details of pay, hours and conditions and take notes (see the section on Contracts below). Often there are disappointing discrepancies between what is promised in the early stages and what is delivered; at least if these things have been discussed at interview, you will be in a stronger bargaining position if the conditions are not met.

If you are offered a job by an agent and are worried about what kind of employer the school will be, you could phone the local British Council office to find out whether the school enjoys a good local reputation. Occasionally an embassy or consulate will assist, as in the case of the US Embassy in Seoul which keeps a file of language schools about which they have received persistent complaints. More commonly, someone will have set up a web-page where this kind of inside information can be obtained (again, common in Korea).

ON THE SPOT

It is almost impossible to fix up a job in advance in some countries, due to the way the TEFL business operates. For example, written applications to the majority of language schools in Bangkok (assuming you could compile a list of addresses) are a waste of time since the pool of teacher-travellers on the spot is appropriate to the unpredictable needs of Thai schools. Even in countries like Spain and Germany for which adverts appear in the UK, the bulk of hiring goes on on-the-spot.

When you arrive in a likely place, your initial steps might include some of the following: transcribing a list of schools from the Yellow Pages consulted in the telephone office, reading the classified column of the local newspapers including the English language papers, checking notice boards in likely locations such as the British Council, US Embassy/Cultural Centres, universities, TEFL training centres,

English language bookshops (where you should also notice which EFL materials are stocked), or hostels which teacher-travellers frequent.

A reconnaisance trip is a good idea if possible. For example Fiona Paton wanted to teach English in France. On her way back from a summer holiday in Spain, she jumped off the train in Vichy for long enough to distribute her CV to several language schools. To her surprise, a letter arrived from one of them once she was at home offering her a job for the academic year, which she subsequently accepted and greatly enjoyed.

After obtaining a list of potential employers and before contacting them, get hold of a detailed map and guide to the public transport network so you can locate the schools. Phone the schools and try to arrange a meeting with the director or director of studies (DOS). Even if an initial chat does not result in a job offer, you may learn something about the local TEFL scene which will benefit you at the next interview, especially if you ask lots of questions. You might also be able to strike up a conversation with one of the foreign teachers who could turn out to be a valuable source of information about that school in particular and the situation generally. It is very common to have to begin with just a few hours a week. Make it clear that you are prepared to stand in at short notice for an absent teacher. The longer you stay in one place, the more hours will come your way and the better your chances of securing a stable contract.

This gradual approach also gives you a chance to discover which are the cowboy schools, something which is difficult to do before you are on the scene. The British Council has called for an EU-wide recognition scheme for language schools, to force rogue schools out of business. But this is a long way off, and in the meantime disreputable schools flourish in Europe just as they do in other parts of the world. It is not always easy to distinguish them, though if a school sports a sign 'Purrfect Anglish' you are probably not going to need an MA in Applied Linguistics to get a job there. Working for a cowboy outfit may not be the end of the world, though it often spells trouble, as the chapter *Problems* will reveal. But without many qualifications you may not have much choice.

Cowboy schools abound

FREELANCE TEACHING

Private English lessons are usually more lucrative than contract teaching simply because the middle man has been cut out. Learners may prefer them as well, not only because of the more personal attention they receive in a private lesson but because it costs them less. As a private tutor working from your own home or visiting pupils in theirs, you can undercut the big schools with their overheads. But at the same time you deprive yourself of the advantages of working for a decent school: access to resources and equipment, in-service training, social security schemes and holiday pay. The life of a freelance teacher can be quite a lonely one. Normally teachers working for a school take on a small amount of private teaching to supplement their income, provided this is allowed in their contracts. Most employers do not mind unless your private teaching is interfering with your school schedule or (obviously) if you are pinching potential clients from your employer.

In order to round up private pupils, you will have to sell yourself as energetically as any salesman. Turn to the section on Freelance Teaching in the Spain chapter for some ideas which have worked in Spain but could work anywhere. It might be possible to persuade companies to pay you to run English classes for employees during the lunch hour or siesta (if appropriate), though you would have to be a confident teacher and dynamic salesperson to succeed. You are far more likely to find one or two pupils by word of mouth and build from there.

Self-promotion is essential. Steven Hendry recommends plastering neatly printed bilingual notices all over town, as he did to good effect in Chiang Mai in northern Thailand. Meanwhile Ian McArthur in Cairo made a large number of posters (in Arabic and English) and painstakingly coloured in the Union Jack by hand in order to attract attention. (Unfortunately these were such a novelty that many posters were pinched.) Putting a notice up on appropriate notice boards (in schools, universities, public libraries, popular supermarkets) and running an advertisement in the local paper are good ideas for those who have the use of a phone or an e-mail address (since few people would reply by post to such an advert). Some have gone so far as to hire a paging device so that they can be contacted anytime. These methods should put you in touch with a few hopeful language learners. If you are any good, word will spread and more paying pupils will come your way, though it can be a slow process.

To counterbalance the advantages of higher pay and a more flexible schedule, freelance teaching has many disadvantages. Everyone, from lazy Taiwanese teenagers to busy Barcelona businessmen, cancels or postpones one-to-one lessons with irritating frequency. People who have taught in Latin countries complain that the problem is chronic. Cancellations among school and university students especially escalate at exam time. It is important to agree on a procedure for cancellations which won't leave you out of pocket. Although it is virtually impossible to arrange to be paid in advance, you can request 24 hours notice of a cancellation and mention politely that if they fail to give due warning you will insist on being paid for the missed lesson. But you can't take too tough a line, since your clients are paying above the odds for your flexibility. Another consideration is the unpaid time spent travelling between clients' homes and workplaces.

If you are less interested in making money than integrating with a culture, exchanging conversation for board and lodging may appeal. This can be set up by answering (or placing) small ads in appropriate places (the American Church in Paris notice board is famous for this). Hannah Start, a school leaver in Merseyside, put up a notice at her local English language school indicating that she wanted to exchange English conversation for accommodation in Paris; a businesswoman on an intensive English course contacted her and invited her to stay with her.

TEFL WEBSITES

More than 100 websites are devoted to EFL/ESL jobs, many in Asia. Most of them have links to Dave Sperling's ESL Café (www.eslcafe.com) which so expertly dominates the field that it is hard to see how others can compete. It provides a job list updated daily and a mind-boggling but well-organised amount of material for the future or current teacher including accounts of people's experiences of teaching abroad (but bear in mind that these are the opinions of individuals). It also provides links to specific institutes and chains in each country.

Here is a brief survey of some of the other key sites:

www.edunet.com – At the time of checking, the ELT job centre section of this education website had over 90 posts advertised in over a dozen countries including China, Greece, Korea, Indonesia, Taiwan, Japan, Italy and Kyrgyzstan. Full job details given for each post. Possible to apply online.

http://store.yahoo.com/alphabetcity – Alphabetcity contains a huge list of schools and TEFL courses worldwide. It is divided into two sections: white pages (school addresses) and yellow pages (jobs and listings). Full details of each vacancy are given.

www.eslworldwide.com – Another site with postings and chatrooms. Also commercial links to bookstore, airlines, etc.

www.eflweb.com – Lots of teaching vacancies posted

www.englishexpert.com – ditto

www.ihworld.com – International House London's website. IH is an established and expanding English Language Teaching organisation with 120 schools worldwide. The recruitment and training sections of the website are accessible to all, while up-to-date details of IH schools are accessible only to IH teachers via a password. Demonstrations of teaching materials will also become available on the site.

http://tefl.com – website of the TEFL Professional Network which publishes ELT Job Source available on subscription only.

www.tefl.net – Jobs listings (231 at the time of checking), free weekly newsletter and Career Helpline (ELT JobLink) also available. Users can apply directly online. It also has a facility which notifies the user how many new job posts have been advertised since the last visit.

Other websites which are country specific e.g. www.ohayosensei.com (jobs in Japan) or www.ajarn.com (teaching in Thailand) are listed in the relevant country chapters.

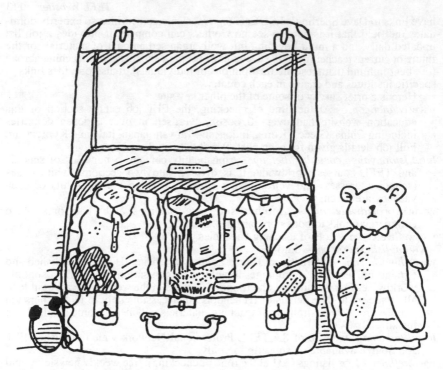

Preparation

The preceding chapters on ELT training and job-hunting set out ways in which you can make yourself more attractive to potential employers. One of the best ways in which to prepare for a stint of teaching abroad is to teach English locally. Relevant experience can usually be gained by volunteering to tutor immigrants in your home town; this is particularly feasible in the US where literacy programmes take place on a massive scale. It might also be a good idea to contact the director of a local commercial language school and ask to sit in on some lessons to see what it's all about and to talk to teachers. A polite note expressing your interest in TEFL would probably meet with a positive response. EFL teachers are like everyone else; they are experts at what they do and don't mind sharing that knowledge with interested outsiders.

More prolonged exposure to TEFL can best be gained by working at a language summer school. This not only provides a chance to find out whether you will enjoy English teaching for a longer period, but may put you in touch with people who are well-informed on overseas possibilities.

UK SUMMER SCHOOLS

Language summer courses take place throughout the British Isles, especially in tourist areas. The short-term nature of the teacher requirements means that schools sometimes have difficulties finding enough qualified staff, though with a recent decrease in the number of language learners coming to Britain, there are fewer jobs floating around. Wages are higher than for most seasonal summer jobs and as a result it is harder to get a job teaching English in Torquay than in Taipei. You may have to use the same wiles as described above in the section on interviews in order to be hired.

It is estimated that there are 600-800 English language schools in operation in Britain during July and August, mainly catering for foreign students, especially from France, Spain, Italy and other EU countries, but increasingly from further afield (e.g. Eastern Europe and Turkey). Many of these schools advertise heavily in the spring, e.g. 'Teach English on the English Riviera'. Quality varies dramatically of course. The more established schools are usually members of ARELS, the Association of Recognised English Language Services, which is trying to raise standards and whose staff are less likely to be novice teachers. The organisation is located at 56 Buckingham Gate, London SW1E 6AG (0207 802 9200; e-mail: enquiries@arels.org.uk) and will send a list of its 200+ members to enquirers. The counterpart in the state sector is BASELT (British Association of State English Language Teaching, Cheltenham & Gloucester College of H.E., Francis Close Hall, Swindon Road, Cheltenham, Glos. GL50 4AZ; www.baselt.org.uk).

While waiting for VSO to find him a teaching placement in Mongolia, Mr. R. Roy taught English for Pilgrims in Canterbury which gave him further experience at the same time as earning him a tidy sum:

> *I worked two three-week courses back to back which left me very little time to myself but also no time to spend any money and of course food and accommodation were included in the deal. It was really intense and tiring but good experience with all the visits and sports and performances and producing videos and magazines and reports. Pilgrims provided a good stock of books and equipment to help teachers prepare their lessons. I'm still in touch with them and would like to work another summer when I'm back in Britain.*

At the other end of the spectrum are the entrepreneurs who rent space (possibly ill-suited to teaching) and will take on almost anyone to teach. Teachers are thrown in at the deep end with little preparation and few materials. Marta Eleniak was not very happy with her employer:

> *I have got nothing good to say about my employer. We were expected to do nearly everything including perform miracles, with no support and pathetic facilities. I can only liken it to being asked to entertain 200 people for 4 hours with a plastic bowl. The pupils got a raw deal too because of false promises made to them.*

She does admit that it was on the basis of this three-week job that she got a job in a Madrid language school.

Schools at both extremes are listed in the Yellow Pages and advertise in the national press. They are located throughout the UK, but are concentrated in London and the South-East, Oxford, Cambridge and resorts like Bournemouth and Blackpool. Recruitment of summer teachers gets underway in the new year and is usually well advanced by Easter. The average starting salary for teachers is £170-£200 per week, though Certificate-qualified teachers should earn £250-£300. Residential schools may pay less if they are providing board and lodging, though some pay the same because the hours are so much longer. Since most schools are located in popular tourist destinations, private accommodation can be prohibitively expensive and the residential option attractive. Without any TEFL background it is easier to get taken on as a non-teaching sports and activities supervisor which at least would introduce you to the world of TEFL. EFL teachers must expect a number of extracurricular activities such as chaperoning a group of over-excited adolescents to a West End theatre or on an art gallery visit.

Two useful websites which list English language schools in Britain are www.EnglishinBritain.co.uk (accredited by the British Council) and www.tlcuk.com

Here is a short list of major language course organisations which normally offer a large number of summer vacancies:

Alexanders International School, Bawdsey Manor, Bawdsey, Woodbridge, Suffolk IP12 3AZ (tel: 01394-411633; fax: 01394 411257. E-mail: english@

alexandersint.demon.co.uk. Employ about 24 teachers for an international summer school for 11-18 year-olds mid-June to late August. Minimum 2 weeks. Activity staff also employed.

Anglo Continental Educational Group, 33 Wimborne Road, Bournemouth BH2 6NA 901202 557414/fax 01202 556156). Up to 100 EFL teachers for adult summer courses and 20 for adolescents.

Anglo-European Study Tours, 8 Celbridge Mews, Porchester Road, London W2 6EU (020-7229 4435/fax 020-7792 8717; e-mail: c.morris@aest.co.uk. Website: www.aest.co.uk). 200+ at centres throughout the UK for 2-6 weeks. £190-£235 per week. No accommodation.

Anglophiles Academic, 34 North End Road, London W14 OSH. Fax 020-7603 2441. E-mail: sutton@anglophiles.demon.co.uk. Teachers/supervisors for French teenagers at Easter, and summer (July and August) in Basingstoke, Boston, Bristol, Bury, Chelmsford, Kings Lynn, Nottingham, Peterborough, Plymouth and Skegness. Some residential.

Concorde International Summer Schools, Arnett House, Hawks Lane, Canterbury, Kent CT1 2NU (01227 765537/fax 01227 762760; e-mail: info@concorde.ltd.uk. website: www.concorde.ltd.uk). 120 teachers. £210 a week depending on the course. Average 15 hours teaching and 20 supervising activities. Full board residential accommodation is provided. Experience and TEFL qualification required. Contact Beth Stavely.

EF Language Travel, Cherwell House, 3rd Floor, Cherwell House, London Place, Oxford OX4 1BD. Tel: 01865-200720. Fax: 01865-243196. E-mail: lt.oxford@ef.com. Website: www.ef.com. 25-30 teachers needed per year and hundreds of group leaders for centres in Hastings, Brighton, London, Cambridge and Oxford. All teachers must be native speakers with TEFL or substantial experience. 3 weeks from 9am-midday or 1.30-4.30pm. £23 per 3-hour session. B&B accommodation can be found with host families. Contact Aneli Oakes.

Elizabeth Johnson Organisation, West House, 19/21 West St, Haslemere, Surrey GU27 2AE. With 35 centres around the UK. 85-90 teachers needed at peak time (July). Two weeks to a month minimum. £185-£270 per week. Three schools are residential.

Embassy CES, Head Office: Lorna House, 103 Lorna Road, Hove, East Sussex BN3 3EL. Tel 01273-322353. Fax 01273-322381. E-mail emb_recruit@bsg.ac.uk. Summer schools from end of June to end of August at 40 centres around the UK. Employs 400 teachers throughout UK and Ireland. Minimum requirement is a TEFL Cert. Accommodation can be provided.

Embassy CES, Highcliffe House, Clifton Gardens, Folkestone, Kent CT20 2EF (01303 258536/fax 01303 851455). One of their many centres (see above). 20+ teachers.

English Language & Cultural Organisation, Lowlands, Chorleywood Road, Rickmansworth, Herts. WD3 4ES (01923 776731/fax 01923 774678). 20-30 EFL teachers to work at several locations in the south of England during the summer.

International Quest Centres, 9 Stradbroke Road, Southwold, Suffolk IP18 6LL; tel 01502-722648 and 50 Oxford Street, Southampton S014 3DP. Tel: 023 80 338858. Fax: 023 80 338848. E-mail: english@internationalquest.co.uk. Website: www.internationalquest.co.uk). 300-400 EFL teachers for 3-6 weeks. 17 hours per week. Wage of £10 per hour. Accommodation is not normally provided except in Oxford and Kent where recruitment is difficult. Contact A. McCarthy.

International Study Programmes, The Manor, Hazleton, Nr. Cheltenham, Glos. GL54 4EB (01451 860379).

Kent School of English, 3,5,10,12 Granville Road, Broadstairs, Kent CT10 1QD (tel 01843-874870); fax 01843-860418; e-mail: enquiries@kentschool.co.uk). Hires 25 teachers at Easter and from late June to August in summer. Must be graduates with either CELTA or TESOL. £210-£270 per week. Supplement for outstanding staff. No accommodation.

Kingswood Group, Linton House, 164-180 Union St, London SE1 0LH (020-7922

1234). Summer camps in southern England needing 40-45 EFL teachers.

Nord-Anglia, 10 Eden Place, Cheadle, Stockport, Cheshire SK8 1AT (0161-491 8477/491 8415/fax 0161-491 4409). 300+ EFL teachers for more than 80 centres around Britain, especially the North. Apply March-June for UK summer work. Also runs TEFL courses in various centres abroad including in Australia and the Czech Republic.

OISE Youth Language Centres, OISE House, Binsey Lane, Oxford OX2 0EY (01865 258350/fax 01865 792706). 500 summer and Easter vacancies in dozens of locations. OISE offer their own training course to tutors.

Passport Language Schools, 37 Park Road, Bromley, Kent BR1 3HJ (020-8466 5925). Employ about 150 teachers for schools in 30 towns in England and South Wales.

SUL Language Schools, Beech Holm, 7 Woodland Avenue, Tywardreath, Par, Cornwall PL24 2PL (01726 814227/fax 01726 813135). E-mail: claire@sul-schools.com. Website: www.sul-schools.com. Employ 200-300 a year with degree and TEFL Cert. Minimum 2 weeks. Mornings only. £22.90-£34 per morning. Residential.

TASIS England American School, Coldharbour Lane, Thorpe, Surrey TW20 8TE. Of special interest to American EFL teachers who want to teach in Britain from late June to late August; only suitably qualified Americans are eligible for work permits.

Thames Valley Cultural Centres, 15 Park St, Windsor, Berks. SL4 1LU (01753 852001/fax 01753 831165). Up to 60 teachers around England.

Torbay Language Centre, Conway Road, Paignton, Devon T04 5LH; tel 01803-558555; fax 01803-559606; e-mail tlc@lalschool.org). Employs about 40 teachers from the last week of June to the third week of August for a minimum of two weeks. Pay is £8.50 per hour; average 22 and a half hours per week. Also runs a small residential centre in North Devon.

YES Education Centres, 12 Eversfield Road, Eastbourne, East Sussex BN21 2AS (01323 644830/fax 01323 726260). EFL teachers for summer courses in Abingdon, Brighton, Hastings, Oxford and Seaford.

Sels College, (64/65 Long Acre, Covent Garden, London WC2E 9SX; 020-7240 2581) has been in business for over 25 years and its owner Y Raiss ran one of the first Cambridge TEFL training centres. Although the school no longer offers training courses it would be an excellent place for the newly qualified teacher to hone his or her teaching skills teaching during the academic year.

Roberta Wedge found that working for a large summer school organisation was not only good preparation for a teaching contract in Italy, but was fun for its own sake:

The big language mills in Britain are a good way to see the country. I signed up with OISE in Exeter because I wanted to tramp the moors. It's possible to spend the whole summer jumping around fortnightly from contract to contract, all arranged ahead of time through the same organisation. Make sure you know what to do about accommodation, though; I have a tent in reserve.

WHILE YOU'RE WAITING

After you have secured a job, there may be a considerable gap which will give you a chance to organise the practicalities of moving abroad and to prepare yourself in other ways. If you are going to a country which requires immigration procedures (the majority of cases unless you're an EU national planning to work in another member state) you can start the visa procedures. In addition to deciding what to take and how to get to your destination, you should think about your tax position and health insurance, plus find out as much as you can about the situation in which you will find yourself.

Many teachers take out a subscription to the *Guardian Weekly* (164 Deansgate, Manchester M60 2RR; 0161-832 7200) to guarantee access to world news, though you might prefer to wait until you arrive to see what newspapers are available. A one-year subscription costs £67 in Europe and North America, £75 elsewhere. Also contact BBC English, the English language teaching arm of BBC World Service, Bush House, London WC2B 4PH (www.bbc.co.uk/worldservice/learningenglish), which also publishes information sheets to go with their programmes and material on their websites. Further enquiries can be made to the BBC World Service (tel 020-7240 3456).

Alternative English language broadcasting organisations are Voice of America, Radio Canada International (PO Box 6000, Montreal, Canada H3C 3A8) and Swiss Radio International (SBC, CH-3000 Bern 15, Switzerland; website: www.swissinfo.org; e-mail: info@sri.ch), all of which will send information about their services. SRI publish a monthly magazine *Swiss World* in English and other languages which would be useful to teachers in Germany and elsewhere in Europe.

ELT professionals should consider joining the International Association of Teachers of English as a Foreign Language (IATEFL, 3 Kingsdown Park, Whitstable, Kent CT5 2FL; 01227 276528/fax 01227 274415/e-mail: IATEFL@compuserve.com/Web-site: http://www.iatefl.org). Membership, which costs £30 to individuals or £90 to institutions, entitles teachers to various services including six newsletters annually and access to special interest groups, conferences, workshops and symposia. Another association to consider joining is BIELT, the British Institute of English Language Teaching, PO Box 1109, Headington, D.O. Oxford OX3 8XR (tel/fax 01865 742086; enquiries@bielt.org). Members have to have a recognised TEFL qualification. BIELT is establishing a job centre (see *Finding a Job*).

The more information you can find out about your future employer the better. Kathy Panton thinks that she would have been a more effective teacher in her first year in the Czech Republic if she had asked more probing questions beforehand:

> *Now that I have a better idea of what to teach I think I could handle it, but a first year teacher should ask a lot of questions; such as, what books the students have used, teacher continuity, very detailed report of what the students can do (as opposed to what they have studied), and most of all what they will be expected to accomplish during the school year. If the report is vague, I don't think anyone should take the job unless they are really confident that they'll be able to develop the framework themselves. I would look for a school that said something like, 'You'll guide the students through Hotline 1 textbook, and also give them extra vocabulary and speaking exercises to supplement the text. You'll also work with a phonics text for a few weeks, because these students have poor pronunciation. You'll probably find it useful to bring some old magazines but the school has several ESL textbooks already.' This would show that the school takes both curriculum and organisation seriously.*

An invaluable source of information is someone who has taught at the school before; ask your employer for a couple of addresses. Past teachers will be in a position to pass on priceless minutiae, not only recommending pubs, bakeries, etc. but (if the accommodation is tied to the job) they can advise you to arrive early and avoid the back bedroom because of the noisy plumbing.

Contracts

This is the point at which a formal contract or at least an informal agreement should be drawn up. Any employer who is reluctant to provide something in writing is definitely suspect. Horror stories abound of the young, unsuspecting teacher who goes out to teach overseas and discovers no pay, no accommodation and maybe even no school. For this reason it is not only very important to sign a contract, but also to have a good idea as to what it is letting you in for.

The following items should be covered in a contract or at least given some consideration:

1. Name and address of employer.
2. Details of the duties and hours of the job. (A standard load might be 24 contact teaching hours a week, plus 3 hours on standby to fill in for an absent teacher, fill all the board markers in the staff room, etc.)
3. The amount and currency of your pay. Is it adequate to live on? How often are you paid? Is any money held back? Can it be easily transferred into sterling or dollars? What arrangements are there if the exchange rate drops suddenly or the local currency is devalued?
4. The length of the contract and whether it is renewable.
5. Help with finding and paying for accommodation. If accommodation is not provided free, is your salary adequate to cover this? If it is, are utilities included? Does the organisation pay for a stay in a hotel while you look for somewhere to live? How easy is it to find accommodation in the area? If it is unfurnished what help do you get in providing furniture? Can you get a salary advance to pay for this and for any rent deposits?
6. Your tax liability.
7. Provisions for health care and sick pay.
8. Payment of pension or national insurance contributions.
9. Bonuses, gratuities or perks.
10. Days off, statutory holidays and vacation times.
11. Paid flights home if the contract is outside Europe, and mid-term flights if you are teaching for 2 years.
12. Luggage and surplus luggage allowance at the beginning and end of the contract.
13. Any probationary period and the length of notice which you and the employer must give.
14. Penalties for breaking the contract and circumstances under which the penalties would be waived (e.g. extreme family illness, etc.)

Obviously any contract should be carefully studied before signing. It is a wise precaution to make a photocopy of it before returning to avoid what happened to Belinda Michaels whose employer in Greece refused to give her a copy when she started to dispute some points. In some cases the only contract offered will be in a foreign language (e.g. Arabic) and you will either have to trust your contact at the school for a translation or consider obtaining an independent English translation.

Health and Insurance

Increasingly, the immigration authorities abroad will not grant a teacher a work permit until they have provided a medical certificate. Many countries now insist on an HIV test and various other health checks including for syphilis and TB. GPs will charge for carrying out these tests, whether you do it before you leave home or after arrival.

Reputable schools will make the necessary contributions into the national health insurance and social security scheme. Even if you are covered by the national scheme, however, you may find that there are exclusion clauses such as dental treatment, non-emergency treatment, prescription drugs, etc. or you may find that you are covered only while at work. Private travel insurance can be very expensive. Most insurance companies offer a standard rate that covers medical emergencies and a premium rate that covers personal baggage, cancellation, etc. Expect to pay roughly £20-£25 per month for basic cover and £35-£40 for more extensive cover. Specialist expatriate policies might be worth investigating. Policies endorsed by American Citizens Abroad (5, bus rue Liotard, CH-1202 Geneva or PO Box 321, 1211 Geneva 12, Switzerland) are available from Abrams Insurance Agency (1051 North George Mason Drive, Arlington, VA 22205, USA). The following UK companies are familiar with insuring expats including EFL teachers:

Bone & Company, 69a Castle Street, Farnham, Surrey GU9 7LP (01252 724140).

Club Direct Travel Insurance, Dominican House, Freepost PT577, Chichester, West Sussex, PO19 1YQ; tel 01243-817766. Website: www.clubdirect.co.uk. Offers special backpacker policies (either basic or comprehensive) for long trips of two months to a year or more. A one-year basic policy costs £179, comprehensive £249.

Dove Insurance Brokers, Green Tree House, 11 St. Margaret's St, Bradford-on-Avon, Wilts. BA15 1DA (01225 864642).

Our Way Travel Insurance, Foxbury House, Foxbury Road, Bromley, Kent BR1 4DG (020-8313 3900/fax 020 8313 3652; ourwayins@aol.com/ www.ourway.co.uk).

If you are British and intending to work in the European Union (Germany, France, Italy, Spain, Portugal, Greece, Austria, Denmark, Sweden, Finland, Netherlands, Belgium, Luxembourg and Ireland), you should acquire form E-111, which is a certificate of entitlement to medical treatment within the EU. The leaflet T6 contains the application form and is available from British post offices. Even if your employer will be paying into a health scheme, cover may not take effect immediately and it is as well to have the ordinary tourist cover for the first three months. An E-111 provides cover for up to 12 months; after that the appropriate form is E-106. Council in New York (address in *Finding a Job* chapter) offers an International Teachers' Identity Card (like a student card) for $22, which includes cover for emergency repatriation.

If your destination is tropical, consult an up-to-date book on health such as *Travellers' Health: How to Stay Healthy Abroad* by Richard Dawood (OUP, £9.99) or the excellent and highly readable general guide *The Tropical Traveller* by John Hatt. British Airways has set up a network of travel clinics throughout the UK which will give advice on specific destinations, administer jabs and prescribe the correct anti-malarials, etc. Telephone advice on immunisations and malaria is available from MASTA (Medical Advisory Service for Travellers Abroad), Keppel St, London WC1E 7HT. The Travellers' Health Line operates on 09068 224 100; after callers leave details of their itinerary, dates of arrival and expected living conditions, a basic MASTA Health Brief will be sent to them, though the call on this premium rate line will cost £2-£3. If a more personalised Health Brief is required, travellers should telephone 023 92 553933 to find out the cost, according to the depth of detail required.

If you are heading off to central Africa or any other place where the incidence of HIV is high, you will be understandably worried about the standards of health care in general and the quality of blood and syringes in particular. Sterile medical packs containing hypodermic needles, intravenous drip needles, etc. are available from MASTA.

Americans should obtain the booklet 'Health Information for International Travel' which includes information on vaccination requirements, malaria prophylactics, etc. The US Public Health Service updates it annually; to obtain a copy of this document, contact the Superintendent of Documents, US Government Printing Office, Washington, DC 20402-9325 and enquire about the current cost.

In 2000, the British government announced that it would set up a 24-hour freephone helpline for all British nationals to contact in a crisis, e.g. robbery, illness or arrest.

National Insurance Contributions and Social Security

If you are a national of a European Economic Area country working in another member state, you will be covered by European Social Security regulations. Advice and the free information leaflet SA29 'Your Social Security Health Care and Pension Rights in the European Community plus Iceland, Liechtenstein and Norway' may be obtained from the Contributions Agency International Services, Longbenton, Newcastle-upon-Tyne NE98 1YX (06451 54811, local rate call). The leaflet explains that payments made in any EEA country count towards benefit entitlement when you return home. The UK also has Social Security agreements with other countries including Croatia, Cyprus, Israel, Jamaica, Malta, Slovenia, Switzerland, Turkey, USA and republics of the former Yugoslavia. If you are going to teach in any of these countries, contact International Services for the appropriate leaflet.

In countries where no Social Security agreement exists, the leaflet NI38 'Social Security Abroad' gives an outline of the arrangements and options open to you. If you fail to make National Insurance contributions while you are out of the UK, you will forfeit entitlement to benefits on your return. You can decide to pay voluntary contributions at regular intervals or in a lump sum in order to retain your rights to certain benefits. Unfortunately this entitles you only to a retirement/widow's pension, not to sickness benefit or unemployment benefit. Since teachers abroad are seldom in a pension scheme, it is usually worth maintaining your right to a UK state pension.

Tax

Calculating your liability to tax when working outside your home country is notoriously complicated so, if possible, check your position with an accountant. Everything depends on whether you fall into the category of 'resident', 'ordinarily resident' or 'domiciled'. Most EFL teachers count as domiciled in the UK since it is assumed that they will ultimately return. New legislation has removed the 'foreign earnings deduction' for UK nationals unless they are out of the country for a complete tax year. Since most teaching contracts operate from September, this means that the vast majority of EFL teachers, including teachers on high salaries in the Middle East or on the Japan Exchange and Teaching scheme which were formerly tax-free, will now be liable to UK tax. If you are out of the country for a tax year, you will be entitled to the exemption, provided no more than 62 days (i.e. one-sixth of the year) have been spent in the UK.

If the country in which you have been teaching has a double taxation agreement with Britain, you can offset tax paid abroad against your tax bill at home. But not all countries have such an agreement (Sweden for example) and it is not inconceivable that you will be taxed twice. Keep all receipts and financial documents in case you need to plead your case at a later date.

Inland Revenue leaflets which may be of assistance are IR20 'Residents and non-residents: Liability to tax in the UK' and IR139 'Income from Abroad? A guide to UK tax on overseas income.' Tax enquiries pertaining to issues of residence and non-residence may be addressed to the Inland Revenue Financial Intermediaries & Claims Office (Non-Residents), St. John's House, Merton Road, Bootle, Merseyside L69 9BB (0151-472 6214/5/6). The Inland Revenue also has a good website which might provide answers to your questions (www.inlandrevenue.gov.uk); it lists the relevant contact offices that deal with specific issues. General enquiries may be directed to 020-7438 6420. A possible source of further information on tax is the annually revised book *Working Abroad* published by Kogan Page in conjunction with the *Daily Telegraph*.

If US citizens can establish that they are resident abroad, the first $80,000 (from the year 2000) of overseas earnings is tax-exempt in the US.

Travel

London is the cheap airfare capital of the world and the number of agencies offering discount flights to all corners of the world is seemingly endless. To narrow the choice you should find a travel agency which specialises in your destination. Those who know their way around the web can find lots of useful information. Start with www.cheapflights.co.uk which allows users to log onto a destination and see a list of prices offered by a variety of airlines and agents. It also has links to other travel-related topics (exchange rates, weather forecast, health advice). Compare the prices posted on www.travelocity.com and other cheap travel websites including www.expedia-msn.co.uk and www.lastminute.com.

Alternatively, consult specialist travel magazines such as *TNT* (which is free in London) plus *Time Out* and the Saturday edition of the *Independent* or other national papers. By ringing a few of the agencies with advertisements you will soon discover which airlines offer the cheapest service. STA and usit-Campus Travel with branches in most university towns can usually be relied on to come up with the best flight options to suit your needs.; STA's telephone sales numbers are 020-7361 6145 for Europe, 020-7361 6144 worldwide and Northern Call Centre 0161-830 4713 and their website is www.statravel.co.uk. usit-Campus can be contacted on 08702-401010 or via their website www.usitCampus.co.uk which also has a free e-mail service so that that travellers can keep in touch while abroad.

In North America, the best newspapers to scour for cheap flights are the *New York Times* (the Sunday edition has a section devoted to travel with cut-price flights advertised), the *LA Times, San Francisco Chronicle-Examiner, Miami Herald, Dallas Morning News, Chicago Sun Times,* the *Boston Globe* and the Canadian *Globe & Mail.* Recommended agencies include Council Travel Services (part of the Council on International Educational Exchange) with branches in most major university towns, and STA with 100 offices worldwide including 15 in the US. If your dates are flexible, contact Airtech, 584 Broadway, Suite 1007, New York, NY 10012 (212-219-7000; www.airtech.com) which advertises its fares by saying, 'if you can beat these prices, start your own damn airline'. One-way transatlantic fares start at $179 from the east coast and $279 from the west. Travel CUTS in Canada sell discounted fares and have offices overseas (e.g. in London at 44 Queensway, Bayswater, London W2 3RS; 020-7792 3770).

Within Europe, rail is often the preferred way of travelling, especially since the months of September and June when most teachers are travelling to and from their destinations are among the most enjoyable times to travel. Good discounts are available to travellers under 26; details are available from Eurotrain (see usit-Campus address above) or www.raileurope.com, which has schedules, fares etc. for European rail passes, Eurostar and for point-to-point tickets throughout Europe. You can also book online.

Maps & Information

Good maps and guide books always enhance one's anticipation and enjoyment of going abroad. If you are in London, visit the famous map shop Edward Stanford Ltd. (12-14 Long Acre, Covent Garden, WC2E 9LP; 020-7836 1321) which also sends maps by post. The Map Shop (15 High St, Upton-on-Severn, Worcestershire WR8 0HJ; 01684 593146) does an extensive mail order business and will send you the relevant list of their holdings. Daunt Books for Travellers (83 Marylebone High Street, London W1M 4DE; 020-7224 2295) organises its holdings according to region, shelving practical guides next to relevant travel literature. The Travel Bookshop (13 Blenheim Crescent, London W11; 020-7229 5260) divides travel books by region and stocks literary titles connected with them. The travel section of the online bookshop www.bol.com is run in conjunction with the Travel Bookshop. Meanwhile www.travellerscompanion.co.uk is an online travel bookshop offering a wide selection of guide books, although it gives only titles and prices. Post and packing are free within the UK.

Browsing in the travel section of any bookshop will introduce you to the range of travel guides. The Rough Guides series is generally excellent, and the very detailed books published by Lonely Planet are also popular. If you want a detailed historical and architectural guide, obtain a *Blue Guide* or a *Michelin Green Guide.*If you are heading for a remote or politically unstable part of the world, it would be worth obtaining up-to-date safety information from the Foreign & Commonwealth Office.

You can ring their Travel Advice Unit on 020-7238 4503 or check their website www.fco.gov.uk which carries up-to-date travel warnings and some visa information.

Learning the Language

Even if you will not need any knowledge of the local language in the classroom, the ability to communicate will increase your enjoyment many times over. After a long hard week of trying to din some English into your pupils' heads, you probably won't relish the prospect of struggling to convey your requests to uncomprehending shopkeepers, neighbours, etc. A refusal to try to learn some of the local language reflects badly on the teacher and reinforces the suspicion that English teachers are afflicted with cultural arrogance.

If there is time before you leave home, you might consider enrolling in a part-time or short intensive course of conversation classes at a local college of further education or using a self-study programme with books and tapes. This will have the salutary effect of reminding you how difficult it is to learn a language. There are a great many teach-yourself courses on the market from the BBC, Berlitz and so on. A course consisting of a couple of course books and a couple of tapes will cost in the region of £30. Linguaphone (0800 282417) which is one of the biggest (and most expensive) recommends half an hour of study a day for three months. Among the more popular self-study courses are *Teach Yourself* published by Hodder and Stoughton, The Routledge Colloquial Language series (Fetter Street, London EC4P 4E6) and Dorling Kindersley's collection (www.dk.com), all of which combine books and tapes.

If you are heading for a remote place, take a language course with you, since tapes and books (including a good dictionary) may not be available locally and your enthusiasm to learn may be rekindled once you are on-location. Of course it is much easier to learn the language once you are there. Some employers may even offer you the chance to join language classes free of charge; if you are particularly interested in this perk, ask about it in advance.

In a few cases, it is a positive disadvantage to speak the language as Jamie Masters discovered in Crete:

> *About speaking Greek. Well, no one told me. I assumed that they'd be quite pleased to have a Greek-speaking English teacher, best of both worlds. It's useful for discipline; the kids can't talk about you behind your back; you can tell when they're cheating on their vocab tests; and, I stupidly thought, you can explain things more clearly, really get them to understand... Well, I was wrong, and was laboriously reprimanded for it when they finally worked out what I was doing. But by that time it was too late: the kids knew I could understand Greek, and so they knew they didn't have to make the effort to speak to me in English. No amount of my playing dumb worked.*

WHAT TO TAKE

The research you do on your destination will no doubt include its climate, which will help you choose an appropriate range of clothing to take. But there is probably no need to equip yourself for every eventuality. EFL teachers normally earn enough to afford to buy a warm coat or boots if required. Be sure to pack enough smart clothes to see you through the academic year; blue jeans are rarely acceptable in the classroom.

Even though you are expecting to earn a decent salary, you should not arrive short of money. It is usual to be paid only at the end of the first month. Plus you may need sizeable sums for rent deposits and other setting-up expenses.

A generous supply of passport photos and copies of your vital documents (birth certificate, education certificates, references) should be considered essential. Recreational reading in English will be limited, so you should take a good supply of novels, etc. It could take time to establish a busy social life, leaving more time for reading than usual. In such circumstances, having access to the World Service can be a godsend. You will need a good short-wave radio with several bands powerful enough to pick up the BBC. 'Dedicated' short-wave receivers which are about the size of a paperback start at £65. If you are travelling via the Middle East or Hong Kong, think about buying one duty-free. A further advantage of having access to the BBC is that you can tape programmes for use in the classroom. Up-to-date details of BBC World Service frequencies are available at www.bbc.co.uk/worldservice/schedules/frequencies/ or similarly, Voice of America's web page (www.voa.gov) has the latest listings of its broadcasting frequencies. The BBC Shop (020-75572576) sells a slide chart (price £3.50) for calculating the main BBC World Service frequencies.

If possible find out from recently returned travellers what items are in short supply or very expensive (e.g. deodorant in Greece, cigarette papers in Scandinavia). Some items which recur on teachers' lists are vitamin tablets, a deck of cards, ear plugs and thermal underwear.

Teaching Materials

Try to find out which course your school follows and then become familiar with it. Depending on the circumstances, there may be a shortage of materials, so again enquire in advance about the facilities. (For example, English texts being used in a few places in Cambodia dated from 1938 and contained such useful sentences as, 'I got this suit in Savile Row'.) If you are going to have to be self-reliant, you may want to write to the major EFL publishers, primarily Oxford University Press, Cambridge University Press, Longman, Heinemann, Penguin and Phoenix to request details of their course books with a sample lesson if possible, and the address of their stockist in your destination country.

Before leaving home, you should visit a good ELT department of a bookshop, or

obtain a detailed catalogue of ELT materials from a specialist EFL bookshop. Waterstones (82 Gower Street, London WC1E 6EQ; tel 020-7636 1577; e-mail: arts@gowerst.waterstones.co.uk) have a large ELT department and will send their 90-page catalogue of ELT publications on request. They also have a worldwide mail order service.

KELTIC is another major specialist EFL bookshop and international mail order service offering an extensive range of materials, information and a free catalogue *The KELTIC Guide to ELT Materials* to teachers and schools worldwide. The London shop is at 25 Chepstow Corner, Chepstow Place, London W2 4XE (tel: 020-7229 8560; fax: 020-7221 7955; e-mail shop@keltic-london.co.uk) and the KELTIC International Order Department is at 39 Alexandra Road, Addlestone, Surrey KT15 2PQ (tel: 01932 820485; fax: 01932 854320; e-mail: keltic@keltic.co.uk; www.keltic.co.uk).

Another major stockist is BEBC the Bournemouth English Book Centre (Albion Close, Parkstone, Poole, Dorset BH12 3LL; 01202 712934; fax 01202 712913; e-mail: elt@bbc.co.uk Website: www.bebc.co.uk). The company supplies books, tapes, videos and ELT software by mail order to teachers worldwide. Orders of more than 15 books are sent postage free within the UK and selected EU countries. For a list of recommended titles, see the following section. Waterstone's in Manchester is strong in the north of England (91 Deansgate, Manchester M3 2BW; 0161-834 7055). GBG Direct is an overseas mail order bookshop from which you can order English language books once you are abroad (24 Seward St, London EC1V 3PB; tel: 020-7490 0900; fax 020-7490 9909; e-mail: gb@gbgdirect.com Website: gbgonline.com).

In North America those looking for TEFL titles can resort to purchasing online from Barnes and Noble (www.barnesandnoble.com) or Amazon.com. There are also a few specialist online bookstores including Alta Book Center (14 Adrian Court, Burlinghame, CA 94010; tel 800 ALTA-ESL or fax 800 ALTA-FAX; e-mail: altaesl@aol.com and website www.altaesl.com) and Delta Systems Co (1400 Miller Parkway, McHenry, IL 60050-7030; tel 800-323 8270; fax 800-909-9901; website: www.delta-systems.com. Both Alta and Delta also do orthodox mail order.

Here is a list of items to consider packing which most often crop up in the recommendations of teachers of conversation classes in which the main target is to get the students talking. Teachers expecting to teach at an under-resourced school might think about taking some of the following: good dual language dictionary, picture dictionary, cassettes (including pop music with clear lyrics such as Pink Floyd, Beatles, Simon & Garfunkel, Tracy Chapman, early Billy Bragg), blank tapes (and a cassette recorder if necessary with spare batteries), games and activities book; illustrated magazines like *National Geographic* or unusual publications like old comic books, teen mags or *The Big Issue* (interesting to many language learners in former communist countries); maps (for example of London), tourist guides to your home country, travel brochures, blank application forms, flash cards (which are expensive if bought commercially; home-made ones work just as well); grammar exercise book; old Cambridge exam papers (if you are going to be teaching First Certificate or Proficiency classes). Postcards, balloons, stick-on stars and photos of yourself as an infant have all been used to good effect. If you know that there will be a shortage of materials, it might even be worth taking general stationery such as notebooks, carbon paper, Blutack, plastic files, large pieces of paper, coloured markers, etc. Most employers would be willing to pay the postage costs if you don't want to carry it all in your luggage. (If you are entering a country without a pre-arranged work visa, bear in mind that teaching aids in your luggage will alert customs officers that you intend to work.)

Richard McBrien, who taught English in China, recommends taking a collection of photos of anything in your home environment. A few rolls shot of local petrol stations, supermarkets, houses, parks, etc. can be of great interest to pupils in far-off lands. It may of course be difficult to anticipate what will excite your students' curiosity. The anthropologist Nigel Barley, who writes amusing books on his fieldwork, describes being enlisted to attend an impromptu English conversation club in a remote corner of Indonesia in his book *Not a Hazardous Sport:*

> *I answered questions about the royal family, traffic lights and the etiquette of eating asparagus, and gave a quick analysis of the shipbuilding industry. At the end of the evening, I fled back to the hotel.*

EFL teachers cannot escape so easily, so you should be prepared to be treated like a guru of contemporary British or American culture.

Recommended Bibliography

There is such a plethora of books and materials that the choice can be daunting to the uninitiated. One valuable resource for English language teachers working abroad is TESOL's *More Than a Native Speaker: An Introduction for Volunteers Teaching Abroad* by Don Snow. The book covers classroom survival skills and includes a 'Starter Kit for Course Planning.' The book also addresses adapting to life in a new culture and ways to teach listening, speaking, reading, writing, grammar, vocabulary and culture. The book costs $29.95 plus 12% postage (or $24.95 plus postage for TESOL members). Orders may be ordered directly from TESOL Inc., 700 South Washington St, Suite 200, Alexandria, VA 22314 (703-836-0774/fax 703-836-7864; e-mail: tesol@tesol.org/www.tesol.org).

Every teacher should have a basic manual of grammar handy, such as one of the following:

Grammar for English Language Teachers: by Parrott (CUP 2000). £12.25.

Practical English Grammar, by A. J. Thomson & A. V. Martinet (OUP, 1990) £9.15.

Exercises available separately: *Practical English Grammar Exercises 1 & 2* and *Practical English Grammar Structure Drills* (both £7.10).

Using English Grammar, by Edward Woods & Nicole McLeod (Phoenix) £9.95.
English Grammar in Use, by Raymond Murphy (CUP). 2000 edition. £8.95. Plus *Supplementary Exercises,* £4.60.
Advanced Grammar in Use, by Martin Hewings (CUP, 1999). £9.45.
English Grammar, (Collins, Gem). £2.99. Genuinely pocket-sized. (Dubbed by at least one novice, 'the Teacher's Friend'.)
Practical English Usage, by M. Swan (OUP). Second edition, £14.40.
A *Practical Handbook of Language Teaching,* David Cross (Phoenix). £15.95. Do-it-yourself guide for teachers with poor resources.

Here is a selected list of recommended books and teaching aids which you could consider; obviously you won't want to buy all of them.
Collins Cobuild English Dictionary (Collins) £15. Collins publish a range of dictionaries for the language learner.
Cambridge International Dictionary of English (CUP, 1995). £12.55 paperback.
Grammar Games & Activities, by Peter Watcyn-Jones (Penguin) £21. Other titles by the same author include *Pair Work, Vocabulary Games* and *Fun and Games.*
Grammar Workbooks 1 and 2 for Beginners and Pre-Intermediate (Penguin). £3.75 each.
Freestanding: by Maurice Jamall (ABAX £11.95). Elementary to Upper Intermediate. Teachers' resource book suitable for children and young adults.
The Grammar Lab by K. Bourke (OUP) £6.30 each. Written for young learners with grammar explanations that are easy for children to understand. 3 books at elementary to intermediate level.
Grammar Practice Activities: by Penny Ur (CUP). For all levels and ages. Includes photocopiable texts and visuals. £13.50.
How English Works: by Swan/Walter. (OUP) £10.65. For intermediate/upper intermediate. Specially suitable for self-study.
IH: Index of EFL Materials: by Acklam. £12.50. A guide containing some of the most useful pieces of teaching materials selected from over 100 tried and tested ELT books and supplementaries. Invaluable as a lesson planning and teaching aid.
An Introduction to English Language Teaching, by John Haycraft (Longman) £11.95. Aimed at unqualified/inexperienced people and less taxing than many EFL books.
Listen and Speak: Situational English: by Hancock (Listen and Speak). Self-study book, classroom book, cassette and CD. £4.75 to £19.99.
Keep Talking: by Klippel. £12.95. Over a hundred fluency activities.
More Grammar Games, by M. Rinvolucri & P. Davis (CUP) £13.25. Includes activities for all levels.
Oxford Advanced Learner's Dictionary, (OUP) £14. Definitions and information about language for upper intermediate level.
The Practice of English Language Teaching, by Jeremy Harmer (Longman) £15.35. A well-known core reference work for teachers. In three parts which deal with the theory of English Language Teaching, Specific techniques and materials and lesson planning and management. From the same author *How to Teach English* (£14.95), a straightforward introduction to the theory and practice of TEFL for new teachers, those with limited experience and those taking the CELTA exam.
Recipes for Tired Teachers, edited by Christopher Sion (Addison-Wesley/Longman) £17.95.
Source Book for Teaching English as a Foreign Language, by Michael Lewis and Jimmie Hill (Heinemann, 1993). £13.15. Practical guide for those with little formal training.
The Resourceful English Teacher: by Chandler/Stone (Delta £12). A teaching companion. Over 200 classroom activities for a wide range of teaching situations.
The Standby Book: Lindstromberg (CUP £13.50). Teacher's resource book of 110

language learning activities for all types of teaching situation.

Lessons from Nothing, by Bruce Marsland (CUP, 1998). £9.50. From the Cambridge Handbooks for Language Teachers series.

Children Learning English: (Heinemann 2000). £15. Introduces the theory behind good classroom practice with examples from around the world.

Learning Teaching: (Scrivener). Useful for teachers in training and as a quick resource of lively lesson ideas.

The Lexical Approach, by Michael Lewis (Language Teaching Publications). £14.50.

Anyone who is likely to be teaching young children might like to request the catalogue of Ladybird's Books for English Learning, since the well known children's publisher has an inexpensive series *Key Words Scheme* for children (Ladybird Books Ltd, 27 Wrights Lane, Kensington, London W8 5TZ; 020-7416 3000). However, customers should order through Customer Services (Penguin Group Distribution Ltd., Bath Road, Harmondsworth, Middlesex UB7 ODA; tel: 020-8757 4000).

If your place of work has an internet connection, you can download teaching materials from the web. Try for example the *Guardian's* www.educationunlimited. co.uk/tefl which provides lesson ideas based on current events. OUP's site (www1.oup.co.uk/elt/mazagine/worksh) has good quality worksheets mostly tied in with its own books.

Problems

Potential problems fall into two broad categories: personal and professional. You may quickly feel settled and find your new setting fascinating but may discover that the job itself is beset with difficulties. On the other hand the teaching might suit but otherwise you feel alienated and lonely. Those who choose to uproot themselves suddenly should be fairly confident that they have enough resources to rely on themselves, and must expect some adjustment problems. Only you can assess your chances of enjoying the whole experience and of not feeling traumatised. Women may encounter special problems in countries where women have little status. A book which will introduce you to potential difficulties and includes chapters on most of the countries of the world is called *More Women Travel*.

PROBLEMS AT WORK

Anyone who has done some language teaching will be familiar with at least some of the problems EFL teachers face. Problems encountered in a classroom of Turkish or Peruvian adolescents will be quite different from the ones experienced teaching French or Japanese business people. The country chapters attempt to identify some of the specific problems which groups of language learners present.

Although you are unlikely to be expected to entertain 200 people for four hours with a plastic bowl, there may be a fairly complete lack of facilities and resources. The teacher who has packed some of the teaching materials listed above will feel particularly grateful for his or her foresight in such circumstances. Some schools, especially at the cowboy end of the spectrum go to the other extreme of providing very rigid lesson plans from which you are not allowed to deviate and which are likely to be uncongenial and uninspiring. Even when reasonable course texts are provided, supplementary materials for role play and games can considerably liven up classes (and teachers). You can obtain extra teaching aids after arrival from the nearest English language bookshop or make them yourself, for example tape a dialogue between yourself and an English speaking friend or cut up magazines or use postcards to make flashcards. If the missing facilities are more basic (e.g. tables, chairs, heating, paper, pens) you will have to improvise as best you can and (if appropriate) press the administration for some equipment.

Problems with Pupils

A very common problem is to find yourself in front of a class of mixed ability and incompatible aims. How do you plan a lesson that will satisfy a sophisticated business executive whose English is fairly advanced, a delinquent teenager and a housewife crippled by lack of confidence? A good school of course will stream its clients and make life easier for its teachers. But this may be left to you, in which case a set of commercially produced tests to assess level of language acquisition could come in very handy. Alternatively you can devise a simple questionnaire for the students to describe their hobbies, studies, family or whatever. This will not only display their use of English but also give you some clues about their various backgrounds. One way of coping with gross discrepancies is to divide the class into compatible groups of pairs and give tasks which work at different levels. Sub-dividing a class is in fact generally a good idea especially in classes which are too large.

In some places you may even have to contend with racial or cultural friction among pupils, as Bryn Thomas encountered in Egypt:

> *One of the problems I found in the class was the often quite shocking displays of racism by the Egyptians towards their dark-skinned neighbours from Somalia. Vast amounts of tact and diplomacy were required to ensure that enough attention was given to the Somalis (who tend to be shy, quiet and highly intelligent) without upsetting the sometimes rowdy and over-enthusiastic Egyptians.*

Your expectations of what teaching is supposed to achieve may be quite different from the expectations of your students. Foreign educational systems are often far more formal than their British or American counterparts and students may seem distressingly content to memorise and regurgitate, often with the sole motivation of passing an exam. But this doesn't always operate. Many teachers have had to face a class who don't seem to care at all about learning any English and merely want to be entertained.

In many countries free discussion is quite alien, whether because of repressive governments or cultural taboos. It is essential to be sensitive to these cultural differences and not to expect too much of your pupils straightaway. The only way of overcoming this reluctance to express an opinion or indeed express anything at all is to involve them patiently and tactfully, again by splitting them into smaller units and asking them to come up with a joint reply.

Discipline is seldom a serious problem outside Europe; in fact liberal teachers are often taken aback by what they perceive as an excess of docility, an over-willingness to believe that 'teacher is always right'. In some cases, classes of bored and rebellious European teenagers might cause problems (especially on Fridays), or children who are being sent to English lessons after school simply as an alternative to babysitting for working mothers. Unfortunately, a couple of troublemakers can poison a class. You may even have to contend with one or two downright uncontrollable students as Jamie Masters did in Crete:

> *At least two of my pupils were very malevolent. There was one, Makis, who used to bring a 'prop' to every lesson, some new way of disrupting the class – an air pistol, a piece of string with a banknote tied to it, a whistle, white*

In classes of mixed ages, you may have trouble pleasing everyone

paint. He used to slap my cheeks, hug me and lift me off the floor, was quite open about not wanting to work... and then claimed I was picking on him when I retaliated. Well, call me a humourless unfeeling bastard, but...

One teacher in Turkey found the majority students 'bouncy, bright, enthusiastic and sharp' but with one class he was always amazed that they walked upright when they got out of their chairs. It often turns out that each class develops a certain character. Some months after Jamie Masters returned home to London, he confessed:

Even now you only have to say the words 'D class Mastamba' to strike terror into my heart. But the A class in the same school was a joy to teach: rowdy, yes, but I had a lot of time for them. Within a class there are different personalities of course but they tend to get subsumed into the personality of the group. So I had good classes and bad classes in all the places I taught. When I left, some classes cheered; others wept and drew hearts all over their vocab tests. The main line of demarcation may in fact be age rather than income: the younger students more or less accept that they have to work; the older ones are beginning to rebel.

Marta Eleniak, who taught in Spain, recommends taking a hard line:

Be a bitch at the start. The kids can be very wicked and take advantage of any good nature shown. Squash anyone who is late, shouts, gossips, etc. the first time or it'll never stop. The good classes make you love teaching. The bad make you feel as if you want to go back to filing.

Each level and age group brings its own difficulties. Anyone who has no experience of dealing with young children may find it impossible to grab and hold their attention, let alone teach them any English. A lack of inhibition is very useful for teaching young children who will enjoy sing-songs, nursery rhymes, simple puzzles and games, etc. A firm hand may also be necessary if Aine Fligg's experience in Hong Kong is anything to go by. She was bitten on the ankle by one of her less receptive students. When the headmaster came in and remonstrated (with Aine!) the child bit him on the nose. The brat was then incarcerated in a cupboard, and emerged somewhat subdued.

Beginners of all ages progress much more rapidly than intermediate learners. Many teachers find adolescent intermediate learners the most difficult to teach. The original fun and novelty are past and they now face a long slog of consolidating vocabulary and structures. (The 'intermediate plateau' is a well-known phenomenon in language acquisition.) Adolescents may resent 'grammar games' (which are a standard part of EFL) thinking that games are suitable only for children.

The worst problem of all is to be confronted with a bored and unresponsive class. This may happen in a class of beginners who can't understand what is going on, especially a problem if you don't speak a word of their language. It can be extremely frustrating for all concerned when trying to teach some concept or new vocabulary without being able to provide the simple equivalent. If this is the case, you'll have to rely heavily on visual aids. Whole books have been written to show EFL teachers how to draw, for example *1000+ Pictures for Teachers to Copy* by Wright from CUP (£15.50). For a very low-level class, you may need to resort to your bilingual dictionary for lesson plans. On the other hand some teachers enjoy the challenge: 18 year old Hannah Bullock found teaching her class of Czech beginners good fun 'because each lesson was like an invigorating game of charades.' Many new teachers make the mistake of doing all the talking. During his year of teaching in Slovenia, Adam Cook, like many others before him, came to the conclusion that silence is one of the teacher's most effective tools.

The best way to inject a little life into a lethargic class is to get them moving around, for example get them to do a relaxation exercise or have them carry out a little survey of their neighbours and then report their findings back to the class. A reluctance to participate may be because the pupils do not see the point of it. In many countries foreign teachers come to feel like a dancing bear or performing monkey, someone who is expected to be a cultural token and an entertainer. If the students are expecting someone to dance a jig or swing from the chandelier (so to speak) they will be understandably disappointed to be presented with someone asking them to form sentences using the present perfect. At the other extreme, it is similarly disconcerting to be treated just as a model of pronunciation, and you may begin to wonder whether your employer might be better off employing a tape recorder.

Problems with Yourself

Of course lessons which fizzle or never get off the ground are not always the fault of the students. One of the most common traps into which inexperienced teachers fall is to dominate the class too much. Conversational English can only be acquired by endless practice and so you must allow your pupils to do most of the talking. Even if there are long pauses between your questions and their attempts to answer, the temptation to fill the silences should be avoided. Pauses have a positive role to play, allowing pupils a chance to dwell on and absorb the point you have just been illustrating. Avoid asking 'do you understand?' since the answer is meaningless; it is much more useful to test their comprehension indirectly.

A native speaker's function is seldom to teach grammar, though he or she should feel comfortable naming grammatical constructions. You are not there to help the students to analyse the language but to use it and communicate with it. It has been said that grammar is the highway code, the catalogue of rules and traffic signs, quite useless in isolation from driving, which gets you where you want to go. Grammar is only the cookery book while talking is cooking for other people to understand/eat. Persuading some students, whose language education has been founded on grammar rather than communication, that this is the priority may be difficult, but try not to be drawn into detailed explanations of grammatical structures.

This is probably not a very great temptation for many teachers who can barely distinguish prepositions from pronouns. Being utterly ignorant of grammar often results in embarrassing situations. You can only get away with bluffing for so long ('Stefan, I don't think it matters here whether or not it's a subjunctive') and irate pupils have been known to report to school directors that their teachers are grammar-illiterate. One useful trick suggested by Roberta Wedge is to reply, 'very good question – we're going to deal with that in the next class.' Normally it will suffice to have studied a general grammar handbook such as *Practical English Grammar* or *Practical English Usage* (see Bibliography above). If you contradict yourself between one lesson and the next, and an eager student notices it, take Richard Osborne's advice and say 'Ah yes, I'm sorry about that. You see, that's the way we do it at home. Bizness is always spelled with a z in Canada.'

The worst fate which can befall a teacher is to run dry, to run out of ideas and steam completely before the appointed hour has arrived. This usually happens when you fail to arrive with a structured lesson plan. It is usually a recipe for disaster to announce at the beginning of the lesson 'tonight let's talk about our travels/hobbies/animals' or whatever. Any course book will help you to avoid grinding to a halt. Supplementary materials such as songs and games can be lifesavers in (and out) of a crisis. If you are absolutely stuck for what to talk about next, try writing the lyrics of a popular song on the board and asking the class to analyse it or even act it out (avoiding titles such as 'I Want Your Body'). Apparently songs which have worked well for many teachers include George Michael's 'Careless Whispers', the Beatles' 'Here Comes the Sun' and 'When I'm 64' and 'Perfect Day' by Lou Reed. Another way of stepping outside the predictability of a course book might be to teach a short poem which you like, or even a short story (e.g. by Saki) if the class is sufficiently advanced.

Get the class to act out the title of a popular song

A very popular way to structure a lesson is in 'notions'; you take a general situation like 'praising' or 'complaining', teach some relevant vocabulary and structures and then have the class put them into practice in role-play situations. Unfortunately repetition is the key to language learning, though you have to avoid boring drills which will kill any interest in the language.

Culture shock is experienced by most people who live in a foreign country in whatever circumstances (see below), but can be especially problematic for teachers. Unthinkingly you might choose a topic which seems neutral to you but is controversial to them. A little feature on the English pub for example would not be enjoyed in Saudi Arabia. A discussion about whaling might make a class of Norwegians uncomfortable. Asking questions about foreign travels would be tactless in many places where few will be able to afford international travel.

One of the hardest problems to contend with is teacher burn-out. If you invariably arrive just as the class is scheduled to begin, show no enthusiasm, and glance at the clock every 90 seconds, you will not be a popular teacher. Getting hold of some new authentic materials might shore up your flagging enthusiasm for the enterprise. If not, perhaps it is time to consider going home (bearing in mind your contractual commitments).

Problems with Employers

All sorts of schools break their promises about pay, perks and availability of resources. The worst disappointment of all, however, is to turn up and find that you don't have a job at all. Because schools which hire their teachers sight unseen often find themselves let down at the last moment, they may over-hire, just in the way that airlines overbook their flights in the expectation of a certain level of cancellation. Even more probable is that the school has not been able to predict the number of pupils who will enrol and decides to hire enough teachers to cover the projected maximum. Whatever the reason, it can be devastating to have the job carpet whipped from under your feet. Having a signed contract helps. It may also be a good idea to maintain contact with the school between being hired and your first day of work. If the worst does happen, you could try losing your temper, threatening to tarnish their good name, and demand a month's pay and your return airfare. Or you could try playing on the guilt of the director and ask him or her to help you get a last-minute job in another school.

Just because a school does not belong to the EFL establishment does not mean that teachers will be treated badly (and vice versa). However the back street fly-by-night school may well cause its foreign teachers anxiety. The most common complaints revolve around wages – not enough or not often enough or both. Either you will have signed a contract (possibly in ignorance of the prevailing conditions and pay levels) or you have nothing in writing and find that your pay packet does not correspond with what you were originally promised. It is probably not advisable to take up a confrontational stance straightaway since this may be the beginning of a year of hostility and misery. Polite but persistent negotiations might prove successful. Find out if there is a relevant teachers union, join it and ask them for advice (though EFL is notorious for being non-unionised). As the year wears on, your bargaining clout increases, especially if you are a half-decent teacher, since you will be more difficult to replace mid-term.

One recourse is to bring your employer's shortcomings to the attention of the British Council or in extreme cases of exploitation, your Embassy/Consulate. If you are being genuinely maltreated and you are prepared to leave the job, delivering an ultimatum and threatening to leave might work. Remember that if there are cowboy schools, there are also cowboy teachers. Many honest and responsible employers have fallen victim to unreliable and undisciplined individuals who break their promises, show up late and abuse the accommodation they are given. Try not to let your employer down unless the provocation is serious.

Language schools must function as businesses as well as educational establishments and in some case the profit motive overtakes everything else. In those cases, teachers soon realise that they matter less to the people in charge than the number and satisfaction of students. You may be asked to conduct a conversation class in a room not much smaller than the Albert Hall. Some employers leave you entirely to your own devices and even look to you for teaching ideas. Others interfere to an annoying degree; we've heard of one school director in Spain who bugged the classrooms to make sure the staff were following his idiosyncratic home-produced course outlines. Jayne Nash worked for a chain of schools in France which use their own method; clients learned basic phrases and words for everyday situations parrot fashion:

Welcome to your conversation class

The courses were aimed at local business people, therefore students learned mostly spoken English to introduce themselves, their company or product, language for meetings, telephone conversations, etc. The method seemed very effective, but can prove extremely tedious for the teacher. After you have repeated a word 10-20 times with 10 students, 4 times a day, 5 days a week...

One of the most commonly heard complaints from teachers concerns their schedule. Eager only to satisfy clients, employers tend to mess around with teachers' timetables, offering awkward combinations of hours or changing the schedule at the last moment, which is extremely stressful. A certain amount of evening work is almost inevitable in private language schools where pupils (whether of school or working age) must study English out-of-hours. Having to work early in the morning and then again through the evening can become exhausting after a while. It can also be annoying to have several long gruelling days a week and other days with scarcely any teaching at all (but still not days off).

One trick to beware of is to find that the 24 hours a week you were told you would be working actually means 32 45-minute lessons (which is much harder work than teaching 24 one-hour lessons). Even if the number of hours has not been exaggerated, you may have been deluded into thinking that a 24-hour week is quite cushy. But preparation time can easily add half as many hours again, plus if you are teaching in different locations, travel time (often unpaid) has to be taken into consideration.

In some situations teachers may be expected to participate in extra-curricular activities such as dreary drinks parties for pupils or asked to make a public speech. Make an effort to accept such invitations (especially near the beginning of your contract) or, if you must decline, do so as graciously as possible. There might also be extra duties, translating letters and documents, updating teaching materials, etc. for which you are unlikely to be paid extra.

PROBLEMS OUTSIDE WORK

Your main initial worry outside your place of employment will probably be accommodation. Once this is sorted out, either with the help of your school or on your own, and you have mastered the essentials of getting around and shopping for food, there is nothing to do but enjoy yourself, exploring your new surroundings and making friends.

Culture Shock

Enjoying yourself won't be at all easy if you are suffering from culture shock. Shock implies something which happens suddenly, but cultural disorientation more often creeps up on you. Adrenalin usually sees you through the first few weeks as you find the novelty exhilarating and challenging. You will be amazed and charmed by the odd gestures the people use or the antiquated way that things work. As time goes on, practical irritations intrude and the constant misunderstanding caused by those charming gestures – such as a nod in Greece meaning 'no' or in Japan meaning 'yes, I understand, but don't agree' – and the inconvenience of those antiquated phone boxes and buses will begin to get on your nerves. Unless you can find someone to listen sympathetically to your complaints, you may begin to think you have made a mistake in coming in the first place.

Experts say that most people who have moved abroad hit the trough after three or four months, probably just before Christmas in the case of teachers who started work in September. A holiday over Christmas may serve to calm you down or, if you go home for Christmas, may make you feel terminally homesick and not want to go back. Teachers who survive this, often find that things improve in the second term as they cease to perceive many aspects of life as 'foreign'.

The best way to avoid disappointment is to be well briefed beforehand, as emphasised in the chapter *Preparation*. Gathering general information about the country and specific information about the school before arrival will obviate many of the negative feelings some EFL teachers feel. If you are the type to build up high hopes and expectations of new situations, it is wise to try to dismantle these before leaving home. English teaching is seldom glamorous.

Even if you are feeling depressed and disappointed, do not broadcast your feelings randomly. Feeling contempt and hostility towards your host country is actually part of the process of adjusting to being abroad. But not everyone seems to appreciate that it has more to do with their own feelings than with the inadequacies (real or imagined) of the country they are in. So if you feel you have to let off steam about the local bureaucracy or the dishonesty of taxi-drivers or the way one simply cannot walk ten yards down the pavement without people crossing the street for the express purpose of bumping into you, at least have the common courtesy to do it in private, in letters or when there are no local people around.

This is especially important if you have colleagues who are natives of the country. They may find some of the idiosyncracies of their culture irritating too but, unlike you, they have to live with them forever. Some native-speaker teachers have found an unpleasant rift between local and foreign staff, which in some cases can be accounted for by the simple fact that you are being paid a lot more than they are. Sometimes new foreign teachers find their local colleagues cliquey and uncommunicative. No doubt they have seen a lot of foreigners come, and make a lot of noise, and go, and there is no particular reason why they should find the consignment you're in wildly exciting and worth getting to know.

Loneliness

Creating a social life from scratch is difficult enough at any time, but becomes even more difficult in an alien tongue and culture. You will probably find that many of your fellow teachers are lots of fun and able to offer practical help in your first few weeks (especially any who are bilingual). If you find yourself in a one-foreigner village, surely there's another lonely teacher across the mountaintop. You could meet for a drink at the weekend to commiserate and to draw up a charter and call yourselves 'The Wonga Plateau EFL Teachers' Association' (and remember to put yourself down as founder the next time you are revising your CV).

You may want to take some positive steps to meet people and participate in activities outside the world of English language instruction. This may require uncharacteristically extrovert behaviour, but overcoming initial inhibitions almost always pays worthwhile dividends.

If you are tired of conversations about students' dullness or your director of studies' evident lunacy, you might want to try to meet other expatriates who are not EFL teachers. The local English language bookshop might prove a useful source of information about forthcoming events for English-speakers, as will be any newspapers or magazines published in English such as the *Bulletin* in Belgium or the *Athens Daily News* in Greece. Seek out the overseas student club if there is a university nearby (though when they discover what line of work you are in they may well have designs on you). Even the least devout teachers have found English-speaking churches to be useful for arranging social functions and offering practical advice. If there is a bar in town which models itself on a British pub or American bar, you will no doubt find a few die-hards drinking Guinness or Budweiser, who might be more than willing to befriend you.

The most obvious way to meet other foreigners is to enrol in a language course or perhaps classes in art and civilisation. Even if you are not particularly serious about pursuing language studies, language classes are the ideal place to form vital social contacts. You can also join other clubs or classes aimed at residents abroad, for example some German cities have English amateur dramatics groups.

Making friends with locals may prove more difficult, though circumstances vary enormously according to whether you live in a small town or a big city, with some gregarious colleagues or by yourself, etc. The obvious source of social contact is your students and their friends and families (bearing in mind that in certain cultures, a teacher who goes out to a bar or disco with students risks losing their respect). As long as you don't spend all your free time moping at home, you are bound to strike up conversations with the locals, whether in cafés, on buses or in shops. Admittedly these seldom go past a superficial acquaintance, but they still serve the purpose of making you feel a little more integrated in the community. Local university students will probably be more socially flexible than others and it is worth investigating the bars and cafés frequented by students. If you have a particular hobby, sport or interest, find out if there is a local club where you will meet like-minded people; join local ramblers, jazz buffs, etc. – the more obscure the more welcome you are likely to be. You only have to become friendly with one other person to open up new social horizons if you are invited to meet their friends and family.

Make an effort to organise some breaks from work. Even a couple of days by the seaside or visiting a tourist attraction in the region can revitalise your interest in being abroad and provide a refreshing break from the tyranny of the teacher's routine.

Coming Home

For some, teaching abroad can be addictive. The prospect of returning home to scour the local job adverts becomes distinctly unappealing as they drink Retsina, eat sushi or spend the weekend at a Brazilian beach. Once you have completed one teaching contract, it will be very much easier to land the next one, and it can be exhilarating to think that you can choose to work in almost any corner of the globe.

By the same token, many people who go abroad to teach English get burned out after a year or two. The majority of English teachers do not think of TEFL as a long-term proposition. They talk about their colleagues who move on to other things as getting a 'proper job,' i.e. one that does not require an early start followed by a long idle morning, where shabby treatment by bosses is not the norm and where you do not have to correct anyone's phrasal verbs.

Homesickness catches up with most EFL teachers and they begin to pine for a pub or bar where repartee is quick and natural and for all the other accoutrements of the culture of their birth. The bad news is that there are few jobs in EFL in Britain except at summer schools. Even professional English language teachers can find it difficult to land a reasonable job in the UK. American teachers will probably fare better due to the growth industry of ESL in the US, though the majority of openings are part-time with few fringe benefits and opportunities for career development. The good news is that a stint of teaching English abroad is an asset on anyone's CV/resumé. Employers of all kinds look favourably on people who have had the get-up-and-go to work at a respectable job in a foreign land. Such experience can always be presented as valuable for increasing self-assurance, maturity, a knowledge of the world, communication skills and any other positive feature which comes to mind. Very few teachers have regretted their decision to travel the world, even if the specific job they did was not without its drawbacks and difficulties.

PART II

Country by Country Guide

General prospects for Teachers
How to Fix up a Job
Pros and Cons
Rules and Regulations
List of Schools

WESTERN EUROPE	**AFRICA**
EASTERN EUROPE	**ASIA**
MIDDLE EAST	**LATIN AMERICA**

Most wages and prices are given in local currencies. For conversion to sterling and US dollars, see *Appendix 1* on page 538.

Embassies and Consulates will normally provide information on working visas to supplement the information provided in this book. A selective list of diplomatic representatives in London and Washington can be found in *Appendix 2* on page 539.

British Council offices abroad are frequently referred to in these chapters. A list of the relevant addresses is provided in *Appendix 3* on page 541.

Schools whose names are italicised in the text are included in the directory of schools which follows each country chapter. Recruitment agencies whose names appear in italics are listed in the appropriate introductory section beginning on page 91.

WESTERN EUROPE

Austria

The attraction to English in Austria is proved by the number of English bookshops with names like Big Ben and Shakespeare & Co. and the popularity of the two English language newspapers *Austria Today* and *Vienna Reporter*. The market for ELT in Austria is largely dominated by English for the business community so teachers with any kind of experience of the business world, even if just temping in an office, have a sharp advantage over those with experience only of teaching general English.

As in Germany and Switzerland, most private language institutes depend on freelance part-time teachers drawn from the sizeable resident international community. An estimated 90% of EFL teachers in Austria are freelancers which means that they do not have a contract with just one school and must pay tax as self-employed workers.

Finding a Job

The British Council in Vienna Austria has a list of about 25 English language institutes in Vienna. This list is annotated so that the kind of English tuition in which the company specialises is given, e.g. executive training, conversation classes, etc. It can be requested by e-mail (information@britishcouncil.at).

Teachers with a professional profile might find it worthwhile contacting the Austrian Cultural Institute in London (28 Rutland Gate, SW7 1PQ; 020-7584 8653/fax 020-7225 0470; culture@austria.org.uk/ www.austria.org.uk). They produce a leaflet which gives the address of the appropriate government department for British teachers interested in teaching in the state sector and can also supply a list headed 'Private Schools in Austria' which are not language institutes but private secondary schools with names like *Gymnasium Sacre Coeur für Mädchen*. Qualified teacher status would be virtually essential for teaching jobs in either sector. The British Council in Vienna also issues a list 'International and Bilingual Schools in Austria' containing 22 addresses.

Most *Volkshochschulen* offer English courses. The co-ordinating office in Vienna should be able to send you a list of the institutes around Austria (Verband Osterreichischer Volkshochschulen, Weintraubengasse 13, 1020 Vienna; 1-216 4226).

The Austrian Embassy in Washington distributes a leaflet *Teaching in Austria* which covers official teacher exchanges but not English language teaching. English Language Teaching Assistants from the UK and US are placed in Austrian secondary schools by the Central Bureau in London and the Fulbright Commission (Schmidgasse 14, 1082 Vienna; fax: 1-408 7765). They are looking for graduates in German and qualified teachers, under the age of 30. The deadline for applications is March 1st for the following academic year. Detailed information and an application form can be downloaded from their website (www.oead.ac.at/fulbright/ applying.htm).

New arrivals in Austria should visit a number of institutes and try to piece together a timetable. It should not be necessary to accept hours at the first one to offer them since there are still a number of cowboy outfits in the field. After working for three or four schools, it is better to cultivate just one or two since it is unrealistic to try to work for any more than this on a longer-term basis. A smart appearance and confident manner are always assets when looking for work teaching within the business community. Most Austrians will have an intermediate or higher level of English.

The rate at reputable institutes starts at AS225 per lesson (normally 45 minutes) and more for 60-minute lessons. This is none-too-generous when the high cost of living in Vienna is taken into account. Life in the provinces is less expensive of course. At the interview stage, always find out whether quoted rates are gross or net, if travelling time is covered and when you will be paid. Some schools pay after the course has finished which will leave you a pauper for an extended period.

Summer Camps

The demand for teachers of children and young people is very strong in Austria as elsewhere in Europe. Summer camps provide scope for EFL teachers, as indicated in the entries for *English for Children, English for Kids* and *Village Camps* of Switzerland. The summer camp organisation *Young Austria Summercamps* runs specialist English language camps in Salzburg (6456-7214) and Obertauern (6456-7249) attended by children aged 9-18. Monitors organise the outdoor programme and help the teachers with the social programme as well as with the lessons.

Some foreign young people who work as au pairs in Austria find that their primary task is to help teenage children with their English, which Maree Lakey from Australia found more taxing than she expected:

I am basically here to help the four children (aged between 11 and 17) with their English learning, although this is not always easy. On the whole, they have little desire to learn and see their lessons with me as more of a chore than anything else, but I guess that is not so unusual. I've found out how hard it is to try to speak correct English with them and to explain grammar rules which I have forgotten. It's also a bit difficult sometimes, as my Australian English is different from what the children have to learn. The children are of course not sympathetic to my difficulties, insisting that I should be infallable [sic] being a native speaker.

Regulations

Austria's full membership of the EU simplifies the red tape for British and Irish teachers. This, together with new laws governing social security, make it next to impossible for non-EU citizens to obtain teaching work. As Rebecca Chapman, Manager of the *Business Language Center* explains:

New laws mean that English teachers qualify for health care (extremely good) and contribute to the pension scheme which is reciprocal with the UK. Teachers therefore have to pay social security contributions which should be taken off at source. Reputable schools will register you and you'll receive a social security card and number. Because the schools register you and also have to pay part of the contributions for you, they are only allowed to take on EU citizens.

Registered teachers can expect to lose about 30% of their gross earnings in contributions.

Other nationalities may be able to find freelance work without having a work permit. It is generally accepted that as long as the number of hours worked per week does not exceed ten, a work permit is not required.

Austria (again like Germany) has many bureaucratic layers. New arrivals need to register with the police, organise a bank account (into which their wages will be paid directly) and get a tax number from the local tax office.

LIST OF SCHOOLS

BERLITZ AUSTRIA GMBH
Graben 13, 1010 Vienna. Tel: (1) 512 82 86. Fax: (1) 587 99 25. E-mail: wien01@berlitz.at. Website: www.berlitz.com.
Number of teachers: fluctuates with demand. Teachers work freelance. Recruits for Slovenia and Slovakia as well as Austria.

Preference of nationality: UK, Ireland, USA, Australia.
Qualifications: minimum 23 years old. Degree or equivalent; good general education. Knowledge of German not necessary.
Conditions of employment: freelance part-time basis. Most teaching takes place mornings and evenings.
Salary: AS185 per 40-minute lesson.
Facilities/Support: pre-service training given. No assistance with work permits or accommodation.
Recruitment: newspaper ads, word of mouth.
Contact: Joe Zeigler, Instructional Supervisor Austria/Slovenia/Slovakia, Berlitz, Mariahilferstrasse 27, 1060 Vienna (1-587 99 24/586 56 93; fax 1-587 99 25).

BFI/BERUFSFOERDERUNGSINSTITUT WIEN
Kinderspitalgasse 5, 1090 Vienna. Tel: (1) 404 35 114. Fax: (1) 404 35 124. E-mail: sprachen.bat@bfi-wien.or.at. Website: www.bfi-wien.or.at/bfi-wien.
Number of teachers: about 20.
Preference of nationality: English native speakers.
Qualifications: TEFL qualification (CELTA preferred).
Conditions of employment: freelance basis. Students are attending BFI (Vocational Training Institute of Vienna).
Salary: AS250-AS400 per 45 minute unit.
Facilities/Support: no assistance with finding accommodation.
Recruitment: local interviews essential.

BRI BOU
Barichgasse 26/3, 1030 Vienna. Tel: (1) 512 01 90/710 88 29. Fax: (1) 512 01 90.
Number of teachers: about 10 freelancers.
Preference of nationality: British, Canadian.
Qualifications: teaching experience and EFL certificate. Knowledge of German would be useful.
Conditions of employment: depends on the seminars. Standard length of course is 10-12 weeks. Daytime and evening classes.
Salary: AS275 per hour.
Facilities/Support: help with accommodation given if possible. No help available for obtaining work permits.
Recruitment: via British Council and university.
Contact: Mag. Brigitte Bouvain, Director.

BUSINESS LANGUAGE CENTER
Charles La Fond & Co. KEG, Trattnerhof 2, 1010 Vienna. Tel: (1) 533 70 010. Fax: (1) 532 85 21. E-mail blc@blc.co.at. Website: www.blc.co.at.
Number of teachers: 15.
Preference of nationality: none, but must be native speaker of English.
Qualifications: university degree, CELTA or equivalent, experience preferred, an interest in the business world.
Conditions of employment: minimum stay 12 months. Teachers work on freelance basis and must sort out their own visa and tax requirements. No guarantee of fixed number of hours.
Salary: starting fee of AS225 per 40 minute lesson, net of VAT (not including 30% approx. deduction at source for social security contributions).
Facilities/Support: monthly training, continuous pedagogical support but also chance to work independently. No assistance with accommodation.
Recruitment: personal interview necessary.
Contact: Rebecca Chapman, Pedagogical Manager.

ENGLISH FOR CHILDREN/EFC
English Language Day Camp/ELDC, Kanalstrasse 44, Postfach 160, 1220 Vienna. Tel: (1) 282 77 17. Fax: (1) 282 77 177. E-mail: english.for. children@eunet.at.

Website: http://members.eunet.at/english. for.children.
Number of teachers: varies according to need.
Preference of nationality: none, but must be English native speaker.
Qualifications: minimum age 21. Experience of working with children.
Conditions of employment: freelance 10-month contract (Sept-June). Minimum 4 h.p.w. Summer camp run during month of July.
Facilities/Support: need to be resident in Austria. Full training given free of charge before and during contract. All course materials provided. Housing not provided.
Recruitment: direct applications, local advertising and interviews.
Contact: Yolanda Reischer-Bohanec.

ENGLISH FOR KIDS
A. Baumgartnerstr. 44/A 7042, 1230 Vienna. Tel: (1) 667 45 79. Fax: (1) 667 51 63. E-mail: magik@e4kids.co.at. Website: www.e4kids.co.at.
Number of teachers and camp counsellors: 6-8 for residential summer camp.
Preference of nationality: EU or others with work permit for Austria.
Qualifications: CELTA or Trinity Certificate (minimum grade B) and some formal teaching preferred/required.
Conditions of employment: 6-8 weeks in July and August. Pupils aged from kindergarten to age 8 at level one and from 9 to 15 at level two. Also run language camp in the UK for pupils aged 15-17. Full-immersion courses with in-house methods following carefully planned syllabus and teachers' manual, supplemented with CD-Roms, etc.
Salary: varies depending on qualifications. From AS20,000 plus full board and accommodation for 6 weeks.
Facilities/Support: good standard of accommodation and full board provided for teachers.
Recruitment: personal interviews essential, sometimes held in UK.
Contact: Irena Kästenbauer, Principal.

ENGLISH LANGUAGE CENTRE HIETZING
In Der Hagenau 7, 1130 Vienna. Tel/fax: (1) 879 7548. E-mail: elch@xpoint.at
Number of teachers: 3-4.
Preference of nationality: none.
Qualifications: CELTA and degree (preferably in languages/humanities) Experience advantageous especially of children's classes.
Conditions of employment: 10 month contracts September to June. No fixed hours since teachers work on freelance basis.
Salary: AS260-400 per 60 minutes, depending on size of class. Health insurance and pension contributions. Teachers responsible for paying their own income tax.
Facilities/Support: no help with accommodation.
Recruitment: personal interview necessary.

LINGUARAMA SPRACHENINSTITUT
Concordiaplatz 2, 1010 Vienna. Tel/fax: (1) 533 0879. E-mail: vienna@ linguarama.com.
Number of teachers: 25-70.
Preference of nationality: native speakers only.
Qualifications: university degree or equivalent plus a basic TEFL qualification e.g. CELTA. Experience teaching Business English is preferred, but must have at least a keen interest in business.
Conditions of employment: mixture of contract and freelance teachers. Early morning and evening work.
Salary: depends on experience.
Facilities/Support: all teachers are given an induction course and paid training is held monthly. Help given to contract teachers to find accommodation and obtain permits.
Recruitment: freelancers hired locally; contract teachers normally via Linguarama

Group Personnel Department, 89 High St, Alton, Hants. GU34 1LG, UK; personnel@linguarama.com.

SPIDI (Spracheninstitut der Industrie)
Mariahilferstrasse 32, 1070 Vienna. Tel: (1) 524 17 17/40. Fax: (1) 524 17 17/540. E-mail: kitty.loewenstein@mdi-spidi.at. Website: www.spidi.at.
Number of teachers: about 50.
Preference of nationality: EU citizens.
Qualifications: minimum CELTA plus 1 year's experience.
Conditions of employment: freelance only. Flexible hours.
Salary: AS300-350 per hour, depending on qualifications and experience.
Facilities/Support: no assistance with accommodation. Teachers' room with PC and library. Induction course in mid-September. Monthly teacher development sessions/workshops.
Recruitment: local interview essential.
Contact: Kitty Loewenstein, Director of Studies.

TALK PARTNERS
Fischerstiege 10/16, 1010 Vienna. Tel: (1) 535 9695. Fax: (1) 533 3073. E-mail: talk.partners@telecom.at.
Number of teachers: 50.
Preference of nationality: none.
Qualifications: minimum CELTA, university degree plus business experience.
Conditions of employment: most trainers are freelance. Hours vary.
Salary: minimum rate is AS230 for 45 minutes.
Facilities/Support: assistance with accommodation may be given if necessary.
Recruitment: local adverts in EFL journals and via British Council. Interviews essential; sometimes available in UK.
Contact: Christian Almásy, Director of Studies.

VERBAND WIENER VOLKSBILDUNG/WIENER VOLKSHOCHSCHULEN
Hollergasse 22, 1150 Vienna. Tel: +43 1 89 174. Fax: +43 1 89 174 65. E-mail: info@vwv.at. Website: www.vhs.at.
Number of teachers: varies according to demand. All teachers are freelance.
Preference of nationality: none.
Qualifications: CELTA or university training, or extensive experience of language teaching in adult education.
Conditions of employment: self-employed freelancers. 4-8 months. Maximum 11¹/2 lessons a week; minimum commitment 15 weeks. Hours are 9-12am and 6-9pm, including weekends.
Salary: AS215 per 50-minute lesson.
Facilities/Support: workshops and other training available. Library and media facilities available.
Recruitment: courses planned 6 months in advance. Local interview essential.
Contact: Thomas Fritz or Inge-Anna Koleff, Languages Department.

VILLAGE CAMPS
14 rue de la Morache, 1260 Nyon. Switzerland. Tel: (22) 990 94 05. Fax: (22) 990 94 94. E-mail: personnel@villagecamps.ch. Website: www.villagecamps.com/ staff/staff1.htm.
Language summer camp at Zell am See and multi-activity camps in Austria.
Preference of nationality: none; must be native speaker.
Qualifications: EFL qualification and experience required. Knowledge of a second European language needed. Minimum age 21 for language monitors, 23 for teachers.
Conditions of employment: five to seven weeks during the period of work from mid or end of June to mid-August teaching children aged 10-12 years. 3-5 hours teaching per day. Additional duties include supervising sports, activities and excursions.
Salary: English teachers earn 300 Swiss francs per week plus room and board and

insurance provided.

Recruitment: direct application (to Dept. 850), via adverts, websites, international schools and universities.

Contact: Rebecca Meaton, Personnel Manager.

YOUNG AUSTRIA SUMMERCAMPS
Ferienhöfe GmbH, Alpenstrasse 108a, A-5020 Salzburg. Tel: (662) 62 57 58-0. Fax: (662) 62 57 58-2. E-mail: office@camps.at. Website: www.camps.at.
Summer language and sports camps near Salzburg.

Number of teachers: 30 teachers and monitors.

Preference of nationality: British.

Qualifications: teachers must have teaching experience. Monitors should have had experience of working with children.

Conditions of employment: 3-4 hours of work per day for 2 weeks in summer.

Salary: AS4,420 for teachers (for 2 weeks); AS3,120 for monitors in their first year. Free board and lodging and a lump sum payment of AS2,000 for travel expenses.

Recruitment: application forms available from above address; these must be in by end of February.

Contact: Andrea Brunnhauer.

Other Schools to Try

Note that these schools did not confirm their teacher requirements for this edition of *Teaching English Abroad.* Upper case entries marked with an asterisk had entries in the last edition (1999); addresses without asterisks have been taken from various sources, such as British Council lists and the *Yellow Pages.*

International School Kaprun, Alpine Sports & Ski Racing Academy, Postfach 47, 5710 Kaprun (tel/fax 6547 7106). Young graduates to supervise English and sports in exchange for room and board and ski pass.

English Language Services Network, Reichergasse 59/C, 3411 Klosterneuburg

Alpha Sprachinstitut Austria, Schwarzenbergplatz 16/Canovagasse 5, 1010 Vienna (office@alpha.at; www.alpha.at)

Amerika-Institut, Operngasse 4, 1010 Vienna (aaie@magnet.at)

*AUSTRO-BRITISH SOCIETY, Wickenburggasse 19, 1080 Vienna (tel/fax 1-406 11 41)

Didactica Akademie f. Wirtschaft und Sprachen, Schottenfeldgasse 13 15, 1070 Vienna

English Language Services, Kaposigasse 106/5/11, 1220 Vienna (ELS_Austria@ compuserve.com

inlingua Sprachschule, Neuer Markt 1, 1010 Vienna (wien@inlingua.at)

Institut CEF, Strozzigasse 4, 1080 Vienna (cefw@cef.at)

International Language Services, Getreidemarkt 17, 1060 Vienna (tel/fax 1-585 53 47; delphin@dolphin.at)

Multi Lingua, Hardtgasse 5/2, 1190 Vienna (MLingua@compuserve.com)

Private Institut Venetia, Grosse Neugasse 8/19, 1040 Vienna (office@venetia.co.at; www.venetia.co.at)

Sprachstudio J.J Rousseau, Untere Viaduktgasse 43, 1030 Vienna

Super Language Learning, Florianigasse 55, 1080 Vienna (pearl@ping.at)

Benelux

BELGIUM

The list of language schools in the Brussels Yellow Pages runs to four pages, under the heading *Langues (Ecoles de)/Talensholen* and prospects for business-oriented language teachers are very good in Belgium. Several language teaching organisations are represented in more than one Belgian city, especially *Berlitz* which employs upwards of 150 freelance teachers in ten branches. The starting pay at most schools is BF600-BF650 an hour. Linguarama Belgium is constantly recruiting freelance teachers with a TEFL qualification and one year's experience (rue Lincoln 64, 1180 Brussels; 2-343 14 56; brussels@linguarama.com).

As one of the capitals of the European Union, there is a huge demand for all the principal European languages in Brussels. Yet, despite the enormous amount of language teaching in Belgium, there is no real shortage of teachers. In addition to the many Belgian teachers, there are also well-qualified expatriate spouses who take up teaching. One area in which a shortage does exist, however, is primary teaching in the private sector.

The Education Office of the British Council in Brussels (which is responsible for Luxembourg as well as Belgium) distributes a list of 20 private language schools. If possible, get hold of the special 'Schools Guide' edition published in April by the weekly English language magazine *The Bulletin* (1038 Chaussée de Waterloo, 1180 Brussels; www.XPATS.com). *Newcomer* is a free bi-annual publication from the publishers of *The Bulletin* which contains information and contact addresses of interest to the newly arrived teacher including a listing of major language schools. Occasionally the classified ads include some requests for live-in helpers willing to teach English, or you can of course advertise yourself, though there will be plenty of competition from highly qualified teachers.

The casual teacher will probably steer clear of the schools which undertake to teach senior EU bureaucrats, but there are plenty of other schools. Telephone teaching has caught on in Belgium, especially among French learners of English; see entry for *Phone Languages*.

As throughout continental Europe, children attend summer camps which focus on language learning. Companies like Kiddy & Junior Classes (see entry for *Brussels Language Studies*), *Kids' Computer Club* and *Call International* organise holiday English courses; the latter company has centres in Waterloo, Antwerp and Tournai. One organisation which sometimes advertises in the UK for teachers is *Pro Linguis,* where Philip Dray worked one summer:

> *The school mainly caters for French boys and girls between 12 and 18. They come to Thiaumont for a course of one or two weeks. They sleep in dormitory-like accommodation in somewhat spartan conditions. I am employed in a freelance capacity to work 90 days between April and mid-September. The salary is £60 a day (paid monthly). The hours are very long: 8 per day with sometimes 7 days in a row though you are compensated by the fact that some days you are completely free. Travel is a great incentive in this part of Belgium (although you need a lot of money for the sky-high prices). For my keep (in a sort of hotel room) I have to check the dorms twice a week, which means enforcing an 11pm curfew, which so far has not been too bad since most kids have been co-operative.*

If you intend to stay in Belgium some time, it might be worth contacting your local *commune* (municipal council), which may offer adult education language courses.

Freelance

The British Council keeps a register of individuals who teach English privately. Private tutors charge BF900-1,000 an hour. In order to be included on their list of private tutors of English, you must provide documentary evidence that you have a CELTA or 100-hour equivalent plus either teacher certification or two years' TEFL experience. A typical listing would be for a teacher with a BA (Hons) in modern languages, a PGCE and a TEFL qualification from International House. If your past attainments fall short of these, it is quite feasible to put up notices in one of the large university towns (Brussels, Antwerp, Gent, Leuven, Liège, etc.) offering conversation practice.

Almost all foreign teachers who begin to work for an institute do so on a freelance basis and will have to deal with their own tax and social security. Officially they should declare themselves *indépendants* (self-employed persons) and pay contributions which usually amount to about one-third of their salary. In fact many English teachers take their gross salary without declaring it, and don't work long enough to risk being caught. Once a teacher has worked black *(en noir/in het zwart)* it is difficult to regularise his or her status, since they then have to declare all previous earnings. Therefore anyone who plans to spend more than a few months teaching in Belgium should consider this question.

LIST OF SCHOOLS

ANTWERPSE TALENAKADEMIE C.V.
Karel Govaertsstraat 23-25, 2100 Deurne. Tel: (3) 366 11 92. Fax: (3) 321 93 50.
Number of teachers: 7.
Preference of nationality: British.
Qualifications: any TEFL qualification and relevant experience.
Conditions of employment: variable; courses last from 1 to 30 weeks. Evening hours 7pm-10pm. Children and adult classes.
Salary: BF600-700 per hour, depending on client.
Facilities/Support: some assistance with finding accommodation and obtaining work permits if necessary.
Recruitment: interviews in Belgium required.
Contact: Rita Stevens.

BERLITZ LANGUAGE CENTERS
Avenue de Tervueren 265, 1150 Brussels. Tel: (2) 763 08 30. Fax: (2) 771 01 70. E-mail: joke.vandaele@berlitz.be.
Number of teachers: about 50.
Preference of nationality: British or Irish.
Qualifications: university degree.
Conditions of employment: employee contract. Trial period of 3 months. Flexible hours (mornings, evenings plus Saturday morning).
Salary: BF321 per 40 minute teaching unit. Contracts of 100 units BF32,700 minimum.
Facilities/Support: no assistance with accommodation. In-house training lasts 12 days.
Recruitment: via adverts and direct applications.
Contact: Joke Van Daele, Area/Country Instructional Supervisor.

BRUSSELS LANGUAGE STUDIES (BLS)
Rue du Marteau 8, 1210 Brussels. Tel: (2) 217 23 73. Fax: (2) 217 64 51. E-mail: info@kiddyclasses.net. Website: www.kiddyclasses.net.
Number of teachers: about 30.
Preference of nationality: none, but should be native speaker.
Qualifications: must have TEFL teaching experience. Experience of teaching children desirable.
Conditions of employment: temporary job as freelancers. School hours are 8.30am-8pm. Children's courses are 6 h.p.w., adults more.
Salary: varies.
Facilities/Support: none.
Recruitment: via internet, newspaper.
Contact: Madame Drablier, Manager.

CALL INTERNATIONAL
Boulevard de la Cense 41, 1410 Waterloo & Avenue des Drapiers 25, 1050 Brussels. Tel: (2) 644 95 95. Fax: (2) 644 94 95. E-mail: callinter@skynet.be.
Number of teachers: 40.
Preference of nationality: none.
Qualifications: degree. Experience an advantage. Good communication skills needed.

Conditions of employment: freelance. Flexible hours. BF650-BF1,000 per hour.
Facilities/support: no assistance with accommodation.
Recruitment: via local newspapers.
Contact: Parick Wauquier, Director.

CERAN LINGUA INTERNATIONAL S.A.
16 Avenue du Château, 4900 Spa. Tel: (87) 791 545. Fax: (87) 791 185. E-mail: human.resources@ceran.be. Website: www.ceran.com.
Number of teachers: 15 for this residential school.
Preference of nationality: must have work permit or EU nationality and be native English speaker.
Qualifications: university degree or relevant work experience and some teaching experience. TEFL background not essential.
Conditions of employment: open-ended after 6-month trial. 9am-5.30pm and occasional evenings and weekends. (Residential courses commence on Sunday evenings.)
Facilities/Support: accommodation provided for first 6 months. In-house training available.
Recruitment: newspaper and magazine adverts, website (www.jobs-career.be) and word of mouth.
Contact: Ms. Vicky Bryant, Head of English Department or Ms. Gelica Dalon, Human Resources Department.

DIALOGUE
Head Office, 55, route du Tonnelet, 4900 Spa. Tel: (87) 79 30 10. Fax: (87) 79 30 11. E-mail: dialogue@arcadis.be. Website: www.dialogue-languages.com.
Number of teachers: 5.
Preference of nationality: none.
Qualifications: business experience.
Conditions of employment: freelance. Usual hours 9am-4pm.
Salary: £16 for 60 minute lessons.
Facilities/Support: no assistance with accommodation.
Recruitment: advertising.
Contact: M. Godard, President.

EURO BUSINESS LANGUAGES
Leuvensesteenweg 325, 1932 Zaventem. Tel: (2) 720 15 10. Fax: (2) 720 25 80. E-mail: euro.business.languages@skynet.be.
Number of teachers: 22.
Preference of nationality: none.
Qualifications: university degree and several years of work experience (preferably teaching English to adults) required.
Conditions of employment: all teachers are freelancers. Variable hours between 8am and 6pm or evening classes until 10pm. Students are all business people. Teachers choose their own course books (but need not pay for these). All courses are custom-made; emphasis on role plays relevant to client's profession.
Salary: starting hourly rate of BF750. Travelling allowance paid if course given at client's office.
Facilities/Support: assistance given to teachers who want to establish legitimate freelance status. Can sponsor non-EU applicants for work permit if appropriate. Training given plus three refresher meetings a year.
Recruitment: personal interview necessary.
Contact: F. Valentin, Director.

KIDS' COMPUTER CLUB
Avenue René Gobert 31, 1180 Brussels. Tel: (2) 374 27 08. Fax: (2) 374 75 87. E-mail: secretariat@kidscomputer.be. Website: www.kidscomputer.be.
Number of teachers: 3.

Preference of nationality: British.
Qualifications: paedagogical degree.
Conditions of employment: Wednesday 1pm-5pm; Friday 4pm-7pm; Saturday 9am-1pm and school holidays 9-12am and 1.30pm-4.30pm.
Facilities/Support: no assistance with accommodation.
Recruitment: spontaneous applications.
Contact: Marie-Claire Bodart, Manager or Anne Zerard, English Teacher.

MAY INTERNATIONAL TRAINING CONSULTANTS
55 rue de Bordeaux, 1060 Brussels. Tel: (2) 536 06 70. Fax: (2) 536 06 80. E-mail: info@mayintl.com.
Number of teachers: approximately 50.
Preference of nationality: none.
Qualifications: TEFL qualification, minimum 1 year's teaching experience with adults.
Conditions of employment: self-employed, no contracts, but minimum commitment of 1 year. Mostly day-time work, although evening work is available. Pupils are all adults, and mostly in business/professions. ISO 9001 Quality System in operation.
Salary: minimum BF700 per hour. Higher rates depending on experience/performance.
Facilities/Support: assistance in finding accommodation. Informal training/assistance given.
Recruitment: internet and local newspaper adverts. Interviews essential, usually local but sometimes held in UK.
Contact: Valerie McConaghy, Director.

PETERS SCHOOL
87 rue des Deux Eglises, 1210 Brussels. Tel: (2) 280 00 21. Fax: (2) 280 00 21.
Number of teachers: 10-15.
Preference of nationality: none. Majority British but Americans and Australians welcome to apply.
Qualifications: linguistic and paedagogical qualifications and some teaching experience. Personality very important.
Conditions of employment: freelance. Contracts last from 1 week to 1 year. School is open daytime and evenings.
Salary: BF700 per hour.
Recruitment: speculative applications by post and in person; word of mouth. Interview or test given.
Contact: Françoise Poncelet, *Responsable Pédagogique*.

PHONE LANGUAGES
Rue des Echevins 65, 1050 Brussels. Tel: (2) 647 40 20. Fax: (2) 647 40 55. E-mail: belgium@phonelanguages.com. Website: www.phonelanguages.com.
Number of teachers: 80 throughout Belgium (including 20 English teachers).
Preference of nationality: all nationalities, especially English and American.
Qualifications: BA preferably with TEFL diploma. Must be on-line at home.
Conditions of employment: all teachers are freelance and teach in cycles of 10, 30, 50 or 100 half-hour lessons over the phone. Flexible hours of work between 8am and 10pm; the favourite times are 8am-10am, lunchtime and 5pm-8pm. Pupils are all adults (usually business people). Teachers work from their own homes over the telephone and no longer need to be in Belgium to work. All teachers must have a telephone and e-mail and internet access at home.
Salary: from £10 per hour.
Facilities/Support: no assistance with accommodation. Free training given for 8-10 half-hours. Course books supplied free of charge.
Recruitment: send CV and accompanying letter to Virginia Czwakiel who visits London twice a month.

PRO LINGUIS
67 Place de l'Eglise, 6717 Thiaumont. Tel: (63) 22 04 62. Fax: (63) 22 06 88. E-mail: secretariat@prolinguis.be. Website: www.prolinguis.be.
Number of teachers: 14 (freelancers) to work near Arlon.
Preference of nationality: British.
Qualifications: EFL training, BA (Hons) in English or business.
Conditions of employment: minimum 1 year contracts or 2 month contracts in summer. 7 hours a day, 4-5 days per week.
Salary: BF3,300-3,500 per day plus full board and lodging on campus.
Facilities/Support: details on website.
Recruitment: personal contacts. Phone interviews.
Contact: Christiane Maillart or Melanie Fröhlking.

SKI TEN INTERNATIONAL
Chateau d'Emines, 5080 Emines (Namur). Tel: (81) 21 30 51. Fax: (81) 20 02 63. E-mail: ski-ten-goffinet@skynet.be.
Number of teachers: 1.
Preference of nationality: none.
Qualifications: experience with children. Some knowledge of French useful.
Conditions of employment: student contract for July and August. 6 hours of work per day including teaching and 'animation' i.e. supervising camp activities.
Salary: 1,000 euros per month.
Facilities/Support: board and lodging provided at camp.
Recruitment: university exchanges, word of mouth.
Contact: Martine Goffinet, Directrice.

Other Schools to Try

Note that these schools did not confirm their teacher requirements for this edition of *Teaching English Abroad*. Upper case entries marked with an asterisk had entries in the last edition (1999); addresses without asterisks have been taken from various sources, such as British Council lists and the *Yellow Pages*.

Berlitz Language Centre, Meir 21, 1st Floor, 2000 Antwerpen
Berlitz Language Centre, Britselei 15, 2018 Antwerpen

American Language School, 92/94 Square E. Plasky, 1030 Brussels (2-743 22 59/fax 2-736 75 66)
Amira, 251 Avenue Louise, 1050 Brussels
Berlitz Language Centre, Avenue Louise 306-310, 1050 Brussels (info@berlitz.be)
Berlitz Language Centre, Avenue des Arts 36, 1040 Brussels
CCLM, 29 rue Abbé Jean Heymans, 1200 Brussels
CPAB Language School, Galerie de la Toison d'Or, 4th Floor, 29-31 Chaussée d'Ixelles, 1050 Brussels
European Language Center, 141 rue Champ du Roi, 1040 Brussels
Eurospeak, Rue de Stassart 49, 1050 Brussels (2-511 89 12)
Fondation 9, 412 Avenue Louise, 1050 Brussels
*LANGUAGES UNLIMITED, 77 Chaussée de Charleroi, 1060 Brussels (2-534 76 84)
Language Workshop, Ave A Blaivie 4, 1950 Kraain (2-782 18 50)
Liren International Institute, 13 rue du Beau-Site, 1000 Brussels
LTC, Rue Willems 14, bte. 308, 1040 Brussels (2-230 98 10)
Mitchell School, Rue Louis Hap 156, 1040 Brussels (2-734 80 73/fax 2-732 63 35; mitchell@planetinternet.be)

Berlitz Language Centre, Kouter 177, 9000 Gent
Inlingua School of Languages, UCO-Toren/6de Verdieping, Bellevue 9/10, 9050 Gent (Ledeberg)

Practicum, Reep 24, 9000 Gent
Berlitz Language Centre, rue du Pont d'Avroy 2/4, 4000 Liège
Access bvba Taalbureau, Abdijstraat 40, 2260 Tongerlo

LUXEMBOURG

With only a handful of private language schools in the country, Luxembourg does not offer much scope for ELT teachers. *Phone Languages* in Belgium have a network of telephone teachers in Luxembourg, but run the operation from the Brussels office. Another possibility is the Centre de Langues Luxembourg (80 Boulevard G. Patton, L-2316 Luxembourg; 403941/fax 403930).

The national employment service *(l'Administration de l'Emploi)* at 10 rue Bender, L-1229 (352-478 53 00; www.etat.lu/ADEM) has a EURES adviser who may have information about language teaching openings. Informal live-in tutoring jobs are possible. Luxembourg Accueil Information (10 Bisserwee, L-1238 Luxembourg-Grund; 241717) is a centre for new arrivals and temporary residents. They provide a range of services on their premises, including workshops and language courses, and might be able to advise on teaching and tutoring possibilities. The British-Luxembourg Society promotes British culture and the English language in Luxembourg, and they also might be a source of information. The English language newspaper is the *Luxembourg News* (25 rue Philippe II, L-2340 Luxembourg).

NETHERLANDS

Urban Dutch people have a very high degree of competence in English after they finish their schooling. Educated Dutch people are so fluent in English that the Minister of Education once suggested that English might become the main language used in Dutch universities, a suggestion which caused an understandable outcry. This is not a country in which any old BA (Hons) has much chance of stepping into an ELT job.

What private language schools there are tend to provide business English and to be looking for teachers with extensive commercial or government experience as well as a teaching qualification. So many British people have settled in the Netherlands, attracted by its liberal institutions, that most schools depend on long-term freelancers. The British Council in Amsterdam maintains a list of more than 80 language institutes throughout the country which prepare candidates for the Cambridge exams. Highly qualified teachers or those with expertise in tutoring in an executive context should contact these language institutes. The *British Language Training Centre* in Amsterdam, which offers the CELTA course (see *Training* chapter) and employs a number of ELT teachers itself, may be able to give advice to qualified job-seekers and recommend other institutes to try for work. CPLS Training (Vestdijk 55a, Eindhoven 5611 CA; 40-244 57 73; www.cplsnet.com) is a typical training company employing project based trainers to deliver business-to-business programmes all over the Netherlands. Applicants should be qualified and with a good track record of training business clients. Similarly Linguarama Nederland is expanding in the business-training field with centres in Amsterdam, the Hague and Soesterberg; enquiries may be sent to Linguarama, Bleijenburg 1, 2511 VC Den Haag.

Another possibility is the network of *Volksuniversiteit,* the northern European institution of 'folk universities'. Branches can be found in Amersfoort, Delft, Groningen, Haarlem, Hertogenbosch, Hilversum, Leiden, Rotterdam, Utrecht and several others as well as Amsterdam. When Andrew Boyle wrote to a selection of the addresses on the British Council list, the ones that replied were able to offer only the possibility of part-time work.

Outside the mainstream language institutes, it might be possible to arrange some telephone teaching. Village Camps (see chapter on Switzerland) has a language camp operation in the Netherlands which takes on a few English teachers and monitors.

LIST OF SCHOOLS

BOGAERS TALENINSTITUUT B.V.
Groenstraat 139 155, 5021 LL Tilburg. Tel: (13) 536 21 01. Fax: (13) 535 81 99. E-mail: bogaers@xs4all.nl. Website: www.bogaerstalen.nl.
Number of teachers: 3.
Preference of nationality: British.
Qualifications: degree and TEFL Cert. Experience in teaching conversational and business English preferred.
Conditions of employment: from one week to 9 months. Lessons last one and a half hours.
Salary: from 40 guilders per hour.
Facilities/Support: will help with accommodation if needed.
Recruitment: speculative CVs and applications.

BRITISH LANGUAGE TRAINING CENTRE
Oxford House, N.Z.Voorburgwal 328E, 1012 RW Amsterdam. Tel: (20) 622 36 34. Fax: (20) 626 49 62. E-mail: bltc@bltc.nl. Website: www.bltc.nl.
Number of teachers: 20.
Preference of nationality: UK.
Qualifications: CELTA, DELTA. From 2 years' experience for full-time, ESP experience, Business English experience.
Conditions of employment: various.
Salary: varies depending on qualifications and experience.
Facilities/Support: no assistance with accommodation. CELTA training centre.
Recruitment: application with CV followed by an in-person interview.
Contact: C. O'Gorman, Director.

FEEDBACK
Lassusstraat 9a, 1075 GV Amsterdam. Tel: (20) 671 67 09. Fax: (20) 662 05 51. E-mail: feedback@wxs.nl.
Number of teachers: 8.
Preference of nationality: none but must be native speakers.
Qualifications: TEFL Cert. Business or technical experience highly valued.
Conditions of employment: contract from September to June. 15-25 hours of classes per week. Lessons last 1¹/2-2 hours.
Salary: 35-48 guilders per hour.
Facilities/support: 60 hours compulsory in-house training.
Recruitment: personal interview essential.
Contact: Bill Wohlrab.

FRANGLAIS TAALBUREAU
Molenstraat 15, 258 VW, The Hague. Tel: (70) 361 17 03. Fax: (70) 361 17 34. E-mail: learn@franglais.nl. Website: www.franglais.nl.
Number of teachers: 10.
Preference of nationality: none.
Qualifications: teaching experience, preferably with a business background. No specific teaching degree necessary, but it is helpful.
Conditions of employment: 12 weeks or 16 weeks renewable. From 3 hours a week up to a maximum of 30 per week. Opportunities also available to edit texts by non-native speakers; pay is 10 cents per word.
Salary: 50 guilders per hour plus transport costs.
Facilities/Support: no assistance with accommodation.
Recruitment: advertisements in newspapers and on-the-spot interviews.
Contact: Sarah MacMillin, Director.

INSTITUT DE WESTER
Postbus 1020, 1810 KA Alkmaar and Ruusbroechof 37, 1813 Alkmaar. Tel: (72) 540 55 43. Fax: (72) 540 55 42. E-mail: talen@dewester.com.
Number of teachers: 5.
Preference of nationality: none, but British accent preferred.
Qualifications: business and teaching experience appreciated. Should have completed language studies.
Conditions of employment: 1 year. Flexible timetable. Freelance basis.
Salary: 45-70 guilders per hour.
Facilities/support: no assistance with accommodation.
Recruitment: CVs on spec and contacts.
Contact: Dr. F. A. Martynse-Visser, Director.

THE LANGUAGE ACADEMY
Spuistraat 134, 1012 VB Amsterdam. Tel: (20) 525 46 37. Fax: (20) 525 43 08. E-mail: info@thelanguageacademy.nl. Website: www.thelanguageacademy.nl.
Number of teachers: 10 per year on short-term contracts.
Preference of nationality: British, American.
Qualifications: none specified.
Conditions of employment: usually 10-week contracts, i.e. duration of an English course. Most courses taught in the evenings; some daytime hours too.
Salary: average 40-60 guilders per hour gross.
Facilities/Support: no assistance with accommodation or work permits.
Recruitment: teachers submit CVs; face-to-face interviews required.
Contact: Mrs. P. Andriessen, General Manager.

PIMENTEL COMMUNICATIONS INTERNATIONAL
Bachlaan 43, 1817 GH Alkmaar. Tel: (72) 512 11 90. Fax: (72) 511 64 09. E-mail: info@pcitalen.nl. Website: www.pcitalen.nl.
Number of teachers: 20+.
Preference of nationality: mostly British.
Qualifications: experience in business and technical writing essential.
Conditions of employment: freelancers working in-company all day. Evenings rarely.
Salary: starts at 50 guilders per hour.
Facilities/Support: most teachers are already living in the Netherlands.
Recruitment: advertisements, word-of-mouth and recommendations.
Contact: Iona de Pimentel.

SUITCASE TALEN
Operetteweg 104, 1323 Ve Almere. Tel: (36) 536 74 82. Fax: (36) 536 72 64. E-mail: info@suitcase.nl. Website: www.suitcase.nl.
Number of teachers: 3.
Preference of nationality: none, but should be native speaker.
Qualifications: good paedagogical ones.
Conditions of employment: 3 months.
Salary: freelance per hour.
Facilities/Support: no assistance with accommodation.
Recruitment: on spec application. Interview essential.
Contact: Mrs. M. E. A. Kwakerhaak.

A selection of other schools to try (towns in alphabetical order):
BERLITZ, Rokin 87-89, 1012 KL Amsterdam (20-622 13 75/fax 20-620 39 59).
   Employs about 60 teachers but according to Berlitz website (www.berlitz.com) Berlitz in Amsterdam is not normally looking to hire teachers.
English Language Institute, Postbus 75209, 1070 AE Amsterdam
Schoevers Opleidingen, Stadhouderskade 60, 1072 AC Amsterdam
The Workshop, Rostocklaan 38, 7315 HM Apeldoorn

English Language Institute, Berkenweg 46, 3741 BZ Baarn
All-English Institute, Iepenlaan 96, 2061 GN Bloemendaal
Dutchess English Language Centre, Schoutenstraat 86, 1623 RZ Hoorn
Schoevers Opleidingen, Kromme Nieuwe Gracht 3, 3512 HC Utrecht

France

The French used to rival the English for their reluctance to learn other languages. A Frenchman abroad spoke French as stubbornly as Britons spoke English. But things have changed, especially in the business and technical community. French telephone directories contain pages of language institutes.

Since the 1970s, the law has put pressure on companies to provide on-going training to staff. The *Droit de Formation Continue* stipulates that companies devote at least 1% of their salary budget to training. English and computing are the most popular objects of investment, and therefore many private language institutes cater purely to the business market. In fact a quick browse through the entries in the List of Schools at the end of this chapter will lead you to the conclusion that all adult language training in France is business-oriented, with most of it taking place on-site and the rest taking place in business and vocational schools. In this setting the term *formateurs* or 'trainers' is often used instead of English teachers. Private training companies involved with *formation continue* seem to produce very glossy brochures which look more like the annual report of a multinational corporation than an invitation to take an evening course. Many offer one-to-one tuition.

The French government does not neglect the less privileged, either: there is a scheme in place in some regions whereby the unemployed can take free English lessons at private schools. A considerable number of town councils *(mairies)* and *Chambres de Commerce et d'Industrie* (CCI) have their own Centres d'Etude des Langues. The main CCI in Paris (1-55 65 55 65) should be able to refer enquirers to other centres involved in English teaching; contact their Bureau pour l'Information et l'Orientation Professionnelle on 1-55 65 60 00 between 1.30pm and 5pm.

Teaching young children is left mostly to French teachers of English, though native speakers might find a freelance opening. Some municipalities have introduced projects to teach English to four-year-olds. The most popular times are Wednesdays (when state schools are closed) and Saturdays. The fashion for telephone teaching, a concept invented by a Parisian yuppie (or so it is said), seems to be waning somewhat.

Prospects for Teachers

Advanced ELT qualifications seem to be less in demand in France than solid teaching experience, particularly in a business context. But an increasing number of schools require a relevant educational background, e.g. B.Ed., PGCE, CELTA or DELTA. Fewer schools accept candidates on the basis of being a native speaker alone than once was the case, and candidates may be asked to provide an *attestation de durée d'études* to show the educational level they have reached. However, anyone who has a university degree in any subject and who can look at home in a business situation has a chance of finding teaching work, particularly if they have a working knowledge of French. Having your own transport is a huge advantage as Helen Welch reported. She arrived in the Toulouse area (from Thailand) in August, was offered two jobs almost straightaway and immediately got a car which she claims is 'absolutely necessary for teaching here'.

In some circles it is fashionable to learn American English which means that, despite the visa difficulties for non-EU nationals, it is possible for Americans to find work as well. Twice as many schools listed at the end of this chapter claim to have no preference as to the country of origin of their native-speaker teachers as mention EU or British nationality.

France is such a popular and obvious destination for British and Irish people and also with North Americans that a speculative job hunt from abroad can be disappointing. Major language teaching organisations receive speculative CVs every day and can't promise anything until they meet the applicant.

FIXING UP A JOB

In Advance

A list of English language institutes in France is hard to come by. If you want to find the addresses of private language schools, consult the *Pages Jaunes* (Yellow Pages; www.pagesjaunes.fr) under the headings *Enseignement: Langues* or *Ecoles de Langues*.

The British Council in Paris (9-11 rue de Constantine, 75007; 1-49 55 73 00/fax 1-47 05 77 02) has a small but growing Young Learners Centre which employs specialist teachers. It also has a library (1-49 55 73 23) which would be of assistance to people already teaching in France but which cannot offer individual help to job applicants or deal with CVs. The Paris library is open weekdays from 11am to 6pm (till 7pm on Wednesdays). Unfortunately the Paris Council no longer distributes information on teaching English and a list of language schools as it once did.

The British Council in Bordeaux (Université Victor-Segalen, 3 place de la Victoire, 33076 Bordeaux; 5-57 57 19 52; Alison.Edge@britishcouncil.fr) has no Teaching Centre but it might know of local teaching vacancies. The Bordeaux office is open Monday to Friday 11am-1pm and 2pm-5pm. Both British Council offices are closed between mid-July and early September.

For addresses of other language schools, try the Franco-British Chamber of Commerce (41 rue de Turenne, 75003 Paris). The British Council recommends consulting *Dicoguide de la Formation* published by Génération Formation (27 rue du Chemin Vert, 75011 Paris: 1-48-07-41-41). However this is not very practical advice since the book retails for F2,500. The website www.ressources-web.com/rh/formation/themes/formation-langues.htm has a small selection of language training companies for business.

The *Central Bureau for International Education & Training Language Assistants Team* at the British Council (10 Spring Gardens, London SW1A 2BN; 020-7389 4764) sends a large number of undergraduates studying French at UK universities (and recent graduates) to spend an academic year as language assistants in secondary and primary schools in France. They receive a gross allowance of F5,734 a month for seven months, beginning October 1st. Similar posts are also available in other francophone countries, i.e. Belgium, Quebec (Canada) and Switzerland.

The *Alliance Française* has centres throughout the world, with more than 60 in the UK and 100 in the US. Anyone who can converse in French might find it useful to make contact before leaving home. Most centres have a notice board where requests for tutors, au pairs, etc. are occasionally posted. In London, the Alliance Française of Grande Bretagne is located at 1 Dorset Square, NW1 6PU (020-7224 1865) and in New York at 22 E. 60th St, New York, NY 10022 (212-355-6100/fax 212-935-4119; www.fiaf.org).

Other federations and associations which might be able to provide contacts to qualified teachers are listed below. If writing to them, be specific in your request:
Fédération française des organisations de séjours culturels linguistiques (FFOSC), 108 bd Péreire, 75017 Paris (1-40 54 86 99).
Séjours linguistiques associés (SELIA), rue de l'Eperon, 75006 Paris (1-44 32 16 86)
L'Union nationale des organisations de séjours linguistiques (UNOEL), 15-19 rue des Mathurins, 75009 Paris (1-49 24 03 61)

L'Union nationale des organisations de séjours longues durée à l'étranger (UNSE), 46 rue du Commandant-J.-Duhail, 94120 Fontenay-sous-Bois (1-48 76 65 12).

Adverts for teaching jobs in France seldom appear in the UK press and virtually never in American journals. One organisation seen advertising vacancies in France repeatedly is Eurotemp, 37 Greenhill St, Stratford-upon-Avon, Warwickshire CV37 6LE. French newspapers carry few teaching ads though there is no harm in trying *Le Figaro* especially on Mondays and Tuesdays and also the Paris edition of the *International Herald Tribune*.

When applying to a training organisation, try to demonstrate your commercial flair with a polished presentation including a business-like CV (omitting your hobbies) preferably accompanied by a hand-written letter in impeccable French. Andrew Sykes felt that he owed the success of his job-hunt to his misguided and unsuccessful accountancy training rather than to his TEFL Certificate:

> *I wrote to more or less all the schools from your book in France and elsewhere that didn't stipulate 'experience required' and was fairly disheartened by the few, none-too-encouraging replies along the lines of 'if you're in town, give us a call.' Sitting in a very cheap hotel bedroom halfway down Italy in early November feeling sorry for myself and knowing that I was getting closer and closer to my overdraft limit and an office job back in the UK, I rang the schools that had replied and so picked up the phone and rang through to BEST in Tours. 'Drop in,' the voice said, 'and we will give you an interview'. So I jumped on the next train, met the director on Monday and was offered a job on the Tuesday morning, initially on an hour-by-hour basis and then in December on a contract of 15 hours which was later increased to 20 hours a week.*
>
> *OK, I was very lucky. I have since learned that the school receives several phone calls and letters per week; it's an employer's market. What got me the job was not my TEFL certificate nor my very good French. It was the fact that I was an ex-accountant. I had been one of the thousands enticed by the financial benefits of joining an accountancy firm after graduation. But I hated the job and failed my first professional exams. Ironically the experience gained during those two and a half years of hell was invaluable. Whereas in Italy they want teaching experience, in France they want business experience.*
>
> *You will in the end be teaching people not objects, and any experience you can bring to the job (and especially the job interview) will help. However ashamed you may be of telling everyone in the pub back home that you were once a rat catcher, it may be invaluable if the school's main client is 'Rent-o-kill'.*

The technique of making a personal approach to schools in the months preceding the one in which you would like to teach is often successful. On the strength of her Cambridge Certificate from International House, Fiona Paton had been hoping to find teaching work in the south of France in the summer but quickly discovered that there are very few opportunities outside the academic year. On her way back to England, she disembarked from the train in the picturesque town of Vichy in the Auvergne just long enough to distribute a few self-promotional leaflets to three language schools. She was very surprised to receive a favourable reply from one of them once she was home, and so returned a few weeks later for a happy year of teaching.

Teaching English in exchange for room and board is very widespread and is normally arranged on the spot, but can also be set up in advance. While looking for something to do in her gap year, Hannah Start was put in touch with a French bank executive who had done an English language course in Hannah's home town and who wanted to keep up her English at home in Paris by having someone to provide live-in conversation lessons. So, in exchange for three hours of speaking English in

If the school's best business client is Rentokil it may be invaluable

the evening (usually over an excellent dinner), Hannah was given free accommodation in the 17th *arrondissement*.

On the Spot

The *British Institute* in Paris has a notice board advertising occasional teaching vacancies as well as live-in tutoring and au pair jobs. Among the services cut back by the Paris British Council is its notice board.

Prospective teachers should not automatically head for Paris but bear in mind that provincial cities have many language schools too. Not only is it hard to find work but of course rents are very high in the capital. If you do decide to give it a go in Paris, watch for adverts in the *métro* for English language courses, since these are usually the biggest schools and therefore have the greatest number of vacancies for teachers. Certain streets in the 8th *arrondissement* around the Gare St. Lazare abound in language schools.

Berlitz has a sizeable presence in Paris and 18 centres throughout the country, with the French head office located at 15 rue le Louis Grand, 75002 Paris (1-44 94 50 25). *inlingua* has multiple centres in France, while Linguarama has centres in the Paris region, Dijon and Lyon as well as the one in Grenoble (see entry and website www.linguarama.com/centres/france.htm).

Non-EU nationals are bound to encounter problems (see section on Regulations) as Beth Mayer from New York found:

I've tried to get a job at a school teaching, but they asked for working papers which I don't have. I checked with several schools who told me that working papers and a university degree were more important than TEFL qualifications.

Freelance

As is increasingly common in many countries, schools are often reluctant to take on contract teachers for whom they would be obliged to make expensive contributions for social security (19%-22% of gross pay). So there is a bustling market in freelance teachers. Self-employed workers *(travailleurs indépendants)*, however little they earn, are obliged to register at the social security office (URSSAF de Paris, 3 rue Franklin, 93100 Montreuil; 1-49 20 10 10; www.urssaf-parisp.fr). The hourly fees *(honoraires)* paid to freelance teachers should be significantly higher than to contract workers *(salariés)* since they are free of deductions. It is very difficult to earn a professional living as a freelancer especially in Paris, since competition is ferocious, the market saturated, and taxes and social charges very high.

However at a more casual level, language exchanges for room and board are commonplace in Paris; these are usually arranged through advertisements or word-of-mouth. You can also offer English lessons privately in people's homes, which often pays F100 a session. In addition to the British Institute notice board mentioned above, there are many other *panneaux* which might prove useful to someone looking for private tutoring. This is especially appealing to Americans who do this without worrying too much about visas.

There are expatriate grapevines all over Paris, very helpful for finding teaching work and accommodation. The one in the foyer of the CIDJ at 101 Quai Branly; 1-44 49 12 00 *(métro* Bir-Hakeim) is good for occasional student-type jobs, but sometimes there are adverts for a *soutien scolaire en Anglais* (English tutor). It is worth arriving early to check for new notices (the hours are Monday-Friday 9.30am-6pm and Saturday 9.30am-1pm).

The other mecca for job and flat-hunters is the American Church at 65 Quai d'Orsay *(métro* Invalides) which has very active notice boards upstairs, downstairs and outside. There is a charge for posting a notice (e.g. for au pair jobs and accommodation) and they are kept up to date. In the basement, the free corkboard is much more chaotic; it can take about half an hour to rummage through all the notices.

The American Cathedral in Paris (23 ave. George V; www.us.net.amcathedral-paris) near the *métro* stations Alma Marceau and George V, also has a notice board featuring employment opportunities and housing listings. The Cathedral even offers career forums for job-seekers. The two British churches may be of assistance: St. Georges at 7 rue Auguste Vacquerie in the 16th *arrondissement* and St. Michael's at 5 rue d'Aguesseau in the 8th *(métro* Madeleine). The notice board of St. Michael's carries notices of accommodation both wanted and available, as well as very occasional ads for conversation exchanges (e.g. English for French). The church administrator says she often gets asked if she can help with finding jobs, but really is unable to offer any assistance. She adds that people are welcome to come and look at the noticeboard but that it is entirely separate from the church's activities. The church is open Monday, Tuesday, Thursday, Friday and Sunday between 10am and 5.30pm.

Although the notice board at the Alliance Française (101 Boulevard Raspail; *métro* Notre Dame des Champs) is for the use of registered students of French, you may be able to persuade a student to look at the adverts for you, many of which involve free lodging in return for babysitting and/or teaching. The notice board is in the annexe around the corner at 34 rue de Fleurus (near the *métro* Notre Dame des Champs). The Alliance Français can be contacted at 1-45 44 38 28/www.alliancefrancaise.fr. As mentioned the British Institute at 11 rue de Constantine has a notice board.

Most of the above expat meeting-places distribute the free bilingual newsletter *France-USA Contacts* or *FUSAC* (www.fusac.com) which comes out every other Wednesday. It can also be picked up at English language bookshops like W.H. Smith near Place de la Concorde or Attica, the largest language learning bookseller in Paris (www.attica-langues.com). *FUSAC* comprises mainly classified adverts including some for English teachers which are best followed up on the day the paper appears. It is possible to place an ad before your arrival in France. An advert in *FUSAC* costs US$20 for 20 words, and can be e-mailed to franceusa@aol.com or sent in the US to France Contacts at PO Box 115, Coopers Station, New York, NY 10276; 212-777-5553/fax 212-777-5554). Ask to place your ad under the heading 'Work wanted in France'. Alternatively you can pay $15 to have a notice posted at the magazine's Paris office for ten days.

During Beth Mayer's first year in Paris she found that advertising in *FUSAC* was very effective:

> *I placed an ad to teach English and offer editing services (I was an editor in New York City before moving here) and received many responses. I charged F80 per hour but found that after I had spent time going and coming, I earned only F40 an hour. So perhaps it would have been better to have the lessons at your apartment (if centrally located). I not only 'teach' English but offer English conversation to French people who don't need a teacher but more a companion with whom to practise. I've met a lot of nice people this way and earned money to boot.*

It may be worth including a reminder here that anyone who advertises their services should exercise a degree of caution when arranging to meet prospective clients.

REGULATIONS

For Britons, the same situation pertains as throughout the EU, and the bureaucratic procedures can be just as protracted as they are in other member states. French bureaucracy is legendary. EU nationals must apply for a residence permit *(carte de séjour de ressortissant de l'Union Européenne)* from the Aliens Department of the police *(Préfecture)* or at the *Mairie* (town hall) within three months of arrival or as soon as work is found. This application should be made in the area in which you are living. You are entitled to work as soon as the application has been lodged; the document typically takes six to nine months to come through.

The documents needed to accompany your application for a *carte de séjour* are your passport and birth certificate, either the original or a certified and translated copy (which costs about F100 at the British Embassy in Paris but may be cheaper if you do it before you leave home). You will also need a *Déclaration d'Etat Civil* from your consulate, on presentation of your birth certificate. In some areas you may also be asked to submit the originals of your diplomas or certificates, photographs, three salary slips, rent receipts and a medical certificate, e.g. from the *Médicine du Travail* centre in Paris. If you are applying before you find a job you may have to show proof of adequate funds (F1,000 and a credit card should be enough). A social security number *(sécu)* will be assigned to you so that employers can start paying contributions for you. No claims can be made before working 120 hours in one month or 200 hours in three months, so it is wise to have private insurance initially. Tax is not deducted in your first year of employment but must be paid in arrears from your second year onwards. The tax year runs from February. Most schools estimate that an annual tax bill for a full-time teacher will be the equivalent of between one month's salary and one and a half month's salary.

It is worth pointing out that anyone with a *carte de séjour* may be able to reduce their rent bill significantly, provided their earnings two years prior to applying were low. The benefit is administered by the Caisse d'Allocations Familiales (CAF), as Andrew Sykes explains:

> *If your income two years before applying was low (e.g. if you worked as a campsite courier as I did), a substantial part of your rent (anything up to 65-70%) may be paid by the French government. At first glance, getting hold of*

all the paperwork may seem a drag (and expensive in the case of official translations of documents) but it is financially beneficial if they decide you are eligible. As an indication of how much they pay out, the rent that I pay for a large town centre studio is F2,300 per month and the benefit I receive is F1,341 (just under 60%).

In order to apply, it is necessary to furnish the CAF with a signed/stamped declaration from your landlord, a declaration of income for the calendar year preceding the year of benefit, a *Fiche Individual d'Etat Civile* and various other bits and pieces.

Documents published by the CIDJ (www.cidj.asso.fr) could be of help when sorting out the paper work as well as when hunting for a job. To obtain the CIDJ catalogue of information leaflets *(fiches)* by post, send four international reply coupons to CIDJ at 101 Quai Branly, 75740 Paris Cedex 15 (1-44 49 12 25/fax 1-40 65 02 61). Most *fiches* cost F10 if picked up in person or F20 or 6 IRCs if requested by post, e.g. 5.5702: *Travailler en France: ressortissants de l'Union Européenne*; and 3.01: *Rechercher un emploi*.

Non-EU Nationals

In France, it is bordering on the impossible for Americans, Canadians, Australians and all other non-EU nationalities to get a work permit. Even with a job offer, applicants are not granted work permits unless they are married to a French national. Non-EU nationals must obtain work documents before they leave their home country, either a *carte de séjour temporaire salarié* (valid for one year and specifying where and in what sector they may work) or a *carte de résident* (valid for ten years and for any activity anywhere in continental France). The only way to get either visa is to have a signed contract in hand and to obtain authorisation from the French Department of Employment. A handful of employers are willing to tackle the bureaucracy which involves applying to the *Direction Départementale du Travail, de l'Emploi et de la Formation Professionelle* for permission to hire a foreigner. If granted, the applicant must undergo a medical examination by an appointed doctor.

Note that the TEFL training organisation WICE (20 Boulevard du Montparnasse, 75015 Paris; 1-45 66 75 50), which is affiliated to Rutgers University in the US, runs occasional information evenings for Americans on how to get working papers. In its standard letter E7, the CIDJ writes in no uncertain terms about the difficulty of obtaining working papers. It might also be worth obtaining fiche 5.5701 *Travailler en France: législation pour êtrangers*. Also, the Public Affairs Section of the American Embassy runs an English Teacher's Resource and Information Centre (2 rue de Constantine, 75001 Paris; 1-43 12 22 22).

One of the language schools which corresponded with this book phrased the situation rather brutally:

Unless US citizens have priority work or are married to a French national and have French nationality themselves, they will NOT be able to work in France, even if they have a job offer. Those who are looking for a full-time regular job without satisfying those requirements are wasting their time sending CVs to France. It is very unfortunate but it is the LAW.

In fact thousands of Americans (and other nationalities) are teaching English in France on a part-time basis. If they have student status and are registered in the second year of a university course, they are allowed to work for a limited number of hours, usually ten but up to 20 in some cases. As mentioned in the introductory chapter 'Finding a Job,' Council Exchanges (633 Third Ave, 20th Floor, New York, NY 10017-6706; 1-888-COUNCIL) arranges work permits for qualifying US students for up to three months. Similarly Canadian students can enter France as part of the SWAP scheme (Travel CUTS, 45 Charles St East, Suite 100, Toronto, Ontario M4Y 1S2). The CIEE office in Paris (1 Place de l'Odéon, 75006 Paris; 1-44 41 74

69; info@councilexchanges-fr.org/ www.councilexchanges-fr.org) is very supportive of its *Work in France* programme participants and assists them in finding jobs. Apparently, about 10% of the students enrolled in the programme teach English in France.

The French Cultural Service (972 Fifth Avenue, New York, NY 10021; fax 212-439-1455/1482; new-york.culture@diplomatic.fr; www.info-france-usa.org/culture) runs an English Teaching Assistantship programme called SCULE which runs from October 1st to April 30th. A working knowledge of French is required so French majors are encouraged. The assistants in France receive a stipend of about F6,000 a month.

One possibility open to some Americans with Irish or Greek ancestry is to obtain an EU passport. An easier route is to teach on a voluntary basis. The Amity Volunteer Teachers Abroad programme (see *Finding a Job for North Americans*) has recently been sending young people to France to live with a family for nine months, enrol in some French classes and teach English at a local language school.

CONDITIONS OF WORK

Teaching 'beezneezmen' is not everyone's cup of tea, but it can be less strenuous than other kinds of teaching. Provided you do not feel intimidated by your pupils' polished manners and impeccable dress, and can keep them entertained, you will probably be a success. As mentioned above, one-to-one teaching is not uncommon, for which ELT training (including the CELTA or Trinity Certificate) do not prepare you. However, if you develop a rapport with your client, this can be the most enjoyable teaching of all. As mentioned earlier, language schools which offer this facility to clients may well expect you to drive, perhaps even own, a car so that you can give lessons in offices and private homes. Most schools pay between F100 and F150 (gross) per lesson.

Salaried teachers should be covered by a nationally agreed and widely enforced *Convention Collectif* which makes stable contracts, sick pay, holiday pay, etc. compulsory as well as guaranteeing a monthly salary. The annual holiday allowance for full-time teachers is five weeks plus an extra five days.

Telephone and internet teaching are popular for their convenience and anonymity. For many people, making mistakes over the phone is less embarrassing than face-to-face. Apparently this method of teaching is great fun for teachers since the anonymity prompts people to spill out all their secrets. Many have been surprised by the good results. It is not necessary to be able to speak French and possibly even an advantage to be monolingual, so you won't be tempted to break into French in frustration. The standard rate of pay for telephone teaching is about F50 for half an hour plus telephone expenses.

Split shifts between 8am and 8pm are the norm, with the usual average of 24 contact hours per week. An unusual feature in France is that some schools calculate the salary according to a certain number of teaching hours per 9 or 12 months, and will pay overtime for hours worked in excess of this. Obviously the total can't be calculated until the end of the contract, which is a drawback for anyone considering leaving early.

Partly because of France's proximity to a seemingly inexhaustible supply of willing English teachers, working conditions in France are seldom brilliant. Although Andrew Boyle enjoyed his year teaching English in Lyon and the chance to become integrated into an otherwise impenetrable community, he concluded that even respectable schools treated teachers as their most expendable commodity, a view corroborated by the veteran traveller Jayne Nash who lasted only three months in Le Havre:

While I was wined and dined at the interview, I was left completely to my own devices after I arrived in Le Havre on a Saturday morning, having only the weekend to find somewhere to live. If I had not had my own vehicle and spoken fluent French, it would have been a nightmare. As it turned out I signed a contract for an apartment which was double the rent paid by my

*The newest concept in English teaching
is teaching by telephone*

colleagues. Not once did anyone ask if I needed help, advice, a meal.

Thirty plus hour weeks (not including preparation time), irregular hours at any time between 8am and 8pm with last-minute classes to cover for absent colleagues, and classes of mixed ability, soon took their toll. The money wasn't that good either. I felt my employer cared little for his employees. After three months I found myself under so much stress that I was obliged to leave, although I am normally not someone to shun a challenge or responsibility.

Similarly, after spending the better part of a decade teaching English in the Far East, Helen Welch decided against accepting the jobs offered her in France. She too realised that she had been cheated by her landlady and couldn't face starting from scratch again, teaching-wise, in a new country for notoriously low wages.

By contrast, Fiona Paton was well looked after and had no trouble finding a comfortable and affordable flat in Vichy (which is often easy in popular holiday resorts outside the summer season). Her impression was that flat-sharing is not as commonplace in France as in other countries.

Despite some negative reports, the chance to eat and drink and live in France outweighs the disadvantages for a whole range of Francophiles.

LIST OF SCHOOLS

AC3
38 rue du Temple, 75004 Paris. Tel: (1) 40 29 97 40. Fax: (1) 40 29 09 16. E-mail: ac3international@ac3.fr. Website: www.ac3.fr.
Number of teachers: 12.
Preference of nationality: British or Irish or others who have work permits.
Qualifications: degree (preferably in English or a language related subject), CELTA, experience of teaching in companies. Excellent inter personal skills. Smart appearance.
Conditions of employment: temporary contracts. Hourly paid work. Varying hours between 8 and 20 hours per week.
Salary: starting wage of F120/hr.
Facilities/Support: extensive training provided.
Recruitment: send/fax/e-mail CV and cover letter. Interviews will take place in Paris.
Contact: David Valente, Head of Language Department.

ANGLESEY LANGUAGE SERVICES (A.L.S.)
1 bis Avenue Foch, 78400 Chatou. Tel: (1) 34 80 65 15. Fax: (1) 34 80 69 91. E-mail: ALS_sarl@compuserve.com.
Number of teachers: 10.
Preference of nationality: EU.
Qualifications: CELTA plus 2 years' experience preferred but possibilities for trainees.
Conditions of employment: one year contract. 15-25 h.p.w. Pupils are adults and many are taught in their workplaces. Recent expansion, so group lessons at all levels offered in evenings and during the day.
Salary: negotiable.
Facilities/Support: some help with accommodation possible. No training provided.
Recruitment: personal contacts or via UK partner organisation: Ditto 93 Ltd., 3 Kingsmead, Lon Towyn Capel, Treaddur Bay, Angelsey, Gwynedd, North Wales (tel/fax 01407 861331). Contact Mike Webster.

AUDIO-ENGLISH
44 allées de Tourny, 33000 Bordeaux. Tel: (5) 56 44 54 05. E-mail: christian.labat@worldonline.fr. Website: http://perso.worldonline_FR/AAF.
Number of teachers: 3-4.
Preference of nationality: British preferred, others considered (English mother tongue).
Qualifications: BA or equivalent, and good French. No previous experience necessary, but people who have already lived/worked in France, and who hold a clean driving licence are preferred. Pleasant personality, strong motivation and teaching talent important.
Conditions of employment: minimum 6 month contracts, but 10 months or more preferred. Full-time teachers work 34 h.p.w. including preparation and report-writing time. Part-time work also available. Hours of work between 8am and 8pm. Teachers expected to work 2 evenings a week. Mostly adults but some classes of young children.
Salary: F6,700-6,800 per month (gross) less 22% in deductions.
Facilities/Support: no assistance with accommodation. Training provided.
Recruitment: through direct application and adverts, e.g. in *TES*. Interviews essential; occasionally held in UK.
Contact: Christian Labat, Director.

AXIEL-R.2001
85 Boulevard Pasteur, 75015 Paris. Tel: (1) 43 21 59 39. Fax: (1) 42 79 89 96.
Number of teachers: fluctuates seasonally.

Preference of nationality: native speakers.
Qualifications: university degree (Education, Psychology or Business) plus TEFL qualification and teaching experienc. Working knowledge of French an advantage.
Conditions of employment: variable periods of work to suit teachers. Clients are mainly professional people taught in their workplaces.
Salary: high hourly rate.
Facilities/Support: no help with accommodation.
Recruitment: via British Council and word-of-mouth. Personal interview necessary.

BRITISH INSTITUTE IN PARIS (UNIVERSITY OF LONDON)
11 rue de Constantine, 75340 Paris Cedex 07. Website: www.bip.lon.ac.uk.
Number of teachers: 36 tutors.
Preference of nationality: none.
Qualifications: BA, serious TEFL qualification, at least 5 years' experience and experience in teaching French adults.
Conditions of employment: one semester (15 week) contracts. 4-8 hours per week between 8.30am and 8.45pm.
Salary: F270 per hour.
Facilities/Support: no assistance with accommodation or training. Support given for research projects.
Recruitment: local interviews essential.

CITYLANGUES
Immeuble les Saisons, La Défense 1, 92036 Paris la Défense Cedex. Tel: (1) 55 91 96 70. Fax: (1) 55 91 96 76. E-mail: contact@citylangues.com. Website: www.citylangues.com.
Number of teachers: 15.
Preference of nationality: none, but employ only teachers resident in Paris.
Qualifications: degree and TEFL certificate.
Conditions of employment: teaching represents 70% of total paid hours.
Salary: according to profile.
Facilities/Support: no assistance with accommodation. Training available.
Recruitment: local interviews essential.
Contact: Stefan Wheater.

LE COMPTOIR DES LANGUES
63 Rue la Boétie, 75008 Paris. Tel: (1) 45 61 53 53. Fax: (1) 45 61 53 30.
Number of teachers: 50.
Preference of nationality: British, plus American, Canadian and Australian if they have valid working papers.
Qualifications: university degree and at least 2 years' teaching experience in a school.
Conditions of employment: 1 year contracts, 4-6 hours work per day between 8am and 9pm within Paris, between 9am and 8pm in the suburbs. All clients are business executives.
Salary: starting salary is F90 per hour (gross) including paid holiday.
Facilities/Support: no assistance with accommodation. Training provided.
Recruitment: adverts in French and British newspapers. Interviews essential and sometimes held in London.
Contact: Philippa Dralet, Quality Control.

EXECUTIVE LANGUAGE SERVICES
20 rue Sainte Croix de la Bretonnerie, 75004 Paris. Tel (1) 44 54 58 71. Fax: (1) 48 04 55 53. E-mail els@mail.codix.fr.
Number of teachers: 40.
Preference of nationality: none.
Qualifications: minimum TEFL grade B for a beginner or 1 year minimum

experience.
Conditions of employment: 1 year minimum.
Salary: 10,500-13,000 francs per month. 22% deductions for tax and social security.
Facilities/Support: school places adverts for accommodation and sometimes helps with a partial loan for the initial payment. Work permits complicated for non EU citizens.
Recruitment: interview after CV and handwritten letter, observation of a class and demo in Paris.

IFG LANGUES
37 quai de Grenelle, 75738 Paris Cedex 15. Tel: (1) 40 59 31 35. Fax: (1) 45 78 96 66. E-mail: ifglangues@wanadoo.fr.
Number of teachers: 110 for four centres; the other three are located near the World Trade Centre in La Défense, in Marne la Vallée next to Disneyland Paris and Neuilly.
Preference of nationality: EU or others with permission to work in France.
Qualifications: minimum BA, CELTA or equivalent, and experience. Prefer TOEFL or DELTA qualification plus 2 years' experience.
Conditions of employment: contracts of 897 to 1075 teaching hours a year. Students are professional adults from large and small firms, the French Civil Service etc.
Salary: from F95,000 to F128,100 per year (gross) depending on number of hours and teaching experience. 8 weeks paid holidays. Possibility of extra hours, luncheon vouchers, health and life insurance and pension schemes.
Facilities/Support: assistance sometimes given with accommodation. Advisory and administrative staff number 34. Training ongoing.
Recruitment: adverts in *Guardian* and French newspapers. Interviews and demonstration class held in Paris.
Contact: Ingrid Foussat.

IMPAQT
Head Office: Téléport IV, Futuropolis IV, B.P. 186, Futurscope Cedex. Tel: (5) 49 49 63 80. Fax: (5) 49 49 63 81. E-mail: hq@impaqt.net. Website: www.impaqt.net.
UK office: Neave House, Windsmore Lane, Abingdon, Oxfordshire OX14 5BY. Tel: 01235 533 7709. Fax: 01235 533 7714.
Number of teachers: 20.
Preference of nationality: none.
Qualifications: degree, TEFL qualification and some additional experience other than in education. Must be open and curious.
Conditions of employment: minimum contract 2 years. Teaching hours are during normal office hours.
Salary: £12,000-£14,000 per annum.
Facilities/Support: first two weeks accommodation are paid for and two days are allowed off for finding own accommodation.
Recruitment: normally through newspapers.
Contact: Jane Legoff, Director of Relations.

INLINGUA PARIS
109 rue de l'Université, 75007 Paris. Tel: (1) 45 51 46 60. Fax: (1) 47 05 66 05. E-mail: rivegauche@inlingua-paris.com.
Number of teachers: 30.
Preference of nationality: none.
Qualifications: TEFL plus 2 years' experience.
Conditions of employment: minimum 12 months. Flexible hours.
Salary: F100-138 per hour.
Facilities/Support: assistance with accommodation, work permits and training.
Recruitment: adverts in *Guardian*. Interviews essential in UK or France.
Contact: Antoine Faure, Director.

LINGUARAMA
Mini Parc Alpes Congrès, 6 rue Roland Garros, 38320 Eybens. Tel: (4) 76 62 00
18. Fax: (4) 76 25 89 60. E-mail: grenoble@linguarama.com.
Number of teachers: 15.
Preference of nationality: none.
Qualifications: one-week TEFL certificate plus minimum 1 year's experience or 4-week Certificate plus minimum 3 months' experience. Driving licence essential.
Conditions of employment: full-time teachers work 25 h.p.w. September to June.
Part-time teachers work flexible hours. Most teaching is business English, taught in-company and at school.
Salary: F9,000 per month.
Facilities/Support: advice on accommodation given. Training available.
Recruitment: via Linguarama in England and also locally.

STUDY GROUP INTERNATIONAL/ILC FRANCE
13 Passage Dauphine, 75006 Paris. Tel: (1) 44 41 80 20. Fax: (1) 44 41 80 21. E-mail: ilcfrance@studygroupintl.com. Website: www.studygroupintl.com or www.ilcfrance.com.
Number of teachers: 30.
Preference of nationality: must be native speaker.
Qualifications: CELTA or approved equivalent. Experience of business world needed.
Conditions of employment: teaching hours between 8.30am and 7pm. No standard length of contract.
Salary: variable.
Facilities/Support: assistance with accommodation, work permits and training. ILC offers the CELTA course (see *Training* chapter).
Recruitment: spontaneous CVs and local adverts. Interviews in Paris essential.

SUL LANGUAGE SCHOOLS
7 Woodland Avenue, Tywardreath, Par, Cornwall, UK PL24 2PL. Tel 01726 814227. Fax 01726 813135. E-mail: claire@sul-schools.com. Website: www.sul-schools.com.
Number of teachers: 1 each year.
Preference of nationality: British.
Qualifications: preferably TEFL qualified and French-speaking.
Conditions of employment: 2 months (July & August) to work in France.
Salary: £900 gross. Teacher pays own transport cost to Paris.
Facilities/Support: board and lodging are free.
Recruitment: usually word-of-mouth.
Contact: Claire Pomeroy, Teaching Administration.

SYNDICAT MIXTE MONTAIGU-ROCHESERVIERE
35 Ave. Villebois Mareuil, 85607 Montaigu Cedex. Tel: (2) 51 46 45 45. Fax: (2) 51 46 45 40. E-mail: julie_legree@yahoo.co.uk.
Number of teachers: 5.
Preference of nationality: British.
Qualifications: French A level, experience of staying in France, interest in teaching and aged 18-25.
Conditions of employment: 1 October to 31 May either to teach 9-11 year-olds in 8 different primary schools in rural areas in the Vendee or to teach as an *assistant(e)* in a Collège and Lycée (14-21 year-olds). 20 hours a week teaching. Wednesdays, weekends and school holidays free.
Salary: 1,800 francs per month allowance.
Facilities/Support: free meals and board and lodging with local family. Full training given. Opportunity to learn French. Local government scheme approved by French *Education Nationale.*
Recruitment: websites and mailings.
Contact: Julie Legree.

TRANSFER
Three schools: 15 rue de Berri, 75008 Paris. Tel: (1) 56 69 22 30. Fax: (1) 56 69 22 35. E-mail: dmachat@transfer.fr. Also: 20 rue Godot de Mauroy, 75009 Paris and 303 Square des Champs Elysees, Evry.
Number of teachers: 80.
Preference of nationality: none.
Qualifications: either professional or technical experience (law, finance etc.) or solid teaching experience, Cambridge TEFL and degree.
Conditions of employment: short term, long term or permanent. Teaching takes place generally from 9am to 6pm and some evenings.
Salary: between 108 and 140 francs per hour depending on experience, permanent salaries between 11,000 and 15,000 francs per month. About 20% is deducted for tax and social security.
Facilities/Support: Americans must have their own work papers as no assistance is given with arranging these. Assistance to EU citizens to get a residence permit.
Recruitment: direct application and CV. Interview.
Contact: Dorothy Machat.

VILLAGE CAMPS
14 rue de la Morache, 1260 Nyon. Switzerland. Tel: (22) 990 94 05. Fax: (22) 990 94 94. E-mail: personnel@villagecamps.ch. Website: www.villagecamps.com/staff/staff1.htm.
Language summer camp in the Ardèche.
Preference of nationality: none.
Qualifications: EFL experience of teaching children required. Also a knowledge of a second European language needed. Minimum age 21 for language monitors, 23 for teachers.

Conditions of employment: 5-7 weeks between mid or end of June to mid-August teaching children aged 10-12 years. 3-5 hours teaching per day. Additional duties include supervising sports, activities and excursions.

Salary: English teachers earn 300 Swiss francs per day (£175 per week). Room and board and insurance provided.

Recruitment: via adverts, internet, international schools, universities, etc.

VS LANGUES
16 rue Christophe Colomb, 75008 Paris. Tel: (1) 45 49 90 30. Fax: (1) 45 49 90 32. E-mail: vs.langues@wanadoo.fr.

Number of teachers: 15 approximately.

Preference of nationality: none.

Qualifications: university degree and teaching experience required (of adults preferable). Must have nice personality.

Conditions of employment: minimum 6 month contracts. Variable hours between 7am and 10pm weekends included.

Salary: approximately F100-130 an hour (gross).

Facilities/Support: unable to help with accommodation.

Recruitment: personal interview necessary.

Other Schools to Try

Note that these schools (towns in alphabetical order) did not confirm their teacher requirements for this edition of *Teaching English Abroad*. Upper case entries marked with an asterisk had entries in the last edition (1999).

METROPOLITAN LANGUAGES, 151 rue de Billancourt, 92100 Boulogne (1-46 04 57 32/fax 1-46 04 57 12)

FONTAINEBLEAU LANGUES & COMMUNICATION, 15 rue Saint-Honoré, B.P. 27, 77300 Fontainebleau (1-64 22 48 96/fax 1-64 22 51 94; flccalv@club-internet.fr). 18 teachers.

DIRECT ENGLISH, Ferme de Rambure, 76270 Mesniers en Bray (2-35 94 56 26/fax 2-35 94 51 20). Branches also in Rouen and Montdidier.

Business & Technical Languages (BTL), 82 Boulevard Haussmann, 75008 Paris (1-42 93 45 45/fax 1-42 93 99 19). 25 teachers.

IAL, Centre de Formation de la Chambre de Commerce Franco-Britannique, 41 rue de Turenne, 75003 Paris (tel/fax 1-44 59 25 10; ial@calva.net). 35 teachers.

Regency Langues, 1 rue Ferdinand Duval, 75004 Paris (1-48 04 99 97/fax 1-48 04 34 96).

UNILANGUES, La Grande Arche, 1 le Parvis-Paroi Nord, 92044 Paris la Défense Cedex 41 (1-47 78 45 80/fax 1-49 00 03 16; info@unilangues.com)

Wall Street Institute, 21 Avenue Victor Hugo, 75116 Paris (1-45 00 59 60/fax 1-45 01 22 64)

INLINGUA, B.P. 156, F-76144 Petit Quevilly, Cedex (2-35 69 81 61/fax 2-35 69 81 59; rouen@inlingua.fr). 30 teachers for centres in Normandy and Picardy.

LINGUISTIC SERVICES, 2 rte. Vierge à la Lisseuse, 33210 Pujols sur Ciron (5-56 76 66 44).

CENTRE DE FORMATION DE ST OMER, Centre d'Etude des Langues, B.P. 278, Z.I. du Brockus, 62504 St. Omer (3-21 88 13 03/21 93 78 45).

BEST-ISF (Business English Service & Translation), 24 Bd. Béranger, 37000 Tours (2-47 05 55 33/fax 2-47 64 40 27)

ISES, 104 Avenue Maginot, Tours 37100 (2-47 54 76 79/fax 2-47 54 30 67). 15 teachers, preferably North American or Australian.

Germany

The excellent state education system in western Germany ensures that a majority of Germans have a good grounding in English, so very little teaching is done at the beginner level. If German students want exposure to a native speaker they are far more likely to enrol in a language summer course in Britain than sign up for extra tuition at a local institute. Furthermore, many secondary schools in Germany (including the former East) employ native speakers of English to assist in classrooms (programme details below). English is also offered at *Volkshochschulen* or 'folk high schools', where various subsidised adult education courses are run.

The reunification of Germany created a huge demand for English in the eastern *Länder* which has now eased off to some extent. Cities like Leipzig, Dresden and Erfurt are less popular destinations for job-seeking teachers than Munich and Freiburg, and may therefore afford more opportunities. As in the west, many private institutes have an American bias.

The greatest demand for English in Germany continues to come from the business and professional community. The current difficulties in Germany's economy mean that some companies are cutting back EFL programmes, though government incentives are in place to encourage companies to provide training to their employees, with one of the most popular options being English language training. This means that there are many highly paid in-company positions for EFL and ESP teachers, as well as a number of agencies and consultancies which supply teachers to their clients.

The reduction in in-company opportunities has been somewhat offset by the continuing demand from former East Germans, especially those who have migrated to Frankfurt and elsewhere, who view privately paid-for English classes as an important investment in their job futures.

Prospects for Teachers

Any graduate with a background in economics or business who can speak German has a chance of finding work in a German city. A TEFL Certificate and a university degree have less clout than relevant experience, as Kevin Boyd found when he arrived with his brand new Cambridge Certificate in September:

> *I was persuaded by a teaching friend to go to Munich with him to try to get highly paid jobs together. As he spoke some German and had about a year's teaching experience, he got a job straightaway. Every school I went to in Munich just didn't want to know as I couldn't speak German and only had four weeks teaching experience. After two days of this I decided to try my luck in Italy.*

Experience in business is often a more desirable qualification than an ELT qualification. The question is not so much whether you know what a past participle is but whether you know what an 'irrevocable letter of credit' or a 'bank giro' is. Many schools offer *Oberstufe,* advanced or specialist courses in, for example, Banking English, Business English, or for bilingual secretaries, etc. Full-time vocationally-oriented courses in languages for business and commerce are called *Berufsfachschule* and this is still a buoyant part of the market. For none of these is a Cambridge or Trinity Certificate or even a Diploma the most appropriate training.

Very few schools are willing to consider candidates who can't speak any German. Although the 'direct method' is in use everywhere (i.e. total immersion in English), the pupils will expect you to be able to explain things in German. If the school prepares its students for the Chamber of Commerce exams (known as LCCI), the teacher will be expected not only to understand the syllabus but to interpret and teach it with confidence. Some schools employ the now unfashionable 'contrastive' method, again making a knowledge of conversational German essential.

Wages for teachers and trainers (as for most professions in Germany) are very high, which means that there is less turn-over of staff than elsewhere. On the other hand, there is a definite tax advantage for British and American nationals if they work for less than two years (see *Regulations* below) which frees up vacancies on an on-going basis. One further requirement of many employers is a driving licence, so that teachers can travel easily from one off-site assignment to another.

FIXING UP A JOB

Posts for English-speaking *Helferen* (classroom assistants) are normally reserved for students of German who apply through the Assistants Department of the Central Bureau for International Education & Training (Language Assistants Team, The British Council, 10 Spring Gardens, London SW1A 2BN; tel 020-7389 4764). The Central Bureau sends a large number of undergraduate students (and recent graduates) from the UK to spend an academic year as language assistants in German schools. Limited posts as English-speaking *Helferen* are also available for gap year students with A level (or an equivalent) in German. Language Assistants like Sarah Davies (who was sent to a small town in the east) advises against agreeing to teach in a small village where conditions may be primitive and the sense of isolation strong.

Similarly for US graduates, the US Department of State's Fulbright Program (administered by the Institute of International Education, 809 UN Plaza, New York, NY 10017-3580) places 50 teaching assistants in German high schools. Candidates planning to go on to become teachers of German are strongly preferred for this programme, which pays a monthly stipend of DM1,150 in addition to free flights and insurance. For general information about academic opportunities in Germany, Americans can contact the German Academic Exchange Service, the NY office of the Deutscher Akademischer Austauschdienst (DAAD), 950 Third Avenue, 19th Floor, New York, NY 10022; 212-758-3223; fax 212-755-5780; daadny@daad.org/ www.daad.org). However this office does not offer a teaching programme. It might be worth contacting the Goethe Institute or the *Padagogischer Austauschdienst*, Nassestr. 8, Postfach 22 40, 53012 Bonn; 228-501-0/fax 228-501 301 for information on teaching assistant programmes.

University students and graduates can often find out about possible employers from their university careers office or local English schools, as happened to Catherine Rogers. She wrote on spec to a number of local language schools to get some experience before working abroad and ended up being interviewed by two British contacts of a government scheme for teaching English to unemployed engineers and secretaries operating in the Dresden area of the former East Germany.

Like so many embassies, the German Embassy in London is not noted for its helpful attitude to aspiring teachers or other job-seekers. The German Information Centre (34 Belgrave Square, London SW1X 8QB 020-7824 1300; infoctr@german-embassy.org.uk/ www.german-embassy.org.uk) does, however, distribute a short information sheet headed 'Teaching in Germany'. Apart from directing students to enquire about the exchange programme run by the Central Bureau and providing addresses of the state Ministries of Education, it recommends applying to the Zentralstelle für Arbeitsvermittlung, Villemombler Strasse 76, 53123 Bonn (228-7130/fax 228-713 10 35). This is the Central Placement Office of the Federal Department of Employment, which has a special department for dealing with applications from abroad. A letter addressed to one of the 184 *Arbeitsamter* (job centres) around the country will be forwarded to the Zentralstelle for processing. A personal visit to an *Arbeitsamt* is more likely to produce results, though you are likely to be told that there are far more qualified teachers and translators than there are vacancies.

The five British Council offices in Germany are on the whole efficient and helpful to people enquiring about English teaching work. The Information section of the British Council in Berlin co-ordinates ELT enquiries on behalf of the offices in Berlin, Hamburg, Köln, Leipzig and Münich, and will send photocopies of local *Sprachenschulen* from the Yellow Pages *(Gelbe Seiten)*. The British Council in Munich also has its own one-page list of about 40 English language schools and furthermore recommends the English-language magazine *Munich Found* (www.munichfound.com), which carries regular TEFL vacancies.

As usual, it is much more difficult to arrange a job by sending written applications and CVs from the UK than by presenting yourself in person to language school directors and training companies, CV in hand. Determination, qualifications, experience and being on the spot are often deciding factors when an employer has to choose between large numbers of similarly qualified applicants.

All the major language school chains have a significant presence in Germany including Berlitz, Bénédict (with nearly 40 German branches), Language Link, inlingua (with 50 schools), Linguarama which specialises in language training for business in eight cities and Wall Street Institutes (see chapter *Finding a Job* for their websites). Teachers looking to work for Berlitz can contact their German headquarters on imke.finke@berlitz.de or fax (6169) 400506. In addition to the entry for *Linguarama Deutschland* in Munich in the directory section, Linguarama schools in Germany are as follows:

Steinstr. 30, 40210 Düsseldorf (211-867 6990/fax 211-13 20 85).

Linguarama Haus, Geotheplatz 2, 60311 Franfurt am Main (69-28 02 46/fax 69-28 05 56).

Hopfenburg, Hopfensack 19, 20457 Hamburg (40-33 50 97/fax 40-32 46 09).

Marzellenstr. 3-5, 50667 Köln (221-160 99 0/fax 221-160 99 66).

Lipsia-Haus, Barfüssgässchen 12, 04109 Leipzig (341-213 14 64/fax 341-213 14 82).

Leuschnerstr. 3, 70174 Stuttgart (711-22 19 36/fax 711-226 18 820.

Throughout Germany, more than 1,000 adult education centres or *Volkshochschulen* teach the English language (among many other courses) to adults. Native speakers with teaching experience might find a role within this institution (see entry for *Deutscher Volkshochschul-Verband e.V.* In addition to their homepage (www.vhs.de), they also provide an internet service whereby candidates seeking teaching opportunities can place their résumés and where *Volkshochschulen* can register their vacancies for lecturers and part-time instructors. The Europe-wide International Certificate Conference (ICC) is based in Germany (Hansaallee 150, 60320 Frankfurt; www.icc-europe.com) and acts as an umbrella organisation for adult education associations like VHS, working on teaching foreign languages in Europe but it cannot send a list of addresses.

Interviews

Most schools and institutes in Germany cannot under normal operating circumstances hire someone unseen merely on the basis of his/her CV and photo. Applicants should arrange for a face-to-face interview and make themselves available at a moment's notice. Professional presentation is even more important for securing work in the German business world than elsewhere. Vacancies occur throughout the year since businessmen and women are just as likely to start a course in April as in September. Germans tend to be formal, so dress appropriately and be aware of your manners at an interview. Also good references *(zeugnisse)* are essential.

A good starting place is Frankfurt am Main, known to locals as 'Bankfurt' or 'Mainhattan'. Frankfurt has the highest concentration of major banks and financial institutions in the country (nearly 400) and a correspondingly high number of private language schools. It is helpful, though not essential, to have some basic knowledge of German and business experience. In a job interview with a language school director, demonstrating a detailed knowledge of a handful of commonly used textbooks may be more important than business experience. Nathan Edwards, a Canadian who spent two years teaching in dozens of banks and multinational companies, recommends *Build Your Business English* by J. Flower, *The Language of Meetings* by M. Goodale and *International Business English* by L. Jones and R. Alexander.

You can also impress a potential employer by showing some familiarity with current major Germany business news (bank mergers, etc.). This can easily be done by scanning the English language press or listening to the BBC World Business Report on a short-wave radio. Language schools are looking for teachers who can pose intelligent questions to business students about their jobs. There is a considerable demand from the business community for guidance on conducting 'small talk' in English, which is crucial in building rapport with clients and colleagues.

If asked about permits, visas, etc. (especially in the case of non-EU nationals), reassure the interviewer that you are waiting for your paperwork to be finalised.

Freelance Teaching

The majority of native speakers teaching for commercial institutes are not on contracts but are employed as freelancers *(Honorarvertrag)* who work for between two and 20 hours per week. In some cases deductions are made for tax and social security but in most cases freelance teachers are left to deal with these themselves. Some consider this to be an advantage, while others consider it exploitative.

If you want to find private pupils, you could attend a meeting of an Anglo-German club of which there are many. The Deutsch-Englische Gesellschaft meets regularly in most major cities, including Hamburg, Bonn, Düsseldorf and Cologne: details are available from the British Council. Americans might be able to make contact with English teachers at US cultural centres such as the JFK-Haus Library in Darmstadt (Kasinostr. 3, 64293 Darmstadt; 6151-25924). Check adverts in local magazines such as *Zitty, TIP* or *Zweite Hand* in Berlin.

Upon successful completion of a Trinity TESOL Certificate course in England, Ann Barkett from Atlanta went to Munich to look for freelance work, but found it tough going:

> *During the period December to March, I was putting up flyers for private and group lessons but received no response. I finally answered an ad for a private student whom I taught for a few weeks, but there just wasn't enough work or money coming in and I was tired of trying at that point.*

Many freelance teachers find themselves for the first time required to design an ESP course (English for Specific Purposes), individually tailored to the needs of their businessmen and women students. Nathan Edwards found that he got better at this:

> *Experience has shown me that such a syllabus must be flexible, open to change and short-term adjustment so as to accommodate the complex and evolving needs of students who are also full-time working professionals. Students and their employers must be given the assurance of a clearly structured course outline, but this must be partly generated by an ongoing negotiated process with all the participants. Finally don't forget that the students themselves can be a valuable source of ESP course material such as authentic English fax or e-mail messages, business letters and company brochures from their offices.*

REGULATIONS

EU nationals are free to travel to Germany to look for work but are still subject to the labyrinthine bureaucracy. The first step is to register your address with the local authority *(Einwohnermeldeamt)* or at the local registry office *(Meldestelle)*, as German citizens must also do. For this you will need proof that you are living or working locally, e.g. your landlord's or future employer's countersignature.

Only after doing this is it possible to apply for a residence permit *(Aufenthaltserlaubnis)* from the residence office *(Landeseinerwohneramt)* or from the aliens' authority *(Ausländerbehorde)* probably located in the *Rathaus* or the *Kreisverwaltungsreferat* (Area Administration Centre). You may find that you are granted a five-year residence permit immediately, or you may be given three months in the first instance during which time you are expected to find employment. You normally have to surrender your passport for up to six weeks while your application is being processed, though if you have the stamina you can do battle with the bureaucracy and do it in a day or two. Procedures should be standard throughout Germany, though in the eastern *Länder* where fewer foreigners go, it can be more difficult to get definitive advice.

American English is strongly in demand in Germany since so many companies have branches or clients in North America, and many students in Germany prefer the American to the British accent. Americans can arrange teaching jobs in Germany more easily than in Spain, Italy or France. Some organisations which offer English courses, especially in the former East Germany, may be prepared to assist in the lengthy process of getting work permits, provided they are otherwise short of teachers. An American who finds an employer while still in the US might seek advice on documentation from the Carl Duisberg Society (CDS International, 871 United Nations Plaza, 15th Floor, New York, NY 10017-1814; 212-497-3500; www.cdsintl.org) which specialises in arranging six-month business internships.

As soon as a teacher from outside the EU obtains a promise of employment, he or she should take steps to get the permits. The teacher must first register his or her name and address (as for EU nationals) and then report to the Ausländersamt (foreigners' office). There they must present a contract or letter from a school claiming that you are the best candidate for the job (difficult) or else request a *Freimitarbeiter Urlaubnis,* the freelancer's permit given to *Honorarvertrag* (freelancers) which may need to be backed up by a letter from an employer. Further requirements include a certificate of good conduct (notarised by the US Embassy for a fee), proof of address and health insurance and also a health certificate from a German doctor. If approved, a one-year residence permit will be affixed to the passport, with a hand-written explanation that the bearer is allowed to work as an English teacher in private language schools only. All of this will take between three and six weeks and cost at least DM75, renewable for three years for a further fee.

The American Ann Barkett did not find the procedures in any way straightforward. After being enrolled in a Berlitz training course by a director who claimed that there was a desperate need for English teachers, Ann thought employment would automatically follow. But despite passing the course, Ann was not given any teaching hours and could not ascertain the reason for this, especially since her fellow trainees were working an absurd 40 hours a week. She wondered whether it had something to do with her non-EU status, though the Arbeitsamt in Munich had told her that freelancers didn't need a work permit.

Unfortunately Canadians, Australians, New Zealanders and other nationalities experience more difficulties since they require a resident visa which has been applied for in their country of origin. If within the three months of their tourist stay they manage to obtain a formal written offer of employment, they must return to their home country in order to apply for a working visa at the German Consulate. The application process takes up to one month and there is always a risk that the application will be refused. Successful applicants are issued with a one-year renewable work visa. Not all employers are willing to wait one month for a new teacher to begin working and may prefer to hire British or Irish teachers in the meantime.

Tax and Contributions

Since the majority of English teachers in Germany work freelance and are self-employed, they must be sure to put enough aside from their gross wages to cover sickness insurance and pension contributions which are very expensive. In 2000 old legislation concerning compulsory state pension contributions began to be enforced among the large population of British freelance teachers, estimated at 25,000. Teachers were suddenly sent bills, as high as £8,000+ for five years of arrears, which drove many of them to leave Germany. A survey done in June 2000 by the English Language Teachers Association of München indicated that two-thirds of British teachers were planning to quit because of the change. At last report lobbyists were planning to contest the legislation in the European Court of Justice.

Foreigners working in Germany should obtain a *Lohnsteuerkarte* (tax card) or a *steuernummber* (tax number) from the local *Steueramt*. The earnings threshold for paying tax is about DM12,500; after which the rates of tax are high, at least 30%. However, according to a tax treaty between Great Britain or the US and Germany (DBA1964/70), professors and teachers who teach at a school for less than two years and have a permanent address in their home country are exempt from tax. However, most will have about 13%-20% deducted for social security and pension contributions.

CONDITIONS OF WORK

You can almost guarantee that you will be teaching adults (since school children receive such a high standard of English tuition at school), and usually before or after office hours. Contracts for full-time work are normally at least a year long, often with a three-month probation period.

Wages are undoubtedly among the highest anywhere. DM20-30 per 45-minute lesson is standard and DM50 not impossible. A working week of 30 hours could consist of 40 45-minute lessons, which would be a very heavy workload. Off-site teaching hours often incur a premium of about DM5 to compensate for travel time.

If you are depending solely on one employer for your income try to find an institute which guarantees a monthly minimum number of hours. Monthly salaries are usually between DM2,500 and DM3,000 gross, with the possibility of paid overtime. Considering that a one-bedroom flat in one of the big cities can easily cost DM1,000 per month, salaries need to be high. Quite a few schools assist with accommodation. Teachers often turn to agencies though their fees can be very steep, as much as two or three months rent plus VAT. Try answering ads in the local paper, or look up *Wohnung* (apartments/flats) in the phone book or try the local *Mitwohnzentralen* which charges a more reasonable fee (usually one month's rent) for finding flats, though they may charge less if you end up renting a room or flat from owners who are temporarily absent. It is customary to pay your rent directly out of a bank account, so open a basic savings account as early as you can. By law, the deposit you pay (usually three months rent) is put in a bank account and will earn you interest.

Working and living conditions in the former GDR are gradually coming into line with those in the west and are much improved since the early days of reunification when Catherine Rogers went there:

> *Accommodation was provided in 'outer Siberia', five miles from the factory where I was teaching. The temperature fell so low that the inside of the window was completely frozen. The wages were very good and I was able to save half my salary. I tried to sort out the red tape but was told by my boss that the local officials were not really geared up for that sort of thing. The students were extremely helpful and generally thrilled to have a native English speaker. They loved grammar and games, but role plays usually fell flat. Success was virtually guaranteed if I put them in teams since they were*

very competitive. Most of them went to considerable lengths to help me. The hospitality and kindness were amazing. But I still felt isolated because my German is rather basic and there were no other foreigners around.

Some teachers in the new *Länder* have found it difficult to control their classes. After years of very strict discipline, it is not surprising that pupils are keen to take advantage of the new liberality. But like Catherine Rogers, Sarah Davies met nothing but a friendly welcome in the east (and no reports have been received to indicate that her pessimistic prediction about the future has come to pass):

The easterners are different and everyone has been tremendously friendly and supportive. They are used to pulling together as a community. For instance, before my money came through, the teachers at my school literally passed the hat round for me and gave me a present of cash. I know it's inevitable that they will change as soon as they become materialistic; it seems a shame, but that's progress.

LIST OF SCHOOLS

ACADEMY OF BUSINESS COMMUNICATION (ABC)
Marienstr. 41, 70178 Stuttgart. Tel: (711) 607 49 25. Fax: (711) 607 49 27. E-mail: info@abc-stuttgart.de
Number of teachers: approx. 50. New ABC schools are opening so numbers may increase.
Preference of nationality: none.
Qualifications: teaching experience or business background plus university degree in any subject.
Conditions of employment: mostly freelance; some contracts available. Academy open Monday to Saturday.
Facilities/Support: advice on finding accommodation. Assistance given to non-EU teachers in obtaining permits. Regular training. Teachers can obtain ABC's own teaching certificate if they attend course and pass test/observation (after approx. one year).
Recruitment: adverts in UK and personal recommendations. Interviews preferred and are occasionally available in UK.
Contact: Mrs. Joy Zeller, Director.

ADVANX SCHOOL OF LANGUAGES
Hauptstr.88, 42651 Solingen. Tel: (212) 224 25 22. Fax: (212) 224 26 80. Website: www.advanx.de.
Number of teachers: 5/6.
Preference of nationality: none.
Qualifications: TEFL Cert.
Conditions of employment: from short contracts for 4-6 weeks to long-term contracts up to 2 years. 25 contact hours per week, plus overtime.
Salary: DM3,000.
Facilities/Support: one teacher's flat and accommodation can be found for future teachers.
Recruitment: *Guardian* newspaper, website.
Contact: Nathan Spruce, Partner/School Manager.

AMERICAN LANGUAGE ACADEMY
Charlottenstrasse 65, 10117 Berlin. Tel: (30) 20 39 78 11. Fax: (30) 20 39 78 13. E-mail: info@ala-germany.de. Website: www.ala-germany.com.
Number of teachers: 70 freelancers in 5 centres.
Preference of nationality: none (native speakers only).
Qualifications: CELTA, TEFL, TESL, university certification. Also opportunities for native speakers with practical experience, especially of business English

(banking, civil engineering).
Conditions of employment: minimum contract period of 10 weeks. Variable hours, generally between 7.30am and 9pm.
Salary: rate for 45 minute lesson starts at DM25.
Facilities/Support: library supply of teaching materials.
Recruitment: advertisements. Local interview necessary.
Contact: Academic Director.

ARTES SPRACHEN & BILDUNG
Paul-List-Str. 8, Leipzig. Tel/fax: (341) 211 12 82 & (341) 2111211. E-mail: artes@planet-interkom.de.
Number of teachers: varies according to client demand.
Preference of nationality: British, American, Irish, Australian.
Qualifications: fluent German, teaching experience, business English and profound IT knowledge.
Conditions of employment: 3-6 month contracts; longer possible.
Salary: DM20-40 per hour (varies with clients).
Facilities/Support: can advise on accommodation in Leizig.
Recruitment: interviews not essential.
Contact: Jorg Eckhardt, Managing Director.

AUSLAND SPRACHENDIENST GmbH
Postfach 10 22 22, Frankfurter Strasse 114, 63268 Dreieich bei Frankfurt/M. Tel: (6103) 34113. Fax: (6103) 34783.
Number of teachers: 2.
Preference of nationality: British, Irish.
Qualifications: TEFL qualification with at least 2 years' experience, business English for in-company training, German (not essential).
Conditions of employment: 10-month contracts (September to June). 27 hours per week. All students are company employees.
Salary: DM3,300 per month, tax free (equivalent of DM4,000 gross salary).
Facilities/support: assistance with finding accommodation, use of company restaurant (full subsidised meal at present costs DM4.50).
Recruitment: written application with CV and recent photograph.

BENEDICT SPRACHSCHULE
Goebenstr. 6/Hügelstr. 56-58, 41061 Mönchengladbach. Tel: (2161) 81498-0. Fax: (2161) 81498-22.
Number of teachers: 3-5.
Preference of nationality: none.
Qualifications: language teaching experience.
Conditions of employment: long-term (3-5 years). Hours between 8am and 4.15pm.
Salary: negotiable.
Facilities/Support: no assistance with accommodation, training or visas.
Contact: Rainer Jakobs, Deputy Head.

BERLIN SCHOOL OF ENGLISH
Dorotheenstrasse 90, 10117 Berlin. Tel: (30) 229 04 55. Fax: (30) 229 04 71. E-mail: info@berlin.school-of-english.de. Website: www.berlin.school-of-english.de.
Number of teachers: from 20.
Preference of nationality: none.
Qualifications: university degree plus TEFL/CELTA Certificate and minimum one year's experience.
Conditions of employment: minimum one year on freelance basis. Between 16 and 30 h.p.w.
Salary: approximately DM42 for 90 minute teaching session.

Facilities/Support: in house training provided.
Contact: John Wills, School Manager.

DEUTSCHLAND GmbH (LEIPZIG)
Petersstrasse 39-41, 04109 Leipzig. Tel: (341) 2 11 48 17. Fax: (341) 2 11 50 10.
Number of teachers: 15-20.
Preference of nationality: EU or American native speakers preferred.
Qualifications: teaching experience and TEF(S)L helpful; academic background and ability to work with people needed.
Conditions of employment: open-ended contract. Flexible hours between 8am and 9.30pm.
Salary: DM22-24 per 45-minute lesson.
Facilities/Support: after the first year, 1 week intensive training given (materials, methods, teaching aids). Assistance with accommodation and work permits given.
Recruitment: adverts and personal referral.
Contact: M Mikolaiczak, Language Centre Director.

BERLITZ DEUTSCHLAND GmbH (MAGDEBURG)
Hasselbachplatz 3, 39104 Magdeburg. Tel: (391) 541 46 88. Fax: (391) 541 46 45.
E-mail: imke.finke@berlitz.de.
Number of teachers: 5.
Preference of nationality: none (British, American, Canadian, Australian, New Zealand, etc.) as long as native speakers of English.
Qualifications: university degree.
Conditions of employment: freelance only. 30-40 h.p.w.
Salary: DM22-24 per unit.
Facilities/Support: assistance given with accommodation and work permits.
Recruitment: via internet, job centres and universities. Interviews in UK, US and locally.

CAMBRIDGE INSTITUT
Hildegardstr. 8, 80539 München. Tel: (89) 22 111 15. Fax: (89) 290 47 38. E-mail: info@cambridgeinstitut.de
Number of teachers: approximately 20.
Preference of nationality: British.
Qualifications: PGCE (preferably in modern languages) or in some cases TEFL certificate may be acceptable.
Conditions of employment: 11 month contracts, renewable for a further 11 months. 26 h.p.w. Lessons 9-11.40am and 5.30-9.15pm.
Salary: DM3,700 per month less social security payments of about DM765.
Facilities/Support: assistance with accommodation. One-week induction course and ongoing workshops.
Recruitment: interview essential in Germany or sometimes UK.
Contact: Philip Moore, Co-Director.

CHRISTOPHER HILLS SCHOOL OF ENGLISH
Sandeldamm 12, 63450 Hanau. Tel: (6181) 15015. Fax: (6181) 12121. E-mail: info@c-hills.com. Website: www.c-hills.com.
Number of teachers: 5.
Preference of nationality: EU passport holders preferred. Must be native speaker.
Qualifications: minimum CELTA plus two years of full-time TEFL experience.
Conditions of employment: one year (extendable thereafter). Teaching hours mainly late morning to evening.
Salary: DM3,400-4,000 per month depending on experience and qualifications.
Facilities/Support: the school will advertise for and inspect suitable accommodation and make the necessary arrangements.
Recruitment: press, internet, recommendations.
Contact: Christopher Hills, Director.

COMMUNICATION SERVICES ROLAND LUKE
Schiller Prom. 2, 12049 Berlin. Tel: (30) 62709580. E-mail: r-luke@mailcity.com.
Number of teachers: 4.
Preference of nationality: none, but should be native speaker.
Qualifications: TEFL Certificate minimum.
Conditions of employment: freelance, varies from project to project.
Salary: approximately DM30-40 for a 45-minute lesson.
Facilities/Support: none.
Recruitment: personal contact or via English Language Teachers' Association.
Contact: Roland Luke, Director.

CONTEXT SPRACHENDIENSTE GmbH
Elisenstr. 4-10, 50667 Köln. Tel: (221) 925 45 612. Fax: (221) 925 45 616. E-mail:
context@contextinc.com. Website: www.contextinc.com.
Number of teachers: 15-20.
Preference of nationality: none.
Qualifications: must be native speakers with academic education and experience.
Conditions of employment: freelance basis. Hours vary between 8am and 8pm.
Salary: varies according to qualifications and experience and degree of difficulty of class taught.
Facilities/Support: accommodation and visas are responsibility of teachers. Some training given.
Recruitment: newspaper adverts, followed by local interviews.
Contact: Patrick O'Sullivan, Project Manager.

DAVID BERRY LANGUAGES
Weinbergsweg 3, 10119 Berlin. Tel/fax: (30) 449 90 25. E-mail dbl@bln.de
Number of teachers: 10-15.
Preference of nationality: none.
Qualifications: TEFL Certificate, business teaching experience needed.
Conditions of employment: freelance.
Salary: DM25+ per hour.
Facilities/Support: no assistance with accommodation. Training provided.
Recruitment: direct application. Local interview essential.
Contact: David Berry, Director of Studies.

DESK
Blumenstr. 1, 80331 München. Tel: (89) 26 33 34. Fax: (89) 260 56 00. E-mail:
desk.sprachen@t-online.de. Website: desk-sprachkurse.de.
Number of teachers: 20.
Preference of nationality: none.
Qualifications: degree. Experience teaching English as a foreign language to adults.
Conditions of employment: duration of contract to suit. Teaching hours early mornings and evenings.
Salary: DM33-37 per 45 minute lesson.
Facilities/Support: no help with accommodation.
Recruitment: CV and interview.
Contact: Erwin Schmidt-Achert, Owner.

DEUTSCHER VOLKSHOCHSCHUL-VERBAND
Obere Wilhelmstrasse 32, 53225 Bonn. Tel/fax: (228) 975 69 20. E-mail:
buero@dvv-vhs.de. Website: www.vhs.de.
Number of teachers: opportunities in more than 1,000 associated *Volkshochschulen*; addresses listed on website.
Preference of nationality: British, American, Canadian, any English-speaking nationality.
Conditions of employment: one semester renewable contracts. Most positions are part-time.

Salary: variable hourly rates. Income from part-time teaching will not necessarily cover living expenses.
Facilities/Support: no assistance with finding accommodation. Help can be given with work permits, in the form of a letter testifying that no EU national is equally qualified. Continuing staff training is available through the German Institute for Adult Education (DIE) in Frankfurt.
Recruitment: must apply to individual *Volkshochschulen*. Local interviews required.

ENGLISH FOR BUSINESS (E4B)
Graacher Strasse 10, 12247 Berlin. Tel/fax: (30) 7667 7241. E-mail: eforb@compuserve.com. Website: www.E4B.de.
Number of teachers: 20.
Preference of nationality: none, but should be native speakers.
Qualifications: TEFL Certificate and one year teaching experience (business English), and German speaker.
Conditions of employment: varies from freelance to full-time. Hours depends on client.
Salary: DM60-DM100 per hour (freelance).
Recruitment: applications arrive regularly via the Yellow Pages and word-of-mouth.
Contact: Evan Frendo, Manager.

ENGLISCHES INSTITUT KOLN
Gertrudenstr. 24-28, 50667 Köln. Tel: (221) 257 82 74/5. Fax: (221) 25 54 50. E-mail: nc-enginst@netcologne.de
Number of teachers: 20-25.
Preference of nationality: none, though ease of obtaining work permit helps.
Qualifications: BA, TEFL Certificate and at least 2 years' EFL experience.
Conditions of employment: part-time and full-time. Courses offered mornings (including Saturdays) and evenings. Some in-company teaching.
Salary: depends on hours contracted. Standard German deductions of about 25% in total.
Facilities/Support: good teacher resources, optional workshops.
Recruitment: direct application.
Contact: D. Sutherland.

ENGLISH FOR EVERYBODY
1 Schenfeld 2, Rissener Strasse 58, 22880 Wedel/Hamburg. Tel 4103-702468. Fax: 4103-702469; also at: Theodor-Storm-Str. 1, 22869 Schenefeld. Tel: (40) 830 99 009. Fax: (40) 830 99 019. E-mail: efe.lowe@debitel.net
Number of teachers: 20.
Preference of nationality: none.
Qualifications: TEFL plus experience, business background.
Conditions of employment: one year contracts. Various hours Monday to Friday mornings and evenings.
Salary: DM30 per hour.
Facilities/Support: assistance given with accommodation. Training.
Recruitment: via adverts, agencies, internet and word of mouth.
Contact: Kerstin Lowe, Owner.

EURO-SCHULEN ERFURT
Bahnhofstrasse 44, 99084 Erfurt. Tel: (361) 6 46 10 90. Fax: (361) 64 6 10 93. E-mail: erfurt@eso.de. Website: www.erfurt.eso.de.
Number of teachers: 35 including 3 English teachers.
Preference of nationality: none.
Qualifications: TEFL.
Conditions of employment: 26-30 h.p.w.

Salary: according to qualifications.
Facilities/support: assistance with accommodation or training.
Recruitment: written applications or local interviews.
Contact: Dr. Ulrike Hippe, Director.

EURO FREMDSPRACHENSCHULE
Esplanade 36, 85049 Ingolstadt. Tel: (841) 17001. Fax: (841) 17193. E-mail: euro-ingolstadt@t-online.de.
Number of teachers: 25.
Preference of nationality: British, American, Canadian.
Qualifications: at least a BA (including German studies). PGCE preferred. At least 5 years experience.
Conditions of employment: permanent contracts. Part-time work possible. 30 h.p.w.
Salary: based on German state salary scale.
Facilities/Support: assistance given with accommodation and work permits.
Recruitment: interview in Ingolstadt necessary.
Contact: Stuart Wheeler.

FOKUS LANGUAGE SCHOOL
Brienner Strasse 48, 80333 München. Tel: (89) 52 31 43 47. Fax: (89) 52 31 47 51. E-mail: fokussprachen@t-online.de. Website: www.fokusspachen.de. Also schools in Frankfurt: Gartenstrasse 56, 60596 Frankfurt (69-61 99 03 84/fax 69-61 99 03 85) and Stuttgart: Sigmaringer Strasse 41, 70567 Stuttgart (711-719 6270/fax 711-719 6280).
Number of teachers: 20-25.
Preference of nationality: none, but no dialects.
Qualifications: university degree plus TEFL.
Conditions of employment: flexible contracts and hours, mornings and evenings.
Salary: DM30-35 per 45 minutes.
Facilities/Support: assistance with accommodation and work permits. No training.
Recruitment: adverts in UK and local interviews.
Contact: Monika Vibert, Director.

GERMAN AMERICAN INSTITUTE TUEBINGEN
Karlstrasse 3, 72072 Tübingen. Tel: (7071) 34071. Fax: (7071) 31873. E-mail: mail@dai-tuebingen.de. Website: www.dai-tuebingen.de.
Number of teachers: 15.
Preference of nationality: American.
Qualifications: BA or MA from an American university.
Conditions of employment: freelance only. 3-9 h.p.w. Mostly adult students.
Salary: hourly wage.
Facilities/Support: no help with accommodation. Limited training given.
Recruitment: local interview essential.
Contact: Carolyn Murphey Melchers, Language Program Co-ordinator.

HAMBURG SCHOOL OF ENGLISH
Eppend. Landstr. 112a, 20249 Hamburg. Tel: (40) 480 21 16/9. Fax: (40) 480 73 67. E-mail: info@hamburg.school-of-english.de. Website: www.hamburg-school-of-english.de.
Number of teachers: 24-28.
Preference of nationality: none.
Qualifications: university degree plus TEFL Certificate and minimum one year's experience.
Conditions of employment: minimum one year on freelance basis. Between 16 and 30 h.p.w.
Salary: DM44-60 for 90 minute teaching session.
Facilities/Support: assistance given with finding accommodation and obtaining

work permits. Some training given.
Recruitment: via local interviews.
Contact: Bill Cope, Director of Studies.

ICC SPRACHSCHULE
Villa Rosental, Liviastr. 8, 04105 Leipzig. Tel: (341) 980 40 59. Fax: (341) 980 54 74. E-mail: villa-rosental@t-online.de. Website: www.villa-rosental.de.
Number of teachers: 20.
Preference of nationality: none.
Qualifications: CELTA (or one-month equivalent) and/or 6 months TEFL experience.
Conditions of employment: 9 month contracts. 20 h.p.w. including lots of evening courses.
Salary: DM25 per hour (45 minute lessons).
Facilities/Support: assistance with accommodation and work permits for non-EU teachers. Monthly training sessions.
Recruitment: walk-ins. Local interview essential.
Contact: James Parsons, Director of Studies.

INLINGUA SPRACHSCHULE FRANKFURT
Kaiserstrasse 37, 60329 Frankfurt. Tel: (69) 242 92 03. Fax: (69) 23 48 29. E-mail: inlingua-schwarz@t-online.de.
Number of teachers: 30.
Preference of nationality: none, but must be native speaker.
Qualifications: university degree, TEFL qualification and driving licence preferred.
Conditions of employment: 18 month contracts. 30-35 h.p.w. Pupils aged 18-60. Peak hours are 7.30am-1pm and 5.20pm-8.30pm.
Salary: approximately DM3,400 per month (gross). DM28 per lesson.
Facilities/Support: free accommodation for first two weeks and assistance with more permanent accommodation (average rent DM700 per month). Newcomers guide given on arrival, covering housing, medical and leisure services, etc. Training provided. Possibility of free German lessons. 35 days of paid holidays included in contract.
Recruitment: direct.
Contact: Anne Ellard.

INLINGUA SPRACHSCHULE HANNOVER
Andreaestrasse 3, 30159 Hannover. Tel: (511) 324580. Fax: (511) 363 2931. E-mail: inlingua.Hannover@t-online.de.
Number of teachers: 10.
Preference of nationality: English, American.
Qualifications: EFL and 1 year of teaching experience.
Conditions of employment: 12 months. Minimum 25 hours per week; 30-40 lessons are more usual.
Salary: monthly minimum DM2,200 (gross) guaranteed or DM23 per hour freelance rates. Taxes, etc. amount to approximately 20%.
Facilities/Support: contact with landlords and property inspection to assist with finding accommodation.
Recruitment: via newspaper adverts and internet.
Contact: Heike Gleichmann, School Manager.

INLINGUA SPRACHSCHULE MUNCHEN
Sendlinger-Tor-Platz 6, 80336 München. Tel: (89) 231 15 30. Fax: (89) 260 99 20. E-mail: paedagogik@muenchen.inlingua.de. Website: www.inlingua.de/muenchen.
Number of teachers: 30.
Preference of nationality: none.
Qualifications: minimum BA or BSc.
Conditions of employment: long-term contracts only, minimum 3 years.

Recruitment: written applications enclosing short CV.
Contact: Britta Klawitter (M.A.), Director of Studies.

LINGUA FRANCA
Pfalzburger Strasse 51, 10717 Berlin. Tel: (30) 86398080. Fax: (30) 86398082. E-mail: lingua_franca@compuserve.com. Website: www.lingua-franca.de.
Number of teachers: 40.
Preference of nationality: none.
Qualifications: university degree plus TEFL experience and/or certificate. Experience in ESP preferred.
Conditions of employment: freelance only. Can generally give good teachers as many lesson hours as they want.
Salary: DM26-DM30 per 45-minute lesson.
Facilities/Support: no help with accommodation. Will write the necessary letter to the employment office to support work permit application. In-house training available.
Recruitment: local interviews.
Contact: Charles Arrigo, Director.

LINGUARAMA SPRACHENINSTITUT DEUTSCHLAND
Rindermarkt 16, 80331 München. Tel: (89) 260 70 40. Fax: (89) 260 240 61. E-mail: munich@linguarama.com. Website www.linguarama.com.
Number of teachers: from 25 in the smaller Linguarama schools to 70 in the larger ones; Linguarama schools located in Berlin, Düsseldorf, Frankfurt, Hamburg, Köln, Leipzig, München and Stuttgart (addresses given in text of chapter).
Preference of nationality: native speakers only.
Qualifications: minimum university degree or equivalent and a basic TEFL qualification (e.g. CELTA). Experience of teaching business English is preferred but at least teachers should have a keen interest in business.
Conditions of employment: mixture of contract and freelance teachers. Freelance teachers work variable hours, usually early mornings and evenings. Contract teachers usually contracted for 1 year, extendable to 2 years, but occasionally shorter contracts available. 20 days paid holiday per 12 month contract.
Salary: depends on experience.
Facilities/Support: contract teachers are given an initial 2 week accommodation entitlement and assistance with finding permanent accommodation. Travel expenses to the city are paid from the UK if recruitment is through head office. Help is given with obtaining a residence permit, etc. All teachers are given an induction course and paid training is held monthly.
Recruitment: normally local interviews for freelance teachers. Contract staff are sometimes recruited locally or via Linguarama Group Personnel Department, Oceanic House, 89 High St, Alton, Hants. GU34 1LG (see introductory chapter *Finding a Job*).
Contact: Rosemary Annandale, General Manager, Linguarama Deutschland.

LINGUS DAS SPRACHINSTITUT
Bertolt-Brecht-Allee 24, 01309 Dresden. Tel: (351) 3199 3080. Fax: (351) 3199 3081. E-mail: lingus@businesspark-dresden.de
Number of teachers: 10.
Preference of nationality: none.
Qualifications: fully trained.
Conditions of employment: freelance. Number of hours depend on courses: 10-20 p.w.
Salary: DM25 per hour (gross) less about 25% deductions.
Facilities/Support: assistance with accommodation if necessary. No training.
Recruitment: direct. Interviews occasionally held in UK.
Contact: Mr. Karsten Uhl, Director of Studies/Owner.

LTC (LANGUAGE TRAINING CENTER)
Grosse Bleichen 32, 20354 Hamburg. Tel: (40) 357 11038. Fax: (40) 357 11049. E-mail: LTC.Hamburg@t-online.de

Number of teachers: about 50.
Preference of nationality: none.
Qualifications: CELTA or equivalent and some experience.
Conditions of employment: freelance. Early mornings, late afternoons and evenings.
Salary: from about DM35 per hour (net).
Facilities/Support: assistance with accommodation or work permits if necessary.
Recruitment: word of mouth. Local interview essential.
Contact: Nicole Willock, Director of Studies.

MUNCHNER VOLKSHOCHSCHULE
Fachgebiet Englisch, Postfach 801164m 81611 München. Tel: (89) 480 06 165. Fax: (89) 480 06 253.

Number of teachers: 150 freelancers, all native speakers.
Preference of nationality: none. Also employ some non-native speakers.
Qualifications: CELTA or equivalent plus some experience or extensive experience and informal training.
Conditions of employment: freelance only. Applications not considered until teachers are resident in Munich area.
Facilities/Support: extensive programme of free seminars and training.
Recruitment: local interview essential.
Contact: Briony Beaven, Director of Studies for English.

DIE NEUE SCHULE
Sprachen und Mehr, Gieselerstrasse 30a, 10713 Berlin. Tel: (30) 873 03 73. Fax: (30) 873 86 13. E-mail: info@neueschule.de. Website: www.neueschule.de.

Number of teachers: 15-20.
Preference of nationality: British, American.
Qualifications: Cambridge or TEFL Certificate and teaching experience needed. Mostly adults (ages 25-40) in small groups of no more than 8.
Conditions of employment: open-ended freelance contracts. Variable hours in the mornings (9-12am) and evenings (6-9.15pm).
Salary: DM26 per 60-minute lesson.
Facilities/Support: no help with accommodation.
Recruitment: personal interview necessary.

PLS LERNSTUDIO
Drächslstr. 14, 81541 München. Tel: (89) 651 80 54. Fax: (89) 664947. E-mail: info@pls-lernstudio.de

Number of teachers: 30.
Preference of nationality: none.
Qualifications: experience in teaching English.
Conditions of employment: 1 year or more. Hours between 10am and 7pm.
Salary: DM40 per hour (net).
Facilities/Support: no assistance with accommodation or work permits. In-house training in Superlearning.
Recruitment: local interview essential.
Contact: Brigitte Braun, Manager.

PROFESSIONAL ENGLISH TRAINING (P.E.T.)
Wittelsbacherstrasse 13, 80469 München. Tel: (89) 202 386 55. Fax: (89) 202 386 54. E-mail: pet.firmenkurse@gmx.de.

Number of teachers: 30 freelancers.
Preference of nationality: none.
Qualifications: TEFL qualification and/or degree preferable, as are business

experience and and friendly, outgoing disposition.
Conditions of employment: travelling to companies to hold in-company courses on a freelance basis.
Salary: DM45-55 per teaching unit (45 minutes).
Facilities/Support: no assistance with accommodation. Materials support given. Teachers' workshops held.
Recruitment: direct applications. Local interviews necessary.

SPRACHSCHUL-CENTRUM DREIEICH
Frankfurter Strasse 114, 63268 Dreieich. Tel: (6103) 373931; Fax: (6103) 34783.
Number of teachers: 9.
Preference of nationality: Irish, British.
Qualifications: TEFL qualification with one year's experience, German (not compulsory).
Conditions of employment: 9 or 10 months contract (September/October-June), 27 h.p.w. Students all adults, max. 8 per group, some in-company courses.
Salary: DM2,600 per month, tax-free (equivalent of DM3,300 gross salary).
Facilities/Support: studio apartments available for rent in walking distance.
Recruitment: written application with full CV and recent photograph.

SPRACHE UND WIRTSCHAFT
Sternwartenstr. 4-6, 04103 Leipzig. Tel: (341) 25 77 127. Fax: (341) 25 77 127. E-mail: sprache.wirtschaft@t-online.de.
Number of teachers: about 40.
Preference of nationality: none.
Qualifications: TEFL Certificate.
Conditions of employment: freelance. At least 20 hours teaching per week.
Salary: varies.
Facilities/Support: no assistance with accommodation.
Recruitment: through word-of-mouth, the telephone directory.
Contact: Kathrin Taubert, Managing Director.

STEVENS ENGLISH TRAINING
Rüttenscheiderstr. 68, 45130 Essen. Tel: (201) 787091-93. Fax: (201) 793783. E-mail: MStevens@stevens-english.de. Also Kaiser-Wilhelm-Ring 14-16, 50672 Köln.
Number of teachers: approx 50 full and part-time.
Preference of nationality: native speakers of English.
Qualifications: TEFL Certificate or business experience.
Conditions of employment: 2 year contracts. Hours between 7.30am and 8.45pm Monday to Friday. 80% of teaching is in-company with high element of ESP.
Salary: paid on points system per 45-minute session.
Facilities/Support: furnished flats available near the school for trainers recruited from the UK. Extensive workshop training programme for trainers. Opportunity to take the LCCI exam 'Foundation Certificate in Teaching Business English' (FTBE). Extensive library of teaching materials.
Recruitment: interviews essential and regularly held in London.
Contacts: Sigrid and Michael Stevens, Managing Directors.

TARGET GmBH
Türkenstrasse 66, 80799 München. Tel: (89) 280 92 35. Fax: (89) 280 04 16. E-mail: info@t-english.com. Website: www.t-english.com.
Number of teachers: 15.
Preference of nationality: none (native English speakers).
Qualifications: Cert TEFL is essential. Minimum 3 years experience with business English. Diploma preferred.
Conditions of employment: freelance only. Trainers must be prepared to stay for 18 months.

Salary: minimum 25 Euros per 45-minute lesson.
Facilities/Support: advice and help given finding accommodation when needed. Regular workshops. Will contribute up to 50% of external training fees.
Recruitment: word of mouth and adverts in regional newspapers. Local interview essential.
Contact: John Sydes.

WALL STREET INSTITUTE BERLIN
Friedrich Str. 118/119, 10117 Berlin. Tel/fax: (30) 283 99 510. E-mail: zena@proeducation.de. Also at Kurfurstendamm 71, 01711 Berlin. Tel: (30) 32 77 040. Fax: (30) 32 77 94 10.
Number of teachers: 4-5 per school. 2 schools in Berlin, with plans to open more.
Preference of nationality: none.
Qualifications: TEFL Cert.
Conditions of employment: freelance. 30 hours of teaching a week.
Salary: DM27 per hour.
Facilities/Support: no assistance with accommodation.
Recruitment: frequent unsolicited applications.
Contact: Zena Davidson, Service Manager or Murray Venance, Director.

WALL STREET INSTITUTE FREIBURG
Humboldtstr. 2, 79098 Freiburg. Tel: (761) 207 110. Fax: (761) 207 1120. E-mail: s.lersch@wallstreetinstitute.de.
Number of teachers: 2-4.
Preference of nationality: none.
Qualifications: native speaker of English, Teaching Certificate, teaching experience preferred.
Conditions of employment: fixed contracts. 20-40 h.p.w.
Salary: DM20-DM27 per hour.
Facilities/Support: training.
Recruitment: local interviews essential.
Contact: Giuseppe Provenzano, Director.

WALL STREET INSTITUTE FRANKFURT
Kaiserstr. 44, 60329 Frankfurt/Main. Tel: (69) 92 91 95 90. Fax: (69) 0201 05 03.
Same conditions as above.
Contact: Thomas Witt, Director.

WALL STREET INSTITUTE MUNICH
Nymphenburgerstr. 21, 80335 Munich. Tel: (89) 599 885 30. Fax: (89) 24 83 75 33. Also at Rosental 5, 80331 Munich. Tel: (89) 236 905 0. Fax: (89) 236 905 20.
Same conditions as above.
Contact: Todd Theisen, Director.

WALL STREET INSTITUTE STUTTGART
Christophstr. 7, 70178 Stuttgart. Tel: (711) 24 83 750.
Same conditions as above.
Contact: Achim Gniffke, Director.

Other Schools to Try (cities and towns in alphabetical order)
Note that these schools did not confirm their teacher requirements for this edition of *Teaching English Abroad.* Upper case entries marked with an asterisk had entries in the last edition (1999); addresses without asterisks have been taken from various sources, such as British Council lists, the *Yellow Pages,* etc.

SpracheDirekt, Breite Strasse 69, 56626 Andernach
Saxon College of English, Markt 15, 09573 Augustusburg
Accent Business Languages, Sächsische Str. 7, 10707 Berlin
Akademia fur Fremdsprachen GmbH, Postfach 104, 10663 Berlin

Berlitz, Kurfürstendamm 74, 10709 Berlin
Didactica, Kaiser-Friedrich Str. 76, 10585 Berlin
Flying English, Bachestr. 3, 12161 Berlin
inlingua Sprachschule Berlin, Ludwigkirchstr. 9A, 10719 Berlin
Protea Sprachschule, Klingsorstr. 7, 12167 Berlin
ABC English, Zwickauer 297, Chemnitz
European Language School, Hansastr. 44, 44137 Dortmund
Berlitz, Wilsdruffer Strasse 11, 01067 Dresden
Fremdsprachen Institut Angelika Trautmann, Schweriner Str. 56, 01067 Dresden
Die Sprachwerkstatt, Grossenhainer 99, 01127 Dresden
inlingua Sprachschule, Königstrasse 61, 47051 Duisburg (203-30 53 40)
Berlitz-Sprachschle, Markt 11, Erfurt
Euro Schulen Gera, Friedrich Engels 10, 07545 Gera
Albis Sprach-Institut, Colonnaden 18, 20354 Hamburg
Anglo English School, Gänsemarkt 43, 20354 Hamburg
Sprachenschule Klisa, Agrippinaufer 6, 50678 Köln
inlingua, Nikolaistrasse 36, 04109 Leipzig
Euro-Schulen-Sachsen Anhalt, Fuchsberg 5, Magdeburg
A.S.S. München, Leopoldst. 62, 08082 München
*LERNEN IM ZENTRUM, Lehrinstitut R. Cerny, Sendlinger Strasse 47, 80331
    München (89-260 90 34/fax 89-260 52 97)
English Language Centre, Bieberer Strasse 205, 63071 Offenbach am Main (69-85
    87 87/fax 69-85 72 02)

Greece

The huge ELT industry in Greece predates Greece's full membership in the
European Union, and continues to increase. Of all the candidates worldwide who sit
the Cambridge First Certificate and Cambridge Proficiency examinations, about one
quarter are in Greece, i.e. more than 130,000. English language teaching in Greece
has been described as an exam industry. The British Council estimates that there are
between 5,000 and 6,000 private language schools (*frontisteria*) in the country,
almost all of them teaching children of secondary school age. This creates a huge
demand for native speakers. Standards at *frontisteria* vary from indifferent to
excellent, but the run-of-the-mill variety is usually a reasonable place to work for
nine months, even if *frontisterion* owners are primarily business people rather than
educators.

Frontisteria come in all shapes and sizes. In a town of 30,000 inhabitants, it
would not be unusual to find ten English *frontisteria*, three or four of which would
be big enough to employ one native English speaker. The city of Patras alone has
400. The Greek Ministry of Education imposes a quota on language schools,
stipulating that there can be no more than one foreigner for every nine Greek
teachers.

Any Greek who has passed the Cambridge Proficiency exam is legally permitted
to open his or her own private school. These are often in buildings which were not
designed to be schools and facilities can be very basic. Secondary school pupils in
Greece are obliged to study 15 subjects, all of which they must pass before being
allowed to proceed to the next year. In most areas the teaching of English in state
schools is considered inadequate so that the vast majority of pupils also attend
frontisteria, and it is not uncommon for a 15 year old to have two or three hours of
lessons a day (in other subjects as well as English) in one or more private
establishments to supplement the state schooling. Not surprisingly, the students are
not always brimming over with enthusiasm; in fact, quite often they are not even
awake.

Prospects for Teachers

At the beginning of the 21st century, the employment situation for teachers is still booming with a number of agencies busily recruiting EFL teachers throughout the summer for the following academic year. Prospects for EU nationals with a university degree are good, particularly outside Athens. Though an increasing number of *frontisteria* are looking for other teaching qualifications like a Cambridge or Trinity Certificate. Few school employers insist on experience. The government stipulates that in order to obtain a teacher's licence, English teachers must have at least a BA in English language and literature or education, so that all but the most dodgy schools will expect to see a university certificate. Having a TEFL qualification, as always, will make the job hunt easier. Given the size of the ELT market in Greece, it is surprising that so few training centres offer the CELTA or the Trinity TESOL Certificate in Greece.

Americans and other non-EU nationals will find it difficult to find a school willing to hire them, purely because of immigration difficulties. The government imposes stiff penalities on employers who break the rules, and few will risk it, as Tim Leffel found out: 'We had planned on teaching in Greece, but as Americans, we were not exactly welcomed with open arms in Athens; they told us to try the countryside.' Tim moved on to Turkey instead. A further complicating factor is the high number of Greek emigrés to North America and Australia who have returned (or whose children have returned) to Greece. In many cases, they are virtually native speakers of English but because of their ancestry do not use up the one-in-nine allocation of foreigners mentioned above. Of course there will always be schools prepared to hire Americans and others if well qualified, such as the Hellenic American Union (22 Massalias Street, 106 80 Athens; 1-362 9886/ admin@hau.gr) which has one of the largest programmes in adult EFL in Athens.

One reason why EU nationals with basic qualifications can expect to land a job in Greece is that wages are not high enough to attract a great many highly qualified EFL teachers. Greece tends to be a country where people get their first English teaching job for the experience and then move to more lucrative countries. Also, few schools place any emphasis on staff development or provide in-house training, so serious teachers tend to move on quickly.

The majority of advertised jobs are in towns and cities in mainland Greece. Athens has such a large expatriate community that most of the large central schools at the elite end of the market are able to hire well qualified staff locally. But the competition will not be so keen in Edessa, Larissa, Preveza or any of numerous towns of which the tourist to Greece is unlikely to have heard.

FIXING UP A JOB

In Advance

Unless you elect to register with a recruitment agency (which deal primarily with Certificate-qualified teachers), it may not be worthwhile trying to fix up a job in advance, since so much in Greece is accomplished by word of mouth. Getting a list of language schools from outside Greece is not easy. A considerable proportion of *frontisteria* belong to the Pan-Hellenic Federation of Language School Owners (PALSO, 2 Lykavitou St & Akadimias St, 106 71 Kolonaki, Athens; 1-364 0792/363 6052/Fax 1-364 2359; www.palso.gr). Unfortunately they do not distribute regional lists of their 5,000 member schools nor are the addresses posted on their website. Note that PALSO Thessaloniki has its own website at http://users. otenet.gr/~palsothes/federation_en.html which does contain the addresses of its members though few corresponded with this book. The British Council in Athens does not maintain a list of English schools, though the Teaching Centre Director at the British Council in Thessaloniki can send a long list of addresses in and around Greece's second city, only partially transliterated into the English alphabet. If you do manage to get hold of a list of *Frontisteria* from the Yellow Pages, note that you will have to be conversant with the Greek alphabet unless you find the *Athens Blue Pages*, an English version of the Yellow Pages.

The internet is not as widely used in Greece as in some other countries, though occasionally a Greek school will post a vacancy on www.eslcafe.com or www.englishclub.net, usually specifying that applicants must have an EU passport. The server www.forthnet.gr handles a few language schools and the category Education can be worth checking. Most schools do their hiring for the following academic year between March and June. Obviously the major chains of schools offer the most opportunities, and it is worth sending your CV in the spring to organisations like the *Strategakis Group* with about a hundred schools in northern Greece.

Adverts for Greek schools continue to appear, especially in the *TES*. Few seem to go in for lavish display adverts, but there is a sprinkling of four-line adverts along the lines of 'English teachers required. Good salary and housing. Fax your CV and a photo to Frontisterion X.' There are also occasional adverts for live-in tutors. The spring is the best time to look, though inevitably some schools who are let down by contracted teachers place rather panicky ads in August and into September. Often independent language school owners do their own interviewing in London over the summer; for example the director of the Hatzinikolaou on Kos (fax 242-26566).

Fortunately there are several active recruitment agencies which specialise in Greece with offices in Greece and/or Britain. These recruitment agencies are looking for people with at least a BA and preferably a TEFL qualification and/or experience (depending on the client school's requirements). All client employers provide accommodation. Complaints about a lack of back-up are occasionally heard, so do not expect to be nannied along after placement. The following undertake to match teachers (with EU nationality) with *frontisteria* and do not charge teachers a fee:

Anglo-Hellenic Teacher Recruitment, PO Box 263, 201 00 Corinth (tel/fax 741-53511; jobs@anglo-hellenic.com/ www.anglo-hellenic.com). Dozens of posts in wide choice of locations for university graduates from the UK, preferably with a CELTA or Trinity TESOL. Interviews are conducted in London, Athens or Corinth throughout the summer. 9-month contracts pay the going rate of about £300 per month (net) plus bonuses, 4 weeks' paid holiday and accommodation in a furnished flat. A four-page contract will be provided by agency (specimen copy available beforehand). Anglo-Hellenic also take care of the bureaucratic essentials, with the exception of the health certificate, and encourage meetings and exchange visits of their teachers and provide interactive web-based facilities for information, opinion and social chat. Professional development is also provided including ongoing training to obtain further qualifications, and progressively more responsibility in placements. Training courses are run in collaboration with City College Manchester (see entry in *Training: Trinity College Certificate Courses*).

Cambridge Teachers Recruitment, 33A Makryanni St, New Halkidona, 143 43 Athens (tel/fax 1-258 5155). UK contact address of main interviewer during the summer: Andrew MacLeod-Smith, 53 Green Acres, Parkhill, Croydon CRO 5UX; tel/fax 020-8686 3733; macleod_smith_andrew@hotmail.com. One of the largest agencies, placing 80-100 teachers per year in vetted schools. Applicants must have a degree and in most cases a TEFL Certificate, a friendly personality and conscientious attitude. Comprehensive interviews are conducted between mid-June and the end of August; applicants can expect to receive a wealth of information about working in Greece.

i-to-i, 1 Cottage Road, Headingley, Leeds LS6 4DD. Tel: 0870-333 2332. Fax: 0113 274 6923. E-mail: info@i-to-i.com. TEFL training organisation which has links with schools in Greece and can arrange employment.

NET (Native English Teachers), 72 Windsor Road, Worthing, West Sussex BN11 2LY. Tel: (01903) 218638. Agency run by Susan Lancaster, who interviews British teachers for up to 20 vacancies in *frontisteria*. Selection is based on qualifications, merit and good references. (No help can be given to North Americans because of visa restrictions.) Provides orientation which includes information on cheap air fares and on how to show respect for Greek customs.

When discussing your future post with an agency, don't be lulled into a false sense of security. It is wise to check contractual details for yourself and verify verbal promises. Check to see whether you are entitled to any compensation if the employer breaks the contract and similarly whether you will have to compensate the school if you leave early. Find out if there will be any other native speaker teachers in the area, and ask about the possibility of contacting your predecessor in the job.

On the Spot

So many *frontisteria* rely on agents to find teachers for them, that it can be difficult to walk into a job. After gaining a lot of on-the-ground experience of Greece, Jane McNally from County Derry in Ireland concluded that knocking on school doors can be discouraging, a view corroborated by Jain Cook when she was Director of Studies at the Koutsantonis School of Languages in Patras (35 Gounari Avenue, 262 21 Patras; 61-273925/fax 61-224496):

> There do not seem to be as many vacancies for teachers as there used to be in the Peloponnese. I have interviewed about 15 British teachers in the past few weeks, all of whom have stressed the difficulty of finding work in this area. They were all personable, smartly dressed, well qualified and experienced, but as yet have received no definite job offers.

The majority of schools have filled all their vacancies by June, so September is normally too late for prospective teachers to be looking for work. One of the best times to look is January. Greece is far less attractive in mid-winter than in summer, and many foreign teachers do not return to their posts after Christmas. Finding work in the summer is virtually impossible; most English language summer courses in resorts or on the islands are staffed by people who have taught for an academic year.

Yet in the more remote corners of Greece, native speakers can locate jobs on-the-spot and negotiate a position. Sarah Clifford had no trouble lining up part-time work at a *frontisterion* in the Peloponnesian village of Kynoryrias, with 'no experience, no teaching qualification, no degree and no knowledge of Greek'. The catch was that the hourly wage was lower than average, but she enjoyed rural Greece more than cosmopolitan Athens. Note that teaching in Greece without a degree is against the law.

Little can be reliably accomplished by post, e-mail or even by telephone. Larry Church describes the unpredictable way in which his second teaching contract was arranged:

> While on a weekend holiday to Athens from Orestiada, my second teaching job (in Alexandroupolis) occurred through a chance meeting on the airplane with a frontisterion owner. The job offer came during a shared taxi ride into Athens. Taking care of business at the last possible minute being a normal procedure in Greece, a contract was signed in June at the airport, ten minutes before our plane was due to take off for our return trip to America for the summer. At the same time my wife was promised some part-time hours in the school, although she had no teaching experience.

Although Jamie Masters knew that October was not prime time for job-hunting, that is when he arrived in Heraklion to look for work:

> I advertised (in Greek) in the Cretan newspapers, no joy. I lowered my sights and started knocking on doors of frontisteria. I was put onto some guy who ran an English-language bookshop and went to see him. Turned out he was a lynch-pin in the frontisterion business and in fact I got my first job through him. Simultaneously I went to something which roughly translates as the

'Council for owners of frontisteria' and was given a list of schools which were looking for people. The list, it turned out, was pretty much out of date. But I had insisted on leaving my name with the Council (they certainly didn't offer) and that's how I found my second job.

Once you arrange an interview, be sure to dress well and to amass as many educational diplomas as you can. This will create the right aura of respectability in which to impress the potential employer with your conscientiousness and amiability. Decisions are often taken more according to whether you hit it off with the interviewer than on your qualifications and experience. Jamie Masters found that no one cared a fig about his PhD in Latin.

Check the adverts in the English language daily *Athens News* or *Greek News* or the weekly *Hellenic Times* where *frontisteria* sometimes advertise, though they normally ask for qualifications. These papers are probably more useful if you are looking for a more informal arrangement: many Greek families are looking for live-in or part-time tutors for their children. You can read the *Athens News* Situations Vacant ads on the internet at http://athensnews.dolnet.gr/ or you can place your own 15-word advert in the *Athens News* for dr2,200; contact them at 3 Christou Lada, 102 37 Athens; 1-33 3404/fax 1-322 3746.

When you elicit interest from a language school owner or a family, take your time over agreeing terms. Greece is not a country in which it pays to rush, and negotiations can be carried out in a leisurely and civilised fashion. On the other hand, do not come to an agreement with an employer without clarifying wages and schedules precisely. Make sure you read your contract very carefully so that you are familiar with what you should be entitled to.

Freelance

Private lessons, at least in the provinces, are very easy to find. Some people estimate that between a third and a half of all English language teaching that goes on in Greece takes place privately. The going rate is dr2,500-3,000 an hour for First Certificate teaching, dr5,000 for Proficiency. Rates in Athens are more likely to be in the range dr5,000-10,000. For example at the time of writing the Betsis School in Athens (betsis@globalnet.co.uk) was advertising jobs which paid £600 a month for combining 20 hours a week of English teaching with ten hours of working in an ELT publishing house.

Most teachers in *frontisteria* do at least three or four hours a week of private tutoring, since the basic salary is increasingly difficult to live on, at least if you are on your own instead of part of a teaching couple. Private tutoring jobs seem to materialise either from the language schools (whose directors seldom seem to mind their teachers earning on the side) or from conversations in a *kafeneion*.

Trading English lessons for board and lodging is a common form of freelance teaching in Athens and elsewhere. Sometimes contracted teachers are offered free accommodation in exchange for tutoring their boss's children. In Athens, the rich suburbs of Kifissia and Politia are full of families who can afford to provide private English lessons for their offspring. The suburbs of Pangrati and Filothei are also well-heeled as is the more central suburb of Kolonaki. It is also possible to start up private classes for children, provided you have decent accommodation in a prosperous residential area, though this will normally be too expensive if your only source of income is private teaching. Leah White solved her accommodation problem in Athens by approaching managers of blocks of flats to see whether they could arrange for her to have a rent-free flat in exchange for teaching their children. (This way she avoided the problem that plagues live-in tutors, a lack of privacy.)

REGULATIONS

English teachers must first obtain a teacher's licence and then a residence permit, and the bureaucratic procedures involved can be stressful even with a supportive employer. The two documents needed for a teacher's licence are a health certificate and a degree certificate. The Ministry of Education considers a BA or higher degree in English literature or a degree in Education a sufficient qualification though a TEFL Certificate strengthens your application of course. You must have your degree certificate officially translated and notarised, either before you leave home (which is usually cheaper) or in Greece (ask the British Council for advice). The health certificate can be obtained only in Greece, and involves a chest X-ray and in some cases a blood test.

English speakers of Greek ancestry find it much easier to obtain a teacher's licence and are generally more attractive prospects, as explained by Jain Cook:

> *Australian, Canadian, South African and American Greeks are classed as native speakers because English is their first language, but their Greek surnames helps the one-in-ten Greek/foreigner ratio. They do all their own bureaucratic paperwork, have family and relatives in Greece, fewer accommodation and financial problems and are reliable, very rarely leaving for reasons other than pregnancy. Usually they come back after their maternity leave as they have family to look after the baby. Since February I have interviewed over a hundred such teachers, the majority from Canada. Although many have no teaching experience or qualifications, they have already obtained a teacher's licence and therefore school owners are more than willing to consider them.*

Many choose to take out citizenship, which involves getting a Greek Identity Card. This entitles them to a teacher's licence valid for life, exempting them from having to renew it annually as other foreigners do. However, the downside is that as a citizen you may become liable for military service.

When the teacher's licence arrives from Athens, the teacher must take it along with his or her passport, photos and a lot of patience to the police station to apply for a residence permit, which should come through in about a month. The health certificate and residence permit must be renewed annually, though if you protest loudly enough you can usually get away with just having a chest X-ray. You will however have to take your IKA book (see below) to renew your residence permit and a form from your employer which shows the length of your term of employment. The first residence permit is normally valid for just six months, subsequent ones for one to three years. Keep photocopies of all forms.

Some teachers simply extend their tourist visa (as long as they can provide plenty of currency exchange slips to prove that they are self-supporting) or leave the country every three months to renew their tourist stamp. Unfortunately this is expensive and time-consuming if you are in a remote corner of Greece. Also the second term is normally longer than three months and if you have to be replaced for the last few weeks of term, you may find that you are not welcomed back.

Frontisteria usually tend to leave all the bureaucratic legwork to the teachers because hiring a foreigner, especially those coming from outside the EU, is extremely complicated. Employers will take on the necessary transactions only if they are convinced that a candidate will be an asset to their school. Non-EU teachers often find that the Ministry of Education delays and even turns down their applications for a teacher's licence. Officially they must obtain a letter of hire from a language school which must be sent to an address outside Greece. The teacher takes the letter to the nearest Greek consulate and applies for a work permit; the procedures take at least two months.

It is mandatory for Greek employers to register employees with the Greek National Health Insurance scheme (IKA) and pay employer contributions which amount to 27.97% of the salary; the employee's contribution is 15.89%. Be sure to find out ahead of time whether the salary quoted is before or after the IKA deduction. You should go with your employer to the local IKA office in order to apply for an IKA book 60 days after starting to pay contributions; thereafter you are entitled to free medical treatment and reduced cost prescriptions on production of the book. If you suspect that your employer is not in fact paying contributions on your behalf, ask to see the stamps. If he or she will not show you, threaten to expose him or her to the authorities. (Once you have paid IKA and tax for two consecutive years, you are entitled to unemployment benefit; some teachers have been known to claim over the summer when they are out of the country, though the authorities may clamp down on this.) Very few teachers declare their private earnings for tax purposes.

CONDITIONS OF WORK

Standards vary enormously among *frontisteria*. Although there is specific legislation which is meant to regulate the operation of language schools, this is seldom enforced. The way to recognise a good *frontisterion* is by its exam results and by its ability to retain staff.

In general the large chains like *Strategakis* are better, probably for no other reason than that they have a longer history of employing native English speakers. You also have some back-up if you have been hired through a mediating agency. Some of the small one-man or one-woman schools are cowboy outfits run by barely qualified entrepreneurs who have had little contact with the English language; their teaching techniques involve shouting (usually in Greek) at their students and getting them to recite English irregular verbs parrot fashion. In fact this kind of school is on the decline, helped by the fact that foreigners are now allowed to run language schools in Greece which has had the effect of raising standards.

The minimum hourly rate of pay is about dr2,000 gross, dr1,650 net. Anyone with some training or experience should be able to ask for at least dr2,200. No teacher should accept less than the legal rate. Depending on the number of holidays (unpaid) in a month, your take-home pay can fluctuate alarmingly and be barely enough to live on, especially if you are paying rent for your accommodation; the average is equivalent to about a quarter of a teacher's net salary, but can be higher. In theory, teachers should be paid for an extra ten hours of marking a month but almost no one receives this.

Always keep a copy of your contract safe in case difficulties arise, as they did in the case of Belinda Michaels while working at a *frontisterion* in Patras:

> *In November, the school owner told me that the students wanted me back after Christmas. On January 29th the following year, she dismissed me with no notice and no holiday pay. Her excuse was that there was low student attendance during the university exam period. The next day the landlady was very rude to me saying that I had left the school. I had to pay dr46,000 for my January electricity bill which I never saw. She also asked for dr13,000 for the water bill and a month's rent in advance. I immediately left the accommodation. When I went into the school to ask for one month's severance pay to which I was legally entitled, the owner started attacking me verbally and ordered me out of the school. She refused to give me a copy of my contract, nor had the UK agent given me a copy.*

The basic salary should be augmented by compulsory bonuses at Christmas, Easter and summer. Teaching unions have negotiated some reasonable conditions, though not all schools offer them. Bonuses, holiday pay and health insurance should all be stipulated, plus employers may not fire teachers during the school year. The majority of employers offer eight or nine month contracts from September and allow two paid fortnight holidays at Christmas and Easter (remember that the Greek Easter is usually later than elsewhere). Bonuses are calculated according to the number of days worked. For every nine days you have worked before Christmas you get one day's pay (i.e. five hours). For every 13 days worked between January 1st and April 30th you get two days pay. This usually approximates to an extra month's pay at

Christmas and half a month's pay at Easter. If you have queries about the collective labour agreement, contact the Greek Labour Office (OEAD) at Ethnikis Antistasis 8 str, 16610 Ano Glyfada; 1-9989 0000/ www.oead.gr).

You also get a lump sum at the end of your contract which is not in fact a bonus. It is two weeks' holiday pay and two weeks' severance pay (both tax-free). Beware of employers who pay for your accommodation out of your gross salary and then try to calculate your bonuses as a percentage of your net salary. This is illegal. Employers who have suffered from staff desertions in the past may hold back some of your monthly pay as a bond *(kratisi)* against an early departure. The indignity of this niggled away at Jamie Masters (plus he needed the dr5,000 per month) until he complained and the practice was discontinued.

The working week in a *frontisterion* may be longer than in most countries; the average is 25 contact hours per week. The usual maximum is 32 hours, excluding preparation time and the minimum is 18 hours. Teachers working fewer than 18 hours do not have a fully paid up National Insurance contribution. Split shifts are common especially in areas where the state schools operate a shift system where students attend mornings one week and afternoons the next. A *frontisterion* schedule of 9am-11am and 5pm-10pm means late nights and early starts. The state school system is changing gradually, so that in some areas students attend only morning classes, which in turn means that private schools are offering English tuition only in the evenings, thereby cutting down the potential number of hours a teacher can work.

It is not unusual to be expected to teach in two or more 'satellite' sites of the main school in villages up to ten miles away. Local bus services are generally good and cheap but you could find yourself spending an inordinate amount of (unpaid) time in transit and standing around at bus stops.

All areas have a local Workers' Office where you can go if you are in dispute with your employer or fear that you are being ripped off. They are gradually becoming more efficient and are obliged to investigate every complaint.

Pupils

Most native English speakers are employed to teach advanced classes, usually the two years leading to Cambridge exams. Because of the Greek style of education, pupils won't show much initiative and will expect to be tested frequently on what they have been taught. Andrew Boyle found the prevailing methodology of 'sit 'em down, shut 'em up and give 'em lots of homework' was moderately successful.

Another problem is that there is a great deal of pressure to assign pass marks just to retain the students' custom. Some school owners are so profit-motivated, they have drachmas for eyeballs. Students expect to be told the answers and bosses want their teachers to be lenient with the marking so that the students all pass and parents will re-enrol them.

As a consequence of this leniency, discipline can also be a problem. Miss C. Warren-Swettenham from Oxfordshire worked at a *frontisterion* in Trikkala in Northern Greece:

> As regards the teaching, everything is running smoothly, although at the best of times trying to inspire rowdy adolescent Greek kids with totally unsuitable outdated English books is enough to give you a nervous breakdown. Suggesting a possible alternative to my boss is something I have tried, but to no avail. Basically their idea of English is what they have in grammar books, accompanied by dreary written exercises, conjugating verbs. Any attempt to introduce TEFL teaching where the emphasis is on communicaiton falls on deaf ears.

Jamie Masters came to the conclusion that cheating is a national pastime and hated his role as policeman. He expended a lot of energy on outwitting their strategies, when all he wanted to do was to get them to learn something. He had to teach pupils who had been promoted because of parental pressure, notably one girl in a third year class who didn't understand one word of English and yet turned in perfect compositions, done by other people.

Accommodation

Since most schools provide a flat or at least help in finding a flat, teachers are often not too concerned about their living arrangements. Placements arranged by the recruitment agencies listed above all come with accommodation, which at best is spartan (consisting of a bed, chair, table, baby belling and shower) and at worst revolting. Andrew Boyle described his flat in Tripolis as a 'particularly vile, subterranean cavern with an almost non-existent window and stomach-turning plumbing' but found that anything more congenial was ridiculously expensive. Another problem with tied flats is that you may not be consulted over rent increases. If your employer pays your rent directly out of your salary, you may be helpless to object.

If your employer provides your accommodation, it is definitely worth checking in advance about furnishings. Many flats, especially in Athens, are unfurnished which is a serious nuisance for someone on a nine-month contract. Also check which (if any) utility bills are included in the rent. Many people are shocked at how cold Greece gets in the winter, and at how expensive electricity is. The cost of electricity continues to rise as have water and telephone charges. Jain Cook and her husband had a bill of £250 for two months, using only lights, hot water, iron and TV. Make sure you have plenty of warm clothes and a hot water bottle, so that you don't use up your entire budget on heating.

LEISURE

Teachers in Athens should have no trouble constructing a social life. The monthly paper *The Athenian* available from kiosks in Omonia Square among other places contains details of clubs and events of interest to expats. Outside Athens, the social order is still fairly conservative. A further problem is the enormous language barrier in a country where it will take some time to learn how to read the alphabet. Watching Greek television is a good way to learn the language plus Greek lessons are run free of charge in many locations. Larry Church and his wife were among only five native English speakers in Orestiada and the only Americans; at times they felt like the town oddities, but well-loved ones. Most teachers find the vast majority of Greek people to be honest, friendly and helpful and are seldom disappointed with the hospitality they receive.

As anyone who has visited Greece knows, the country has countless other attractions, not least the very convivial and affordable tavernas. Eating out, wine and cigarettes are more or less the only things that have not become expensive. Cafés *(kafeneions)* are a largely male institution in which women teachers may not feel comfortable. Travel, particularly ferry travel, is relatively cheap and a pure delight out of season.

When people think of Greece they automatically think of sun-soaked Mediterranean beaches, but it is quite a different story in the inland towns of northern Greece in the winter. Erica Jolly and Paul Robinson soon exhausted the possibilities of their northern town:

> There were very few facilities other than bars and a few restaurants. The cinema did show undubbed British and American films but was too cold to sit in in winter. Sports facilities were non-existent and adults were not allowed to use the town's swimming pool. Fortunately we had brought our car and were able to see quite a lot of Greece. We even took the car over to Corfu at Easter. Insurance was not cheap but was easily obtainable.

The cost of living is higher than it used to be. All imports are expensive, for

example cosmetics, shoes and clothes. Don't expect to have much left out of your £400 or so take-home pay for saving or splurging.
Despite all the hassles, most people enjoy a year in Greece, as Philip Dray did:

> *I have many happy memories of working in northeastern Greece, even though we were asked to work 32 hours a week (and that was too much for £90) and had a boss who was out to exploit from the start. But the town was great, the children superb and I also had friendly colleagues.*

LIST OF SCHOOLS

ATHANASOPOULOS LANGUAGE SCHOOLS
6 Einstein St & Nikis, 18 757 Keratsini-Piraeus. Tel: (1) 43 14 921/40 01 226. Fax: (1) 43 18 241. Branch school at 30 & 34 Ipsilantou St, 187 58 Keratsini (1-43 23 947). E-mail: athanasopoulos@acropolis.gr.
Number of teachers: 9-10.
Preference of nationality: British, American, Canadian.
Qualifications: BA (English) or equivalent. Cambridge Certificate valued.
Conditions of employment: 8 month extendable contracts. Morning and/or afternoon work. Pupils aged 9-24.
Salary: £450 per month plus £450 summer bonus.
Facilities/Support: subsidised accommodation offered. Free British Council seminars arranged.
Recruitment: through newspaper adverts and TEFL training centres. Interviews essential and are held locally or abroad.

ENGLISH LANGUAGE SCHOOL
66 Tepeleniou Street, New Liossia, 13123 Athens, Greece. Tel: (1) 501 4000. E-mail: jackyschool@ath.forthnet.gr. Website: jackyschool.homestead.com/init.html.
Preference of nationality: EU.
Qualifications: BA in English literature required. EFL qualification an advantage. Ages 22-30, Should have happy, outgoing personality and be genuinely interested in living in Greece.
Conditions of employment: period of work mid-September to May. Hours by arrangement Monday-Friday. Students are mainly teenagers in a school with easy access to the city centre and beach.
Salary: according to qualifications. National insurance covered and holidays paid.
Facilities/Support: extensive training given to inexperienced teachers.
Contact: Jacky Wilson-Vamvaka.

HELLENIC AMERICAN UNION
22 Massalias Street, 106 80 Athens. Tel: (1) 362 9886. Fax: (1) 363 3174. E-mail: admin@hau.gr. Website: www.hau.gr (in English).
Number of teachers: 45.
Preference of nationality: EU plus American, Canadian, Australian, etc.
Qualifications: MA preferred (50% of their teachers have an MA).
Conditions of employment: most students are adults but also offer EFL courses for children and adolescents.
Contact: Deputy Director of Education.

HERCULES LANGUAGE SCHOOL
L. Saronidas 28-30, 19013 Saronida. Tel/fax: (291) 60707. E-mail: karengallo@ath.forthnet.gr.
Number of teachers: 3 for school situated on coast 45 miles from Athens.
Preference of nationality: none; must hold EU passport.
Qualifications: university degree and TEFL Certificate needed; experience an advantage but not essential.
Conditions of employment: 10 month contract from September. Maximum 30 contact hours p.w. (afternoons and evenings) teaching beginners to advanced.

Salary: dr200,000 net per month. Deductions total approximately dr40,000 per month.
Facilities/Support: accommodation provided in one-bedroom furnished flat, 10 minutes walk from school. Bills extra. Possibility of free flights to and from London. 3 weeks paid holiday and insurance provided.
Recruitment: adverts in *TES* or websites (e.g. www.englishclub.net). Interviews sometimes held in UK as well as Greece.
Contact: Karen Gallo, Director of Studies.

KARANTZOUNIS INSTITUTE OF FOREIGN LANGUAGES
41 Epidavrou St, 104 41 Athens. Tel: (1) 514 2397. Fax: (1) 524 5479.
Number of teachers: 5 at 3 schools (Tertipi 31 & Papanastasiou 82, 104 45 Athens; and Odysseus & Troias 17, 121 33 Peristeri).
Preference of nationality: British, American.
Qualifications: BA.
Conditions of employment: 1 academic year contracts from September to June. 25-28 h.p.w. mainly evening work. Pupils aged 8-16.
Salary: dr150,000-170,000 per month.
Facilities/Support: small independent furnished and equipped apartment provided free of charge. Training provided.
Recruitment: interviews in Athens essential.

D. KOUTOUGERA-KORRE FOREIGN LANGUAGES CENTER
4 Smyrnis St, Nea Filadelfeia, 143 41 Athens. Tel: (1) 25 18 281/25 20 854. Fax: (1) 25 11 657.
Number of teachers: 4 (two couples).
Preference of nationality: British, Irish.
Qualifications: BA/Higher diploma in English/TEFL qualification.
Conditions of employment: minimum 8¹/2 month contracts. 25 h.p.w. Pupils aged 8-18.
Salary: dr230,000 per month plus holiday bonuses totalling dr2,300,000.
Facilities/Support: accommodation available: 1 bedroom furnished flat offered to each couple. Training provided.
Recruitment: adverts in *TES*. Interviews sometimes carried out in UK as well as in Athens. Photo and CV necessary.

LORD BYRON SCHOOL OF ENGLISH
104 Tsimiski St, 54622 Thessaloniki. Tel: (31) 278804/268647. Fax: (31) 234598.
Number of teachers: 22.
Preference of nationality: Greek, British and other EU.
Qualifications: university degree and TEFL certificate.
Conditions of employment: 8 month contracts (October to May). Students from ages 7 to 70.
Salary: varies according to experience and age (dr2,600-dr3,000 per hour).
Facilities/Support: no assistance with accommodation. Training given.
Recruitment: via British universities and TEFL training centres. Interviews essential and sometimes available in the UK.
Contact: Harry Nikolaides, Director of Studies.

OMIROS ASSOCIATION
52 Academias St, 106 79 Athens. Tel: (1) 36 22 887. Fax: (1) 36 21 833. E-mail: omiros@omiros.gr. Website: www.omiros.gr.
Number of teachers: an average of 10 at each of the Association's 120 schools in Greece.
Preference of nationality: British.
Qualifications: BA and experience of TEFL.
Conditions of employment: 8-10 month contracts. About 20 h.p.w. Pupils range in age from 9-16.

Salary: on application.
Facilities/Support: assistance with accommodation provided in most cases. Teacher training facilities available in Athens (tel: 1-36 33 242).
Recruitment: adverts in Athens newspapers. Local interviews only between early June and the end of August.

M. PERDIKOPOULOU-NEARCHOU SCHOOL OF FOREIGN LANGUAGES & F.E.
25 Saranta Ekklision, 671 00 Xanthi. Tel: (541) 65010-11. Fax: (541) 78616. E-mail: perd-near@xan.forthnet.gr. Website: www.forthnet.gr/perd-near.
Number of teachers: 2.
Preference of nationality: British, Irish.
Qualifications: experienced TEFL teachers.
Conditions of employment: 1 academic year contracts from 1st October to the end of May. 26-28 h.p.w. Pupils range in age from 8 to 17.
Salary: above the collective labour agreement rate.
Facilities/Support: furnished flat provided.
Recruitment: through *TES*. Interviews not essential.
Contact: Mary Perdikopoulou.

STRATEGAKIS SCHOOLS, FOREIGN LANGUAGES AND COMPUTING
24 Proxenou Koromila St, 546 22 Thessaloniki. Tel: (31) 264276. Fax: (31) 228848. E-mail: stratkey@compulink.gr.
Number of teachers: 25 in 100 schools all over northern Greece.
Preference of nationality: British, Irish only.
Qualifications: BA/MA, PGCE (or equivalent). TEFL qualifications welcomed but not required.
Conditions of employment: 1 academic year renewable contracts. 28 h.p.w. Pupils mainly aged 9-17 although there are also some adult groups.
Salary: dr240,000 per month.
Facilities/Support: accommodation arranged; teacher pays rent. Training provided.
Recruitment: through advertising and UK universities and colleges. Interviews essential and are held in UK, usually in May. Note that the Strategakis School in Athens (6 George St, Canningos Square, 106 77 Athens; 1-36 11 496/36 12 858; fax 1-36 13 251) is a completely separate operation.
Contact: G. A. Tavridi, Assistant General Director.

SYCHRONO SCHOOL OF ENGLISH
20 Konitsis St, Veria 591 00. Tel/fax: (331) 29384. E-mail: bouksyche@otenet.gr.
Number of teachers: 1 or 2.
Preference of nationality: British, Irish.
Qualifications: BA or BSc with TEFL Certificate. Must be in perfect health and less than 30.
Conditions of employment: 8 month contracts from mid-September to May. 25-30 h.p.w. Also run summer courses in August and September.
Salary: dr2,200 per hour, less 18% deductions.
Facilities/Support: free accommodation provided (bills payable by teacher). Help with working papers.
Recruitment: personal interview not necessary.
Contact: Mrs. Helen Bakaloudi, Owner.

EVA TSOPANAKOS-VENIZELOU FRONTISTERIA
19 Yiannitsi St, 341 00 Chalkis. Tel: (221) 77744. Fax: (221) 85523. E-mail: venipan@otenet.gr
Number of teachers: 6.
Preference of nationality: British, American.
Qualifications: degree plus Cambridge Cert. or equivalent minimum.
Conditions of employment: minimum 2 year contracts. 20-25 h.p.w. Pupils from 7 years.

Salary: negotiable.
Facilities/Support: assistance given with accommodation and training.
Recruitment: adverts. Local interviews essential.

Other Schools to Try

Note that these schools did not confirm their teacher requirements for this edition of *Teaching English Abroad*. Upper case entries marked with an asterisk had entries in the last edition (1999); addresses without asterisks have been taken from various sources, such as British Council lists and the *Yellow Pages*.

Michalopoulos School of English, 30 E. Antistasis, 593 00 Alexandria (333-22890/fax 333-26601; micheng@compulink.gr)

Sandra Hays-Papageorgiou, 32004 Aracova, Viotias (267-32045)

C. Petalas English Institute, 3 Tzanetou St, 471 00 Arta (681-24414)

Athens College, PO Box 65005, 15410 Psychico, Athens (1-671 4621/fax 1-647 8156). US-biased institute

Hambakis Institutes, Kar Servias 12-14, 105 62 Athens (1-322 7531-5). Employ 30 teachers in three Athens schools.

Eva Chryssanthopoulou, 6 Ploutonos and Nisi St, Kalamaki, 174 55 Athens (1-983 10 91/931 26 16)

Zoula Language School, A. Andreadi 5, Sanroco Square, 491 00 Corfu (661-39330/35334/fax 661-35894)

Trehas Language Centres, 20 Koundouriotou St, Keratsini (1-43 20 546)

LINDA LEE-NIKOLAOU SCHOOL OF FOREIGN LANGUAGES, 12 P. Tsaldari St, Xylokastro, 204 00 Korinthias (743-24678/61276)

Zavitsanou Language Centre, 3 Mitropoleos St, 311 00 Lefkada (645-24514/fax 645-24877)

Kotanitsi English School, Metsovo   (656-42530/fax   656-42514; julietownsend@hotmail.com)

*KOUTSANTONIS SCHOOL OF LANGUAGES, 35 Gounari Avenue, 262 21 Patras (61-273925/fax 61-224496)

A. Lymberopoulos English Language Institute, 29 Pindarou St, 322 00 Thebes (262-29191)

Italy

After a decline in the Italian EFL industry in the 1990s, language schools in the big cities are once again thriving as Italians have embraced the internet generation. Opportunities for native speaker teachers are again abundant, especially in towns and cities which cannot boast leaning towers, gondolas or coliseums. Small towns in Sicily and Sardinia, in the Dolomites and along the Adriatic have more than their fair share of private language schools and institutes, all catering for Italians who have failed to learn English in the state system. (English teaching in Italian schools is generally acknowledged to be inadequate.)

Prospects for Teachers

A complete range of language schools can be found in Italy, as the Yellow Pages will confirm. At the elite end of the market, there are the schools which belong to AISLI, the Associazione Italiana Scuole di Lingue, which is administered from the *Cambridge Centre of English* in Modena (Via Campanella 16, 41100 Modena). The Secretariat can send a list of the 34 AISLI members (e-mail: aisli@tiscalinet.it; www.eaquals.org/aisli/aisli.htm). Prospective teachers should apply directly to the schools and not to AISLI.

Very strict regulations mean that only ultra-respectable schools can become AISLI members so there are thousands of good schools outside the Association.

AISLI schools normally expect their teachers to have advanced qualifications and in return offer attractive remuneration packages and conditions of employment.

At the other end of the spectrum, there is a host of schools which some might describe as cowboy operations, though these are decreasing in number. The CELTA is very widely recognised and respected in Italy (unlike in France, for instance). US qualifications are much less well known for the simple reason that work permits are virtually impossible for non-EU citizens to obtain.

Finding a job is difficult, whatever the qualifications you have to offer, especially in the popular cities. Sandeha Lynch describes the change he witnessed while working at a language school in Bologna for five years:

> *As the economic crisis of the 1990s began to bite, we found that we could no longer offer contracts but only occasional freelance work. This meant that few of the teachers who came could afford to stay very long (Bologna is notoriously expensive especially for rent). Year by year we gradually received more and more applications by post, from the UK, Ireland, North America, Australasia and even Japan. Some were highly qualified or at least had some experience. We were receiving more than a hundred applications a year. None of them received a reply. In my experience the ones who make it as English teachers are the lucky ones. There are, I think, too many teachers for the capacity of the market and not enough students, for the schools themselves are often under threat of closure. My own school is due to close this winter.*

Not all reports are as gloomy as this one, and a healthy number of schools wanted their job vacancies to be registered in this book and can be seen advertising on the main TEFL websites and relevant journals.

A further problem has been caused by strict employment regulations in Italy which make small companies very reluctant to offer full-time contracts. One expatriate language school owner went so far as to write, 'Unfortunately there are no longer proper jobs in EFL in independent schools as the cost of employment is prohibitive'. Compulsory contributions for social security and expensive perks (such as the compulsory severance pay of one month's pay) make hiring a member of staff very costly. The majority of English teachers in Italy work on a freelance basis with no job security, which is acceptable for those who only want to spend one or two years in the country.

FIXING UP A JOB

In Advance

There is no single compendium of the hundreds of language school addresses in Italy. The British Council offices in Rome, Milan, Naples, Turin and Bologna may be willing to photocopy the relevant Yellow Pages *(Pagine Gialle)*; better still is to go to the Yellow Pages website *www.paginegialle.it* and search under *Scuole di Lingue* in the cities and towns in which you're hoping to work. Make sure you use the Italian version of the name, e.g. Napoli, Venezia, etc. In some cases there will be a link to an advert for a language school possibly with e-mail address.

International language school groups like Benedict Schools (with 19 Italian outlets), Linguarama, Berlitz and inlingua are major providers of English language teaching in Italy. International House has 22 affiliated schools throughout the country. Wall Street Institutes now have about 50 centres in Italy and actively recruit native speakers; the headquarters are in Udine at Via Maniago 2; 0432-481464/ www.wsi.it.

Several Italian-based chains of language schools account for a large number of teaching jobs. But because many of them operate as independent franchises, it is difficult to get a master list of addresses. Chains include the British Schools Group with 70 member schools who carry out a lot of their recruitment through *Saxoncourt & English Worldwide Recruitment.* Another major chain is British Institutes with 50+ and *Oxford Schools* with 15 schools in north eastern Italy (see entry). If you are in Italy, go into a branch of the student tourist bureau CTS, for example at Via Genova 16, 00184 Rome, and ask for the leaflet listing all the British Institutes in Italy. (Most language schools in Italy seem to incorporate the word British, English, Oxford or Cambridge randomly combined with Centre, School or Institute, which can result in confusion.) Individual schools advertise their own job vacancies in the *Guardian, TES* or *EL Prospects* in the spring and summer. For example the Italian Language School in London (53/54 Haymarket, London SW1Y 4RP; 020-7930/fax 020-7930 3714; tefl@italianlanguageschool.co.uk) was repeatedly advertising recently for mother tongue English teachers with experience and a driving licence to teach English in Italy.

The following training centre in Italy also acts as a recruitment agency for state and private schools in Italy: BC English Language Training, C.P. 685, 59100 Prato (0574-21179/fax 0574-443630; bcelt@exnet.it). The director, Claudia Beccheroni, interviews teachers in London in July and September.

On the Spot

The heading *Scuole di Lingue* in the Yellow Pages is the best source of possible employers. There is a useful *English Yellow Pages* but it covers only the north (including Milan, Rome, Florence and Bologna). When Bruce Nairne and Sue Ratcliffe went job-hunting in Italy a few years ago, they relied on the Yellow Pages as a source of potential employers:

> *Rather unimaginatively we packed our bags and made for Italy in the middle of the summer holidays when there was no teaching work at all. Nevertheless we utilised the Yellow Pages in the SIP telephone office in Syracuse and proceeded to make 30 speculative applications, specifying our status as graduates who had completed a short course in TEFL. By the end of September we had received four job offers without so much as an interview.*

Unfortunately the jobs in Bari which they chose to accept never materialised and so they once again resorted to the Yellow Pages, this time in Milan railway station, where they managed to secure the interest of three or four establishments for part-time work.

As mentioned above, part-time work is the best that most can hope for initially. Often a few hours teaching can gradually be built up into a full-time job by those willing to say 'Yes'. If you're there when they need you, you can usually get something. Most find that the longer they stay, the more hours they get, though there is still no job security working this way. The importance of having a firm base from which to look for teaching work and to wait for the hours to accumulate is also stressed by Sandeha Lynch who again is describing the situation in Bologna:

> *Teachers arriving to look for work on the off-chance would camp in tents, hoping that the promise of lots of lessons would become a reality. The unlucky ones caught flu and returned home in debt. The luckier ones managed to work during the peak period of November to February. Those who were taken on temporarily by my school were the ones who had already solved the major problem of accommodation and had ample funds to tide them over until the work began.*

Although it is difficult to get work without TEFL training it is not impossible. Laurence Koe visited all the language schools in Como and Lecco, some of them on several occasions, and was told that he needed a qualification or that he was there at the wrong time (October). After three weeks of making the rounds he was asked to stand in for an absent teacher on one occasion, and this was enough to secure him further part-time work. After a few more weeks he found work teaching an evening class of adults. He began to attend the weekly English Club and was offered a few thousand lire to answer questions on the plot after the showing of a James Bond film. Most towns have an English Club *(Associazione Italo-Britannico)* which may offer conversation classes and employ native speakers on a casual basis.

Scouring adverts in English language newspapers has worked for some. Try the fortnightly publications in Rome *Metropolitan* and *Wanted in Rome*, and also the Italian-language classified ads paper *Porta Portese*. (If you happen to see a request for 'mothers only', this means that they are looking for someone whose mother tongue is English not a female with small children.)

Freelance Teaching

Another possibility is to set up as a freelance tutor, though a knowledge of Italian is even more of an asset here than it is for jobs in schools. You can post notices in supermarkets, tobacconists, primary and secondary schools, etc. In Rome, the notice board at International House's training centre (Accademia Britannica, Viale Manzoni 22, 00185 Rome) displays requests for teachers. Also in Rome, check out the notice boards at English language bookshops like the Lion Bookshop on Via Babuina and the Economy Bookshop on Via Torino, or frequent the right pubs such as Ned Kelly's near Palazzo Valdassini and Miscellania near the Pantheon. University students looking for private tuition might consult the notice boards at the Citta Universitaria.

Porta Portese is also a good forum in which to advertise your availability to offer English lessons in Rome; adverts placed by women should not betray their gender and meetings with prospective clients should not take place in private homes. It cost Dustie Hickey about £15 to advertise in four editions of the free paper in Rimini. As long as you have access to some premises, you can try to arrange both individual and group lessons, though competition is so cut-throat in some places that hourly fees are less than they used to be, starting at about L14,000 and going up to L45,000 an hour in Rome.

Whatever way you decide to look for work, remember that life grinds to a halt in August, just as in France. Competition is keenest in Rome, Florence and Venice, so new arrivals should head elsewhere. Peter Penn recommends Trieste where he was offered two jobs with no experience.

Universities throughout Italy employ foreigners as *lettori* (readers/lecturers) who teach English as well as other subjects such as business and science in English. There are probably around 1,000 *lettori* on yearly contracts (maximum three years) earning about the same as EFL teachers in private institutes. Although personal recommendation often plays a part in getting this work, it may be worth contacting various faculties directly and asking for work, preferably in September/October. After flouting EU legislation for many years, Italian universities have recently come into line and are starting to accord the same status and benefits to foreign teachers as to Italian ones.

REGULATIONS

The bureaucratic procedures for EU nationals have become easier in recent years. Teachers must take their passport and letter of employment to the local *Questura* (police department) to obtain a *permesso di soggiorno* (residence permit). Ideally, they will also obtain a *libretto di lavoro* (work permit) from the local *Ispettorato del Lavoro* and/or *Ufficio Collocamento* which generally involves much queuing and a wait of several months. It is helpful if you have with you your university diploma, Cambridge or Trinity Certificate and birth certificate (originals rather than copies, and preferably authenticated by the Italian Consulate in your home country).

As mentioned above, non-EU citizens have very little chance of getting their papers in order unless they get a firm offer of a job while they are still in their home country. According to the Italian Embassy in Washington, language teachers from the US need a visa for *lavoro subordinato*. To qualify they must first obtain from their employer in Italy an authorisation to work issued by the Ministry of Labour or a Provincial Office of Labour *(Servizio politiche del lavoro)* plus an authorisation from the local *Questura*. The originals of these plus a passport and one photo must be sent to the applicant's nearest Embassy or Consulate.

Tax is a further headache for long-stay teachers. As soon as you sort out the work documents, you should obtain a tax number *(codice fiscale)*. The rate of income tax *(Ritenuta d'Acconto)* is usually about 20% in addition to social security deductions of up to 10%.

CONDITIONS OF WORK

A good salary for a full-time timetable would be about L2,000,000 net per month (roughly £600) though many novice teachers earn less. Staff on a *contratto di collaborazione* are paid by the hour, normally ranging from L18,000 to L25,000 net. Always find out if pay scales are quoted net or gross, since the two figures are so different. Take-home pay is not as high as might have been expected because of the high cost of compulsory national insurance, social security and pension contributions. Salaries tend to be substantially higher in northern Italy than in the south to compensate for the much higher cost of living. Some teachers in Rome, Milan, Bologna, etc. have had to reconcile themselves to spending up to half their salaries on rent.

Only professional teachers will benefit from the *Contratto Collettivo Nazionale del Lavoro* (CCLN) which sets a high salary for a regulation 100-hour working month. Many schools hiring native-speaker teachers claim that they offer a 'British contract,' i.e. one that is not subject to Italian legislation. Because of the high costs of legal employment, there is still a lot of dubious practice in Italy and prospective teachers should try to talk to an ex-teacher before committing themselves, especially if offered a job before arrival. Rhys Sage was disappointed at the discrepancy between what he had been promised by a language institute in Chivasso near Torino and what he found when he arrived:

> *They had given a glowing description of the locality and of the cost of living, of the flat they were offering and of the high wages. Upon arrival, it transpired that the wages were minimal, the prices quite high and the flat shoddy. The toilet didn't work and neither did the heating. The school also wanted L500,000 in advance for the first month and would then deduct from my salary for the rent. When I discovered the extent to which I'd been told a tissue of lies, I regretted going to Chivasso and left. In the end my Italian trip turned into a holiday.*

Few teachers complain about their students. Even when pupils attend English classes for social reasons (as many do in small towns with little nightlife) or are generally unmotivated, they are normally good-natured, hospitable and talkative in class. In contrast to Greece, many language school directors are British rather than local.

LEISURE TIME

Italian culture and life style do not need to have their praises sung here. A large number of teachers who have gone out on short-term contracts never come back – probably a higher proportion than in any other country. While rents are high, eating out is cheap and wonderful and public transport is quite affordable. Women teachers should be prepared to cope with some Mediterranean *machismo,* particularly in the south.

Compared to many languages, Italian is easy to learn, though courses are expensive. It may be possible to swap English lessons for Italian ones, which might lead to further freelance teaching.

LIST OF SCHOOLS
ACCADEMIA BRITANNICA
Merry del Val 2, Piazza Pio X1 62, 00165 Rome. Tel: (06) 662 6722. Fax: (06) 660 13006. E-mail: mdv2@iol.it.
Preference of nationality: none, but must be native speakers.
Qualifications: CELTA minimum.
Conditions of employment: work is on a freelance basis and involves teachers working for more than one school. Teachers are employed generally during the period from late September to the following June.
Salary: varies.
Facilities/Support: no assistance provided with accommodation.
Recruitment: teachers should send CV prior to September. The school is closed during the month of August.
Contact: Audrey Jones, Director of Studies.

A.C.L.E. – SUMMER & CITY CAMPS
Via Roma 54, 18038 San Remo. Tel/fax: (0184) 506070. E-mail: info@acle.org. Website: www.acle.org.
Number of teachers: 60+ for both day camps and residential camps.
Preference of nationality: all native English speakers.
Qualifications: minimum age 18. Must have experience working with children and ability to teach English through the use of drama and outdoor activities. A fun-loving personality and genuine interest in children, high moral standards and a flexible attitude to work required.
Conditions of employment: 4, 8 or 12 weeks in summer. May involve working in different parts of Italy. Long working hours, including organising activities, lessons, sports and arts. Half-day or full day off each week.
Salary: approximately £400 per month plus full board and performance-related bonus. Travel within Italy paid for.
Facilities/Support: a combined distance and intensive 3-day introductory TEFL course. £30 registration fee plus £120 course fee, inclusive of board and lodging, deducted from wage at end of teaching period. (See entry in *Directory of Introductory Training Courses*). TEFL certificate issued at end of working period.
Recruitment: adverts, internet, word of mouth. Interviews held in UK.

BENEDICT SCHOOLS
Via Crispi 36A, 80122 Naples. Tel/fax: (081) 081 803 83 98. E-mail: benedictschool@libero.it. Also schools at Piazza Primavera, 80038 Pomigliano d'Arco and Via Roma, 72 80021 Afragola.
Number of teachers: 10-15 full-time teachers and freelancers.
Preference of nationality: none (no assistance given with work permits).
Qualifications: university degree, TEFL and minimum 1 year's experience.
Conditions of employment: 9 month contracts. 100 h.p.m.
Salary: L800,000 per month, plus free accommodation and utilities, Italian course and flight home at end of contract.
Facilities/Support: training in the Benedict method given.
Recruitment: via agency or direct.
Contact: Carmen Elsa Clemente, Manager.

BENEDICT SCHOOL
Via Salara 36, 48100 Ravenna. Tel: (0544) 38199. Fax: (0544) 38399. E-mail: benedict@linknet.it. Website: www.romagna.com/benedict.
Number of teachers: 5 full-time, some freelancers.
Preference of nationality: British but other nationalities considered.
Qualifications: university degree plus CELTA or equivalent required. Minimum 2 years experience.
Conditions of employment: minimum 6 month contracts, renewable. 25-30 h.p.w.

Salary: according to experience and qualifications.
Facilities/Support: assistance with finding accommodation. Training available.
Recruitment: via agencies, ads in *TES*r training schools in UK or CVs received directly. Interviews necessary and are sometimes held in the UK.
Contact: Mirella Pin, Director.

BRITISH INSTITUTES
Via Leopardi, 8, 20123 Milan. Tel: 02 4390041. Fax: 02 43 90031. E-mail: info@British.Institutes.it. Website: www.Britishinstitutes.org.
Number of teachers: 10-20.
Preference of nationality: none.
Qualifications: TEFL Cert. and teaching experience.
Conditions of employment: 9-10 months (scholastic year). Varied hours from 9am to 9.20pm during which opening times contract workers do 28 hours teaching per week.
Salary: contract workers L1,800,000 per month; freelance L21,000-L26,000 net per hour.
Facilities/Support: flats can be provided and the rent is deducted directly from the salary.
Recruitment: word of mouth, advertising in Italy and UK, direct recruiting in the UK.
Contact: Jennifer Ferlez.

THE BRITISH INSTITUTES
Via Aurelia 137, Rome. Tel: (06) 393 75 966 (5 lines). Fax: (06) 393 75 804. E-mail: britishroma@euol.it.
Number of teachers: 70 per year (including part-time teachers).
Preference of nationality: none.
Qualifications: university degree plus serious TEFL course and experience. Knowledge of Italian is valuable.
Conditions of employment: minimum one academic year. Lessons offered 8am-9pm Monday-Saturday.
Salary: varies according to experience, normally L18,000 per hour net.
Facilities/Support: assistance with accommodation. No assistance with residence/work permits. One-week pre-service training course held last week of September or first week of October.
Recruitment: word of mouth. Most candidates are interviewed in person.
Contact: Tina Conte D'Amico, Director.

BRITISH SCHOOL OF MONZA
Via Zucchi 38, 20052 Monza (MI). Tel: (039) 389803. Fax: (039) 230 2047. E-mail: Risales@tin.it.
Number of teachers: 5.
Preference of nationality: EU.
Qualifications: university degree plus CELTA required.
Conditions of employment: 10 month UK contracts. 25 h.p.w.
Salary: L1,500,000 per month.
Facilities/Support: assistance with finding accommodation. Training given.
Recruitment: via UK recruitment agency, so interviews can take place in UK as well as locally.
Contact: Richard Sales, Director.

BRITISH SCHOOL, VICENZA
Viale Roma 8, 36100 Vicenza. Tel: (0444) 542190. Fax: (0444) 323444. E-mail: elsa@protec.it. Other schools: British Centre, Piazza Lamarmora 12, 10015 Ivrea. Tel: (0125) 641618. Fax: (0125) 40242; British Centre, Via Tripoli 27, 15100 Alessandria. Tel/fax: (0131) 263475.
Number of teachers: 15 for three schools.

Preference of nationality: must have an EU passport.
Qualifications: degree, Cert TEFL and 1-2 years experience plus good Italian.
Conditions of employment: Sept 15th to June 15th. 25 h.p.w. Mainly evening work (to 10pm).
Salary: L1,800,000 (net) per month plus L2,700,000 (net) in bonuses over the contract period.
Facilities/Support: school accommodation available in Vicenza (though not always available to new teachers). In other locations, school advertises and contacts accommodation agencies on teacher's behalf.
Recruitment: via *Guardian* adverts and Saxoncourt & English Worldwide recruitment agency. Most teachers are interviewed in London.
Contact: John Byrne, Director.

BRITISH s.r.l.
Via XX Settembre 12, 16121 Genoa. Tel: (010) 593591/562621. Fax: (010) 562621.
Number of teachers: 12.
Preference of nationality: EU only.
Qualifications: BA plus CELTA and minimum experience. Italian useful.
Conditions of employment: 25+ h.p.w. between mid-September and mid-June. Most pupils aged 18-30.
Salary: variable according to hours worked.
Facilities/Support: assistance given with accommodation, teaching materials and course programming.
Recruitment: interviews not essential, but usually take place in Italy.
Contact: Daniela Multari, Director of Studies.

BYRON LANGUAGE DEVELOPMENT
Via Sicilia 125, 00187 Rome. Tel: 06 42 01 44 36. Fax: 06-42012537. E-mail: byron.lang@flashnet.it. Website: www.byronschool.it.
Number of teachers: 30.
Preference of nationality: none.
Qualifications: degree and Cert. TEFL. Minimum of three years' teaching experience.
Conditions of employment: indefinite. Usually freelance.
Salary: L29,000 (net). 24 hours teaching per week average.
Facilities/support: no assistance with accommodation.
Recruitment: CV, interview and test.
Contact: Jayne Chivers.

CAMBRIDGE CENTRE OF ENGLISH
Via Campanella 16, 41100 Modena. Tel: (059) 241004. Fax (059) 224238. E-mail: norris@tin.it. Website: www.cambridgecentre.com.
Number of teachers: 8.
Preference of nationality: British.
Qualifications: BA plus TEFL certificate and 2 years' experience.
Conditions of employment: permanent full-time or part-time. Pupils of all ages from 8.
Salary: from L1,850,000 (gross) per month. 14 months pay. 9 weeks paid holiday and social security increments for higher qualifications and experience.
Recruitment: through recommendation and direct application, often via other AISLI schools. Interviews sometimes held in UK.

CAMBRIDGE INSTITUTE
Viale Cappuccini 45, 66034 Lanciano (CH). Tel: (0872) 710291. Also branch at Corso Garibaldi 38, Ortona (085-906 4010).
Number of teachers: 4-7.
Qualifications: TOEFL/TEFL qualification.
Conditions of employment: one year contracts. 15-30 h.p.w.

Salary: L1,600,000 per month net.
Facilities/Support: assistance with accommodation and work permits. Training available.
Recruitment: adverts in *Guardian* and via word of mouth. Interviews can sometimes be arranged in UK, and are not always essential.
Contact: Principal.

CAMBRIDGE SCHOOL
Via Mercanti 36, 84100 Salerno. Tel: (089) 228942. Fax: (089) 252523. E-mail: annadem@box.1.tiu.it.
Number of teachers: 5.
Preference of nationality: British.
Qualifications: BA plus CELTA (grade B) plus 12 months' experience.
Conditions of employment: 9-10 month renewable contracts. 25 contact h.p.w. Pupils aged 6-60. Authorised centre of University of Cambridge Local Examinations Syndicate.
Salary: competitive and augmented with accommodation allowance.
Facilities/Support: assistance with accommodation. Regular in-house training.
Recruitment: direct. Interviews essential.

THE CAMBRIDGE SCHOOL
Via San Rocchetto 3, 37121 Verona. Tel: (045) 800 3154. Fax: (045) 801 4900. E-mail: info@cambridgeschool.it. Website: www.cambridgeschool.it.
Member of AISLI.
Number of teachers: 12-15.
Preference of nationality: none, but should be native speaker.
Qualifications: CELTA (or similar), degree and preferably two years' experience.
Conditions of employment: 9 months for 10/15 or 20 hours per week. Hours are mainly evenings from 5-10pm.
Salary: depends on hours, qualifications and experience.
Facilities/Support: the school has one apartment which can be shared by two teachers, otherwise assistance given with finding accommodation. School runs CELTA courses (see *Training*). On-going assistance and training.
Recruitment: on presentation at the school.
Contact: Paul Childs, Director of Studies.

CENTRO LINGUISTICO BRITISH INSTITUTES
Corso Umberto I, 17 - 62012 Civitanova Marche (MC). Tel/fax: (0733) 816197 and via Carducci 21, 62100 Macerata. Tel/fax: 0733 231364. E-mail: bidimccm@tin.it/centrolimc@tiscalinet.it.
Number of teachers: 10.
Preference of nationality: British.
Qualifications: BA essential (MA preferred) and TEFL Certificate or Diploma.
Conditions of employment: 8 month contracts from October. 20 h.p.w. minimum.
Salary: L1,700,000 per month.
Facilities/Support: training available, free Italian lessons, assistance with finding accommodation.
Recruitment: phone interviews are possible.
Contact: Loretta Muzi, Director.

CLM-BELL (Centro di Lingue Moderne/Bell Educational Trust)
Via Pozzo 30, 38100 Trento. Tel: (0461) 981733. Fax: (0461) 981687. E-mail: clm-bell@eclipse-net.it. Website: www.pegasomedia.it/clm-bell.
Member of AISLI and EAQUALS.
Number of teachers: 22 (including German, French and Spanish).
Preference of nationality: EU.
Qualifications: university degree, CELTA, DELTA.
Conditions of employment: permanent contracts (full/part-time). 22 contact h.p.w.

Pupils aged from 5.
Salary: from £840 per month.
Facilities/Support: assistance given with finding accommodation.
Recruitment: direct application.

COFIMP
Consorzio per la Formazione e lo Sviluppo delle Piccole e Medie Imprese, Via Sebastiano Serlio 24/2, 40128 Bologna. Fax: 051 360757. E-mail: languages@cofimp.it. Website: www.cofimp.it.
Number of teachers: 15.
Preference of nationality: UK and US.
Qualifications: BA degree plus a TEFL Cert. minimum.
Conditions of employment: 40 teaching hours per course.
Salary: approx. L2,000,000 for a 40-hour course.
Facilities/Support: no assistance with accommodation.
Recruitment: usually those who are already resident in Italy. Interviews are essential.
Contact: Prof. G Mattioli.

DARBY SCHOOL OF LANGUAGES
Via Mosca 51, Villino 15, 00142 Rome. Tel: 06-51962205; Fax: 06-51965012. E-mail: darbyschool@tin.it.
Number of teachers: 30-40.
Preference of nationality: none, but must be native speaker.
Qualifications: TEFL Cert.
Conditions of employment: freelance. Teachers can choose their hours which normally are an average of 20-25 hours per week. More hours available if wanted.
Salary: the average salary of about 2 million lire is sufficient and more to live on in Italy.
Facilities/Support: new teachers are helped to find accommodation.
Recruitment: relevant CVs and friendly personality. Interviews.
Contact: Gilda Darby.

THE ENGLISH CENTRE
via P. Paoli 34, 07100 Sassari. Tel: 079 23 21 54. Fax 079 232 180. E-mail: theenglishcentre@tin.it.
Number of teachers: 8.
Preference of nationality: British.
Qualifications: Cambridge Cert. plus 2 years' experience.
Conditions of employment: 10 months contract. 25 teaching hours per week.
Salary: L1,700,000-L2,200,000 net.
Facilities/Support: shared flat available for 2 new teachers.
Recruitment: through Saxoncourt agency in London.
Contact: Paul Rogerson.

ENGLISH INSTITUTE
Piazza Garibaldi 60, 80142 Naples. Tel: (081) 287002. Fax: (081) 5548745. E-mail: sadra@iol.it. Website: www.paginegialle.it/sadra.
Number of teachers: 4.
Preference of nationality: English.
Qualifications: TEFL Cert.
Conditions of employment: 10 month contracts. Timetable between 9am and 9pm, depending on demand.
Salary: L20,000 per hour net.
Facilities/Support: assistance with finding accommodation and obtaining permits. Training available.
Recruitment: direct application with CVs and TEFL Certificates. Interviews essential.

Contact: Al Sacco, Director of Studies.

THE ENGLISH INSTITUTE
Corso Gelone 82, 96100 Siracusa. Tel/fax: (0931) 60875. E-mail: englishb@tin.it.
Number of teachers: 5.
Preference of nationality: British, American or others with English as mother tongue.
Qualifications: minimum 1 but preferably 2 years' experience in EFL teaching.
Conditions of employment: 8½ months from September/October. 27 h.p.w. mostly in early evening (4-9pm). Some morning work but no weekends. Children's classes (from age 6) and adult classes up to First Certificate level.
Salary: L1,100,000 per month (net).
Facilities/Support: free accommodation. Training available.
Recruitment: adverts in *TES*. Phone interviews possible.
Contact: Mr. Armand Giardina, Director.

ENGLISH SCHOOL
Via dei Correttori 6, 89127 Reggio Calabria. Tel/fax: (0965) 899535.
Belongs to British Schools Group.
Number of teachers: 4.
Preference of nationality: none, though procedures are easier for EU nationals.
Qualifications: minimum requirements are degree, CELTA and 1 year's experience.
Conditions of employment: UK employment contract. UK PAYE and National Insurance contributions paid in the UK by the employer. 9-month renewable contracts (October-June). 28 h.p.w. Children, teens and adults divided into 8 different levels.
Salary: approximately £500 per month (net).
Facilities/Support: assistance given with accommodation. No training.
Recruitment: advertisements and recruitment agencies. Interviews are sometimes held in the UK, but are not essential.
Contact: Maria A. Rizzo, Director.

THE ENGLISH SCHOOL
Viale Roosevelt 14, 67039 Sulmona (AQ). Tel/fax: (0864) 55606.E-mail mdicio@arc.it.
School is authorised by the Ministry of Education.
Number of teachers: 3-4.
Preference of nationality: none.
Qualifications: university degree and TEFL certificate required. 1-2 years' experience working abroad.
Conditions of employment: 8-month contracts October to May. Mainly afternoon and evening classes. Students aged 7-70 (mainly adults).
Salary: minimum £6-£7 per hour (net).
Facilities/Support: assistance with finding accommodation. Training available. CD Rom, computers, etc.
Recruitment: adverts in newspaper. Telephone interviews possible.
Contact: Tania Pugielli.

GREYHOUND LANGUAGE SCHOOL
Via Castellani 9, 15100 Alessandria (AL). Tel: (0131) 31 70 19. Fax: (0131) 23 47 87. E-mail: ghound@tin.it.
Number of teachers: 2/3.
Preference of nationality: none; must be native speaker.
Qualifications: university degree, CELTA (equivalent or higher).
Conditions of employment: full-time and part-time contracts. Maximum 7 hours per day in 2 of 3 possible blocks. Pupils range from children to adult professionals.
Salary: negotiable (according to experience and qualifications)
Facilities/Support: assistance with accommodation.

Recruitment: via network of contacts. Interviews essential in Italy or UK.
Contact: Robert Hunter, Director.

INTERLANGUAGE POINT
Corso Vittorio Emanuele 14, 84100 Salerno. Tel: (089) 275 3581. Fax: (089) 275 3581.
Number of teachers: varies.
Preference of nationality: none, but should be native speaker.
Qualifications: CELTA or similar with some experience if possible. Knowledge of Italian language useful but not essential.
Conditions of employment: teaching children and adults. 20 hours weekly with possibility of additional hours.
Salary: L1,200,000 per month minimum for 20 hours teaching per week.
Recruitment: via the internet (e.g. www.jobs.edunet.com).

INTERLINGUE SCHOOL OF LANGUAGES
Via E.Q. Visconti 20, 00193 Rome. Tel: (06) 321 5740/321 0317. Fax: (06) 323 5709. E-mail: interlingue@interlingue-it.com.
Number of teachers: about 15 teachers per year.
Preference of nationality: none.
Qualifications: English degree or B.Ed. and/or TEFL Cert. Teaching experience is definitely appreciated but not essential.
Conditions of employment: teachers stay for an academic year. Part-time contract 15/20 hours a week. Full-time contract 30/35 hours per week.
Salary: L18,750-L25,000 (gross) per hour.
Facilities/Support: no assistance with accommodation.
Recruitment: on spec applications and CVs. Prior to the final selection, there are three interviews, one of which is a trial lesson. Assistance can be given with work permits for North Americans; however, the procedure is lengthy.
Contact: Liddia Socci.

INTERNATIONAL BRITISH SCHOOL
Via Argine destro Annunziata, 13, 89121 Reggio Calabria. Tel : (0965) 20024. Fax: (0965) 28000. E-mail: ibs@diel.it.
Number of teachers: 4.
Preference of nationality: none.
Qualifications: university degree plus CELTA.
Conditions of employment: 9 month contracts; some UK, some Italian contracts. 25 h.p.w.
Salary: L1,400,000 per month (net).
Facilities/Support: assistance with finding accommodation. British School training courses available.
Recruitment: via agency, adverts and internet. Interviews are available in UK.
Contact: Cristina Willauer, Principal.

INTERNATIONAL HOUSE (CAMPOBASSO)
Via Zurlo 5, 86100 Campobasso. Tel/fax: (0874) 63240/481321. E-mail: britannica@moldat.molisedati.it.
Number of teachers: 10-15 (for summer camp in Campitello in the Apennines).
Preference of nationality: British.
Qualifications: TEFL qualification essential, and experience on summer camps and/or teaching children and teenagers. Interest in sports and outdoor activities valuable asset.
Conditions of employment: contract of 6 weeks from end of June to early August. 4 hours teaching per day plus 2 afternoons per week for activities and evening activities. Pupils aged 8-16.
Salary: approximately £800.
Facilities/Support: accommodation provided with all meals.

Recruitment: through IH London or direct application.
Contact: Mary Ricciardi.

INTERNATIONAL HOUSE (PALERMO)
Via Gaetano Daita 29, 90139 Palermo. Tel: (091) 584954. Fax: (091) 323965. E-mail: ihpa1@gestelnet.it.
Number of teachers: 12-13.
Preference of nationality: British; others considered (preferably European passport).
Qualifications: degree and CELTA (minimum grade 'B'). School interested in career teachers only.
Conditions of employment: 9 month contracts. 25 h.p.w. normally 1-9.30pm.
Salary: L1,800,000 (net) plus increments.
Facilities/Support: assistance with finding accommodation. Weekly seminars and workshops. School will subsidise in-service Diploma course by distance learning for suitable candidates.
Recruitment: via IH London or directly. Interviews essential.

INTERNATIONAL HOUSE (SEREGNO)
Accademia Britannica Srl, Via Gozzano 4/6, 20038 Seregno (MI). Tel: (0362) 230970. Fax: (0362) 328278. E-mail: ih_seregno@galactica.it.
Member of AISLI.
Number of teachers: 10.
Preference of nationality: British.
Qualifications: degree and CELTA with 1-2 years' experience minimum. DELTA preferred.
Conditions of employment: 1-2 year renewable contracts. 24 h.p.w. Pupils of all ages. Some in-company teaching (for which driving licence is needed).
Salary: approximately L1,500,000 (net) per month.
Facilities/Support: assistance given with accommodation, though it is expensive and difficult to find. Training given.
Recruitment: via IH London.
Contact: Marcella Banchetti.

INTERNATIONAL LANGUAGE SCHOOL
Via Tibullo 10, 00193 Rome. Tel: (06) 68 30 77 96. Fax: (06) 68 69 758. E-mail: ILS@ggg.it. Website: www.ggg.it/ils.
Number of teachers: 20.
Preference of nationality: none.
Qualifications: degree and CELTA or similar.
Conditions of employment: 2 year contracts. Hours of teaching normally 1-9pm.
Salary: L1,460,000 per month.
Facilities/Support: assistance given with accommodation if needed. Training given.
Recruitment: by direct application. Interviews sometimes held in UK.
Contact: Giuseppina Foti, Director.

THE INTERNATIONAL SCHOOL
Via Garibaldi 4, 07026 Olbia, Sardinia. Tel/fax: (0789) 21578. E-mail: xischool@tin.it.
Number of teachers: 7-8.
Preference of nationality: none.
Qualifications: university degree plus good TEFL course and teaching experience. Must have EU passport.
Conditions of employment: all teachers subject to *Contratto Nazionale* between October 1st and May 31st.
Salary: L1,700,000 per month (net) plus bonuses, travel allowance, health insurance and pension plan.

Facilities/Support: pre-service training course given. Complete assistance with work permits and affordable accommodation given.
Recruitment: direct application with CV and photo.
Contact: Christina Starr Bonacossa.

KEEP TALKING
Via Roma 60, 33100 Udine. Tel: (0432) 5015256. Tel/fax: (0432) 505016. E-mail: info@keeptalking.it. Website: www.keeptalking.it.
Number of teachers: 10 in 2 schools.
Preference of nationality: none but must be native speakers.
Qualifications: university degree and CELTA or equivalent required plus minimum 1 year of experience.
Conditions of employment: 9 month contracts (*contratto di collaborazione*). Min. 700-800 hours per year. 25 h.p.w. Lessons mostly at lunchtimes and evenings till 9.30pm and Saturday mornings.
Salary: starting hourly wage of L25-28,000 (net); monthly L2,080,000-L2,330,000 depending on qualifications and experience.
Facilities/Support: training seminars once a month. Excellent facilities. Income tax, pension, medical/accident insurance paid by employer.
Recruitment: adverts in the *Guardian* and via internet (www.eslcafe.com).

THE LANGUAGE CENTRE
Vicolo Becchini 2, 42100 Reggio Emilia. Tel: (0522) 451622. Fax: (0522) 442801. E-mail: oise@pronet.it.
Number of teachers: 10.
Preference of nationality: British.
Qualifications: degree with CELTA plus lots of enthusiasm.
Conditions of employment: contract from end September to end June. 25/30 hours per week, mornings, afternoons and evenings.
Salary: L30,000 per hour less 20% tax and 12% pension contributions.
Facilities/Support: assistance with finding accommodation.
Recruitment: *The Guardian* newspaper, TEFL Website, internet.
Contact: Susan Morrison, Director of Studies.

LIVING LANGUAGES SCHOOL
Via Magna Grecia 2, 89100 Reggio Calabria. Tel/fax: (0965) 330926.
Number of teachers: 7.
Preference of nationality: mother tongue speakers of English.
Qualifications: TEFL, CELTA.
Conditions of employment: 9 month renewable contracts. Teaching hours from 3-9pm Monday to Friday.
Salary: L1,400,000 (net) per month.
Facilities/Support: help given with accommodation.
Recruitment: via adverts. Interviews sometimes carried out in UK.

LORD BYRON COLLEGE
Via Sparano 102, 70121 Bari. Tel: (080) 523 2686. Fax: (080) 524 1349. E-mail: lordbyron@mail3.clio.it/ johncredico@lordbyroncollege.com.
Number of teachers: 32.
Preference of nationality: British.
Qualifications: should be aged 24-29. Degree plus TEFL Certificate or PGCE needed plus one year's teaching experience abroad and knowledge of a foreign language.
Conditions of employment: 1 or 2 year renewable contracts. 27¹/2 h.p.w. 1,200 students of all ages and levels but mainly aged 19-30.
Salary: from approximately L1,600,000 (net) per month.
Facilities/Support: free basic Italian course and free in-house Trinity College TESOL Diploma course. Large self-access centre with videoclub and CD ROM.

Recruitment: adverts in *Guardian* or apply directly with full CV, photo, references, copies of degree/TEFL certificates. Interviews and hiring mainly in June and December.
Contact: John Credico, Director of Studies.

OXFORD INSTITUTE
10/12 Via Adriatica 10/12, 73100 Lecce. Tel: (0832) 390312. Fax: (0832) 390312.
Number of teachers: 15.
Preference of nationality: none.
Qualifications: CELTA plus 2 years' experience.
Conditions of employment: 9-month contracts October to June. 30 h.p.w.
Salary: L1,300,000 (net).
Facilities/Support: free accommodation provided. Help given with obtaining all necessary documents. Training available.
Recruitment: adverts in *Guardian* and interviews in London.
Contact: Elizabeth Blackwood, Director of Studies.

OXFORD SCHOOL OF ENGLISH s.r.l.
Administrative Office, Via S. Pertini 14, 30035 Mirano, Venice. Tel/fax: (041) 570 23 55. E-mail: oxseitad@mi.sctrade.it. Website: www.oxforditalia.it.
Number of teachers: 20-30 for 15 schools in northeast Italy of which 10 are independent franchises (60-70 teachers employed altogether).
Preference of nationality: British.
Qualifications: degree, TEFL and knowledge of Italian needed.
Conditions of employment: 9 month contracts or longer. 22 h.p.w.
Salary: varies according to hours and length of contract. Deductions of 20% for tax.
Facilities/Support: accommodation at teacher's own expense, but school will help to find it.
Recruitment: interviews in London from mid-May or Italy.
Contact: Philip Panter, Administrator.

OXFORD SCHOOL OF LANGUAGES
Via Garibaldi 108, 06034 Foligno. Fax: (0742) 357430. E-mail: italiaum@tin.it.
Preference of nationality: EU.
Qualifications: TEFL qualification and experience.
Conditions of employment: full-time contract October-May.
Salary: L2,000,000 per month.
Recruitment: adverts in the *Guardian*.

PROLINGUA
via Angelo Ranucci 5, 00165 Rome. Tel: (06) 39367721. Fax: (06) 393 67723. Tel: info@linguapro.com. Website: www.linguapro.com.
Number of teachers: 15.
Preference of nationality: none, but should be native speaker.
Qualifications: a teaching certificate and/or several years' experience.
Conditions of employment: initial contract is 3 months. School hours are 9am-1pm, 1pm-5pm and 5pm to 9pm.
Salary: depends on experience.
Facilities/Support: the school has a department which deals with housing.
Recruitment: newspaper advertisements.
Contact: Damien O'Farrell, Marketing Director.

REGENCY SCHOOL
Via Arcivescovado 7, 10121 Torino. Tel: (011) 562 7456. Fax: (011) 541845. E-mail: regency@tin.it. Web-site: www.regency.it.
Number of teachers: 30.
Preference of nationality: none.
Qualifications: university degree essential plus CELTA or equivalent or DELTA or equivalent.

Conditions of employment: full-time and part-time contracts. Maximum 7 hours per day in 2 of possible 3 blocks. Pupils range from young children to adult professionals.
Salary: negotiable (according to experience and qualifications).
Facilities/Support: regular seminars and workshops for teachers.
Recruitment: through network of contacts or internet (e.g. www.tefl.net). Interviews essential in Italy or UK.
Contact: John Lewell.

SHENKER INSTITUTE
Via S. Gerardo dei Tintori 1, 20052 Monza. Tel: (039) 386861. Fax: (039) 388905. E-mail: info@shenker.it. Website: www.shenker.it.
Number of teachers: 5.
Preference of nationality: none, though prefer those with permission to work in Italy.
Qualifications: good general education, especially in English. TEFL if possible.
Conditions of employment: minimum 1 year. Timetable varies according to needs.
Salary: varies.
Facilities/Support: assistance with finding accommodation. Training available.
Recruitment: local adverts and interviews.
Contact: Pauline Austin, Managing Director.

SUMMER CAMPS
Via Roma 54, 18038 San Remo. Tel/fax: (0184) 506070.
See entry for A.C.L.E. above.

THE TRAINING COMPANY
Via XX Settembre 34111, 16124 Genova. Tel: 010 540964. Fax 010 5533167. E-mail: enquiry@thetrainingcompany.org. Website: thetrainingcompany.org.
Number of teachers: 12.
Preference of nationality: none.
Qualifications: CELTA and a year's experience.
Conditions of employment: 8 months. 100 hours per month.
Salary: L1,700,000-L2,100,000 (net).
Facilities/Support: help with finding accommodation given.
Recruitment: internet. Face to face interviews sometimes, but not essential.
Contact: Rita Scontrino.

THE UNITED COLLEGE
Ronco a Via Von Platen 16/18, 96100 Siracusa. Tel/fax: (931) 22000. E-mail: united.college@tin.it.
Number of teachers: 8.
Preference of nationality: none.
Qualifications: degree plus Certificate (Cambridge or TESOL).
Conditions of employment: October-June. Hours between 3pm and 9pm.
Salary: approximately £500 p.m.
Facilities/Support: assistance given with finding accommodation and with obtaining visas (provided teachers bring a copy of their degree and teaching certificate).
Recruitment: via adverts in *Guardian* and *TES*.
Contact: Carolyn Davies, Director of Studies.

WALL STEET INSTITUTE (BERGAMO)
Via Brigata Lupi 6, 24122 Bergamo. Tel: (035) 224531/235442. Fax: (035) 238759. E-mail: emma@uninetcom.it.
Number of teachers: 8-10.
Preference of nationality: EU nationals.
Qualifications: qualified teachers with EFL experience. Business English preferred.
Conditions of employment: October-June. 24 h.p.w.. Extra hours when required.

In-house and in-company teaching between Monday and Saturday morning.
Facilities/Support: assistance with accommodation if needed. One-week teacher training course at beginning of academic year.
Recruitment: casual enquiries, personal recommendation and direct application. Interviews in Bergamo compulsory.
Contact: Emma Roberts.

WALL STREET INSTITUTE (FERRARA)
Piazzetta Combattenti 6, 44100 Ferrara. Tel: (0532) 200231. Fax: (0532) 209597. E-mail: g.b.italia@fe/nettuno.it.
Number of teachers: 6-7.
Preference of nationality: British.
Qualifications: CELTA or other TEFL qualification; teaching experience, knowledge of Italian.
Conditions of employment: 9 month contracts (October-June). 25 h.p.w. Mostly adults.
Salary: approx. L1,600,000 per month.
Facilities/Support: assistance with finding accommodation and obtaining working papers. No training.
Recruitment: direct application and recruiting agencies.

WALL STREET INSTITUTE (MILAN)
Corso Buenos Aires 79, 20124 Milan. Tel: (02) 670 3108. E-mail: wsi@wsi.it.
Number of teachers: 45.
Preference of nationality: EU countries or those from elsewhere who already have work permits.
Qualifications: CELTA.
Conditions of employment: contracts run until end of June or mid-July. 25 contact h.p.w. teaching adults.
Salary: L1,650,000-L2,400,000 (net) per month.
Facilities/Support: assistance is given finding accommodation. A limited amount of training is available.
Recruitment: through application in person only. Interviews occasionally held in UK.

WASHINGTON SCHOOL
Via del Corso 184, Rome 00186. Tel: (06) 679 3785. Fax: (06) 678 1512. E-mail: informatik@iol.it. Website: www.washingtonschool.it.
Number of teachers: 6-25 (depending on demand for company work).
Preference of nationality: British, Irish.
Qualifications: university degree, CELTA or equivalent, 1 year's experience. Basic Italian useful.
Conditions of employment: freelance teachers only, with hours varying from 4 to 25 p.w.
Salary: L19,000-L21,000 per hour (net) depending on location. Teachers are responsible for paying their own social security.
Facilities/Support: no assistance with accommodation.
Recruitment: local interviews essential.
Contact: S. R. Barley, Director of Studies.

Other Schools to Try (cities and towns in alphabetical order)

Note that these schools did not confirm their teacher requirements for this edition of *Teaching English Abroad.* Upper case entries marked with an asterisk had entries in the last edition (1999); addresses without asterisks have been taken from various sources, such as British Council lists, the AISLI list, *Yellow Pages,* etc.
British Institute of Augusta, Sicily, 0931-521882/fax 0931-978071; britaug@qsconsul.it. Teaching year starts at beginning of October. Contact Ms.

Scicluna. Must have EU passport.

School of Europe, Bari (bmolloy@iol.it)

Anglo American School, Piazza S Giovanni in Monte 9, Bologna (tel/fax 051-238028)

Arts Language B.C., Via Salvini 12, Bologna (tel/fax 051-512634)

Benedict School, Via N. Sauro 1/ 2, Bologna (051-264 788/fax 051-238436; british@posta.alinet.it/ www.paginegialle.it/benedictsc)

Berlitz, Via C Battisti 21, Bologna (0511 261034/051-222336)

Ditchfield & Rossit English Services S.N.C., Via della Ghisiliera 16/A, 40131 Bologna (tel/fax 051-523906; drenglish@bo.flashnet.it/ www.nconsult.com/ drenglish)

English Language Institute, Via Marconi 29, 40122 Bologna (051-236527)

International House (Tradint), Via Jannozzi 6, 20097 San Donato Milanese (02-527 91 24/fax 02-556 00 324; tradint@mv.itline.it). 15 teachers for suburban locations around Milan.

In Lingua, Via Testoni 2, Bologna (051-238022/fax 051-237087)

Modern English Study Centre, Via Borgonuovo 14, 40125 Bologna (051-227523/fax 051-225314; modernenglish@bo.flashnet.it)

Piccadilly School, (051-371065; www.cduno.it)

Politzer School, Via Amendola 16, 40121 Bologna (tel/fax 051-249063)

Victoria Language Centre, Viale G. Fassi 28, 41012 Carpi (Modena) (059-652545/fax 059-652499; victoria@carpi.nettuno.it)

British School of Gorizia, Corso Italia 17, 34170 Gorizia (gorizia@british-fvg.net). AISLI member

International House La Spezia, Via Manzoni 64, 19100 La Spezia (ihspezia@cdh.it). AISLI member

British School of Monfalcone, Via Duca d'Aosta 16, 34074 Monfalcone (monfalcone@british-fvg.net). AISLI member

Callan Method School, Central Milan (nino.casimo@barclays.net)

Connor Language Services, 8 p. Piemonte, 20145 Milan (02-469 5819/fax 02-469 5807; connor@comm2000.it)

Into English, Via Cadorna 5, 20037 Paderno Dugnano (MI) (02-990 43 215/fax 178 223 5867; into.english@tiscalinet.it), 15 minutes north of Milan. Must be available for interview in Milan.

Regent Italia s.r.l., Via Fabio Filzi 27, 20124 Milan (02-670 70516/fax 02-670 73625). Summer, year-long and part-time contracts available.

American Studies Center, 36 V. D'Isernia, Naples (081-550562/ ascnaples@na.nettuno.it)

British Language School, 73 V. Diaz, Portici (NA) (081-480240)

CLM Bell Pergine, Viale Dante Alighieri 1, 38057 Pergine Valsugano (tel/fax 0461-532858; clm-bell@pn.itnet.it). AISLI member

International House Pisa, Via Risorgimento 9, 56126 Pisa (tel/fax 050-44040; ihpisa@alet.it). AISLI member

The Language Centre, Reggio Emilia (oise@pronet.it). General and in-company teaching.

Centro Linguistico Rimini, C. so DiAugusto 144, 47900 Rimini (0541-56487)

CLM-Bell, Via Canella 14, 38066 Riva del Garda (tel/fax 0464-554121). AISLI member.

L'Ateneo Centro Studi Rome, fax 06-231 1945; lateneo@tiscalinet.it or c.studilateneo@mclink.it

British Institute of Rome, Via 4 Fontane 109, 00184 Rome (06-488 1979/fax 06-481 5549). AISLI member

CDC English Language School srl, Via Aureliana 53, 00187 Rome (06-420 03046).

*BERLA B.N.F. de Neil, Ursula & Forte Lucia S.N.C., Vicolo Biscaro 1, 31100 Treviso (tel/fax 0422-544242)

Portugal

Relations between Portugal and Britain have always been warm and the market for English tuition is as buoyant as anywhere in Europe, especially in the teaching of young children. Most schools cater for anyone over the age of seven, so you should be prepared to teach little ones. In fact some schools organise courses in nursery schools for children from the age of four. Furthermore Portugal's economy has taken considerable strides over the past ten years which has created a bigger demand for English for Special Purposes, especially business. One school has even run an 'English for footballers' course.

The vast majority of British tourists flock to the Algarve along the southern coast of Portugal, which means that many Portuguese in the south who aspire to work in the tourist industry want to learn English. Schools like the Wall Street Institutes in Portimao and Faro, the *Centro de Linguas* in Lagos and *Interlingua* in Portimao cater for just that market. But the demand for English teachers is greatest in the north. Apart from in the main cities of Lisbon and Oporto, both of which have British Council offices, jobs crop up in historic provincial centres such as Coimbra (where there is also a British Council) and Braga and in small seaside towns like Aveiro and Póvoa do Varzim. These can be a very welcome destination for teachers burned out from teaching in big cities or first-time teachers who want to avoid the rat-race. The British Council has a fourth office in Parede and English language centres in Almada, Alverca, Cascais (the prosperous seaside suburb of Lisbon), Foz, Faia, Maia, Miraflores and Queluz.

FIXING UP A JOB

Most teachers in Portugal have either answered adverts in the educational press or are working for International House which has nine affiliated schools in Portugal. About three-quarters of all IH students in Portugal are children, so expertise with young learners is a definite asset. Outside the cities where there have traditionally been large expatriate communities, schools cannot depend on English speakers just showing up and so must recruit well in advance of the academic year (late September to the end of June).

Although the *Bristol School Group* is associated with South West English near Bristol (see entry), they prefer to handle applications themselves. (This is the only possibility of which we have heard for working in the Azores, so if you want to work in the most isolated islands in the Atlantic Ocean – over 1,000km west of Portugal – this is your chance.)

Small groups of schools, say six schools in a single region, is the norm in Portugal. A number of the schools listed in the directory at the end of this chapter belong to such mini-chains. One of the most well-established is the *Cambridge Schools* group which every year imports around 100 teachers. Of the international chains, Wall Street Institutes are well represented with 32 centres throughout Portugal; their central telephone number is 800-20 20 40 and e-mail wsi@ mail.telepac.pt.

The British Council offices may have lists of local English language schools in their region, but they probably won't be willing to send them to enquirers. Many schools are small family-run establishments with fewer than ten teachers, so sending off a lot of speculative applications is unlikely to succeed.

As is true anywhere, you might be lucky and fix up something on the spot. In addition to calling at the British Council, check the English language weekly newspaper *Anglo-Portuguese News* which occasionally carries adverts for private tutors (Apartado 113, 2766-902 Estoril; 21-466 1551/apn@mail.telepac.pt). Young people looking for an opportunity to exchange English conversation for room and board with a family might investigate the International Friendship League (R Ruy de Sousa Vinagre 2, 2890 Alcochete; fax 21-234 1082/ifl.por @mail.telepac.pt).

The Cambridge CELTA is widely requested by schools and can be obtained at International House in Lisbon (or part-time in Oporto). At present the Trinity College Certificate course is not offered anywhere in Portugal.

REGULATIONS

The red tape for EU nationals working in Portugal is refreshingly painless. All that is required (as throughout the EU) is to obtain a residence permit after an initial three month stay by taking documents to show proof of accommodation, health insurance and means of support. If they are employed they must show that they have been registered in the social security system and are not being paid less than the Portuguese minimum wage, i.e. 61,300 escudos per month. These must be presented to the local authorities, i.e. any office of the *Serviço de Estrangeiros e Fronteiras* (SEF) or Aliens Office. The headquarters are at Rua Conselheiro José Silvestre Ribeiro 4, 1600-007 Lisbon (21-711 5000).

Although Portugal has been a full member of the European Community since 1992, it has also been possible for Americans and other nationalities to work legally in Portugal (unlike in neighbouring Spain). When the American Richard Spacer was encountering red tape difficulties teaching in Greece, he made enquiries at the Portuguese Embassy in Athens and was told that once he secured a teaching job in Portugal he could apply for the appropriate permits locally. In fact Portuguese regulations have tightened up since then, though some schools (notably the *American Language Center*) do manage to obtain work permits for their non-EU staff.

At present a non-EU citizen must take a contract of employment to an SEF (for the Lisbon region the address is Avenida António Augusto Aguiar 20; 21-315 9681). The document obtained here is sent off together with the contract of employment to the Ministry of Labour. The final stage is to take a letter of good conduct provided by the teacher's own embassy to the police for the work and residence permit.

Since most teachers working for nine months are working on a freelance basis, they are responsible for paying their own taxes and contributions, which amount to about 20% of gross salary. Tax is paid on a sliding scale and most teachers on nine-month contracts with no other source of income will not necessarily be liable for tax. By law, all employers must insure their employees against work-related accidents. For eventualities outside work, teachers should insure themselves.

CONDITIONS OF WORK

The consensus seems to be that wages are low, but have been improving at a favourable rate in view of the cost of living. On the positive side, working conditions are generally relaxed. The normal salary range is 145,000-185,000 escudos per month. Full-time contract workers are entitled to an extra month's pay after 12 months. Some schools pay lower salaries but subsidise or pay for flights and accommodation. Several provide free Portuguese lessons. Salaries in Lisbon are significantly higher than in the small towns of northern Portugal. Teachers being paid on an hourly basis should expect to earn about 2,000 escudos, but they will not be eligible for the thirteenth month bonus or paid holidays.

Contracts are for a minimum of nine months though some are for a calendar year. Several International House schools have flats for their teachers. On average teachers spend about a quarter of their net salary on rent which is lower than in some other European countries. Accommodation in the greater Lisbon area will not be less than 65,000 escudos per person per month.

LIST OF SCHOOLS

AMERICAN LANGUAGE CENTER
Rua José Falcão 15-5° Esq, 4050-316 Oporto. Tel: (222) 058 127. Fax: (222) 085 287. E-mail: americanlangctr@mail.telepac.pt.
Number of teachers: 5-6.
Preference of nationality: American, Canadian.
Qualifications: minimum CELTA or equivalent plus one year's full time teaching experience. MA in TEFL with experience preferred.
Conditions of employment: 9-month contracts October to June, with possibility of renewing for a second year. Average 18-21 h.p.w. with both day (morning and afternoon company classes) and evening (6.30-9.30/10pm) schedules. Students are university students and professional adults.
Salary: 2,500-3,000 escudos per hour in local currency.
Facilities/Support: historic centre of city, sunny classrooms with views; informal assistance with housing and working papers.
Recruitment: on-site interviews preferred but applications accepted by correspondence, picture and telephone interview.

BELMONTE SCHOOL
Rua Pedro Alvares Cabral, No. 111, 6250-085 Belmonte. Tel: (275) 913397. E-mail: mgadb@teleweb.pt.
Number of teachers: 2-4.
Preference of nationality: British, American.
Qualifications: Certificate in TEFL for adults or children plus relevant experience.
Conditions of employment: 1-9 months. Up to 25 h.p.w. Timetable varies; includes some Saturday and evening work.
Salary: hourly rates.
Facilities/Support: assistance can be given with finding accommodation.
Recruitment: via adverts in press and by word of mouth.
Contact: Gloria Baia, Director.

BRISTOL SCHOOL
Instituto de Lingua Inglesa, Lda., Avenida da Republica, 1622–1°E, 4430-193 Vila Nova de Gaia. Tel: (22) 379 2002. Fax: (22) 3792002. E-mail: bsgaia@bristolschool.pt. Website: www.bristolschool.pt.
Number of teachers: 5.
Preference of nationality: British.
Qualifications: BA and TEFL Cert.
Conditions of employment: minimum period of work is October to June. Students from age 8.
Salary: 185,000 escudos net per month plus outward flight, Christmas and holiday bonuses.
Facilities/Support: assistance given with accommodation.
Recruitment: advertising in *TES*, interviews held in Portugal and the UK and recruitment agencies. Interview essential and can be held in the UK.
Contact: Mr Rui Fonseca.

BRISTOL SCHOOL GROUP
Instituto de Línguas da Maia & Ermesinde, Trav. Dr. Carlos Pires Felgueiras, 12-3°, 4470 Maia. Tel: (22) 948 8803/972 2761. Fax: (22) 960 6460/972 2761.
Comprises a group of 8 small schools: 4 near Oporto, 2 in the Azores and 2 inland (Castelo Branco and Fundão).
Number of teachers: 22.
Preference of nationality: British only (couples preferred).
Qualifications: BA and TEFL qualification. 1 year's experience essential.
Conditions of employment: minimum period of work October-June, 25 h.p.w. Pupils aged from 8 to Proficiency level.

Salary: 190,000 escudos net per month plus Christmas bonus of 50,000 escudos and end-of-contract bonus of 120,000 escudos.
Facilities/Support: assistance with accommodation given. No training.
Recruitment: direct application preferred. Also via adverts in *TES* and via South West English, Pill, Bristol BS20 0AA.
Contact: Idalina Meireles, Director.

CAMBRIDGE SCHOOL
Avenida da Liberdade 173, 1250-141 Lisbon. Tel: (21) 312 4600. Fax: (21) 353 4729. E-mail: cambridge@mail.telepac.pt. Website: www.cambridge.pt.
Portugal's largest private language school with 8 centres in Lisbon and other major cities.
Number of teachers: 90-110.
Preference of nationality: EU citizens preferred.
Qualifications: BA plus CELTA, Trinity College TESOL or equivalent.
Conditions of employment: initial contracts for 9 months from 1st October to 30th June.
Facilities/Support: authorised Cambridge/UCLES CELTA centre. All schools have 2 or 3 senior staff.
Recruitment: adverts in *TES* and *Guardian*. Applicants should send CV, recent photograph, contact telephone number and copies of degree and EFL Certificate. Interviews are usually held in London in early May and possibly other times depending on requirements. Visitors to Portugal can be interviewed in Lisbon by prior arrangement.
Contact: Jeffrey Kapke, General Director of Studies.

CENTRO DE INGLES DE FAMALICAO
Edificio dos Correios, no 116-4° andar, Praça do Bombeiro Voluntário, 4760 V.N.

Famalicão. Tel/fax: (252) 374233. E-mail: cif@esoterica.pt.
Number of teachers: 4.
Preference of nationality: EU preferred.
Qualifications: degree and CELTA essential; experience an advantage. CELTA grade A or B preferred.
Conditions of employment: 9 month renewable contracts. 24 contact hours p.w.
Salary: 161,000 escudos per month (net).
Facilities/Support: fully-furnished flat near school provided rent-free. Help given with work permit procedures. Lessons are regularly observed and feedback given.
Recruitment: via adverts in the *Guardian*. Interviews essential, normally in London.
Contact: David Mills, Director of Studies.

CENTRO DE INGLES DA TROFA
R. Pornão Magalhães, 193, Apartado 35, 4786 Trofa. Tel/fax: (252) 415036.
Number of teachers: 3.
Preference of nationality: British.
Qualifications: BA plus TEFL Cert. and a minimum year's experience of teaching at all levels.
Conditions of employment: 9-10 months. 30 hours per week.
Salary: approximately £500 per month net.
Facilities/Support: school owns flat for teacher use.
Recruitment: *The Guardian* newspaper.
Contact: Henrique Fragata, Director.

CENTRO DE LINGUAS DE LAGOS
Rua Dr. Joaquim Tello 32, 1° esq, 8600-583 Lagos. Tel/fax: (282) 761070. E-mail: cll@mail.telepac.pt.
Number of teachers: 4.
Preference of nationality: none (must be native speaker).
Qualifications: degree in education or arts subject plus a recognised TEFL qualification required.
Conditions of employment: freelance basis. Between 8 and 25 h.p.w. Mainly late afternoons and evenings. Most students work in tourist-related businesses or are school children. Possibility of work on summer courses for children and teenagers.
Salary: 2,150 escudos (£7) per hour.
Facilities/Support: assistance with finding accommodation.
Recruitment: applications from September 2001. Personal interview necessary.
Contact: Maureen McKeeve, Principal.

CITANIA CENTRO DE INGLES
Av. Conde de Margaride 543, Sala 34, 4810 Guimãraes. Tel: (253) 513757. Fax: (253) 415633.
Number of teachers: varies (for three centres near Guimarães.
Preference of nationality: must be native English speaker with a passport from the European Union.
Qualifications: TEFL Certificate or a general teaching qualification e.g. PGCE.
Conditions of employment: teaching all ages 16 classes per week (approx. 20 hours). Possibly also business English, exam classes and university support classes. Regular attendance at staff meetings and preparation time extra.
Salary: 145,000,00 escudos monthly, plus one-off travel allowance.
Facilities/Support: good staff support. Possible assistance with finding accommodation if requested.
Recruitment: via the internet and other adverts.

ENCOUNTER ENGLISH
Av. Fernao de Magalhaes 604, 4350-150 Oporto. Tel: (225) 367916. Fax: (225) 366 339. Also at Avenida Boavista 80, 5°-D-s-38, 4050-112 Oporto. Tel: (226) 095 410.

Fax: (226) 003 453.
Number of teachers: 14.
Preference of nationality: British.
Qualifications: CELTA plus 1 or 2 years experience.
Conditions of employment: contracts last from 15th September to 30th June. Up to 24 lessons per week lasting 50 minutes. Mostly evenings and Saturday mornings.
Salary: 150,000-180,000 escudos (net) per month.
Facilities/Support: assistance given with finding accommodation. Training available.
Recruitment: via adverts in *Guardian*. Interviews held locally or in England.
Contact: Director.

INSTITUTO BRITANICO DE BRAGA
Rua Conselheiro Januario 119, Apartado 2682, 4701-908 Braga. Tel: (253) 263298. Fax: (253) 619 355. E-mail: efl.IBB@mail.telepac.pt. Website: http://welcome. to/ibbraga.
Number of teachers: 9.
Preference of nationality: English speaking countries.
Qualifications: degree plus TEFL Cert, CELTA etc. and experience of teaching.
Conditions of employment: one school year. 22 contact hours per week.
Salary: 180,000 escudos.
Facilities/Support: no assistance with accommodation.
Recruitment: direct application. Interview at the school essential.
Contact: Dr. Vergilio Rodrigues.

INSTITUTO DE LINGUAS DE S. JOAO DA MADEIRA
Largo Durbalino Laranjeira S/N, 3700 S. João da Madeira. Tel: (256) 833906. Fax: (256) 835887. E-mail: institutodelinguas@mail.telepac.pt.
Preference of nationality: British.
Qualifications: DELTA/COTE plus 2 years experience.
Conditions of employment: 9 month contracts from October.
Salary: dependent on qualifications.
Facilities/Support: no help given with accommodation, work permits or training.
Recruitment: interview essential.
Contact: Dr. Helena Borges, Director.

INTERLEARNING CENTRE (ILC)
Rua Capitão Mouzinho de Albuquerque, 62-64 Edificio Alice, 1° Andar, 2400-193 Leiria. Tel: (244) 830950. Fax (244) 830959.
Number of teachers: 6.
Preference of nationality: none
Qualifications: must have TEFL Cert. and experience.
Conditions of employment: September to June contract. 25 contact hours.
Salary: 125,000 escudos per month.
Facilities/Support: no assistance with accommodation, but help with residence permit.
Recruitment: usually through newspaper adverts.
Contact: Sergio Gomes, Director, or Linda Martins.

INTERLINGUA INSTITUTO DE LINGUAS
Lg. 1° de Dezembro 28, 8500 Portimao. Tel: (282) 427690. Fax: (282) 416030. E-mail: interlingua@mail.telepac.pt.
Number of teachers: 4.
Preference of nationality: British.
Qualifications: TEFL Cert. able to teach children (6-10 years) as well as adults.
Conditions of employment: 9 months to a year.
Salary: £8 per hour or £365 per month.
Facilities/Support: assistance with finding accommodation.

Recruitment: letters of application. Interviews in Portugal not essential but preferred.
Contact: Zita Segall Neto, Director.

INTERNATIONAL HOUSE (AVEIRO)
Rua Domingos Carrancho 1-1°, 3800 Aveiro. Tel: (234) 426923/384497. Fax: (234) 423983. E-mail: ihaveiro@mail.teleweb.pt.
Also recruit for International House (Ilhavo), Largo do Municipio 16-1° Dto, 3830 Ilhavo. Tel/fax: (234) 325605.
Number of teachers: 15 (some part-time).
Preference of nationality: EU.
Qualifications: BA plus CELTA (Grade 'B') plus 2 years experience.
Conditions of employment: usually 9 month contracts. 24 h.p.w. Pupils aged 7-70, though majority are young learners. Some company teaching and evening teaching.
Salary: from 180,000 escudos.
Facilities/Support: school flats provided (45,000 escudos each in shared flat). In-service training given.
Recruitment: through IH, London and locally.

INTERNATIONAL HOUSE (LISBON)
Rua Marquês Sá da Bandeira 16, 1050-148 Lisbon. Tel: (21) 315 1496/4/3. Fax: (21) 353 0081. E-mail: ihlisbon@mail.telepac.pt. Website: www.international-house.com.
Number of teachers: 18.
Preference of nationality: British.
Qualifications: CELTA minimum.
Conditions of employment: standard length of stay 9 months. Flexible working hours to include evening and Saturday work. Pupils range in age from 8 to 80.
Salary: 244,700 escudos per month for first year teachers.
Facilities/Support: assistance with accommodation. CELTA and CELTYL courses offered regularly (see *Training* chapter).
Recruitment: through local adverts and by IH, London.
Contact: Colin McMillan, Director.

INTERNATIONAL HOUSE (PORTO)
Rua Dr. Sousa Rosa 38-1°, 4150 Porto. Tel: (222) 617 7641. Fax: (222) 616 9828. E-mail: ihporto@iname.com. Web-site: http://members.nbci.com/ihporto. Also Leça da Palmeira, Rua Oliveira Lessa 350, 4450 Matosinhos. Tel: (22) 995 9087. Fax: (22) 995 6084.
Number of teachers: 10.
Preference of nationality: British, Irish but also American.
Qualifications: CELTA.
Conditions of employment: 1-year contracts. 22 h.p.w. Pupils aged from 7.
Salary: depending on qualifications and experience.
Facilities/Support: assistance with accommodation. Portuguese lessons available. Training provided.
Recruitment: direct application.
Contact: Leslie Hughes, Director.

INTERNATIONAL HOUSE (TORRES VEDRAS)
Rua Miguel Bombarda 3-1°, 2560 Torres Vedras. Tel/fax: (261) 324421. E-mail: ihtorresvedras@mail.telepac.pt.
Number of teachers: 5.
Preference of nationality: EU.
Qualifications: CELTA (Grade 'A' or 'B').
Conditions of employment: 9 month contracts (October-June). 20 h.p.w. Pupils are children (6-14) and adults.
Facilities/Support: assistance given with accommodation. Regular seminars,

observations and help with lesson-planning given. Newly recruited teachers are expected to attend a development course in teaching younger learners. DELTA course offered in alternate years.
Recruitment: via IH, London and locally.
Contact: Diana England, Director of Studies.

INTERNATIONAL HOUSE (VISEU)
Rua dos Casimiros 33, 3510-061 Viseu. Tel: (232) 420850. Fax: (232) 420851. E-mail: ihviseu@mail.telepac.pt. Website: www.international-house.com/viseu
Number of teachers: 10.
Preference of nationality: EU passport-holders preferred.
Qualifications: minimum CELTA (grade 'B'), Preferably a degree.
Conditions of employment: 9-12 months contract. Maximum 24 contact h.p.w. Pupils aged 8-60, but majority children and adolescents.
Salary: from 185,000 escudos per month.
Facilities/Support: three school flats available; rent is about 40,000 escudos per person. Strong emphasis on teacher development and in-service training provided.
Recruitment: through Human Resources Dept. at IH, London. Interviews required.

LANCASTER COLLEGE
Praceta 25 de Abril 35-1°, 4430 Vila Nova de Gaia. Tel: (22) 377 2030. Fax: (22) 377 2039. E-mail: info@lancastercollege.pt. Website: www.lancastercollege.pt.
Also at Covilhã, Estarreja, Santa Maria da Feira, Fafe, Oeiras, Arcozelo, Vizela and Estoril (phone, fax and e-mail numbers on website).
Number of teachers: 10-20 for 8 schools plus franchised schools in Póvoa de Varzim, Arrifana and Esmoriz.
Preference of nationality: EU (British and Irish preferred).
Qualifications: CELTA, Trinity Cert or equivalent (minimum).
Conditions of employment: 9 month contracts. 16-20 contact h.p.w.; 25 hour working week.
Salary: 1,750 escudos per hour (net for first year).
Facilities/Support: assistance given with finding accommodation. Training given when possible.
Recruitment: via internet and EFL press.
Contact: Personnel Manager.

LINGUACULTURA INSTITUTO DE LINGUAS DE SANTAREM LDA
Apartado 37, 2001 Santarém Codex. Tel: (243) 309140. E-mail: Linguacultura@Linguacultura.pt. Headquarters for a number of schools, e.g. Linguacultura, Avenida Dr. José H Vareda 22, 1-°-D, 2430 Marinha Grande. Tel: (244) 560 952. Also in Alcanena (249-891040), Loures (219-830714), Portalegre (245-331471) and Batalha (244-766414).
Number of teachers: 50 in several schools.
Preference of nationality: British.
Qualifications: CELTA plus minimum 1 year of TEFL experience.
Conditions of employment: period of work from mid-September to end of June. 21 h.p.w. Hours include morning and late evening work.
Salary: 1,650 escudos per hour plus accommodation allowance.
Facilities/Support: assistance with finding accommodation. Further training with workshops throughout the year.
Recruitment: adverts in *TES*. Interviews held in Portugal and UK.

MANITOBA INSTITUTO DE LINGUAS
Apartado 184, 4491 Póvoa de Varzim Codex. Tel/fax: (252) 683014.
Number of teachers: 10-12 in 2 schools (other one is in Vila do Conde).
Preference of nationality: American, Canadian, British, Australian, etc.
Qualifications: B.Ed./MA plus TEFL qualifications and experience.
Conditions of employment: 1-2 year contracts. 25 h.p.w. Pupils aged 7-60.

Salary: above average for Portugal.
Facilities/Support: assistance with finding accommodation. Training provided.
Recruitment: applicants should send proof of degrees and other certificates, at least two references and a recent photograph. Interviews not always necessary.
Contact: Isobel Loureiro, Pedagogic Director.

NEW INSTITUTE OF LANGUAGES
Rua Cordeiro Ferreira, 19C 1° Dto, 1750-071 Lisbon. Tel/fax: (217) 590 770. E-mail: nilportugal@mail.telepac.pt.
Number of teachers: 15/16.
Preference of nationality: British.
Qualifications: experienced and inexperienced graduates who have successfully completed a TEFL course.
Conditions of employment: 9/10 months, renewable at the end. 20-25 contact hours per week.
Salary: depends on experience.
Facilities/Support: secretarial and administrative help with residence permit and finding and renting accommodation. The school acts as guarantor for rentals.
Recruitment: *TES* and website advertising followed by London interviews in June and September.
Contact: John Rudall, Owner, Director of Studies.

NEW INSTITUTE OF LANGUAGES
Urb. da Portela Lt. 197-5° B/C, 2685-223 Sacavém. Tel/fax: (21) 943 5238. E-mail: nilportugal@mail.telepac.pt.
Number of teachers: 15.
Preference of nationality: English.
Qualifications: graduates with 1 week preparatory course. Experience welcome but not necessary.
Conditions of employment: 10-month contracts. 20-25 h.p.w.
Salary: varies.
Facilities/Support: secretarial and administrative help given while looking for accommodation. School acts as guarantor.
Recruitment: interviews held in London between June and September.
Contact: Mr. Randall, Director of Studies.

POMBALINGUA
Rua 1° de Maio, 6-1° dto., 3100-477 Pombal. Tel: (236) 214319. Fax: (236) 211064.
Number of teachers: 2.
Preference of nationality: British.
Qualifications: minimum TEFL Cert.
Conditions of employment: October to end June. 25 hours per week – mostly after 6pm.
Salary: 2000 escudos per hour (200,000 per calendar month). The salary is net.
Facilities/Support: assistance given in finding room/flat to rent.
Recruitment: teachers resident in Portugal.
Contact: Robert Carter, Director.

ROYAL SCHOOL OF LANGUAGES
Av. Lourenco Peixinho 92-2° andar & Rua José Rabumba 2, 3810-125 Aveiro. Tel: (234) 429156. Fax: (234) 382870.
Number of teachers: 28-33 in group of 8 schools.
Preference of nationality: British and South African, plus a few Canadians and Americans.
Qualifications: university degree plus TEFL Certificate (Trinity, Cambridge or equivalent).
Conditions of employment: 9 month contracts. 25-27 teaching hours p.w.
Salary: 150,000-170,000 escudos per month less 20% deductions.

Facilities/Support: assistance with accommodation and working papers. Training given.
Recruitment: via CVs or interviews which sometimes take place in UK.
Contact: Rosa do Céu Ramos Amorim, School Director.

SINTRALINGUA CENTRO DE LINGUAS LDA
Avenida Movimento das Forças, Armada 14-1° Dto, 2710 Sintra. Tel/fax: (21) 923 4941. E-mail: sintralingua@mail.telepac.pt
Number of teachers: 15.
Preference of nationality: British; must be native speaker.
Qualifications: minimum BA plus CELTA and 2 years experience.
Conditions of employment: 10 or 11 month contracts. Part-time hourly work also available. Lots of evening teaching (5.30pm-9.30pm) but other times possible.
Salary: 205,000 escudos per month full-time. 2,100 escudos per hour part-time (rates due to rise for 2001/2).
Facilities/Support: assistance given with finding accommodation. Feedback programme and observation.
Recruitment: via adverts in *Guardian* and interviews in UK or locally.
Contact: James. E. Scott, Director.

SPEAKWELL ESCOLA DE LINGUAS
Praça Mário Azevedo Gomes, Lote 12-1°, 2775-240 Parede. Tel: (21) 456 1771. Fax: (21) 456 1771. E-mail: speakwell@speakwell.pt. Website: www.speakwell.pt.
Number of teachers: 6 full-time and 5-10 part-time.
Preference of nationality: none, but must be native speakers.
Qualifications: TEFL preferably plus some business experience.
Conditions of employment: guarantee basic 10 hours a week October to June. School opening times are four weekdays and Saturday morning.
Salary: above the average hourly rate for Portugal.
Facilities/Support: nothing formally, but will help people to find accommodation through contacts etc.
Recruitment: local advertising and word-of-mouth.
Contact: Emer Nowlan Roberts, Director of Studies.

Other Schools to Try

Note that these schools (in alphabetical order according to town) did not confirm their teacher requirements for this edition of *Teaching English Abroad*. Upper case entries marked with an asterisk had entries in the last edition; addresses without asterisks have been taken from various sources, such as British Council lists and the *Yellow Pages*.

Atrio-Centro Linguas, ISLA, Apartado 224, 5300 Bragança
Instituto Bragança, Apartado 38, 5300 Bragança
Chaves English Centre, Av Pedro Alvares Cabral, 5400 Chaves
The English Centre, R Eng. Custodio Guimaraes, 4740 Esposende
Wall Street Institute Faro, Av. 5 de Outuburo 29, 8000-077 Faro
Associaçao Luso-Britanica Felgueiras, Praceta Aniceto P Ferreira, 4610 Felgueiras
British Education Europe, R Bombeiros Voluntarios, 4610 Felgueiras
Linguaterra, Loteamento Rebordão, Iote 24-r/c Dir, 6230-291 Fundão
CD-Complemento Directo, Av. Gen. Humberto Delgado 1022, 4420 Gondomar
Instituto Linguas Gondomar Lda, Praça Manuel Guedes, 240-1° Esq, 4420 Gondomar
Greenwich Instituto de Linguas, Rua 25 de Abril 560, S. Cosme, 4420 Gondorem (tel/fax 22-483 6429)
Citania Centro de Ingles, Lda, Av Conde Margaride 543, 4810 Guimaraes
Instituto Britanico, Rua Gravador Molarinho 29, 4800 Guimaraes

IF-Ingles Funcional, R. Comdte Almeida Henriques, 32-1°, 2400 Leiria (244-568351)

IPFEL - Linguas e Informatica, Rua de S Francisco 9, 4° Dt°, 2400 Leiria(244-815253)

*AMERICAN LANGUAGE INSTITUTE, Avenida Duque de Loulé 22-1°, 1050-148 Lisbon (21-315 2535/fax 21-352 4848)

Cial Centro de Linguas, Av. da Republica, 14-2°, 1000 Lisbon (21-533733/fax 21-352 3096). 9 teachers for Lisbon, 3 for Oporto, 3 for Faro.

Wall Street Institute Avenidas, Av. Praia de Vitoria, 71 3°C, 1050-183 Lisbon (fax 21-316 0553)

Wall Street Institute, Av. da Liberdade 166 R/C, 1250-146 Lisbon

IPFEL-Centro Estudos, R Barao S Cosme 166-2° Esq, 4000 Oporto

ISAI (Instituto Superior de Assistentes e Interpretes), Rua Alvares Cabral 159, 4050 Oporto (e-mail: isai@mail.telepac.pt)

Academia Estudos Paredes, R Dr Jose Cabral, 4580 Paredes

Instituto Linguas Paredes, Av Republica 401-c/v, 4580 Paredes

Wall Street Institute Portimao, Rua do Comércio no. 39, 8500-633 Portimao

Communicate Language Institute, Pcta Joao Villaret 12B, 2675 Póvoa de St Adriao (e-mail: cli@esoterica.pt). Prefer teachers experienced with young learners to teach in suburban Lisbon primary schools.

Escola Inglesa, R Visconde, 2097 3700 S. João Madeira

Scandinavia

Certain similarities exist in ELT throughout Scandinavia. The standard of English teaching in state schools is uniformly high, as anyone who has met a Dane or a Swede travelling abroad will know. Yet many ordinary Scandinavians aspire to fluency so keep up their English by attending evening classes, if only for social reasons. Sweden, Denmark and Norway have excellent facilities for such people, which are variations on the theme of 'folk university', a state-subsidised system of adult education. Classes at such institutions are the ideal setting for enthusiastic amateur teachers.

But as elsewhere in Europe the greatest demand for the English language comes from the business community, particularly in Finland. Enthusiastic amateurs tend to be less in demand in this setting than mature professionals. Yet Scandinavia is not a very popular destination for such teachers, despite its unspoilt countryside and efficient public transport. So there is scope for most kinds of teacher to work in Scandinavia, particularly in Finland, whose language schools sometimes advertise in the British press.

Since Finland and Sweden joined the European Union in 1994, the red tape has become much easier for EU teachers. But even in Norway, whose people voted by a referendum not to join, the formalities are straightforward for EU nationals and language institutes employ foreign teachers.

DENMARK

There is little recruitment of English teachers outside Denmark, apart from the *Cambridge Institute Foundation* which is Denmark's largest EFL institution with 38 branches and which specialises in English for business.

Many schools expect their teachers to speak Danish, and there seems to be almost enough fully bilingual candidates resident in Denmark to satisfy this requirement. It is worthwhile for any native speaker with an appropriate background who is staying in Denmark to enquire about part-time openings.

Like Scandinavians generally, Danes are enthusiastic self-improvers which means that evening classes in English (and hundreds of other things) are very popular. These are purely recreational and are meant to be fun and informal (*hygge* in Danish). *Folkehøjskoler* (folk high schools) offer residential courses of varying lengths where working conditions are generally so favourable that there is very little turnover of teaching staff. The tradition of voluntary organisations including trade unions running courses is still strong in Denmark. It might be worth tracking down one of the voluntary organisations which run evening classes countrywide:

Arbejdernes Oplysnings Forbund (AOF), Teglvaerksgade 27, 2100 Copenhagen Ø.
Folkeligt Oplysnings Forbund (FOF), Frederiksborggade 20, 1360 Copenhagen K
Frit Oplysningsforbund (FO), Landsforbundet, Fredriksberggade 21, 1459 Copenhagen K (fo@fo.dk/ www.fo.dk)
Hovedstadens Oplysnings Forbund (HOF), Købmagergade 26, 1150 Copenhagen K
Studieskolen, Antoniagade 6, 1106 Copenhagen K

Addresses of the Danish Folkeuniversitet can be found on its website at www.folkeuni.dk or you can e-mail sekr@fu.dk.

Wages in Denmark are set by law and teaching English is no exception. The minimum is about kr150, and that is what most new arrivals earn. However once you're established you can expect to earn £25 an hour teaching in the state sector (which is much better funded and resourced than its UK counterpart). Denmark has among the highest taxes in the world, i.e. 50%.

FINLAND

Although Finland's second language is Swedish, English runs a close second. Finns are admirably energetic and industrious in learning foreign languages, possibly because their own language is so impenetrable (belonging to the Finno-Ugric group of languages along with Hungarian and Estonian). English is taught in every kind of educational institution from trade and technology colleges to universities, but especially in commercial colleges (*Kauppaloulu*) and in Civic and Workers' Institutes. Private language schools flourish too and traditionally have not been too fussy about the paper qualifications of their native speaker teachers. Children start their primary education at age seven, and many children between the ages of three and seven are sent to private kindergartens, many of which are English (as well as German, American, etc.) These often welcome a native English speaker with experience of teaching children. (The only skill which concerned one of these nurseries-cum-kindergartens looking to hire a young British graduate was singing.)

Fixing up a Job

The Education Adviser at the British Council in Helsinki (www.britishcouncil.fi) will send a list of 21 private schools, taken from the Helsinki Yellow Pages and not endorsed by them. One of the key organisations in Finland is the Federation of Finnish-British Societies (Puistokatu 1 b A, 00140 Helsinki; +358-9-687 7020/fax +358-9-687 70210/ finnbrit@finnbrit.fi/ www.finnbrit.fi) which takes on a few mostly experienced teachers for its teaching centres in Helsinki and Jakobstad/Pietsaari (Ostermalmsgatan 29B, 68600 Jakobstad). The 12 other societies have given up on teaching in the face of stiff competition from commercial institutes and because of lack of staff and time for teaching, which was largely done on a voluntary basis in the past. Any teacher who is hired at an English Club usually finds that it is considered compulsory to participate in regular social evenings, for example giving a talk about British life, or accompanying classes on excursions and ski trips.

Another big player in the provision of English language teaching is *Richard Lewis Communications* with offices throughout Finland and Sweden as well as England (see entry). RLC draws most of its students from senior management in both the public and private sector, and also provides cross-cultural training in Finland.

An employer which advertises at regular intervals is Linguarama. Graduates of Linguarama's introductory training courses in Britain are often encouraged to consider Finland for their posting abroad; their head office in the UK (Oceanic House, 85 High St, Alton, Hants. GU34 1LG) handles some recruitment, or you can contact the growing Helsinki operation on +358-9-680 3230/fax 603118; helsinki@linguarama.com.

According to the Director of *Talk Shop Communications*, the situation in Turku is flourishing:

We have changed our operating model and now only employ freelance teachers. Most of the Finnish market has now gone this way. There is a significant demand for these in Turku as a whole. The pay is reasonable and anyone coming here would have no problem finding work.

Teachers without European nationality will encounter more problems, though they can apply to participate in an organised exchange through the American-Scandinavian Foundation (58 Park Avenue, New York, NY 10016; 212-879-9779/fax 212-249-3444; trainscan@amscan.org/ www.amscan.org). The ASF arranges for TEFOL (Teachers of English as a Foreign Language) teachers to teach in a variety of educational establishments including state schools, institutes and private organisations for a period of between three months and one academic year. Teachers are paid US$900-$1550 monthly. Accommodation is arranged, but must be paid for by the teacher at $180-$270 per month. Flights, insurance and internal travel are also at the teacher's expense. The application deadline is February 1st for placement the following autumn.

In Finland, short-term paid training posts are available in a range of fields including language teaching. The Centre for International Mobility (CIMO, PO Box 343, SF-00531 Helsinki; +358-9-7747 7033/fax 7747 7064; cimoinfo@cimo.fi/ http://finland.cimo.fi or www.cimo.fi) co-ordinates an International Trainee Exchange programme whereby students and graduates work in their field for a named Finnish employer for between one and 18 months. The academic year lasts from the end of August or beginning of September until the end of May. Of course most schools prefer their native speaker teachers to stay for the whole year though one-term positions are possible. Salaries average about FIM6,500 per month. The formalities are minimal for EU teachers but the programme is also open to other nationalities who are granted a residence permit.

There is also demand for private tutoring which you could fix up by advertising in the usual way.

Conditions of Work

Freelance arrangements have largely replaced contracts which means that fewer institutes pay travel expenses and arrange accommodation for their teachers. A teaching unit of 45 minutes is the norm, with less evening work than elsewhere. Wages are high, but so is the cost of living. Teachers paid by the lesson can expect to earn between FIM100 and FIM130 for 45 minutes. Some schools compress the teaching into four days a week, leaving plenty of time for weekend exploration of the country.

Deductions will be significant from a gross monthly salary of FIM8,500. Taxes are high and are usually the responsibility of the teacher, whereas contributions should be paid by the employer; social security and unemployment insurance deductions will amount to at least 6% of the salary.

The Finnish Embassy in London distributes a detailed booklet produced by the Ministry of Labour entitled 'Are You Planning to Move to Finland?' which is worth reading. Helsinki has about 35 museums and art galleries plus a high density of sports facilities, ice rinks, etc. The long dark winters are relieved by a wide choice of cheerful restaurants, cafés, bars and clubs in the cities, and saunas almost everywhere.

NORWAY

The trend in Norwegian EFL is similar to that in Denmark, and most schools rely on a pool of native speakers already resident in Norway. Most jobs are for part-time work and of course do not offer accommodation. At least things are easier from an immigration point of view than they used to be. Although Norway is not a member of the EU, it does allow the free reciprocity of labour so that EU nationals are allowed to work in Norway without a work permit. Immigration restrictions on non-EU teachers remain stringent.

The British Council in Oslo does not keep a list of language schools, though it has the Yellow Pages for Oslo, Bergen, Stavanger, Trondheim and others. The Yellow Pages for Norway are on-line at www.gulesider.no, though typing in *Sprakinstitut* produced nothing.

As throughout Scandinavia, the Folkuniversity of Norway plays an important role in language tuition and hires many native speakers, mostly on an occasional basis; the main office is at Chr. Krohgsgt. 34, Oslo (22 98 88 00; info@fu.no/ www.fu.no). There are branches in 300 Norwegian municipalities with fairly major teaching operations in Stavanger, Skien, Kristiansand and Hamar. *Berlitz* hires native-speakers with no TEFL background including students and trains them in their method.

The basic hourly wage is about kr140, though this can double for high-level business teaching. Expect to lose about a third in deductions.

Casual opportunities may crop up in unpredictable places. David Moor was simply intending to spend a month on holiday skiing in Norway. However he saw an advert in a local supermarket for a native English teacher and jumped at the chance:

> *A teacher put me up and fed me. I'd intended to stay in the hostel or a cheap hotel, but was finding Norway expensive. I was just working for keep, teaching three days a week, so I had lots of spare time. I had a fantastic time, much better than a normal holiday.*

SWEDEN

The Folkuniversity of Sweden has a long-established scheme (since 1955) by which British and other native English speakers may be placed for nine months (one academic year) at a time in a network of adult education centres throughout the country. There are five trusts closely linked to the universities of Stockholm, Gothenburg, Lund, Uppsala and Umea, with branches in many smaller towns. Anyone interested in teaching in Sweden on this scheme should contact the programme co-ordinator, Peter Baston, Folkuniversitetet, Box 2116, S-22002 Lund; 46-19 77 00/fax 46-19 77 80; peter.baston@folkuniversitetet.se; www. folkuniversitetet.se. Interviews can be held in the UK at the Salisbury School of English (36 Fowler's Road, Salisbury, Wilts. SP1 2QU; 01722 331011).

Originally the teaching at the Folkuniversity consisted of evening classes called a 'Study Circle', an informal conversation session. Circumstances have changed, however, and the range of pupils can be very varied from unemployed people to business executives, as well as people who want to prepare for Cambridge examinations. Business people are coming to dominate the FU's clientele, and light-hearted evening 'study circles' have been mostly replaced by hard-headed company courses.

The FU in Stockholm runs English summer courses from June to August for which it looks to hire teachers and group leaders. Most of these are drawn from native speakers already in Sweden with the FU who would otherwise be idle all summer (or, more likely, looking for work at a summer school in the UK).

Fixing up a Job

With approximately 80 jobs a year, mostly from September but also from January, Folkuniversitetet offers the best chance to anyone aged 22-40 of fixing up work in Sweden. They now look for candidates with a first degree or recognised teaching qualification or initial TEFL certificate and two years experience. Classroom experience is essential and experience in other fields is an advantage. Paul Greening found that his interviewer was more concerned to establish that he would be willing to stick it out in northern Sweden for a year than to see his ELT qualifications, so adaptability and stamina are also important.

Anyone who does not want to work through the FU will find it more difficult unless they have experience of teaching or working in a business context. Advertisements seldom appear in the educational press. Teachers with a solid ELT background might try the main state universities who put on English courses or the language schools listed in the Yellow Pages of Stockholm, Malmö, Gothenburg, Orebro and Uppsala. Charlotte Rosen decided to do a TEFL course in London before going to Sweden to be with her Swedish fiancé:

> *I had visited Sweden several times before going to Gothenburg to work. After I'd been in Sweden for about six weeks, I looked through the Yellow Pages for language schools and sent off my CV in English which wasn't a problem because everyone speaks English really well. I was offered several interviews, including by the British Institute. Many of them said they were interested but the terms only start in September and January so you have to time your applications quite carefully.*

Making a breakthrough as a freelancer is also difficult without a knowledge of the Swedish labour market and a functioning network of contacts. Some FU teachers do teach privately to supplement their incomes, though technically this is forbidden by the terms of their visa.

Conditions of Work

Folkuniversitetet guarantees 720 hours of work (lessons are 45 minutes long) over the nine-month contract. Hours in excess of this figure of approximately 80 hours per month are paid extra and some more lucrative courses are paid at a higher rate. The teaching schedule varies enormously from place to place but is not normally onerous, though it may involve up to four evenings a week and some travelling, perhaps even to neighbouring towns. It may also include some promoting of KV courses to increase enrolment. The journey from Britain to Sweden is paid, as is the return journey at the end of each of the two contract years.

Folkuniversitetet pays Kr13,500 (£950) per month basic plus supplements. This is reasonable to live on, but makes it difficult to save. Paul Greening found it difficult to make ends meet on his salary:

> *The accommodation which was provided was good but expensive. I always had to think about prices and look for the cheapest. I was able to save money only because I started a large number of teenage courses for which I was paid extra.*

Teachers must pay tax in Sweden on a scale which varies according to the municipality. Swedish income tax is notoriously high, and the FU estimates that teachers lose about 30% in deductions. Expect to earn from £8-£10 per hour net.

Constructing a lively social life is a challenge. Most find Swedes fairly reserved, a problem that is not helped by the fact that there are few places to meet the locals outside the classroom, since drinking and eating out are so expensive. Ann Hunter points out that it can be difficult to make Swedish friends:

The only Swedes you meet regularly are your pupils and the professional relationship can make it awkward to socialise, though after your first term you can get to know ex-pupils quite well. Learning Swedish, if it is possible, is a good way to meet people, though your fellow students are foreigners of course.

Andrew Boyle had mixed feeling about Sweden and Swedish people:

Sweden is a pleasant place to live, if a little dull at times. It is a generally liberal place, although the increasingly multicultural nature of society is causing Swedes to have to face up to their own prejudices. The students are generally of a high level and although initially quiet not unfriendly and even chatty after they know you a little better.

Still, you have to be independent and comfortable with your own company for long periods to enjoy Sweden, especially in the north of the country during the seven months of the winter when the locals either hibernate or devote all their leisure to skiing. Anyone who enjoys outdoor activities will probably enjoy a stint in Sweden, especially ramblers and hill-walkers, who take advantage of the *Allemannsrätt*, the law which guarantees free access to the countryside for everyone.

LIST OF SCHOOLS

Denmark

BABEL SPROGTRAENING ApS
Hyldegardsvej 2, 2920 Charlottenlund. Tel: 39 64 23 20; Fax: 39 64 20 84. E-mail: Daniel.King@babel-sprog.dk.
Qualifications: the school hires language instructors interested in living in Denmark long-term. Age range mainly 28-38 and should have either business or teaching background and preferably both. Clients are business people taught in classes or privately and can have demanding standards.
Contact: Daniel King.

CAMBRIDGE INSTITUTE FOUNDATION
Vimmclskaftet 40, 1161 Copenhagen K. Tel: 33 13 33 02. Fax: 33 13 33 23. Website: www.cambridgeinstitute.dk.
Number of teachers: 53 in various schools in the Copenhagen area.
Preference of nationality: British, Irish.
Qualifications: BA, TEFL qualification and at least 1 year's TEFL experience abroad.
Conditions of employment: 8 month renewable contracts (October-May). Minimum 20 h.p.w. Students aged 18-70.
Salary: approximately £20 per teaching hour.
Facilities/Support: assistance with accommodation. Training given.
Recruitment: through adverts in UK newspapers.
Contact: Richard Philp, Principal.

SANWES SPROGINSTITUT APS
Kokholm 1, 6000 Kolding. Tel: 75 51 74 10. Fax: 75 51 74 90. E-mail: sanwes@sanwes.dk. Also branches at Horsensvej 39C, 7100 Vejle (75 72 46 10) and Fredericia Uddannelsescenter, Mosegardsvej, 7000 Fredericia (75 94 14 11).
Number of teachers: 8-10.
Preference of nationality: British, American, Australian.
Qualifications: should have some business background, be open-minded, cheerful and have lots of initiative.
Conditions of employment: freelance; preferred minimum period 6 months. Daytime hours; total number depends on clients.
Salary: approximately kr130 per hour.

Facilities/Support: no assistance with accommodation. Pre-service training from other teacher. Help given with work permits.
Recruitment: local interviews.
Contact: Lone von der Sandt, Director.

STUDIESKOLEN
Antonigade 6, 1018 Copenhagen. Tel 33 18 79 13. Fax 33 14 81 45. E-mail: grundy@studieskolen.dk. Website: www.studieskolen.dk.
Number of teachers: 19.
Preference of nationality: none.
Qualifications: BA/B.Sc and TEFL qualification minimum.
Conditions of employment: no fixed contracts.
Salary: kr209 per hour.
Facilities/Support: no assistance with accommodation.
Contact: Mark Grundy.

A selection of other schools to try (towns in alphabetical order):
FOF (Folkeligt Oplysnings Forbund), Sønder Allé 9, 8000 Arhus C (86 12 29 55/fax 86 19 54 35).
Berlitz International, Vimmelskaftet 42A, 1161 Copenhagen
Master-Ling, Sortedam Dossering 83, 2100 Copenhagen Ø
Elite Sprogcentret, Hoffmeyersvej 19, 2000 Frederiksberg
Babel Sprogtraening, Naverland 2, 10, 2600 Glostrup
AIS Language Training Centre, Kongevejen 115, 2840 Holte
BS Sprogservice, Birkevej 3, 2830 Virum
Lingua Dan, Høtoften 4, 2830 Virum

Finland

AAC – OPISTO OY
Kauppaneuvoksentie 8, 00200 Helsinki. Tel: (+358-9) 4766 7800. Fax: (+358-9) 4766 7810. E-mail: info@aac.fi. Website: www.aac.fi.
Number of teachers: 250 (75 native English speakers) in 8 centres (Helsinki: Lauttasaari and Pitäjänmäki, Tampere, Turku (fax +358-2-469 1240), Jyväskylä, Kuopio, Vaasa and Oulu).
Preference of nationality: British, American, Canadian.
Qualifications: degree plus CELTA, or degree plus business background; teaching experience preferred.
Conditions of employment: 9 month contracts. 80-100 hours per month. Students are business people who want to learn business and/or technical English.
Salary: FIM95-100 per lesson.
Facilities/Support: one-way air fare paid, housing arranged. Training provided on different teaching methods and materials.
Recruitment: direct application, newspaper ads (*Guardian*), internet.
Contact: Craig Stocks.

GREENWICH MERIDIAN TRAINING
Lumikintie 6 A 40, 00820 Helsinki. Tel/fax (+358-9) 7279 4370. E-mail: Jeremy.Dallyn@gmt.fi. Website: www.gmt.fi.
Number of teachers: 3-4.
Preference of nationality: none.
Qualifications: CELTA or equivalent.
Conditions of employment: 1 or 2 years. 28 contact h.p.w. Lessons last 45 minutes.
Salary: FIM8,500 per month minimum, according to qualifications and experience, less taxes, social security (4.7%) and unemployment insurance (1.5%).
Facilities/Support: assistance given with accommodation, work permits and training. Chances to become involved in sales and marketing and developing the school's online training system.

Recruitment: direct. Telephone and e-mail contact is sufficient.
Contact: Jeremy Dallyn, Director.

KIELIAVAIN
Kaisaniemenkatu 3, 00100 Helsinki. Tel: (+358-9) 684 0730. Fax: (+358-9) 6840 7320.
Number of teachers: 2-3.
Preference of nationality: American, British.
Qualifications: degree and TEFL experience.
Conditions of employment: from September to end May. 20-30 lessons.
Salary: FIM 90-120 gross per lesson.
Facilities/Support: no assistance usually with finding accommodation. Virtually impossible to get permits for citizens not from the European Union.
Recruitment: in-person interview.
Contact: Sam Einsalo, Director.

KIELIPISTE KAUPPAKAARI OY
Kaisaniemenkatu 4A, 00100 Helsinki. Tel: (+358-90) 622 6190. Fax: (+358-90) 6226 1999. E-mail: Anja.strom@keilipiste.fi. Website: www.kielipiste.fi.
Number of teachers: 30-40.
Preference of nationality: none.
Qualifications: CELTA or BA/MA in TEFL plus experience teaching adults and preferably a business background. Some positions also open for ESP teachers of legal (EC) English, technical English, etc.
Conditions of employment: freelance work only. Indeterminate number of hours (2-40) between 8am and 8.15pm. Students are all adults.
Salary: FIM105-121 per 45-minute lesson.
Facilities/Support: no assistance with accommodation.
Recruitment: local interview essential (by appointment only).
Contact: Anja Ström, Training Consultant.

LINGUALINK OY
Yliopistonkatu 24 A 18, 20100 Turku. Tel: (358-2) 251 9025. Fax: (358-2) 251 2128. E-mail: lingualink.turku@lingualink.fi. Website: www.lingualink.fi. Also LinguaLink Centre in Tampere: Kuninkaankatu 30A, 33200 Tampere; 3-222 8422; lingualink.tampere@lingualink.fi.
Number of teachers: 9.
Preference of nationality: English, American, Canadian.
Qualifications: university degree, TEFL (or equivalent). Minimum 2 years experience.
Conditions of employment: 10 month contracts. Hours of teaching between 7am and 9pm.
Salary: 8,500 markka per month. Deductions of 18%.
Facilities/Support: help teachers to locate subsidised accommodation.
Recruitment: locally and through partner school Linguarama International.
Contact: Stephen Viola, Managing Director or Paula Haapanen, Language Teacher.

RICHARD LEWIS COMMUNICATIONS
Länsituulentie 10, 02100 Espoo (Helsinki). Tel: (+358-9) 4157 4700. Fax: (+358-9) 466 592. E-mail: info@rlcglobal.com. Website: www.crossculture.com. Offices also in Turku, Tampere, Lahti, Oulu, Jyväskylä and Kuopio; and in the UK: Riversdown House, Warnford, Southampton, Hants. SO32 3LH. Tel: 01962 771111.
Preference of nationality: British.
Qualifications: university degree and TEFL preferred.
Conditions of employment: 9 month contracts (September till the third week in June). Possibility of summer work in England.
Facilities/Support: assistance with finding accommodation. New teachers are given training in RLC's methods.
Recruitment: direct application to Michael Gates, Managing Director (mobile

phone +358-40 751 7299).

TALK SHOP COMMUNICATIONS
Yliopistonkatu 23A, 20100 Turku. Tel: (+358-2) 277 5100. Fax: (+358-2) 277 5110.
E-mail: alex.frost@talkshop.fi. Website: www.talkshop.fi.
Number of teachers: 3 (freelancers only).
Preference of nationality: American, British.
Qualifications: Cert. TEFL and experience, especially in corporate training.
Conditions of employment: hours between 8am and 4pm.
Salary: FIM9,500+ per month, less about 25% deductions.
Facilities/Support: no assistance with accommodation; applicants should be living locally. Training given.
Recruitment: interviews necessary.
Contact: Alex Frost, Managing Director.

TYOVAEN AKATEMIA/WORKERS' ACADEMY
Vanha Turuntie 14, 02700 Kauniainen. Tel: (+358-9) 5404 2412. Fax: (+358-9) 5404 2444. E-mail: toimisto@akatemia.org. Website: www.akatemia.org.
Number of teachers: 1-4.
Preference of nationality: none (must be native speakers).
Qualifications: TEFL diploma.
Conditions of employment: freelancers teach 15-30 lessons per month for 6-12 months.
Salary: FIM120-130 per lesson.
Facilities/Support: training given in Finnish.
Contact: Ms. Heidi Mäkäläinen, Language Co-ordinator.

A selection of other schools to try (towns in alphabetical order):
Alpha Communications Oy, Kaisaniemenkatu 4 A, 00100 Helsinki
Arkadi Oy, Töölönkatu 8, 00100 Helsinki
Bellcrest Language Services Oy, Luotsikatu 1 A, 00160 Helsinki
Berlitz, Kaivokatu 10 A, 00100 Helsinki
FINTRA, PL 50 (Kaupintie 2),00441 Helsinki
Habil Oy Helsinki, International House, Ritarikatu 7A, 00170 Helsinki (+358-9-135 7104/fax 278 3632). 5 teachers.
*INSTITUTE OF MARKETING, Töölöntullinkatu 6, 00250 Helsinki (+358-9-47361/fax (+358-9-241 4794)
Josbel Oy Kieliopisto, Vuorimiehenkatu 20, 00150 Helsinki
Kieli-instituutti Languista, Annankatu 29 A, 00100 Helsinki
Kielikoulu Small Talk, Annankatu 31-33 B, 00100 Helsinki
LinguaBella, Vuorikatu 16 A, 00100 Helsinki
Linguarama Kielopisto, Annankatu 26, 00100 Helsinki (fax +358-9-603118; e-mail linguarama.hki@linguarama.com).
Optimi Training Oy, Ludviginkatu 3-5 B 21, 00130 Helsinki
*REFERICON OY, Miniatontie 4 E 23, 02360 Espoo (Helsinki) (+358-9-813 3507/fax +358-9-801 8801; raija.ikonen@refericon.fi). Not hiring in 20000/2001 but may need teachers in the future.
Lansi-Suomen Opisto, Loimijoentie 280, 32700 Huittinen (+358-2-567866/fax 566409)
*IWG KIELI-INSTITUUTTI LTD, Hämeenkatu 25 B, 33200 Tampere (3-389 1002/fax 3-389 1003)

Norway
BERLITZ A/S
Akersgt.16, 0158 Oslo. Tel: 22 33 10 30. Fax: 22 33 10 03. E-mail: instruction@berlitz.no. Website: www.berlitz.com.
Number of teachers: varies.

Preference of nationality: none.
Qualifications: graduates, also students. The most important thing is to be energetic, outgoing and creative.
Conditions of employment: freelance basis. Instructors choose their hours of availablility between 8am and 9pm which are the opening hours. Trainee teachers receive an initial training course in the Berlitz Direct Method.
Salary: to be negotiated.
Facilities/Support: no assistance with accommodation given
Contact: Nieves Aurora Ponta, Instructional Supervisor.

FOLKEUNIVERSITETET/FRIUNDERVISNINGEN OSLO
Torggata 7 (P.B. 496 Sentrum), 0105 Oslo. Tel: 22 47 60 00. Fax: 22 47 60 01. E-mail: info@fu.oslo.no.
Number of teachers: 2 full-time, 15-20 part-time.
Preference of nationality: none.
Qualifications: TEFL experience and qualifications preferred. Prefer native speakers already resident in Norway.
Conditions of employment: no contracts. Students aged 18-65.
Salary: varies from course to course.
Facilities/Support: no assistance with accommodation. Some training given.
Recruitment: local interviews only.
Contact: Elinor Stang Lund.

INTERNATIONAL LANGUAGE SCHOOL
Markveien 35B, 0554 Oslo. Tel: 22 35 10 70/22 35 40 05. E-mail: ils.oslo@online.no.
Number of teachers: 10-15.
Preference of nationality: none.
Qualifications: pedagogical or English language degree and teaching experience.
Conditions of employment: freelance basis. School hours are from 9am-6pm.
Salary: varies.
Facilities/Support: limited assistance with finding accommodation. School only hires those already in possession of a valid work visa.
Recruitment: adverts in local paper and the university career centre. CV and interview essential for on spec applications.
Contact: Melisa Bonvik.

NELTEC
Molbakken 17, 5035 Bergen. Tel: (55) 952000. Fax: (55) 950100. E-mail: richardn@online.no. Website: www.neltec@sol.no.
Number of teachers: 2.
Preference of nationality: none.
Qualifications: TEFL, especially in business or technical fields.
Conditions of employment: three months contract. 10 hours per week.
Salary: hourly rate approx £17.
Facilities/Support: can help with accommodation in special cases.
Recruitment: CV and interview essential.
Contact: Richard Nelson, Manager.

NORSK SPRAKINSTITUTT
Kongensgt. 9, 0153 Oslo. Tel: 23 10 01 10. Fax: 23 10 01 27. E-mail: snorsk@online.no.
Number of teachers: 7 (but varies).
Preference of nationality: British or American without marked accent.
Qualifications: TEFL, etc. and teaching experience. Work experience in other fields such as business is a valuable asset. Must be resident in Oslo.
Conditions of employment: freelance only. Hours vary according to course requirements.

Salary: hourly rate. Holiday pay based on previous year's earnings.
Recruitment: direct contact.

POLARIS INSTITUTE AS
P.O. Box 628, Skoyen, 0214 Oslo. Tel: 22 55 46 11. Fax 22 55 49 60. E-mail: polaris@polarisinstitute.no.
Number of teachers: 3.
Qualifications: Business experience, native speaker, experience in education.
Conditions of employment: standard contract is 2 years.
Salary: 190 kroner per hour.
Contact: Richard Stevenson.

A selection of other schools to try (towns in alphabetical order):
Allegro A/S Spraktjenester, Strandkaien 6, 5013 Bergen
*LILLEHAMMER OVERSETTING, Postboks 54, 2601 Lillehammer (61 26 47 60/fax 61 25 61 14)
Atlas Sprakreiser, Postboks 191, Vindern, 0319 Oslo
Kommunike Sprakinstitut, Jacobaalsgt. 17A, 0364 Oslo (22 69 97 10/fax 22 69 26 75)
*SPRAKSKOLEN AS, Karl Johansgat. 8, 0154 Oslo (22 42 00 87/fax 22 42 32 94)
English Language Centre, Løkkev. 16, 4008 Stavanger
Folkeuniversitetet Rogaland, Kongsg. 58, 4012 Stavanger
Noricom Spraktjenester, Batstadstien 4, 4056 Tananger
Noricom Spraktjenester, Kjøpmannsg.11, 7001 Trondheim

Sweden

THE BRITISH INSTITUTE
Hagagatan 3, 11348 Stockholm. Tel: (8) 341200. Fax: (8) 344192. E-mail: info@britishinstitute.se
Number of teachers: 12.
Preference of nationality: British.
Qualifications: CELTA or DELTA.
Conditions of employment: short-term or permanent contracts. 1,760 hours per year.
Salary: kr12,500-19,000 per month for permanent staff; kr130-240 per lesson for term staff. Deductions of 30%-35% for tax and contributions.
Facilities/Support: no assistance with accommodation. Training provided.
Recruitment: local interview essential.
Contact: Mrs. Barbro Kjellson, Principal.

RICHARD LEWIS COMMUNICATIONS
Head Office, Norevägen 9, Box 3, 18205 Djursholm. Tel: (8) 753 2222. Fax: (8) 763 0967.   E-mail: (general)   rlc@telia.com   or   (local   manager) sally_kennedy@rlc.com. Website: www.crossculture.com.
Number of teachers: approx. 10 including freelancers.
Preference of nationality: must be native English speakers.
Qualifications: an EFL qualification, teaching experience in Business English/adult contact and some personal business experience.
Conditions of employment: varies. Daytime regular hours are 8am-5pm.
Salary: negotiable.
Facilities/Support: provides teachers with accommodation on a temporary basis, but they have to find their own accommodation eventually.
Recruitment: through networking, references and first-time applicants who send their CVs to RLC Head Office. Interviews are essential and can be arranged in the UK.
Contact: Sally Kennedy, Centre Manager, Stockholm Region.

TBV
Box 4401, 10268 Stockholm. Tel: (8) 615 5725. Fax: (8) 6155710. E-mail: birgitta.thulin@tbv.se. Website: www.tbv.se.
Number of teachers: 100 every summer.
Preference of nationality: none, but must be native speaker.
Qualifications: degree plus TEFL Certificate.
Conditions of employment: one semester. 3-30 hours per week freelance.
Salary: about £11 per hour and social costs.
Facilities/Support: no assistance with accommodation.
Recruitment: contacts, advertisements, agencies.
Contact: Birgitta Thulin, Head of Languages.

A selection of other schools to try (towns in alphabetical order):
All-International Language Center AB, Morbydalen 25, 182 52 Danderyd (8-753 6000)
ABC Engelsk o. Amerikanska Sprakundervisning, Säfflegatan 7, 7 tr, 123 44 Farsta
(8-605 3918)
Berlitz International Sweden, Apelbergsg.57, 111 37 Stockholm (8-412 1300)
Cambridge Language Service, Kocksg.56, 116 29 Stockholm (8-716 7567)
Language for Business, Ekbakev. 16, 181 46 Lidingö, Stockholm (8-765 8890)
Speak Right AB, Linneg. 6, 114 47 Stockholm (8-661 9049)
Viewpoint Communications, Lundagatan 36A, 117 27 Stockhom (8-668 1833)
Uppsala Sprakcenter, Havsörnsv.3, 756 52 Uppsala (18-32 18 65)

Spain

The late 20th century was a period of unprecedented economic growth in Spain as business and industry forged ahead, prodding Spanish schools and businesses into a frenzy of English language learning. Few job interviews would have omitted the question, 'How much English can you speak?' But the emphasis has shifted to adapt to changing conditions in the market. The majority of language academies are now involved with the teaching of children starting with the pre-school age group. There is a national push to introduce English early; it is compulsory in state schools from the age of nine, and the Spanish Ministry of Education in conjunction with the British Council has been recruiting experienced EFL teachers to work in nearly 50 participating primary schools. This trend has filtered through to private language providers, some of whom organise summer language camps for adolescents. As in Greece, many children are enrolled in private English lessons to improve their chances of passing school exams. Language centres which dealt more or less exclusively with company personnel for a decade are suddenly asking their teachers to organise sing-songs and games for young children.

Despite a decline in the adult market, there are still thousands of foreigners teaching English in language institutes from the Basque north (where there is a surprisingly strong concentration) to the Balearic and Canary Islands. The entries for language schools occupy about 18 pages of the Madrid Yellow Pages and 585 listings in the on-line Yellow Pages (see below). Almost every back street in every Spanish town has an *Academia de Ingles*. Technically *academias* are privately run and largely unregulated and *institutos* teach children 16 to 18.

Spain has always been a popular destination for EFL teachers. Who can fail to be attracted to the climate, scenery, history and culture? And yet, many new arrivals in Spain soon realise that Spain and the Spanish people of their imagination bear little resemblance to what they find, at least in the major cities. All this economic expansion and increased prosperity has not only led to pollution and over-development, but also to greed and corruption at many levels. Due to recession, the ELT business has become cut-throat with academy owners doing their best to squeeze out every last peseta of profit, which can lead to poor working conditions.

Another myth which is soon exploded is that life in Spain is cheap. Although it is still possible to enjoy a three-course meal with wine for a few pounds and to travel on the metro for a few pence, Madrid is considered to be one of the most expensive cities in the world, and Spain as a whole suffers from high inflation and expensive accommodation. Teaching wages rarely allow more than a tolerably comfortable lifestyle. These are points to bear in mind when visions of *paella* and beaches dance before your eyes.

Prospects for Teachers

The days are gone when any native speaker of English without a TEFL background could reasonably expect to be hired by a language academy. Many schools in the major cities echo the discouraging comments made by the director of a well-established school in Barcelona who said that he has found that there is a large supply of well-qualified native English speakers on hand so that his school cannot possibly reply to all the CVs from abroad that they receive as well.

Other schools report that the number of applications from candidates with a TEFL Certificate has soared simply because so many more centres in the UK and worldwide are churning them out. (One claims to have noticed a decline in standards, at least from the level of literacy displayed in CVs and applications.) Opportunities for untrained graduates have all but disappeared in what can be loosely described as 'respectable' schools, though there are still plenty of more opportunistic language academy directors who might be prepared to hire someone without qualifications, particularly part-time. A great many schools fall into this category. To take a random example, the expatriate director of a well-established school in Alicante estimated that of the 20 or so schools in town, only four operate within the law (i.e. keep their books in order, pay social security contributions for their staff, etc.)

Many Britons and Irish people with or without TEFL qualifications set off for Spain to look for work on spec, preferably in early September. A high percentage of schools, especially those which have been termed 'storefront' schools, depend on word-of-mouth and local walk-ins for their staff requirements. Anyone with some experience and/or a qualification should find it fairly easy to land a job this way. With a knowledge of Spanish, you can usually fill one of the many vacancies for teachers of children (with whom the total immersion method is not always suitable). The usual process is to put together a timetable from various sources and be reconciled to the fact that some or all of your employers in your first year will exploit you to some degree. Those who stay on for a second or further years can become more choosy.

The situation for Americans has become almost impossible if they want to work legally (see section on *Regulations* below).

FIXING UP A JOB

Because schools run the whole gamut from prestigious to cowboy, every method of job-hunting works at some level. The big chains like Wall Street Institutes (with 140 academies in Spain), inlingua (with up to 40), Berlitz and Linguarama mostly hire locally, though it may be worth enquiring at their headquarters (see chapter *Finding a Job*). They are probably a good bet for the novice teacher on account of the stability of hours they can offer. Anyone hired by Berlitz receives a free week-long training course in the Berlitz Method. Similarly, Wall Street Institutes (whose head office in Spain is at Rambla de Catalunya 2-4, 08007 Barcelona; 93-412 0014/412 5736/fax 93-412 3803; www.wsi.es) are always looking for teachers, including relatively inexperienced ones whom they train in their own method. Another chain is Opening Schools based in Barcelona (central office 93-241 8900/

cwesterman@ openingschool.com), which employs 450 teachers at its schools in Spain.

In Advance

Candidates who know that they want to teach in Spain should consider doing their TEFL training with an organisation with strong Spanish links such as *Languages Training & Development* in Oxfordshire, *Windsor Schools* or *Oxford House College.* The latter has a partner school in Barcelona at Avinguda Diagonal 402, 08037 Barcelona (93-458 0111). (See *Training: Trinity College TESOL Courses.*) Better still, do your training in Spain, for example *CLIC Seville* and *International House* in Barcelona and Madrid regularly offer CELTA courses and *Next Training Espana* in Barcelona offers the Trinity TESOL course. An independent training organisation whose courses are patronised mainly by Americans is the International Career Center (ICC) in Barcelona; in the US ring 888-256-2519 or look at www.teflbarcelona.com for details of their monthly courses which come with on-going job assistance and advice on obtaining work visas.

For a listing of English language schools in Spain, a good place to start is the Education Department of the Spanish Embassy (20 Peel St, London W8 7PD; 020-7243 8535/020-7727 2462; asesores@dial.pipex.com/ www.cec-spain.org.uk). As well as sending an outline of Spanish immigration regulations and a one-page handout 'Teaching English as a Foreign Language', it can send a list of the 350 members of FECEI, the national federation of English language schools *(Federación Española de Centros de Enseñanza de Idiomas)*, though they may not always have the most up-to-date list available. FECEI is concerned with maintaining high standards, so its members are committed to providing a high quality of teaching and fair working conditions for teachers. In order to become a member, a school has to undergo a thorough inspection. Therefore FECEI schools represent the elite end of the market and are normally looking for well qualified teachers. The presidency of FECEI is a rotating one. At present the contact is Mr. Frank Spain, Calle Miguel Servet 1, 13500 Puertollano, Ciudad Real (926-42 7537). FECEI comprises 16 regional associations integrated in ACADE (Asociación de Centros Autónomos de Enseñanza Privada, Calle Ferraz 85, 28008 Madrid; tel 91 5500102; fax 91 5500122/ acade@acade.es/ www.acade.es).

The book *Teaching English in Spain* by Jenny Johnson (Head of Teacher Training at International House Barcelona) contains a list of about 40 schools and also a lot of detailed information about finding work as well as working and living in Spain. The book (published in April 1998) can be ordered by e-mailing orders@combook.co.uk or through bookshops or www.amazon.com (ISBN 1 873047 12 6, £11.99).

Otherwise it will be a matter of consulting the Yellow Pages *(Las Paginas Amarillos)* on the internet or at specialist libraries. Although fewer jobs are advertised in the British educational press than formerly, there is a good sprinkling. Searching for *Escuela Idiomas* on www.paginas-amarillas.es will produce lists of schools in the places you search, some with e-mail and internet addresses.

Most of the regional British Council offices in Spain maintain lists of language schools in their region (which partially duplicates FECEI lists) apart from Madrid which does not keep a register of schools. The Seville office has separate lists for the eight provinces of Andalucia (Seville, Cadiz, Cordoba, Huelva, Malaga, Granada, Jaén and Almeriá). The offices in Valencia, Bilbao, Barcelona and Palma de Mallorca also produce useful lists.

British or Irish nationals with a TEFL qualification or PGCE might want to make use of a recruitment agency, whether a general one or one which specialises in Spain such as English Educational Services (Alcalá 20-2°, 28014 Madrid; 91-532 9734/531 4783/fax 531 5298; e-mail: movingparts@excite.com). The owner Richard Harrison recommends that candidates with just a degree and CELTA come to Spain in early September and contact his agency on arrival. He works in conjunction with schools all over Spain. Another agency ESS (English and Spanish Studies, Otterburn House, Bromley Road, Beckenham, Kent BR3 5JE; 020-7937 3110) is less active but recruits for a few posts in Catalonia each year. The jobs are for an academic year.

The American organisation, InterExchange (161 Sixth Avenue, New York, NY 10013; 212-924-0446 ext. 109/fax 212-924-0575; info@interexchange.org/ www.interexchange.org) arranges language assistant programmes in Spain for a placement fee of $400-$600.

On the Spot

Most teaching jobs in Spain are found on the spot. With increasing competition from candidates with the Cambridge or Trinity Certificate (now considered by many language school owners a minimum requirement), it is more and more difficult for the under-qualified to succeed. The best time to look is between the end of the summer holidays and the start of term, normally October 1st. November is also promising, since that is when teachers hand in their notice for a Christmas departure. Since a considerable number of teachers do not return to their jobs after the Christmas break and schools are often left in the lurch, early January is also possible.

The beginning of summer is the worst time to travel out to Spain to look for work since schools will be closed and their owners unobtainable. There are some language teaching jobs in the summer at residential English camps for children and teenagers, but these are usually more for young people looking for a working holiday as camp monitors than for EFL teachers.

The experiences of Jon Loop from Hampshire during his successful job hunt in Madrid in October illustrate that persistence is the key:

> *I travelled to Madrid from Bordeaux in October. I had given a few English lessons in France, but basically I had no experience and no qualifications. I copied down lots of addresses from the Madrid Yellow Pages under the heading 'Academias de Enseñanza Idiomas' and just went round all of them leaving my CV. I got three hours a week after 45 schools and a further three hours after number 75. I visited five more then gave up and waited for the two schools to give me more hours.*
>
> *At the interviews, they asked the usual questions about experience, teaching methods (always say you use media materials), etc. I just looked them in the eye and lied. However I was fairly confident that I could teach English. Since I had been to so many schools previously these interviews were easy, and I had managed to build up a very good CV.*

When knocking on doors, bear in mind that most language academies will be closed between 2pm and 4pm when directors are invariably away from their desks. Try to leave a contact telephone number (most pensions won't mind). A serious director will probe into any claims of experience and will soon weed out any bogus stories. Other directors are just checking to see that you are a reasonable proposition or at least not a complete dud.

A more probable scenario for the untrained is that they will elicit some mild interest from one or two schools and will be told that they may be contacted right at the beginning of term and offered a few hours of teaching. Spanish students sign up for English classes during September and into early October. Consequently the academies do not know how many classes they will offer and how many teachers they will need until quite late. It can become a war of nerves; anyone who is willing and can afford to stay on has an increasingly good chance of becoming established. After going a certain distance in looking for a teaching job, George Kelly lost his nerve and abandoned the fray (though his job-hunt was made considerably more difficult since he has a US passport):

> *I arrived in September and spent about two weeks in Madrid looking for an*

English teaching job. I contacted about 40 schools and had received only one firm offer when I left Spain on September 21st. Many schools told me that they would contact me if they ended up needing teachers, and I believe at least a few of them would have called me.

If in Madrid, try to locate a copy of the Blue Pages, a directory organised by street. It is possible to pick out language schools in selected neighbourhoods this way, i.e. near where you are staying. It also includes a useful grid map of the Madrid metropolitan area. Alternatively, of course, you can simply wander the streets looking for schools. The density is so high that you are bound to come across several.

Other sources of job vacancy information includes the Madrid daily *El Pais* which usually has a few relevant classifieds under the heading *Trabajo – Idiomas*. Also try *Ya, ABC* or *Segundamano,* Madrid's classified ad paper (published Monday, Wednesday and Friday) which usually carries a good selection of relevant ads under the heading *Empleo* (rather than *Idiomas – Inglés*). Local magazines may advertise the possibility of *intercambio* which means an exchange of English for Spanish or Catalan conversation practice. As usual, English language bookshops sometimes have a notice board with relevant notices.

Although the majority of job-seekers head for Madrid or Barcelona, other towns may answer your requirements better. There are language academies all along the north coast and a door-to-door job hunt in September might pay off. This is the time when tourists are departing so accommodation may be available at a reasonable rent on a nine-month lease.

Live-in Positions

If you want a base from which to look for work and some contact with the kinds of Spaniards who are eager to learn English, you might like to consider a live-in position with a family who wants an English tutor for their children or a voluntary position as an English assistant on summer language/sports camps. Further details may be sought from Relaciones Culturales, the youth exchange organisation at Calle Ferraz 82, 28008 Madrid (91-541 71 03/fax 559 1181), which also places native speakers with Spanish families who want to practise their English in exchange for providing room and board. Two other agencies involved in making this sort of live-in placements are GIC, Pintor Sorolla 29, Apdo. 1080, 46901 Monte Vedat (Valencia) and Castrum, Ctra. Ruedas 33, 47008 Valladolid (983-222213/ www.terra.es/personal2/castrumspain). The latter makes placements in Castille and Leon whereby participants undertake to spend three or four hours a day teaching English to members of the family and to enrol in a Spanish course (minimum five hours a week). The placement fee is pta25,000.

Michelle Manion from the US was happy with the language exchange arranged for her by Elena Garcia Perez of Castrum:

I would recommend the programme to anyone in my situation, i.e. anyone who wants to live in Spain but not as an au pair and is not entitled to a work permit. I was placed with a family with two boys aged 11 and 14. In the morning I went off for my Spanish lesson and then gave a lesson to the boys in turn. Spanish boys are notorious for being spoilt and impossible to control, but also for possessing wonderful personalities and great senses of humour. Carlos and César were typically Spanish and always managed to be both delightful and infuriating. Anyone interested in undertaking this venture should try to ascertain the children's level of English before arriving in Spain and to bring textbooks, magazines and children's books to work with, since English books are difficult to find in Spain. Also, when you arrive in Spain try to make as many friends and take up every opportunity you're given as this is the best way to learn Spanish.

Freelance Teaching

As usual, private tutoring pays better than contract teaching because there is no middle man. According to Glen Williams, the going rate in Granada starts at about pta1,500 for individuals and from pta2,000 for teaching three or four at once. Freelance rates in Madrid are potentially higher (pta3,000) but travelling time has to be taken into consideration. Stuart Britton easily found private pupils to supplement his school income in a small town in the untouristy north of Las Palmas de Gran Canaria. However when his employer found out, he was told to drop them or risk being sacked, even over the summer when the school was closed and Stuart had no other source of income. He resented this so much that he advises not bothering with small schools, and simply concentrate on obtaining private students.

As always, it is difficult to start up without contacts and a good knowledge of the language; and when you do get started it is difficult to earn a stable income due to the frequency with which pupils cancel. The problem is particularly acute in May when school pupils concentrate on preparing for exams and other activities fall by the wayside. Spaniards are fond of taking off the days between a mid-week fiesta and the weekend known as *puente* meaning bridge.

Getting private lessons is a marketing exercise and you will have to explore all the avenues which seem appropriate to your circumstances. Obviously you can advertise on notice boards at universities, public libraries, corner shops and wherever you think there is a market. Major stores are a good bet, for example Jumbo and Al Campo in Madrid. A neat notice in Spanish along the lines of *'Profesora Nativa da clases particulares a domicilió'* might elicit a favourable response. Send neat notices to local state schools asking them to pin it up broadcasting your willingness to ensure the children's linguistic future. Compile a list of addresses of professionals (e.g. lawyers, architects, etc.) as they may need English for their work and have the wherewithal to pay for it. Try export businesses, distribution companies, perhaps even travel agencies. Make the acquaintance of language teachers who will know of openings. Place adverts in free papers (like *El 18*) and in advertising papers (like *Almoneda* in Granada).

Because private classes are so much better paid than institute teaching, they are much in demand, including by contract teachers, most of whom are engaged in some private tutoring. The ideal is to arrange a school contract with no more than 15 or 20 hours and supplement this with private classes which are lucrative though unstable.

REGULATIONS

Patience is required to deal with the paperwork required by EU nationals after starting work. In order to obtain a residence permit *(residencia)*, employees must take a copy of their contract (in Spanish and officially stamped) to the *Oficina de Extranjería* or, if there isn't a local foreigners' registration office, the *Comisaría Provincial de Policía*. It will also be necessary to queue in various offices to obtain a foreigners' identity number (NIE) from the police and a fiscal identity number (NIF) from the tax office *(Hacienda)*. When the *residencia* is eventually granted, it is valid for five years. Many foreigners engage a specialist lawyer called a *gestoria* to assist. Further details are contained in the Notes *Settling in Spain* available from the British-Consulate in Spain (c/ Marqués de la Ensenada 16-2°, 28004 Madrid; 91-308 5201).

The immigration situation for people from outside Europe has become increasingly difficult. Most of the schools which once hired large numbers of North Americans now refuse to tackle the lengthy procedures involved in obtaining work permits. As the director of one school explained:

> *The Spanish authorities have rejected all the applications we have made in the past year, using Spain's high unemployment rate as their justification. An appeal now takes at least two years and costs a small fortune in legal fees.*

This means that we will be employing fewer non-European Union citizens in the future. Candidates have to be very qualified for us to consider them in the first place. Many Americans have now caught on to this problem and apply for Irish or Italian nationality if they are eligible.

This pessimistic view of the chances for Americans and Canadians was voiced by so many schools that it seems almost superfluous to describe the procedures. Briefly, work permit applications must be lodged and collected in the applicant's country of residence. The application must include a formal job offer from an employer in Spain, a recent medical certificate, *antecedents penales* (police certificate of good character), notarised degree certificate and seven passport photographs. The future employer then applies for the work and residence permits.

None of this means that there aren't any Americans or other nationalities teaching in Spain. Jon Loop's fellow teachers in Madrid were mainly Americans who had no permits whatsoever. According to Jon, many post-Hemingway Americans go to Spain for a year to learn Spanish and 'find themselves man' (or maybe even find themselves a man).

Social security *(seguridad social)* contributions are between 4% and 7% of earnings; 6.4% is typical. Under EU legislation, language schools must give contracts and make contributions for all staff, whether full-time or part-time. In practice, this does not always happen. After a few months of teaching for one academy, Jon Loop asked for a contract and was given a special 11-hour contract (though at the time he was teaching 20 hours a week). Contracts for less than 12 hours a week do not require more than minimal social security contributions. Joanna Mudie from the Midlands describes the situation which results from this:

There's a great deal of uncertainty and insecurity about all aspects of work: hours, days, rates of pay, insurance, etc. Contracts (if you're lucky enough to get one) are a load of rubbish because employers put down far fewer hours on paper to avoid paying so much insurance, and also to protect themselves if business dwindles... My advice is, forget your English sense of honesty and obeying the law. 'When in Rome...' Relax and simply don't worry about the legalities. It usually seems to work out okay, and if not, well, it's a nice life in the sun.

Tax deductions of about 12% are paid in arrears and do not normally affect teachers on nine-month contracts, though in some cases a small percentage is withdrawn at source *(retenciones)*. Technically any person who spends more than 183 days a year in Spain is considered a resident and is liable to pay Spanish tax, though Spain has a double taxation treaty with the UK.

Schools that sidestep the regulations to maximise profits and who do not pay contributions to cover their employees' social security might well be the ones willing to employ non-Europeans and pay cash-in-hand. Anyone who works on a tourist visa will have to renew it every three months by leaving the country. Weekend trips to France or Portugal can be organised for this purpose.

CONDITIONS OF WORK

Salaries are not high in Spain and have not increased significantly over the past decade. A further problem for teachers in Madrid and Barcelona is that there is not much difference between salaries in the big cities where the cost of living has escalated enormously and salaries in the small towns. The minimum net salary is about pta100,000 per month, though most schools offer pta120,000 to pta140,000 for a minimum of 25 hours a week. David Bourne found this sufficient in the town of Gijon in Asturias where he taught for nine months:

Prices and rents here are not as bad as they are in the big cities like Madrid, Seville and Barcelona, so most teachers live quite happily on their take-home wages. I have been able to save pta230,000 without having to live too stringently for example.

The best paid hourly wage, say pta2,000, is paid to teachers who are sent out to firms or those teaching short courses which are funded by the European Union, typically of unemployed professionals in their 20s.

Spanish TEFL is no different from TEFL in other countries in that there are lots of employers offering low pay, long hours and exploitative conditions. For example teachers have discovered that pay has been deducted when they have been unavoidably absent or that their bonuses have been withheld with no explanation. As always, you can gain an idea of an employer's integrity by talking to other teachers as well as by using your intuition at the interview. Asking lots of questions is a good idea since then you can find out your pay and maximum hours so that you will be in a stronger position to argue should your employer try to mess you around. But realistically, most new arrivals are exploited at least in some respects in their first year. Laura Phibbs was spared the possibility of being exploited, since her promised job evaporated overnight:

The Madrid school director rang me to inform me that I had got the job and I was to start nine days later. When, as instructed, I rang to confirm the arrival time of my plane, I was told that there was no job for me after all since the school had gone bankrupt. I think what really made me angry was that I had rung him rather than the other way round. He did not even say sorry or sound in the least remorseful.

The same school continues to be listed by the Association of Private Language Schools (ACADE), so it may be that pleading bankruptcy was just an excuse in the face of insufficient pupils.

Increasingly schools do not offer full-time work. Those that do tend to work their teachers very hard, expecting them to teach around 30 hours; the legal maximum is 33. Considering that preparation and travelling is extra, this can result in a gruelling schedule. Dennis Bricault refers to the notoriously uncongenial timetable of most EFL teachers (and not just in Spain) as a 'bookend schedule', whereby you might have to teach between 8am and 10am, then again through the evening. Most teachers put up with the late finishing time without too many murmurs because they are not deprived of Spanish nightlife even if they have to work until 10pm.

According to Spanish law, workers are not entitled to paid holiday until they have been working for 12 months, hence the near-universality of nine-month contracts. Most teachers find it impossible to save enough in nine months to fund themselves abroad for the rest of the year. Most pay agreements also take account of bonuses *(pagas extraordinaria)* of which there are two or three a year. Legal schools will pay *finiquito* (holiday pay) at the end of a contract which should work out to be about £50 for every month worked.

If the terms of a contract are being breached and the employer does not respond to the teacher's reminders, recourse can be taken to a *denuncio*, which involves informing the authorities (either in person or via a union, such as the Commissiones Obreros) that your school is not complying with tax and social security rules or fire regulations or whatever. The *denuncio* can effectively close a school if it is taken seriously and if the school does not have the proverbial friends in high places. In fact the procedure is complicated and time-consuming but the mere mention of it *might* improve your working conditions.

The experience of teaching at a summer camp is entirely different. The pay is fairly good (say, pta100,000-120,000 for a four-week stint plus free board and accommodation), though some organisations offer little more than accommodation, meals and pocket money. Glen Williams describes his summer job at a summer language camp in Izarra in the Basque Country:

The children learned English for three hours in the morning with one half
hour break (but not for the teacher on morning snack duty trying to fight off
the hordes from ripping apart the bocadillos*). Then we had another three or*
four hours of duties ranging from sports and/or arts to shop/bank duty. For
many of us, inexperienced with dealing with groups of kids, there were a few
problems of discipline. It was the kids' holiday and they quickly cottoned on
that we English teachers in general were a bunch of hippies.

Pupils

For reasons which remain obscure, Spaniards have the reputation for being hopeless at languages, possibly as a result of unreasonable expectations. This is more tolerable in the adults who are fairly well motivated, but often hard-going with children (unless you are especially fond of kids). This was one of David Bourne's biggest problems and one which he thinks is underestimated, especially as a higher proportion of English teaching in Spain is now of children and teenagers:

I have found that a lot of the younger students only come here because their
parents have sent them in order to improve their exam results. The children
themselves would much rather be outside playing football. There are days
when you spend most of the lesson trying (unsuccessfully in my case) to keep
them quiet. This is especially true on Fridays. I have found it very hard work
trying to inject life into a class of bored ten year olds, particularly when the
course books provided are equally uninspiring.

In such cases it might be a good idea to change your aim, from teaching them English to entertaining them (and paying your rent). If students don't want to learn, you will only break your heart trying to achieve the impossible.

A good knowledge of Spanish is helpful if not essential when teaching junior classes as Peter Saliba, Director of the Cross School in Malaga, explains:

We need teachers with a fluent command of Spanish, not the typical grasp of
elementary phrases which may get them by in a social context. On a limited
two or three hour per week teaching timetable, there simply is not time for
cumbersome English explanations of English grammar and vocabulary. It is
worse still with young learners and teens, who will 'run riot' or at the very
least run circles round non-Castilian speaking teachers.

Classes differ enormously as Jon Loop found during his year of teaching at an academy in Madrid:

A lot of my groups were civil servants. They were excruciating because they
didn't want to be there. The government has to spend its language training
budget and picks people at random. I taught other classes of university
students who were very enthusiastic and were great to work with. I taught a
group of technicians at the meteorological office who were keen because it
was directly linked to their work. Then I taught groups from companies who
were not very keen to start with, but by the end of the year we were having a
great time. It's classes like this that make teaching worthwhile.

Jon recommends making good use of your students, since so many Spaniards are friendly and eager to help. If you are having trouble with a recalcitrant landlord, perhaps a letter from a trainee lawyer you happen to be teaching might solve the problem. Students may lend you an unoccupied holiday house or put you in touch with friends looking for private English lessons. In Jon's case, a student arranged for him to spend the harvest at a family vineyard and another helped him to fix up work editing technical papers.

Needless to say, Spaniards are a nation of talkers. If things seem to be going awry in your classes, for example students turning up late or being inattentive, don't pussyfoot around. Make your feelings known, just as Spaniards do.

Accommodation

Rents usually swallow up at least a quarter of a teacher's income, more in the big cities and much more if you don't share. In small towns, it is not uncommon for schools to arrange accommodation for their teachers at least for an initial period. Many Spanish students want to live with English students so check university notice boards for flat shares, especially in the *Facultad de Filosofia y Letras* which includes the Department of English. Some teachers even arrange to share a flat rent-free in exchange for English lessons.

If renting a flat expect to pay a month's rent in advance, plus one or two months' rent as deposit. Since your first pay cheque may not arrive until November, you should arrive with between £800 and £1,000 to tide you over. Try to avoid using a *finca* (property agency) which will charge a further month's rent (at least). In Madrid many people use the free ads paper *Segundamano;* if you do decide to compete for a flat listed in this paper, get up early since most flats are gone by 8am.

LEISURE TIME

Once you acquire some Spanish, it is very easy to meet people, since Spaniards are so friendly, relaxed and willing to invite newcomers out with them. Of course there is also a strong fraternity of EFL teachers almost everywhere. With luck you will end up socialising with both groups in bars, at parties, *romerías* (pilgrimages), fiestas, etc.

Spain is a good country for wine-drinking film-goers but not so good for gadget-addicts with poor teeth. Eating, drinking, smoking, entertainment and transport (including taxis) are all still cheap, though this advantage is cancelled out for some by the high cost of other things such as clothes, cars and electrical items, not to mention contraceptives, standard chemists' products and dental care. The cost of living gets lower the longer you stay and discover where the locals get their bargains.

If you're looking for traditional Spanish culture, don't go to Madrid, and certainly don't look for it in Barcelona which is not Spanish at all but Catalan. Seville, Granada and Valencia are lovely Spanish cities. While teaching in Andalucia, Joanna Mudie appreciated the chance to learn about the traditional but still very much alive dances of Spain, e.g. Sevillanas, Malagueras and Pasadoble. If you're looking for an idyllic Mediterranean climate don't go to northern Spain in mid-winter. After teaching in Segovia north of Madrid for a year, Eleanor Sedgwick concluded that it rained more there than in Manchester. But most teachers have little fault to find with the climate. Stuart Britton, who paints, was thrilled by the glorious blue light in which to paint historic castles and colourful narrow streets lined with gorgeous balconies.

Glen Williams describes his spare time activities in Madrid, a city he was clearly enjoying to the full:

> *Madrid is a crazy place. We usually stay out all night at the weekend drinking and boogying. During the gaps in my timetable (10-2 and 4-7) I pretend to study Spanish (I'm no natural) and just wander the back streets. I suppose I should try to be more cultural and learn to play an instrument, write poetry or look at paintings, but I never get myself in gear. I think most people teach English in Spain as a means to live in Spain and learn the Spanish language and culture. But there is a real problem that you end up living in an English enclave, teaching English all day and socialising with English teachers. You have to make a big effort to get out of this rut. I am lucky to live with Spanish people (who do not want to practise their English!).*

A few schools offer free or subsidised Spanish lessons as a perk to teachers. Otherwise investigate the government-run *Escuela Oficial de Idiomas*.

So many kinds of people find themselves teaching English in different situations that there is no average profile. Jon Shurlock worked alongside both reformed alcoholics whose lives had fallen apart and the usual middle class 'jolly nice' people taking a year or two out. While one teacher finds the locals cold and hostile and money-grubbing, another finds them warm and supportive. If the idea of teaching in Spain appeals at all, it is almost always a rewarding and memorable way for people with limited work experience to finance themselves as they travel and live abroad for a spell.

LIST OF SCHOOLS

All schools prefer their teachers to have European Union nationality (and most will not consider applicants without it) and to have a university degree, Cambridge Certificate (or equivalent) and knowledge of Spanish. Although some may be prepared to consider less, especially from candidates with some business experience or experience teaching children, the ever-increasing number of qualified applicants means that the occasions when schools need to do so are diminishing.

The standard negotiated contract is about pta130,000 per month for a 21-hour-a-week full-time teacher, though gross salaries tend to fluctuate between pta125,000 and pta150,000 depending on number of hours worked. The average range for an hourly wage is pta1,500-2,000, though a few schools still try to pay pta1,000 an hour and pta100,000 a month. Rates are usually higher in Madrid and Barcelona. The best plan is to pick out the schools in the city or province which appeals to you, and write off for details enclosing a CV, photograph and international reply coupons. Most schools carry out their selection procedure of new teachers between April and July, though if you arrive in person to look for a job in September at one of the listed schools, your chances of success are reasonable.

Because of the shift from a teachers' to an employers' market over the past ten years, quite a few schools are reluctant to publicise expected job vacancies for fear of being inundated with applications. The following list of schools is divided into the ones that actively encourage TEFL-trained job-seekers to contact them and those others which may have vacancies from time to time. Bear in mind that a personal visit is always more likely to lead to success than an unsolicited CV by mail.

Instead of including full entries for the schools, we have provided a skeletal list of names and addresses of schools willing to consider applications, followed by the number of native speaker teachers which they expect to employ each year and in some cases some brief annotations. Note that the country prefix to Spanish telephone numbers is 34. Schools are listed alphabetically by city or town except those in the Balearic Islands which are listed by island.

LANGUAGE CENTRE IDIOMAS: C/ Convento No. 5, 46970 Alamas (Valencia). Tel: (96) 150 6760. Fax: (96) 150 6760. 2 per year with degree and TEFL or one year experience and a knowledge of Spanish. Contact Carmen Ros.

ALGINET ENGLISH CENTRE: Reyes Catolicos No 52, 2 PtA 4, Alginet, 46240 Valencia. Tel: (961) 752747. Fax: (961) 772854. 4 teachers with TEFL Cert. and if possible one year's experience. Contact Carol Luscombe.

CENTRO FRANCES: C/Isilla 3, 09400 Aranda de Duero. Tel: (947) 50 51 17. Fax: (947) 51 05 51. E-mail: 3aconsul@wanadoo.es. 2 teachers with BA and TEFL Cert. Help with finding accommodation. Contact Mercedes Calvo.

EL CENTRO DE INGLES: C/Calderos 7, Andujar (Jaen). Tel: (953) 506821. Fax: (953) 506821. E-mail: med 014469@nacom.es. 7 teachers with degree and TEFL qualification. School is a teacher training centre. Contact Julie Hetherington.

CENTRE CULTURAL: C/Tarrega 27, 25600 Balaguer. Tel: (973) 445429 or (973) 443627. E-mail: info@centrecultural.com. 1-2 teachers needed. Help given with finding apartment or family to stay with. Contact Carles Pedra.

BRIGHTON IDIOMAS: Rambla Catalunya 66, 08007 Barcelona. Tel: (93) 488 3060. Fax: (93) 216 0747. E-mail: curriculum@brighton-idiomas.com. Summer and academic year vacancies in Barcelona and Madrid. BA plus 2 years' experience required. Contact Paul Henderson.

CAMBRIDGE SCHOOL: Plaza Manel Montanya 4, 08400 Granollers, Barcelona. Tel: (93) 870 2001. Fax: (93) 879 5111. E-mail: sarah@cambridgeschool.com. Website: www.cambridge.school.com. 30 teachers with CELTA, DELTA and primary or secondary school experience an advantage. Contact Sarah Edge.

CIC: Via Augusta 205, Barcelona 08021. Tel: (93) 200 1133. Fax: (93) 209 2960. E-mail: idiomes@iccic.edu. Website: www.iccic.edu. 20 teachers with Cambridge Certificate and 1 year's experience. Contact Tom Walton.

ENGLISH CENTRE: Plaza Paradis 2, 08500 Vic (near Barcelona). Tel: (93) 889 05 78. Fax: (93) 889 1969. E-mail: englishcentre@teleline.es. 10 teachers with degree, recognised EFL Cert. and some experience. Can assist with finding accommodation. Contact Rowland Norris.

EUROLOG IDIOMAS: Pl. Lesseps 4, 08023 Barcelona. Tel: (93) 415 99 44. Fax: (93) 415 33 42. E-mail: eurolog@eurolog. Website: www.eurolog.es. 30 teachers with CELTA and minimum one year's teaching experience. Contact Jon Green.

INTERNATIONAL HOUSE, Calle Trafalgar 14, 08010 Barcelona. Tel: 93-268 4511. Fax: 93-268 0239. E-mail: webmaster@bcn.ihes.com. www.ihes.com/bcn. (15-20 teachers). Run CELTA course and hire teachers who have passed the CELTA. Maximum 20 h.p.w. Pta157,000 per month (gross).

MERIT SCHOOL: Campo Florido 54-56, 2a, Barcelona. Tel: 93-408 15 50. Fax: 93-408 24 53. E-mail: dos@meritschool.com. 30-40 teachers with Cambridge Cert and a minimum 3 years' experience. Contact Anna Cole.

OPENING SCHOOL International: Plaza Francesc Macia, 7,13°, 08029 Barcelona.

OPENING SCHOOL SPAIN: Central Offices, via Augusta 238, 08021 Barcelona. Tel: +34 (93) 241 89 00. Fax: +34 (93) 241 89 10. E-mail: cwesterman@openingschool.com. CVs for all Opening schools in Spain can be sent to this address. 34-hour working week. 2,100,000 pesetas plus per year.

WALL STREET INSTITUTE: Font Vella 50, 08221 Terrassa, (Barcelona). Tel: (93) 7843131. Fax: (93) 784 33 22. 3 teachers with degree and TEFL/equivalent. Contact Joanne Bowler.

YOUR HOUSE: Pl. Nova 15, 08570 Torello, Barcelona. E-mail: yhouse@cconline.es. Website: www.osonaweb.com/yourhouse. 5-6 teachers; TEFL qualification not essential. Furnished flat provided. Contact: J Ferrau Perez.

SECOND LANGUAGE: Autonomia, 26-6°A, 48010 Bilbao. Tel: (94) 444 8062. Fax: (94) 444 8066. E-mail: second@secondlanguage.net. Website: www.secondlanguage.net. 15 teachers with in-company training and Cambridge Cert.

EL CENTRO INGLES: Ctra. Fuentebravia, Km.1, 11500 El Puerto de Santa Maria, Cadiz. Tel: (956) 850560. Fax: (956) 873804. E-mail: C_ingles@arrakis.es. 35 teacher trained graduates with PGCE and TEFL and specialities: art, music, P.E., I.T. etc. Contact Linda Randell.

OLMARES, Basieda-Lomeña, 39574 Canabria. Tel: (942) 735102. Fax: (942) 735102. E-mail: ingles@olmares.com. Website: www.olmares.com. 5 teachers with CELTA plus 2 years' experience. 1 year contract. All-day residential school meals included. Min. pta100,000 net plus accommodation on-site. Contact Richard Beazley.

THE ACADEMY OF LANGUAGES: Paseo Alfonso XIII, 47 y 49, 30203 Cartagena. Tel: (968) 52 09 42. Fax: (968) 52 19 88. E-mail: theacademy@ctv.es. 8 teachers with BA/BSc and CELTA. 9-month contracts. 25 h.p.w. Pta160,000 per month. No assistance with accommodation.

ESCUELA DE IDIOMAS: Miguel Servet No 1, Puertolland, Ciudad Real. Tel: (926) 427537. Fax: (926) 427537. E-mail: spain@canal21.com. 12 teachers with degree and PGCE. 1st month's rent paid on accommodation. Contact: Frank Spain.

EXETER SCHOOL: C/Uria 15-1° A, Eiton 33202. Tel/fax: (985) 330070. 4-6 teachers with degree plus EFL Cert. Spanish experience preferred. 25 hours per week. Pta120,000-140,000 per month. Contact Colin Lyne.

THE ENGLISH COLLEGE: Carrer Empedrat 4, 03203 Elche, Alicante. Tel: (965) 458401. Fax: (965) 452 302. E-mail: cnglishcoll@teleline.es. 3-5 teachers with degree and TEFL Cert and 1-2 years experience of similar kind of teaching. Some knowledge of Spanish desirable but not essential. 9-month contract. 29 hours per week. Pta130,000 per month. School has its own flat to rent. Contact Mark Harper, Director.

KENSINGTON CENTROS DE IDIOMAS: Avda. Pedro Muguruza 8, 20870 Elgoibar. Tel: (943) 740236. Fax: (943) 743512. 4 native speakers, BA and CELTA minimum. Help with finding accommodation. Contact Mark Sutter.

THE ENGLISH SCHOOL: Calle Bacia 7, 17001 Girona. Tel: (972) 211856. Fax: (972) 493129. London interviews in June.

INSTITUTE OF MODERN LANGUAGES: Puerta Real 1, 18009 Granada. Tel: (958) 225536. Fax: (958) 221455. E-mail: Jonathan@moebius.es. 12 teachers with degree and TEFL qualification and relevant experience. Contact Jonathan Baum.

EUROPEAN LANGUAGE STUDIES: Edificio Edimburgo, Plaza Nina, Huelva. Tel: (959) 263821. Fax: (959) 280778. E-mail: inforec2@teleline.es. 15 teachers with CELTA plus one year's experience. Interviews in London end of June. The school helps finding flats. Contact Jaqueline Buchanan.

CAMBRIDGE ENGLISH STUDIES: Avenida de Arteijo, 8-1°, 15004 La Coruña. Tel: (981) 160216. Fax: (981) 145694. E-mail: camcor@alehop.com (12-14) with recognised EFL qualification and one to three years' experience. Contact Nick Shaw.

LORD'S LANGUAGE CENTRE, Lamereo, Asturias. Tel: (985) 682850. Fax: (985) 682050. E-mail: Lords@fade.es. 4 teachers.

SAM'S ACADEMY: Dres. Castroviejo 29 1°, 26003 Logrono, La Rioja. Tel: (941) 25 91 25. 2 teachers with Cambridge qualification. Experience not essential. Contact Amparo Busto.

LA ACADEMIA DE INGLES: Avda. de Moratalaz 139, (Lonja Comercial), 28030 Madrid. Tel: (91) 430 5545. E-mail: laacaddein@neko.es. Approx 20 teachers with degree in modern languages, preferably Spanish. Contact Ana M Aparicio.

AMERICAN LANGUAGE ACADEMY: c/ Rodriquez San Pedro, 2, 28015 Madrid. Tel: (91) 445 5511. Fax: (91) 445 5800. E-mail: efl@americanlanguage.es. Website: www.americanlanguage.es. 20 teachers with degree and TEFL training. Contact Jeffrey Locey.

ASTEX: Hnos. Becquer 7-6°, 28006 Madrid. Tel: (91) 590 3477. Fax: (91) 563 8466. E-mail: selem@astex.es. Website: www.astex.es. 24 teachers with CELTA, TESOL and experience with young learners and business people. 1,600-1,800 pesetas per hour. Contact: David Warner.

BETA GROUP: Paseo Castellana no. 210-10° - 5, Madrid. Tel: (91) 345 2452. Fax: (91) 345 1701. E-mail: thebetagroup@train.es. Website: www.betagroup.com. 30 teachers with degree plus TEFL experience. Typically 23 hours per week; pta125,000 a month. Business English. Help given with finding accommodation.

BRITISH LANGUAGE CENTRE: Calle Bravo Murillo 377-2° 28020 Madrid. Tel: (91) 733 07 39. Fax: (91) 314 50 09. E-mail: ted.blc@cospa.es. Website: www.cospa.es/blc. 40 or more teachers with CELTA minimum. Also offers CELTA/DELTA courses. Teacher interviews in Spain essential. Can help with finding accommodation. Contact Alistair Dickinson.

CAMBRIDGE HOUSE: C/Lopez de Noyos, 95, 1°A, 28002 Madrid. Tel: (91) 519 4603. Fax: (91) 528 5078. E-mail: academia@cambridge-house.com. Website: www.cambridge-house.com. 25 teachers with degree and EFL Cert. and minimum 6 months experience. Contact Penny Rollinson.

THE ENGLISH CENTRE: Calle Nunez de Balboa 17, 28001 Madrid. Tel: (91) 57791 22. Fax: (91) 577 97 43. E-mail: engcent@teleline.es. 40 teachers with minimum CELTA qualification or equivalent and a year's experience. Contact Julia Hoare.

ENGLISH EDUCATIONAL SERVICES: C/Alcala, 20-2°, 28014 Madrid. Tel: (91) 531 4783. Fax: (91) 531 5298. E-mail: movingparts@excite.com. Agency recruiting 80-110 annually with degree and TEFL qualification. Contact Alan Crisp.

T.E.C. ENGLISH: Guzmán el Bueno 7, 28015 Madrid. Tel/fax: (91) 543 9271. 6 teachers with degree and EFL Cert and at least a year's experience. Applications processed in April/May. Contact Anne Sainz.

INTER-COM ENGLISH: Paseo General Martinez Campus 28, 28010 Madrid. Tel: (91) 308 28 22. Fax: (91) 308 47 75. E-mail: info@inter-com.com. Website: www.inter-com.com. 25 teachers with degree and DELTA or equivalent. Contact Alan Crisp.

LINGUACENTER: c/Rafael Calvo 8, 28010 Madrid. Tel: (91) 447 0300. Fax: (91) 4470781. E-mail: steven@linguacenter.es. Website: www.linguacenter.es. 100+ teachers mainly for company classes in the Madrid area. CELTA and 1 year's experience required. Contact Steven Pragnell.

CROSS SCHOOL OF LANGUAGES: C/Esperanto 19, 29007 Malaga. Tel: (95) 228 01 48. Fax: (95) 228 01 48. E-mail: crossidiomas@hotmail.com. 2 teachers employed directly from unsolicited applications. Modern languages degree, TEFL Cert. and fluent Spanish essential.

NUMBER NINE – THE ENGLISH LANGUAGE CENTRE: C/Sant Onofre 1, Ciutadella de Menorca, Menorca, Balearic Islands. Tel: (971) 384058. Fax: (971) 484001/384058. E-mail: number9@supersonik.com. 3 native and 2 non native speakers with degree preferably in modern languages and min Cert. TEFL (prefer Dip.). Contact James R Easton.

THE AMERICAN CENTER: Manuel Llaneza 26, 33600 Mieres (Asturias). Tel: (985) 461 454. Fax: (985) 794 870. E-mail: americancenter@hotmail.com. 3-4 teachers with experience of ESL teaching preferred but not essential. Some Spanish needed. Contact Ibrahim Hag-Omer.

CENTRO BRITANICO: Avda Rodriguez Acosta , P.O. Box 201, 18600 Motoril (Granada). Tel: (958) 83 3641. Fax: (958) 600937. 4-6 teachers with degree, TEFL Cert. Contact Javier-Luis Guardia Olmedo.

APPLE IDIOMAS: C/Agüera 2, 30001 Murcia. Tel: (968) 211038. Fax: (968) 218164. E-mail: apple.idiomas@wanadoo.es. 16 teachers with degree, TEFL Cert. and a knowledge of Spanish. Contact Duncan McBain.

ALCE IDIOMAS: C/Nogales 2, 33006 Oviedo. Tel: (985) 254543. Fax: (985) 254543. E-mail: alceidiomas@fade.es. 3 teachers with a degree and at least two year's teaching experience of some kind. Contact Mrs. S. Valles.

BRIAN SCHOOL: Magdalena 19, 33009 Oviedo. Tel: (985) 220408. E-mail: brianschool@fade.es. 3-4 native speakers with EFL qualifications. Sometimes teachers without experience are accepted if they are really keen and talented. American teachers require a vast amount of Spanish bureaucracy so they have got to be outstanding to make it worthwhile.

YORK IDIOMAS: C/Munoz Degrain, 9, 33007 Oviedo. Tel: (985) 241341. Fax: (985) 24 13 41. yorkidiomas@fade.es (12) with degree, TEFL, knowledge of Spanish, 1 year's (minimum) experience. Two nights accommodation provided. Contact Carmen Valledor.

PROGRESO CENTROS DE IDIOMAS: Plaza del Progreso 12B, 07013 Palma de Mallorca (Balearic Islands). Tel: (971) 734555. Fax: (971) 731664. (15-20). CELTA plus 2 years' experience or a PGCE, TEFL after a BA in Spanish. Contact Agnes Howard.

LEAP LANGUAGES: Inigo Arista 18, Entla. 31007 Pamplona. Tel: (948) 277904. Fax: (948) 271572. E-mail: info@leapnet.net. Website: www.leapnet.net (4) with degree, internet experience, experience in communication and if possible a knowledge of Spanish. 2 year contract. Help with finding accommodation.

Contact David Escott.

EIDE SCHOOL OF ENGLISH: Genaro Oraa 6, Santurce 48980. Tel: (94) 493 7005. Fax: (94) 461 5723. E-mail: eide@eide.es. Website: www.eide.es. 4 teachers with BA plus teaching experience if possible. Contact Maria Soledad Largo.

KENT IDIOMAS: C/ Tejedores 26, El Carmen, 40004 Segovia. Tel: (921) 43 4423. Fax: (931) 43 44 23. E-mail: kent-id@teleline.es. 2-3 teachers with degree and 1 year experience minimum. Good command of Spanish needed. Help with finding accommodation with families or renting apartments. Contact José Miguel Arranz.

BRITISH INSTITUTE OF SEVILLE: Federico Rubio 14, 41004 Seville. Tel: (954) 220240. Fax: (954) 211145. E-mail: mlawson@britinsev.com/ bisev@sistelnet.es. 20 teachers with CELTA/DELTA plus degree and 2 years experience. 9-month non-renewable and 12 month renewable contracts. 2¹/2-3 million pesetas per year gross. Affiliated to Bell Schools.

ENGLISH LANGUAGE INSTITUTE: Avda Eduardo Dato 36, 41005 Seville. Tel: (954) 640026. Fax: (954) 649503. E-mail: eli@eli.es. Website: elicentral@eli.es. 30 teachers with TEFL qualification. Interviews essential (in Seville and occasionally the UK). Help given with finding accommodation. Contact: Bridget Buckley.

ENGLISH ONE: Marques del Nervion, 41005 Seville. Tel: (954) 64 20 98. E-mail: english@arrakis.es. Website: www.arrakis.es/~english1. 5 teachers with degree and TEFL Cert or Diploma and some experience with children, teenagers and adults. Assistance with finding accommodation given. Contact Jennifer Fricker.

BRITISH SCHOOL: Pl. Ponent 5, 2, 43001 Tarragona. Tel: (977) 211 605. Fax: (977) 211605. E-mail: british@bstarragona.com. Website: www.bstarragona.com. 6 teachers with degree, TEFL qualification and minimum one year's experience teaching English abroad. Contact Bernard Tingle.

MANGOLD INSTITUTE: Av. Marques de Sotelo, Valencia. Tel: (96) 35227714. Fax: (96) 3514556. E-mail: mangold.idiomas@-es.com. 10-15 teachers with degree and TEFL Cert. 9 months. 30 hours weekly. Contact M. Enriques.

CENTRO DE IDIOMAS SANTA ANA: Calle Pasion 10, Valladolid. Tel/fax: (983) 358242. 3 teachers with degree plus TEFL Cert. Interview in Spain essential. Contact Beatriz Martinez.

EUROPEAN LANGUAGES SCHOOLS: Regueiro 2, 36211 Vigo. Tel: (986) 291748. Fax: (986) 291 748. E-mail: euroschools@moriartys.com. 15-16 teachers with degree in English or Spanish, TEFL qualification, some experience preferred. Candidates need references, knowlege of Spanish, outgoing, friendly personality. Contact John Moriarty.

VIGVATTEN NATUR KLUBB: Apartado 3253, 01002 Vitoria-Gasteiz; 945-281794. 15 teachers and monitors needed for language and sports summer camps in the Basque country, Pyrenees and Sierra de Urbion (near the town of Soria). Payment is pta35,000 plus board and lodging per fortnight.

THE BRITISH SCHOOL OF ARAGON: Carretera Valencia, km 8.5, 50410 Cuarte de Huelva, Zaragoza. Tel: (976) 505223. Fax: (976) 505253. E-mail: cba@virtualsw.es. Website: www.britanico-aragon.edu. 11 teachers with B.Ed. or BA with P.G.C.E in the relevant areas. Practical experience. Assistance given with finding accommodation. Contact Andrés Cirujano Pita.

Other Schools to Try (cities and towns in alphabetical order)

Note that these schools did not confirm their teacher requirements for this edition of Teaching English Abroad.

CAMBRIDGE SCHOOL IDIOMAS: Dos de Mayo, 26, 46960 Aldaya.

STANTON SCHOOL OF ENGLISH: Angel Lozano, 10-3° izq, 03001 Alicante. Tel: (96) 520 7581. Candidates must teach a demonstration class and take a test in English.

ENGLISH CENTRE: College of Languages, C/ José Artés de Arcos 34, 04004 Almeria. Tel: (951) 234551. Fax: (951) 272738. (96-7 British or Americans). Prefer teachers with experience of teaching children.

CAMBRIDGE CENTRE: Avda. Santos Patronos 25, 46600 Alzira (Valencia). Tel/fax: (96) 241 18 79. (5-7). BA plus minimum 2 years experience wanted.

BUSINESS LANGUAGE CENTER, C/ Enric Granados 113, 08008 Barcelona (93-218 2658)

ENGLISH CENTRE: Paseo Manual, Girona 12, 08034 Barcelona.

ENGLISH LANGUAGE INSTITUTE: Via Augusta 59 4t, 08006 Barcelona.

EUROLOG IDIOMES: Plaza Lesseps 4, 080023 Barcelona.

ICL: Av. Joseph Tarradellas 106 2° 3a, 08029 Barcelona.

INSTITUTE MANGOLD: Rambla Catalunya 16, 08007 Barcelona.

INSTITUTE OF NORTH AMERICAN STUDIES: Via Augusta 123, 08006 Barcelona. Tel: (93) 209 2711. Fax: (93) 202 0690. (85-100). Americans and Canadians. MA plus minimum 2 years' overseas experience.

LANGUAGE CLUB IDIOMAS, Rosalia de Castro 63, 08025 Barcelona

LINGUARAMA: Gran Via de Carlos III 98, 2°, Edificios Trade, 08028 Barcelona.

NATIVE NATION LANGUAGE ACADEMY, Via Laietaana 48-A, 1°, 3a, 08003 Barcelona (93-319 7172/fax 93-319 6191; NNation@bcn.servicom.es)

OPEN ENGLISH INTERNATIONAL GROUP, Rambla Catalunya 38, 08007 Barcelona. Tel: (93) 488 3601. 42 branches in Spain.

PHONE LANGUAGES, Francoli 11, 08006 Barcelona

WINDSOR SCHOOL: Av. Diagonal 319, pral, 4a, 08009 Barcelona

YOUR HOUSE LANGUAGE SCHOOL: Pl. Nova 15, 08570 Torelló, Barcelona. Tel/fax: (93) 859 2704. (5-10).

SKILLS CENTRO DE IDIOMAS: Trinidad 94-1°, 2002 Castellon. Tel: (964) 242668. (4). Majority of teaching to children.

THE ENGLISH HOUSE ACADEMY: C/ Iglesia 36, 2°, 15402 Ferrol. Tel: (981) 354223. (92).

EIS ESCOLA D'IDIOMES: Girona (e-mail: tracuceis@grn.es). Must speak Spanish or Catalan and be aged 25-35.

THE LANGUAGE CENTRE: Girona. Fax: (972) 201401. E-mail: tlc@bbs.grn.es.

DUNEDIN COLLEGE: Recogidas 18-1° Izq. 18002 Granada. Tel: (958) 255018. Also: C/ Rector Marín Ocete 8, 18014 Granada.

TEC ENGLISH CENTRE: C/ Pedro Frances 22A, 07800 Ibiza (Baleares). Tel: (971) 315828. Fax: (971) 191725. Also in Ibiza at C/ del Sol, Es Mercat, Santa Eulalia; tel: (971) 332070, and C/ San Vicente 21 1°, 07820 San Antonio; tel: (971) 345403. (10). Must have university degree and TEFL.

TEN: CENTRO DE INGLES: C/ Caracuel 24, 11402 Jerez de la Frontera (Cadiz). Tel: (956) 324707. (3).

HARRIS ENGLISH STUDIES, La Coruña (Galicia). Tel: (981) 557434. E-mail: harris@terra.es. 25 h.p.w. Contact Richard Harris.

ENGLISH CENTRE FOR LANZAROTE: C/ Canalejas 1-1°, Arrecife, Lanzarote (928-816156). Also C/ Fraternidad 23, Tias, Lanzarote. Tel: (928) 833519.

LANZAROTE LANGUAGE SCHOOL: fax (928) 802685. Summer jobs at children's camp and year-long vacancies from October.

TRELAND ANGLO-WORLD: Mayor 15-7°, 48930 Las Arenas (Vizcaya). Tel: (94) 463 1926/464 8989. Fax: (94) 464 2438. (9).

OXFORD SCHOOL: C/ Aleixandre s/n, 33400 Las Vegas (Corvera de Asturias). Tel: (985) 57 75 75. (1).

ACADEMIA VICTORIA: Gran Via 3, 26002 Logroño (La Rioja). Tel: (941) 242038. Fax: (941) 256711. (4).

CEE IDIOMAS: C/ Carmen 6, 28030 Madrid.

CENTRO DE IDIOMAS CONCORDE: C/ Gral. Moscardó 12, 28020 Madrid.

CHESTER SCHOOL OF ENGLISH: Jorge Juan 125, 28009 Madrid. Tel: (91) 40 25879. Fax: (91) 431 5054. E-mail: chester@bitmailer.net. Website:

www.chester.es. 25 teachers with degree and Cert. TEFL. Help with finding accommodation. Contact Sandra Bradwell.
COLON: Gran Via 55, Madrid.
EUROCENTRES: pa Castellana 194, 28046 Madrid.
IBERLENGUA: Torpedero Tucuman 26, 28016 Madrid. Tel: (91) 350 7297. (6-8). Two years' experience and liking for children's classes.
INLINGUA MADRID S.L.: Calle Arenal 24, 28013 Madrid. Tel: (91) 541 3246/7. Fax: (91) 542 8296. (25).
KING'S COLLEGE: Serrano 44, 28001 Madrid (kennedy@kingsgroup.com).
KURSOLAN: C/ Sandalo 5, 28042 Madrid. Tel: (91) 320 7500. Fax: (91) 320 7136. (40). Runs 2 summer camps outside Madrid for Spanish boys and girls. Teachers work long hours (teaching and activity/sports programme) from mid-June to September.
LANGUAGE HOUSE: Avda. de Brasilia 7, 28028 Madrid. Tel: (91) 726 1844. (1-2).
LANGUAGES STUDIES INTERNATIONAL: Luchana 31, 1°, 28010 Madrid.
LISTEN AND LEARN: C/ Narváez 14, 28009 Madrid.
LIVERPOOL, CENTRO DE IDIOMAS: Libreros 11-1°, 28801 Alcalá de Henares (Madrid). Tel: (91) 881 3184. Fax: (91) 881 35 84. (14). Run summer school programme in Barcelona for which they hire 15 EFL teachers.
PHONE LANGUAGES, Velázquez. IJ-6° ozqiierde, Madrid 28001 (91-426 0177/fax (91) 426 0178).
THAMESIS, SA: C/ Castelló 24, bajo Dcha, 28001 Madrid. Tel: (91) 575 8949/431 9635. Fax: (91) 575 6597. (25-30).
WALL STREET INSTITUTE: Centro Comercial Cuesta Blanca, Local 12, 2° Planta, la Moraleja, Alcobendas, 28100 Madrid. Tel: (91) 650 7602. Fax: (91) 650 8246. (4). 6-month contracts (renewable). 2 week training course given.
WALL STREET ESPANA Sa, Calle Lopez de Hoyos 153m 28002 Madrid. Tel: (91) 519 4907.
MALACA INSTITUTO: Calle Cortada 6, Cerrado de Calderon, 29018 Malaga. Fax: (95) 229 6316; e-mail: espanol@malacainst.ch.es.
THE AMERICAN CENTER: Hevia Aza 36, 33630 Pola de Lena; tel: 549 2513, and Plaza de la Iglesia 2, 33670 Moreda; tel: 548 2811. (6).
ACADEMIA MURCIA: fax (968) 2346514. E-mail: CATS@arrakis.es.
BILINGUE NORMINGTON: Calle Vinadel 11-15, 30004 Murcia. Tel: (968) 213262. Fax: (968) 628439. (1-2).
BUSINESS ENGLISH ACADEMY: Paseo Mutilnova 55, 31192 Navarra (e-mail: richard.lander@pna.servicom.es). Teachers for Pamplona.
IDIOMAS BLAZEK: Llinàs 2, 07014 Palma de Mallorca (Baleares). Tel: (971) 457260. Fax: (971) 284674. (1-2).
NORFOLK SCHOOL IDIOMAS: Aparejador Monzó 11, 46930 Quart de Poblet.
INTERNATIONAL HOUSE: Llovera 47, 43201 Reus (Tarragona). Tel: (977) 343562. Fax: (977) 340021. (7).
ACADEMIA LACUNZA/INTERNATIONAL HOUSE: Urbieta 14-1°, 20006 San Sebastián.
INLINGUA IDIOMAS: Larramendi 23 bajo, 20006 San Sebastián.
THE SMITHS' SCHOOL: Maestro Guridi s/n, 20008 San Sebastián. Tel: (943) 211028. (10).
AULA 57: Paseo de Canalejas 57, 39004 Santander. Fax: (942) 282028. Fluent Spanish needed.
OPEN ENGLISH ACADEMY, Rbla Generalitat 15-25, Entl., 17220 Sant Feliu de Guíxols, Girona (OPENENGL@teleline.es).
SCHOOL OF ENGLISH: Genaro Oraá 6, 48980 Santurce (Vizcaya). Tel: (94) 461 9555. Fax: 461 5723. (5).
ENGLISH 1: C/ Santa Maria Mozzarello s/n, Seville.
ENGLISH SCHOOL MACARENA: Dr. Jimenez Diaz 20, 41009 Seville. Tel: (95)

435 6134. (16).
ESCUELA UNION PACIFIC: Virgen de Luján 30A, 41011 Seville. Tel: (95) 445 5515. (15). Mostly part-time work in 5 centres located in Madrid (2), Barcelona, Bilboa and Seville.
LONDON CENTRE: C/ Asunción 52, Seville.
APPLE IDIOMAS: C/ Aben Al Abbar 9, 46021 Valencia. Tel: (96) 362 2545.
INLINGUA: C/ Gregorio Fernandez 6, 47006 Valladolid. Tel/fax: (983) 35 86 97. (5-6). Week long training course given in September.
ENGLISH CENTRE: Calle Bruselas 9, 50003 Zaragoza. Tel: (976) 283246. Mostly teaching children.
TECHNICAL COLLEGE OF ENGLISH: C/ Maria Lostal No. 22, 50008 Zaragoza. Tel: (976) 227909. Fax: (976) 233676. (12). Runs summer courses in the Pyrenees (Cerler and Jaca). Spanish to university level and an interest in children and sport required.

Switzerland

Prospects are gloomy for people who fancy the idea of teaching the gnomes of Zürich or their counterparts in other parts of Switzerland. Immigration regulations are very restrictive for all but the ultra-qualified, though a recently signed bilateral treaty on free movement between EU citizens and Switzerland will come into force in 2001 which may simplify the red tape. It is predicted that the main obstacles to free movement will be completely abolished in 2003 though it is unlikely that Switzerland will suddenly welcome an army of foreign language teachers. The Swiss economy is not as invincible as it was once considered to be as the director of a *Sprachschule* in Basel explained:

> *As a small language school in a country and region which has been experiencing severe withdrawal symptoms (from full employment, job and financial security), it is unlikely that we will be recruiting staff from outside Switzerland, especially as there is a large reservoir of potential candidates here in the Basel region and work permits for staff from outside Switzerland are now a rarity.*

Very few native speakers are recruited abroad except at a very advanced level. Those schools that do not insist on very advanced qualifications, for example the network of adult education *Ecoles Club Migros* have club schools in all the major cities but generally hire only teachers who already have a 'B' residence permit for Switzerland.

There are 14 Wall Street Institutes in Switzerland; a list of addresses and e-mail contact numbers is available at http://wsi.ch. One of the biggest is the one in Lausanne at Rue du Simplon 34, 1006 Lausanne (21-614 66 14/ caubort@wallst.ch). If you are hired by a Swiss language school, wages are high, ranging from SFr30 to SFr60 for a 50-minute lesson.

Regulations

Visa enquiries can be made at the Swiss Embassy in London between 3pm and 4pm on 020-7616 6000. A free booklet called *Living and Working in Switzerland* can be obtained from the Swiss Embassy in London or consulted on the web (www.swissembassy.org.uk or www.swissinfo.org) which briefly outlines the types of permit available. Like most official embassy literature, it implies that only people who are filling the kind of high-level vacancies that cannot be filled by someone already resident are eligible to obtain a residence permit. The only two possibilities are *Permis A,* reserved for seasonal employment in the building, hotel and holiday industry, or *Permis B* which is valid for a specific job for a year and can be renewed.

Even people who have been offered work by private institutes (teaching business English, for example) have failed to be granted a permit, often on the grounds that the employer cannot guarantee a minimum number of hours. The only other visa possibility is the *Frontalier*. To qualify, you must commute from a French or German town within 10km of the Swiss border where you have been resident for at least six months.

One possible avenue to explore is the approved trainee exchange scheme which operates between English-speaking countries and Switzerland. To qualify to become a *stagiaire* (trainee) with a Swiss employer, you must be aged 18-30 and have trained in the field in which you wish to work. The permit is valid for a year but can be renewed for a further six months. Details are available from the Swiss Federal Aliens Office (BFA Bundesamt für Ausländerfragen), Sektion Auswanderung und Stagiaires, Quellenweg 9, CH-3003 Bern (31-322 42 02).

Vacation Work

More possibilities for teaching English exist at summer camps than in city language institutes, as can be seen from the three programmes listed in the Directory below. There are a number of international schools in Switzerland, some of which run English language and sports summer schools. The Swiss Federation of Private Schools produces a leaflet called 'Language Courses in Switzerland' which lists the names and addresses of scores of private schools, with a code showing which ones teach English. The *Service Scolaire* (Advisory Office) is unwilling to send this leaflet to job-hunters, so if you do want to request it, it is best to impersonate a rich person looking for a summer language school on behalf of someone else and preferably enclose international reply coupons. The address is Service Scolaire, 16 rue du Mont-Blanc (PO Box 1488), 1211 Geneva 1.

Watch for occasional ads or, if you are in Switzerland, make local enquiries. Susanna Macmillan hitch-hiked from Italy to Crans-Montana in the Swiss Alps in the autumn and within three days had arranged a job as a *monitrice* at the International School there. The job, which was to teach English and sport, came with room and board and paid an additional SFr850 per month. (Perhaps one reason the job was so easy to get was because of the 60-hour weeks and compulsory overtime with no compensation.)

In addition to the organisations with entries below, the following organisations offer summer language courses between June and September and may need teachers or monitors (or some combination of the two):

Aiglon Summer School, 1885 Chesières.

Beau Soleil Holiday Language Camp, EPTA Organisation, CH-1884 Villars-sur-Ollon.

Institut Le Rosey, Camp d'Eté, Route des Quatre Communes, CH-1180 Rolle. Winter address January-March: CH-3780 Gstaad (30-435 15). Qualified or experienced EFL teachers for co-educational summer camps with sports coaching on Lake Geneva. Teachers must be capable of carrying out boarding school duties.

Institut le Vieux Chalet, CH-1837 Chateau d'Oex.

Institut Monte Rosa, 57 Avenue de Chillon, CH-1820 Montreux.

Leysin American School in Switzerland, CH-1854 Leysin. Tel: (24) 493 37 7. Fax: (24) 494 15 85.

St. George's School in Switzerland, 1815 Clarens/Montreux.

Surval Mont-Fleuri, Route de Glion 56, CH-1820 Montreux 1.

TASIS (The American School in Switzerland), Summer Language Programs, 6926 Montagnola-Lugano. Tel: (91) 994 64 71. Fax: (91) 993 1647. E-mail: administration@tasis.ch. Employ Americans.

LIST OF SCHOOLS

BERLITZ
Steinentorstr. 45, 4051 Basel. Tel: (61) 281 6200. Fax: (61) 226 9041/281 6206.
Number of teachers: 15.
Preference of nationality: must have work permit.
Qualifications: BA or professional experience, e.g. business, banking.
Conditions of employment: no limit on contract length. Flexible hours of work. Pupils are adults whose average age is between 30 and 40.
Salary: SFr22.50 per 40-minute lesson plus 10-20% supplements for some programmes.
Facilities/Support: no assistance with accommodation. Training provided.
Recruitment: through adverts. Local interviews essential.

ECOLE CLUB MIGROS
rue Hans Fries 4, 1700 Fribourg. Tel: (26) 347 40 60. Fax: (26) 322 70 18. E-mail: daniella.hind@gmnefr.migros.ch.
Number of teachers: about 120 for branches in Neuchâtel and La Chaux de Fond.
Preference of nationality: none, provided they have a *Permis B*.
Qualifications: university degree, adult education certification (if possible), experience teaching adults.
Conditions of employment: open-ended contracts. Mostly evening work.
Salary: SFr35-60 per hour depending on classes, levels and specialities.
Facilities/Support: no assistance with accommodation. Training available.
Recruitment: via unsolicited applications and newspaper adverts.
Contact: Daniella Hind, Language Department Counsellor.

HAUT-LAC INTERNATIONAL LANGUAGE AND LEISURE CENTRE
1831 Les Sciernes. Tel: (26) 928 42 00. Fax: (26) 298 42 01. E-mail: info@haut-lac.ch. Website: www.haut-lac.ch.
Number of teachers: teacher/monitors needed for summer and winter language camps for adolescents.
Preference of nationality: language teachers must be mother-tongue.
Qualifications: must have qualifications and experience in language teaching. It is also useful to have experience in sports, drama, art or games organisation.
Conditions of employment: summer (June to August) and winter (January to April).
Facilities/Support: board and lodging provided in single rooms.
Recruitment: send for an application form or send a CV. Only successful applicants will receive a reply.

VILLAGE CAMPS
14 rue de la Morache, 1260 Nyon. Tel: (22) 990 94 05. Fax: (22) 990 94 94. E-mail: personnel@villagecamps.ch. Website: www.villagecamps.com.
Language summer camps at Leysin near Lake Geneva in French-speaking Switzerland (also in Austrian Alps and Sussex in the UK).
Number of teachers: 10. Also need German and French teachers.
Preference of nationality: European, North American, Australian, New Zealand.
Qualifications: TEFL/TESOL certificate (minimum 4 weeks) and experience of teaching children required. Also knowledge of a second language advantageous.
Conditions of employment: period of work from end of June to mid-August. Additional duties supervising sports, activities and excursions.
Salary: allowance of £120 per week worked for language teachers.
Facilities/support: room and board and accident and liability insurance provided.
Recruitment: via adverts, *TESOL Placement Bulletin*, international schools, etc. To apply go to the Village Camps website for information and an application form, or send a request by e-mail or fax.

The Rest of Europe

Outside the mainstream European nations, demand for native speakers of English obviously exists though immigration problems often occur. Before turning to this miscellany of European countries, there is one organisation which employs people to tour all over Europe trying to bring the English language alive for Euro-teenagers.

BIG WHEEL THEATRE IN EDUCATION
P.O. Box 18221, London EC1R 4WJ. Tel: 020-7689 8670. Fax: 020-7689 8671. E-mail: info@bigwheel.org.uk. Website: www.bigwheel.org.uk.
Number of teachers: 10 per year to join theatre-in-education workshops touring in Europe: Benelux, Germany, Switzerland and Scandinavia.
Preference of nationality: EU national (usually British).
Qualifications: teaching and performance skills. No particular qualifications. Must be able to drive well. Fun and spontaneous personalities.
Conditions of employment: 3-month tours. 40 h.p.w. (early starts).
Salary: £200 p.w. plus all expenses (accommodation and touring allowance).
Facilities/Support: some training provided.
Recruitment: adverts in *Guardian* and *TES*. Interviews in UK essential.
Contact: Jeni Williams.

ANDORRA

Andorra lies in the heart of the Pyrenees between Spain and France, and can be seen as an extension of both countries, though it has its own elected government. It is too small to have many language schools, but the one listed here is a possibility (and you would be there over the skiing season).

CENTRE ANDORRA DE LLENGUES (CALL)
15 Carrer del Fener, Andorra-la-Vella, Andorra. Tel: +376 80 40 30. Fax: +376 82 24 72. E-mail:centrandorra.lang@andorra.ad.
Number of teachers: 3-5.
Preference of nationality: none.
Qualifications: BA plus TEFL qualification or 2-3 years' experience abroad most welcome. A good knowledge of French or Spanish can help. Non-smokers preferred.
Conditions of employment: 9-10 month renewable contract which runs from October to June. 27 h.p.w. 5 days a week. Teaching hours 4pm-9.30pm. Teaching very young learners (6-7 years) and all other ages including professionals.
Salary: £750 per month (plus overtime).
Facilities/Support: board and lodging available from £200 per month. Work permit arranged by the School.
Recruitment: via adverts and direct application. Send CV and photo.
Contact: Claude Benet.

CROATIA

This republic of the former Yugoslavia is making strides to recover from its recent history and is building on its strong indigenous English teaching infrastructure. Private language schools flourish in Zagreb, Varazdin and Karlovac, as well as in other towns. For many schools, the idea of employing a native speaker teacher is very attractive. However there is little tradition of doing this and teachers who go to work in Croatia may find themselves breaking new ground in their place of employment. Partly because of their novelty value, teachers would be likely to find themselves being made very welcome and treated well. Salaries are quoted in

Deutsch marks, the currency to which the Croatian kuna is tied.

The market for private teaching is very strong with few native speakers on hand to supply it. Many authentic materials are available locally. If a job is fixed up ahead of time, the school can send a labour permit to be presented at the Croatian Embassy in London or Washington. But it may also be possible to obtain authorisation after arrival.

The British Council in Zagreb can offer informal assistance to prospective teachers by sending a brief list of contacts including a few private language schools and academic institutions. They should be able to put you in touch with the Association of Croatian Teachers of English (HUPE) which organises teacher development activities but can't help foreign teachers to find jobs.

The voluntary placement organisation Services for Open Learning (see *Eastern Europe: Finding a Job* below) sends teachers to Croatia but reports that posts are dependent on a highly unpredictable Ministry. The procedures for acquiring a work permit are complex and take about three months to complete.

AGENCIJA 'F'
Trg Frane Petrica 4, 51557 Cres. Tel: (51) 571 616. Fax: (51) 571 616. E-mail: agencija-f@ri.tel.hr.
Number of teachers: 1.
Preference of nationality: British.
Qualifications: BA Hons. and TEFL Certificate.
Conditions of employment: contract for an academic year. Teaching children from 8 to 17 years in small groups.
Salary: DM1,000.
Facilities/Support: free accommodation provided, own apartment in a private house.
Recruitment: via internet and telephone contact.
Contact: Ana Boca-Velcic, Director.

LANCON ENGLISH LANGUAGE CONSULTANCY
Kumiciceva 10, 10 000 Zagreb. Tel: (1) 485 4985/6. Fax: (1) 485 4984. E-mail: lmo@lancon.hr. Web-site: www.lancon.hr/lancon.
Number of teachers: 10.
Preference of nationality: must be native speaker of English (from UK, USA, Australia, Canada or South Africa).
Qualifications: university degree, a TEFL qualification and 2 years' experience. Knowledge of Business English useful.
Conditions of employment: 1 academic year contracts, renewable. 24 teaching hours (45 minutes) a week.
Facilities/Support: assistance with finding accommodation. Teachers can enter on a visitor's visa and the school will arrange a work permit on arrival. Weekly training sessions.
Recruitment: via the internet and direct application. Interviews in Zagreb or by telephone.
Contact: Martin Doolan.

SKOLA STRANIH JEZIKA KEZELE
A. Cesarca 10, 42000 Varazdin. Tel: (042) 215055. Fax: (042) 213036. E-mail: ssj-kezele-co@z.tel.hr
Number of teachers: 1.
Preference of nationality: British, Irish, American.
Qualifications: experience of preparing candidates for exams (TOEFL, PET, FCE, CAE).
Conditions of employment: one-year contracts. 22 lessons p.w. Teaching all ages from pre-school to teenagers and adults.
Salary: DM1,000 per month.
Facilities/Support: assistance with accommodation given. Training available.

Recruitment: by word of mouth or personal recommendation. Interviews essential.
Contact: Ann Kexele.

A selection of other Croatian schools to try:
SKOLA ZA UCENJE STRANIH JEZIKA, L. Bezeredija 41, 40000 Cakovec (tel/fax
40-311625)
Lingua Centar, d.o.o., Miroslava Krleze 4c, 47000 Karlovac; and Davorina
Trstenjaka 1, 47000 Karlovac (tel/fax 47-621900/611899).
Linguae, Radiaeeva 4, 51000 Rijeka
Long Foreign Languages, R Strohala ?, 51000 Rijeka
Centar za strane jezike, Trg Republike 2/1, 21000 Split
Langlia, A Staieeviaea 19b, 23000 Zadar
Centar za Strane Jezike, Vodnikova 12, 10000 Zagreb
Skola Stranih Jezika, Varsavska 14, 10000 Zagreb

CYPRUS

A visitor to (Greek) Cyprus will be struck by the similarities with Greece – cuisine,
architecture, landscapes and culture – but then surprised at the relative prominence
of English. Signs are printed both in Greek and English, many local people even
outside the cities speak some English, and the British influence can be noticed
everywhere. Because of the longstanding relationship between Cyprus and Britain,
the English language is given a much higher profile in the state educational system.
As a result the density of *frontisteria* is not as high as it is in Greece, though there
are still a considerable number of private institutes preparing children for external
examinations.

The British Council at 3 Museum St does not have a teaching operation in
Nicosia and cannot be of much assistance though may be prepared to send the list of
'Schools – Private' and 'Schools – Language' from the Yellow Pages. Of the schools
circularised in 2000 for this edition, none replied.

If you wish to advertise your services as a tutor in the English language press of
Greek Cyprus, contact the *Cyprus Mail* (PO Box 1144, Nicosia;
Cyprus.Mail@cytanet.com.cy/ www.cyprus-mail.com) or the *Cyprus Weekly*
published by Cyweekly Ltd. (2 Grypari Street, Trust House Suite 102, P.O. Box
24977, 1306 Nicosia; 2-666047/fax 2-668665; weekly@spidernet.com.cy or
adweekly@spidernet.com.cy/ www.cyprus.weekly.com.cy).

There are no private schools or registered institutes in the Turkish Cypriot sector.
Since the demand for English is so great in mainland Turkey, it is not obvious why
this would not be the case in Turkish Cyprus, except that there is much less need for
English to participate in the tourist industry. Since so few English speakers go to
northern Cyprus even as tourists, perhaps an enterprising EFL teacher would be able
to create a demand, at least for private tuition, provided he or she was willing to
compete with the relatively large number of expatriate English speakers who reside
in the Turkish Republic of Northern Cyprus (TRNC).

The majority of native English speakers employed by language schools in
Cyprus are expatriates (predominantly British) who have settled in Cyprus
permanently. In 1998, Cyprus commenced negotiations for accession to the EU,
though full membership is a very distant prospect at the moment, and all foreign
nationals including EU citizens who wish to work in Cyprus need a work permit for
paid and unpaid work. Recently it has become possible to apply for this from within
Cyprus at the Migration Department of the Ministry of the Interior, 1457 Nicosia (2-
804411). Government regulations require that all English teachers, whether Cypriot
nationals or not, must have a degree in English literature in order to be employed in
state schools. Of course it is possible to be employed without one in the private
sector.

One major English institute, the Forum Language Centre (P.O. Box 25567, Nicosia 1310; e-mail forum1@cytanet.com.cy), which offers English at all levels, offers the Trinity CTESOL part-time (see entry in *Training* chapter). They are not able to help graduates find work locally.

MALTA

Although somewhat off the beaten track and although English is the first language of the tiny island, English as a Foreign Language is booming in Malta. A number of private language schools cater to groups coming from other Mediterranean countries on short courses in the spring, summer and at other times. Even the National Tourist Office of Malta distributes a leaflet 'Learning English in the Sun' though the list of ten licensed schools they send is not up-to-date. Their interests are represented by FELTOM, the Federation of English Language Teaching Organisations Malta (Foundation for International Studies, Old University Building, St. Paul St, Valletta VLT 07; website: www.go-ed.com/feltom).

The following schools are members of FELTOM (contact details given below) though there are many others on this island nation: *inlingua*, English Language Academy, English Communication School, Institute of English Language Studies and the International English Language Centre all in Sliema; elsewhere: Sprachcaffe Languages Plus (St. Andrew's), European Centre of English (Ta' Xbiex, Masida), NSTS English Language Institute (Valletta and Sliema), Lasalle Institute (Floriana, Valletta), Global Village (St. Paul's Bay) and B.E.L.S. (Gozo).

The British Council in Valletta (housed with the British High Commission) can send a list of language schools but does not recruit teachers nor advise on local employment prospects unless a prospective teacher pays a personal call. The problem with working in Malta has always been the difficulty of obtaining a permit, as Philip Dray from Ireland described a few years ago, 'I tried many times to get a teaching job in Malta but was thwarted by the paranoia surrounding work permits. The annoying thing is that there is a shortage of teachers.' The language academies who have been similarly thwarted in hiring foreign teachers are pinning their hopes on a possible future entry of Malta into the European Union. In the meantime it may be possible to teach for the summer season without obtaining a Maltese working permit.

The procedure for obtaining an employment licence is to obtain a signed form from your prospective employer, who must prove that the position cannot be filled by a skilled Maltese national, and send it to the Department for Citizenship and Expatriate Affairs (3 Castille Place, Valletta CMR 02; 2-50868/fax 2-237513; citizenship@magnet.mt). According to the Department, although employment licences are issued at any time of year, the bulk of applications are in the summer from May to October when the number of foreign students who go to Malta to learn English increases sharply. These are normally valid for one year in the first instance. Further details may be requested from the Malta High Commission in London (Malta House, 36-38 Piccadilly, London W1V 0PQ; 020-7292 4800/fax 020 7734 1832; tony-bonnici@magnet.mt) or direct from the Department for Citizenship and Expatriate Affairs in Malta.

The NSTS English Language Institute (220 St. Paul St, Valletta VLT07; 246628/fax 230330; www.nsts.org) markets its English courses in conjunction with sports holidays for young tourists to Malta. NSTS run weekly vacation courses from June to August, and it might be worth approaching them for a job, particularly if you are a water sports enthusiast. NSTS was keen to hire Robert Mizzi from Canada once they learned that he was half Maltese:

> *I was offered a job quite casually when NSTS found out I was volunteering conversational English in the main youth hostel in Valletta. Perhaps one reason they wanted to hire me was they knew the visa would not be a problem. However I was surprised by how relaxed the offer was. It was just*

mentioned in passing rather than at an actual interview. I guess it is the Maltese way: once you are one of them, then everything is gravy.

EDUCATIONAL ENGLISH CULTURE LANGUAGE CENTRE
'Villa Monaco', Sliema Road, Kappara SGN 06. Tel: 313033. Fax: 314523.
Number of teachers: 3.
Preference of nationality: British.
Qualifications: TEFL trained teachers.
Conditions of employment: ?-4 months. Hours of teaching 9am-1pm.
Salary. M£3.25 per hour (net).
Facilities/Support: accommodation and training arranged.
Recruitment: personal contact. Personal interview not essential.
Contact: Renato Valente, Principal.

INLINGUA SCHOOL OF LANGUAGES
9 Triq Guzè Fava, Tower Road, Sliema SLM 15. Tel: 336384/313158. Fax: 336419/318903. E-mail: inlingua@digigate.net. Website: www.digigate.net/inlingua.
Member of FELTOM.
Number of teachers: 15 (out of a total of 100).
Preference of nationality: Maltese (or foreigner if work permit is in hand).
Qualifications: 'A' level English and TEFL qualification minimum.
Conditions of employment: casual and freelance employment only.
Salary: depends on qualifications.
Recruitment: local interviews essential.
Contact: Ms. Kathleen Cremona, Director.

A selection of Maltese schools to try:
B.E.L.S. Ltd., Torri Kercem, Qasan San Paul, Kercem VCT 113, Gozo (tel/fax 564 333; bels@maltanet.nct/ www.jagrove.com/bels)
English Communication School, 10 St. Pius V Street, Sliema SLM06 (332 861)
English Language Academy, 9 Tower Lanc, Sliema SLM15 (346 264; ela@sms.com.mt)
European Centre of English Language Studies, 13 Paolo Court, Guze Call Street, Ta' Xbiex, Masida MSD14 (319 303/4; info@ccenglish.com)
Global Village, St. George's St, St. Paul's Bay SPB 02 (573 417; bvmalta@globalvil.com)
Institute of English Language Studies, Matthew Pulis Str., Sliema SLM15 (320 381/3; iels@lalschool.org)
International English Language Centre, 78 Tigne Street, Sliema SLM11 (335 367; sttsltd@keyworld.net)
Lasalle Institute, 105 St. Thomas St, Floriana, VLT14 (230 257; lasalle@maltanet.net)
Sprachcaffe Languages Plus, Sprachcaffe Club Village, Pembroke STJ14 (373 574/5; sprachcaffe@maltanet.net)

SLOVENIA

The former Yugoslav republic of Slovenia remained uninvolved in the Balkan conflict throughout, which allowed its economy to flourish. It is in the group of countries at the head of the queue to join the European Union. As in Croatia, there are a good many private schools and many opportunities can be created by energetic native speakers both as freelance teachers for institutes or as private tutors.

The English Studies Resource Centre at the British Council in Ljubljana has a long list of private language schools throughout the country which it updates constantly; see their web page www.britishcouncil.si. The Council remains closely in touch with language schools and will refer qualified candidates to possible employers. There is also a British Council Resource Centre in Maribor located in the university library.

The average hourly wage is 2,000 Slovenian tolars net. According to most schools, it is not essential for foreign teachers to go through the complex and lengthy procedures for obtaining a work permit during their first year in Slovenia. Language assistants on the Central Bureau's scheme are paid the equivalent of about £300 per month for teaching 15 hours a week in addition to free accommodation.

After answering an advert in the *Guardian*, Adam Cook spent a year working at a *Gimnazija* in the town of Ajdovscina. He was hired with a BA plus an introductory TEFL certificate from the Language Project in Bristol (see entry in *Training* chapter).

The work is great and Slovenia is a fabulous country: good standard of living, good wages. My contract stipulates 20 hours a week but I work more, to save myself from boredom if nothing else. I'm paid by the Slovene Ministry of Education but am answerable to the British Council who recruited me in the first place. Slovene students are great and I have no discipline problems.

Teachers should (theoretically) obtain a temporary residence permit for working in Slovenia; the Embassy in London (www.embassy-slovenia.org.uk) handles applications for both British and Irish nationals; the average processing time is one month. The processing fee is £50 (non-refundable) plus £7 per document if you ask the Embassy to certify the required papers. Your school will have to obtain a work permit and give you a written statement in Slovene confirming your appointment.

BERLITZ LANGUAGE CENTER
Gosposvetska 2, 1000 Ljubljana. Tel: +386 (61) 133 13 25. Fax: + 386 (61) 133 20 42. E-mail: gregor.sergan@berlitz.si. Website: www.berlitz.com. Berlitz Austria GMBH, Graben 13, 1010 Vienna. Tel: (1) 512 82 86. Fax: (1) 587 99 25.
Also recruits teachers for Slovenia (see *Austria* chapter).
Number of teachers: 13.
Preference of nationality: none.
Qualifications: sound educational background, good communication skills, professional attitude and appearance.
Conditions of employment: minimum 1 year. 4-8 teaching hours per day.
Salary: 2,000 tolars per unit (40 minutes).
Facilities/Support: try to assist teachers with accommodation. Compulsory training in Berlitz method. Regular support through observations and workshops.
Recruitment: adverts and personal recommendation. Interviews necessary in most cases, occasionally held abroad.
Contact: Sergan Gregor, Director.

BERLITZ AUSTRIA GMBH
Graben 13, 1010 Vienna, Austria. Tel: (1) 512 82 86. Fax: (1) 587 99 25. E-mail: wien01@berlitz.at. Website: www.berlitz.com.
Number of teachers: fluctuates with demand. Teachers work freelance. Recruits for Austria and Slovakia as well as Slovenia.

BLED SOLA TUJ JESKIK
c.Svobode 15, Bled. Tel: +386 (64) 745 880. Fax: +386 (64) 745 881. E-mail: bredav@siol.net.
Number of teachers: 4.
Preference of nationality: Britain.
Qualifications: Pedagogical, TEFL.
Conditions of employment: 8-10 months. 20-24 teaching hours per week.
Salary: DM20 per hour (lessons last 45 minutes). The school pays the required taxes.
Facilities/Support: addresses of agents provided to find own accommodation. Arranging a work permit is the responsibility of the teacher.
Recruitment: interview necessary.

Contact: Breda Viekelj.

EUROPA BLED d.o.o.
Alpska 7, 4260 Bled. Tel/fax: +386 (64) 741 563. Tel: (41) 644 988.
Number of teachers: 1-2.
Preference of nationality: none.
Qualifications: experience essential. Teacher training course for TEFL required.
Conditions of employment: school year from October to May. Minimum 30-40 lessons a month.
Salary: starting salary of 1,500 tolars (about £4.50 net) per 45-minute lesson.
Facilities/Support: help is given with finding accommodation but the rental charge is borne by the teacher.
Recruitment: contacts through the British Council.
Contact: Cilka Demsar, Manager.

GLOTTA NOVA
Poljanska 95, 1000 Ljubljana. Tel: +386 (1) 52 00 675. Fax: +386 (1) 52 00 676. E-mail: glotta-nova@siol.net. Website: www.glottanova.si.
Number of teachers: 23.
Preference of nationality: British.
Qualifications: BA English teacher or at least TEFL training certificate.
Conditions of employment: part-time up to 2 years. Hours 9am to 7pm for the intensive language courses lasting for 4 consecutive days (40 school hours) from Thursday to Sunday.
Salary: DM20 per school hour.
Facilities/Support: no assistance with accommodation. Advice can be given on work permits. All teachers are given the opportunity to be trained for teaching foreign languages according to the Global Learning Method.
Recruitment: adverts, interviews, probationary period.
Contact: Tatjana Dragovie, Teacher Trainer.

ICM JEZIKOVNA SOLA
Kadilnikova 3, 1000 Ljubljana. Tel: +386 (1) 568 2406. Fax: +386 (1) 565 7860. E-mail: info@icm-js.si. Website: www.icm-js.si.
Number of teachers: 6.
Preference of nationality: UK, USA, Canada.
Qualifications: teacher of business and general English with experience.
Conditions of employment: 1 year.
Salary: DM19 net (general English); DM21 net (Business English) per hour. 5-30 hours per week.
Recruitment: CV, appraisal interview, teacher prepares one-to-one lesson before the agreement is signed.
Contact: Klaudija Kosmac, Deputy Manager.

KRONA PLUS
Trzaska 2, 1000 Ljubljiana. Tel/fax: +386 (0) 142 61266. E-mail: krona.plus@siol.net.
Number of teachers: 1.
Preference of nationality: none.
Qualifications: TEFL and relevant teaching experience.
Conditions of employment: long-term contract preferred. Hours by agreement.
Salary: DM20 per hour.
Facilities/Support: help can be given with finding accommodation.
Recruitment: applicant observes classes and then teaches a demonstration one and is hired depending on the outcome.
Contact: Tatjana Vuzen.

LJUDSKA UNIVERZA KRANJ
Cesta Staneta Zagarja 1, Kranj. Tel: (64) 28 04 815. Fax: (64) 20 12 891. E-mail:

simona.krizaj@lu-kranj.si and mateja.nlinar@lu-kranj.si.
Number of teachers: 1 native English speaker and 8 Slovene English teachers.
Preference of nationality: none.
Qualifications: qualified teachers of English sought. Some experience in ELT preferred.
Conditions of employment: 2-3 month contracts. Teaching hours are either mornings (8am-9.30am) or afternoons/evenings (5pm-9pm).
Salary: 2,000 tolars (net) per lesson of 45 minutes minimum.
Facilities/support: help teachers to find lodgings. Training and assistance with work permits given.
Recruitment: word of mouth. Local interviews essential.
Contact: Simona Krizaj Pochat and Mateja Mlinar.

NISTA LANGUAGE SCHOOL
6 Smarska C.5D, 6000 Koper. Tel: +386 (0) 56250 400. Fax: +386 (0) 56258 440. E-mail: nista@siol.net.
Number of teachers: 7.
Preference of nationality: New Zealand, England, Scotland, Australia.
Qualifications: BA (hons.) and TEFL Cert. plus a year's teaching experience. Business background useful.
Conditions of employment: minimim ten months (preferably longer). Usual 24-26 hours contact time per week.
Salary: 2,000 tolars per hour. No tax or social security deductions.
Facilities/support: the school finds accommodation for teachers and provides necessary documents for obtaining a temporary visa which the teacher has to obtain.
Recruitment: e-mail, newspaper adverts, internet, on spec applications.
Contact: Alenka Rajeic, Director and Susie Dickinson, Director of Studies.

PANTEON COLLEGE
Vojkova 1, 1000 Ljubljana. Tel: (61) 43 61 828. Fax: (61) 23 62 347. E-mail: info@panteon.si. Website: www.panteon.si.
Number of teachers: as many as required.
Preference of nationality: none (though no assistance with work permits).
Conditions of employment: freelance basis: contracts, hours and salaries vary according to course demands.
Facilities/Support: no assistance with accommodation.
Recruitment: direct application and interviews.
Contact: Mr. Andres Toporosic, Director.

PIONIRSKI DOM, CKM
Vilharjeva 11-15, 1000 Ljubljana. Tel: +386 01 2310967. Fax: +386 01 2311530. E-mail: info@pionirski-dom.si. Website: www.pionirski-dom.si.
Number of teachers: 2-5.
Preference of nationality: none
Qualifications: degree and TEFL Cert and/or ability and willingness to teach teenagers and you adults in preparation for all Cambridge exams.
Conditions of employment: part-time for a school year from mid-September to mid-June. At least 6-8 hours a week (2 hours per group).
Salary: 2,400-2,800 tolars net.
Recruitment: personal contacts and recommendation.
Contact: Lucka Franceskin, Head of Language Dept.

SIBON D.O.O.
Ljubljanska 76, 1230 Domzale. Tel: +386 (1) 7220 240. Fax: +386 (1) 7220 245. E-mail: sibon.office@siol.ne. Website: www.sibon.si.
Number of teachers: 1.
Preference of nationality: none.
Qualifications: English language degree.

Conditions of employment: 6-9 months. 6 hours per week.
Facilities/Support: no accommodation assistance.
Recruitment: through Slovenian Philanthropy Society.
Contact: Mrs. V Dermitz.

YURENA
Glavni trg 11, 8000 Novo Mesto. Tel: (7) 337 2100 and 733 72102. Fax: (7) 337 2101. E-mail: yurena@siol.net.
Number of teachers: 3.
Preference of nationality: British.
Qualifications: university degree in TEFL preferred; otherwise a TEFL/TESOL Certificate.
Conditions of employment: 10 month contracts from September. 26 h.p.w. Mostly afternoon teaching of children and adults.
Salary: approximately £580 per month net.
Facilities/Support: assistance given with accommodation and work permits.
Recruitment: direct.
Contact: Kati Golobic, Director.

Other Schools to Try

Note that these schools (in alphabetical order according to town) did not confirm their teacher requirements for this edition of *Teaching English Abroad*. The majority are taken from the British Council list which included nearly 100 addresses. Upper case entries marked with an asterisk had entries in the last edition (1999).

Bled, Sola za Tuje Jezike, Breda Vukelj s.p., Kajuhova c. 11, 4260 Bled
Selih Kozelj d.n.o., Studio za Ucenje, Miklosiceva 9, 3000 Celje
*SPEKTRA JAMEKS, Malgajeva 10, 3000 Celje (63-63 443 192/fax 63-443 191; jamex@siol.net)
Accent On Language d.o.o., Ljubljanska c. 36, 1230 Domzale
Dude d.o.o. English Language Center, Slamnikarska 1, 1230 Domzale
ISCG Domzale, Kolodvorska c. 6, 1230 Domzale
Poliglot d.o.o., Ljubljanska 110, 1230 Domzale
Speak It, Heintzman and Heintzman, Trubarjeva ul. 4, 1230 Domzale
Altera d.n.o., Kettejeva 23, 1241 Kamnik
Little England Club d.o.o., Medvedova ul. 6, 1241 Kamnik
Eurocenter, Lilijana Durdevic s.p., Kidriceva ul. 46, 6000 Koper
Pharmagan d.o.o., Straziska ul 7, 4000 Kranj
Progress Jezikovni Tecaji d.o.o., Seljakovo n. 33, 4000 Kranj
Most d.o.o., Kovinarska ul. 9, 8270 Krsko
Jezikovni Studio Kotar Sonja,s.p., Cesta na Svetino 10, 3270 Lasko

Abis d.o.o., Kantetova ul. 2, 1000 Ljubljana
Alpha d.o.o., Brodarjev trg 14, 1000 Ljubljana
Candor Delavnice Tujih Jezikov, Mirje 1, 1000 Ljubljana
Dialog d.o.o. Sola za tuje jezike, Celoska 61, 113 Ljubljana
Gromar d.o.o., Gola Loka 8, 1210 Ljubljana Sentvid
Izobrazevalni Center Horizont, d.o.o., Bezenskova ul. 35, 1000 Ljubljana
Jezykovni Center International, Gornji Trg 4, 1101 Ljubljana (61-125 5317/fax 61-226167).
Jezikovni Center Palatin, Dunajska 7, Ljubljana
Mint d.o.o. Ljubljana, Jeranova ul. 1c, 1000 Ljubljana (61-133 8456/fax 61-126 1206).
Modrin d.o.o., Staniceva ul. 21 (and Jesenkova ul. 7), 1000 Ljubljana
Pengvin, Popoviceva ul. 16, 1113 Ljubljana
Skilltraining d.o.o., Vegova 2, 1000 Ljubljana
SOLT, Cesta 27. Aprila 31, 1000 Ljubljana
Stratos English Ljubljana, Business English Professional

AS Asistent d.o.o., Glavni trg 17B, 2000 Maribor
Dialog d.o.o. Jezikovna Sola, Terceva ul. 39, 2000 Maribor
Multilingua d.o.o., Ulica bratov Hvalic 16, 5000 Nova Gorica
New College d.o.o., Med ogradami 11A, 5000 Nova Gorica
Athena d.o.o., Kolodvorska c. 17, 6230 Postojna
Ontario d.o.o., Miklosiceva ul. 5, 2250 Ptuj
Candor Dominko k.d., Turnovse 19, 1360 Vrhnika

YUGOSLAVIA

Even when the old Yugoslavia was a popular tourist destination, the ELT industry was not highly developed. When the country was ravaged by war, English dropped off most people's agenda. Now that the situation has become more stable, many people in Belgrade and other cities in what remains of Yugoslavia, after the former Yugoslav provinces of Bosnia-Hercegovina, Croatia, Slovenia and Macedonia have separated, are once again showing an interest in learning English. The number of language schools has grown so rapidly that it is very difficult for most of them to attract a native speaker. However, morale is slower to recover as indicated by Nada Djordjevic, Director of the Forum school in Pancevo:

> *I personally doubt that anybody would like to come and work in Yugoslavia, but being mentioned in your book gives me the wonderful feeling that I am a part of the rest of the world – a feeling so rare and precious here these days, thank you.*

In order to get a residence/work permit for Yugoslavia, you must submit a contract of employment and a translated copy of your diploma.

Connect Youth International at the British Council (10 Spring Gardens, London SW1A 2BN; 020-7389 4030/ www.britcoun.org/education/connectyouth) sends young volunteers from England to teach English to teenagers at summer language clubs in Macedonia. Volunteers work for five hours in the morning for at least two weeks in July/August. Food, accommodation, insurance are all provided and airfares are subsidised. The deadline for applications is mid-March.

ABC SCHOOL OF ENGLISH
Sultana Ciuk 7, 26300 Vrsac. Tel: (13) 813 144. Fax: (13) 817 370. E-mail: jatacad@Eunet.yu.
Number of teachers: none at present.
Conditions of employment: 6-12 months. 4-6 hours per day.
Salary: hourly rate.
Facilities/Support: assistance with accommodation, work permits and training.
Recruitment: interviews essential.
Contact: Gradimir Duncic, Principal.

FORUM
Jna 1/5, TC 'Trubac', 26000 Pancevo. Tel: (13) 518 713, (63) 8113-679. E-mail: nadadj@panet.bits.net.
Number of teachers: 1.
Preference of nationality: none.
Qualifications: TEFL, one or more years' experience, nice personality.
Conditions of employment: 1 year; shorter contracts possible (September-December or February-June).
Salary: 30% of total income of groups taught by the teacher.
Facilities/Support: assistance with accommodation and permits.
Recruitment: on recommendation. Personal interview not essential.
Contact: Mrs. Nada Djordjevic, Director.

GALINDO SKOLA (SAVA CENTAR)
Milentija Popovica 9, 11070 Novi Beograd. Tel: (11) 311 4568. Fax: (11) 455785. E-mail: galindo@net.yu.
Number of teachers: 3.
Preference of nationality: none.
Qualifications: BA in English and TEFL, TESL or TESOL qualification. Knowledge of some Serbo-Croatian would be an advantage. Should be active, enthusiastic and responsible.
Conditions of employment: minimum period 3 months during academic year. 6-7 hours per day, 5 days p.w. teaching children, adolescents and executives.
Salary: £250 per month.
Recruitment: direct application.
Contact: Nada Gadjanski.

NEW VISIONS SCHOOL
79 Narodnog Fronta, 21000 Novi Sad. Tel/fax: (21) 368 766. E-mail nvsadm@EUnet.yu
Number of teachers: 2-3.
Preference of nationality: British, American, Australian.
Qualifications: TESOL qualifications.
Conditions of employment: 1 year. 20-25 h.p.w.
Salary: £500 per month.
Facilities/Support: assistance with accommodation, work permits and training.
Recruitment: interviews essential, sometimes held in England.
Contact: Dragana Djurkovic, Principal.

OLYMPOS
16 Batinska Street, 25000 Sombor. Tel: (25) 34057. Fax: (25) 34940. E-mail: paskal@sombor.net
Number of teachers: 1.
Preference of nationality: none.
Qualifications: TEFL. Minimum 2 years experience.
Conditions of employment: 1 year contract. Possibility of teaching in Hungary.
Salary: negotiable. Payable per hours of work.
Facilities/Support: assistance with accommodation.
Recruitment: CV and letter reference. Interview preferred.
Contact: Karlo Hameder, Director of Studies.

RAINBOW
Kolo Srpskih Sestara 8, 21000 Novi Sad. Tel/fax: (21) 363960. E-mail: rainbow@eunet.yu
Number of teachers: 1-2.
Preference of nationality: UK, USA, Canadian.
Qualifications: TEFL certificate. 1-year of experience.
Conditions of employment: one-year contract with a possibility of extension. 18 teaching hours p.w. plus 4 on stand-by. Pupils from 6 years to adult, mostly teenagers.
Salary: DM500 per month (net).
Facilities/Support: assistance with accommodation and work permits given. Lessons are observed once a week and seminars are held once a month.
Recruitment: adverts in *Guardian*. Interviews not always essential but can be carried out in UK.

SPEAK UP ENGLISH LANGUAGE SCHOOL
ul. Visnjiceva 31, 34000 Kragujevac. Tel: (34) 67472. E-mail: speakup@ptt.yu.
Number of teachers: none at present.
Preference of nationality: British.
Qualifications: experience of working with children as well as some teaching experience. Must be reliable and patient with children (aged 5-18).

Conditions of employment: minimum 6 months. 15-20 h.p.w. Opportunities to work at summer schools by the seaside and winter schools at ski resorts.
Salary: equivalent of £100 per month in Deutsch marks. Deductions of about 35% only if teacher requests it.
Facilities/Support: assistance with accommodation and training given.
Recruitment: recommendations from resident native speakers. Interviews essential.
Contact: Mirjana Milovic, Director of Studies.

A selection of Yugoslav schools to try, mostly taken from the British Council's list:
Anglia, Carli Caplina 37 A, 11000 Beograd
Hello, Partizanske avijacije 25, 11070 Novi Beograd
*INSTITUT ZA STRANE JEZIKE, Gospodar Jovanova 35, 11000 Beograd (11-623 034/623 022/fax 11-625 525)
Kent School of English, Hilandarska 29/II, 11000 Beograd
Lingua English Language Services, Vinogradski venac 12/15, 11030 Beograd
Oxford Centar, Dobracina 27/III, 11000 Beograd
Polyglot, Jevrejska 2, 11000 Beograd
Robertson, Kondina 11, 11000 Beograd
Sunny Days School, Jurija Gagarina 205/76, 11070 Novi Beograd
Tom & Emma School of English, Petra Martinovica 26/28, 11030 Beograd
YBS Language School, Simina 19/II, 11000 Beograd
English Teaching Centre, Ljubicka 48, 32000 Cacak
ELC Language School, Nikole Pasic 8/52, 34000 Kragujevac
Inlingua, Ratka Pavlovica 13 (Vinogradi), 34000 Kragujevac
Oxford Centar, Vojvode Putnika 48, 34000 Kragujevac
*ENGLISH WORLD, Ul. Partizanska Br. 36, 11300 Smederevo (26-227 643)
*ABC CENTAR, D. Obradovica 38, 21205 Sremski Karlovci (21-881 533/fax 21-881 491; radmil@eunet.yu)

MACEDONIA

ST. GEORGE'S SCHOOL
Partizanski odredi 3-315, 1000 Skopje. Tel: (91) 212 916/125 280. Fax: (91) 212 916. E-mail: stevedan@mol.com.mk.
Number of teachers: 2-6.
Preference of nationality: British.
Qualifications: degree and Cert. TEFL (Cambridge/Trinity).
Conditions of employment: 9 months, renewable. 25 contact h.p.w. (afternoon).
Salary: DM550 per month plus expenses paid.
Facilities/Support: accommodation provided; all bills paid. Help given with obtaining a work permit.
Recruitment: directly from colleges and via internet. Interviews necessary.
Contact: Mrs D. Milkova-Broadbent, Owner.

A selection of other Macedonian schools to try, taken from a list prepared by the British Council in Beograd with about 40 addresses.
Centar Stojkovski D.O.O., M. Tito 72, 96250 Kicevo
Language School, Vangel Nikoloski 33, 96000 Ohrid
ABC, Kosta Veselinov 6 A, 91000 Skopje
Funschool, Jane Sandanski 67, 91000 Skopje
Get Ready, Ul. Gemidziska 4/2/6, 91000 Skopje
Globe Language Studio, Sv. Kliment Ohridski 23/1, 91000 Skopje
Hello, Boro Kancevski 8, 91000 Skopje
*LETIKOM PLUS, Bojmija 8, 91000 Skopje (91-126 017)
Lifebridge, Palmira Toljatija 13, 91000 Skopje

EASTERN EUROPE

The transition to a market economy throughout the vast area of Eastern and Central Europe has resulted in a huge demand for professional assistance at all levels, especially when it comes to improving the skills of communication. The dramatic changes which have taken place in the former Communist Bloc since 1989 mean that in every hotel lobby, office boardroom and government ministry from Silesia to Siberia, deals are being struck, export partnerships forged and academic alliances developed between East and West. The lucky East Europeans benefitting from this new commerce tend to be the ones who have acquired the English language.

While Russia has been wrestling with its political and economic demons, the more stable Central European states of Hungary, Poland, the Czech Republic and Slovakia have gained an increasing level of autonomy from the West. There has been a mild backlash in some quarters against what has been seen as a selling out to the West, especially in the major capitals which are now swarming with foreigners. School directors are now perfectly aware of the English-speaking foreigner who masquerades as a teacher but really intends to indulge in cheap beer and all-night discos. They are suspicious of anyone projecting this hidden agenda, disliking the fact that so many foreigners used the region as an extended party venue early on.

In the years just after the revolution, teachers up and down the countries of Eastern Europe chucked their ancient textbooks and joyfully embraced the new communicative methodologies. The enthusiasm for learning English was unprecedented. Everybody craved English lessons, assuming that to learn was to earn, parents as well as children and teenagers. Many foreigners, some representing religions like the Mormons and Bahai, arrived and set up schools. The people thought that knowing English would make them happy and rich. It didn't. Furthermore, they learned that learning a language is very difficult, and much of that initial enthusiasm has subsided.

Yet despite having moved past making 'Western' synonymous with 'desirable,' they are still remarkably welcoming to British and American ELT teachers. On most street corners, private language schools employ native speaker teachers. Working in Central and Eastern Europe may not seem as sexy as it did just after the 'revolution', but thousands of Britons and Americans continue to fall under the spell of Prague, Budapest and Kraków. Even those who find themselves in the less prepossessing industrial cities normally come away beguiled by Central European charm.

Even if ordinary people no longer see English as their salvation or even as an automatic passport to higher wages and a better life, they have not stopped wanting to learn it. The English language teaching industry in those countries has grown up, and is now much more likely to hire teachers with proven experience or an appropriate qualification. Massive amounts of money have been invested in Poland, Hungary and the former Czechoslovakia in retraining local teachers for the teaching of English in state schools and these programmes have been largely successful. Yet, demand continues for native speakers in state schools, private language schools and universities, often for native speakers with a sophisticated understanding of linguistic methodology. There is no question now of walking straight into a job in these countries merely because you were born an English-speaker.

Yet outside the major centres, the need remains great. Since the fall of Communism in the region, the quality of schooling has fallen sharply, according to a Unicef report published at the end of the 1990s. While the wealthy elite can afford to pay for extra tuition in English (and other subjects), most citizens must endure smaller education budgets in their local schools and resulting cuts in quality. It is worth bearing these issues in mind when considering where to head to teach EFL, as emphasised by Steve Anderson from Minneapolis who spent two years teaching in Hungary, the first in a well resourced urban school, the second in an impoverished rural one which he found much more fulfilling.

The explosion in the number of training centres for TEFL/TESL teachers in all English-speaking countries means that the pool of available teachers has vastly increased since the early days, and so the balance of supply and demand has shifted. Teachers who can claim to specialise either in teaching young learners or in teaching Business English are especially attractive since both these areas of ELT are booming. Tourism training colleges in Hungary, the Czech & Slovak Republics and the Baltics are especially keen on encouraging conversational English. Failing that, the easiest way to become more employable is to acquire a TEFL qualification which could prove especially useful (and incidentally cheaper) if obtained in Eastern Europe. For example *International House* in Prague, Budapest, Kraków and Wroclaw all offer the CELTA course while *ITC Prague* has its own 4-week certificate courses and *New World Teachers* offer occasional courses in Budapest (see 'Training Courses Abroad' in the *Training* chapter).

As schools and language training organisations have become more choosy, so too the governments have made visas more difficult to obtain. For example the work visa for teachers in Poland must be obtained in your country of origin and will cost more than £100. Even in countries where English native speakers are sought after, the red tape can be off-putting. For example in Russia, visas and residence permits are specific to a given employer. When a pre-arranged job turns out to be less satisfactory than expected, foreign teachers who find a much better job encounter difficulties in switching employers. Officially, it is always necessary to obtain a work visa outside the country though in some cases employers can fix up the red tape after you arrive. In most cases you can enter the country and stay for three months as a tourist.

A future problem which may arise for North Americans is that a few former Eastern bloc countries (viz. Hungary, Slovenia and the Czech Republic) are well on their way to joining the European Union, at which time the immigration regulations will heavily favour English teachers from Britain and Ireland. But this is still several years away. Note that former Yugoslav republics (i.e. Slovenia, Croatia and Macedonia) are included in the previous chapter 'The Rest of Europe', though some placement organisations mentioned here include them as part of Central & Eastern Europe.

One of the first language teaching organisations to break into Eastern Europe has continued to be one of the most active and energetic in the region, International House. Of the countries in which vacancies were being advertised at the time of writing, more than half were countries included in this chapter. In the past few years a number of International House affiliated schools have opened in Belarus, Macedonia, Lithuania, Ukraine and Poland. The affiliation agreement with all International House schools states that the schools can employ only teachers who have passed the CELTA course. Similarly the British Council was looking for suitable candidates to fill vacancies in its teaching centres in Azerbaijan, Bulgaria, Romania and Ukraine, among others worldwide.

Local salaries can seem absurdly low when translated into a hard currency. A few schools pay a dollar supplement in addition to a local salary; others pay what is usually a generous salary by local standards but which can leave little after paying for food and accommodation. A typical package would include a monthly net salary of between £150 and £400 in addition to free accommodation and possibly some other perks such as a travel stipend. The best paid jobs are for firms which teach in-company courses, especially in Poland.

A host of private language schools which are either independent or part of larger language teaching organisations are represented in Eastern and Central Europe. Most of the Central European schools listed in the Directory are well established and offer above average working conditions. Some mainstream schools in the stable democracies have delegated to specialist recruiters the task of finding teachers. But in the more volatile climate of Russia and former Soviet republics (which are several years behind the Central European nations), schools come and go, and tend to choose their teachers from the pool of native English speakers on the spot, who also come and go. Intrepid travellers visiting the Central Asian Republics with no intention to work are still often invited to stay a while and do some English teaching, as was happening in off-the-beaten track towns in Poland and Czechoslovakia ten years ago.

One interesting option for those who do not wish to commit themselves for a full academic year is to work at one of the many language summer camps which are offered to young people, usually in scenic locations from Lake Balaton in Hungary to Lake Baikal in Siberia.

Conditions of Work

The financial rewards of working in the old Russian Empire are usually so negligible that trained/experienced teachers cannot be enticed to teach there unless they are supported by a voluntary organisation like VSO or the Soros Foundation. The problems attendant on the economic crisis in Russia have been made worse by inflation and sudden price rises which will eat away at a salary that was marginal to begin with. Ironically 'volunteers' with the major agencies are comparatively well off since they benefit from the standard package which includes free travel, insurance and other benefits. Other voluntary programmes arrange for eager but unqualified volunteers in search of a cultural experience who on the whole will be out-of-pocket at the end of a short stint of teaching in the Ukraine, the Baltics, etc. The role of native speaking volunteers is to conduct practical English classes (i.e. conversation classes) to supplement grammar taught by local school staff.

The scarcity of accommodation in the major cities of Eastern Europe is less acute than it was but it is still difficult to find something affordable and comfortable. Fortunately many employers of native-speaker teachers supply accommodation. Be prepared for cramped quarters, perhaps a small room in a student dormitory or family flat.

A certain level of hardship is inevitable, especially for vegetarians, anyone who has forgotten to bring winter boots and those who have breathing problems, since the pollution in many Eastern European cities can be choking. A further problem is the difficulty in communicating, though most people who have spent time in these countries find that they are well looked after by the local people.

It should not be surprising to learn that in the case of some countries and some ELT programmes there is considerable uncertainty and confusion. The dire shortage of English teaching facilities through the past decades cannot be reversed instantaneously. The emergence of these countries into the 'real world' has been attended by problems and pitfalls such as an absence of co-ordinated educational policies and the possibility of shoddy or exploitative working conditions for teachers, not to mention price rises, unemployment and a dramatic increase in crime.

While opportunities vary from place to place and while the future is uncertain due to the speed of change, it is true to say that there will be a great demand for native English teachers for many years ahead. And though these may not be the best paid EFL jobs in the world, Eastern Europe can offer historic and beautiful cities, genuinely friendly people and a unique chance to experience life in the 'other Europe'.

FINDING A JOB

A range of vacancies in Central and Eastern Europe, particularly in Poland, continues to be advertised in the educational press. A certain number of commercial recruitment agencies are involved with filling vacancies in Eastern Europe, including agencies which charge untrained volunteer teachers a fee for the arrangements to be made on their behalf.

Many British and American programmes that were set up in the wake of the 1989 revolution have now been cancelled, a loss to the state schools in much of Eastern Europe, and also to the many young Britons and Americans who would still be willing to spend a year earning very little. The need for native speakers in state schools hasn't disappeared, but the number of mediating agencies has certainly diminished.

As has been stressed elsewhere, the possibility of creating your own job in this region is very strong. Much of what takes place happens by chance, and protocol is often given a back seat to friendly encounters. Obtaining work often comes down to the right (or wrong) hairstyle or whether you've got any Polish/Lithuanian/Slovak/Azerbaijani ancestry. Looking professional, being persistent and asking as many questions as you are asked, rather than sitting back on your heels, usually pays off.

But if you want to arrange a position through a mediating organisation, here are the main ones in the UK which continue to recruit teachers for more than one country in the region. (Organisations that deal only with one country are included in the relevant chapter.) Note that a number of general ELT recruitment agencies included in the introductory chapter *Finding a Job* have vacancies in Eastern Europe, such as i to i's *i venture* programme (Russia, Georgia, Uzbekistan), *EF English First* (Lithuania, Poland, Russia) and *Saxoncourt & English Worldwide* (Russia, Poland, etc.).

Central Bureau for International Education & Training – Assistants Team at the British Council (10 Spring Gardens, London SW1A 2BN; 020-7389 4764) places native English-speaking recent graduates from a UK university, who are interested in a career in TEFL or who have an initial TEFL qualification, and are seeking some practical experience. Posts are for an academic year in Bulgaria, Hungary, Romania, Russia or Slovenia, at primary, secondary and vocational schools or at universities. Interviews are held in London.

East European Partnership, see *VSO* below.

English for Everybody, ITC, Kaprova 14, 110 00 Prague 1. Tel: 2-2481 4791. Fax: 2-2481 7530; E-mail: EFE@itc-training.com (Subject EFE). Agency matches clients with suitable posts in the Czech Republic and elsewhere in Eastern Europe Candidates must have a university degree and either a TEFL Certificate or relevant experience. Assistance fee US$450. (Further details in chapter on the Czech Republic.)

Language Link, 21 Harrington Road, London SW7 3EU. Tel: 020-7225 1065. Fax: 020-7584 3518. E-mail: languagelink@compuserve.com. Website: www.languagelink.co.uk. Mainly active in Russia (see entry) and Slovakia (see entry for *Akademia Vzdelavania*) but also have positions in their network of schools in other parts of East & Central Europe including Poland, the Czech Republic and Ukraine. Accept newly qualified teachers.

Services for Open Learning (SOL), North Devon Professional Centre, Vicarage St, Barnstaple, Devon EX32 7HB. Tel: (01271) 327319. Fax: (01271) 376650. E-mail: sol@enterprise.net. Website: www.sol.org.uk. Non-profit-making organisation which annually recruits about 60 graduates (preferably with degree in languages or education and with recognised TEFL Certificate) to teach in schools in the state sector in most Eastern and Central European countries (Belarus, Croatia, Czech Republic, Hungary, Romania and Slovakia). The SOL programme is open to all native speakers of English, though interviews take place only in Britain (March and June) and in Eastern & Central Europe. Contracts are with each school and are for a complete academic year (September to June), though a handful of posts may arise in January. All posts include free independent housing. Some financial assistance may be available to volunteers going to Romania.

The Soros Professional English Language Teaching Program (SPELT)
is seeking English as a Foreign Language (EFL) Teachers and Teacher
Trainers for teaching assignments in the following countries:
Azerbaijan, Bosnia-Herzegovina, Georgia, Haiti, Kyrgyzstan, Mongolia,
the Volga region in Russia, Tajikistan, Uzbekistan, and Yugoslavia.

Master's Degree in TESL or RSA Certificate + teaching experience
required. For further details, go to **www.soros.org/spelt**
or email Laureen Phillips at **lphillips@sorosny.org**.
Inquiries may also be sent to 400 W. 59th St., 4th Floor, Ny, NY 10019

Soros Professional English Language Teaching Program (SPELT), Open
Society Institute, 400 West 59th Street, 4th Floor, New York, NY 10019. Tel: (212)
548-0136. Fax: (212) 548-4650. E-mail: spelt@sorosny.org. Open Society
Institute's English Language Program places instructors at universities and teacher
training colleges in Azerbaijan, Bosnia and Herzegovina, Croatia, Georgia,
Kyrgyzstan, Mongolia, Russia, Tajikistan, Uzbekistan and Yugoslavia. An MA in
Linguistics or TESOL is required in most cases, although EFL certification will be
considered. Prior teaching experience is required. US nationality is not necessary.
Also sends instructors to Haiti.

Teachers for Central & Eastern Europe, 21 V 5 Rackovski Blvd,
Dimitrovgrad 6400, Bulgaria. Tel/fax: (391) 24787 in Bulgaria or 707-276-4571 in
the USA. E-mail: tfcee_klim@skat.spnet.net or tfcee@usa.net. Website:
www.tfcee.8m.com. US contact is InterExchange (address below). TFCEE Inc.
appoints about 80 native speakers of English per year to teach English (or other
disciplines) at English language secondary schools, secondary schools of natural
sciences and universities in Bulgaria, Czech Republic, Hungary, Poland and
Slovakia (further details about Bulgaria in respective chapter). Most participants are
from universities in the US, Canada, UK and Australia. Candidates must send
original of transcript/university record, notarised copies of university diplomas, CV
and 3 letters of academic reference. TEFL certification and experience not generally
required but are strongly recommended. Most appointments are for an academic
year though one-semester placements are possible (i.e mid-September to mid-
January or February to mid-June). Summer programme in July and August at Black
Sea resorts. Typically, English teachers in this region are given a lot of independence
so they will enjoy their role more if they are confident in planning their own lessons
and syllabus. Contact hours are 20 classes of 40 minutes over a 4-day working week.
Salaries are universally low though foreign teachers receive higher pay than local
teachers. Benefits include free furnished accommodation with all bills paid by the
host school, 60 days of paid leave per academic year, multiple entry/exit visa free,
free internet access, etc.

Teaching & Projects Abroad, Gerrard House, Rustington, West Sussex BN16
1AW. Tel: (01903) 859911. Fax: (01903) 785779. E-mail: info@teaching-
abroad.co.uk. Website: www.teaching-abroad.co.uk. Recruits volunteers to work as
English Language Teaching Assistants for the summer or during the academic year
in Ukraine and Russia (Moscow, St. Petersburg and Siberia). No TEFL background
required. Packages cost from £795 for Ukraine (excluding travel) to £1,495 for
Siberia (including travel from UK). Prices include placement, board and
accommodation and back-up. Flexible starting dates and durations for up to three
months; extensions can be arranged for a further fee.

Travellers, 7 Mulberry Close, Ferring, West Sussex BN12 5HY. Tel/fax: 01903
502595. E-mail: teach@travellersworldwide.com. Website: www. travellersworldwide.

com. Paying volunteers teach conversational English in Russia (Moscow, St. Petersburg and Siberia) and the Ukraine (Kiev and Crimea). Placements last from 2 weeks and costs vary depending on the country. Sample prices for 2-3 months: Ukraine £775 and Russia £895 including food and accommodation. Travel to destination can be arranged at extra cost. Longer stays can be arranged for an extra monthly fee.

Travel Teach, St James's Building, 79 Oxford St, Manchester M1 6FR. Tel: 0870 789 8100. Website: www.travelteach.com. Working holiday opportunities, teaching conversational and comprehensive English in two former republics of the Soviet Union: Lithuania and Moldova. English is taught in schools, summer schools and organisations to kindergarten and school children as well as to adults. Flexible periods of teaching from 2 weeks in Moldova/7 weeks in Lithuania to 12 months, including the summer vacation. Open to graduates, undergraduates or gap year students. All-inclusive programme fee includes return air travel, visas, board and lodging throughout with a host family, language learning and organised visits and excursions every three weeks. Orientation, teacher training and materials provided as well as advice on travelling in the region. The programme fee is £445 for Moldova and £495 for Lithuania (with 15% reduction for individuals with a TEFL qualification or Qualified Teacher Status).

VSO, 317 Putney Bridge Road, London SW15 2PN. E-mail: depstein@vso.org.uk. VSO aims to meet the short-term needs for skills in East and Central Europe and Russia. VSO recruits qualified professionals with a minimum of two years post-qualification experience to work in education as well as other sectors. Placements are for one to two years in Albania, Macedonia, Bulgaria, Romania, Slovakia, Czech Republic, former Soviet Union, Latvia and Lithuania. At present they are developing programmes in Kazakhstan and the former Yugoslavia. They offer a salary in line with local salaries, free flights, training and insurance. Note that the East European Partnership (EEP) has been subsumed in VSO.

For North Americans

Several US organisations are actively involved in teacher recruitment for the region:

Bridges for Education: 94 Lamarack Drive, Buffalo, NY 14226. Tel: 716-839 0180. Fax 716-893 9493. E-mail: jbc@buffalo.edu. Website: www.bridges4edu.org. Recruits 180 volunteer English teachers for peace camps organised with the Ministries of Education and UNESCO. Camps are held for three weeks in July followed by one week of travel in Romania, Poland, Hungary, and Belarus. Teen and adult participants come from 20 countries including Kosovo, Albania, Georgia, Mongolia, Serbia, Armenia, Lithuania, Ukraine, Germany, Italy and Switzerland. Volunteers train in basic ESL before departing in a group from North America. Summer teachers are sometimes offered longer jobs. Participants pay their own airfare and participation costs.

Central European Teaching Program/CETP, Beloit College, 700 College St, Beloit, WI 53511, USA. Tel: (608) 363-2619. Fax: (608) 363-2449. E-mail: dunlopa@beloit.edu. Website: www.beloit.edu/~cetp. CETP places over 90 native speakers of English in Hungary, Poland and Romania and plans to expand into Lithuania and the Czech Republic. The position offered is as an English Conversation Teacher in elementary, high school or college state education establishments. Conversation teachers merely enhance oral fluency since local teachers teach formal grammar. Normal class hours are 7.45am to 2.10pm. Teachers have 18-22 class meetings per week; each class lasts 45 minutes. This is a year-long programme (September to June) for graduates with overseas TEFL or teaching experience (TEFL Certificate not essential). The placement fee is US$2,000 which helps to maintain an extensive network of offices, full-time country co-ordinator, orientation, weekend opportunities for professional development. Accommodation (but not food) is provided free and monthly pocket money of about US$200 is paid in local currency which is enough to cover basic living and in-country travel expenses. International airfares not included in the programme. Applicants are interviewed by telephone and the deadline of 1st April is extended if there are still vacancies to be filled. In past years applicants have come from the USA, Canada, the UK, Australia and Jamaica.

It was through CETP that Steve Anderson arranged his year of teaching in Hungary, and he was impressed:

CETP is a professional yet personal organisation. They maintain in-country contacts for the duration of the contracts and will kindly hammer out any kinks in a teacher's experience (whether it be work-related or otherwise). They purposely keep the directorship in the hands of a young, returning teacher in order to keep administration close to what the organisation actually does.

Steve goes on to lament the need to introduce such a substantial fee, but recommends it to anyone who can afford it.

InterExchange, 161 Sixth Avenue, New York, NY 10013. Tel: (212) 924-0446 ext. 109. Fax: (212) 924-0575. E mail: info@Interexchange.org. Website: www.interexchange.org. Arranges teaching assistantships in Bulgaria, Poland, Russia and Ukraine. Placement fee of $400-$600.

Peace Corps, Room 803E, 1111 20th St NW, Washington DC 20526. Tel: (toll-free) 1-800-424-8580. Web-site: www.peacecorps.gov. Provides volunteer teachers on the usual 27-month contracts to the former USSR. Must be US citizen, over 18 and in good health. They recruit people to teach at both secondary and university level and to become involved with teacher training and curriculum development.

The rest of this chapter is organised by country. Bulgaria, Czech Republic, Hungary, Poland and Romania are followed by Russia and its former satellite states and finally by Slovakia.

Albania barely figures in the literature about ELT in Eastern Europe. Not only does it lack the infrastructure taken for granted in most of Europe, it is considered by many to be downright dangerous. Where once Albanians wanted to learn Italian (in order to understand the illicit Italian television transmitted from across the Adriatic) or French or German, English is now the favoured foreign language and is compulsory from the fifth grade through to university. (There are about 37 English lecturers at the University of Tirana.) There are no private schools in Albania, though English is taught up to 12 hours a week in certain selective schools. There might be a market for private tuition if Albanians had any disposable income, but most do not earn enough to feed and clothe themselves adequately. Many Albanians live in abject poverty, and there is an acute shortage of teaching materials in the country.

The Albanian Youth Club (whose motto is 'We work for a better world for young people') would welcome any voluntary input, whether as teachers of one of their eight classes of children and adults (especially in the summer) or as donors of ELT books and cassettes (hand-me-down photocopiers and computers very welcome...) The Club President, Selami Percja, says that volunteers do not need to be trained teachers, just ordinary people willing to come at any time of the year. More details are available from the AYC, PO Box 1741, Tirana, Albania.

Bulgaria

Teaching positions for native speakers in Bulgarian state schools are organised by the Ministry of Education & Science. Specialist foreign language secondary schools in Bulgaria employ native speaker teachers on one-year renewable contracts from September through the Bulgarian Ministry of Education & Science. The Bulgarian educational system could never afford to attract teachers on its own since public expenditure on education in Bulgaria has been reduced by three-quarters over the past decade according to a Unicef report.

The Sofia-based organisation Teachers for Central and Eastern Europe, 21 V 5 Rakovski Boulevard, Dimitrovgrad 6400 (see above for fax, e-mail and contact names in Bulgaria and the US) is most active in Bulgaria. Since 1993 TFCEE has been recruiting native speaker teachers on behalf of the Ministry of Education. With 80 native speaker teachers placed in Bulgarian schools annually, TFCEE is second only to the Peace Corps. Participants are sent to English medium secondary schools or schools of natural sciences in cities of over 50,000 for an academic year, though one-semester placements are possible (i.e. mid-September to mid-January and 1st February to mid-June).

The weekly teaching load is 19 40-minute classes per four-day week. The salary in Bulgarian leva is equivalent to $150 (which is nearly a third higher than that of the host school's principal). Benefits include free furnished accommodation and all utility bills, 60 days of paid holiday, paid sick leave, free Bulgarian language instruction, free health care and free multiple-entry visa and work permit.

In conjunction with the Ministry of Education, English language summer courses are held at mountain and seaside resorts. Teachers can stay from between one and three months. Monthly remuneration exceeds $200 as accommodation is free of charge.

Political change in Bulgaria has been much less dramatic than elsewhere in the former Eastern Bloc, and in fact the Communist party is the elected government. The private sector is still relatively undeveloped, and placement of teachers in state schools is centralised by the Ministry of Education. As a result, there is not much point in contacting individual schools, even if you do obtain a list from the British Council in Sofia. The British Council is responsible for recruiting *lektors* for universities in Bulgaria, who have to have a strong academic background. Most of the main voluntary organisations like the Soros Foundation are active in Bulgaria.

According to the Bulgarian Embassy in London, people who have found employment should apply with a letter from their employer for a multiple entry visa (at a cost of £42) which will be valid for three months. Longer-term work and residence permits can be arranged with the local authorities after arrival.

Neither of the schools which had entries in the last edition of this book confirmed this time:

ALLIANCE FOR FOREIGN LANGUAGES, 3 Slaveikov Square, Sofia 1000 (2-880238/fax 2-882349)

PRIVATE SCHOOL FOR BANKING AND BUSINESS, 83 Bogomil Street, Plovdiv (32-68 14 14/fax 32-27 48 80)

Czech Republic

Because of the worldwide increase in the number of trained EFL teachers as well as the popularity of Prague and the Czech Republic, the standard of native speaker teacher has improved. Gone are the days when an English speaker could walk into a school and be offered a position complete with reasonable salary and accommodation, simply by opening his or her mouth. There is still some scope for novices outside Prague. But in Prague, it continues to be difficult to obtain either employment or accommodation because of the competition from so many other foreigners. Some of the smaller Czech towns including some rather uninspiring places in the steel-producing heart of the country and the Moravian capital Brno offer interested teachers much more scope for employment than the tourist-clogged capital.

Teaching private lessons is the most lucrative but the most difficult to fix up for new arrivals. Private lessons now go as high as 300 crowns an hour for businesses, but most earn the teacher about half that. A good way to attract pupils initially is to charge at the lower end of the scale but to teach in groups of three or four.

FIXING UP A JOB

Most schools express no preference for nationality, and prefer a mixture of accents. Americans are still in the ascendancy (it has been estimated that there are between 20,000 and 30,000 in Prague alone) but Canadians, Britons, etc. are all welcome. Australians are generally well received partly because of the large number of Czechs (about 20,000) who emigrated to Australia.

State Schools

Qualified teachers are recruited to teach in Czech primary and secondary schools, usually on a one-year contract with low-cost or free accommodation and a salary of 7,000-10,000 Czech crowns net per month. The centralised contact is the *Academic Information Agency (AIA)* in Prague (see entry). AIA is part of the Ministry of Education, and distributes its literature through Czech Embassies abroad. In the UK write to the Cultural Section, Czech Embassy, 26 Kensington Palace Gardens, London W8 4QY; 020-7243 1115/fax 020-7727 9654; london@embassy.mzo.cz.

The AIA assists people interested in teaching English at primary and secondary state schools. Most of the teaching positions are at schools in smaller towns. The school year runs for ten months from September 1st to June 30th, though some vacancies occur in January between semesters. Although the minimum requirement is a BA/MA in English/Applied Linguistics, additional teaching qualifications (TEFL or PGCE) and experience give an applicant priority. Applications should be submitted before the end of April. The AIA simply acts as a go-between, circulating CVs and applications to state schools which have requested a teacher. Schools then contact applicants directly to discuss contractual details.

Kathy Panton is just one of the AIA's satisfied customers: 'I really recommend the AIA; they helped me out of a bad hole when I moved from Liberec to Prague and tried harder than I had any right to expect to get me out of another one, when I was assigned flea-ridden and expensive accommodation.'

Another important Czech organisation for TEFLers is the *Akademie J.A. Komenského* which actively recruits native speakers to participate in the Czech adult education programme. Americans should contact *InterExchange* in New York which cooperates with the international exchange organisation APEX in Prague (Pod Juliskou 4, 160 00 Prague 6; tel/fax: 2-311 9158) to place Americans in state schools for the 10-month academic year. The programme is open to graduates who either have a teaching certificate or solid experience of teaching, preferably ESL. The fee is $450 and the deadline is April 15th.

As mentioned in the introduction to this chapter, the organisation based in Bulgaria *Teachers for Central & Eastern Europe* co-operates with the Ministries of Education of the countries in which it is active (including the Czech Republic) in order to place native speakers for an academic year in state schools.

The growth of a free market economy means that the role of voluntary organisations has diminished. Although *SOL* (see introduction to Eastern Europe) is more active in Romania and Hungary, it is able to place EFL teachers in Czech state schools for an academic year, as it did for Brian Farrelly:

I taught in two state schools in the Czech Republic and had a really great time in both. I felt really privileged to teach the students there. My first job in a 'gymnazium' secondary school in a small town called Sedlcany south of Prague was arranged by SOL. The staff and students made me tremendously welcome. I also greatly enjoyed the freedom to teach as I saw fit, although I felt initially very daunted by the lack of guidance regarding what I should be doing with the students. My next job was found by the AIA in Prague. After visiting, I was offered a number of schools and I chose another gymnazium in another small town called Jevicko, north of Brno.

Private Schools

The private sector has matured enormously in the past few years so that there is now a wide range of well-established schools offering high standards of instruction. The main international chains of language schools like Linguarama, Berlitz and International Language Centres (formerly International House) have large established operations in the country. Most teachers are recruited locally, often via notice boards for example at the British Council and the Globe English language bookshop. Others recommended by the *Prague Post* (see below) are the notice boards at Radost FX, Laundry Kings and the Meduza Café. The internet site www.jobs.cz is aimed primarily at Czech job-seekers and, although there is a section in English, it contains only occasional teaching vacancies.

Most schools in Prague can count on receiving plenty of CVs on spec from which to fill any vacancies that arise. Anyone who is well qualified or experienced should have few difficulties in finding a job on the spot and obtaining a work permit. The Yellow Pages (*Zlaté Stránky*) are an excellent source of addresses under the heading *Jazykove skoly*. Looking at all the glossy ads for English language schools, both Western backed and locally owned, it is hard to believe that just a decade ago, Czechoslovakia was still a Communist country.

Some private recruitment agencies in Britain (such as *Language Link* mentioned in the introduction to this chapter on Eastern Europe) can place qualified applicants in teaching posts in the Czech Republic. The agency *English for Everybody* is in a strong position to match clients with suitable posts in Prague and elsewhere in the Czech Republic. Candidates must have a university degree and either a TEFL Certificate or relevant experience. According to the Director Iva Brozova, newly arrived English teachers in Prague need more than just a job-finding service. They need a practical orientation and someone to turn to with questions and problems, so she maintains regular contact with her clients after they have started work. The assistance fee charged is US$450. English for Everybody may be contacted at ITC, Kaprova 14, 110 00 Prague; 2-2481 4791/fax 2-2481 7530; e-mail: EFE@itc-training.com (Subject EFE).

However most people wait until they arrive in Prague before trying to find teaching work, which is what Linda Harrison did:

The best time to apply is before June. I arrived in September which was too late, but if you persevere there are jobs around. A lot of teaching work here seems to be in companies. Schools employ you to go into offices, etc. to teach English (though not usually business English). After a short job hunt, I was hired by Languages at Work which paid well and provided food and travel vouchers as well as helping with accommodation.

In Prague, keep your eyes open for small notices. M. J. Hinton answered an ad in a coffee shop, phoned up and was invited for an informal interview, which resulted in a good job that involved only seven hours of teaching a week and 11 hours of administration.

Those without qualifications or experience will find it very difficult. Even with a year and a half of teaching experience in a Czech town, Kathy Panton got turned down in Prague because she didn't have a TEFL Certificate. She warns that you can't count on picking up work for at least a month, though living expenses shouldn't be much more than £200 during that time. Unlike state schools, private schools in Prague do not necessarily offer accommodation, and will give preference when hiring to anyone who already has accommodation fixed up.

There are quite a few advertisements for teaching jobs in the local English press, primarily *The Prague Post* (Stepanska 20, 110 00 Prague 1; 2-9633

4411/4400). The classifieds can be read on-line at www.praguepost.cz. At the time of writing several language schools were advertising using only telephone or e-mail numbers (e.g. 2-2481 0627 and dos@eminenc.cz). It is very cheap to place your own advert; if you send 25 words or less to classifieds@praguepost.cz you will pay just $1 a day for a minimum of ten days. Heather Mayes noticed an ad placed here by an American businesswoman looking for EFL teachers to work at a private school in Brno. It may be worth advertising your speciality as an English tutor (e.g. marketing, law, etc.) ahead of time. Kathy Panton suggests enlisting the help of a Czech friend:

> *A better way to find work is to get someone (the Czech embassy will probably do it if you catch them on a slow day) to translate 'Native speaker will tutor English to intermediate or advanced students starting... phone/write...' and send it to a newspaper like* Mláda Fronta Dnes *or* Annoncé *with a £5 note maybe.*

REGULATIONS

A new Residency Law came into force on January 1st 2000 making it necessary to apply for a long-stay Czech visa before arrival in the country. Full details are available from the Czech Embassy in London (020-7243 1115/fax 020-7243 7988) or Washington (www.czech.cz/washington). Anyone who intends to work or for any other reason stay in the Czech Republic for longer than 90 days must obtain the visa in advance. This requires gathering a raft of documents including a work permit issued by the employer, proof of accommodation, etc. all presented in the original or a notarised copy. In the summer of 2000, Nicole Rosenleaf Ritter left an editorial job in Massachusetts to live and work in Prague:

> *The big news in Prague is the change in residency laws which makes it impossible to apply for a long-stay visa from Prague. All applications now must be done at Czech embassies abroad and can take up to six months. What I've found out is that many Americans are still following the old system and waiting until they arrive to get everything in order and then simply taking the train to Dresden or Vienna and applying there. (Considering that the application requires proof of a year's lease, a Czech criminal history report, etc., it's almost impossible to do before you arrive.) It's one more painful thing about getting legal there, but there is talk of trying to simplify it because of the complaints they're getting.*

The work permit must be obtained from the local employment office (*Urad práce*) by your future employer. They will need a signed form from you plus a photocopy of your passport and the originals or notarised copies of your education certificates.

All of this is quite a palaver and (realistically) takes at least three months. The necessity of conforming with these procedures puts some candidates off according to the head of the English Department at the *Státní Jazyková Skola*:

> *I must say that quite a lot of teachers inquire about positions available here but what they usually do not like is a long period necessary for arranging the work and residency permits. As a state school we cannot employ anybody illegally. Therefore if the teacher is not in the country, it means a lot of correspondence. All the procedures may take about three months.*

The President of APEX (mentioned above) blames the cumbersome red tape for the relatively small number of teacher placements his organisation is able to make, and APEX is lobbying for the Czech government to give official cultural exchange programmes special dispensation so that they can bypass the normal immigration procedures.

CONDITIONS OF WORK

Most English teachers agree that working conditions in state schools are generally better than in private schools. People teaching at private institutes in Prague where there is a definite glut of foreign teachers, attracted by the cultural chic of the city, have been called the 'sweat shop labourers' of the TEFL world because of the low wages employers can get away with paying. The guaranteed salary at state schools, even if you're sick or there is a holiday, is a definite advantage. If you are lucky enough to be teaching mostly final year students, your working hours in the exam month of June will be minimal. A drawback of state school teaching is the 8am start, but of course there is no evening or weekend work as in private schools.

Compared to the monthly wage in state schools of 7,000 crowns, private sector wages are normally more like 8,500-10,500 crowns (also net). But this does not include accommodation which will account for between a quarter and third of a teaching salary. Hourly fees start at 100 crowns net, though a more usual wage is 150 crowns less 20%-25% for tax and deductions. A full-time salary should be adequate to live on by local standards but will not allow you to save anything, unless you take on lots of private tutoring.

The majority of private language school clients are adults who are available for lessons after work, so most teaching takes place between 4pm and 8pm Monday to Thursday. (Some schools do specialise in teaching children, for which a basic knowledge of the Czech language is essential.)

Accommodation is generally in very short supply, and housing problems were made worse by a relaxation of the regulations. Very little rental accommodation is available on the open market in Prague and, unless you have contacts or your employer undertakes to help you (as many do), you will have severe problems. If you have a friend to translate for you, you can try the accommodation listings in *Annoncé,* the Prague free ads paper. Most employers are prepared to help newcomers to find accommodation, usually a room in a small shared flat or university hostel. Registered students are eligible for very cheap housing and therefore, not surprisingly, it is not at all easy to register as a student. Many teachers in Prague have no choice but to live in a concrete jungle of soulless *paneláks* (monolithic apartment buildings) a long commute away (where the suicide rate is triple the national average).

Students are reported to be 'a delight to teach, alert, intelligent, fun-loving, keen and interested'. Although textbooks are now widely available, teachers would be advised before setting out to check on the availability of supplementary materials in the school where they are going to teach and to take along their own favourites. Many English teachers avail themselves of the excellent resource centres run by the British Council in Prague (where the joining fee is 300 crowns), Brno, Ceske Budejovice, Olomouc, Ostrava, Pardubice, Plzen and Usti nad Labem.

One of the strongest motivations among secondary school *(Gymnazium)* students to learn English is the prospect of the 'Maturity' exam. At the beginning of the year they are given 25 topics (e.g. the British Royal Family, the influence of the media) and at the end of the year they must talk in English about one topic (chosen at random) for 15 minutes. This is a very good incentive for class participation.

Leisure Time

The cost of living continues to creep up; the cost of cinema and concert tickets has doubled over the past few years. But you can still afford to buy an awful lot of the truly excellent Czech beer out of a teacher's wage, if not fund much travelling round the region. (A dual pricing system operates so that those without a Czech passport pay more for hotel rooms and transport.)

Prague has a vibrant nightlife with clubs and cafés, cinema, opera, poetry and dance. There is so much expat culture, that a new arrival serious about getting into Czech culture will encounter difficulty. There is also something of a backlash among

Czechs against western 'good-for-nothings' who spend Czech currency as if it were Monopoly money. In Prague theft is a serious problem, though walking the streets is still safe.

In small towns, however, English teachers are still likely to be treated as honoured guests with many offers of hospitality and invitations, for example to join skiing trips (which are very cheap), as Hannah Bullock from Oxford discovered in her year out between school and university in the town of Strakonice:

I've got some great Czech friends here. A colleague of mine has been very kind (as I've found most Czechs are) and has been like a mentor-cum-grandpa to me, taking me to visit castles, nearby towns, beautiful little villages and to walk in the mountains which border Germany. Most of this would have been very difficult without a car (the trains go very infrequently and at unsociable hours). I've spent many weekends in Prague since it's only one and a half hours by bus. I had to do double takes on hearing English spoken and seeing the Guardian *being passed round the bars. Now instead of seeing Prague as the opening to Central Europe with its old-fashioned trams and cobbled streets as I did when I first arrived in September, I now think of it as the door back to westernisation.*

One final tip: if you play a musical instrument, take it with you since it's a great way to make local friends.

LIST OF SCHOOLS

ACADEMIC INFORMATION AGENCY (AIA)
Dum zahranicních sluzeb MSMT, Senovázné nám. 26, P.O Box 8, 110 06 Prague 1. Tel: (2) 2422 9698. Fax: (2) 2422 9697. E-mail: aia@dzs.cz. Website: www.dzs.cz/aia/lektori.htm.
Number of teachers: many teachers needed for state schools throughout the Czech Republic.
Preference of nationality: native speakers.
Qualifications: university degree in relevant subject required (e.g. English or Linguistics) or BA in other subject plus TEFL/TESL qualification. Previous experience in TEFL highly valued.
Conditions of employment: 10-month contracts September-June. 24 h.p.w.
Salary: 7,000-10,000 Czech crowns per month (net).
Facilities/Support: accommodation provided (free or subsidised). Work and residence permits organised before arrival.
Recruitment: direct application via AIA or Czech Embassy. Deadline for applications is end of April.
Contact: Karla Benesová.

AGENTURA EDUCO
Veletrzni 24, 170 00 Prague 7. Tel: (2) 2039 7368. E-mail: info@educo.cz.
Number of teachers: 6.
Preference of nationality: none.
Qualifications: BA in English. TEFL and teaching experience preferred. Knowledge of economics, business, banking and other fields useful.
Conditions of employment: 1 year contracts possible. From 4 hours per week.
Salary: 120 crowns per teaching unit (45 minutes). Teachers are expected not just to conduct conversation but to teach vocabulary and grammar.
Facilities/Support: no help with accommodation given. No training.
Recruitment: notices in the British Council, Globe Bookstore & Café.

AKADEMIE J.A. KOMENSKEHO
Trziste 20, Mala Strana, 118 43 Prague 1. Tel: (2) 5753 1476. Fax: (2) 5753 4054. E-mail: akademie@login.cz. Website: www.akademie.cz.
Number of teachers: many posts in 50 adult education centres and schools

throughout the Czech Republic.
Preference of nationality: British.
Qualifications: native speakers. Gap year students may be hired.
Salary: 8,000 crowns per month (net).
Facilities/Support: free accommodation provided. Short pre-service training course is compulsory.
Recruitment: applications to Recruitment Officer should include fax, telephone or e-mail addresses of two referees.

AKCENT INTERNATIONAL HOUSE PRAGUE
Bitovska 3, 140 00 Prague 4. Tel: (2) 6126 16 38/6126 16 75. Fax: (2) 6126 18 80. E-mail: brian@akcent.cz.
Number of teachers: 50+.
Preference of nationality: none.
Qualifications: CELTA or equivalent (minimum).
Conditions of employment: 12 months from 1st September. 1,060 54-minute teaching hours per year, approximately $26^{1/2}$ X 45 minutes a week. Mostly teaching general English to adults but a few students aged 5-14. Half on-site and half in-company.
Salary: 8,000-14,000 crowns (net) per month plus free accommodation and up to 1,400 crowns in benefits.
Facilities/Support: free private health insurance (BUPA) and 40 days paid holidays per full school year. Contribution made to cost of travelling to Prague.
Recruitment: *Guardian* adverts and locally. Teachers can apply through Human Resources Dept of IH London.
Contact: Brian O hEithir.

ANGLICTINA EXPRES
Korunní 2, 12000 Prague 2. Tel/fax: (2) 2251 3040. Tel: 2-2425 1482. E-mail: kelly@anexpres.cz.
Number of teachers: 15-20.
Preference of nationality: none.
Qualifications: university degree and some teaching experience preferred.
Conditions of employment: 1 year contracts. Morning and evening work.
Salary: hourly rate.
Facilities/Support: no help with accommodation. Some training available. Materials produced in-house.
Recruitment: direct application by e-mail. Detailed information about the school in English is at www.anexpres.cz
Contact: Milena Kelly.

BELL SCHOOL
Nedvezská 29, 100 00 Prague 10. Tel: (2) 78 15 342. Fax: (2) 78 22 961. E-mail: info@bellschool.cz
Number of teachers: 25 (full-time and part-time).
Preference of nationality: British, American.
Qualifications: DELTA or CELTA or equivalent, plus 2 years' teaching experience.
Recruitment: local interviews essential.
Contact: Steve Button, Director of Studies.

THE CALEDONIAN SCHOOL
Vltavská 24, 150 00 Prague 5. Tel/fax: (2) 573 13 650. E-mail: jobs@ caledonianschool.com; www.caledonianschool.com.
Number of teachers: 80.
Preference of nationality: none.
Qualifications: BA plus CELTA or equivalent.
Conditions of employment: 10 month contracts from mid-September. 20-24 45-minute lessons p.w. School teaches adults and young adults, in-school and in-company.

Salary: 15,000 crowns per month for qualified teachers. Free local transport pass. Free health care plan. Contract completion bonus.

Facilities/Support: accommodation usually offered in Hotel Dum ('Teachers' House') or Hotel Tourist for 4,300 crowns per month or school arranges a shared flat. School arranges and pays for flats for teachers who teach at out-of-Prague sites (including school at Bratislava, Slovakia). Regular, usually twice a month teacher development workshops held. Library has over 3,000 EFL titles, photocopiers and free e-mail and internet access for teachers. Social committee organises excursions and events for staff.

Recruitment: direct application. School hires year round. Recruiters: Paul Davies, 8 Temple Road, Windsor, Berkshire SL4 1WH, UK (01753-840967; Caledonian1@compuserve.com) and Thomas Norris, 6 Greenmount Court, Toronto, Ontario, Canada M8Y 1Y1 (416-231-9546/fax 416-231 1730; norrcal@sympatico.ca).

Contact: Paul Michel, Director of Studies.

DAVID'S AGENCY
Stefánikova 2888, 76001 Zlín. Tel: (67) 37505. E-mail: DavidsAgency@iol.cz.
Number of teachers: 15.
Preference of nationality: none.
Qualifications: university degree and TEFL.
Conditions of employment: 10 month contracts. Hours are 8am-noon and 1pm-4.30pm.
Salary: 16,000 crowns (gross) less about 25% for tax, health insurance and social security.
Facilities/Support: accommodation arranged for 3,000 crowns per month. Assistance with work permit process. Training given in Czech language and culture.
Recruitment: via adverts in the *Guardian*. Interviews compulsory and are held in England in the summer (David's Agency, c/o 18 Low Mill, Lancaster Road, Canton, Lancaster LA2 9HX).
Contact: David Catto, Director (Davidsagency@hotmail.com).

EASY ENGLISH
Botanicka 13, 60200 Brno. Tel: (5) 742318. Fax: (5) 742318. E-mail: info@easy-english.cz. Website: www.easy-english.cz.
Number of teachers: 3.
Preference of nationality: UK, American.
Qualifications: degree, preferably in TEFL.
Conditions of employment: 10 month contracts. Hours are 8am-1pm or 3pm to 8pm.
Salary: depends on education and experience. Taxes of 15% and social security payments 12.5%.
Facilities/Support: assistance given with finding accommodation. Work permit arranged by school.
Recruitment: on spec applications, word of mouth.

ENGLISH HOUSE
Vysehradská 2, 128 00 Prague 2. Tel/fax: (2) 293141.
Number of teachers: 15.
Preference of nationality: British preferred for convenience.
Qualifications: EFL certificate and some experience required.
Conditions of employment: 10 month contracts September-June. Lessons are 45 minutes, held Monday-Friday between 8am and 8pm.
Salary: approximately 13,000 crowns per month.
Facilities/Support: accommodation provided, public transport pass provided and paid. Professional development workshops held twice a month.
Recruitment: personal interview necessary, possible either in London or Prague.
Contact: Jaroslava Fricová, School Manager.

ENGLISH LANGUAGE SERVICES/ELS
Rooseveltova 9, 301 14 Plzen. Tel/fax: (19) 723 6699. E-mail: els@pm.bohem-net.cz. Web-site: www.kadel.cz/els
Number of teachers: 2.
Preference of nationality: English, Scottish, Canadian.
Qualifications: standard TEFL and good all-round education.
Conditions of employment: 1 academic year. 30 h.p.w.
Salary: 18,500 crowns (gross) and 8,500 crowns net after deductions for rent, social security and tax.
Facilities/Support: flat provided. Full assistance with work permits. Training provided.
Recruitment: directly or via agency. Phone interviews sufficient.
Contact: Director.

ENGLISH LINK
Na Berá 2, 160 00 Prague 6. Tel: (2) 360380; Fax: (2) 2281 2229. E-mail: elink@mbox.vol.cz. Website: www.englishlink.cz.
Number of teachers: 10.
Preference of nationality: none.
Qualifications: degree plus CELTA or equivalent.
Conditions of employment: 1 year, September to June. 24 contact hours per week.
Salary: performance related. Approx. 15,000 crowns per month.
Facilities/Support: assistance given with accommodation and work permits.
Recruitment: advertising in the local Czech press, adverts on various internet bulletin boards, and through the English Link website. Direct contact welcome. Interview in person essential. Can be done in the UK if requested.
Contact: Caralyn Bushey, Director of Studies.

ET CETERA LANGUAGE SCHOOL
Dusni 17, 110 00 Prague 1. Tel: (2) 231 3062. Fax: (2) 71 77 04 05. E-mail: etc-praha@post.cz. Website: www.etc-praha.cz.
Number of teachers: 4-5.
Preference of nationality: none.
Qualifications: TEFL/TESOL/2 years' teaching experience.
Conditions of employment: 1 year contract. Usually 20 h.p.w. (minimum 16, maximum unlimited).
Salary: 150 crowns per lesson.
Facilities/Support: assistance given with accommodation. No training.
Recruitment: direct application and local interviews.
Contact: Dagmar Kouchá.

INTERNATIONAL HOUSE BRNO
Sokolska 1, 602 00 Brno. Tel: (5) 41 24 04 93. Fax: (5) 41 24 59 54. E-mail: ihbrno@sby.cz. Website: www.ihbrno.cz.
Number of teachers: 7-10.
Preference of nationality: British.
Qualifications: CELTA Pass A or B preferred, experience an advantage.
Conditions of employment: end of September to end of June. 25 hours per week; 21 maximum contact hours per week.
Salary: 9,100 crowns gross per month, food vouchers (about 1,300 net per month), sterling payment, travel allowance, 4 weeks paid holiay.
Facilities/Support: accommodation is provided free by the school. The school deals with the work permit process.
Recruitment: internet and International House recruitment services.
Contact: Sona Vranova, Director.

INTERNATIONAL LANGUAGE CENTRES, PRAGUE
Lupácova 1, 130 00 Prague 3. Tel: (2) 697 4513/9000. Fax: (2) 231 8584. E-mail:

ihprague@telecom.cz. **Website: www.ilcgroup.com or www.studygroupintl.com.**
Part of ILC Group (formerly International House).
Preference of nationality: must be native speaker of English.
Qualifications: minimum CELTA.
Conditions of employment: 9 month-1 year renewable contracts.
Facilities/Support: accommodation and in-service training provided. Full-time CELTA courses offered regularly.
Recruitment: locally or via Study Group International (Embassy CES), Lorna House, 103 Lorna Road, Hove, East Sussex BN3 3EL; tel 01273-207481; fax 01273-208527.
Contact: Sian Adler, Director.

INTERTEXT SERVIS KAREL NAVRATIL
Anglická 24, 360 09 Karlovy Vary. Tel/fax: (17) 323 0436. E-mail: knavratil@iol.cz.
Number of teachers: 2.
Preference of nationality: none (e.g. British, American, Canadian).
Qualifications: BA plus CELTA/TESOL, plus preferably some teaching experience.
Conditions of employment: 1 year contracts. 16-20 h.p.w. Teachers expected to teach vocabulary and grammar (Cambridge English) and to conduct conversations.
Salary: 100 crowns net per teaching hour (45 minutes).
Facilities/Support: assistance given with accommodation. On-going assistance with lesson planning.
Recruitment: direct application, personal contact.
Contact: Karel Navrátil, Director.

JAZYKOVA SKOLA
456 Boleslavska, Nymburk. Tel: (606) 83 42 55. E-mail: jazykova@hotmail.com.
Number of teachers: varies.
Preference of nationality: none, but must be native speaker.
Qualifications: degree and TEFL Cert. minimum. Must be dedicated to students.
Conditions of employment: 1 year contract.
Salary: from 8,200 crowns net per month with increases dependent on ability and student feedback.
Facilities/Support: accommodation provided and health insurance which goes into effect 60 days after the start date of the contract.
Recruitment: via the internet.
Contact: William Sullivan.

LANGUAGES AT WORK
Na Florenci 35, 110 00 Prague 1. Tel/fax: (2) 248 11 379. E-mail: employment.atwork@login.cz. Website: www.atwork.cz.
Number of teachers: 35 full and part-time.
Preference of nationality: none, but must be native speaker.
Qualifications: preferably CELTA or equivalent, or with teaching experience, particularly in ESP since certain clients require business, banking, law, computer or other knowledge.
Conditions of employment: 1 year contracts. Approximately 20 h.p.w. (more if requested).
Salary: from 170 crowns per hour. Pay rise of 5-10 crowns given each semester. Deductions amount to 33%.
Facilities/Support: local travel benefits, bonuses, computers, internet and other benefits. Assistance with finding accommodation. Basic health care provided. Methodology seminars.
Recruitment: interviews conducted in Prague. Initial contact welcomed by e-mail. Candidates not available for interview must write a short essay and describe a teaching scenario.
Contact: Katerina Krizkova, General Director.

LINGUA VIVA LTD.
Spalena 21, 11000 Prague 1. Tel: (2) 24920675. Fax: (2) 2492 1142. E-mail: info@linguaviva.cz. Website: www.linguaviva.cz.
Number of teachers: approximately 10.
Preference of nationality: none.
Qualifications: TESOL, TEFL etc. certificates (minimum).
Conditions of employment: 1 term (half of a year). Teaching hours are all day, mostly in the afternoons and evenings.
Salary: 150 crowns gross per 45 minute lesson, less taxes of 20% minimum.
Facilities/Support: assistance is not usually given with accommodation. Help with work permit.
Recruitment: on spec applications. In-person interview essential so applicants are often already in the Czech Republic.
Contact: Hana Brezinova.

LONDON SCHOOL OF MODERN LANGUAGES
Francouzská 30, 120 00 Prague 2. Tel: (2) 242 53 437. Fax: (2) 242 54 259. E-mail: feakins@lsml.cz.
Number of teachers: 25.
Preference of nationality: none.
Qualifications: CELTA required.
Conditions of employment: 1 year contract. Teaching mornings and afternoons 26 hours per week.
Salary: 8000-11,000 crowns net per month.
Facilities/Support: accommodation provided and paid for. Work permit arranged by the school.
Recruitment: graduates of local training courses or *Times Educational Supplement* adverts and interviews in the UK.
Contact: J. Feakins, Assistant Director of Studies.

ST JAMES LANGUAGE CENTER
Namesti Miru 15, 120 00 Prague 2. Tel: (2) 2251 7869. Fax; (2) 2251 7870. E-mail: kacin@stjames.cz or tasker@stjames.cz. Website: www.stjames.cz.
Number of teachers: about 20.
Preference of nationality: must be native speaker.
Qualifications: minimum requirements are university degree and a recognised TEFL certificate (CELTA/Trinity). Formal EFL teaching experience is valued and teachers with experience can expect a higher salary. Must have a professional attitude, smart appearance and enthusiasm to teach.
Conditions of employment: 10-12 month contracts. 20 60-minute lessons per week. Teaching adults only, mainly in-company general and business English.
Salary: 14,000-17,000 crowns (gross). 1,000 crown performance bonus per month.
Facilities/Support: free accommodation provided (worth about 5,000 crowns), vacation pay (4 weeks per 12-month contract), internet access, monthly city travel pass, health insurance and assistance with visas.
Recruitment: application form available on website. School recruits year-round but main recruiting months are September and January.
Contact: Roman Kacin or Tom Tasker.

SPUSA EDUCATION CENTER
Rytirská 10, 110 00 Prague 1. Tel: (2) 421 0813. Tel/fax: (2) 421 3859. E-mail: spusa@mbox.vol.cz.
Non-profit organisation.
Number of teachers: 25.
Preference of nationality: none.
Qualifications: TEFL or equivalent certificate and preferably one or more year's teaching experience.
Conditions of employment: 1 year contracts. 20-25 45-minute lessons p.w. On- and

off-site teaching of adults.
Salary: starting salary from 15,000 crowns per month.
Facilities/Support: advice given on finding accommodation. Help with work and residence permits. Health and dental insurance provided. Training workshops held. Non-profit organisation.
Recruitment: direct application. Applicants must submit references, sample lesson plans and copies of diplomas and teaching certificates.
Contact: Neil Cairns, Lynda Mallinger.

STATNI JAZYKOVA SKOLA BRNO
Kotlárská 9, 611 49 Brno. Tel/fax: (5) 412 49 001. Tel: (5) 412 48 999. E-mail: pilarova@sjs-brno.cz. Website: www.sjs-brno.cz.
Number of teachers: 5-7.
Preference of nationality: British.
Qualifications: must have TEFL qualification.
Conditions of employment: 1 academic year (September-June). Approximately 20 h.p.w.
Salary: about 10,000 crowns per month (gross) less 30% in deductions.
Facilities/Support: assistance with finding accommodation, full help with work permits and training available at staff meetings.
Recruitment: liaise with other schools.
Contact: Marie Pilarová, Deputy Head.

STATNI JAZYKOVA SKOLA PRAGUE
Skolsá 15, 116 72 Prague 1. Tel: (2) 222 32 237 (English Department). Fax: (2) 222 32 236. E-mail: ao@sjs.cz or sjs@sjs.cz. Website: www.sjs.cz.
Separate state language school with similar conditions at Buresova 1130, 182 00 Prague 8 (Ladvi); 2-85 88 028.
Number of teachers: 45 teachers of English, usually 12 of them native speakers.
Preference of nationality: none.
Qualifications: BA in English, TESOL or Cambridge Cert., TEFL, TEFLA, or teaching experience.
Conditions of employment: 10 months from September 1st. 19 45-minute classes per week between 8am and 8pm.
Salary: starting salary 10,500 crowns per month (gross) plus at least 2 bonuses a year.
Facilities/Support: centrally located accommodation can be arranged for about 4,000 crowns a month (a small contribution towards accommodation of 1000 crowns a month). Subsidised meal coupons. Six free Czech lessons (or another language) per week.
Recruitment: contact by mail or in person. Interviews not always necessary, though trial lesson at school preferred.
Contact: Eva Zahradnícková, Head of the English Department (Prague 1); Ruth Vacková, Head of the English Department (Prague 8).

VIA LINGUA PRAGUE
Thamova 7, Prague 8 18600. Tel: (2) 217 02 100. Fax: (2) 217 02 102. E-mail: vialingua@mbox.vol.cz. Website: www.via-lingua.cz.
Runs its own 4-week TEFL certificate course (see entry in *Training Courses Abroad*).
Number of teachers: 25.
Preference of nationality: none.
Qualifications: TEFL Cert and or experience.
Conditions of work: average 24 class hours per week.
Salary: 220 crowns per hour.
Facilities/Support: help with work permits and accommodation can be provided.
Recruitment: locally and through the internet. Interviews preferred but not essential.
Contact: Franciscus Brakkenhof.

VISTA WELCOME
Konevova 210, 130 00 Prague 3. Tel/fax: (2) 69 77 492. E-mail: vista@iol.cz.
Website: www.vista-welcome.cz.
Number of teachers: 9 native speakers.
Preference of nationality: British, Canadian, American.
Qualifications: TEFL Cert. and/or proven ELS teaching experience. Mature teachers preferred, though enthusiasm important. School does not want to hire people who are just looking for a way to see the world. Experience in teaching Business English a plus.
Conditions of employment: 1-year contract minimum. Teaching hours vary. Full-time teachers guaranteed 20 lessons (45 minutes each) per week minimum. Courses aimed at firms and organisations looking for in-house courses. Teachers often work for more than one school to get enough teaching hours.
Salary: 210 crowns per hour if the school pays medical and social insurance; 280 crowns without insurance.
Facilities/Support: no accommodation provided though advice may be given to new arrivals.
Recruitment: adverts in the local English-language newspaper for expats *(Prague Post)*, the internet and via other schools in Prague.
Contact: Ela Struzkova, Principal.

Other Schools to Try

Note that these schools (in alphabetical order according to town) did not confirm their teacher requirements for this edition of *Teaching English Abroad*. Upper case entries marked with an asterisk had entries in the last edition (1999); addresses without asterisks have been taken from various sources, such as British Council lists and the *Yellow Pages*.

Albion Travel, Milady Horákové 14-16, Brno (tel/fax 5-452 40 911)
Berlitz, Starobrnenská 3, Brno (5-422 13 729)
Brno English Centre, VUT Kravi hora 13, 602 00 Brno (tel/fax 5-4121 2262)
Colourful English, námesti Svornosti 8, Brno (5-412 13 306)
Ability Language School, Lipova Laznia Mountain Spa Resort (tel/fax 2-627 21986). Summer school.
Aliance, Malická 4, 301 11 Plzen
Dum Technicky, Sady Petatrlcátníku 6, 301 24 Plzen
JAP, Slovenská alej 24, 307 04 Plzen
Jazyková skola Evropa, Tylová 15, 301 25 Plzen 1
Language Link, Kopeckého sady 15, 301 36 Plzen
Ability Jazyková Agentura, Levského 3203, 13-16 hod, Prague 4 (tel/fax 2-401 07 71)
Aha Jazyková Agentura, Kourimská 11, 130 00 Prague 3 (Vinohrady) (2-673 15 737/fax 2-717 32 127; aha@ini.cz)
Berlitz Language Centre, Vlkova 12, 130 00 Prague 3 (2-277101/270559)
Berlitz School of Languages, Hybernská 24, Prague 1 (2-212 5550-3)
British School, Tynska 19, 110 00 Prague 1 (tel/fax 2-480 8243). Recent advert in *Prague Post.*
Cosmolingua, Zdarilá 8, 140 00 Prague 4 (Nusle) (2-612 25 690/1; praha@cosmolingua.cz)
Elvis Jazyková Skola, Dacického 8, 140 00 Prague 4 (tel/fax 2-420044; info@elvis.cz)
*ENCOUNTER ENGLISH, Azalková 12, 100 00 Prague 10-Hostivar (tel/fax 2-758773)
Exellent, Stepánská 13, 120 00 Prague 2 (tel/fax 2-291063)
European Language Institute, Na Porici 17, Prague 1 (tel/fax 2-248 12 474)
Klub Maldych Cestovatch (KMC), Karoliny Svetlé 30, 11 000 Prague 1.

International summer workcamps which may involve teaching English to children.
Kolumbus Language Club, Zahrebska 9, 120 00 Prague 2 (900 58 481).
Linguarama, Srobárova 1, 130 00 Prague 3 (2-744889)
Prague Language Centre, V Jame 8, 110 00 Prague 1 (2-22 23 29 32; plc@mbox.vol.cz). Advertising for full and part-time teachers in *Prague Post* September 2000 offering possibility of accommodation.

Hungary

English is compulsory for all Hungarian students who wish to apply for college or university entrance, and university students in both the Arts and Sciences must take courses in English. Apart from the much-hated Russian, the second language of Hungary was traditionally German, a legacy of the old Austro-Hungarian Empire. But in most contexts German has been overtaken by English.

The Hungarian education system has much to be proud of, not least the efficacy with which it retrained its Russian teachers as English teachers after the return to democracy in 1989. The network of bilingual secondary schools *(gimnazia)* has produced a large number of graduates with a sophisticated knowledge of English. The vast majority of private language schools are owned and run by Hungarians rather than expats. Because of the calibre of Hungarian teachers of English, native speakers do not perhaps have the cachet that they have in other central European countries. Furthermore, the Hungarian language is so difficult for non-Hungarians to master, many schools prefer native Hungarians as English teachers.

Despite this, a demand for qualified native speakers continues unabated, especially in the business market. The invasion of foreigners in Budapest was never as overwhelming as it was (and is) in Prague, but still Budapest has a glut of teachers, among them some who have fled over-crowded Prague. The opportunities that do exist now are mostly in the provinces. Even in the more remote parts of the country, formal academic qualifications are important. It is a legal requirement that the bilingual schools employ a native speaker as lector. Most *gimnazia* liaise with the Fulbright Commission or the *Central European Teaching Program* and take on Americans, though Britons are also eligible.

Teachers are poorly paid in Hungary, aside from in the top-notch private schools and the British Council. Although the wage in forints has risen over the past three years, the exchange rate has dropped by more than a third. Rents in Budapest are high and take a major proportion of a teacher's salary; some schools help by subsidising accommodation, or it may be possible to arrange accommodation in return for English lessons. Low as the salaries may seem, native speakers can console themselves with the thought that they are usually better paid than Hungarian university lecturers.

FIXING UP A JOB

Very few jobs in Hungary are advertised in the UK and only one or two UK sending organisations (notably Services for Open Learning) include Hungary in their list of destinations. More opportunities exist for gap year students since the main organisations make placements in Hungarian schools (see *Conditions of Work* below).

In the US, recruitment of teaching assistants takes place via the *Central European Teaching Program* (see entry). The programme offers 'cultural immersion through teaching' and is open to anyone with a university degree, and preferably some experience of TEFL and overseas teaching/study experience. CETP liaises with the relevant government department in Hungary to place teachers in state schools throughout the country.

After Arrival

The British Council in Budapest may be willing to advise personal callers. You can request their list of nine Dual Language Secondary Grammar Schools and consult the 'Book of Lists' from the *Budapest Business Journal* which contains about 40 addresses of private language institutes. The regional resource centres in Győr, Miskolc, Pécs and Szombathely may be more helpful. They should have a list of primary and secondary schools which teach English in the region.

Of interest to Americans is the Regional English Language Office located in the Public Diplomacy section of the US Embassy (Szabadság tér 7-9, 1054 Budapest; 1-475-4328). The Regional office does not run its own English teaching programme but provides some assistance to Hungarian teacher training programmes by providing access to English language materials. From the autumn of 2000 a small lending/resource collection of professional ELT materials is available to professionals in the field in the Information Resource Center in the Embassy's Public Affairs section.

The professional journal *English Teaching Forum* produced by the English Language Programs office in Washington D.C. can be obtained through IATEFL Hungary. Back issues can be found on the ELP's web page www.exchanges.state.gov/education/engteaching. Other information can be found on the Public Affairs web page: www.usis.hu/ or by calling the Regional English Language Office.

A personal approach to potential employers will certainly have more chance of success than writing speculative letters, although anyone in Hungary on a tourist visa will find it difficult to change status (see below). Introducing yourself in the staff room has led to more than one job offer in the past. Steve Anderson returned to the places where he had taught on the CETP scheme in the spring of 1998 and came away convinced that initiative would be rewarded:

> *I believe it's still possible to hook up work upon arrival simply by walking the beat. Of course the trick is to get out of Budapest, where the supply of MATESOL and other substantially qualified teachers runs at a surplus. The provincial cities and town (particularly in the impoverished northeast close to the Ukrainian border) would still welcome an energetic and dedicated native-speaking teacher. A student from the university in Szeged in southern Hungary assured me that I could obtain work as a part-time English lecturer after arriving, solely on the basis of my two years' EFL experience in Hungary and my one semester of an MATESOL. Apparently many teachers work their way into full-time positions after proving themselves by this method. Numerous native speaking teachers (from the US, Canada, UK and Australia) have passed through this university to teach for a bit.*

State Schools

Native English speakers are sought by many state schools. English is available to pupils at the Dual Language Secondary Schools (a small percentage of the total), in the Gimnázium schools (more academic 'grammar schools', with 20% of total pupils), in technical and vocational schools *(szakközépiskola)* and in ordinary secondary schools throughout the country. The World Bank Program for the Development of Eastern Europe supports about 60 schools in the country and there are many perks for native speaker teachers employed by them such as field trips outside the school.

In the early days of the post-Communist period, the Hungarian Ministry of Education actively sought native speaker teachers for schools throughout the country, mainly through the English Teachers' Association of Hungary. This is the way Brian Komyathy, who describes himself as a New York suburbanite, fixed up his job a few years ago at a vocational school of economics, foreign trade and banking in Szolnok in central Hungary. However the placement of foreign teachers has mostly been delegated now to the foreign organisations mentioned above.

I found out after the fact that my query to the English Teachers' Association was forwarded (along with 24 others) to my current employer. They selected eight finalists whom they contacted, and when the dust settled, I was seen to have gone the distance. The eight Hungarian teachers of English here liked my credentials. I was rather surprised at how effortlessly I was able to arrange the job considering my lack of any previous teaching experience, only a BA in East European and Russian studies. Apparently the department (who have all been to Russia) thought I might have had some common experiences and would fit in as one of the gang, so to speak.

Most positions in Budapest schools are filled from the pool of available expats. The university towns of Debrecen, Miskolc, Szeged and Pécs are all better bets. You might be able to arrange at least part-time work assisting in English classes for university students. A further advantage is that universities normally can provide cheap housing in students' halls of residence.

Private Schools

Private institutes have mushroomed, primarily to meet the needs of the business community but also for children whose parents are keen for them to supplement the English teaching at state schools. It is estimated that there are over 100 private language schools in Budapest alone and 300 around the country, both very fluid numbers since schools open and close so quickly. Many private schools use native speakers as live commercials for the schools, though nowadays they want to advertise the qualifications of their teachers too.

Anyone with a recognised TEFL Certificate has a good chance of finding at least some hourly teaching after arrival in Budapest or elsewhere. British and American accents are both in demand. *International House* offers one-year contracts for qualified teachers of both adults and children and (according to Dennis Bricault) 'a wonderful social and professional atmosphere'.

To find the less well established schools on the spot, check the 'Book of Lists' mentioned above, try to decipher the Yellow Pages, keep your eyes open for the flyers posted in the main shopping streets or check out the English language weeklies. To find out what new institutes have opened or expanded, look at Hungarian papers like *Magyar Nemzet* or the free ads paper *Hirdetes* to see if any courses in *Angol* are being advertised at *Nyelviskola* (language schools).

Private tutoring provides one way of supplementing a meagre salary. Freelance teachers may find a developing market for their linguistic expertise in companies. Many executives need English for business as Hungary seeks to integrate with the economies of the West and attract foreign investors. The Department of Commerce, for example, employs teachers to train bankers, traders and top electrical engineers. Many professionals now need English as part of their work and are both able and prepared to pay for it. If you have a contact at International House in Budapest or Eger, you might enquire whether you can attend the fortnightly Angol Club which holds social events attended by learners and teachers, or perhaps the Executive Club for company clients. This would be a good place to meet potential private students.

REGULATIONS

Hungary was the first country in the former Eastern Bloc to clamp down on the untrained casual English teacher and to bring in work permit regulations. Employing schools must obtain a labour permit for their foreign teachers from the appropriate Hungarian labour office *(Munkaügyi Központ)* stating that no Hungarian national is available to do the job. The application for a labour permit must include originals (notarised copies will not suffice) of your university diploma, TEFL certificate (if applicable) and medical report stating that you have no communicable diseases (including HIV). The costs involved in having all these tests done in Hungary is about $100. All documents must be officially translated into Hungarian, which is much more cheaply carried out by the Central Translation Office in Budapest than by the Embassy abroad; the Washington Embassy charges $15 just for the official stamp, never mind the translating service.

British nationals who have found a Hungarian employer willing to go through all this and obtain a work permit do not need to apply to the Embassy for a work visa. Instead they must report to the Hungarian police within 15 days of arrival and obtain a residence permit for the period covered by the work permit. General information for Britons is available on the Embassy website http://dspace.dial. pipex.com/huemblon/front.htm or by ringing 09001 171204.

Americans and other nationalities (excluding Britons, as mentioned) must obtain a work visa from the Hungarian Embassy or Consulate in their country of residence. To apply for the work visa, the applicant must have a labour permit from the appropriate Hungarian labour office. Work visas are issued for multiple entries (one year extendable to a maximum of three). Within one month of starting your job, you should go to the local police, accompanied by an official from your place of work to get a temporary residency permit stamped in your passport which is proof that you have both a work permit and a work visa. The fee of 4,000 forints is normally paid by the teacher.

Deportation is said to be a real possibility for those who continue to teach for more than 90 days without a labour permit, though a more likely scenario is that the casual teacher with no prospect of getting a work permit will find it very difficult to find an employer in the first place. A foreign employee cannot get paid (at least not legally) until he or she has a labour permit.

CONDITIONS OF WORK

Salaries vary, but currently teachers in the state sector can expect between 30,000 and 50,000-60,000 forints (net) a month for teaching 20 hours a week. The hourly rate at commercial centres is normally in the range 1,400-1,700 forints while a full-time position should earn a teacher about 70,000 forints (net). It is essential to find out whether pay is net or gross since Hungarians lose about a quarter of their already meagre wages on tax and contributions.

Money is not the point for gap year students looking for an interesting way to spend the year before university. Some gap students end up providing conversational English practice for the older classes in secondary schools, which means they are teaching people nearly the same age as they are, as happened to Trudie Darch who spent a year teaching in Hungary through *GAP Activity Porjects*:

I had been there three weeks and with very little notice I was told that I'd be teaching on my own for one whole week. This was the scariest thing that had happened so far. Virtually unprepared, I walked into a classroom full of 18 year olds (I was 19) and had to teach. The first lesson was not very good and I had some difficulties getting them to listen to me. It was hard to get over the fact that these were my students not people who were supposed to be my friends. However I overcame this and learnt that to be a more professional teacher, I had to distance myself from trying to be their friend. The school was basic, the food was interesting (pasta and icing sugar was one I hated) and my accommodation left a lot to be desired. But even the bad things I wouldn't swap because they taught me a lot.

Helen Fagan did not have to work to gain her pupils' respect in her gap year placement in a remote Hungarian village:

Arriving at the children's home where I was to teach is one of my most treasured and vivid memories. As we pulled up outside this very grand old building, the youngest boy from my group met me with a bunch of flowers and a kiss. As I proceeded down the stairs, all 50 children were holding small bunches of flowers which they presented to me individually with a kiss, a traditional Hungarian welcome. The low point of my placement in Hungary was definitely the day I had to leave.

Brian Komyathy spells out the advantages of working for the state rather than private enterprise:

I personally would recommend seeking a teaching position in a public school, especially if you're doing it for the experience. At my school, for instance, what made my job of interest to me (in addition to the classroom aspect) was the atmosphere of the school: visitors from abroad, school trips, sporting events, holiday celebrations, student performances, etc. At my school's expense I accompanied students to Budapest and Romania (on a skiing and English camp). Even though I only understood every eighth word, I rather enjoyed attending local festivals and historical celebrations. (I always showed my face because I felt that I was an unofficial American ambassador.)

Although the wages in money will be low, schools try to shower as many perks as they can on their foreign teacher in addition to free furnished accommodation, e.g. use of a bicycle and travel discounts.

The American Steve Anderson was the first foreigner to work at his school in the 1000-strong village of Vaja in northeastern Hungary close to the Ukrainian border. It was obvious to him that the northeastern reaches of Hungary were most in need of teachers, and he found teaching there more rewarding than he had in a well-resourced school in Western Hungary. Writing in *Transitions Abroad* magazine, he described why he prefers teaching off the beaten track:

Though I initially rode the wave of native English speakers who rolled in to teach in Budapest and other larger cities, I am glad that I jumped ship to work in the poorer provinces. Activities like preparing spicy fish soup over an open fire and swaying to folk songs fiddled by the village gypsy don't happen in less traditional urban centres... The students of Vaja, lacking the luxuries of computers and up-to-date text books, had less developed English skills than those I had encountered the year before. I rewound all the way to the ABCs with my younger class and was forced to develop creative teaching methods I hadn't needed in my more advanced school, where audio and visual materials did the work for me.

Inexperienced teachers are used by state schools for language and cultural enhancement through conversation classes, while the nitty-gritty teaching of grammar and reading is usually done by Hungarian teachers. This team-teaching approach seems to work well although obviously some of the Hungarian teachers have quite a struggle with English and depend heavily on their 'big shot' foreigner to adjudicate on points of grammar and British versus American usage. Don't expect any training facilities; it is more likely to be the other way round with the Hungarian teachers expecting you to do the training, even if you have few qualifications.

Teachers in private schools must expect to teach everything from grammar to conversation, with variable materials. Students are generally keen and no problem to teach. Dennis Bricault, who taught at IH in Budapest for a year, describes pupils as a 'teacher's dream: hard-working, generally competent and with a good idea of what it takes to learn languages'. Some pupils may find modern teaching methods strange as they are used to a more teacher-centred approach, and more creative techniques may take some getting use to.

LIST OF SCHOOLS

ATALANTA BUSINESS AND LANGUAGE SCHOOL
Visegradi u. 9, 1132 Budapest. Tel/fax: (1) 339 8913/339 8549. E-mail: market.atalanta@qwertynet.hu.
Number of teachers: 60.
Preference of nationality: none.
Qualifications: college degree plus TEFL or TESOL certificate.
Conditions of employment: contracts given for length of course, 60-240 hours. Full-time teachers work minimum 14 h.p.w.
Salary: 1,400-2,000 forints per hour (net).
Facilities/Support: help provided with obtaining work permits and costs of work permits are fully reimbursed. No assistance with accommodation. Regular lesson observation and feedback by qualified mentors plus fortnightly workshops.
Recruitment: local advertisements and interviews. Candidates can also submit sample teaching materials at interview.
Contact: Eva Malomsoki, Director of Studies or Magda Kimmel, Assistant Director of Studies.

BABILON NYELVSTUDIO
Károly krt. 3/a IV.em, 1075 Budapest. Tel: (1) 269 5531. Fax: (1) 322 6023. E-mail: bab@mail.datanet.hu.
Number of teachers: 3-5.
Preference of nationality: British, American.
Qualifications: BA plus TEFL or TESL certificate and experience.
Conditions of employment: minimum one year. 12-18 h.p.w. between 8am and 11am, 3pm and 5pm and 5pm and 8pm.
Salary: 1,200 forints per hour (net).
Facilities/Support: no assistance with accommodation. Help given with work permits. Training available.
Recruitment: local interviews only.
Contact: Eva Babai, Director or Katalin Jonas, Director of Studies.

BELL ISKOLAK
Tulipán u. 8, 1022 Budapest. Tel: (1) 212 4324, 326 8457/326 5257. Fax: (1) 326 5033. E-mail: bellisk@bell.hu.
Part of the *Bell* Language Schools.
Number of teachers: 45.
Preference of nationality: British.
Qualifications: BA, CELTA or DELTA and a few years' teaching experience.
Conditions of employment: 20 h.p.w. for full-timers. Also part-time vacancies available. Pupils include young children, secondary school students, adults and business people.
Salary: 1,700 forints for 45-minute lesson. Earnings taxed at rate of 25%.
Facilities/Support: seminars held; training and professional assistance given. Good library and resources.
Recruitment: direct application with CV.
Contact: Eszter Timár, Director of Studies.

BUSINESS POLYTECHNIC
Vendel u. 3, 1096 Budapest. Tel: (1) 215 4900. Fax: (1) 215 4906. E-mail: titkar@mail.poli.hu.
Number of teachers: 3.
Preference of nationality: none.
Qualifications: teaching experience in secondary schools.
Conditions of employment: one year in first instance. Hours 8am-2pm.
Salary: negotiable.
Facilities/Support: assistance with accommodation if necessary. Help with work

permits and training given.
Recruitment: word of mouth. Local interviews necessary.
Contact: Adrienne Varga, Head of Foreign Language Department.

CENTRAL EUROPEAN TEACHING PROGRAM (CETP)
Beloit College, 700 College St, Beloit, Wisconsin 53511, USA. Tel: (608) 363-2619. Fax: (608) 363-2449. E-mail: dunlopa@beloit.edu. Website: www.beloit.edu/~cetp.
Number of teachers: 60 English conversation teachers for state schools only throughout Hungary (and 30 more for Romania, Poland and Lithuania).
Preference of nationality: native speakers of English.
Qualifications: BA or BSc required before departure. Classroom teaching in English or ESL needed either before or after application. Must demonstrate flexibility, patience, cultural sensitivity and maturity. Ability to teach German as well as English in great demand.
Conditions of employment: 10-month contracts from September 1st. 18-22 classes (45 minutes) p.w.
Salary: forint equivalent of US$200 per month.
Facilities/Support: free furnished private accommodation provided. Regional contacts arrange initial get-togethers for programme participants. Periodic workshops and some language training.
Recruitment: via college visits and ads. Phone interviews are sufficient. Placement fee of $2,000. Application deadline is April 1st though it can be extended if vacancies exist.
Contact: Alex Dunlop, CETP Director.

EUROPAI NYELVEK STUDIOJA
Muzeum Krt. 39, 1053 Budapest. Tel: (1) 317 1302. Fax: (1) 266 3889. E-mail: els@mail.datanet.hu
Number of teachers: 5-10.
Preference of nationality: British, American.
Qualifications: Cambridge Diploma or TEFL Certificate.
Conditions of employment: 30-week contracts (September-May). At least 16 h.p.w.
Salary: 1,700 forints per hour (net).
Facilities/Support: assistance with work permit but not accommodation. Training sessions once a month.
Recruitment: word of mouth. Local interviews necessary.
Contact: Ms. Judit Varadi, Director of Studies.

INTERNATIONAL HOUSE
Language School & Teacher Training Institute, PO Box 92, 1276 Budapest. Tel: (1) 212 4010, ext 20. Fax: (1) 316 2491. E-mail: dos@ih.hu. Website: www.ih.hu.
Number of teachers: 100 in centres around Hungary. 60 teachers working in the main school in Budapest.
Qualifications: minimum Cambridge CELTA.
Conditions of employment: contracts are for 20 contact hours per week including in-company teaching, groups, one-to-one and special projects.
Salary: 95,000 forints per month (net) and flat allowance and monthly travel card.
Facilities/Support: assistance given with finding accommodation. In-service teacher development.
Recruitment: through direct application and IH, London. Interviews essential.

KARINTHY FRIGYES GIMNAZIUM
Thököly utca 7, Pestlorinc, 1183 Budapest. Tel: (1) 291 2072. Fax: (1) 291 2367. E-mail: BA@karinthy.hu. Website: www.karinthy.hu.
Number of teachers: 4-6 for a bilingual high school.
Preference of nationality: none (must be native speaker of English).

Qualifications: MA (English) or BA plus TEFL experience.
Conditions of employment: 1 academic year contracts. Hours of work 8am-2pm.
Pupils aged 14-19 studying all academic subjects in English at bilingual school and in the International Baccalaureate programme.
Salary: average for Hungary.
Facilities/Support: free accommodation provided plus heating/electricity costs. No training given.
Recruitment: directly or via the Fulbright Commission.
Contact: Dr. Aniko Bognar.

KOLCSEY FERENC GIMNAZIUM
Rakoczi u. 49-53, 8900 Zalaegerszeg. Tel: (92) 324 285. Fax: (92) 311 144. E-mail: suli703@zala.sulinet.hu. Website: www.kfgz.sulinet.hu.
Number of teachers: 1 lector.
Preference of nationality: native speaker.
Qualifications: EFL teacher with secondary school experience. Majors: English or/and other subjects, preferably history.
Conditions of employment: one year, extendable. 20 lessons a week.
Salary: 50,000 forints net per month after deductions 1.5% for unemployment, 8% pension contribution and 3% health insurance.
Facilities/Support: furnished apartment provided by the school. Assistance with obtaining work permit.
Recruitment: through organisations such as the Central European Teaching Program. Interviews not essential.
Contact: Fehervaryne Harvath Katalin, Coordinator of the bi-lingual programme.

LIVING LANGUAGE SEMINAR
Fejér György u. 8-10, 1053 Budapest. Tel: (1) 326 5251/317 9644. Fax: (1) 317 9655. E-mail: elonyelv@mail.matav.hu.
Number of teachers: 3-5.
Preference of nationality: British, American, Canadian.
Qualifications: a great deal of ESL teaching experience, registered Pitman, Oxford examinations centre. Preparation for Cambridge and local exams, TOEFL, Business English.
Conditions of employment: contracts from 3 months. Negotiable hours. Mainly teaching adults (aged 16-40).
Salary: high by local standards.
Facilities/Support: no assistance with accommodation at present.
Recruitment: through adverts. Interviews required.

LONDON STUDIO
Villányi út. 27, 1114 Budapest. Tel: (1) 385 0177. Fax: (1) 209 1244. E-mail: londonstudio@mail.datanet.hu.
Number of teachers: 10-15.
Preference of nationality: British, American, Canadian, Australian.
Qualifications: MA, BA or LTCL TESOL/DELTA/CELTA.
Conditions of employment: 10-week, year round contracts. Hours are 8-9.30am, 4.30-6pm and 6.30-8pm plus 8-12am on weekends.
Salary: 1,400-2,500 forints per 45 minute lesson, depending on quality of work and demonstration lesson.
Facilities/Support: addresses of accommodation agencies are provided. In-house training once a month.
Recruitment: interview and demonstration lesson in Budapest essential.
Contact: Katalin Sziegl Terescsik, Director of Studies.

NOVOSCHOOL NYELVISKOLA
Ullöi út. 63, 1091 Budapest. Tel: (1) 215 5480. Fax: (1) 215 5488. E-mail: novoschool@mail.matav.hu. Website: www.novoschool.nyelviskola.hu.

Number of teachers: 2-3.
Preference of nationality: British.
Qualifications: university degree and teaching experience in ESL.
Conditions of employment: 1 or 2 years. 5 h.p.w. in first instance, rising to 10 or 20 if satisfactory.
Salary: freelance teachers invoice school for negotiated hourly rate.
Facilities/Support: no assistance with accommodation. Help given with work permits. Workshops held for all teachers.
Recruitment: direct. Interviews are essential. Applicants observe classes, then teach on trial basis before being taken on.
Contact: Kati Németh, Head of English Section.

PROSPERO TRAINING AND CONSULTING
1055 Budapest, Falk Miksa u. 28 III/2. Tel: (1) 302 3032. Tel/fax: (1) 353 1220. E-mail: prospero.training@mail.matav.hu.
Number of teachers: 6.
Preference of nationality: British or American.
Qualifications: EFL and/or Business English qualifications plus some experience in business.
Conditions of employment: 6 month contracts, renewable. About 20 h.p.w.
Salary: negotiable.
Facilities/Support: assistance with accommodation and work permits if required. Training available.
Recruitment: CV and interview. Interviews sometimes available in UK or, if not, by telephone.
Contact: Gyöngyi Köteles, Director of Studies.

TUDOMANY NYELVISKOLA
Vörösvári út. 1 I/1, 1035 Budapest. Tel: (1) 368 1156. Tel/fax: (1) 388 5072. E-mail: info@tudomanynyelviskola.hu. Website: www.tudomanynyelviskola.hu.
Number of teachers: 4-5.
Preference of nationality: British and American.
Qualifications: TEFL/TESL preferred.
Conditions of employment: 10 month contracts. Hours vary.
Facilities/Support: assistance with accommodation not normally given. Training sometimes available.
Recruitment: local interviews essential.
Contact: Tamás Lógrádi, Director.

VACI STREET DEVELOPMENT CENTRE
Teréz Krt. 47, 1067 Budapest. Tel/fax: (1) 353 3274. E-mail: kirstin@whereutoday.com.
Number of teachers: 15.
Preference of nationality: none.
Qualifications: TEFL/TESOL certification and/or teaching experience.
Conditions of employment: minimum 3 months; part-time/full-time positions available (10-20 contact hours per week). VSDC specialises in Anglo-American corporate training including sales, presentation skills and specialised courses for the hotel and customer service industry.
Salary: varies.
Facilities/Support: assistance in finding accommodation and settling in Budapest. Weekly training sessions.
Recruitment: CV and interview, year-round hiring.
Contact: Kirstin Biehl, Language Training.

VARGA KATALIN GIMNAZIUM
Szabadság ter. 6, 5000 Szolnok. Tel: (56) 512240. Fax: (56) 420310. E-mail: molnar@varga-szolnok.sulinet.hu.

Number of teachers: 1 for teaching English and 1 for teaching mathematics.
Preference of nationality: British or American.
Qualifications: diploma for teaching English/Mathematics.
Conditions of employment: 1 year. 20 lessons a week.
Salary: between 30,000 and 60,000 forints per month, depending on age.
Facilities/Support: possible to give help with finding accommodation. Assistance with work permits given.
Recruitment: via organisations like Soros, Fulbright and CETP. Interviews not essential.
Contact: László Molnár, Assistant Principal.

Other Schools to Try

Note that these schools did not confirm their teacher requirements for this edition of *Teaching English Abroad*. Addresses have been taken from various sources such as the *Book of Lists* published by the *Budapest Business Journal.*

Ameropa, Móricz Zsigmond krt. 14 IV/1, 1117 Budapest
Arany János Languages School, Csengery u. 68, 1067 Budapest
Berlitz, Váci u. 11/b, 1052 Budapest
Big Ben Languages Studies, Csepreghy u. 4, 1085 Budapest
Budapest Language School for Children, Szász Károly u. 2, 1027 Budapest
Concord, Németvölgyi út. 34, 1126 Budapest
Danubius, Bajcsy-Zsilinszky köz. 1, 1065 Budapest
Dover, Bécsi u. 3, 1052 Budapest
Fast English Alternative Language School, Vigszínház u. 5, 1137 Budapest
Fókusz, Böszörményi út. 8, 1126 Budapest
Foreign Trade Education Center, Falk Miksa u. 1, 1055 Budapest
Interclub Hungarian Language School, Bertalan Lajos u. 17, 1111 Budapest
International Language School, Pf. 64, 1363 Budapest
Katedra Language School, Fövám ter 2-3, 1114 Budapest
Lingua School of English, Szent István krt. 7, 1055 Budapest
LT Lingvearium, Lajos u. 1, 1023 Budapest
Pasaréti Language School, Csévi út. 7, 1025 Budapest
TIT Globe, Múzeum krt. 7, 1088 Budapest
*IHH A NYELVISKOLA, International Holiday House, Teleki u. 18, 9022 Györ (96-315444/30-363195/fax 96-315665; nagyotto@ihh.hu). 20 teachers.
Oxford Nyelviskola, Ikva u. 52, Györ

Poland

Prospects for English teachers in Poland, western Poland in particular, remain more promising than almost anywhere else in the world. Even the major cities like Warsaw, Wroclaw, Kraków, Poznan and Gdansk are promising destinations, especially for people looking for in-company work. As in the Czech and Slovak Republics there are numerous possibilities in both state and private schools. School directors are often delighted to interview native English speakers who present themselves in a professional manner. The reverence for 'native speakerhood' still runs very high in Poland. However, as British and American native speakers of English have become less of a rarity, the EFL public has become more selective. It is no longer possible to quit at one school, walk next door and start work the next day. The change in visa regulations which requires foreigners to apply in their home country prevents the employment situation from being as fluid as it used to be. Yet it still seems that TEFLers with initiative can create jobs for themselves with hours and a location to suit.

The craving for English does not seem much diminished since the heady days immediately after the collapse of the Communist Party in 1990. The private language school market continues buoyant. Poles seem to have adjusted to their new era with confidence, especially since the 'new zloty' has had a stabilising effect on the economy (though teachers' salaries are often quoted in US dollars or sterling). Inflation is now less than 10% and falling while the economy is growing.

There is a continuing demand for English from the state sector which, due to a shortage of resources, depends very heavily on the steady stream of volunteer teachers supplied by various agencies. The old state exam in English has been replaced by the Cambridge First Certificate creating a large demand for British teachers of English who have some experience of those exams.

Foreign teachers normally find their students unfailingly friendly, open and keen to learn more about the world. Discussion classes are likely to be informed and lively, with students well up to date on developments and very well motivated to practise their English. In some companies, promotion depends on the level of English achieved, which spurs students from the business world to be especially committed. On the other hand, if the company is paying for an employee's lessons, there may be little incentive to attend regularly or with enthusiasm.

FIXING UP A JOB

Interested teachers should not expect to be snapped up by every high quality school to which they apply unless they have at least a TEFL certificate and some sort of teaching experience.

English native speakers in the UK interested in TEFL teaching in Poland can contact the Polish Cultural Institute, Education Office (34 Portland Place, London W1N 4HQ; 020-7636 6032/fax 020-7637 2190). Obviously this office cannot act as an employment agency but it can attempt to refer enquirers to appropriate organisations such as the Anglo-Polish Universities Association. APASS continues to recruit native speakers to work at summer language camps (see section below) and also for year-long appointments.

Placements in state schools were once overseen by the Ministry of National Education at Al. J. Ch. Szucha 25, 00-918 Warsaw, but the Ministry is no longer involved in this activity. The Director of the department of International Cooperation suggests that teachers should apply directly to headteachers of Polish schools. Lists of addresses are available from the regional offices of superintendents of education *(Kuratoria)*. Teacher training colleges *(Nauczycielskie Kolegium Jezyków Obcych* or NKJOs) continue to recruit one or two native speaker teachers each though nowadays they are looking for high academic qualifications.

International House has a big presence in Poland with schools in Bielsko-Biala, Bydgoszcz, Katowice, Kielce, Koszalin, Kraków, Lódz, Opole, Poznanz, Torun and Wroclaw, some of which are listed in the Directory. The Bell Educational Trust has an Associate Network of schools in Poland in Gdansk, Gdynia, Bydgoszcz and Szczecin (see entry for *ELS Bell*), in Warsaw (*UEC-Bell*), Poznan (*Program-Bell*) and Kraków (see *Gama Bell*). These high profile ELT organisations are founding members of PASE, the Polish Association for Standards in English which promotes ethical practices in the private sector.

The TEFL pages of the *Guardian* and the main ELT job search websites probably carry more advertisements for schools in Poland than for any other country. Ads in British newspapers often provide a contact address in the UK where interviews can be scheduled over the summer. Contacting private schools ahead of time may produce some interest, though in most cases they will want to interview you before making any commitment. Commercial recruitment agencies like *TEFLNet* and *Saxoncourt & English Worldwide* are often asked to fill vacancies in private language schools; the latter even hosts occasional 'Poland days' in the summer.

If you have a Polish speaking contact, ask them to help you navigate around the relevant websites like www.angielski.com.pl which has links to language schools in Warsaw.

On the Spot

Semesters begin on October 1st and February 15th, and the best time to arrive is a month beforehand. After arrival, try to establish some contacts, possibly by visiting the English department at the university. Although some school directors state a preference for British or American accents, many are neutral.

Private language schools catering for all kinds of English teaching sprang up everywhere as soon as private enterprise was legally possible. The Warsaw Yellow Pages carry several pages under the heading *Jezykowe Kursy, Szkolenia*. The very busy British Council in Warsaw (near Central station) and the smaller British Council Libraries in Kraków, Wroclaw, Gdansk and seven other cities may be able to assist personal callers. The Gdansk office has a list of the dozen biggest private language schools. In Kraków ask for the comprehensive list of language schools ('Jezyki Obce') in the region compiled annually by a Kraków newspaper (*Gazeta W Krakowie*) for the benefit of Polish readers wanting to compare courses. After obtaining some addresses, would-be teachers should dutifully 'do the rounds' of the *Dyrektors*.

When you fix up interviews with private language schools, it is often very useful to have an interpreter present, since even the directors of such schools do not always speak fluent English. In some cases, you will be offered a certain number of hours but these will only materialise if enough paid-up clients materialise first.

If you base yourself in Warsaw and wish to advertise your availability for private English tuition, try placing a notice just to the right of the main gate of Warsaw University or in one of the main dailies, *Gazeta Wyborcza* or *Zycie Warszawy*. A further idea is to visit the Irish pub on ul. Miodowa near the castle which many English speakers use as their watering-hole.

Most Polish teachers of English work 'on the side' and it may be possible to work in partnership with one of them as a teaching aid, earning a reasonable wage for speaking as instructed (and incidentally picking up some teaching ideas for future use). Freelancing is very popular, and lately there has been a huge increase in demand for tailor-made one-to-one courses. Banks are likely clients and often pay very well by Polish standards. For this work, teachers should have enough ELT awareness to be able to devise their own syllabus.

Academic Institutes

As mentioned above, NKJOs (foreign language teacher training colleges) of which there are 60, are eager to hire qualified, experienced teachers, yet they cannot pay a very high salary. University institutes of language learning called *Studia* run in partnership between the British Council and universities in Warsaw, Wroclaw, Gdansk, Kraków, Poznan, Lódz, Katowice, Gliwice and Szeczecin.

Virtually every institute of higher education (universities, medical academies, technical universities, economics academies, art schools, etc.) has a *Studium Jazyków Obcych* (Foreign Language Department) which is where the students who aren't language majors fulfil their foreign language requirements. The learners are less advanced and possibly less motivated in English than at the NKJOs, and they may be prepared to accept less well qualified native speaker assistants while offering the attractions of an academic setting.

Holiday Language Camps

The Anglo-Polish Universities Association (APASS) is a non-profit fraternity of students, graduates, teachers and others willing to teach EFL in Poland. Contact details are APASS, UK North, 93 Victoria Road, Leeds LS6 1DR; telephone for emergencies only (8am-10am and 4pm-6pm) 0113-275 8121 or 0113-2744363; they have no fax or website. There are two schemes which are run in the summer only and require about 320-350 volunteers. One is for English language instructors and assistants (minimum age 16 years with parental permission) who must be English native speakers. Applicants can be young people but older teachers and mature students from British universities are also welcome to spend one month (end of July to end August) in Poland. ELT experience is of course welcomed but not essential. Furnished accommodation and food is provided for three weeks 'teaching' and there is one week allocated for a tour of Poland. All expenses and pocket money of up to £18 a week in zloties are paid by the Polish host.

There is also an APASS scheme for family/group placements (assisted travel available). Teaching experience is welcomed but not essential as the scheme requires 12-15 hours per week of mainly conversation classes. Hospitality and activities are included. APASS produces a detailed information pack, available from mid-March onwards at a cost of £3 plus 9in X 6in s.a.e. (40p stamped) which will indicate the current placement fee. Reports have been received that details of these summer placements are finalised not long before departure, so be prepared to endure some suspense. Wayne Stimson feels that this excellent scheme is not widely enough known:

I had often wanted to teach English and, as a politics student, I also had an interest in the history and politics of the former Eastern Bloc states. I got the opportunity last summer to combine these two when APASS arranged for me to spend seven weeks in a village near the Czech border called Dusniki Zdroj. Here I worked on two camps that gave children an activity-based holiday alongside English teaching. The children were mainly from middle class, professional backgrounds and their English skills were often quite developed so teaching and general communication was not difficult. I tried to teach a little about the customs, culture and politics of the UK. I was treated very graciously by my hosts and found Polish people to be very warm and friendly.

Many private language teaching organisations run short-term holiday courses which require native speakers, including several in the Directory (*English School of Communication Skills, ELS Bell*, etc.). Will Gardner was full of praise for the camp where he worked one summer:

I spent one month working for ESCS at their summer camp on Poland's Baltic Coast. The camps were well organised and great fun. As an experienced teacher who has worked in several different countries for a range of schools, I would just like to say what a pleasure it was to work with such a well organised group of people and for a school that completely lived up to its promises. The school supplied a wide range of resources to assist teachers, although a lot of emphasis was placed on originality. The focus was always on communication and fun. The camp facilities were perfect for the situation. Food and accommodation were supplied and the weather was beautiful. Although the students were attending lessons daily, a holiday atmosphere prevailed over all activities.

A summer camp in Siennica (50km southeast of Warsaw) was looking for volunteer teachers to teach conversational English; interested people should write to Earl & Annmarie Adreani, 77 Gayland Rd., Needham, MA 02492, USA (Annmarie_Adreani@Needham.K12.ma.us).

REGULATIONS

A work visa (Visa 06) must be applied for in your country of origin, as for Hungary and Slovakia. The required documents must be presented in person to a Polish Consulate: a promisory work permit from your Polish employer, your passport, two photos, a completed application form and the current fee for a work visa (which exceeds £100). In order for your employer to obtain permission to employ a foreign teacher, he or she will have to submit originals or notarised copies of your degree diploma and TEFL Certificate (if applicable) with official translations. Most schools will assist with the documentation and the majority promise to reimburse all or part of the cost on completion of a contract.

CONDITIONS OF WORK

Generally speaking, private language schools in Poland offer reasonable working conditions, with fewer reports of profit-mongers and sharks than in other countries experiencing a TEFL boom. Instead of hearing complaints from teachers of employers, it tends to be more often the other way round, as the Director of Studies of a private language school makes clear:

> *My boss, who has been employing British native speakers for seven years and who has proved to be a very patient person, could provide you with some hair-raising stories of teachers signing their contracts and withdrawing at the very last minute (having probably found a more lucrative job in Japan), teachers returning a couple of days late after the Christmas break without presenting any adequate excuse (or not returning at all), not to mention the state of flats and equipment which, after being used for nine months, is often left in a wrecked condition.*

Wages are not high but they go further than they used to. If your accommodation is reasonably priced and you resist the temptation to shop and party to excess, it is even possible to save. The terms of service are seldom exploitative. It is not uncommon for overtime to be paid to teachers for hours worked in excess of the contracted number (typically 24). Erica Jolly and Paul Robinson describe the situation in Gdansk:

> *The big schools in and around Gdansk all seem similar. They are well equipped but don't pay that well. Class sizes are around 12-15 students and hours are usually a minimum of 18 teaching hours per week. The director in charge of teaching is an experienced EFL teacher and teacher-trainer herself, and is always available to help and advise. My only criticism is the propensity towards paperwork: each teacher is obliged to complete forms after each lesson giving details of everything covered, comments, etc.*

The current average gross salary in the private sector is about £5 an hour or 1,200-1,600 zloties (£175-£235) per month. The standard deduction is 21% for taxes and contributions. It is possible to live on 120zl (£17) a week provided your rent is paid and you have fairly ascetic inclinations, though foreign teachers earn at least twice this and sometimes six times as much as this. Most foreigners supplement their basic income by doing some one-to-one tutoring. The cost of living has been rising though many staples remain exceedingly cheap, for example a pint of beer costs 4zl and a loaf of bread 2zl. However some groceries (especially fruit and vegetables) are nearly as expensive as they are in Britain. One unforeseen expense Erica mentioned was the high cost of replacing windows on their car which was broken into on several occasions. Her conclusion was that it would be better to stick to public transport if spending a year in Poland.

Heidi Rothwell-Walker enjoyed company teaching, which was a contrast with the basic adult education she had been doing in Britain:

> *I was expected to work any time from 7am to 6pm. Sometimes the early hours (especially in the long winter) can get you down, but you will be rewarded financially for starting at 7am. There was a lot of travelling and waiting at bus stops, but working conditions in the companies were excellent. Not every company gave you access to a white board, overhead projector or cassette player but they could be made available upon request.*

Once you are working either in the public or private sector, you may be approached with various proposals, from 'verifying' English translations of scientific research papers or restaurant menus, to coaching actors and singers preparing for English performances and doing dubbing or voice-overs for films and TV.

As throughout Eastern Europe, accommodation is a major problem, though there are fewer complaints about the high rents and low quality than elsewhere. If you don't mind living with a family in what will almost certainly be cramped conditions, it is possible to get free accommodation in exchange for giving English conversation lessons.

Despite a considerable amount of disorganisation at many schools, no one complains of a lack of hospitality from the Poles. Once they get to know the teacher, students will offer whatever services they can from mending shoes to giving large quantities of home-preserved fruit. Marta Eleniak especially enjoyed her experience teaching children:

> *Teaching in the primary school was really enjoyable as the little kids make you feel so appreciated by giving you flowers, drawing pictures for you and performing songs, poems or dances for you. They always wanted to continue after the bell had gone. One class was so keen that they invited themselves for a lesson even though it was my break.*

All of this makes a refreshing contrast with the lot of the EFL teacher in many other parts of the world. Poles even seem to have the ability to crack jokes in English when their English is very elementary, so lessons are not usually dull. On the whole they are also very well-motivated and hard-working, including adolescents. The number of Polish women looking for Western husbands has declined, at least according to the manager of a big Warsaw language school (who has just married a Pole).

State Schools

Anyone who likes kids, wants to do good, feel needed and suffer a little will enjoy a year in a state school. Novice teachers can be useful at public schools, though many find it a rude awakening. Shortages of materials and basic classroom equipment are less common than they were five years ago, but classroom facilities in many cases are still sadly lacking. Even the best-hearted of Polish teachers is generally so overworked and underpaid that they are not in a position to spend time advising foreign teachers. A large measure of independence and self-reliance is therefore essential. Novices who are not prepared for all this soon become miserable and embittered, resulting in a lot of unnecessary bad feelings on both sides.

Jobs attached to universities usually offer stability and a light workload, say 12-15 classroom hours a week during the two 15-week semesters. The salary is paid over 12 months and includes full health insurance, housing perks and discounts on train travel. Bear in mind that if you are tutoring some of them privately, this income will vanish over the summer vacation.

LEISURE TIME

Poland offers no shortage of sights to see, pubs to visit, museum, theatres and parks to enjoy. Films are usually in English with Polish subtitles. Travelling is fairly cheap and easy. The transport system in Warsaw and some other cities looks complicated at first glance but is in fact straightforward. People in shops and so on can seem rude and abrupt, though this should not be taken personally.

Heidi Rothwell-Walker is convinced that she made the right decision when she chose to work for a school in Poland rather than at one of the other schools around the world that offered her a job:

> *Poland can seem a bit of a backwater, but it's a tremendous experience. It'll*

*change your thinking completely and you'll either love it (like 98% of people)
or hate it, but you must try it. I have just renewed my contract for another year
because I have been very impressed by them and am very happy here.*

LIST OF SCHOOLS

ABILITY TRAINING CENTRE
Ul. Mazwiecka 12, 00-048 Warsaw. Tel: (22) 827 69 41. Fax: (22) 827 6941. E-mail: ability@pol.pl.
Number of teachers: 8.
Preference of nationality: none.
Qualifications: TEFL Cert. or equivalent. Experience preferred but not essential.
Conditions of employment: from October to June. 25 45-minute lessons a week.
Salary: depends on experience. Newly qualified teachers are paid about £110; those with 1 year experience about £120 (net) per week.
Facilities/Support: the school has a number of flats which it rents to teachers and acts as their landlord, i.e. deals with bills and any problems. As much assistance as possible is given with work permits which are at the school's expense.
Recruitment: by interview (in person if possible). Sometimes teachers are required to give a demonstration lesson and are offered a job on the basis of this.
Contact: Owen Doherty, Assistant Director of Studies.

AGENCJA LEKTOR SCHOOL OF ENGLISH
ul. Sloneczna 39, 11-700 Mragowo. Tel/fax: (89) 741 4141. E-mail: lektor@mck.pl. Website: www.lektor.w.pl.
Number of teachers: 2-3.
Preference of nationality: British.
Qualifications: BA (preferably English) plus CELTA or equivalent. English native speakers with good communications skills and ability to work independently and unsupervised.
Conditions of employment: 9-10 month contracts. Teaching General English from beginner to upper intermediate and Cambridge Exam courses in small groups of up to 15 per class. 25 contact hours per week; normal timetable runs from Monday to Friday, 3pm to 8pm.
Salary: sufficient for a comfortable living in Poland, i.e. 1800 zloties per month (gross) and up to 30% in bonuses.
Facilities/Support: free single accommodation with all household facilities. Travel expenses and work visa refunded at completion of contract. Free Polish lessons.
Recruitment: internet and newspaper adverts. Interviews not essential.
Contact: Lucja Mlynarczyk.

ALBION LANGUAGE SERVICES
ul Noakowskiego 26/26, 00-668 Warsaw. Tel/fax: (22) 628 8992. Tel: (22) 696 15 76 77; E-mail: languages@albion.com.pl.
Number of teachers: 30.
Preference of nationality: none.
Qualifications: interesting teaching methods, friendly attitude required.
Conditions of employment: open-ended.
Salary: approx. US$10 per 45 minutes.
Facilities/Support: assistance with accommodation and visas.
Recruitment: direct. Local interview essential.
Contact: Dorota Krajewska, Owner.

AMERICAN ENGLISH SCHOOL
3/5 Foksal, Warsaw 00-366. Tel: (22) 827 26 54. Fax: (22) 827 26 54. E-mail: ames@polbox.com.pl. Website: www.americanenglishschool.com.pl.
Number of teachers: 15.

Preference of nationality: none.
Qualifications: degree.
Conditions of employment: October to June. 20-30 hours per week.
Salary: 35-45 zloties per 45 minute lesson.
Facilities/Support: help with finding accommodation.
Recruitment: newspaper adverts.
Contact: John McKenzie.

ANGLOSCHOOL
ul. Ks. J. Popieluszki 7, 01-786 Warsaw. Tel/fax: (22) 664 7700. E-mail: angloschool@angloschool.com.pl. Website: www.angloschool.com.pl.
Number of teachers: 15.
Preference of nationality: none.
Qualifications: CELTA or equivalent and a degree. Teaching experience preferred.
Conditions of employment: yearly contract. Teaching hours from 3pm-8.30pm Monday to Friday. Some morning classes 8.30am 10am and in-company classes. 25-30 lessons (45 mins) weekly.
Salary: 2,200 zloties net per month. School pays taxes and social security (45%) weekly.
Facilities/Support: accommodation is provided by the school in the form of two or three roomed shared flats or single rooms in a house. Accommodation includes all necessary facilities i.e. furniture, a phone, cable TV, a washing machine, kitchen with necessary equipment.
Recruitment: cooperates with schools running CELTA, TEFL courses which provide a job placement service. Advertising in newspapers, TEFL webpages and recruitment agencies. Direct application with CV welcomed.
Contact: Agnieszka Heintze.

BELL – see ELS-Bell, Gama-Bell, Program Bell and UEC Bell.

BERLITZ POLAND
Waly Piastowskie 24, 80-855 Gdansk. Tel: (58) 305 1613. Fax: (58) 305 1614.
Number of teachers: 15.
Preference of nationality: UK, USA or Canada.
Qualifications: degree plus good personality.
Conditions of employment: freelance agreement for a minimum one year. Hours are flexible, full-time or part-time.
Salary: 37-49 zloties per lesson unit There are deductions for tax and social security.
Facilities/Support: arranges accommodation.
Recruitment: advertisements in the local and national press, e-mail, personal recommendation. In-person interview preferred.
Contact: Malgorzata Bankewicz.

BPP INTERNATIONAL POLAND
ul. Widok 8, 00-023 Warsaw. Tel: (22) 6906720. Fax: (22) 6906729. E-mail: warsaw@bpp.com.
Formerly Linguarama Poland.
Number of teachers: 30.
Preference of nationality: EU citizens.
Qualifications: hold or be working towards DELTA or Dip TEB.
Conditions of employment: 9 month contracts. Split shifts, before and after business hours.
Salary: commensurate with qualifications and experience.
Facilities/Support: business training sponsorship. The School specialises in Business English intensive courses.
Recruitment: via Linguarama Group Personnel in England (01420 80899).
Contact: Danny Coughlan.

BRYTANIA SCHOOL OF ENGLISH
Ul. Ogrodowa 12, 39-200 Debica. Tel/fax: (14) 670 3811. E-mail: brytania_school@onet.pl. Website: www.brytania.com.pl.
Number of teachers: 5-7.
Preference of nationality: British, American, Canadian.
Qualifications: BA or MA degree in humanities plus recognised TEFL Certificate.
Conditions of employment: academic year. 20-24 hours per weeek, mainly in the afternoons.
Salary: about £4 per hour.
Facilities/Support: accommodation provided; the school finds apartments for teachers.
Recruitment: advertises in *The Guardian, EL Gazette* and Polish newspapers.
Contact: Bozena Kula.

CAMBRIDGE SCHOOL OF ENGLISH
ul. Konwiktorska 7, 00-216 Warsaw. Tel: (22) 635 24 66. Fax (22) 635 66 14. E-mail: cambridge@cambridge.com.pl. Website: www.cambridge.com.pl.
Number of teachers: 35 for 1,800 students, all levels and ages.
Preference of nationality: native speakers.
Qualifications: CELTA/TESOL and university degree. Experience in lieu considered.
Conditions of employment: 9 month contracts (September to June). Working hours are Monday to Thursday (3pm-8pm), with reduced workload on Fridays. Generally 2 or 3 morning starts during the week. No weekend teaching. 25 hours contact time per week. Teachers should be prepared to teach children (aged 7-10) and adults (14+), carry out exam preparation courses (FCE, CAE, CPE) and give lessons to individuals and companies.
Salary: about £100 per week (net).
Facilities/Support: weekly training seminars, one senior staff member per five teachers for advice and help. Established course syllabus to use if required. Guaranteed accommodation (about one third of salary), return travel from the UK at beginning and end of contract. Coach trip back to England for Christmas. Work permit paid for.
Recruitment: via adverts in *Guardian* or direct through the school.
Contact: Simon Clare, School Manager.

CELT – CENTRE OF ENGLISH LANGUAGE TRAINING
Konarskiego 2, 30-049 Kraków. Tel: (12) 415 1732.
Number of teachers: varies.
Preference of nationality: none.
Qualifications: any teacher training course.
Conditions of employment: one-year contracts. Afternoon and evening work.
Salary: average hourly rate.
Facilities/Support: no assistance with accommodation or work visas.
Recruitment: interviews essential.

CONRAD S.C.
Osrodek Nauczania Jezyków Obcych s.c., ul Orlowicza 8/104, 10-684 Olsztyn. Tel/fax: (89) 542 72 75. E-mail: school@conrad.olsztyn.pl. Website: www.conrad.olsztyn.pl.
Number of teachers: 2-3.
Preference of nationality: British, American.
Qualifications: BA/MA in Humanities (English); CELTA/TEFLA.
Conditions of employment: 18 hours a week, with a fixed schedule, co-teaching youngsters and adults from beginner to advanced with Polish teachers. 10-12 month contract September to June (including 2 week induction in September). Renewal opportunities.
Salary: 1,800 zloties per month (net).

Facilities/Support: accommodation arranged and paid for. Assistance given with obtaining visa and work permit. Olsztyn has a population of about 180,000 and is known as The Land of 100 Lakes (the northeast). It is industrial and academic with a growing British colony of TEFL teachers. The school is located in a state-owned building in which 1,500 young people learn at three different schools.
Recruitment: adverts in *Guardian* and private contacts. Interviews essential in the UK or Poland, can also be arranged by telephone at Conrad's expense.
Contact: Krzysztof Kowalscy.

EF ENGLISH FIRST
ul Smolna 8, 00-375 Warsaw. Tel: (22) 826 8206. Fax: (22) 826 0871. E-mail: steve-allen@ef.com. Website: www.ef.com.
Number of teachers: approx 12 in Warsaw and others in EF centres elsewhere in Poland: Lodz, Bydgoszcz, Wroclaw, Katowice, Poznan, Zielona Gora).
Preference of nationality: none but must be native speaker.
Qualifications: minimum CELTA/TESOL Cert. or equivalent.
Conditions of employment: 9-12 month renewable contract. Teaching 30-36 40-minute work periods per week.
Salary: 3,850-4,750 zloties (net) per month.
Facilities/Support: visa arranged. Help with accommodation: temporary accommodation provided in a hotel on arrival then agent to assist with flat finding.
Recruitment: directly through Warsaw school or through EF offices worldwide including North America, UK or Australia.
Contact: Stephen Allen, Academic Co-ordinator.

ELS-BELL SCHOOL OF ENGLISH
ul. Polanki 110, 80-308 Gdansk. Tel: (58) 554 8382. Fax: 58 554 83 88. E-mail: elsbell@poczta.onet.pl.
In association with Bell Educational Trust of Cambridge.
Number of teachers: 20 for several centres in Gdansk, Gdynia, Bydgoszcz and Szczecin.
Preference of nationality: British and American.
Qualifications: CELTA or equivalent plus university degree. Experience preferred.
Conditions of employment: September to June. Up to 25 lessons a week (45 minutes each). Annual workload is 680 hours, teaching mainly afternoons and evenings. Also run summer camps for young learners (aged 9-18).
Salary: 1,950 zloties net, plus end-of-contract bonus of one month's salary.
Facilities/Support: assistance with accommodation. Cost of obtaining work permits is reimbursed by school. In-house teacher development programme. Centre also runs CELTA and DELTA courses.
Recruitment: ads in *Guardian* and on internet. Interviews necessary, occasionally by phone. Interviews sometimes take place in London.
Contact: Ludka Kotarska, Head of Schools.

EMPIK
Szkola Jezyków Obcych, ul. Dlugi Targ 28/29, 80-830 Gdansk. Tel: (58) 301 4719. Fax: (58) 301 4034. E-mail: sjo.gdansk@empik.com.
Number of teachers: 3 in this branch though Empik is a chain of 30 schools throughout Poland.
Preference of nationality: British preferred, North American considered.
Qualifications: 5 years TEFL experience or appropriate qualifications (e.g. DELTA).
Conditions of employment: one year renewable contract. 24 h.p.w. mostly between 4pm and 9pm. Possibility of morning and weekend work.
Salary: equivalent of £600 per month. Deductions about 20%.
Facilities/Support: assistance with work permits and accommodation.
Recruitment: mostly word of mouth.
Contact: Tadeusz Wolanski, Consultant Methodologist.

ENGLISH HOUSE
Kryniczna 12/14 apt.5, 03-934 Warsaw. Tel: (22) 616 2276/832 2792; Fax: (22) 616 2284. E-mail: english.house.usa.net. Website: www.english_house.com.pl.
Number of teachers: 3-6.
Preference of nationality: none, but should be native speaker.
Qualifications: degree in teaching or TEFL Cert. and teaching experience.
Conditions of employment: September to June. School hours are 8am-12am (in company courses) and 3-9pm (other courses).
Salary: 40-50 zloties per 45-minute lesson (£6-£7.50).
Facilities/Support: the school owns a two-bedroomed apartment for the use of teachers. Otherwise help with finding accommodation in Warsaw will be given.
Recruitment: internet, newspaper, posters. References essential. Interview and demonstration lesson. For overseas applicants telephone/internet interview.
Contact: Alexsandra Gelner, Director of Studies.

ENGLISH LANGUAGE CENTRE
University of Silesia, Plac Sejmu Slaskiego 1, 40-032 Katowice. Tel: (32) 256-1296. Fax: (32) 255-2245. E-mail: elc@homer.fil.us.edu.pl.
Number of teachers: 13.
Preference of nationality: British, Irish.
Qualifications: CELTA plus experience.
Conditions of employment: 1 year renewable contracts (September till the end of June). 18 h.p.w (full-time job).
Salary: approximately 1,200 zloties per month (possibility of overtime).
Facilities/Support: free accommodation in teachers' hostel. Access to British Council training seminars. Paid holidays.
Recruitment: CVs and applications welcome by post. Interviews and a trial lesson in Poland.
Contact: Witold Falkowski, General Manager.

ENGLISH SCHOOL OF COMMUNICATION SKILLS (ESCS)
ul. Bernardynska 15, 33-100 Tarnów. Tel/fax: (14) 621 37 69. E-mail: personnel@escs.pl.
Number of teachers: 65 for 4 schools in southern Poland (Kraków, Tarnów, Nowy Targ and Myslenice). Also hold summer courses and summer camps at Polish seaside.
Preference of nationality: English as mother tongue.
Qualifications: degree level of education plus EFL methodology certificate or ESCS's own training course offered in September.
Conditions of employment: one-year contracts. 20 h.p.w. 600 teaching hours per school year (October-June) plus 36 project hours. Teaching all ages (6-60). Pre-selected course books, standardised tests and many extracurricular activities for students (baseball, drama club, video club, etc.)
Salary: hourly rate; base salary 2,000 zloties per month; varies according to experience and qualifications.
Facilities/Support: seminars and workshops held. Teacher resource centre includes videos, cassettes and supplementary material. Photocopying and computers on-site.
Recruitment: via universities. Interviews held whenever possible. Applications should be sent to the Personnel Department.
Contact: Monika Tajchner, ESCS Personnel Dept.

ENGLISH UNLIMITED
Podmlynska 10, 80-855 Gdansk. Tel/fax: (58) 301 3373. E-mail: kamila@eu.com.pl. Website: www.eu.com.pl.
Number of teachers: 10-15 for seven centres around the Tri-City (Gdansk, Gdynia and Sopot) and in Poznan, Bydgoszcz and Szczecin.
Preference of nationality: none; must be native speakers.
Qualifications: Cambridge Cert. or Dip. plus experience of overseas teaching.

Conditions of employment: 9 month contracts from September. Hours of teaching normally 4.30-8pm. Courses offered in ESP (e.g. business English).
Salary: £300-£350 per month (net).
Facilities/Support: accommodation arranged. Training provided.
Recruitment: adverts in the *Guardian*. Interviews in Poland or UK essential.
Contact: Kamila Anflink, Director of Studies.

EUROPA 2000
Szola Jezyków Obcych, ul. Dabrowskiego 24, 40-032 Katowice. Tel: (32) 25510 53. Also: Szkola Jezyków Obcych, ul de Gaulle'a 8, 43-100 Tychy. Tel: (32) 73483. E-mail: e2000@box43.gnet.pl.
Number of teachers: 2-4.
Preference of nationality: British, American.
Qualifications: MA, BA, experience in English teaching and leading courses.
Conditions of employment: 1-3 years. Usual hours 3pm-8pm.
Salary: £7-£10 per hour less 21% income tax.
Facilities/Support: assistance with finding accommodation and obtaining permits. Insurance provided.
Recruitment: word-of-mouth. Interviews not essential.
Contact: Edyta Stasiak-Ulfik, Language Centre Manager.

GAMA-BELL SCHOOL OF ENGLISH
ul. Sw. Krzyza 16, 31-023 Kraków. Tel: (12) 421 97 55/421 97 22. Fax: (12) 421 73 79. E-mail: gamabell@bci.krakow.pl.
Number of teachers: 10.
Preference of nationality: British.
Qualifications: BA plus CELTA.
Conditions of employment: 9-month contracts. 20 h.p.w. Students from age 10.
Salary: from £5 per hour.
Facilities/Support: assistance with finding accommodation given only to teachers on long-term contracts. Monthly teacher development seminars and workshops (organised by school and by IATEFL Poland).
Recruitment: interviews essential.
Contact: Elzbieta Jarosz, Director of Studies.

GREENWICH SCHOOL OF ENGLISH
ul. Gdanska 2/3, 01-633 Warsaw. Tel: (22) 833 2431. Fax: (22) 833 36 02. E-mail: school@greenwich.edu.pl. Website: www.greenwich.edu.pl.
Number of teachers: 30.
Preference of nationality: British or any native English speaker.
Qualifications: accredited EFL teaching certificate and preferably a BA.
Conditions of employment: one school year contract e.g. 2 October 2000 to 30 June 2001. Guaranteed minimum 20 hours per week plus up to 5 hours overtime. Sick and holiday pay at 70%.
Salary: £100-£130 basic (guaranteed) depending on experience, qualifications and ability. Plus end of contract bonus.
Facilities/Support: accommodation found by school, normally in shared flats. Rent is approximately $250. Assistance with work permits (before teachers arrive in Poland). Regular programme of lectures, seminars and observations.
Recruitment: adverts in the *Guardian*. Interviews essential and held in various locations in the UK in July.
Contact: Andy Edwins, Director of Studies.

INTERNATIONAL HOUSE – BIELSKO BIALA
Ul. Krasinskiego 24, 43-300 Bielsko Biala. Tel: (33) 11 02 29.
Number of teachers: 25.
Preference of nationality: none.
Qualifications, conditions of employment, etc.: same as for International House

Katowice (below).

INTERNATIONAL HOUSE – BYDGOSZCZ
Ul. Dworcowa 81, 85-009 Bydgoszcz. Tel/fax: (52) 322 35 15. E-mail: bydgoszcz@inthouse.pl. Website: www.inhouse.pl/bydgoszcz.
Number of teachers: 17.
Preference of nationality: English-speaking countries.
Qualifications: CELTA or equivalent.
Conditions of employment: September to end of June. 20 clock hours p.w.
Salary: 1,485 zloties per month.
Facilities/Support: shared flat provided free; all bills paid by school apart from phone bill. Teachers must obtain visa in their own country but school covers cost.
Recruitment: via Human Resources Department, IH London or phone interview for applicants in the US.
Contact: Julian L'Enfant, Director of Studies (lenfant.bydgoszcz@inthouse.pl) or Mr. Marek Tukaszewski, Director.

INTERNATIONAL HOUSE – KATOWICE
Ul. Sokolska 78/80, 40-128 Katowice. Tel/fax: (32) 59 99 97. E-mail: katowice.dos@ih.com.pl. Website: www.ih.com.pl.
Number of teachers: 40+.
Preference of nationality: none.
Qualifications: minimum CELTA or equivalent.
Conditions of employment: 9 month contracts. 20 contact hours per week, plus one and a half hours standby and one and a half hours administration input. Students are all ages and there are several in-company contracts.
Facilities/Support: accommodation provided rent free and normally shared. Possible to opt out. Assisted DELTA and Young Learners Certificate courses available.
Recruitment: via IH Central Department (London) or direct to the school.
Contact: Mike Cattlin, Director of Studies.

INTERNATIONAL HOUSE – KRAKOW
ul. Pilsudskiego 6, lp, 31-109 Kraków. Tel: (12) 421 9440/422 6482. Fax: (12) 430 1000. E-mail: admin@ih.pl. Website: www.ih.pl.
Number of teachers: 30.
Preference of nationality: none.
Conditions of employment: one year contracts. 24 contact hours per week. Students from nine years up. Classes may include in-company Business English for suitably qualified/experienced teachers.
Salary: basic 1,400 zloties per month.
Facilities/Support: assistance given with accommodation. Fortnightly training workshops plus regular developmental observations. In-house intensive courses for teaching young learners and Business English. Support for those wishing to take the DELTA course run annually.
Recruitment: locally or via IH Central Department (London) and other training centres.
Contact: Peter Moran, Director of Studies.

INTERNATIONAL HOUSE – OPOLE
Ul. Kosciuszki 17, 45-062 Opole. Tel/fax: (77) 4 54 66 55. E-mail: sekret@pol.pl.
Number of teachers: 20.
Preference of nationality: none.
Qualifications: B pass CELTA or C pass plus a year's experience.
Conditions of employment: Approximately 6 weeks holiday and bank holidays per year (3 days per month worked).
Salary: on a sliding scale dependent on qualifications and experience. B pass/C pass

plus one year, 1,500 zloties p.m. plus shared flat plus travel allowance of £40 for every month worked.
Facilities/Support: accommodation and travel allowance provided.
Contact: Rod Fricker, Director of Studies.

INTERNATIONAL HOUSE – WROCLAW
Ul. Leszczynskiego 3, 50-078 Wroclaw. Tel/fax: +48 (0)71 372 3698. E-mail: ttcentre@id.pl. Website: www.ih.com.pl.
Number of teachers: 20.
Preference of nationality: none.
Qualifications: minimum CELTA or Trinity Cert, grade B (or Pass plus 1 year's experience).
Conditions of employment: 20 contact hours per week.
Salary: 1,200-1,750 zloties per month net (in first year).
Facilities/Support: shared accommodation provided free. Work permit paid. School runs CELTA courses (see entry in Training Directory) with attractive terms for those who are later employed by IH in Wroclaw, Katowice, Opole or Bielsko Biala. In-house teacher support includes induction, regular observation and feedback, weekly seminars. Subsidies sometimes available for courses in YL, DELTA and Teaching English for Business.
Recruitment: via IH Human Resources in London or direct at e-mail address above.
Contact: Elisa Jaroch.

INTERNATIONAL LANGUAGE SCHOOL
ul, Krakowska 51, Opole. Tel: (44) 774 531 597. E-mail: ils@ils.pl. Website: www.ils.pl.
Number of teachers: about 9.
Preference of nationality: British.
Qualifications: TEFL/TESOL Cert. Newly qualified teachers are considered.
Conditions of employment: nine months. 24 contact hours per week.
Salary: 1,500 zloties per month.
Facilities/Support: shared accommodation provided and all bills except telephone paid. School organises and pays for all visas and permits. Teachers are expected to visit the Polish embassy in their own country.
Recruitment: agency/recommendation.
Contact: Martin Shepherd, Director of Studies.

JDJ COLLEGE
ul. Bninska 26, Poznan. Tel: (61) 827 71 24. Fax: (61) 827 71 99. E-mail: jdj@ikp.atm.com.pl. Alternative address: ul. Gronowa 22, 61-655 Poznan.
Number of teachers: 35-45 for various schools.
Preference of nationality: British, American, Australian, New Zealand; must be native speaker.
Qualifications: minimum one year's experience in teaching; CELTA or equivalent.
Conditions of employment: contract is for an academic year. Usual 20-28 hours teaching per week and one standby slot and attendance at workshops and meetings. Students are all ages from 6 to 65 and there are several in-company contracts. 17 days paid holiday (Christmas and Easter).
Salary: 28-45 zloties per teaching hour (salary base is 2,000-3,500 zloties a month (£300-£530).
Facilities/Support: JDJ has flats for teachers in some towns. If there is no school flat, the School Manager can find a flat or room if requested by the teacher. The flat is paid for by the teacher.
Recruitment: CVs to JDJ Service and interviews are organised in London or by telephone.
Contact: Karolina Domagalska, College Co-ordinator in JDJ Headquarters in Poznan.

LANG LTC
Al Niepodleglosci 217/8, 02-087 Warsaw. Tel: (22) 825 3940. Fax: (22) 825 2273.
E-mail: lang@lang.com.pl. Website: www.lang.com.pl.
Number of teachers: 15.
Preference of nationality: none, but should be native speaker.
Qualifications: degree and TEFL Cert.
Conditions of employment: 10 months/12 months. 20 teaching hours per week.
Salary: approx. US$1000 a month.
Facilities/Support: help with finding accommodation.
Recruitment: internet, advertisements.
Contact: Jayne Freeman, Director of Studies.

LINGUARAMA
Correspondence address: ul. Sniadeckich 17, Warsaw. E-mail: aniamalmska@ linguarama.com. Website: www.linguarama.com.
Number of teachers: 3.
Preference of nationality: none, but must be native speaker.
Qualifications: minimum Cert. TEFL, preferably with experience.
Conditions of employment: 9 months. School hours are 7.30am to 4pm.
Salary: dependent on contract and experience.
Facilities/Support: 2 weeks in a hotel if coming from the UK.
Recruitment: centrally through Linguarama UK or locally.
Contact: W Nowlan, Director of Studies.

LEKTOR INTERNATIONAL HOUSE
ul. SW Marcin 66/72, Poznan 61-807. Tel/fax: (61) 8516171. E-mail: grantbutler.dos.IHPoznan@poczta.fm
Number of teachers: 25.
Preference of nationality: none.
Qualifications: minimum CELTA or recognised equivalent.
Conditions of employment: 1 year. 18 contact hours per week.
Salary: 1600 zloties for a teacher with a CELTA Cert. and no experience.
Facilities/Support: free one bedroom flat with all bills paid (except telephone). Visa to be obtained in teacher's home country (school pays for visa).
Recruitment: recruits from own CELTA courses, IH in London and from teachers locally.
Contact: Grant Butler.

LEKTOR SZKOLA JEZYKOW OBCYCH
ul. Olawska 25, 50-123 Wroclaw. Tel/fax: (71) 343 2599/372 52 92. E-mail: biuro@lektor.com.pl.
Number of teachers: 30.
Preference of nationality: British, American.
Qualifications: Certificate in TEFL required.
Conditions of employment: one-year contracts. 20-25 lessons/week. Students are young adults.
Salary: from 50 zloties/£7.50 per hour.
Facilities/Support: assistance with finding accommodation and obtaining work permit.
Recruitment: personal interviews essential.
Contact: Sylwia Sikora.

LINGUA NOVA
ul. Basniowa 3, pok. 412, 00-349 Warsaw. Tel: (22) 668 7674. Fax: (22) 668 8559.
E-mail: linguanova@linguanova.com.pl. Website: www.linguanova.com.pl.
Number of teachers: 12.
Preference of nationality: native speaker.
Qualifications: TEFL/CELTA.

Conditions of employment: as agreed. School hours are from 7am-10am and 3pm-9pm.
Salary: hourly. Rate as agreed. Deductions of 16%.
Facilities/Support: could assist with accommodation if requested.
Recruitment: advertisements in local newspapers.
Contact: Grazyna Szyve, Director.

LINGUA STUDIUM JEZYKOW OBCYCH
Ul. Jasnogórska 6, 42-200 Czestochowa. Tel/fax. (34) 361 1763.
Number of teachers: 4.
Preference of nationality: British.
Qualifications: degree in modern languages/literature plus CELTA or Trinity Cert (TESOL).
Conditions of employment: initial contract for academic year. 24 lessons p.w. (45 minutes) mainly afternoons and evenings.
Salary: 1,100 zloties per month net.
Facilities/Support: furnished accommodation, rent and utility bills paid by the school. All the necessary permits and National Insurance provided. In-service teacher training. Access to the latest ELT publications.
Recruitment: adverts in the *Guardian*. Detailed CV and references may be sufficient when interview cannot be arranged.
Contact: Beata Marszalek, Director of Studies.

MACPHERSON SZKOLA JEZYKA ANGIELSKIEGO
ul. Dworcowa 12, 66-400 Gorzow Wlkp. Tel: (95) 720 3578. Fax: (95) 720 5389. E-mail: english@page.pl.
Number of teachers: 6.
Preference of nationality: UK.
Qualifications: TEFL/TESOL Cert. Experience is welcomed but not a must.
Conditions of employment: 9 months.
Salary: 27 zloties net per hour.
Facilities/Support: arranges for an English-speaking agent to arrange accommodation with landlords. Sometimes the school makes a direct deal with landlords. Cost of work visa is reimbursed on arrival at school.
Recruitment: via internet.
Contact: Renata Szumilas.

MTA LANGUAGE CENTRE
Pl. Teatralny 6, Wroclaw. Tel: (71) 372 13 34. Fax: (71) 343 44 54.
Number of teachers: 10.
Preference of nationality: none.
Qualifications: Cambridge Certificate/Diploma, TOEFL and other certificates welcome.
Conditions of employment: 2 month contracts. 16-20 h.p.w.
Salary: £600 per month less 20% taxes.
Facilities/Support: assistance with finding accommodation and obtaining work permits given.
Recruitment: interviews not always essential.

NKJO – KRAKOW
ul. Kanonicza 14, 31-002 Kraków. Tel: (12) 422 7955. Fax: (12) 423 2318. E-mail: NKJO@merlin.in.uj.edu.pl.
Number of teachers: 3.
Preference of nationality: British, American, Canadian.
Qualifications: minimum MA in education, applied linguistics or English literature, plus diploma in TEFL and at least one year's experience of teaching in secondary school or college.
Conditions of employment: 12 month contracts from October 1st. 26 contact h.p.w.

Variable hours between 9am and 8pm.

Salary: about £3,000 per year.

Facilities/Support: only 2 university flats available for which the rent would be about £1,000 per year to be shared between two. Computer facilities, etc. available.

Recruitment: British Council and direct application. Local interviews encouraged.

NKJO – LESZNO
pl. Kosciuski 5, 64-100 Leszno. Tel: (65) 520 3607. Fax (65) 5295798. E-mail: koleszno@ids.pl. Website: www.ko.Leszno.ids.pl.

Number of teachers: 3.

Preference of nationality: British, American, Canadian.

Qualifications: MA or BA.

Conditions of employment: minimum stay one year. 12-18 h.p.w.

Salary: 1,600 zloties per month.

Facilities/Support: free accommodation in dormitory or shared flat. Some training through the University of Poznan to which this NKJO is affiliated.

Recruitment: via voluntary organisations and direct application. Interviews not essential.

Contact: Anna Geremek.

NKJO – WROCLAW
ul. Skarbowców 8A, 53-025 Wroclaw. Tel: (71) 339 8551. Fax: (71) 339 85 51. E-mail: biuro@home.nkjo-wroc.edu.pl.

Number of teachers: 5 out of a staff of 30 in the English Department.

Preference of nationality: British, American or other.

Qualifications: BA, MA or PhD in TEFL, British and American literature, history or languages. Sufficient experience of teaching English at higher level, e.g. institutes of higher education.

Conditions of employment: one-year contracts. Full-time contract is 12 h.p.w. (mornings only).

Salary: 800 zloties per month (net).

Facilities/Support: assistance with finding accommodation and work permit given. Possibility of attending professional development conferences, etc.

Recruitment: local interviews essential.

Contact: Anna Karp, Director.

OXFORD STUDY CENTRE
ul. 25 Czerwca 60, 26-600 Radom. Tel/fax: (48) 360 2166. E-mail: oxford@ats.net.pl. www.oxfordstudycentre.com.pl.

Number of teachers: 14.

Preference of nationality: the majority tend to be British but teachers from the USA, Canada and New Zealand have also been taken on.

Qualifications: Cambridge/Trinity Certificate or equivalent plus a degree.

Conditions of employment: contract from September to June; 2 year contracts and summer jobs also possible. Teaching 22 lessons per week. General English, Business English and exam classes. All ages.

Salary: from 1,450 zloties per month (net). Paid overtime 18 zloties per hour.

Facilities/Support: visa and work permit arranged, return travel between the UK and Poland, private medical insurance. Fully furnished accommodation a short distance from the school. Teacher development programme. Subsidies for further qualifications like DELTA available for teachers who commit themselves to stay on.

Recruitment: via e-mail as above. Interviews held every June and July in Oxford.

Contact: Inga Gorzkowska, Recruitment Co-ordinator.

POLANGLO
Szkola Jezyków Obcych, ul. Nowowiejska 1/3, 00-643 Warsaw. Tel: (22) 825 7733. Fax: (22) 825 3747. E-mail: polanglo@polbox.pl. Website: www.polanglo. polbox.pl.

Number of teachers: 5.
Preference of nationality: British.
Qualifications: BA plus CELTA or DELTA.
Conditions of employment: minimum 8-12 h.p.w for one semester. General and business English for adults.
Salary: 45-55 zloties per 45 minute lesson.
Facilities/Support: candidates must apply in advance if assistance with work permits is needed. No help with accommodation
Recruitment: local adverts. Local interviews essential.
Contact: Jolanta Dobrowolska, Director, Justyna Martin, Director of Studies.

PREMIERE SCHOOL OF ENGLISH
Ul. Trubadurow 4, 80-205 Gdansk. Tel/fax: (58) 3444003. E-mail: mark@premiere.zsl.gda.pl. Website: www.premiere.zsl.gda.pl.
Number of teachers: 3.
Preference of nationality: British/Irish.
Qualifications: CELTA or BEd.(Primary) and/or 2 years' TEFL teaching experience.
Conditions of employment: one or two years. 15-20 clock hours per week.
Salary: 2,500-3,000 zloties per 4 weeks (£400-£500). No deductions.
Facilities/Support: help with finding accommodation. Temporary accommodation always secured at the beginning. Teachers are given a work visa (no cost to them).
Recruitment: language schools in the UK and Poland.
Contact: Mark Czekalski, Director of Studies.

PROGRAM-BELL
ul. Fredry 7, pok. 22-26, 61-701 Poznan. Tel: (61) 853 6972. Fax: (61) 853 0612. E-mail: office@programme-bell.edu.pl.
Number of teachers: 4-5.
Preference of nationality: British, American.
Qualifications: Cambridge Cert. or Dip. with experience of teaching young children.
Conditions of employment: 9 month contracts. 16 h.p.w. Pupils of all ages including classes for 7-10 year olds. Summer and winter language camps also organised.
Facilities/Support: assistance given with accommodation. Good choice of teaching materials.
Recruitment: newspaper adverts. Interviews held in London in March.
Contact: Anna Gebka-Suska, Head of School.

STUDIUM JEZYKOW OBCYCH PROJECT
ul Szholezerow 5B/10, 66-400 Gorzow Wlkp. Tel: (95) 722 9880. Fax: (95) 722 9009. E-mail: monach@polbox.com.
Number of teachers: 4.
Preference of nationality: British
Qualifications: Bachelor or MA degree and TEFL qualification.
Conditions of employment: 10 months. Afternoon and evening classes. About 20-22 lessons per week.
Salary: 20-24 zloties per hour net.
Facilities/Support: accommodation is provided free – a shared, furnished apartment equipped with satellite TV and a telephone. All paperwork for work permits is carried out and paid for by the school.
Recruitment: e-mail applications and advertising in *EL Gazette*.
Contact: Krystyne Monach, Director.

TARGET PROFESSIONAL ENGLISH CONSULTANTS
Ulica Polna 50, 7th floor, 00-644 Warsaw. Tel: (22) 870 35 57. Fax: (22) 870 35 27. E-mail: info@target.it.pol. Website: www.target.it.pl.

Number of teachers: 55 of whom 5 are full-time teacher support staff (i.e. experienced teachers) who do not regularly teach but instead help the less experienced teachers.
Preference of nationality: English as native language although the work permit situation is easiest for UK and Ireland and those with ancestry visa status.
Qualifications: CELTA or equivalent. As many clients are companies, mature teachers are especially welcome. Business experience is helpful but not essential.
Conditions of employment: 9-12 months. 25-30 h.p.w.
Salary: £450-£650 per month (gross). Salary does not depend on hours taught.
Facilities/Support: the school rents accommodation and sublets to teachers at a subsidised price. Money for first month's rent can be loaned and repaid in instalments. Work permits arranged and paid for by the school including the cost of picking them up in the UK. Work permits are valid a year. Extensive support for newly qualified teachers.
Recruitment: through recommendation locally or Saxoncourt & English Worldwide in London. Interviews essential, but in some cases conducted by telephone if backed by suitable references. Saxoncourt arranged UK interviews. No USA contact (yet).
Contact: Michael Gardom, General Manager (mike@target.it.pl)

TELA SCHOOL OF ENGLISH
ul. Krakowskie Przedmiescie 6 IIIp, 00-325 Warsaw. Tel: (22) 828 12 11. Fax: (22) 828 12 11.
Number of teachers: approx 15.
Preference of nationality: none.
Qualifications: TEFL/TESOL/TESL or equivalent depending on country of origin.
Conditions of employment: 2 semesters from 1st October to the end of June. Extension possible. Approx. 24-30/34 hours per week.
Salary: negotiable. If accommodation is provided, there is a salary deduction to cover this.
Facilities/Support: accommodation can be provided in shared flats (one bedroom per teacher), or teachers can be assisted to find their own accommodation in the central part of Warsaw. Assistance given with finding work permits.
Recruitment: through agencies and direct application.
Contact: Veronica Omeni, Director of Studies.

UEC-BELL
Plac Kzech Krzyzy 4/6, 00-499 Warsaw. Tel: (22) 625 4792. Fax: (22) 628 4167. E-mail: efl.jobs@uec-bell.pl. Website: www.uec-bell.pl.
Number of teachers: approx. 20.
Preference of nationality: none, but should be native speaker.
Qualifications: TEFL Cert. minimum. Experience preferred but not essential.
Conditions of employment: 9 months. Extendable.
Salary: 24 units of 45 minutes per week.
Facilities/Support: three days of free accommodation on arrival and help with arrangements for more permanent accommodation (rent payable by the teacher).
Recruitment: *The Guardian*, internet and local press. Telephone interviews.
Contact: Angus Baird, Director of Studies.

UNIVERSITY OF SZCZECIN
Department of English, Al. Piastow 40B, 71-065 Szczecin. Tel/fax: (91) 433 3161. Website: www.univ.szczecin.pl.
Number of teachers: 1.
Preference of nationality: none.
Qualifications: PhD/MA in humanities (cultural studies, literature, history, linguistics) and teaching experience, preferably at tertiary level.
Conditions of employment: one academic year with renewal possibility.

Salary: starting at 1,200 zloties per month. No tax deduction for the first two years of employment.
Facilities/Support: Accommodation in hall of residence at 150 zloties per month.
Recruitment: direct application.
Contact: Julitta Rydlewska, Head, Dept. of English.

WARSAW STUDY CENTRE
Ul. Rasynska 22, 02-026 Warsaw. Tel: (22) 822 1412. Fax: (22) 822 1412. Website: www.wsc.edu.pl.
Number of teachers: 15.
Preference of nationality: none.
Qualifications: degree plus TEFL Cert.
Conditions of employment: 10 months contract. 24 teaching hours per week.
Salary: approx US$1,100 per month.
Facilities/Support: temporary hostel accommodation provided initially and then assistance in negotiating with landlords for accommodation.
Recruitment: newspapers, internet, word-of-mouth.
Contact: Marzena Fryckowska.

WORLDWIDE SCHOOL
27 Berezynska str. apt. 1, Warsaw. Tel: (22) 617 3474. Fax: (22) 617 34 74. E-mail: urbanasiewicz@post.pl.
Number of teachers: 13 (others are employed in fives centres including in-company department).
Preference of nationality: British.
Qualifications: degree and CELTA. Experience plus business background are advantages.
Conditions of employment: 1 year (2 years preferable). School is open 7.30-9am and 4pm-6pm. 20 hours per week minimum. Some early mornings.
Salary: standard rates plus benefits and transport (negotiable).
Facilities/Support: assistance with accommodation. School pays for work permits. Continuous training and development. The School is a member of PASE (Polish Association for Standards in English). Opportunities to attend outside seminars and conferences.
Recruitment: locally and possibility of UK and telephone interviews.
Contact: Maria Banasiewicz.

YES SCHOOL OF LANGUAGE
ul. Reformacka 8, 35-026 Rzeszów. Tel/fax: (17) 852 0720. Tel: (17) 852 0723. E-mail: info@yes.pl. Website: www.yes.pl.
Number of teachers: 10 full-time, plus 14 positions at the summer programme in the mountains.
Preference of nationality: British.
Qualifications: university degree and CELTA (or equivalent) required. At least one year's experience is usually required.
Conditions of employment: 10-month contract (September to June); teaching 20 45-minute lessons a week between 4 30 and 8pm; occasional daytime hours; all levels and ages.
Salary: 37 zloties per 45 minute lesson net (approximately £5.50).
Facilities/Support: assistance with finding accommodation given.
Recruitment: adverts in teacher training colleges, internet and direct applications.
Contact: Danuta Balanda, Managing Director.

YORK SCHOOL OF ENGLISH
ul. Mackiewicza 12, 31-213 Kraków. Tel: (12) 415 1818/415 1444. E-mail: york@kraknet.pl. Website: www.york.edu.pl.
Number of teachers: 7 (full-time).
Preference of nationality: British, also American, Canadian, Irish.

Qualifications: minimum BA or MA (preferably in languages). TEFL certificate (UCLES, Trinity). 1-3 years' teaching experience in EFL.
Conditions of employment: one year (September to June). 25 h.p.w. mainly afternoons/evenings.
Salary: 2,800-3,000 zloties a month (about $7 per 45 minutes).
Facilities/Support: accommodation in school flat for two teachers to share (rent is 600 zloties). Help given with permits. Possibility of bonuses.
Recruitment: adverts in the *Guardian*. Interviews carried out in UK. Regular workshops, conferences and staff meetings.
Contact: Ewa Krupska.

Other Schools to Try

Note that these schools did not confirm their teacher requirements for this edition of *Teaching English Abroad*. Upper case entries marked with an asterisk had entries in the last edition (1999); addresses without asterisks have been taken from various sources, such as British Council lists and the *Yellow Pages*. No attempt has been made to transcribe Polish accents accurately.

NKJO-Bialystok, ul. Liniarskiego 3, 15-420 Bialystok (tel/fax 85-424371).
European College, ul. Konarskiego 4, 85-066 Bydgoszcz (52-22 10 80). 5 teachers, British or Irish preferred.
College of Linguists/Wyzsza Szkola Lingwistyczna, ul. Zwirki i Wigury 9/11, 42-200 Czestochowa (tel/fax 34-365 48 59/324 4859; e-mail: cel@cel.czest.pl). Group of language schools in constant need of English teachers.
*NKJO – ELBLAG, ul. Czerniakowska 22, 82-300 Elblag (55-324797/fax 55-326188)

Fluent Szkola Jezyków, ul. Fiszera 14, 80-231 Gdansk
Maryland Kursy i Obozy Jezydowe, Slaska 66b, 80-389 Gdansk
Oswiata Lingiwista, Malczewskiego 51, Gdansk
London School, ul. Abrahama 27/1, Gdynia

Bénédict School, Ul. Sienkiewicza 23, 40-039 Katowice
English Club, Kielce (fax 41-368 1384/e-mail panpol@complex.com.pl
*PROLOG, Szkola Jezykow Obcych, ul. Kosciuszki 24, 30-105 Kraków (tel/fax 12-227228)
*STAIRWAY SCHOOL OF ENGLISH, Ulica Dunajewskiego 6/415, 31-133 Kraków (tel/fax 12-422 1836)
School of English, ul. P. Skargi 74A m 14, 95-200 Pabianice
TEST, ul Oginskiego 18, 05-820 Piastów (tel/fax 22-723 6000; takrachela@pf.pl).
Advertising summer 2000 on yahoo's alphabetcity website for graduates to teach small groups of children and adults in a Warsaw suburb on a semi-voluntary basis.
*SZANSA, Prywatny Zaklad Oswiatowy, ul. Lubowska 6a, 60-433 Poznan (61- 848 8176)
Stamford School of English, ul. Boh. Monte Cassino 10, 81-775 Sopot
Proficiency Szkola Jezyków Obcych, ul. Grottgera 6/8, 81-809 Sopot
Stanley's Szkola Jezyków Obcych, al. Niepodleglosci 817/2, Sopot
Brytania School of English, Tarnów (14-670 3811).
NKJO-Walbrzych, ul. Kombatantów 20, 58-302 Walbrzych (tel/fax 74-78695)

A & B American and British School of English, Swietokrzyska 1, 00-360 Warsaw
Archibald Szkola Jezyka Angielskiego, Szpitalna 8/19, Warsaw
British Council Warsaw Studium, Warsaw University of Technology, ul. Filtrowa 2, 00-611 Warsaw (tel/fax 22-25 82 87)
Context Language Centre, ul. Hoza 62/1, 00-680 Warsaw (tel/fax: 22-622 5860

English Language College, Mokotowska 12, Warsaw
English Language School, ul. Mazowiecka 12 IIIp, 00-048 Warsaw (tel/fax 22-827
  6941/827 2029; teachers@ability.com.pl)
LEXIS Szkola Jezyków Obcych, Marszalkowska 60, Warsaw
Linguae Mundi Szkola Jezyków Obcych, Zlota 61, 00-819 Warsaw
Lingwista, Marszalkowska 83, 00-683 Warsaw
New School of English, Madalinskiego 22, Warsaw
Peritia Szkola Jezyków Angielskiego, Bednarska 2.4, 00-310 Warsaw
SUCCESS, Osrodek Nauczania Jezykow Obcych, ul. Agawy 5/9, 01-158 Warsaw
  (22-623 39 40/fax 22-20 55 03)
English Language Centre, University of Wroclaw, Kuznicza 21, 50-138 Wroclaw
  (71-402955)
English Evening School – Radom, ul. Jagielly 10, 26-700 Zwollen (tel/fax 48-676
  4115; ees@poczta.onet.pl). Advertising on www.tefl.net in 2000 for young
  enthusiastic certified teachers with 1 year's proven TEFL experience.

Romania

The downfall of Ceaucescu in 1989 and the collapse of communism in Eastern
Europe led to Romania seeking closer links with the West. English was barely taught
before (French was the second language) but now there is a growing demand as the
country seeks to attract foreign investment and to modernise antiquated industries.
Unfortunately the weak state of the Romanian economy, legacy of the ruinous
Ceaucescu era, means that development has been slow. The Ministry of Education
(Strada Gen Berthelot 28-30, 70749 Bucharest; 1-615 7430/614 2680/614 4588/fax
1-312 4819) does not recruit EFL teachers directly, though it co-operates with the
British Council to improve standards of local teachers and place volunteers. It has
recently made an English exam compulsory for graduating from school and
university.

The vast majority of English teaching is carried out by Romanian teachers. In
recent years, Romania has had the highest pass rate in the Cambridge exams
worldwide. The British Council has been very active in promoting English in
Romania at all levels and in 2000 opened its own Teaching Centre in Bucharest. The
British Council Romania web-page (www.britcoun.org/romania) has relevant
information including a link to 'Volunteer Teachers'. The Council works with
volunteer placement organisations like *Services for Open Learning* and the *Central
Bureau* (see chapter introduction). SOL teachers in Romania are often asked to teach
a subject such as geography alongside English. The American organisation *Central
European Teaching Program* (Beloit College, 700 College St, Beloit, WI 53511)
supplies teachers to schools, particularly in the Hungarian-speaking areas of
Transylvania. The Cultural Counsellor at the Romanian Embassy in London
(Arundel House, 4 Palace Green, W8 4QD; 020-7937 8125) deals with education
and can advise on contacting the Ministry of Education or regional education
departments, by whom all teaching jobs in state schools must be processed.

QUEST Romania (www.quest.ro), the Romanian Association for Quality
Language Services, operates as a quality control system on the basis of an inspection
scheme. The Language Centre members of QUEST employ well-qualified teachers
(most of them Romanian) and operate as private language schools registered as
NGOs and recognised by the Ministry of Education. The addresses of its seven
founder members and one other are available from QUEST's website or from its
office at the Prosper-ASE Language Centre (prosper1@prosper.ro). Under the
heading *Limbi Straine – Cursuri* in the Yellow Pages there are about 24 addresses
though these are unlikely to employ a native speaker. The *Pagini Nationale*
(Romanian Directory 2000) also lists language schools.

International House's school in Timosoara (birthplace of the 1989 revolution) was the first private language school in the country when it opened in 1992. The gradual arrival of Western investment and companies like McDonald's and Hilton Hotels is creating more demand for commercial English.

Wages will be equivalent to those earned by Romanian teachers, from US$100 a month. Of all the countries to which *Services for Open Learning/SOL* sends teachers, Romania is the only one in which the estimated monthly wage falls below £100. Accommodation is normally provided; if it isn't, it takes a good part of a teacher's salary. Rent for a one-bedroom flat in a provincial city can even take all of a local salary, though teachers may receive an extra allowance to help cover this. Plumbing, heating and standards of construction do not match those of Western European countries. Resident foreign teachers are eligible to obtain an AVIZ card, which in theory entitles them to pay the Romanian rate for hotels, etc. (a quarter of the tourist rate) though many hoteliers insist on charging the higher rate. Obviously it is possible to live on the salary earned but not if a teacher indulges in western luxuries in high-price supermarkets catering to privileged Romanians.

Pupils are lively and curious about life in the West, and children are often up-to-date with the latest Western fashions and music from MTV. Photocopiers are scarce and paper is in short supply, if available at all. Outside British Council supported projects and universities, language laboratories and videos are rare teaching aids. Teachers would be advised to take as many teaching materials as possible, e.g. magazine articles, postcards, language games, photos, pictures. Information about the teacher's home town always goes down well. The voluntary organisation Youth Action for Peace (Victor Babes St 11/3, 3400 Club Napoca) arranges for a few foreign volunteers to teach English to village children in the mediaeval town of Sighisoara; enquiries should be made to partner organisations e.g. YAP UK (01983 752557/ www.yap.uk.org).

If going to Romania to teach, request the information sheet 'Employment Visas and Work Permits for Foreign Citizens' from the Romanian Embassy (visa@roemb.demon.co.uk). Teachers must apply for a work permit from the Ministry of Employment and Social Security; the current processing fee is US$200. As usual applicants will have to provide a sheaf of documents including originals of their teacher training certificate and university degree, documentation from the local or national police indicating that they have no criminal record, a medical certificate and contract. If going to Romania on a preliminary visit, Britons must purchase a visitor visa valid for three months (fee £33) while US nationals can enter without a visa for up to one month.

INTERNATIONAL HOUSE TIMISOARA
Bl. Republicii 9, 1900 Timisoara. Tel/fax: (56) 190593. E-mail: rsocoliuc@ih.dnttm.ro.
Number of teachers: 15 in Timisoara and 3-4 in Arad 40kms away.
Preference of nationality: none.
Qualifications: tertiary education degree plus CELTA (minimum grade B). Experience of teaching young learners and/or business English preferred. Interest in eastern Europe.
Conditions of employment: one year contracts August to October. 24 h.p.w. including Saturday mornings.
Salary: from $120 (in local currency) plus US$50 a month.
Facilities/Support: free accommodation in flats; utilities paid for by school (except phone). Return flight paid. One-week orientation. Social security and health insurance paid according to Romanian labour laws.
Recruitment: normally through International House, London.
Contact: Rodica Socoliuc or John Anderson, Director of Studies.

OPEN DOORS SCHOOL OF ENGLISH
Str. L. Blaga 4, 1900 Timisoara. Tel: (56) 092 302 201. E-mail: carmenod@

mail.dnttm.ro.
Number of teachers: 5.
Preference of nationality: none.
Qualifications: university degree and a recognised TEFL/TESL qualification.
Conditions of employment: 10 or 11 months from September. 24 h.p.w. maximum.
Salary: depends on experience.
Facilities/Support: accommodation is provided free; teachers only pay for telephone.
School pays translation costs for work permit application, and contributes DM50 per month worked towards a flight allowance, paid at the end of the contract. Training seminars conducted at school.
Recruitment: via teacher training programmes, internet and word of mouth.
Contact: Carmen Botis, Director.

Other Schools to Try

Prosper-Transilvania Language Centre, Iuliu Maniu 32, 2200 Brasov (tel/fax 68-475447)
Linguarama, 51 Delea Verne Str, BL 46, 9th Floor, Sector 2, Bucharest
Prosper-ASE Language Centre, Calea Grivitei 2-2A et. 2s, Bucharest 1 (tel/fax 1-211 7800/prosper1@prosper.ro)
Access Language Centre, Str. Tebei 21, 3400 Cluj-Napoca (tel/fax 64-420476; ovidiu@access.ro)
CLASS (Constanta Language Association), Str. Mircea cel Batran 103, 8700 Constanta (tel/fax 41-612877; class@impromex.ro)
EuroEd, Str. Florilor 1C, 6600 Iasi (acolib@ilc.iasi.osf.ro)
Professional Language Centre, Selimbar 4/1, Tg. Mures 4300 (tel/fax 65-254401; acotoara@netsoft.ro)
RALEX Linguistic Centre, Str. Buna Vestire 35, 1000 Ramnicu-Valcea (tel/fax 50-740032; ralex@unet.ro)
Soros Educational Centre, Florilor 9, III PO Box 40, Miercurea Ciuc 4100 (tel/fax 66-171799; office@cemc.topnet.ro)
Yes Language Centre, Colegiul Pedagogic Andrei Saguna, Str. Gen. Magheru 34, 2400 Sibiu (69-241266/fax 69-225222; liasb@starnets.ro)

Russia

The popularity of the English language has continued to increase and English teaching centres have appeared all over Russia at a rate far too fast for the British Council to keep track of. Yet two years ago, Russia was undergoing its worst political and economic crisis since 1991. The rouble was in free fall, banks and businesses were failing, unemployment was increasing, the price of real estate was dropping and confidence was at yet another all time low. Most companies, including language schools, were forced to restructure and cut costs. A year later, fear of a second financial crisis loomed on the horizon, compounded by the conflict in Dagestan and all-out war in Chechnya, and forcing the business community to undergo a period of economic soul-searching. This was especially true for those language schools that hired native English-speaking teaching staff. Two years of uncertainty and a flagging economy gave many of these schools the impetus to use local English teachers (much cheaper than expats) and to rely more on technology-based methodologies such as CALL. As a result the number of full-time job opportunities for native English-speaking teachers decreased. Similarly, those teachers who were offered full-time employment were also offered smaller salary and benefit packages.

Although the picture this paints may seem discouraging for the average TEFL teacher, the situation at the beginning of the 21st century is not unalloyed gloom and doom. There are still ample English teaching opportunities for those wishing to experience the real Russia. The average benefit package may have shrunk but it is still more than sufficient to live on and to enjoy the best of what Russia has to offer. Less expensive home-grown foodstuffs have replaced high priced foreign imports while domestically produced products now vie for their share of the market. Of equal importance, the rouble is and has been stable for some time now and financial analysts, though still cautious, have stopped predicting a renewed crisis round every corner. President Putin, stronger and more confident than his predecessor, has taken office and appears committed to pushing through reforms which should help gradually strengthen the economy. So at the time of writing, most schools of English were sounding more upbeat in their appraisal of the future.

Many Russians maintain a passionate interest in English, especially among students at secondary school and university. Many are already fairly competent in the language and want not only to improve their linguistic skills but to become more conversant with western culture, particularly American music.

Paper qualifications in ELT are something of a rarity in Russia. One estimate has been made that of the more than 150 language schools in Moscow, only about 20 employ native speaker teachers, the majority of whom are probably working without qualifications. Apart from the qualified teachers working for the major foreign-owned language chains, i.e. Language Link, Benedict and EF English First, the majority of English teachers in Russia and its Republics, including the Baltics, Central Asian Republics and Ukraine, have come through voluntary placement organisations or are students of Russian language and culture. But Russians are becoming more aware of standards and demanding better value for money. Robert Jensky, Director of Language Link Russia, who generously provided much of the information in this chapter, is convinced that high standards are essential:

> *I have personally seen many unqualified teachers fail because they did not fully realise the difference between speaking English and teaching English. Although Russians can vary in temperament and personality, they share a respect for education. Russians who under Communism did not have to pay for education have come to accept the fact that it is now necessary to do so. There is little debate among Russians as to the significance of the English language both domestically and globally. Their only concern is that they get their full money's worth from each and every lesson. Russian students are demanding and place high expectations on their teachers, and so do the companies which employ them (including those which hire EFL teachers illegally). Given these circumstances, it is strongly recommended that any teacher coming to Russia has with him or her a good grammar book, a dictionary and a concise guide to TEFL methodology.*

FINDING A JOB

As the largest country in the world, Russia covers eleven time zones, every imaginable kind of geography and a huge ethnic diversity. Temperatures can range from 40° above zero to 40° below. On the urban front, not all Russian cities were created equal and it is essential that teachers give careful consideration when choosing a teaching job and destination. EFL teachers would be advised to research school locations for the availability of facilities which are deemed of personal interest such as theatres, museums, parks, tourist attractions, medical services and the like. Finally don't be fooled into believing that just because you choose to work for a chain school, you are going to be working in either a large school or one staffed by native English-speaking teachers. Many major chains operate small teaching operations in far-flung locations.

A second consideration is the type of teaching that you will be expected to do. Teachers who are capable of performing in a variety of EFL classroom settings (young learners, adults, general, business English, examination preparation) are in the greatest demand. Likewise, teachers who are prepared to be flexible with regard to teaching schedules will find a far greater number of employment opportunities. This is especially true in the great metropolitan areas where the number of both business and one-to-one clients is on the rise, many of whom want to be taught before or after the working day.

Few schools can afford to advertise and recruit teachers abroad, thus internet advertising is becoming increasingly important. The most popular sites among Russian companies are www.tefl.com, www.eslcafe.com, elsworldwide.com, globalesl.net and www.goabroad.com. But anyone with contacts anywhere in the region or who is prepared to go there to make contacts should be able to arrange a teaching niche on an individual basis, always assuming money is no object. Most educational institutes are suffering such serious financial hardship that they can't attract local teachers, let along Western ones. Only in a handful of cases (like the Institute of International Law & Economics in Moscow) are qualified EFL teachers employed and paid accordingly, e.g. US$15-$20 per class. The helpful Information Officer at the British Council in Moscow maintains lists of institutes of higher education in the Moscow and other regions (in the Cyrillic script) but not lists of commercial language schools.

Those who are not deterred by the prospect of earning virtually nothing can contact the International Department of the Education Committee in Moscow which is responsible for the allocation of teachers to state schools. In order for an individual to be considered, he or she should be able to provide a relevant qualification, a health certificate and references.

Private lessons will be less easy to fix up than they were a few years ago when 'New Russians', those who were made relatively rich by the change to a free market, were willing and able to pay up to an outrageous US$30 an hour for one-on-one tuition, sometimes even in hard currency. While spending six months as a student of Russian in the beautiful and historic town of Yaroslavl, Hannah Start found private pupils very easily. She decided to accept only high school students to diminish the risk of crime; apparently if you are teaching in your own accommodation, it is wise to refrain from displaying any expensive Western items.

The main language chains recruit heavily abroad; both *Language Link* and *Benedict* have active departments in the UK which screen and interview candidates (see entries) for their schools throughout Russia. *EF English First's* several schools in Moscow and elsewhere in Russia rely heavily on EF in the UK (EF House, 1-3 Farman Street, Brighton, BN3 1AL; 01273 747308/fax 01273 746742). EF recruits for Russia on reasonable terms with return flight, medical insurance and visa costs included. *Saxoncourt Recruitment & English Worldwide* fill vacancies in Moscow and Siberia on behalf of IH-affiliated schools, among others; *Oxford Crown* recruits for its school in Moscow while *Nord Anglia* recruits for its member school Polyglot.

The International Exchange Center (2 Republic Square, 1010 Riga, Latvia; fax: 371-8830257; e-mail: iec@mail.eunet.lv) recruits ELT teachers for summer language camps and courses in Russia as well as Latvia. It offers between 20 and 40 hours of teaching in return for a salary equivalent to local rates or free board and lodging. The application fee is US$150.

A thriving English language press has established itself in Moscow and St. Petersburg. Check adverts in the *Moscow Times, Moscow Tribune* and the weekly *St. Petersburg Press*. Look out also for the free ads paper *Iz Ruk v Ruki* in about 15 towns in Russia.

UK Organisations
A number of voluntary and cultural exchange organisations place English language assistants in the former Soviet Union primarily the *Central Bureau for International Education & Training* (address in the introduction to this chapter). Such

organisations are recommended since they are a way of getting something organised in a country which is notoriously disorganised. In addition to the ones listed, *GAP Activity Projects* has a sizeable programme in the region and both *i-to-i* and *Teaching & Projects Abroad* run schemes by which paying volunteers are placed mostly in state schools.

The Central Bureau's Assistants Scheme, open only to graduates who have studied Russian, is now well established in sending students to linguistic universities and paedagogical institutes. In addition to the negligible wage paid to all university employees, the Central Bureau pays a monthly top-up of about US$200 to enable assistants to have a decent standard of living.

Chris Jones had a wonderful year as a teaching assistant in Nizhny Novgorod (seven hours from Moscow) with the Central Bureau and his experiences are representative of others' who have gone through a mediating organisation to teach in the Russian state system:

> *I had no relevant teaching experience, but the fact that I had been to Russia several times before seemed to be a big selling factor; I obviously knew what I was in for. During the interview, discussion concentrated on how you thought you would cope with living in Russia for nine months.*
>
> *My institution was very conscious of not over-burdening me with work and I regularly had to press for more hours. I was expected to concentrate on phonetic and conversational practice but was allowed almost to do my own thing once they realised that I was competent. I used articles from newspapers and magazines for listening and reading comprehensions and made extensive use of popular songs.*
>
> *There were problems with resources. There were only two video recorders in my university and these had to be booked well in advance. Hand-outs are virtually unheard of in university teaching in Russia and getting photocopying done for lessons was very difficult. Certainly all copies had to be handed back in at the end of each lesson and saved for other groups to use. Sometimes I paid for photocopies myself, as the official channel for using the photocopier (there was only one) involved much wearisome justification to those in authority.*

US Organisations

Several organisations in the USA offer volunteers the chance to teach English at any level from university to businesses. The Teacher Internship Program run by Project Harmony (6 Irasville Common, Waitsfield, VT 05673; 802-496-4545/fax 802-496-4548; www.projectharmony.org) arranges for recent college graduates and experienced teachers to work in host schools and institutions in Russia and Odessa in the Ukraine for six months or a year. The placement fee of $2,250 includes everything including airfares from the US but not health insurance. Accommodation is provided, normally sharing with a host family. Project Harmony has offices in St. Petersburg, Moscow and Petrozavodsk.

Another cultural exchange programme which sends volunteer teachers to Russia is the Petro-Teach Program (named for St. Petersburg where placements are made, rather than for Russia's petro-chemical industry). The application procedure should be started in February/March for year-long placements beginning on September 1st. The public and private schools where participants teach are located throughout central St. Petersburg and host families are scattered around the city. An intensive pre-teaching Russian course and on-going lessons in Russian are given at the Institute of Foreign Languages. Further details of the Petro-Teach Program are available from Professor Wallace J Sherlock, Dept. of Curriculum and Instruction, University of Wisconsin, Whitewater, WI 53190 (sherlocw@mail.uww.edu/ www.semlab2. sbs.sunysb.edu/Users/jbailyn/Petro.html).

WORKING AND LIVING CONDITIONS

Anyone who has seen television news programmes will be aware of the privations of life in Russia, where in some cases teachers and other professionals have been forced to grow vegetables in order to survive. The unregulated housing market makes it very difficult for foreign teachers to find independent accommodation. Employers normally arrange accommodation for their teachers in small shared flats, with host families or in student hostels where conditions are very basic. Many teachers lodge with landladies, of whom there is no shortage considering how many widows there are trying to make ends meet on vanishingly small pensions.

With a serious shortage of teaching aids in many places, resourcefulness will be necessary as Hannah Start demonstrated. She happened to find a cucumber and some milk one day in a shop and so hastily organised an impromptu English afternoon tea. Not surprisingly, the younger generation seems more willing to embrace new communicative teaching methods than the older one, according to Elena Pershakova of the English School Sunny Plus:

> *Adults cause headaches. They get upset with grammar. Many of them can't easily accept modern methods of teaching. The progress is very slow. For many weeks they can't understand a teacher. They demand changing him. Their pronunciation is terrible, but during classes they keep silent.*

Regulations

For people participating in established international exchanges, the red tape is usually straightforward. Russia is still a place where the rules change weekly. In the commercial sector, work permits are more problematic, mainly because so few Russian companies have been given the right to invite and employ foreigners legally. Obtaining this right is a time-consuming and lengthy process. For language schools this involves having the support of the Department or Ministry of Education, the Mayor's Office and Tax Inspection. To date, only four or five language companies have received the necessary permission both to invite and employ native English-speaking teachers. As a consequence, the vast majority of businesses and schools operate outside the law. Put simply, if you are an ex-pat and want to teach English in Russia, you must have permission to work and only the company that has invited you to Russia (the visa sponsor) has the right to obtain this for you.

Language schools which are unable to provide teachers with legal working status usually elect to use the services of any one of a number of firms which specialise in inviting 'foreigners' to Russia (as distinct from employing foreigners in Russia). This is most often accomplished through the issuance of a one-year multiple entry visa. As these firms only have the right to invite foreigners, they can only register visas with the local UVIR office, and this is not the same as obtaining permission to work. Nevertheless, the process takes about a month from the time the visa-sponsoring firm applies to the Ministry of Foreign Affairs for an invitation. To apply for the visa, the applicant will need to bring the original invitation, a completed visa application form (obtainable from the Russian Consulate or downloadable from www.russianembassy.org), passport, photocopy of the details' page of the passport, three photos, and proof of recent HIV test to the Russian Consulate. The cost is approximately £100. Unless you are actually going to be working for the firm which invited you to Russia, you cannot obtain a work permission.

By contrast, language schools with the right to invite and employ foreigners apply to the Ministry of Foreign Affairs for a telex number which is obtainable on the same day that the application is made. This number is given to the applicant who must then bring the documents as above to the Russian Consulate and pay the fee of £20. The visa issued will be valid for three months. After entering Russia, the visa sponsor has 90 days to arrange for a work permission to be issued by the Federal Migration Service (FMS). This can be issued only after the teacher has been HIV-tested in an authorised clinic or hospital and after the visa sponsor has posted a sizeable bond with FMS. After the issuance of a work permit, the visa sponsor can extend a three-month visa for up to a year. Should the teacher wish to leave Russia for the holidays or in the event of an emergency, the visa sponsor can arrange for special exit-entry visas.

It is worth noting that British-based recruitment companies and their clients have acted in ignorance of the regulations and as a result foreign teachers have received substantial fines for visa violations. Teachers should be wary of language teaching companies which refuse to give contracts bearing an official stamp. Their suspicions should also be aroused if salaries are paid in a currency other than the rouble as this is absolutely illegal. Cities like Moscow abound in stories of ex-pats who have been prevented from sending money out of the country when they were unable to provide legal proof as to how the hard currency was obtained.

Numerous foreigners do work without proper authorisation, but run a constant risk of being fined or even deported. Rhys Sage became suspicious of a language school which sent him the wrong visa:

> *After a fiasco in Latvia, it has become apparent to me that if a company is not willing to obtain the proper visa then they must be up to something dodgy. When I negotiated my contract with a school in Novosibirsk, they accepted some pretty excessive demands on my part which made me suspicious that the contract was worthless. This, combined with the fact that they sent me a visa form for a transit visa claiming it was a work visa, resulted in my complete loss of interest in them. A transit visa means nothing. It just means that you have permission to cross Russia, and therefore you have no redress if the employer decides to withhold your wages.*

LIST OF SCHOOLS

AMERICAN ACADEMY OF FOREIGN LANGUAGES – MOSCOW
17 Bolshoi, Cheremushkinskaya, Moscow. Tel: (095) 123 46 33. Fax: (095) 129 41 11. E-mail: aafl@rui.ru/cj@rui.ru. Website: http://aafl.rui.ru/e/Jobs.html.
Number of teachers: 35+ (full-time and part-time).
Preference of nationality: native speaker with awareness of differences between American and British English. Must be citizen of USA, Great Britain, Canada, Australia or New Zealand.
Qualifications: EFL teaching experience. Knowledge of business world useful.
Conditions of employment: 1 year contracts. Hours vary; peak times are before 10am and after 6pm.
Salary: approximately $1,200-$1,500 net for full-time timetable.
Facilities/Support: assistance with home search and visa support given.
Recruitment: internet, adverts.
Contact: Craig Jackson or Irina Mozheiko.

BENEDICT SCHOOL
Business and Language School, Of. 315, 41 Arotchnaia, Kemerovo 650099. Tel: (3842) 23 00 69. E-mail: 230069@kmr.kuzbass.net.
Number of teachers: 1/2.
Preference of nationality: British.
Qualifications: degree and teaching qualification or experience.
Conditions of employment: from September/November until May. 24-26 hours per week.
Salary: depending on qualifications. Minimum US$500 per month.
Facilities/Support: assistance with finding accommodation which costs about US$30-$40.
Recruitment: teachers must produce their certificates, diplomas, recommendation letters, etc. In-person interviews not expected.

Contact: Oxana Klimenko.

BENEDICT SCHOOL
Sibirskaya 31, Office 10, Novosibirsk 630004. Tel/fax: (3832) 173875. Tel: (3832) 170341. E-mail: benedict@online.nsk.su.
Number of teachers: 5 native speakers out of 30.
Preference of nationality: British, American, Canadian.
Qualifications: TEFL background including the Benedict TEFL training. 1 year's experience preferred of teaching intermediate to advanced students, teenagers and some business English.
Conditions of employment: minimum one semester (3 month) stays, though two or three semesters preferred, after trial period of 6 weeks. Hours normally in morning and evening (6pm-8pm, Monday to Saturday).
Salary: US$7 per hour (net) which may increase after 6 months. Return airfare from UK paid (maximum $500).
Facilities/Support: shared flat provided for US$50 a month rent, or host families in some cases. Assistance with visas. Good range of teaching materials because school is regional distributor for OUP, CUP and Longman. Orientation meeting on arrival, and pre-course observations.
Recruitment: directly or via UK agency: International Educational Centre Ltd., 74 Baxter Court, Norwich NR3 2ST (tel/fax 01603 763378).

BENEDICT SCHOOL
23 ul. Pskovskaya, St. Petersburg 190008. Tel: (812) 113 85 68/114 10 90. Fax: (812) 114 44 45. E-mail: benedict@infopro.spb.su or emma@griffin.fsbusiness. co.uk. Web-site: www.fsvo.com/benedict.
Number of teachers: 40-60 for Russia including 18-20 for St. Petersburg (main franchise holder) and others in Novosibirsk (see above), Tomsk, Murmansk and Kemerovo.
Preference of nationality: British, American, Canadian, Australian.
Qualifications: no TEFL background needed for Work-Study programme. TEFL graduates needed for teaching.
Conditions of employment: 3-12 months. 15-25 h.p.w.
Salary: US$400-800 per month (net).
Facilities/Support: work permits not needed for Work-Study Programme; otherwise assistance given. In-house training courses (10-30 lessons) result in international Benedict teachers' certificate
Recruitment: universities, careers centres, website, directly or via UK agency, IEC Ltd. (address at end of previous entry).
Contact: Natalya Rostovtseva, Managing Director.

BKC – INTERNATIONAL HOUSE
Starovagankovsky Peruelok 15, office 1, 121019 Moscow. Tel: (095) 737-52-25. Fax: (095)-737-65-79. E-mail: recruit@bkc.ru. Website: www.bkc.ru.
Number of teachers: 70 throughout Russia, including 50 in Moscow.
Preference of nationality: British, Irish, North American, New Zealand, Australian.
Qualifications: Cambridge CELTA, Trinity TESOL, MA in TESOL.
Conditions of employment: 36 teaching weeks and 25 days paid holiday. 25 contact h.p.w. Typical timetable includes some teen or children's classes as well as adults.
Salary: $500-575 net according to qualifications and experience, plus accumulating bonus paid on completion of contract.
Facilities/Support: airfare subsidy. Shared flats provided. All bills except telephone paid by school. Full visa support (valid multiple-entry business visa); monthly seminars and regular observations; teacher training department Cambridge CELTA and DELTA courses; job offer to successful trainees. Considerable discounts are offered to teachers who are interested in learning Russian.
Recruitment: contact the Recruitment Department, BKC-IH Moscow.

Contact: Anna Naumova, Recruitment Manager.

EF ENGLISH FIRST
125 Brestskaya 1st Street, 5th Floor, 125047 Moscow. Tel: (095) 937 3883. Fax: (095) 937 3889. E-mail: tatiana.shestoperova@ef.com. Website: www.ef.com/GB/hr/virtualtour.
Number of teachers: 25 for 14 schools (10 plus one business school in Moscow, 1 EFL in Vladivostok, 2 EFL in St. Petersburg).
Preference of nationality: British, North American, Australian, New Zealand (due to work permit restrictions).
Qualifications: EFL/ESL Certificate plus a university degree.
Conditions of employment: 9-12 month renewable contract. Schools open from 9am to 9pm Monday to Saturday. 25 real contact hours per week.
Facilities/Support: help with finding accommodation. Visas arranged. Paid holidays. Flights paid. Orientation upon arrival and ongoing training. Emergency medical insurance.
Recruitment: directly through Moscow office or through offices in the UK, USA, Canada or Australia or EF teacher recruitment in worldwide offices (see *Finding a Job*).
Contact: Tatiana Shestoperova in the Moscow office or EF Teacher Recruitment in worldwide offices.

ENGLISH SCHOOL SUNNY PLUS
1-Aeroportovskaya Street, building 1/3, P.O. Box 23, 125057 Moscow. Tel: (095) 151 2500 (3pm-8pm); (095) 126 4977. Tel/fax: (095) 129 7303. E-mail: sunnyplus@glasnet.ru. Website: www.sunnyplus.ru.
Number of teachers: 10.
Preference of nationality: British, American, Canadian.
Qualifications: university degree and teaching experience. Ideally, TEFL qualification.
Conditions of employment: 3-12 months between September and end of June. 4-24 h.p.w. Teaching hours 3-9pm Monday to Friday. Classes for children from age 8 and adults.
Salary: $11-$15 per hour. Taxes paid by school.
Facilities/Support: help with visa. Director of Studies provides in-house training.
Recruitment: interviews essential.
Contact: Elena Pershakova (Director), Sergei Smirnov (Deputy Director).

LANGUAGE LINK RUSSIA
Novoslobodskaya ul. 5, bld. 2, 101030 Moscow. Tel: (095) 250 8935/251 4889. Fax: (095) 234 0703. E-mail: jobs@language.ru. Web-site: www.language.ru.
Number of teachers: 400 throughout Russia (Moscow, St. Petersburg, Volgograd, Samara, Voronezh, Rostov, Ekaterinburg, Krasnoyarsk and Krasnodar).
Preference of nationality: British, also American, Canadian and Australian.
Qualifications: university degree and CELTA or Trinity Certificate/Diploma required.
Conditions of employment: 6 or 9 month (40 week) contracts. 25 teaching h.p.w., normally 4^1/2 hours a day, 5 days a week. Adult classes, children's classes and in-company.
Salary: US$550-$850 (net) depending on location and experience. Return airfare (maximum £280) and local transport paid. 4 weeks of paid holiday and health cover (for teachers on 9 month contracts).
Facilities/Support: all teachers provided with free accommodation in 1-room flat (or 2-room flat for 2 teachers). Paid medical services and full visa/work permission support. Academic support via on-site Director of Studies, inset training, seminars and presentations.
Recruitment: interviews and selection mostly carried out by Language Link in London (21 Harrington Road, London SW7 3EU; 020-7225 1065/fax 020-7584

3518; languagelink@compuserve.com/ www.languagelink.co.uk). Teachers applying from outside UK must be interviewed in Russia.
Contact: Robert Jensky, Director.

LINGUAMIR
Novo Sadovaya 3-429, 443002 Samara. Tel: (8462) 37 17 63. E-mail: apply@linguamir.com. Website: www.linguamir.com.
Number of teachers: 8.
Preference of nationality: British.
Qualifications: degree, TEFL Cert, experience.
Conditions of employment: 10 month renewable contracts. 24-25 hours p.w.
Salary: $400-$600 per month depending on experience.
Facilities/Support: visa invitation sent to relevant Russian Embassy. Free single flat provided.
Recruitment: via internet. Face-to-face interviews not necessary.
Contact: Alexander Golovanov, Deputy Director; Peter Bartley, Director of Studies.

OXFORD CROWN
Room 203, 3/8 Lavrushinski, Pereulok, 109017 Moscow. Tel: (095) 959 4265. Fax: 007 095 951 6439. E-mail: oxfcrown@dol.ru.
Number of teachers: 5.
Preference of nationality: British.
Qualifications: degree plus TEFL Certificate.
Conditions of employment: one year. 8.30am-3pm (and possibly evenings).
Salary: US$1,200 gross.
Facilities/Support: help given to locate a flat and negotiate the rent. US$300 for visa and insurance. Help with local application to immigration authorities.
Recruitment: via adverts in the press and from CELTA training centres.
Contact: Alex Bessey, Chairman (8 Tanner's Court, St. Martin's Close, Norwich NR3 3HB; tel 01603-627886; e-mail: oxfordcrown@oxfordcrown2.demon.co.uk).

RUSSIAN-AMERICAN CENTER
Tomsk Polytechnic University, Room 319, Lenin Avenue 30, 634034 Tomsk. Tel: (3822) 41 55 29. Fax: (3822) 27 91 90. E-mail: push@rac.tpu.edu.ru/or knp@ tpu.ru/or ovp@tpu.ru.
Number of teachers: 1.
Preference of nationality: American or British.
Qualifications: experience in teaching languages to foreign students with emphasis on pronunciation. Training for Cambridge exam and TOEFL.
Conditions of employment: one semester. Conditions vary according to individual contract.
Salary: US$5 per hour.
Facilities/Support: assistance with accommodation given and training if necessary.
Recruitment: candidates normally recommended by US or UK partners. Interview not essential.
Contact: Elena Leontieva, Deputy Director.

ST. PETERSBURG UNIVERSITY OF HUMANITIES AND SOCIAL SCIENCES
Department of Foreign Languages, 15 Fuchika Street, 192238 St. Petersburg. Tel: (812) 269 19 25. Fax: (812) 269 59 66. E-mail: info@uhss.spb.ru. Website: www.uhss.spb.ru.
Number of teachers: 2-3.
Preference of nationality: UK.
Qualifications: TEFL Cert. and 1-2 years of experience.
Conditions of employment: 1-2 years.
Facilities/Support: salary is tax free. Public transport paid for by the university. Hostel accommodation is provided. Own room and all conveniences free of charge. Help with visa provided.

Recruitment: mainly through personal contacts.
Contact: Tatiana Vdovenko, Head of English Language Department.

Baltics

Arguably the most westernised part of the old Russian Empire, the Baltic countries of Lithuania, Latvia and Estonia are looking towards a future as part of Western Europe.

LATVIA

Of the three Baltic states, Latvia is the slowest to change with few commercial language schools and some TEFL possibilities with state organisations. Qualified ELT teachers should make contact with the Latvian Association of Teachers of English (LATE), 11 Novembra Krastmala 29, 1050 Riga (late@acad.latnet.lv). Occasionally, there are advertisements for TEFL vacancies in Latvia especially on the internet. One repeat advertiser recently was International R & V Educational Centre, Meistaru iela 10, 1050 Riga (fax 722 4750/ raimonds11@parks.lv).

Even voluntary opportunities are few and far between. The *International Exchange Center* in Riga runs an EFL teaching programme which places teachers at language schools and summer language centres in Latvia, Russia and Ukraine. Rhys Sage worked at a summer camp through the IEC one summer and, despite finding the food and working conditions barely tolerable, returned to the same camp several summers later after receiving a faxed invitation from the camp director:

> *I spent two months as an English teacher. Well, that's what they called it. I was merely a token English speaker and was not allowed to do any actual teaching or any real assisting. It was a typically Soviet experience where people were not expected to do anything but were paid and criticised for anything they actually did.*

Regulations

The Latvian Embassies in London and Washington can send detailed information about residence permits. People planning to go to Latvia as teachers or researchers need a copy of their education/qualifications and a contract of employment approved by the State Labour Department in addition to the usual documents like proof of health insurance. The process is somewhat easier than it was when Rhys Sage tried to obtain a residence permit after being offered a job by the Defence Academy in Riga:

> *I was given a huge list of things to get, including documents which absolutely do not exist other than in the minds of Latvian bureaucrats. Depending on who you ask and in which office, the regulations vary. In the end I left Latvia as my 90 days were up and I really didn't feel like staying illegally. As a tourist, it's possible to stay in Latvia for no more than 90 days in a calendar year. There is a great quantity of work in Latvia for English teachers, but the difficulties of obtaining a visa are almost insurmountable.*

Rhys Sage went on to explain that the lack of a visa was only one in a catalogue of woes:

> *I arrived in November expecting, as agreed with the Rektor of the military academy, a room and meals, 120 Lats per month, a visa and health insurance. The room turned out to be an old KGB prison cell with bars over the windows. The shower had black mould up the walls and green slime on*

the duckboards. A favourite dish served in the mess hall was sauerkraut which was like compost. I was not surprised that most of my students were inattentive, sleepy and generally lacklustre given the diet they had. In the end I spent most of my time hunting for real food. I was never provided with chalk so had to borrow it from the other teachers. There were photocopiers but no paper.

INTERNATIONAL EXCHANGE CENTRE
2 Republic Square, 1010 Riga. Fax: 7830257. E-mail: iec@mail.eunet.lv.
Number of teachers: various.
Preference of nationality: none, but must have basic knowledge of Russian or Latvian.
Qualifications: TEFL qualification and teaching experience.
Conditions of employment: 3-12 weeks June to August. 20-40 hours per week. There is a placement fee of US$150 and teachers must arrange their own medical insurance.
Salary: depends on the position and working hours, usually either a salary equal to that paid to local specialists, or free accommodation.
Recruitment: directly to IEC Riga or UK applicants can apply through International Student Exchange Centre, Britannia House, Britannia Street, London WC1X 9JD (fax 020-7278 3466; Isecexchange@cs.com).

SATVA ENGLISH LANGUAGE CENTER
Dzirnavu iela 79/85 office 8, 1011 Riga. Tel: 722 6641. Fax: 722 6641. E-mail: satva@mailbox.riga.lv.
Number of teachers: 7.
Preference of nationality: none.
Qualifications: minimum certificate in teaching TEFL/ESL. Minimum 1 year experience in teaching (any discipline).
Conditions of employment: contract from September to May. Teaching afternoons and evenings and occasionally mornings.
Salary: $7 per unit (45 mins) starting salary. $8 per hour for experienced teachers. Minimum of 100 hours per month.
Facilities/Support: assistance given with locating flats, but arrangements are the responsibility of the teacher. Assistance with work permits.
Recruitment: newspapers, internet, direct. Interview not essential but preferred.
Contact: Mike Young, Academic Director.

Other Schools to Try
Jurmala Language Centre, 4 Ogres Str, 2000 Jurmala (2-761188)
Public Service Language Unit, 3/1 Smilsu Str, 1838 Riga (721 2251/fax 721 3780)
International Centre R & V, 10 Meistaru Str, 1050 Riga (tel/fax 722 4750)
'Mirte', 23 Raina Bulv., 1050 Riga (tel/fax 722 2284)
Language Centre Laikmets-SG, Brivibas 58-414, 1050 Riga (728 2863)
Language Centre Meridian, 9-210 Juras Str, 3600 Ventspils (362 6207/fax 362 6817)

LITHUANIA

There is more scope for teachers in Lithuania, to which *Travel Teach* and several other placement organisations send volunteers. Lithuanian schools are so keen to have native speakers that qualifications are not necessary, only a university degree. The Lithuanian Embassy in Washington distributes a list of programmes including teaching programmes. One of the key organisation is the American Partnership for Lithuanian Education (APPLE), PO Box 617, Durham, CT 06422, USA (203-347-7095/fax 203-347-5837). Prospective teachers looking for placement in the state system at secondary or tertiary level are invited to send their resumés to the director.

It is also possible to approach the Ministry of Education & Science directly, as recommended by John Morgan from Dorset:

> *The best way to fix up a teaching post is to go to Vilnius yourself and see the person responsible for placing English language teachers. I did this last year and the supervisor rang some schools to arrange interviews for me. The pay is not good (about $20 a week) so private lessons are necessary (and the school may help you to arrange these). Living with a family is the cheapest accommodation and easiest to arrange.*

He enjoyed his stint in a state school more than teaching in companies which he had done the previous year through Travel Teach, when the hours were unsocial and the clients liable to be more demanding.

Alan Reekie is another Briton who has taught in Lithuania through the Ministry of Education:

> *Successful applicants receive free accommodation either with a family or in a flat, a Lithuanian teacher's salary and a week's course of lectures on teaching in Vilnius. I am teaching 14-18 year olds who are fairly eager to learn, though because they only have an examination when they leave at 18, it can be harder to motivate the lower forms. Everyone is friendly which seems to be the case in most of Eastern Europe. I would say that the possibility of getting work is very good. An American I have met here found work within a few weeks of arriving here on spec (however he claims to be telepathic so this may have helped).*
>
> *The teaching hasn't been too hard so far, as the schools accept enthusiasm instead of skill. It also helps when your lessons are only 15 minutes long due to a heating failure. This is quite a good programme for people with no experience of teaching or travelling abroad, as you don't have to worry overly about the logistics, at the same time gaining some experience of dealing with the inevitable problems – like my landlady.*

The scheme is coordinated by the Department of Foreign Relations at the Ministry (Volano Gatve 2/7, 2691 Vilnius; 2-622483/fax 2-612077; vladislovas. budzinauskas@smm11.ipc.elnet.lt). A letter from the Ministry or a school in Lithuania makes it possible to acquire a special visa which in the case of teachers and aid workers is free of charge.

AMERICAN ENGLISH SCHOOL
Pylimo 20, 2001 Vilnius, Lithuania. Tel/fax: (2) 791011/2. E-mail: ames@takas.lt.
Number of teachers: 4.
Preference of nationality: none.
Qualifications: 3 years teaching' experience.
Conditions of employment: 4 days per week (afternoons mainly). Other conditions negotiable. Pupils aged 8-16 and adults.
Salary: US$6-8 per hour.
Facilities/Support: preliminary training provided.
Recruitment: trial class to be taught before appointment.
Contact: Egle Kesyliene, Director.

EF ENGLISH FIRST
Kosciuskos g.11, 2000 Vilnius. Tel: (2) 791616. Fax: (2) 791646. E-mail: vilnius@ef.lt. Website: www.ef.lt/naujienos.
Number of teachers: approx 15 (5 native speakers).
Preference of nationality: British, Australian, New Zealand or North American.
Qualifications: minimum university degree and certificate in TEFL/TESL and preferred teaching experience of 1 year.
Conditions of employment: 9-12 month contract (renewable) teaching between

7am and 9pm weekdays. 24 contact hours per week.
Salary: local equivalent of US$500 a month, plus generous bonuses and annual review.
Facilities/Support: modern facilities, teacher library, computer lab, guidance of an academic counsellor, opportunities for promotion and transfer to other countries. Return flight from London paid. Assistance with finding accommodation. Visas arranged. Paid holidays. Orientation on arrival, ongoing training, local medical insurance and variety of resources provided.
Recruitment: directly to the Academic Co-ordinator or through English First teacher recruitment in worldwide offices including London and Boston.
Contact: Ross Thomson, Director of Studies.

KLAIPEDA INTERNATIONAL SCHOOL OF LANGUAGES
Zveju 2-511 Klaipeda. Tel: (6) 311190. Fax: (6) 313069. E-mail: kisol@klaipeda.omnikl.net.
Number of teachers 6.
Preference of nationality: British.
Qualifications: minimum CELTA or 12 months experience.
Conditions of employment: 9 month contract. 18-20 contact hours per week.
Salary: US$400 net after accommodation.
Facilities/Support: single furnished flat provided free. School deals with all bureaucracy.
Recruitment: newspaper adverts. Interviews.
Contact: Mark Uribe.

SIAULIAI UNIVERSITY LITHUANIA
P. Visinskio Street 25, 5400 Siauliai, Lithuania. Tel: (1) 429808. Fax: (1) 431417. E-mail: urs1cr.su.lt. Website: www.su.lt.
Number of teachers: 1.
Preference of nationality: British or American.
Qualifications: experience of teaching communicative English, British or American studies.
Conditions of employment: 1-year contract. 15 h.p.w. Students aged 18-25.
Salary: depends on experience and scientific degree.
Facilities/Support: room in student hostel available at cost of approximately $25 per month. Some training and visa assistance provided.
Recruitment: adverts in *TES* and direct application.
Contact: Vita Kusleikiene, Co-ordinator, International Relations Office.

SOROS INTERNATIONAL HOUSE
Ukmerges 41, Korp. A, Vilnius, Lithuania 2662. Tel: (2) 724839/724879. Fax: (2) 724839. E-mail: daiva@ihouse.osf.lt. Website: http://katalogas.nkm.lt/soros.
Number of teachers: about 10.
Preference of nationality: none.
Qualifications: CELTA or equivalent.
Conditions of employment: 9 months or 1 year contract. 24 contact hours plus one hour teacher development seminar per week.
Salary: US$406 after taxes for first year teachers.
Facilities/Support: school rents flats for teachers and pays all bills except telephone. Work permits are arranged and paid for by the school.
Recruitment: through IH transfer system, IH recruitment department, locally and via the internet. Interviews also held at International House London.
Contact: Ausra Januliene, Acting Director of Studies.

R. VOSYLIENE'S SCHOOL
Vosylienes Kalbu Mokymo Centras, Jaunimo g. 4/1. 4520 Marijampolé. Tel/fax: (8) 243 97365.
Number of teachers: 3.

Preference of nationality: native speaker.
Qualifications: some TESL experience.
Conditions of employment: 1st September-31st May. Hours fluctuate according to number of students.
Salary: 20 litas per lesson.
Facilities/Support: assistance with accommodation given.
Contact: Regina Vosyliene, Owner.

Other Schools to Try

The America Center, Pranciskoniu 3/6, 2001 Vilnius
English Language Teaching Centre, Rinktines 28a, 2051 Vilnius
Foreign Language Courses, Kauno 1a, Vilnius
Janinos Zukienes, Foreign Language Courses, Taikos 157, 2017 Vilnius
Kalba Ltd, Foreign Language Courses, Ukmerges str. 10A, 2600 Vilnius (2-750000/fax 2-724248; vytas@kalba.lt/ www.kalba.lt). Interested in applications from native speaker teachers.
Korepetitorius, English and German Language Courses, Maisiogalos 34-28, Vilnius
Lingue et Commercium, Foreign Language and Commercial School, Studentu 39, 2034 Vilnius
Partners for International Education & Training Lithuania, Akmenu g. 1-3, 2009 Vilnius
Poliglotas, Foreign Language Courses, Ozo 17-12, Vilnius
A. Sakalienes Foreign Language School, See and Learn, Zirmunu 37, 2012 Vilnius
Vilnius Pedagogical University, International Relations Department, Studentu 39, 2034 Vilnius
Vilnius University, Educational Advising Center, Universiteto 3, 2734 Vilnius

Educational Information Center, Laisves al. 53, 2nd Floor, 3020 Kaunas

ESTONIA

Estonia is arguably the most progressive of the three Baltic countries, and the British Council in Tallinn will send a list headed 'Major Language Schools in Estonia' with about 30 addresses of universities and private language schools; most are reproduced below but without contact names and telephone/fax numbers. There are no major organised placement schemes from Britain or the States.

After her sister had worked in Estonia with a Christian organisation, Sarah Wadsworth applied to four schools in Estonia and was offered jobs in three of them. She chose to teach at a specialist music school in the country town of Rapla. She recommends looking in *Opetaja Lent*, the teachers' newsletter, for employment leads in state schools. International House in Tallinn employs nine ELT instructors, and the Peace Corps places English teachers in state schools.

Like so many of the former states of the USSR, the visa requirements are confusing as Sarah found. Getting the work and residence permits took a great deal of time and patience, as well as costing about £60. The main problem was finding out what papers were needed.

CONCORDIA INTERNATIONAL UNIVERSITY
Kaluri Tee 3 & 5, Haabneeme, 74001 Harjumaa. Tel: (60) 90077. Fax: (60) 90216.
E-mail: ciue@ciue.edu.ee. Website: www.ciue.edu.ee.
Number of teachers: 7-8.
Preference of nationality: none.
Qualifications: teaching experience and a degree.
Conditions of employment: one academic year. 16 hours teaching per week.
Salary: 20,000 kroons per month.
Facilities/Support: apartments available on campus or in town. Faculty assistant

does work permit procedures.
Recruitment: newspaper advertising.
Contact: Esther Maria Grünberg, Chair of the Dept. of Humanities & Social Sciences.

INTERNATIONAL LANGUAGE SERVICES
Pikk 9, 10123 Tallinn. Tel/fax: (2) 6412475. E-mail: ilsinfo@online.ee. Web-site: www.online.ee/~ilsinfo.
Number of teachers: 8-12
Preference of nationality: none.
Qualifications: minimum CELTA or Trinity Cert; experience preferred.
Conditions of employment: 10-month or 22-month contracts. 96 to 120 45-minute lessons per month.
Salary: about US$500 per month after deductions.
Facilities/Support: free flat provided. Travel allowance. All procedures for work permits handled by school. Regular seminars and teacher development programme.
Recruitment: internet and TEFL/TESOL press. Phone interviews.
Contact: Phil Marsdale, Director.

PARNU LANGUAGE SCHOOL
Malmö 19, Pärnu 80010, Estonia. Tel: (44) 31310. Fax: (44) 44002. E-mail: igshool@estpak.ee and lingo@estpak.ee.
Number of teachers: 1.
Preference of nationality: British.
Qualifications: degree. Teaching experience would be an advantage.
Conditions of employment: one year contract.
Salary: local rates apply. Average monthly salary 5,000-6,000 kroons net (about £200-240). Taxes paid by the company.
Facilities/Support: the school arranges a contract with a landlord to get the best rate. The rent is paid by the teacher. Assistance with the complicated work permit procedure. Further details can be obtained by e-mailing the school.
Recruitment: direct. CV, then interview. Interview essential but can be carried out in the UK or elsewhere in Europe.
Contact: Sirje Nakkurt, Manager.

TALLINN TECHNICAL UNIVERSITY
Language Centre, Ehitajate tu 5, Tallinn 19086. Tel: (2) 620 2700. Fax: (2) 620 2020
Number of teachers: 1.
Preference of nationality: none.
Qualifications: MA or equivalent. Lecturers should have at least 5 years of teaching experience at tertiary level.
Conditions of employment: 5 years. 16 contact hours a week.
Salary: £180 per month. 26% tax and social security is paid by the university.
Facilities/support: visiting lecturers can be housed in university accommodation with up to half the rent paid. Work permit procedure is very complicated and assistance is given only in exceptional circumstances
Contact: Mari Uibo, Director of Modern Languages.

Other Schools to Try

ALF Training Centre Ltd. Rävala pst. 4, Tallinn EE0001
HEDI, Tina 16a, Tallinn EE0001
International House, Pikk 69, Tallinn EE0101
Ko-Praktik, Tondi 1, Tallinn EE0013
Kullerkupp, Pärnu mnt. 57, Tallinn EE0001
Language Learning Service, Tonismagi 3, Tallinn EE0001
LEX, Uus 19, Tallinn EE0001
Lingo Ltd., Väike-Kuke 16, Pärnu, Tallinn EE0001

Mainor Language Centre, Kuhlbarsi tn. 1, Tallinn EE0101. Also Kreutzwaldi 48a
  Tartu EE2400
Multilingua, Mere pst.4, Tallinn EE0001
Old Town Language Centre (Helo), Pühavaimu 7, Tallinn EE0001
Sugesto, Barva mnt. 6-8, Tallinn EE0001
Tallinn Language School, Rendla 22, Tallinn EE0001
Tallinn Pedagogical University, Language Centre, Narva mnt. 29, Tallinn EE0101
TEA, Liivalaia 28, Tallinn EE0001

Audentese, Sopruse pst. 2, Tartu EE2400
Dialoog, Turu 9, Tartu EE2400
Folkuniversitet, Lai 30, Tartu EE2400
Studium Munga 18, Tartu EE2400
Tartu Language School, Lai 22, Tartu EE2400

Ukraine

The vast republic of the Ukraine has a serious shortage of English teachers and many
other things besides. In addition to the British organisations mentioned at the
beginning of this chapter which send volunteers to Ukraine, several emigré
organisations in the US recruit volunteers, warning that teachers must be prepared
to accept a modest standard of living. *Project Harmony* (see description in the
section on Russia is active in the Ukraine; participants pay $2,150 to teach for six
months or a year (including flights from the US).

The International Exchange Centre in Latvia (see entry above) has an ELT
programme in summer (June to August) which charges a participation fee of
US$150 and provides free accommodation or a modest salary at local rates.
Volunteer teachers who take their own chalk, paper clips, sellotape and other
materials are usually glad that they did.

There is some commercial ELT activity, so that recruitment agencies in London
advertise vacancies in Ukraine from time to time. Since the ELT market is in its
infancy, the prospect for tough motivated teachers to rise quickly is excellent.

The British Council in Kyiv has a Teaching Centre (National Technical
University, Building 1, room 258, 37 Prospect, Kyiv 252056; 44-441 1659;
elc@elc.bc.kiev.ua) and can also supply a list of English language institutes of
various kinds.

LIST OF SCHOOLS

AMERICAN ACADEMY OF FOREIGN LANGUAGES KIEV
Dmitreva St 16, Office 16, Kiev, Ukraine. Tel/fax: (44) 227 07 82. E-mail:
melissa@aafl.kiev.ua.
Number of teachers: 6-8.
Preference of nationality: native speaker with awareness of differences between
American and British English.
Qualifications: TEFL certificate and/or 2 years' teaching experience. Prefer
teachers with business background (e.g. marketing, finance, law or public relations).
Conditions of employment: renewable every 3 months. Hours vary, between 6 and
20 p.w. Maximum 30 h.p.w. Peak hours before 10am and after 6pm.
Salary: generally between US$10 and $20 per hour less local income tax.
Facilities/Support: assistance with accommodation and work permits.
Recruitment: teachers normally hired locally after advertising in local English
language press, in trade magazines and on the internet. Interviews not essential;
phone interviews given to establish whether teacher is personable, outgoing and
enthusiastic.

Contact: Colin Jackson, General Manager (cj@rui.ru).

INTERNATIONAL HOUSE – KYIV
7, Vasilevskoy str., p/B 6411, 03055 Kyiv. Tel: (44) 238 98 70. Fax: (44) 236 22 64.
E-mail: school@sihs.kiev.ua or ih@webber.kiev.ua.
Number of teachers: 7-10.
Preference of nationality: none, but must be native speaker.
Qualifications: minimum BA and TEFL Cert.
Conditions of employment: one year contracts. Teach up to 24 hours per week.
Salary: US$500 $600 (net)
Facilities/Support: the school provides the teacher with a single room or shared apartment.
Recruitment: through IH London or locally.
Contact: Esfir Kotyk, Director.

INTERNATIONAL HOUSE – LVIV
109 Zelena Street, 79035 Lviv. Tel: (32) 272 60 68. Fax: (32) 272 60 68. E mail: dos@sihs.lviv.ua or root@sihs.lviv.ua.
Number of teachers: 8.
Preference of nationality: none, but should be native speakers.
Qualifications: CELTA/Trinity Cert.
Conditions of employment: 12 months plus paid holidays. 24 teaching sessions (45 mins each) per week, plus a meeting, seminar.
Salary: approx. US$310 net plus 54 hryvnas for more than a year's IH experience.
Facilities/Support: return flight London-Lviv-London covered by the school. Single, furnished accommodation is provided by the school for up to US$80.
Recruitment: through IH recruitment services and via the internet.
Contact: Kaye Anderson/Olena Antonova.

INTERNATIONAL HOUSE – ODESSA
15 Govorova Street, Odessa, 65063 Ukraine. Tel: (48) 242 97 0/237 06 64. Fax: (48) 242 97 02. E-mail: tslnipol@te.net.ua.
Number of teachers: 11 (mixture of native speaker and local).
Preference of nationality: none, but should be native speaker.
Qualifications: CELTA or Trinity Cert.
Conditions of employment: 12 months including 4 weeks holiday.
Salary: US$400 approx.
Facilities/Support: return flight London-Odessa-London provided. Accommodation in flats provided.
Recruitment: through Human Resources at IH London/via the internet.
Contact: Tatyana Sinipolskaya.

UKRAINIAN NATIONAL ASSOCIATION (UNA)
2200 Route 10, PO Box 280, Parsippany, NJ 07054, USA. Tel/fax: (973) 292-9800.
Co-sponsor in Ukraine is PROSVITA.
Preference of nationality: American, Canadian, European native speakers of English.
Qualifications: qualified teachers.
Conditions of employment: voluntary positions. 4 weeks of conversational instruction between May and August. 5 days a week, 4 hours a day. Teachers may be sent to any of the *oblasts* (provinces) to teach beginning, intermediate and advanced conversational English. Students are older adolescents and adults from variety of backgrounds.
Salary: no stipend. Room and board provided in a homestay.
Facilities/Support: books and teaching materials provided. One-day workshop and reunion organised.
Recruitment: $25 non-refundable application fee.
Contact: Oksana Trytjak, Project Co-ordinator.

Other Schools to Try
MONARCH INTERNATIONAL LANGUAGE ACADEMY, 8 Vorovskogo Str, 252000 Kyiv, Ukraine (44-212 0206/fax 44-212 5683). Links with Nord Anglia (listed in introductory section *Finding a Job*).
UKRAINIAN-AMERICAN HUMANITARIAN INSTITUTE, Wisconsin International University – Ukraine, 9 Pyrogov St, 252030 Kyiv, Ukraine (tel/fax 44-216 0666)
UNION FORUM, 10 Ternopilska St, PO Box 10722, 290034 Lviv (tel/fax 322-759488)

Russian Republics

Even some of the most exotic sounding difficult-to-spell ex-USSR republics like Kazakhstan, Azerbaijan and Uzbekistan have developing ELT industries. The spur in some cases has been the influx of businesses connected with the Caspian oil industry, which has particularly affected Kazakhstan and Azerbaijan and to some extent Turkmenistan. In response to the increased demand, the Peace Corps has sent a substantial number of volunteer English teachers to Kazakhstan within the past two years. Already there are some opportunities with international companies for professional ELT teachers where the salaries are on a par with those of the oil-rich states of the Middle East as Richard McGeough, a 28 year old teacher from Britain, explains:

> *My primary motivation for coming to Baku was the salary my post offered, which was £15,000 a year. The students are highly motivated, well-educated and almost embarrassingly hospitable and generous. I'm working in newly modernised premises now, but until recently we had to contend with alternately unheated and unventilated classrooms and regular power cuts in winter. Baku can be too quiet sometimes, although an acquaintance of mine who lived in Ashkhabad, Turkmenistan for two years says that Baku is like Paris compared to there. What Baku lacks in beauty it makes up for in interest. The centre of Baku – the Oil Town and the Old Town – is rustic and charming, and not at all what I'd expected of the old USSR. Having lived in Istanbul before, historical Baku was like a return to the 1950s before ugly modern apartment buildings were put up.*

However, most English teaching is still delivered by the state; for example the list of English Language Institutions sent by the British Council in the Uzbek capital Tashkent comprises only state universities and paedagogical institutes (i.e. teacher training colleges). *i-to-i* (see introductory chapter on Finding a Job) sends paying volunteers to teach in Uzbekistan or Georgia for a fee of £995/$1,795 for up to three months, excluding travel. The Christian voluntary organisation Aid to Russia and the Republics (PO Box 200, Bromley, Kent BR1 1QF; 020-8460 6046/www.ARRC.org.uk) sends a small number of its volunteers to Armenia where some are involved with teaching English to children.

The beginnings of a private EFL industry are evident in Georgia. The Information & Education Officer at the British Council in Tbilisi sent the following addresses in Georgia:
International Language Academy, 17 Chavchavadze Avenue, Tbilisi 380079
International House Tbilisi, 2 Dolidze St, Tbilisi 380015. (This IH school employs only one or two native speakers).
Public Service Language Centre, 8 Rustaveli Avenue, Tbilisi
Nike, English and Computer Teaching Firm, 8 Jambuli St, Tbilisi 380008.

The British Council in Kazakhstan can send a long list of institutes which are likely to offer English language courses and therefore might be interested in employing part-time or full-time teachers of English. Most are state-owned but there is a growing number of private ones. University faculties often have their own international relations office such as *Pavlodar University* (see entry).

EF ENGLISH FIRST
82/23 A. Alekperov Street, Baku 370141, Azerbaijan. E-mail: ef_baku@azadata.net.
Number of teachers: 4 native teachers and 3 locals.
Preference of nationality: UK, North America, Australia, New Zealand.
Qualifications: EFL/ESL Cert. plus university degree.
Conditions of employment: 9-12 month contract (renewable) Schools open from 7.30am-9pm Monday to Saturday. 24 contact hours per week.
Salary: US$850 per month.
Facilities/Support: modern facilities, teacher library, computer laboratory, guidance and support of academic coordinator, excellent opportunities for promotion and transfer to other countries, flights paid for, paid holiday, orientation and ongoing seminars and development. Medical insurance.
Recruitment: applications through English First (EF) teacher recruitment in offices worldwide.

WEBB ACADEMY
148 Vidadi St, 370000 Baku, Azerbaijan. Tel/fax: (12) 973047. Tel: (12) 941345. E-mail: webb@azeuro.net.
Number of teachers: 3-5.
Preference of nationality: British.
Qualifications: minimum CELTA with or without experience.
Conditions of employment: 1 year renewable contracts (Sept-July). To teach mixture of students from high school pupils to professionals and housewives.
Salary: on application.
Facilities/Support: accommodation, flight, meidical insurance, holiday pay and visa are all provided.
Recruitment: direct application or via UK contact: Mrs. Webb, 4 Chesterfield Close, Canford Cliffs, Poole, Dorset BH13 7DL; tel/fax 01202 709516.
Contact: Berenice Webb.

THE BYRON SCHOOL OF TBILISI
No 2, Griboedov Street, Tbilisi, 380008 Georgia. Tel: (32) 93 15 78. Fax: (32) 221965.
Number of Teachers: 2 British, 2 American.
Preference of nationality: British, American.
Qualfications: TEFL qualifications and experience of teaching English and/or cultural aspects.
Conditions of employment: minimum one year contract. 4-20 hours of classes per week. The school is concerned with teaching English language and cultural studies of Britain and the US: history, literature, politics, religion, geography, education, customs, etc. Collaborates with the International Byron Society in the UK.
Salary: from US$10-$15 per hour. Teachers pay income tax and should arrange private health insurance.
Facilities/support: help with finding accommodation to rent. A year's visa comes with the contract.
Recruitment: send CV. Interview usually necessary.
Contact: Professor Ines Merabishvili, Principal.

PAVLODAR STATE UNIVERSITY
Department of Foreign Languages, 64 Lomov Str. 637003 Pavlodar, Kazakhstan. Tel/fax: (3182) 451110. E-mail: rector@psu.pvl.kz.
Also 3-4 vacancies in Department of International Relations, Gorky Str. 102/4, 637003 Pavlodar. Tel: (3182) 454311. Fax: (3182) 326797. E-mail: kan@psu.pvl.kz.
Number of teachers: 1 per academic year.
Qualifications: Masters or doctorate in Philology or 5 years relevant experience.

Conditions of employment: 1 academic year. 17 h.p.w.
Salary: US$100-$150 per month paid in tenge.
Facilities/Support: assistance given in finding accommodation to rent and drawing up tenant's agreement.
Recruitment: direct or via Peace Corps.
Contact: Alexander Kachanov, Chief of International Relations Department.

Slovak Republic

As the poor cousin in the former Czechoslovakia, the republic of the Slovaks has been somewhat neglected not only by tourists but by teachers as well. As one language school director put it:

> *Many teachers are heading for Prague, which is why Slovakia stands aside of the main flow of the teachers. That's a pity as Prague is crowded with British and Americans while there's a lack of the teachers here in Slovakia.*

The density of private language schools in the capital Bratislava and in the other main cities like Banska Bystrika makes an on-the-ground job hunt promising.

Language Link (21 Harrington Road, London SW7 3EU; 020-7225 1065) is affiliated with the *Akadémia Vzdelávania,* the largest semi-private language school in Slovakia (see entry), and actively recruits ELT teachers from the UK. The Caledonian School in Prague (Vltavská 24, 150 00 Prague 5, Czech Republic; tel/fax 2-573 13 650; jobs@caledonianschool.com) recruits for some vacancies in Slovakia. See their entry in the Czech chapter for contact details in the UK and North America.

American ELT teachers can look to the *City University* based in Washington state for placements in Slovak schools. The three campuses of the City University (in Bratislava, Trencin and Poprad) cater mainly to Slovak students of business who receive intensive English language training alongside their business administration studies.

The Slovakian Embassy (www.slovakembassy.co.uk) can send details of how to apply for a Long-term Stay Permit, valid for one year but renewable. It warns that the entire process takes between three and four months. The procedures are similar to those for the Czech Republic, including a requirement that all documents be officially translated, and that the applicant submit a medical certificate, evidence of accommodation, police clearance and so on. A blood test must be carried out within a couple of weeks of arriving as a pre-requisite for a residence permit. Many employers guide their teachers through the process and pay the fee (currently about £100).

As well as the British Council in Bratislava, there are English Teaching Resource Centres in Banska Bystrica and Kosice. The Information Centre Officer (Petra.Hitkova@britishcouncil.sk) can send a list of about 35 schools mostly in Bratislava. The main English language newspaper is the *Slovak Spectator* published every other Thursday. Occasionally the classified column carries an advert of interest to people looking for teaching work. You might also consider advertising your availability to give private tuition. The cost is 200 crowns for up to 20 words plus 23% VAT; contact Krizkova 9, 811 04 Bratislava.

The wages quoted by some schools may seem negligible. But if a monthly salary of £100/$150 sounds low, remember that a beer costs 15 crowns/20p and a restaurant meal is about £2; plus many schools provide free accommodation. The wages are enough to fund an average lifestyle and do the odd spot of travelling. Budapest, Vienna and Prague are all within easy reach. Slovakia also offers good conditions for mountain walking along thousands of miles of hiking routes (up to an altitute of 2,500 metres) and for mountain cycling.

Stephen Mills from England was very positive about his teaching experiences in Slovakia:

I am currently employed as the native speaker at Ivega Learning Center. (Your book didn't mention many jobs in Kosice.) I was told about the job by a friend who was working here at the time. I have quite a few private pupils and there is never a lack of people wanting to learn English here. As my mornings are free, there is always plenty of time. I charge 150-200 crowns an hour. The school has a friendly atmosphere and I get on really well with the Slovak teachers. The owner has been incredibly helpful and efficient with the various bureaucratic procedures and very supportive when I had medical problems.

LIST OF SCHOOLS

AKADEMIA VZDELAVANIA
Gorkého 10, 815 17 Bratislava. Tel/fax: (7) 5441 0040. E-mail: hviscova@aveducation.sk.
Number of teachers: approximately 65 posts in adult education centres and schools throughout Slovakia.
Preference of nationality: mainly British.
Qualifications: CELTA or other TEFL qualification. Energy, enthusiasm and an interest in people required.
Conditions of employment: 1 academic year. Teachers' contracts are for 40 60-minute hours p.w. of which 27 hours p.w. minimum should be spent in school. Teaching adults and children.
Salary: 9,500 crowns per month in first year; 12,200 crowns in second year. (Note these wages are paid in Bratislava; deduct 500 crowns for other towns.)
Facilities/Support: paid accommodation provided in shared flats. Work and residency permits organised and paid for. Academic and pastoral support, monthly staff development days including seminars and workshops; orientation for new teachers. Travel expenses (price of return coach fare from London) paid at end of contract.
Recruitment: via Language Link in London, 21 Harrington Road, London SW7 3EU (020-7225 1065; languagelink@compuserve.com). Interviews take place throughout the year.
Contact: Edita Hviscova (in Bratislava).

BERLITZ SCHOOLS OF LANGUAGES BRATISLAVA
6 Na Vrsku Street, 811 01 Bratislava. Tel: (7) 544 33 796. Fax: (7) 544 33 800. E-mail: info@berlitz.sk. Website: www.berlitz.sk.
Berlitz Austria GMBH,Graben 13, 1010 Vienna (1-512 82 86/fax 1-587 99 25).
Also recruits teachers for Slovakia and Slovenia (see *Austria* chapter).
Number of teachers: 12 native English speakers.
Preference of nationality: none.
Qualifications: pedagogical qualifications and experience or expert knowledge in business helpful. Right personality essential.
Conditions of employment: standard length of full-time contract is one year, but most teachers are part-time. Teachers are required to be available to teach from 7.30am to 9pm, four days per week.
Salary: starting rate 170 crowns per one 45-minute lesson. All deductions for taxes and social security are made in accordance with Slovak law.
Facilities/support: no assistance with accommodation. Visa arranged by school.
Recruitment: advertising in local media and on the Berlitz website. Interviews and trial lesson essential.

BERLITZ LANGUAGE CENTER
Kukucinova 7, 040 01 Kosice. Tel: (95) 670 61 50. Fax: (95) 670 61 54. Website: www.berlitz.com.
Number of teachers: 8-12.
Preference of nationality: must be native English speaker.

Qualifications: minimum BA degree.
Conditions of employment: usually one year, renewable.
Salary: 21,000 crowns less about 6,000 crowns for tax and social security. The school is open from 8am-8.40pm.
Facilities/Support: help with finding accommodation but teacher has to pay rental cost. Help given with obtaining work permit but cost of about US$200 is borne by the teacher.
Recruitment: via Berlitz website or through Berlitz HQ in Germany or the US. Interview essential but can be by telephone.
Contact: Bibiana Popocova, Director.

CITY UNIVERSITY SLOVAKIA
Language Assistance Programs, 919 SW Grady Way, Renton, WA 98055, USA. E-mail: jflaherty@cityu.edu. Website: www.cityu.edu and www.cityu.sk. Bratislava site: Odbojarov 10, 832 32 Bratislava (tel/fax: 7-566 7646. Trencin site: Bezrucova 64, 911 01 Trencin (tel/fax: 831-529337).
Number of teachers: 30 native English speakers.
Preference of nationality: North American but all native speakers considered.
Qualifications: MATESL or equivalent preferred plus 6 months teaching experience and ability to teach all levels and skill areas. Minimum qualification is BA plus TEFL certification and international living experience.
Conditions of employment: 9 month contracts from mid-September to mid-June. Full-time timetable equivalent to 20 h.p.w. in the classroom plus 4 hours scheduled office hours.
Salary: from US$325 per month plus housing provided and airfares.
Facilities/Support: housing provided (on or off campus) and also medical/dental insurance. Orientation session for all instructors held at beginning of school year. Large English-language library.
Recruitment: hiring begins in spring through Human Resources Department, City University, 335 116th Ave SE, Bellevue, WA 98004 (425-637-1010 ext 4011 or 3973/fax 425-637-9689/e-mail: sanderson@cityu.edu).

ENGLISH LEARNING CENTRE
Slovenskeho 18, 040 01 Kosice. Tel/fax: (95) 644 1701. E-mail: elc@dodo.sk.
Number of teachers: 2-3.
Preference of nationality: British.
Qualifications: TEFL experience or as lector.
Conditions of employment: 1 year contracts, renewable. 6 hours a day.
Salary: 13,000-15,000 koruna per month.
Facilities/Support: assistance with accommodation and work permits, insurance and taxes.
Recruitment: via advertisements. Interviews in UK or locally.
Contact: Dr. Silvia Kalaposova, Director.

EUROTREND 21
Starohorská 2, 813 32 Bratislava. Tel/fax: (7) 524 94 350. E-mail: eurotrend21@isnet.sk
Number of teachers: 3.
Preference of nationality: none, as long as they speak grammatically correct English. No assistance given with work permits.
Conditions of employment: 12 month contracts. Daytime teaching hours.
Salary: US$4-$7 per hour (gross), depending on experience and results.
Facilities/Support: advice can be given on finding accommodation. No training.
Recruitment: personal interviews only.
Contact: Magda Nagyová, Managing Director.

IVEGA LEARNING CENTER,
Moldarvská 8, 040 01 Kosice. Tel: (95) 64 278 64/714 943. Fax: (95) 717 970.

Number of teachers: 1-2.
Preference of nationality: none.
Qualifications: preferably qualified teacher with previous experience. Students of ESL for summer courses.
Conditions of employment: 1 year. Mostly evening classes 2pm-8pm.
Salary: equivalent to £60 per week. Less 15% tax and 12% medical and social insurance.
Facilities/Support: advice given on finding accommodation. Full help given with obtaining work permit; process should be started 3-4 months in advance.
Recruitment: personal contacts. Interviews not essential but useful.
Contact: Gabriela Troskóova, Manager.

SALMIA AGENCY
Karloveská 64, Bratislava. Tel/fax: (7) 65422 744. Website: www.salmia.sk.
Number of teachers: 2.
Preference of nationality: British.
Qualifications: minimum 2 years experience of TEFL.
Conditions of employment: 1 year. Teaching hours in afternoons and evenings.
Salary: according to qualifications. 15% deductions.
Facilities/Support: no assistance given with work permits.
Recruitment: newspaper, magazine and internet advertising.
Contact: Mr. Kollarovits, Director.

S-CLUB
Vojenska 30, 934 01 Levice. Tel: (813) 6314378. Fax: (813) 6314378. E-mail: sclub@ba.telecom.sk.
Number of teachers: 1.
Preference of nationality: British, Irish.
Qualifications: TEFL/TESOL and some experience.
Conditions of employment: academic year (September to the end of June). 25 teaching units of 45 minutes per week in the afternoons.
Salary: 100 crowns (net) per lesson.
Facilities/Support: a furnished flat is provided free by the school. Assistance with obtaining work permit. Translations provided for the teacher to apply for the permit at the Slovak embassy in their own country. Permit costs in Slovakia paid by the school.
Recruitment: via the internet, co-operation with the University of Limerick. Telephone interviews.
Contact: Matej Hasko, Director.

SLOVPRO LANGUAGE INSTITUTE
Stromova 13 83101 Bratislava and also at Robojnicka 6, 97400 Bystrica. Tel: (7) 59 79 1391 or (905) 716 776. Fax: (7) 54 79 1394. E-mail: slovpro@slovpro.sk and armillersk@hotmail.com. Website: www.slovpro.sk.
Number of teachers: 15-20.
Preference of nationality: none, but must be native speaker.
Qualifications: training in TEFL or EFL/ESL Certification.
Conditions of employment: 1 year.
Salary: 140-250 crowns per academic hour, the rate being dependent on education, experience, and the region.
Facilities/Support: assistance to locate accommodation, and in some cases Slovpro subsidises the rent.
Recruitment: via the internet, advertising in newspapers and personal recommendation.
Contact: Andrew Miller, Country Director.

VAGES
Hodzova 25, 94901 Nitra. Tel: (87) 6524098. E-mail: vages@mailviapvt.sk.
Number of teachers: 2.

Preference of nationality: British, American.
Qualifications: TEFL or university students preparing for a career in TEFL.
Conditions of employment: one year (renewable). 20 lessons per week.
Salary: 8,000 crowns per month (approx. £100) less tax of 1,000 crowns. This is the university salary for a beginner teacher.
Facilities/Support: room provided and rent is paid by the school. School also has a flat that can be used by teachers for free.
Recruitment: through the local university, personal contacts and through sister city programme in the USA.
Contact: Elena Vargicova, Head Teacher/Owner.

Other Schools to Try

Note that these schools (in alphabetical order according to town) did not confirm their teacher requirements for this edition of *Teaching English Abroad*.
Albion English School, Skuteckého 8, 974 00 Banska Bystrica (tel 88-415 45 95/albion@gtinet.sk)
English Teaching Centre, Skuteckeho 11, 974 00 Banska Bystrica
Lite, Anglická skola, Partizánska cesta 3m 974 01 Banská Bystrica
*RK CENTRUM UNIVERSA, Horná 65, 974 01 Banska Bystrica (88-414 7007/fax 88-414 2740). 3 teachers from UK, US or Canada. £200 a month.

Enlap, Obchodná 46, 811 06 Bratislava (enlap@mbox.bts.sk)
Eurolingua Jazykova Skola, Drienova 16, 821 03 Bratislava
Europe House, Jazyková skola, Mikovínho 1, 831 02 Bratislava (7-4425 1171)
Jazykova Skola MTD, Metodova 2, 821 08 Bratislava (Jamrichova@gmet.schools.sk)
Lang Slovakia, Safarikove namestie 7, Bratislava (lang@mail.eurotel.sk)
Lengua Agency Jazykova Skola, Galbaveho 3, 841 01 Bratislava
Perspektiva, Ursulinska 11, 812 93 Bratislava
Pro Sympatia, Centrum Studia Cudzich Jaykov, Pribnova 23, 810 93 Bratislava
Top School of Languages Pistek, Galandova 2, 811 06 Bratislava

Bakschool, Independent Language School, Postova 1, 040 01 Kosice
Effective Language Centre, Biela 3, 040 01 Kosice
E-KU, Jazyková skola, Piaristicka 25, 949 01 Nitra (87-25545)
Vzdelavacia nadacia ASPEKT, Akademicka 4, 949 01 Nitra
Lingua Jazykova Skola, Zahradnick 2, 931 01 Samorin
Mestske Kulturne Stredisko, Nam slobody 11, 909 01 Skalica
London House, Krusovska 2093, 955 01 Topolcany
BEA English Studio, Anglicka Jazykova Skola, Hlavna 17, 970 01 Trnava

MIDDLE EAST

Oil wealth has meant that many of the countries of the Middle East have long been able to afford to attract the best teachers with superior qualifications and extensive experience. Most employers can afford to hire only professionals and there are few opportunities for newcomers to the profession.

The main exception is Turkey where thousands of native speaker teachers find work. Despite its adherence to Islam, Turkey does not fit comfortably into a chapter on the Middle East. Despite its aspirations to join the European Union, neither does it fit logically into a section on Western Europe. But whatever its geographical classification, Turkey is a very important country for EFL teachers, whatever their background, and is treated at length later in this chapter.

On the one hand, the wealthy countries of Saudi Arabia, Bahrain, Oman and the Gulf states generally employ teachers with top qualifications. On the other hand, countries like Syria and Jordan may have more casual opportunities. There is growing interest in learning English among the Palestinians scattered throughout the Arab World, and native speaker teachers in this context are likely to be working on a voluntary basis rather than for expatriate salaries.

As Lebanon surges forward in a frenzy of reconstruction after its tragic 17-year civil war, the demand for English is increasing (see section below). Some countries are still off-bounds, namely Iraq, but the recent thawing of relations between Tehran and London may mean that opportunities might arise in Iran in the coming years. As Joe Hancock from North Wales reported from the town of Bojnurd in northeastern Iran, there is no shortage of demand for English in this country which is full of 'friendly, helpful and respectful people':

> I called in at the local English school to ask if I could assist with conversational English and was immediately asked if I could take a 40-hour English course starting tomorrow. After that they wondered if I could go to Tehran to teach, as they require five expat teachers there. Qualifications were mentioned but not dwelt on. I couldn't accept since my work permit is with the petrochemical company I work for. As a courtesy I asked my employer if I could teach in my spare time (four hours a week) but they forbade it saying that once the school advertised that they had an English native teacher, they would have queues around the block.

Teachers who sign contracts in a strict Islamic country should be aware of what they are letting themselves in for. People spend a year or two of their lives in Saudi Arabia for the money not for the fun (certainly) nor for the experience (unless they are students of Arab culture). When the amount of money accumulating back home is the principal or only motivation, morale can degenerate. The situation can be especially discouraging for women.

Yet not everyone is gasping to get home (or even to Bahrain) to freely available alcohol, etc. A surprisingly high percentage of teachers are recruited locally from a stable expatriate community.

FIXING UP A JOB

Unless you are more or less resident in the Middle East, it is essential in most cases to fix up a job in advance. Casual teaching is not a possibility in most countries for a number of reasons, including the difficulty of getting tourist visas, the prohibitively high cost of staying without working and the whole tradition of hiring teachers. There are a few countries which can be entered on a tourist visa (i.e. Qatar, Yemen and the United Arab Emirates) if you want to inspect potential employers, but this would be an expensive exercise. Visa difficulties vary from country to country. In Jordan, for example, schools which would like to hire foreign teachers claim to be unable to do so due to work permit restrictions.

Single women, no matter how highly qualified, are at a serious disadvantage when pursuing high-paying jobs in Saudi Arabia and other strict Islamic countries. The majority of adverts specify 'single status male' or, at best, 'teaching couples'. Another requirement often mentioned in job details which excludes many candidates is experience of the Middle East, in acknowledgment of the culture shock which many foreigners encounter in adapting to life under Islam.

Job adverts regularly appear in the *TES, Guardian, TESOL Placement Bulletin* and *International Employment Gazette*. The largest display ads in the British education press are quite often for Middle East vacancies, many placed by recruitment agencies on behalf of high-spending Saudi clients.

The British Council has Teaching Centres in Bahrain (Manama), Israel (Tel Aviv, West Jerusalem and Nazareth), Oman (Muscat and Salalah), Saudi Arabia (Riyadh, Jeddah and Dammam), Damascus in Syria and the West Bank & Gaza (East Jerusalem). *ELS Language Centers/Middle East* has 11 Centres in the region: Al Ain, Dubai and Abu Dhabi (UAE), two centres in Jeddah (one for men, one for women) plus one in Dammam in Saudi Arabia, Doha (Qatar), Muscat (Oman) and Salmiya (Kuwait), with plans to open a centre in Lebanon soon and in the future to expand into Syria, Jordan and Turkey. These centres employ 20 full-time teachers and many part-time teachers to teach American English (see entry). Possible leads may be available from Amideast, 1730 M St NW, No 1100, Washington, DC 20036 (fax 202-776-7090; mdidon@amideast.org) which recruits for international schools in the region.

There are also American Language Centers in Amman, Damascus and Sana'a. Surprisingly, there isn't a single International House school in the entire region. It is worth writing to the Embassies (particularly of Saudi Arabia and Oman) who occasionally recruit directly on behalf of their Ministries of Education or Defense. The Saudi Embassy in London (30 Charles St, London W1X 7PM) occasionally advertises for teachers with high academic qualifications, as does the Saudi Arabian Defence Office (22 Holland Park, London W11 3TD).

If trying to fix up employment directly with a company in the Middle East, try to be sure that you have a water-tight contract. Even with many years of experience of the region, Peter Feltham experienced difficulties:

> *I am an Arabist and have worked in Bahrain, Oman, Saudi Arabia and Egypt on a 'creative job-search' basis, sometimes with extreme success but mostly with disastrous consequences. For example, in Bahrain, I found that about two-thirds or three-quarters of all job offers had not been thought through, and were bogus. I spent between £1,000 and £2,000 in air fares following up bogus job offers and came to the conclusion that this was partly due to the lack of moral implications of failing to tell the truth within Islam.*

Predictably, there is not a great deal of input by the voluntary agencies. However the Peace Corps sends a number of English teachers to civil service oriented language schools as well as secondary schools and universities, particularly in Yemen.

Recruitment Agencies

In theory, being hired by an established recruitment agency in your own country should offer some protection against the problems described in the quotation above. However this is not always the case. A couple of years ago an educational consultancy with an office in Toronto recruited a large number of EFL teachers to work for the United Arab Emirates military. When a dispute arose between client and recruiter, the teachers were the ones to suffer since they weren't paid promised salaries and their contracts were not honoured.

Here is a short list of agencies, organisations and corporations which have recently been seen advertising (mostly high level) EFL vacancies in the Middle East:

C.C.L. Recruitment International, 298 High St, Dovercourt, Harwich, Essex CO12 3PJ. Tel: 01255 506001. Fax: 01255 506002. E-mail: ccl.recruit@btinternet.com.
Delton Personnel Ltd. Ribblesdale House, 4 Ribblesdale Place, Preston, Lancs. PR1 3NA. E-mail: delton@provider.co.uk. Recent adverts for English language instructors to Abu Dhabi with BA in English and at least 6 years' experience.
QTS, Quality Services for Teachers and Schools, Churchill House, 27 Otley Old Road, Leeds LS16 6HB. Tel: 0113-230 1141. Fax: 0870 056 1164. E-mail: director@qts-worldwide.com. Website: www.qts-worldwide.com. Teacher recruitment worldwide. Qualified teachers with UK experience should send a CV and full details to register on the QTS database. British trained infant, junior and secondary teachers for Middle East schools.
ROBACO, 8 Nesburn Road, Barnes, Wearside SR4 7LR. Tel: 07712 579775. E-mail: rb@robaco.net & admin@robaco.net. Website: www.robaco.net. Recruit for posts abroad, including the Middle East.

LEISURE TIME

The majority of teachers live in foreigners' compounds provided by their employers. Most of these are well provided with sports facilities like tennis courts and swimming pools. In some locations, such as Jubail in Saudi Arabia, water sports are a popular diversion. Some have described expat life in the Middle East as a false paradise.

The principal pastimes are barbecues, reading out-of-date copies of the *International Herald Tribune,* playing with computers (which are cheaply available) and complaining about the terrific heat and the lack of alcohol. (Saudi Arabia and Kuwait are completely dry states.) Others of course try to learn some Arabic and make local friends, always taking care not to offend against Islam. The constraints of living under Islam are well known. For example in some countries anyone found drinking or smoking in a public place during the month of Ramadan could face a jail sentence, large fine and/or deportation.

Contracts often include two or even three free leave tickets per year, which need not be to your home. (Apparently Bangkok is a popular destination for expats seeking R & R.) This is therefore a good chance to see the world at your employer's expense.

BAHRAIN

Bahrain is among the most liberal of the oil states, and one which attracts foreigners, including women because of its tolerance of women in the workplace. The *British Council* will send a list of language schools and may be of assistance in referring a TEFL-qualified teacher to private clients, whether companies, individuals or secretarial colleges. Unlike in Saudi Arabia, it is possible to teach mixed classes of men and women.

ISRAEL/PALESTINIAN GOVERNED AREAS

Because of the large number of English-speaking Jews who have settled in Israel from the US, South Africa, etc. many native speakers of English are employed in the state education system and there is no active recruitment of foreign teachers. There are a number of private language schools for example Wall Street Institute in Tel Aviv (Azrieli Centre No 7, PO Box 150, 67027 Tel Aviv; 3-693 2266/adis@wsi.co.il). Even an Israeli, Shahin Sarsour, who had earned a TEFL Certificate from Transworld Teachers in San Francisco, could not find a job as an English teacher. One might have expected some volunteers on kibbutzim to be involved in teaching English to Hebrew-speaking kibbutzniks, but in fact this does not seem to happen.

The British Council maintains a large presence in Israel and has Teaching

Centres in Tel Aviv, Jerusalem and Nazareth, which recruit qualified EFL teachers mainly from the local English-speaking population. Connect Youth International at the British Council (10 Spring Gardens, London SW1A 2BN; 020-7389 4030/ www.britcoun.org/education/connectyouth) sends young volunteers from England to teach English to teenagers at summer language clubs in northern Israel (as well as Jordan and Macedonia). Volunteers work for five hours in the morning for at least two weeks in July/August. Food, accommodation, insurance are all provided and airfares are subsidised. The deadline for applications is mid-March.

The outbreak of violence in autumn 2000 has put the Peace Process under intolerable pressure and may presage the return of the Intifada which preceded the granting of self-rule to Palestinians on the West Bank. If hostilities continue, it is unlikely that there will be many teaching opportunities in the Palestinian-governed Territories. As well as its own teaching centre in East Jerusalem in the Al-Nuzha Building, 2 Abu Obeida Street (PO Box 19136), the British Council has offices in Gaza City (14-706 Al-Nasra Street, Al-Rimal; PO Box 355), in Hebron (Ein Sarah Street; PO Box 277) and in Nablus (Harwash Building, Rafidia Main Street; PO Box 497).

The charity UNIPAL (Universities' Trust for Educational Exchange with Palestinians), BCM UNIPAL, London WC1N 3XX (tel/fax: 020-7771 7368/ www.unipal.org.uk) operates an educational and cultural exchange with Palestinian communities in the West Bank, Gaza and Lebanon. Volunteers teach children aged 12-15 in the refugee camps mid-July to mid-August. Volunteers must be native English-speakers, based in the UK and at least 20 years old. The approximate cost of the programme is £380. Closing date for applications is the end of February. Written enquiries are preferred.

KUWAIT

Prior to Iraq's invasion of Kuwait there were up to 1,000 English teachers in Kuwait (though most of them were out of the country at the time of the invasion, since it was the summer vacation). Efforts have been made to revive all the operations (many of them managed by expats rather than Kuwaitis), but the overall numbers have diminished, partly because the big money days are over.

Educational standards are variable, as encountered by B. P. Rawlins in Kuwait:

> *There are simply too many schools in Kuwait acting like pigs at a trough, all of them out there for the money. They dare not criticise any anti-social behaviour by pupils, parents or adult students for fear of losing fees in a competitive market. Professionalism is viewed with hostile suspicion in some quarters.*

This negative view is not subscribed to by all who have spent time in the region. Many agree that English learners in Kuwait, as throughout the Arab world, can be a pleasure to teach because they are so eager to communicate, and so unhesitant to speak English in class.

As well as keeping an up-to-date list of the many international and English medium schools in Kuwait, the British Council (P.O.B. 345, Safat 13109; e-mail MaryScrimgeour@kw.britishcouncil.org) employs teachers year round and for July/August summer courses.

LEBANON

As mentioned earlier, Lebanon is struggling valiantly to recover from its long and painful war, and is looking to a prosperous future in which English will overtake French in popularity, much to the chagrin of the French who are pouring in vast resources to prop up their language and the archaic Lebanese baccalaureate, still compulsory in schools. English is gaining ground due to its status as the international language of business and to a strong tradition of Lebanese emigration to the United States and Australia. The British Council in Beirut is increasingly active and is worth contacting for teaching opportunities. One Beirut language centre seen advertising for native English speakers in 2000 gave only an e-mail address: allcs@inco.com.lb.

Increasingly it will be worthwhile investigating possibilities in this tiny but fascinating country. While accompanying her husband on a short-term contract in Lebanon, Anne Cleaver (an early-retired teacher) easily found work (albeit voluntary) at a new Special Needs Centre just outside Beirut:

> *Even during my short period there, I was tentatively offered a full-time post at a neighbouring school and even an opening in Abu Dhabi. There is a real eagerness to learn English in Lebanon. I found Lebanese educationalists, parents and children most welcoming and enthusiastic. Being a British teacher there made me feel more valued, I regret to say, than back in the UK.*

OMAN

Since the 1970s Oman has had to import the majority of its skilled labour including teachers. Teachers of English are employed from Sudan, Sri Lanka, India and North Africa and many of the private language schools are run by Indian ex-pats. Therefore 'native-speaker' teachers from the west have never really had much of a look in. Some positions do become available each year with the British Council in Muscat but the major employers of western teachers are employed by the Ministry of Higher Education, Sultan Qaboos University and *CfBT*.

Despite a fast-expanding EFL market, there's no room at all for visiting jobseekers, since a tight hold is kept on tourist visas. It is essential these days to have an MA in TESOL or Applied Linguistics (or at least be enrolled in a distance learning ELT Master's degree) with at least three years of experience, preferably at university level. The main recruiting season begins in March just prior to the Al-Ain TESOL Arabia conference. Exactly why an MA in TESOL should be necessary is not very clear, at least not to Sandeha Lynch who has just finished a contract there and who has provided some of the information in this section. His wry description of students in higher education could apply equally to students throughout the Middle East:

> *Unfortunately there is a widespread idea that experts in linguistics and the like have what it takes to teach English. It can come as a bit of a shock, therefore, for teachers who have studied phonics, syllabus design, methodology and socio-linguistics to discover that they are teaching 'Headway Elementary' units 1 to 5 to groups of up to 40 students per class. Not exactly what the MA prepares you for. It may also be a bit of a shock to discover that with the same qualifications a teacher can usually earn about 20% more in the UAE, have a greater range of colleges and institutes from which to choose, and even have a social life.*
>
> *One could say that the school-leavers who come to the colleges and higher institutes are ill-prepared. Certainly the school-leaving grades for English don't seem to reflect the true level of the students. Although things are gradually changing and entry to the colleges is becoming more rigorous, the teacher still has to get around the idea that these students have had English at school three hours a week for nine years (900 hours of English?) and still can't distinguish 'he' from 'you' or 'did' from 'do'. Teachers raised on communicative or task-based teaching methodology tend to have a rough time in their first few months as they adapt to the quasi-Victorian teaching style of talk and chalk that the students demand. Somewhat short on personal initiative and motivation, the students believe that each of them has a personal relationship with the teacher, and that in the classroom they have the right to direct and exclusive contact. This goes some way towards explaining why 40 students can all shout out the same question within a 5-minute period and why the teacher is expected to explain the point to each of*

them one at a time. This lack of team-playing does not extend to exams, however, when innumerable devices and intrigues are developed so that the students can help each other.

This is not life in the fast lane of academic endeavour but something of an academic lay-by. If you choose to work in one of the colleges of higher education, you may find that the concept of rigorous academic standards is imperfectly understood, and therefore rarely applied. This will change in the future but, for the moment, teachers and students can relax at weekends safe in the knowledge that low exam marks can always be raised by the administration.

The British Council in Muscat does not maintain a list of English language institutes in Oman but can send a copy of the relevant *Yellow Pages*. The main English teaching centres in addition to *Polyglot* in the Directory are:

Capital Institute, PO Box 936, Ruwi 112 (709336/fax 701070)

College of Administrative Sciences, PO Box 710, Ruwi 112 (751572/fax 751570). Intensive English courses for students at this private college of higher education.

Al-Ghosnain Training Institute, PO Box 1016, Ruwi 114, Oman (601102/fax 605521/ www.weboman.com/ghosnain)

Another possibility is to write to the government of Oman before departure. Sometimes the Military Attaché's Office at the Oman Embassy (64 Ennismore Gardens, London SW7 1NH) can prove helpful. Try also Educational Services Overseas Ltd. (PO Box 2398, Ruwi, Postal Code 112, Sultanate of Oman; fax: 565573) who occasionally advertise for male English language trainers with a PGCE in TEFL or a Cambridge DELTA to teach in the interior of Oman on behalf of the Ministry of Education.

CfBT Education Services LLC, Oman, supplies expertise in Education and Training for various public and private sector clients including the Ministry of Education, the Ministry of Higher Education and Petroleum Development Oman (PDO). With about 20 years in-country, CfBT LLC maintains a project office in Muscat and will be expanding operations to the Gulf Region. Further details are available on their website (www.cfbtoman.com).

Despite Sandeha Lynch's reservations about the job, he clearly enjoyed Oman which he describes as the best place to be in all Arabia, both summer and winter:

Oman is a great place for camping in the desert, picnicking in the mountain valleys or just haring around in a 4WD. The countryside and coasts are stunning and if you can handle the heat and at time the humidity, mountain walking and diving are popular leisure activities. Just try not to get bored with these activities. There are no others, unless you happen to live near Muscat where you can indulge in wandering around glossy shopping malls, watching Hindi movies and eating sushi.

SAUDI ARABIA

The decline in oil prices during the past couple of decades means that fabulously high salaries are no longer earned by EFL teachers in the Kingdom of Saudi Arabia. But expatriate packages are still very attractive, with substantial salaries, free airfares and accommodation plus generous holidays and other perks.

Teaching in a naval academy or petrochemical company while living in a teetotal expatriate ghetto is not many people's idea of fun, especially after a request for an exit visa has been denied. The rare woman who gets a job as a teacher (at a women's college) may live to regret it when she finds that she is prohibited by law from driving a car and must not appear in public without being covered from head to foot.

A sprinkling of companies advertise in the educational press, including Arabian Careers Ltd., Berkeley Square House, 7th Floor, Berkeley Square, London W1X 5LB (020-7495 3285/fax 020-7355 2562; recruiter@arabiancareers.com). They recruit teachers for military personnel and hospital staff. Candidates must normally be single males with PGCE plus TEFL certificate and four years full-time experience.

Note that candidates interested in teaching at the ELC Center in Riyadh should apply not to the Middle East office in Abu Dhabi (see *List of Schools* below) but directly to Susan Matson, Director of Field Operations at ELS's International Division in the US: 400 Alexander Park, Princeton NJ 08540 (609-750 3512/ smatson@els.com).

US-based recruiters are most likely to advertise in the *TESOL Placement Bulletin* or other specialist press. The Hassan A. K. Algahtani Sons Co. of Saudi Arabia (PO Box 195, Al-Khobar 31952) has a US representative based in California: Cheryl Ryan, 6363 Christie Avenue, Suite 2617, Emeryville, CA 94608 (tel/fax 510-655 8295; cryan@saudijobs.com/ www.saudijobs.com).

Professional teachers tempted by the money should bear in mind the drawbacks, as Philip Dray did:

> *I decided against Saudi Arabia. The money was most appealing, but I couldn't think myself into a situation where there was no nightlife, limited contact with women and no culture or history. A year may seem short when you say it fast, but you could get very depressed in a situation like that. Money is nearly everthing but it can't buy you peace of mind. So I opted for a job at a school for boys in the U.A.E. which, from the description, sounds sociable, inviting and accessible.*

After Philip's arrival at the Oasis Residence in Dubai, he was well pleased with his decision, since living conditions in his luxury apartment complex complete with pool, steam room, squash court and gym, were just as lavish as he would have been given in Saudi. High salaries can also be earned in the United Arab Emirates.

Caution must be exercised when considering job offers from the Kingdom of Saudi Arabia. We have heard from several American teachers who have been badly burned by a Saudi employer. Carl Hart, writing from Dammam, cautions against 'unscrupulous bait and switch recruiters' who promise fabulous salaries and benefits knowing full well that when you arrive in the country, the salary and benefits will be significantly less than expected:

> *You'll grudgingly accept the job anyway, thus earning the recruiter his commission. Don't even think of leaving for the Kingdom unless you have an iron clad contract signed by all parties involved, clearly stating the exact salary and benefits you are to receive and when you will receive them. But even a signed contract guarantees nothing. Virtually everything I was promised by the American who recruited me in the US and is incorporated into my contract with a government ministry was a lie. My salary is 6,500 riyals instead of the promised 9,600 riyals. My summer vacation is 45 days instead of 60, and a promised two-week salary settlement allowance and Chicago-Washington airfare reimbursement have not and will never be given. Be aware that work experience is based upon the number of full years of experience after you receive your highest degree (partial years count for nothing).*
>
> *One more caution: the wheels of Saudi bureaucracy turn verrrry slowly, so absolutely do not quit your present job until you have a contract signed by them. I naïvely believed the recruiter when he told me that my wife and I would be in Saudi Arabia 'within three weeks'. Four and a half months later we were still waiting, unemployed and sleeping on the floor of our empty apartment, an experience which sorely tested my sanity and plunged us deep into debt. Nevertheless I'm glad I came. Saudi may not offer the cultural thrill of some other nations, but accommodation and working conditions are excellent and it's a clean modern country, far safer than my old neighbourhood in Chicago. If you can live without beer and ham sandwiches*

for a while, it's a great place to save money and work on your magnum opus.
Despite his reservations, Carl decided to stay on and after two years landed a much
better job with a foreign-owned rather than a Saudi company which prompted him
to write in a far more positive vein:

> *Saudi Arabia is modern and cosmopolitan and not at all the oppressive sun-
> baked hotbed of religious fanaticism that some imagine. The overwhelming
> majority of people here are amazingly normal and not at all rabidly anti-
> Western. There are jobs with good salaries here – some upwards of $47,000
> a year. The important variables are location (will you be in a major city or a
> military base in the middle of the desert?), housing (will it be a spacious
> home in a Club Med-like compound or three guys in a trailer?) and vacation
> (from as little as three weeks a year to as much as three months a year).*

Morris Jensen working for *Elite Training Services* is another teacher who points
to the good things about Saudi Arabia including the hospitality, ease of finding
lucrative private work, excellent sports facilities, shopping and accessibility of
places of interest in the Middle East. He also acknowledges the problems, such as
the religious and cultural clashes which arise in the classroom and the frustrating
bureaucracy. Among the documents required for a work permit are a medical
certificate notarised by the Foreign and Commonwealth Office in London, an
authorisation from the Saudi Ministry of Foreign Affairs, copies of diplomas, a
contract of employment and accompanying letter from the sponsoring company. The
fee of 50 riyals payable before leaving your home country is only the beginning.
Your passport is held by your sponsoring employer while you carry around an
official copy as identification, at least until you are issued with an *iqama* (resident
visa). Every time you want to leave the country you must request an exit and re-entry
visa which is given at the discretion of your employer. Some foreign workers have
reported having to pay more than £130 for an exit visa.

SYRIA

The opportunities in neighbouring Syria are expanding and improving. The
Education Adviser at the small British Council office in Damascus is willing to
advise individual enquirers and has a list of half a dozen ELT institutions in Syria.
The British Council cautions that:

> *Teachers wishing to teach here should make sure of their positions before
> arrival. They should obtain sponsorship from the prospective employer for
> residence purposes and have an agreed written contract.*

There's an enthusiastic demand for private tuition, though Syria is a poor country
and only a small proportion of the population can afford it. The *American Language
Center* in Damascus (see entry) employs about 40 native speakers for a minimum of
three months in its programme of American English courses for adults. Anyone with
a TEFL background has a good chance of getting some part-time hours.
Occasionally they run their own training programme for EFL teachers. They may
also know of individuals who want private tutoring in English.

To enter Syria, you should have an entrance visa from the Syrian Embassy in
your country, and you must also obtain an exit visa every time you leave. (The
journey from Damascus to Beirut takes four hours and costs less than $10.) If you
do teach for one of the schools, it is normally possible to obtain a resident visa after
arrival, which entitles you to stay in hotels at local prices (one quarter of the tourist
price in some cases).

YEMEN

Many people consider Yemen to be the most beautiful and interesting of all Middle
Eastern states. Mary Hall worked for an aid agency there and became familiar with

the teaching scene:

There are more and more places teaching English here, the two main ones being YALI (Yemen American Language Institute) and the British Council, both of whom recruit mostly qualified teachers from England or the US. The others hire any old bod who turns up, not many of whom are qualified TEFL teachers. Unfortunately they don't pay very well. If there is a Yemeni boss, the wages are even less and often not regularly forthcoming. I had a lodger who was teaching at one place for a pittance as the boss took money out of her wages to pay for her lodgings, even after she moved in with me. I think she was getting a couple of dollars an hour. This is something you sort of get used to. It can be very cheap living here, with rent about $50 a month or less if you're not fussy. You can get a three month visa if you pay and are HIV-negative.

Travel restrictions have been imposed in response to the spate of foreigner-kidnappings; in 1998 11 people were abducted in four months, including a British Council English teacher and his family.

LIST OF SCHOOLS

ELS LANGUAGE CENTERS – MIDDLE EAST
PO Box 3079, Abu Dhabi, United Arab Emirates. Tel: (2) 665-1516. Fax: (2) 665-3165. E-mail: elsme@emirates.net.ae. Website: www.els.com.
Number of teachers: 20 full-time plus many part-time in 11 centres throughout the Middle East.
Preference of nationality: American and Canadian, though other nationalities are sometimes accepted.
Qualifications: MA in TEFL/TESL and 2 years' experience preferred. Minimum Cambridge/ELS Language Centers TEFL Certificate with 3 years' experience.
Conditions of employment: 1 or 2 year contracts. 30 contact h.p.w. plus 15 administrative h.p.w. for full-time teachers.
Salary: varies according to qualifications, experience and location, e.g. range in Al Ain (UAE) is US$21,0000-$24,000 per year tax free plus benefits such as housing, airfares and medical insurance.
Facilities/Support: furnished accommodation provided, though teachers may choose to find their own within their housing allowance. Work and residency permits arranged in all countries, usually involving a medical examination and blood test and a notarised and attested copy of the teacher's degree and qualifications. Standard orientation for all new teachers and monthly workshops.
Recruitment: through TESOL USA and TESOL Arabia, and also via the internet. Telephone interviews sometimes sufficient. Face-to-face interviews arranged at annual TESOL clearinghouse in North America.
Contact: Marcia Lewis, Director of Education.

Bahrain

BRITISH COUNCIL – BAHRAIN
Sheikh Salman Highway, PO Box 452, Manama, Bahrain. Tel: 261555. Fax: 258689. E-mail: Amanda.Burrell@britishcouncil.org.bh.
Number of teachers: 11.
Preference of nationality: British.
Qualifications: minimum DELTA or equivalent plus 2 years' overseas EFL experience.
Conditions of employment: 2 year contracts. 36 h.p.w. (24 contact hours). Saturday to Wednesday. Most teaching between 3pm and 9pm.
Salary: 600 dinars per month (net) plus 20 dinars travel allowance.
Facilities/Support: accommodation arranged for 350 dinars plus medical insurance.

Recruitment: via British Council Recruitment Unit in London.
Contact: Amanda Burrell, Director.

CAMBRIDGE INSTITUTE OF BAHRAIN
PO Box 24334, Muharraq, Bahrain. Tel: 962 2212. Fax: 530227. E-mail: ajamsheer@hotmail.com.
Preference of nationality: none.
Qualifications: must be male. BA in English language or humanities plus CELTA or TEFL qualification. 4 years of experience preferred.
Conditions of employment: to teach military and civil adults using Headway books. 1 or 2 year contract. Hours 7am-2pm with a chance to work overtime in the afternoons.
Salary: US$1,200 per month tax free ($1,350 in second year). Overtime paid at $15 an hour.
Facilities/Support: free accommodation in shared furnished flat (or $200 housing allowance per month in lieu), travel expenses including ticket flights to Bahrain and return ticket at mid-term, free medicare.
Recruitment: via internet (TEFL Professional Network).
Contact: Mr. Abdul Aziz Jamsheer.

Iran

AYANDEHSAZAN ENGLISH LANGUAGE CENTRE
P.O. Box 13145/1668, Teheran, Iran. E-mail: info@ayandehsazan.com. Website: www.Ayandehsazan.com.
Number of teachers: 2.
Preference of nationality: British.
Qualifications: BA and MA in English (if non-native speaker) otherwise degree and teaching experience essential.
Conditions of employment: usually one year contract.
Salary: depends on supervisor's report and ability.
Facilities/Support: every effort will be made to provide teachers' accommodation. Assistance given with work permits.
Recruitment: written test, interview and test lesson. Interviews possibly in the UK or USA.
Contact: Ghasem Abbasi, Director of the Board.

Jordan

LONDON EDUCATIONAL CENTRE
PO Box 850272, Amman 11185, Jordan. Tel/fax: (6) 585 4466. Fax: (6) 585 4477.
Number of teachers: 8 in total.
Preference of nationality: none.
Qualifications: TEFL Certificate.
Conditions of employment: 1-year renewable contract. 25 contact h.p.w. plus 5 hours at Centre preparing lessons. Specialise in teaching for business.
Salary: 500 Jordanian dinars (US$700) per month. Additional hours paid at JD 7 ($10) an hour.
Facilities/Support: assistance in locating accommodation; rent will be about JD 150. Emergency insurance provided. Paid holidays and 21 days paid vacation.
Recruitment: via internet (e.g. eslworldwide.com).
Contact: Mr. Darwish Najia, Managing Director.

YARMOUK CULTURAL CENTER
Gardens Street, Amman (next to Middle East Hotel). Tel: (6) 5521447. Fax: (6) 5622857. E-mail: yarmouk4books@hotmail.com.
Number of teachers: approximately 15 employed for the summer months.
Preference of nationality: none, but must be native English speaker.

Qualifications: TEFL Cert and degree in English literature or linguistics.
Employment conditions: non-contract. Classes are held mornings and afternoons during summer and afternoons only in winter.
Salary: hourly, according to experience.
Facilities/support: no assistance with accommodation or work permits.
Contact: Andrea Abousaid, Academic Director.

Kuwait

INSTITUTE FOR PRIVATE EDUCATION & TRAINING (IPETQ)
PO Box 6320, 32038 Hawalli, Kuwait. Tel: 573 7811/2. Fax: 574 2924. E-mail: lizs@ipetq.com.kw.
Anglo Kuwait joint venture under British management.
Number of teachers: about 90.
Preference of nationality: British, Irish, American, Canadian, Australian.
Conditions of employment: 1 year. Hours vary according to project requirements; split shifts are common. 6 weeks paid leave per year plus standard insurance and annual gratuity.
Salary: £14,000-18,000 per year.
Facilities/Support: furnished, air-conditioned accommodation and flights provided. Regular schedule of in-service training.
Recruitment: through the internet or *Times Educational Supplement*. Also through TecQuipment (TQ), Bonsall St, Long Eaton, Nottingham NG10 2AN (0115-972 2611/fax 0115-973 1520). Recruitment booklet available. Staff never hired without interview which is held in UK, Kuwait or Egypt (via the American University in Cairo).

KUWAIT UNIVERSITY LANGUAGE CENTRE
PO Box 2575, 13026 Safat, Kuwait. Tel: 481 0325/484 1741. Fax: 484 3824.
Number of teachers: 10-15 new teachers each semester.
Preference of nationality: American, British.
Qualifications: MA in TEFL/TESL or Applied Linguistics plus minimum 3 years' teaching experience.
Conditions of employment: one year renewable contracts. 15 contact h.p.w.
Salary: 652-703 dinars per month tax-free based on experience.
Facilities/Support: free furnished accommodation or housing allowance of 250 dinars. Return air fares and approximately 8 weeks summer leave.
Recruitment: adverts in US and UK, where interviews are conducted.
Contact: Dr. Suad A Al-Bustan, Director.

Oman

CfBT EDUCATION SERVICES
PO Box 2278, PC 112 Medinat Qaboos, Muscat, Oman. Tel: 607236. Fax: 692537. Website: www.cfbtoman.com.
Number of teachers: 40 approx.
Preference of nationality: British, N. American, Australian, New Zealand.
Qualifications: usually MA TESOL.
Conditions of employment: 1 year. Teaching hours normally from 8.30am to 4.30pm.
Salary: approximately US$16,432 per annum plus tickets, insurance. Tax-free.
Facilities/Support: accommodation and work permit are provided.
Recruitment: normally through *TES*, internet, agents abroad.
Contact: Dr. Patricia Groves, Development Advisor.

POLYGLOT INSTITUTE
PO Box 221, Ruwi, Oman. Tel: 773 1261. Fax: 773 4602. E-mail: polyglot@omantel.net.com. Website: www.polyglot.org.

Number of teachers: 15 including part-time teachers.
Preference of nationality: none.
Qualifications: degree and CELTA or equivalent plus 5 years' experience.
Conditions of employment: 2 year contracts. 30 contact h.p.w.
Salary: 600 rials per month (net).
Facilities/Support: accommodation/flights provided. Modern Multimedia centre and good range of resources.
Recruitment: by word of mouth. Interviews (local or telephone) essential.

Saudi Arabia

AL-RAJHI CO
European Centre for Languages and Training, PO Box 60617, Riyadh 11555, Saudi Arabia. Tel: 55 36 31 09. E-mail: euro@zajil_net.
Number of teachers: approx. 100 full-time.
Preference of nationality: none.
Qualifications: DELTA/Trinity Diploma/MA (Applied Linguistics).
Conditions of employment: 3, 6, 10 or 12 month contracts. 27^1/2 contact hours p.w. 40 hours per 5 day week.
Salary: from £1,600 per month (net). Increments for qualifications and length of service.
Facilities/Support: free accommodation and work permits.
Recruitment: direct hire by adverts. Interviews essential.

ELITE TRAINING SERVICES
PO Box 11015, Jubail Industrial City 31961, Saudi Arabia. Tel: (3) 341 5513 & 5808. Fax: (3)-341 1336. E-mail: elite@awalnet.net.sa.
Number of teachers: 7.
Preference of nationality: male UK passport holders.
Qualifications: minimum CELTA or equivalent plus 3 years' experience (1 abroad).
Conditions of employment: contracts from 6 weeks to 1 year (usually the latter). 25 contact h.p.w. plus 15 hours admin.
Salary: about £1,300 per month (net).
Facilities/Support: free furnished single accommodation. Work permits obtained. Free medical insurance.
Recruitment: personal recommendation and via the internet (www.eslcafe.com and www.asktheenglishteacher.com).
Contact: Trevor Hopkins, Managing Director.

ENGLISH LANGUAGE CENTER
King Fahd University of Petroleum & Minerals, Dhahran 31261, Saudi Arabia. Tel: (3) 860 2395. Fax: (3) 860 2341. E-mail: elcrecru@kfupm.edu.sa.
Number of teachers: 80.
Preference of nationality: American, British, Canadian, New Zealander, Australian.
Qualifications: MA in TEFL/TESL/Applied Linguistics or full-time postgraduate diploma in TEFL plus minimum 2 years' overseas experience.
Conditions of employment: 2 year contracts. 20-25 h.p.w. Pupils aged 17-20.
Facilities/Support: accommodation provided. Contract completion bonus.
Recruitment: through adverts in the *Guardian*. Send cover letter and resumé to Dean of Faculty & Personnel Affairs. Personal interviews required.
Contact: Dr. Fahd A. Al-Said, Dean of Educational Services.

INSTITUTE OF PUBLIC ADMINISTRATION ENGLISH LANGUAGE CENTRE
P.O. Box 205, Riyadh 11141, Saudi Arabia. Tel: (1) 476 7305. Fax: (1) 479 2136. E-mail: hobroma@ipa.edu.sa.
Number of teachers: 30.
Preference of nationality: none.

Qualifications: MA in TESOL or Applied Linguistics.
Conditions of employment: one year contract. 22 hours per week.
Salary: US$2,093-$3,026 per month. Tax free.
Facilities/Support: free furnished apartment provided. Help with getting a work visa given.
Recruitment: advertising, TESOL.
Contact: Anwar Hobrom, Director.

JUBAIL INDUSTRIAL COLLEGE
P.O. Box 10099, Madinat Al-Juball Al-Sinalyah 31961, Saudi Arabia. Tel. (3) 340-2018. Fax: (3) 340 2009. E-mail: elc@jic.edu.sa.
Number of teachers: 20.
Preference of nationality: none. Present staff includes Irish, British and American.
Qualifications: minimum one-year full-time postgraduate degree or an MS/MA/MAT in TEFL/TESL or related field. At least 2 years full-time TEFL experience preferably in the Middle East.
Conditions of employment: two-year renewable contract with tax-free competitive salary based on qualifications and experience, plus allowances for transport etc. and end of service bonus, air tickets and education for dependent children. Free accommodation and medical and dental care. 20 hours per week teaching English for Academic Purposes to 800 male students preparing to take courses leading to technical and business diplomas and specialised courses at a higher level.
Recruitment: mail, fax or e-mail cover letter and detailed résumé and recent photograph. Interviews essential.
Contact: Khalifa S. Al-Khaldi, Managing Director.

PRINCE SULTAN COLLEGE FOR TOURISM & HOTEL SCIENCES
P.O. Box 447, Abha, Saudi Arabia. Tel: (7) 231 0800. Fax: (7) 231 0803. E-mail: pscabha@atheer.net.sa.
Number of teachers: 9.
Preference of nationality: American, British, Irish.
Qualifications: BA and ESL credential and experience in Saudi Arabia.
Conditions of employment: 2 year contract. Teaching hours from 8am-10am; 1pm-3pm plus one hour administrative duties.
Salary: depends on qualifications and experience. Tax free.
Facilities/Support: furnished apartment provided per teacher. Help with work permit.
Recruitment: e-mail, internet. Interview essential. Some held in the US.
Contact: Matthew James Schaffer.

YANBU INDUSTRIAL COLLEGE
EFL Center, PO Box 30436, Yanbu Al-Sinaiyah, Saudi Arabia. Tel: (4) 394 6189. Fax: (4) 342 0213.
Number of teachers: 8.
Preference of nationality: none.
Qualifications: degree in English. EFL teaching and Middle East experience.
Conditions of employment: 2 year contract (renewable). Usual hours 7am-4pm.
Salary: US$3,000 per month free of deductions.
Facilities/Support: furnished accommodation provided.
Recruitment: ads followed by interviews (in person or by phone).
Contact: Mr. Bassam Yamani, Managing Director.

Syria

AMERICAN LANGUAGE CENTER
P.O. Box 20, Damascus. Tel: (11) 333 7936. Fax: (11) 331 9327.
Number of teachers: 45.
Preference of nationality: none.

Qualifications: degree and Cert. TEFL.
Conditions of employment: one year or more contract. Flexible hours.
Salary: US$9-13 per hour.
Facilities/Support: no assistance with accommodation but assistance given with work permit.
Recruitment: locally from candidates already in Damascus.
Contact: Steve Bueshaar, Director.

DAMASCUS LANGUAGE INSTITUTE
P.O. Box 249, Damascus. Tel: (11) 4440575. Fax: (11) 3324913.
Number of teachers: varies.
Preference of nationality: UK or US.
Qualifications: teaching diploma and MA (TEFL).
Conditions of employment: 8 months. 12 hours a week in 3 days. Sat. Mon. Wed. (female); Sun. Tue. Thurs. (male). School can help with finding private students for the other three days which can double the salary below. Summer session begins late June ends mid September; winter session starts around mid-October and ends beginning of January.
Salary: $100 per week.
Facilities/Support: financial assistance and help with finding accommodation and paying for it. Work permit arranged.
Recruitment: application followed by an interview.
Contact: Maher Abul-Zahab, Principal.

United Arab Emirates

BRITISH COUNCIL, ABU DHABI
P.O. Box 46523, Abu Dhabi, United Arab Emirates. Tel: (2) 665 93 00. Fax: (2) 666 43 40. E-mail: iain.mackie@britishcouncil.org.ae. Website: www.british.council. org/uae.
Number of teachers: varies.
Qualifications: Cert. level teaching and at least two years' relevant teaching experience.
Conditions of employment: teaching adult and children's courses year round. Also summer intensive programme (June to September).
Contact: Iain Mackie.

HIGHER COLLEGES OF TECHNOLOGY
P.O. Box 47025, Abu Dhabi, United Arab Emirates. Tel: +971 2 681 4244. Fax: +971 2 681 0933. E-mail: ayushee.tomar@hct.ac.ae. Website: www.hct.ac.ae.
Number of teachers: about 450 English Faculty teachers involved in teaching English as a Second Language.
Preference of nationality: none.
Qualifications: first degree and TESOL Diploma or equivalent and 3 years' relevant teaching experience. Experience in curriculum development and student assessment. Knowledge of contemporary teaching practices and computer assisted learning.
Conditions of employment: standard contract is 3 years. 40 hours a week, usually with a class of 20.
Salary: £1,426-£2,707 per month tax free.
Facilities/Support: unfurnished accommodation and a furniture allowance of approximately, £4,975 distributed over three years. Work permit arranged by the college.
Recruitment: conferences, college website, newspaper advertising, posting on the internet, word of mouth. Interviews essential; can be carried out in the UK or the USA.
Contact: Ayushee Tomar.

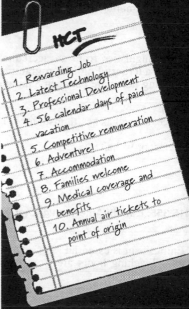

INTERNATIONAL LANGUAGE INSTITUTE
P.O. Box 289, Sharjah, United Arab Emirates. Tel: (6) 5377257. Fax: (6) 5363427.
E-mail: ilishuae@emirates.net.ae.
Number of teachers: 4-5 full-time and some seasonal part-timers.
Preference of nationality: British.
Qualifications: degree plus Cambridge Cert plus 2/3 years teaching experience.
Conditions of employment: 35 hour working week. 24 hours teaching, maximum from Saturday to Wednesday.
Salary: from dhs 6000 (approx. £1000) per month plus accommodation allowance.
Facilities/Support: residence visa and work permit provided.
Recruitment: locally and through press advertising and internet.
Contact: Gillian Knight.

ZAYED UNIVERSITY
English Language Center, P.O. Box 19282, Dubai, United Arab Emirates. Tel: (4) 264 8899. Fax: (4) 264 8690. E-mail: zayed_recruitment@zu.ac.ae. Website: www.zu.ac.ae.
Number of teachers: 300.
Preference of nationality: none.
Qualifications: minimum MA TESOL or applied linguistics from an accredited western institution plus at least 2 years experience in a tertiary English programme.
Conditions of employment: 3-year contract. Teaching hours are between 8am and 5pm, 5 days per week.
Salary: 8,500-15,000 dirhams per month (tax-free).
Facilities/Support: accommodation is provided free, as well as health insurance, 11 weeks of holiday and other subsidies.
Recruitment: via TESOL Inc, *Chronicle, The Times,* or website.
Contact: David M. Walker, Human Resources.

Yemen

AMERICAN SCHOOL
Box 16 003 Sana'a. Tel: (1) 417 119. Fax: (1) 415 355. E-mail: American@y.net.ye.
Number of teachers: 10.
Preference of nationality: none.
Qualifications: various depending on the job. Enthusiasm is essential.
Conditions of employment: one year renewable. Teaching hours are from 8am-2pm.
Salary: $400 to $1000 per month.
Facilities/Support: assistance with housing and airfares.
Recruitment: CV and interview by phone.
Contact: Robert Majuie, Director.

MODERN AMERICAN LANGUAGE INSTITUTE (MALI)
PO Box 11727, Sana'a, Yemen. Tel/fax: (1) 241561. E-mail: MALI1.edu@Y.NET.YE.
Number of teachers: between 9 (winter) and 15 (summer).
Preference of nationality: American, British.
Qualifications: minimum college degree. Prefer experienced ESL/EFL instructors. Should be enthusiastic, motivated and willing to adapt to a different culture.
Conditions of employment: minimum 10 weeks; maximum 1 year renewable.
Salary: US$400-$600 per month depending on experience.
Facilities/Support: single room accommodation provided. There is also an exchange programme of English lessons in return for accommodation and Arabic lessons (two hours daily). Residence visa provided.
Recruitment: phone interviews sometimes sufficient.
Contact: Waleed Maktari, Registrar.

The Vision:

The United Arab Emirates is a small country on the Arabian Gulf with a big goal: expanded higher education for its people. To achieve that goal, the UAE established Zayed University, a new national, English-medium university for women in 1998. With campuses in both Abu Dhabi and Dubai, Zayed University aims to graduate women who are prepared to take on leadership roles in a changing country and a changing world. Graduates are fluent in both English and Arabic and are skilled users of technology in addition to earning degrees from one of its six colleges: Arts and Sciences, Business Sciences, Communication and Media Sciences, Education, Family Sciences and Information Systems.

To ensure that students are well-prepared to undertake academic study in classrooms where English is the language of instruction, the English Language Center offers various courses, labs and activities to further develop their English abilities in its Readiness Program and as they start their general education courses. The ELC also provides English support once students have entered their areas of specialization. The ELC at Zayed University is seeking enthusiastic, student-centered teachers to participate in making the University's vision a reality.

The Profile:

Zayed University invites applications for faculty positions in the English Language Center. Appointments begin in August 2001. Applicants should have a Masters Degree in either TESOL or Applied Linguistics from a fully accredited western tertiary institution and at least 2 years of teaching experience in a tertiary English program. Salary will be commensurate with qualifications and experience. The term of appointment is normally three years.

The Benefits:

The United Arab Emirates is one of the most liberal countries in the Middle East and one of the most rapidly changing countries in the world. Dubai and Abu Dhabi are modern, cosmopolitan cities located on the Arabian Gulf. Salaries are free of tax in the UAE. Housing, healthcare, 56 days annual vacation, annual tickets, furniture allowance and education subsidies for children are also provided.

To Apply:

Please send letter of application with detailed resume to:
David Walker
Human Resources
Zayed University
PO Box 19282
Dubai, UAE
Email: zayed_recruitment@zu.ac.ae

Unforgettable Opportunities

ZAYED UNIVERSITY

YEMEN-AMERICAN LANGUAGE INSTITUTE (YALI)
P.O. Box 22347, Sana'a. Tel: (1) 416-973/4. Fax: (1) 203-251. E-mail: yaliroy@y.net.ye. Website: www.yali.org.ye.
Number of teachers: teaching staff numbers around 30 of which 5 are usually native English speakers.
Preference of nationality: none, but a knowledge of American culture is helpful.
Qualifications: BA degree and CELTA or equivalent, some teaching experience and some experience of living in a developing country.
Conditions of employment: usually 1 year contract, with teaching load of 4 hours per day, five days per week. Terms last five weeks with the sixth week off.
Salaries: hourly rate from $8 to $14, depending on experience and qualifications. Salaries are exempt from Yemeni taxes and other deductions. US citizens may be subject to taxes and deductions.
Facilities/support: YALI can help find accommodation and temporary housing can be provided until teachers find their own. No housing allowance, but local rents are reasonable. YALI arranges visas and work permits at no charge.
Contact: John Scacco, Director of Courses.

YEMEN MODERN SCHOOL
PO Box 13335, Sana'a, Yemen. Tel: (1) 401013. Fax: (1) 401015. E-mail: yms@y.net.ye. Website: http://members.tripod.com/yemenmodernschool.
Number of teachers: 8.
Preference of nationality: none.
Conditions of employment: one academic year contract, renewable. School hours 7.30am-1.30pm Saturday to Wednesday. Teachers are not required to stay after hours. Pupils are bilingual Yemeni children aged 5-19 following a Cambridge syllabus.
Salary: $700-$1,000 (net) a month depending on experience. Return air ticket to country of origin offered at the end of 2 contract years.
Facilities/Support: full assistance given with work permit application. Teacher needs 10 passport photos, CV, qualifications and proof of HIV test (charge is $6). Housing is not provided but advice given on finding accommodation which is very reasonably priced.
Recruitment: local hire, word of mouth, internet and adverts in local papers. Telephone interviews needed to ascertain applicant's accent.
Contact: Stephen and Susan Pahutski.

Other Schools to Try

Bahrain
American Cultural Centre, PO Box 10410, Al Hassam, Bahrain
Capital Computer Institute, PO Box 24893, Al Hassam, Bahrain
Dar Al Ma'aref Centre, PO Box 3714, Al Hassam, Bahrain
Polyglot Institute, PO Box 596, Al Seqaiya, Bahrain
Bahrain Computer School, PO Box 26178, Hoora, Bahrain
Bahrain Languages Centre, PO Box 15066, Hoora, Bahrain
Gulf School International, PO Box 20436 Hoora, Bahrain
Delmon Academy, PO Box 10363, Manama, Bahrain
Informatics, PO Box 1115, Manama, Bahrain
Institute of Private Education, PO Box 26222, Manama, Bahrain
Awal Training Institute, PO Box 28811, Riffa, Bahrain
Bahrain Institute, PO Box 28140, Riffa, Bahrain
English Language Skills Centre, 1427 Road 139, Toobli 701, Bahrain
City Institute, PO Box 15590, Zinj, Bahrain
Iptech Ccomputer Institute, PO Box 5854, Zinj, Bahrain

Kuwait
British Institute of Training and Education (BITE) – 263 6952
ELS Military School of Languages, PO Box 5104, Salmiya 20062, Kuwait (fax 573 3005)
Kuwait American Cultural Center/Kuwaiti American Center of Education – 266 2700
New Horizon – 244 9797

Qatar
Arizona English Language Center, PO Box 7949, Doha
ELS Language Center, PO Box 22678, Doha
Language Institute, PO Box 3224, Doha
Qatar Aeronautical College (malachym@hotmail.com)

Syria
Al Kindi English Language Centre, 29 May Street, Damascus
Al-Kudssi Institute, PO Box 5296, Aleppo

UAE
Al Farabi Language Centre, PO Box 3794, Dubai
Dar Al Ilm School of Languages, PO Box 9399, Dubai
IEI, PO Box 52714, Dubai
Institute for Australian Studies, PO Box 20183, Dubai
Polyglot Language School, PO Box 1093, Dubai
Al-Worood School, PO Box 46673, Abu Dhabi (2-448855/fax 2-449732).

Turkey

The ELT industry at the turn of the new century is perhaps not quite as flourishing as it was in the 1990s but it still absorbs an enormous number of globe-trotting English teachers. Of all the feedback this book receives about all the countries covered, Turkey is the country which has elicited the most and it must be said not all of it positive. By describing the problems which many have encountered on short teaching contracts in Turkey, it is to be hoped that readers can guard against them. Every single one of the teachers who has complained about employers breaking their promises, run-down accommodation, sexual harassment and so on, has concluded by saying that Turkish people are wonderful and the country fascinating.

Prospects for Teachers

Turkey's ambition to join the European Union, together with a remarkable expansion in tourism during the last two decades of the 20th century, means that Turkey's prosperous classes are more eager than ever to learn English. The boom in English is not confined to private language schools *(dershane)* which have mushroomed in the three main cities of Istanbul, Ankara and Izmir. In order to prepare students for an English language engineering, commerce, tourism or arts course, many secondary schools hire native speaker teachers. Hundreds of private secondary schools *(lises)* consider as one of their main priorities the teaching of the English language. Similarly at the tertiary level, some universities, both private and public, use English as the medium of instruction.

Turkey is a good choice of destination for fledgling teachers of any nationality. Not only are there a great many jobs, but these jobs are often part of a package which includes free accommodation and free airfares (London-Istanbul) on completion of a contract. Virtually all of these employers want to see a university degree and a TEFL Certificate of some kind, preferably the Cambridge CELTA or equivalent. Both a degree and a specialist qualification are required by the Turkish Ministry of

Education before it will approve a work permit (see *Regulations* below).

The bias in favour of British English over American is not particularly strong. Many schools claim to have no preference and yet because they advertise in the UK press and are more familiar with British qualifications, there is a preponderance of British teachers. Also the requirement that work visas be applied for in the country of origin makes matters more difficult for teachers from the US, Australia, etc.

FIXING UP A JOB

In Advance

The British Council in Istanbul, Izmir and Ankara have lists of private language schools and *lises*. The up-to-date list of ELT institutions supplied by the British Council in Izmir contains about 25 addresses plus about the same number of *lises* and universities. The Istanbul list (dated November 1999) includes 17 language schools, over 100 *lises* and 17 universities with EFL departments, all in the Istanbul area. The British Council also issues a free one-page 'Information for Foreign Teachers' for prospective and practising teachers.

Bilkent University School of English Language (teacher@bilkent.edu.tr; www.bilkent.edu.tr/busel) in Ankara regularly recruits EFL/EAP instructors through agents or directly. This privately funded English medium university offers excellent facilities and career opportunities together with campus accommodation, fares, etc. Applicants will need to possess as a minimum an honours degree, CELTA and two years' relevant experience, though often they are looking for staff with doctorates. The contact details for Teacher Services are tel 312-290 1712 and fax 312-266 4320.

Many of the recruitment agencies included in the introductory chapter *Finding a Job* have contacts in Turkey, though most of the traffic seems to be from Britain rather than America.

A key agency is *Turkeng Recruitment* based in Antalya in southern Turkey (Ayanoglu Mah, 1284 Sok No 8, Varsak, Antalya; 242-325 2662; fax 242-326 6778; turkeng@angelfire.com/ www.angelfire.com/biz/turkeng). This agency also has a UK branch at 3 Peck Close, Norwich, NR5 9NF (tel/fax 01603 747042). Turkeng recruits about 50 native-speaker teachers for schools in a variety of towns including Istanbul, Bursa, Izmir and Antalya. All schools on Turkeng's books receive a personal visit and inspection from a Turkeng representative. An application can be downloaded from their website which can then be submitted with photo, cover letter, full CV and two references. Turkeng interviews by telephone or in person. Most of their contracts are for 9-12 months. Work permits can be obtained both prior to departure and also once in Turkey. Turkeng can also arrange English teaching jobs in universities for which a degree in English or relevant subject and a PGCE are required.

Another specialist agency is the newly formed Bosphorus Teacher Placement Service, Maresal Cakmak Cad. Incesu Sk., No. 22/4, B.Evler, Istanbul; tel/fax 212-551 0195/mobile 0 532 463 21 58; bosphorus@e-kolay.net. The Recruitment Committee undertakes to find positions for natives speakers aged 21-60 with a university degree and teaching certificate (TEFL, TESOL, CELTA, etc.) The typical package on offer includes one-way travel reimbursement, rent-free furnished apartment, free internet access and a salary of $950-$1,250 for teaching 100-120 hours per month. For the 2000/2001 academic year, they claimed to have about 225 vacancies to fill.

Other organisations can place young people on summer camps in Turkey where the emphasis is on teaching English. For example the *Koparan Summer Camp* operates every year at a purpose-built resort near Erdek on the Sea of Marmara, relying on about 40 native speakers. The Turkish workcamps organisation *Genctur* (see entry) takes on young people to work on their language camps; as well as helping with English teaching, assistants participate in social activities, drama, music, sports and crafts. All expenses are paid except airfares. *i-to-i* (0870 333 2332) supply EFL teachers to a group of language schools in Izmir; most of these teachers are recruited from i-to-i's own training courses (see Introduction).

Among the main indigenous language teaching organisations in Turkey are *International House* with a big operation in Istanbul and the *English Centre* with branches in Istanbul, Ankara and Izmir. *Dilko English, English Times, Interlang* and *Antik English* are all well established. English Fast is another major group of schools, though they did not confirm their teacher requirements for this edition (see end of chapter for their address). Most of the language chains have come in for criticism over the years, with words like 'cowboy,' 'unprofessional' and 'untrustworthy' being bandied about by disappointed teachers.

Many ads for Turkish schools appear in the *Guardian* and *TES* in the spring and right through the summer. If you are considering accepting a job with an advertiser, ask for the name and telephone number of a previous teacher for an informal reference. An even better indication is if they have been able to keep their teachers for two or more years. If the school is reluctant to provide this kind of information, be suspicious. It may also be worth phoning the British Council office in the relevant city, since they keep a file of complaints about language schools.

On the Spot

Although not the capital, Istanbul is the commercial, financial and cultural centre of Turkey, so this is where most of the EFL teaching goes on. On the negative side, there may be more competition from other teachers here and also in Izmir than in Ankara or less obvious cities like Mersin and Diyarbakir. The best starting place in Istanbul is undoubtedly the British Council as Stephen McKeown discovered:

> *The helpful British Council will give you a list of English schools in Istanbul. The addresses read like chemical formulae but you soon get used to them. We were offered jobs by every school we went to and were promised wages of between two and four times the national average.*

You may also find yourself drawn back to the British Council after you have landed a job. The modest joining fee entitles you to use the Council's Teaching Centre with a reference collection of ELT books, video cassettes, seminars, etc.

Given the huge demand for native speaker teachers, Turkey is one country where scouting out possibilities on the ground can pay off, rather than signing a contract at a school you have never seen. After Bruce Lawson had a terrible experience with a private language teaching organisation in Istanbul ('their contract was a fiction that Tolstoy would have been proud of'), he concluded that he could have earned half as much again if he had been hired by a school which hired its teachers in Turkey.

Tim Leffel and Donna Marcus from New Jersey were amazed by the contrast between job-hunting in Greece (where Americans encounter visa problems even when they have a Cambridge Certificate as Tim and Donna had) and Turkey:

> *There's a huge demand for teachers (any nationality really) in Istanbul. We lined up work on our second day of interviews. We interviewed at three schools and all of them offered us positions. We chose English Fast in Bakirköy because there were two jobs available in the same place and we were allowed to wear anything within reason (no ties, no new clothes to buy). They were satisfied that we could only commit ourselves for four months. We did see a lot of applicants turned away, even when there was a need for new teachers, because they lacked TEFL credentials.*

Fewer and fewer schools are willing to employ people with no formal TEFL background.

Freelance

The standard Ministry of Education contract prohibits private teaching outside the bounds of the signed contract. In fact, unless you are blatantly pinching students from the institution that employs you, most employers turn a blind eye. University English departments might be a place to look for private pupils. The top rate of pay is about £10 an hour.

REGULATIONS

It is necessary to apply for a visa before arrival in Turkey as the Vice Consul at the Turkish Consulate General in London (020-7589 0360) clearly explains:

> *Anyone who intends to work in Turkey has to obtain a work visa before departing for Turkey. Otherwise, he/she will not be permitted to take up employment in the country, unless he/she chooses to work illegally. Applications from teachers are usually processed quicker than the other professions. We believe that an application made four weeks before the intended departure would be sufficient. Applications to the Ministry of Education should be done by the prospective employer in Turkey on behalf of the teachers. Written approval of the Undersecretariat for the Treasury also has to be obtained by the Turkish employer.*

The fee for a work visa is £60 at present. Teacher agencies and employers may undertake some of the bureaucratic steps for employers and employees, though for an extra fee.

It is not always clear at what point a teacher has to submit his or her degree and ELT certificate. The Turkish employer needs to send permission from the Ministry of Education that he or she is authorised to employ foreign teachers and a document from the Undersecretariat for the Treasury. Once these have arrived, the teacher takes them with the original contract of employment and completed forms in person to the Consulate to apply for a work visa, preferably six weeks before the proposed departure. (Note that the work and residence permit does not allow you to leave and re-enter the country without paying for a new tourist visa.)

There will always be those who accept work in language schools while on a tourist visa, and this number may now rise with the increased complications in getting a work visa. If working on a tourist visa, you must renew it every three months, either at the immigration office (where you will have to show that you have the means to support yourself; for example having a Turkish friend undertake to support you would help) or more usually by leaving the country and obtaining a new tourist visa, which costs £10 in sterling at the point of entry. Normally people cross the border to Greece, though a trip to Northern Cyprus is more pleasant. If you do this too many times the border officials will become suspicious. If you have overstayed, you become liable for a hefty exit fine of US$250.

All salaries in Turkey are quoted net of deductions which amount to about 25% for contributions and tax. If the school makes social security contributions on your behalf, you will have medical cover from your first day of work. The scheme pays all your doctor's bills and 80% of prescriptions. Once again it is prudent to confirm that your employer keeps any promises he makes. More than one teacher has realised at a critical moment that, despite assurances, insurance premiums have not been paid by the school.

A complication for people who intend to teach English in a *lise* or secondary school is that the Ministry of Education insists that teachers of English have a university degree in English and preferably a PGCE or a B.Ed. with English as a main subject. Barry Wade's degree in philosophy with a minor in English was deemed inadequate to teach English at an Istanbul secondary school, despite what he had been told by an agent in England, and he was fobbed off with having to work for less money at a private language school instead.

CONDITIONS OF WORK

The normal deal is a one-year contract with airfare out and back from London, free or subsidised shared accommodation and a monthly salary in Turkish lire equivalent to £400-£500 in private language schools, more in primary and secondary schools. Hourly employment is not as widely available as in many other countries.

It is probably a mistake to expect Western attitudes towards employees to prevail. In Turkey the manager is the boss and in many cases does not feel it incumbent on him to work efficiently or to look out for the welfare of his staff. Yet some people in the ELT business believe that the situation is gradually improving, among them a Director of Studies at a major Istanbul school:

> *I have worked for approximately four years in Turkey, in Istanbul and in a small remote town in the south. Prospective teachers always hear many horror stories about working in Turkey and to an extent they are well founded. In the past, schools and employers openly abused teachers' rights. But this is definitely changing. There are many good, up-and-coming organisations which can be trusted. Teachers should ask around, be careful about contracts and conditions, and not agree to the first job they are offered without checking out the school, its size, reputation, etc.*

This may well apply to the established chains, but there are still many dodgy operators and swashbuckling and unscrupulous employers. Although one individual's personal experience is not always a good basis for generalising, there has been a lot of duplication in the litany of complaints made about language schools in Turkey which focus on contracts being ignored, late payment of wages (especially irritating when high inflation means that a pay packet in lire is worth considerably less from one day to the next), assigning inflated marks to students to keep or attract custom, and so on. So it is important to remember that some teachers have a marvellous time, as Raza Griffiths had at the first school he worked for, which was in the town of Ordu on the Black Sea coast:

> *It would be no exaggeration to say that as a native English person in a region of Turkey unused to foreigners, I enjoyed celebrity status, with lots of inquiring eyes and lots of invitations to dinner. Although the town did not exactly have a thriving cultural life as we would understand it, this was more than compensated for by the sociableness of the people and their deep desire for communication.*
>
> *Because it was a private school, money was not in short supply and the facilities were excellent with videos, computers, etc. The free furnished flat I was given was large and very comfortable, and there was a free school minibus service that took teachers to the school. On either side of the school there were hazelnut gardens, behind there were mountains and in front the Black Sea, all quite idyllic, especially in summer. The other teachers (all Turkish) were very welcoming from day one, despite the fact that I was less experienced and was getting four times their salary. My salary was the equivalent of £400 per month but went down to about £325 due to spiralling inflation; I could live very comfortably on this and still have a lot left over for spending on holidays and clothes.*

Because of the wild inflation, most schools quote salaries in sterling or dollars and promise quarterly or biannual exchange rate adjustments. Always check whether your salary is to be inflation-linked or pegged against a foreign currency and how often it will be adjusted; October and March pay reviews are common. But even if you are unlucky and see your wages plummet on paper, the important things like beer, doner kebabs and bus tickets remain the same price in lire.

Contracts are usually for 9, 10 or 11 months; some offer 3-month summer contracts. If you want to stay longer than a year you are normally paid over the summer holidays. Do not put too much faith in your contract. Rabindra Roy described his as a 'worthless and contradictory piece of paper.' Private language schools will expect you to work the usual unsocial hours and may chop and change your timetable at short notice, while *lises* offer daytime working hours plus (sometimes onerous) extracurricular duties such as marking tests, attending school ceremonies, etc.

The standard holiday allowance for teachers is four weeks. At inferior schools, national holidays must be taken out of this annual leave, including Muslim holidays like Seker Bayrami, usually celebrated at the end of Ramadan and Kurban Bayrami. Both of these festivals last three days and it is customary to make the bridge to a full week. Christmas is not observed much and you may be offered very little time off as happened to Olivene Aldridge-Tucker from Sheffield who worked for one of the big companies in Istanbul. Her employer proposed giving the staff only one day off but she and her six colleagues stood their ground and got a week in the end. A further problem for Olivene was that she experienced racism due to her Afro-Caribbean origins but found a soul mate (and father of her child) in a Kurdish colleague.

One English teacher with extensive experience of teaching in Istanbul suggests shopping around before accepting a job with a certain school. (Ideally before choosing you'd meet someone like him who could give you the current lowdown):

> *I worked at four different schools in Istanbul. You'll want a school that's professional (with good resources, support and teacher development), offers a good package (salary, accommodation, holiday entitlement) and has a timetable to suit you. Many schools like to boast about how professional they are and ignore their own faults. For example some provide a fake degree to a teacher with no degree, employ teachers without a degree, recruit travellers from youth hostels, fail to pay teachers, gossip about former teachers, and so on.*

The Pupils

The major schools are well equipped with TVs, videos, language labs and course materials. But better than the back-up facilities is the enthusiasm of the pupils who are usually motivated, conscientious and well-behaved, and enjoy role play and group discussions. The friendly openness of young Turks may cause a foreign teacher to forget that Turkey is still an Islamic country where dress is conservative and women, no matter how promising, do not normally go on to higher education. 'Willing if unimaginative' was one teacher's description of her students. One undesirable aspect of Turkish education is that many *lises* are too strongly oriented to exam preparation and university entrance.

Student behaviour differs radically depending on what kind of institution you teach in. Private secondary schools tend to be populated with spoiled and immature kids who do not always respect their teachers. Joan Smith found this hard to stomach at the private school in Kayseri where she taught:

> *Turkish parents indulge their children something rotten. Rich spoilt students abound in my classroom and discipline goes out the window. Foreign teachers are regarded as inferior and are given even less respect than the Turkish teachers.*

Joan did not think that she should have to tolerate some of the innuendos her male students were getting away with, but had little hope of justice if they and their friends denied her allegations.

Others' experiences have been very different. Dick Bird, a veteran EFL teacher in Turkey and elsewhere, describes some of his female and other pupils:

> *I have found women students defer to a far higher level of male chauvinism than would be acceptable anywhere in the West. Turkish women also seem to have exceptionally quiet voices and I can't help feeling that this irritating characteristic is somehow related to their role in society – a case of being seen but not heard until you are very very close perhaps? Sometimes my students know too much grammar to be able to express themselves freely. As*

their own language is radically different to Indo-European languages they have a lot of difficulty adapting to the sentence structure of English: they regard relative clauses as a perversion and are baffled, if not mildly outraged, by the cavalier way English seems to use any tense it fancies to refer to future actions but is puritanically strict about how one may describe present and past events. Another difficulty Turks have is that we EFL teachers like to use a lot of words in our meta-language (i.e. language about language e.g. adjective, verb) which do not have cognates in Turkish as they do in other European languages, for example a teacher may inform their students that 'will' expresses probability, not intention; this will be readily understood by an elementary level Spaniard but is total gibberish to a Turk (as I suspect it is to a great many native speakers of English).

Dick's analysis of Turkish EFL students ends with a light-hearted description of their irrepressible energy and enthusiasm:

Whenever the class is asked a question they would fain prostrate themselves at their teacher's feet were it not that years of instilled discipline keep them penned by invisible bonds within the confines of their desks until the ringing of the bell, whereat pandemonium breaks loose as a thousand berserk adolescents fling themselves across the (highly polished) corridor floors and down the (marble) steps headlong into the playground. (This phenomenon may help to explain why fire drills are not a regular feature of Turkish school life.)

Paul Gallantry, at one time Director of Studies at Dilko English in Bakirköy, agrees that Turkish students are fun to teach but identifies a few of the problems he has encountered:

They have several major problems with English, especially mastering the definite article, the third person singular and the present perfect, none of which exist in Turkish. On the whole, their pronunciation is good, but they do have difficulty with words that have three consonants back to back. (My own surname Gallantry inevitably gets pronounced 'Galilantiree'.) If I have to be criticial of my students, it is that they neither listen to, nor read, instructions; five minutes into an exercise there is always someone asking 'What am I supposed to do?'. Also a recurring problem is that some students merely come to a language school in order to use it as a social club. They're more interested in meeting someone of the opposite sex than learning English, and this can have a demoralising effect in class.

Accommodation

If accommodation is provided as part of your contract, it may be located close to the school in a modern flat which you will have to share with another teacher or it may be some way away, possibly in an undesirable neighbourhood. Fortunately not many teachers are assigned accommodation as gruesome as Philip Dray's in Izmir:

Cockroaches, centipedes, noisy neighbours, a filthy shower room and a fitted kitchen circa 1920, I was slowly adjusting to it all. But one day, while I was having a shower, I saw a rat looking at me from the ventilation shaft and I knew that my patience had run out. I asked for a new flat but they said they couldn't get a new one before May. So, relucantly (as there were some very nice people at the school) I had to leave.

If the school doesn't provide a flat they will certainly help you find one and act as go-between with the landlord. Most provide some kind of rent subsidy, since rents in Turkey are high relative to the cost of living. The situation in over-crowded Istanbul is especially tight. It is usual to bargain over the rent as if you were buying a second-hand car. Flats are advertised through *Hurriyet* newspaper, or there are estate agencies called *emlak* but these tend to charge a month's rent. Rents often seem steep at the outset which may be because they are fixed for a 12 month period. Foreigners are usually considered an attractive proposition as they tend to be undemanding tenants.

In Istanbul, the nicest flats are along the Bosphorus where the air is clean, the views stunning and a lot of the buildings are older properties with a lot of character; this is why they have been snapped up by well-heeled diplomats and multi-nationals. Rents are lower on the Asian side of the city. Although the Asian side has less charm (actually it has no charm at all), it has less pollution and many people prefer it. At the risk of multiplying horror stories, Bruce Lawson describes his situation a few years ago when housed on the Asian side:

> The apartment is a jerry-built five-storey block of 16 rooms which are tiny; six rooms don't have windows. The heating rarely works (it's important to note that Istanbul is very cold in winter), there are no cooking facilities so you eat out, which is expensive, and the place is crawling with cockroaches, the bedding is squalid and very smelly. The area is notorious for prostitutes making it dangerous for women. One colleague of mine (she's leaving tomorrow) has been groped every day in broad daylight. The rent-free accommodation is a misnomer, as a sum is deducted from your wages for utilities, although a bill is never produced.

Ian McArthur chose the opposite situation; his school was in a suburb on the Asian side, but he chose to stay in a cheap hotel in Sultanahmet, partly for the social life:

> I had to commute (from Europe to Asia in fact) for an hour in the morning and evening, but the marvellous views of the sunrise over the domes and minarets from the Bosphorus ferry whilst sipping a much-needed glass of strong sweet tea, made the early rise worth it.

LEISURE TIME

Even if you are earning a salary at the lower end of the scale, you should be able to afford quite a good life, especially if you eat a lot of bread, drink local wines and use public transport. Basic meals and food, transport, hotels and cinemas (most films are subtitled rather than dubbed) are still very reasonable, especially away from the seaside and Istanbul. If out and about, be aware that the police sometimes carry out spot checks for ID, so you should carry some around with you, even if it is only a good photocopy of your passport.

Dick Bird points out the advantages of living in Ankara:

> It's safer than any European capital (except maybe Reykjavik) and although it may not hum at night, there are enough discos etc. to keep you going for a year, plus very cheap classical concerts and cinemas. And the air pollution is not as bad as it was.

Travel in Turkey is wonderfully affordable. The efficiency, comfort and low cost of Turkish bus travel put the coach services of most other countries to shame (though not their safety record). There is very little crime in Turkey. Women will have to learn to handle pestering, which is usually best ignored. Paul Gallantry tries to put the problem into perspective:

> While Turkey is generally an exceptionally safe place, women teachers can expect a certain amount of harassment from a minority of Turkish men, who seem to believe that all foreign females are prostitutes. This attitude leaves a lot of teachers with a thoroughly negative attitude towards Turkey and Turkish people as a whole, which is unfair.
>
> Turkey generally is a great place to live and work. It's a fascinating country, full of contradictions, as befits a land that is the bridge between East and West. Turkey is the ideal country for anyone starting their EFL career.

LIST OF SCHOOLS

ACTIVE ENGLISH
Atatürk Bulvari 127/701, Selcan Han. Bakanliklar, 06640 Ankara. Tel: (312) 418 7973/418 4975. Fax: (312) 425 8235. E-mail: birlesik@acteng.com. Website: www.acteng.com.
Number of teachers: 18-20.
Preference of nationality: British, American, Canadian, Australian.
Qualifications: teaching certificate in English preferably or any university degree plus Cambridge Cert.
Conditions of employment: minimum 8 month contract, otherwise negotiable. 92 hours per month guaranteed. Evening and weekend work. 1 day off per week.
Salary: depends on qualifications and experience.
Facilities/Support: accommodation provided. All books, teachers' manuals, tape recorders, etc. provided by the school.
Recruitment: interviews in Turkey or in London. Send or fax detailed CV and photograph.
Contact: G. C. Ince.

AKADEMI SCHOOL OF ENGLISH
Akkoyunlu Cad. No 22 (P.K. 234), Diyarbakir 21100. Tel: (412) 224 2297/8/9. Fax: (412) 228 8020.
Number of teachers: 3-4.
Preference of nationality: British/American/Canadian.
Qualifications: minimum 4 year degree and CELTA or TEFL Cert (or equivalent).
Conditions of employment: minimum 1 year contracts. 26 h.p.w.
Salary: approximately £700-£900 per month net of all taxes, social security, etc.
Facilities/Support: free airfares. Free furnished shared accommodation provided. Orientation given.
Recruitment: adverts in UK press and recruitment agencies.

ANTIK ENGLISH & B.M.T.
Three Istanbul branches: Istanbul Cad. Kirmizi Sebboy Sokak 10, Bakirköy (European side); 212-570 4847/fax 212-583 7934. Taksim (European side); 212-293 5600/fax 212-244 2396. E-mail: antiktaksim@hotmail.com. Kadikoy (Asian side); 216-349 9920/fax 216-336 2220.
Number of teachers: 40-50.
Preference of nationality: all native English speakers welcome.
Qualifications: degree or further education to HND level plus TEFL Certificate.
Conditions of employment: 9, 10 or 11 month contracts. Up to 24 contact hours per week/32 lessons of 45 minutes, 5 days on/2 days off (not consecutive). Evening and weekend work expected. Closed in August.
Salary: US$800-$1,000 depending on experience. Overtime paid on a monthly basis.
Facilities/Support: subsidised health insurance. Shared accommodation or allowance provided. School assists with work permits. Regular workshops and observations.
Recruitment: via adverts in the *Guardian* and *EL Prospects*, internet links and links with training centres and agencies.
Contact: Director of Studies of each branch.

BEST ENGLISH
Bayindir Sokak No. 53, Kizilay, Ankara. Tel: (312) 417 1819/417 2536. Fax: (312) 417 6808. E-mail: besteng@bnet.net.tr. Website: www.bestenglish.com.tr.
Number of teachers: 30.
Preference of nationality: none.
Qualifications: first degree plus CELTA or equivalent plus experience (overseas experience preferred).
Conditions of employment: 1 year renewable contracts. Teaching load is 26 h.p.w.

Variable hours between 9am and 9pm, 7 days a week, with 2 days off a week. Students mostly young adults.
Salary: varies according to qualifications and experience. Paid in US dollars.
Facilities/Support: shared accommodation provided. Health insurance. One way airfare paid on completion of one year plus three weeks paid leave; return airfare and four weeks paid leave if teacher renews contract. In-house training.
Recruitment: adverts and direct application. Interviews held in UK and Ankara.

CAGDIL ENGLISH LANGUAGE CENTRE
Altiparmak Cad., 2. Otelsokak, 16050 Bursa. Tel: (224) 220 4482. Fax: (224) 220 4482.
Number of teachers: 9.
Preference of nationality: British and Irish.
Qualifications: degree plus TEFL Cert.
Conditions of employment: eight and a half month contract. 23 full hours per week.
Salary: 300-350 million Turkish lira (£300-£350).
Facilities/Support: free furnished flat shared between 2.
Permits are obtained in the teacher's own country.
Recruitment: through advertising and direct.
Contact: Mr Fevzi Carli, Director.

CUKUROVA UNIVERSITY CENTER FOR FOREIGN LANGUAGES
Balcali-Adana. Tel: (322) 338 6084 (switchboard), ext. 2921. E-mail: yadim@mail.cu.edu.tr. Website: www.ekmekci.com.
Number of teachers: 4-5.
Preference of nationality: British, American.
Qualifications: BA or MA in TEFL or Linguistics. Teaching experience in intensive programmes.
Conditions of employment: 1 year renewable contracts. 12 contact h.p.w. 6 h.p.w in office plus regular meetings for staff development.
Salary: approximately TL500,000,000 per month (net).
Facilities/Support: no accommodation or training provided.
Recruitment: interviews held in Turkey.

DILKO ENGLISH
Hatboyu Caddesi No. 16, 34720 Bakirköy, Istanbul. Tel: (212) 570 1270. Fax: (212) 543 6123. E-mail: dilko@superonline.com or denizsen@superonline.com.
Branches also in Kadiköy, Besiktas and Saskinbakkal (Bagdat Caddesi, Kazim Ozalp Sokagi No 15, daire 4, 81070 Saskinbakkal; 216-359 3365).
Number of teachers: up to 30 in Bakirköy and 25-30 in other branches.
Preference of nationality: native speakers.
Qualifications: TEFL certificate or diploma and a 4-year university diploma.
Conditions of employment: 9 month contracts (signing of agreement is compulsory). Minimum 24 h.p.w., maximum 30, including weekend and evening classes. Minimum one day off p.w. Mostly adults, including ESP groups, plus junior groups (ages 11-15) using the *Open Doors* series.
Salary: $750-$1,000 p.m. according to qualifications and experience. Some paid in US dollars in first year, all paid in dollars if teacher renews contract.
Facilities/Support: free accommodation minus utilities bills. Workshops held at least once a month.
Recruitment: direct application mostly; sometimes use agents in England who can interview in London.

DILMER LTC
Unlu Cad. 7, Heykel, Bursa. Tel: (224) 221 4758. Fax: (224) 223 1163.
Number of teachers: 12.
Preference of nationality: British.

Qualifications: university degree plus TEFL certificate.
Conditions of employment: 1 year contracts from October. Teaching adults and children 26 h.p.w. 2 hours p.w. working on resources and materials.
Salary: competitive salary adjusted every 4 months.
Facilities/Support: free flights and accommodation (not shared). Free medical cover.
Recruitment: through adverts in the *Guardian* and via internet (www.edunet.com).
Interviews sometimes in London or, if not, by phone.
Contact: Ruth Tierney.

THE ENGLISH ACADEMY
Head office: 1374 Sokak No. 18/4, Selvili Is Merkezi Cankaya (Izmir). Tel: (232) 446 25 30. Fax: (232) 425 3042. Branch office: 858 Sok Tarancilar Ishani No: 5/4 Konak, Izmir. Tel: (232) 446 25 20. Fax: (232) 425 30 42.
An educational establishment that covers teaching, teacher training, and management of a variety of institutions (private schools, language schools, universities and teacher training colleges). It also runs language summer camps in Turkey.
Number of teachers: 15.
Preference of nationality: British, Australian, New Zealand, Irish, American, Canadian.
Qualifications: minimum degree and TEFL Cert.
Conditions of employment: 9-12 month contracts. 24 h.p.w. working split shift with 2 consecutive days off.
Salary: good local salary according to qualifications and experience.
Facilities/Support: flight paid up to £200. Accommodation provided.
Recruitment: via adverts in *The Guardian*, websites and local recruitment. Interviews preferable and can be arranged in the UK or Ireland.
Contact: Mr. Morgan Finnegan, Founding Director.

THE ENGLISH CENTRE – ANKARA
Selanik Caddesi No. 8, Kat. 5, Kizilay, Ankara. Tel: (312) 435 3094/435 2503. Fax: (312) 434 2738. E-mail: harlock@ada.net.tr.
Number of teachers: 10-12.
Qualifications: degree and CELTA or equivalent.
Conditions of employment: standard contract is 11 months plus holiday; 6-month contracts considered. 24 h.p.w. Mostly adult students but some children's classes.
Salary: $870 per month.
Facilities/Support: Istanbul-London air fare and accommodation provided. Training given.
Recruitment: adverts in *EL Prospects*; direct application by fax/letter/telephone/e-mail.
Contact: Tim Harlock, Director of Studies.

THE ENGLISH CENTRE – ISTANBUL
Rumeli Caddesi 92, Zeki Bey Apt. 4, Osmanbey, Istanbul. Tel: (212) 247 0983. Fax: (212) 225 9173. E-mail: englishcentre@superonline.com / info@englishcentre.com. Website: www.englishcentre.com.
Number of teachers: 55.
Preference of nationality: native speakers.
Qualifications: degree and CELTA essential; DELTA and/or experience preferred.
Conditions of employment: 12 month contracts. 24 contact hours p.w. and 1 hour teacher development meeting. 2 consecutive days off per week. Four weeks paid summer holiday. Some in-company teaching and some young learners classes.
Salary: competitive dollar salary reviewed three times yearly (to compensate for inflation).
Facilities/Support: free accommodation and flights provided. Assistance with DELTA course. Full-time teacher trainer for lesson support. Well-equipped resource rooms, DVD cinema and computer lab.
Recruitment: adverts in the *Guardian* and on the internet. Interviews all year round

in London and Istanbul.
Contact: the Director of Studies.

ENGLISH STAR
Sehit Fethi Bey Cad. No. 79/7, Pasaport, Izmir. Tel: (232) 441 1686. Fax: (232) 483 7851.
Number of teachers: 5-6.
Preference of nationality: British.
Qualifications: minimum university degree plus TEFL certificate. Teaching experience preferred.
Conditions of employment: 1 full year contract. Hours between 9am and 9pm. Guaranteed 60 hours per month.
Salary: hourly rate.
Facilities/Support: assistance with accommodation.
Recruitment: via adverts in the *Guardian* or locally. Phone interviews sufficient.
Contact: Ms. Funda Akgül, School Owner/Director of Studies.

ENGLISH WEST
Cumhuriyet Bulv. No. 36/3, Konak, Izmir. Tel: (232) 425 9208. Fax: (232) 441 8514.
Number of teachers: 8-10.
Preference of nationality: British.
Qualifications: minimum university degree (English preferred) and a teaching certificate.
Conditions of employment: one year contracts. Minimum 15 h.p.w. (usually 5 days p.w.).
Salary: from £360 per month (net).
Facilities/Support: free accommodation provided. Return airfare. Support from Director of Studies.
Recruitment: interviews not essential.
Contact: Mr. Nihat Aksoy, Company Director or Justin Pitt-Bailey, Director of Studies.

EVRIM SCHOOL OF LANGUAGES
Cengiz Topel Caddesi, Kultur Mah. No 10, Camlibel, 33010 Mersin. Tel: (324) 233 9541/233 4825. Fax: (324) 237 0862.
Preference of nationality: British, American.
Qualifications: minimum 2 years teaching, preferably with foreign students. Clear speech and colourful personality are important.
Conditions of employment: 9 month contracts. 30 h.p.w. between 8.30am and 9.30pm weekdays and weekends.
Salary: minimum US$750 per month.
Facilities/Support: in-service training sessions every week.
Recruitment: interviews in Mersin (late June/early July).
Contact: Gelincik Durmaz, Prinicipal.

FONO PRIVATE ELEMENTARY SCHOOL & COLLEGE
Gündogdu Caddesi 49, Merter, 34016 Istanbul. Tel: (212) 641 9900. Fax: (212) 584 2742. E-mail: acikogretim@fono.com.tr. Website: www.fono.com.tr.
Number of teachers: 6 English teachers out of staff of 25.
Preference of nationality: British.
Qualifications: must be qualified to teach elementary school and college students.
Conditions of employment: 1 year contracts. 25 lessons per week. Children aged 7-18.
Salary: twice what local teachers are paid.
Facilities/Support: assistance given with accommodation. No training.
Recruitment: adverts in *TES*. Interviews not essential.

GENCTUR
Istiklal Cad. Zambak Sok. 15/5, Taksim 80080, Istanbul. Tel: (212) 249 25 15. Fax: (212) 249 2554. E-mail: workcamps@genctur.com. Website: www.genctur.com.

Number of teachers: 10.
Preference of nationality: native (or good) English speakers.
Qualifications: experience with children, workcamp or teaching experience is preferred.
Conditions of employment: volunteering for teaching English to children aged 12-17 at workcamps for 2 weeks, through outdoor activities, games and songs.
Salary: free board and lodging.
Recruitment: only through partner voluntary organisations abroad (e.g. International Voluntary Service, Old Hall, East Bergholt, Colchester CO7 6TQ, UK; 01206-298215/ ivs@ivsgbsouth.demon.co.uk; also Concordia (01273-422218) and UNA (02920-223088). CV and 2 references needed; interviews not necessary.

INKUR ENGLISH LANGUAGE INSTITUTE
Ankara Caddesi, Yalihamam Sokak No. 8, Izmit, Kocaeli. Tel: (262) 321 5325. Fax: (262) 322 5391. E-mail: inkur1@superonline.com.
Number of teachers: 5-10.
Preference of nationality: British, American, Australian.
Qualifications: university degree and TEFL certificate.
Conditions of employment: 9-12 month contracts. 28 contact h.p.w.
Facilities/Support: accommodation, return air fare, work permit and health insurance provided and paid for by the School.
Recruitment: advertisements (e.g. in *Guardian*), affiliated schools in England, recommendations and direct applications. Interviews sometimes held in Britain.
Contact: N. G. Dogan, Director.

INTERLANG
Istanbul Cad. Halkçi Sok, Yalçinlar Han. No. 4, Kat 2-5, Bakirköy, Istanbul. Tel: (212) 543 5795/543 9915. Fax: (212) 542 7854.
Number of teachers: 40 (in 3 schools).
Preference of nationality: British, Australian, New Zealand, Canadian, American.
Qualifications: university degree and TEFL certificate.
Conditions of employment: 9-12 month contracts. 5 days p.w.
Salary: competitive. Guaranteed salary.
Facilities/Support: rent-free accommodation and flight benefits given. Resources include TV and video, computer facilities, photocopiers, etc. Regular teacher training workshops and ongoing teacher development. (Interlang is a CELTA centre.)
Recruitment: interviews held in London in July/August. Otherwise faxed application and telephone interviews acceptable.

INTERNATIONAL HOUSE
Nispetiye Cad. Güverein Duragi, Erdölen Ishani 38, Kat 1, Levent Istanbul. Tel: (212) 282 9064/65. Fax: (212) 282 3218. E-mail: info@ihistanbul.com or dos_ihistanbul@hotmail.com.
Number of teachers: 50.
Preference of nationality: none, but must be native speaker.
Qualifications: degree plus CELTA minimum. Experience.
Conditions of employment: 10-12 months. 25 hours per week.
Salary: US$900-US$1,300 per month.
Facilities/Support: helps teachers to find accommodation, usually shared and close to school. Teachers pay their own rent.
Recruitment: internet, via IH transfer scheme, direct application. Interviews essential but can be by telephone.
Contact: Sharon Leach, DOS.

ISIK LISESI (HIGH SCHOOL), ISIK ILKOGRETIM (PRIMARY & MIDDLE)
Tesvikiye Cad. No. 152, Tesvikiye, Istanbul. Tel: (212) 246 6047. Fax: (212) 2313709 (primary), (212) 2401349.
Number of teachers: 10+.

Preference of nationality: native speaker.
Qualifications: English degree and teaching certificate.
Conditions of employment: 1 year contracts (renewable, preferably long-term). About 20 teaching h.p.w.
Salary: £690 per month basic plus £10 for each year of experience up to ten years and overtime hours; two bonuses.
Facilities/Support: furnished accommodation given. Financial assistance with official procedures, service bus from school accommodation. Lunch at school cafeteria.
Recruitment: locally or through agencies abroad.

ISTANBUL LANGUAGE CENTRE
Yakut Sok. no. 10, Bakirköy, Istanbul. Tel: (212) 571 82 84-94. Fax: (212) 571 82 95. E-mail: ilm@ilm.com.tr
Number of teachers: 40 in 4 branches.
Preference of nationality: British, American.
Qualifications: university degree and TEFL certificate.
Conditions of employment: 9-12 month contracts. 28 h.p.w.
Salary: $1,000 (adjusted every 3 months according to the current US$ rate).
Facilities/Support: furnished shared accommodation provided. Training available (Trinity TESOL Cert course offered).
Recruitment: via adverts in the *Guardian* and agency in the UK, i.e. Oxford House College (gail@oxfordhouse.co.uk). Interviews can be held in UK.
Contact: Osman N. Eroglu, School Owner/Founder.

KENT ENGLISH – ANKARA
Mithatpasa Caddesi No. 46 Kat. 3,4,5, 06420 Kizilay, Ankara. Tel: (312) 433 6010/433 6010. Fax: (312) 435 7334. E-mail: kentenglishankara@yahoo.com. Also branch in Bolu: Izzet Baysai Caddesi No. 42, Kat. 3,4,5, Bolu.
Number of teachers: 30+ in Ankara.
Preference of nationality: none, but should be native speaker.
Qualifications: minimum BA plus CELTA or equivalent.
Conditions of employment: 1 year contracts. Minimum 24 contact h.p.w.
Salary: approximately £500 for new teachers (for 24 hours' teaching). Overtime available.
Facilities/support: subsidised, fully-furnished accommodation. Flight refunded and teacher training available.
Recruitment: telephone or local interviews.
Contact: Mick Preece, Assistant Director of Studies.

KENT ENGLISH – ISTANBUL
Bahariye Arayicibasi Sok No. 4, 81300 Kadiköy, Istanbul. Tel: (216) 347 2791/347 2792. Fax: (216) 348 9435. E-mail: kent@veezy.com. Website: www.kent-english.com
Number of teachers: 6 full time; 8 part time.
Preference of nationality: British, American, Canadian, Australian.
Qualifications: degree and TEFL Cert. required. Priority given to teaching experience. Mostly adults.
Conditions of employment: 8, 10 or 12 month contracts. Weekend hours: 9.30am-5pm; weekday hours: 9.30am-12.30pm and 7-9pm.
Salary: average £500 per month.
Facilities/Support: work and residency permits arranged. Some training provided. Paid vacation. Health insurance.
Recruitment: adverts and personal recommendations. Interviews essential.

THE KOC SCHOOL
P.K. 38, Pendik-Istanbul 81481. Tel: (216) 304 1003. Fax: (216) 304 1048. E-mail; chanjo@kocschool.k12.tr. Website: www.kocschool.k12.tr.
Number of teachers: 60.

Preference of nationality: none.
Qualifications: degree and teaching certification in subject field required.
Conditions of employment: 2 year contracts. Teaching hours 8am-4pm.
Salary: $16,000-$40,000 per year (net).
Facilities/Support: housing provided for faculty hired overseas. Training provided.
School takes care of paperwork for work permits.
Recruitment: primarily at recruitment fairs. Interview essential.
Contact: John Chandler, General Director.

KOPARAN LANGUAGE SCHOOL
Istiklal Cad. No. 34, Bandirma 10200. Tel: (266) 714 1414. Fax: (266) 714 5050. E-mail: koparandil@superonline.com.
Number of teachers: 2 or 3 for academic year, 40 in summer.
Preference of nationality: British for long-term staff; no preference for summer camps.
Qualifications: university degree and recognised TEFL certificate essential.
Conditions of employment: 1 year contracts (Sept-Jun). Maximum 26 h.p.w. 35 h.p.w. including meetings and preparation. Summer contract from mid-June (group flight from London) for 10 weeks. Camp is located at purpose-built resort on the Sea of Marmara.
Salary: TL equivalent of £300 per month. Pocket money of £20 per week for summer staff.
Facilities/Support: accommodation provided. Flights reimbursed (including summer flights) at end of contract.
Recruitment: via adverts in the *Guardian*. Often recruit year-round staff from summer crew. Telephone interviews.
Contact: Karen Atis, Director of Studies.

MIMAR SINAN OZEL LISESI
Inönü Caddesi, Mimar Sinan Beldesi, Büyükcekmece 34903, Istanbul. Tel: 212-881 3630. Fax: 212-883 2125. E-mail: kathleen-aytac@hotmail.com or educ@mskolej. k12.tr. Website: www.mskolej.k12.tr.
Number of teachers: 9 for this high school.
Preference of nationality: none.
Qualifications: English degree and PGCE/BEd or equivalent.
Conditions of employment: 10 month contracts or 12 months on renewal. Hours of teaching 8.50am-3.50pm.
Salary: £600-£800 p.m. depending on qualifications and experience.
Facilities/Support: 2-bedroom furnished flat provided; sole occupancy. Electricity, heating, etc. are paid by teacher.
Recruitment: local adverts, word of mouth.
Contact: K. Aytaç, Head of EFL.

NEW KENT ENGLISH
1472 Sokak. No. 32, Alsancak-Izmir. Tel: 0232 4632737. Fax: 0232 4226761.
Number of teachers: 4.
Preference of nationality: British or North American.
Qualifications: degree and TEFL Cert.
Conditions of employment: 8 or 12 months.
Salary: 300 million lira net per month and overtime for 30 teaching hours in a calendar month.
Facilities/Support: shared flat provided for teachers. Own rooms but shared facilities.
Recruitment: CV and interview by telephone.
Contact: Oktan Guner.

ONDER DIL LANGUAGE SCHOOL
Kibris Sehitleri DD. No 43, Eskisehir 26010. Tel: (222) 231 3596. Fax: (222) 233 3356. E-mail: onderdil@onderdil.com.tr. Website: www.onderdil.com.tr.

Number of teachers: 6.
Preference of nationality: British.
Qualifications: university degree and TEFL certificate.
Conditions of employment: 8-12 month contracts. Mostly evening teaching 6pm-9pm and weekends 9am-6pm. Majority of clients are university students.
Salary: TL equivalent of about US$800 per month (net).
Facilities/Support: free accommodation provided. Orientation on arrival and ongoing help given to inexperienced teachers.
Recruitment: via adverts in the *Guardian,* etc. Telephone interviews.
Contact: Mr. Mustafa Koksal, Principal.

OZEL TAN OKULLARI
Yeni Yalova Yolu, 12 Km, 16335 Ovaakça/Bursa. Tel: (224) 267 0072 (Pbx). Fax: (224) 267 0071.
Number of teachers: 3.
Preference of nationality: British, American, South African, Australian.
Qualifications: university degree of English faculty and TEFL teaching certificate.
Conditions of employment: 1 year contracts. 20 h.p.w. (class periods are 45 minutes).
Salary: TL equivalent of £375-£400 per month (net) plus all meals in school canteen.
Facilities/Support: assistance with arranging flat rentals. Assistance with obtaining work permits.
Recruitment: telephone interviews.
Contact: Mr. Sami Ipekboyayan, Head of English Department.

SISTEM ENGLISH COURSE
Arifiye Mah. Kibris Sehitleri Caddesi No 18/1, Eskisehir. Tel: (222) 231 2266. Fax: (222) 230 8681.
Number of teachers: 6.
Preference of nationality: British/American/Canadian.
Qualifications: degree plus EFL Cert. Employ both newly qualified and experienced teachers.
Conditions of employment: 9 month contracts. 30 lessons per week (50 minutes per lesson).
Salary: from TL380,000,000 to TL400,000,000 per month.
Facilities/Support: rent-free, shared flat. Teacher pays for utilities (heating, electricity etc), normally TL40,000,000. Return airfare London-Istanbul. 2 weeks paid holiday in February.
Recruitment: via adverts in the *Guardian* and the Langstar Recruitment agency in the UK. References are essential but interviews are not.
Contact: Durmus Ari, Director.

TURCO-BRITISH ASSOCIATION
Estekar Sokak 32, Avaklidere, 06680 Ankara. Tel: (312) 419 18 44. Fax: (312) 418 5404. E-mail: tba@tba.org.tr. Website: www.tba.org.tr.
Number of teachers: 10.
Preference of nationality: British.
Qualifications: degree plus TEFL Cert. Experience desirable but not essential.
Conditions of employment: 2 years (1 year negotiable). 30 hours per week including evenings and weekends.
Salary: approximately £500 monthly net, payable in the local currency.
Facilities/Support: shared, furnished flat provided free of charge.
Recruitment: via the *Guardian, TES, EL Gazette* and locally.
Contact: Peter Schooley, Director of Studies.

VIDEO ENGLISH
1717 St. 7/202 Karsyoko-Izmir. Tel/fax: (232) 368 8888. E-mail: g-yeliz@hotmail.com or r-nalcioglu@yahoo.com.
Number of teachers: 6.

Preference of nationality: British.
Qualifications: TEFL teaching Certificate minimum.
Conditions of employment: about two years. 6-day week with one day off per week. In summer there is a fifteen-day paid holiday.
Salary: negotiable depending on hours, qualifications etc.
Facilities/Support: accommodation is provided by the school.
Recruitment: via internet and e-mail. Interviews conducted with promising applicants.
Contact: Neslihan Gunduz (Owner), Rahmi Nalcioglu (Director of the school).

Other Schools to Try

Note that these schools (in alphabetical order according to town) did not confirm their teacher requirements for this edition of *Teaching English Abroad*. Upper case entries marked with an asterisk had entries in the last edition (1999).

Berlitz Language Centre, Istanbul (info@berlitz.com.tr). CELTA/Trinity Cert needed.

*BEYKENT UNIVERSITY, Foreign Language School, Beykent Beylikdirisu, 34900 Istanbul (212-872 1125/fax 212-872 2489; herguneg@superonline.com or gherguner@beyu.edu.tr). 10 teachers with an MA in TEFL.

*BRITISH ENGLISH, Cami Duragi Palazoglu Sok. No. 12/2-3-4-5-6, Sisli, Istanbul (tel/fax 216-418 8982). Employ 20 teachers and also at other Istanbul branches in Saskinbakkal and Kadiköy.

Dilfen, Ortabahce Cad. Necil Is Hani No. 11, Besiktas, Istanbul (260 7745/fax 261 2489)

*ENGLISH FAST, Zuhuratbba Cad. 42, Bakirköy, Istanbul (fax 212-561 3231). Language school group with 5 branch schools: 3 in Istanbul, 1 in Ankara, 1 in and Izmir: 440 Sokak No. 5, Konak-Izmir hiring up to 100 teachers.

English Time, Zuhuratbaba Cad. 41, Bakirköy, Istanbul; 212-543 61 60/fax 212-543 61 00; englishtimc@ superonline.com or teachers@ englishtime.com). Advertising regularly in *EL Prospects* in 2000 for native speakers with a Bachelor's degree. $650 per month.

*EYUBOGLU LISESI, Namik Kemal Mah. Dr. Rüstem Eyüboglu Sok. 1, Umraniye 81240, Istanbul (216-329 1614/fax 216-335 7198). 18 teachers with certificates. International Baccalaureate experience preferred.

*KARYA, Dr. Esat Isik Caddesi 110, Moda, 81310 Kadiköy, Istanbul (216-349 9849/fax 216-349 9853; karya@karya.com.tr) 16 teachers.

Kultur Schools, Istanbul (ful.over@veezy.com/ www.kultur.k12.tr). Teachers with BA in English or B.Ed in all subjects; or TEFL qualification plus experience of teaching children aged 5-6 or 11-13.

*LONDON LANGUAGES INTERNATIONAL (LLI), Abide-i Hurriyet Caddesi, Kat. 1, Mecidiyeköy, Istanbul (212-211 7445/fax 212-211 7441). 10 teachers.

*OZEL ORTADOGU LISESI, Spor Cad. No. 26, Yakacik, Istanbul (216-377 2501/fax 216-377 2502)

*THE ENGLISH CENTRE – IZMIR, Cumhuriyet Bulvari No. 125, Kat. 1/D/1, Alsancak, Izmir (232-463 8487/464 3275/fax 232-464 3144). 4-6 teachers.

*GEDIZ PRIVATE COLLEGE, Seyrak Beldesi, Menemen, Izmir (232-844 7444/fax 232-844 7441; baysoy@gediz.kiz.tr).

*EURO CENTER OZEL, Erman Yabanci, Dil Kursu, Mithatpasa Cad. No. 102, Kat. 4, 45300 Salihli (236-712 2330/715 0731/fax 236-713 0612). 3 experienced teachers with clear pronunciation.

*ONLY ENGLISH, Kunduracilar Cad. Dedeoglu Sok. 4/3, Trabzon (462-321 9992/fax 462-321 0223). 4 teachers on 6 or 12 month contracts. Free return flight from UK.

AFRICA

Contradictions abound in a continent as complex as Africa, and one of them pertains to the attitude to the English language. On the one hand the emergent nations of Africa want to distance themselves from their colonial past. Hence the renaming of Leopoldville, Salisbury and Upper Volta to become Kinshasa, Harare and Burkina Faso. On the other hand, they are eager to develop and participate in the world economy and so need to communicate in English.

What makes much of Africa different from Latin America and Asia (vis-à-vis English teaching) is that English is the medium of instruction in state schools in many ex-colonies of Britain including Ghana, Nigeria, Kenya, Zambia, Zimbabwe and Malawi. As in the Indian subcontinent, the majority of English teachers in these countries are locals. But there is still some demand for native speakers in the secondary schools of those countries. The only countries in which there is any significant scope for working in a private language school or institute are the Mediterranean countries of Morocco, Tunisia and Egypt.

The drive towards English extends to most parts of the continent. In 1999, VSO opened a new programme to teach English in Rwanda. It is already supporting an ELT programme in Mozambique, Tanzania, Eritrea, Ghana and Nigeria. Nearly a decade ago, newly independent Namibia decided to make English its official language to replace the hated Afrikaans. A demand for hundreds of native speakers, mainly at the advanced teacher-trainer level, was created overnight, which organisations like the Overseas Development Agency (now the Department for International Development) and VSO attempted to supply. Across southern Africa, the dominant language of business and commerce and the language of university text books is English, leaving Portuguese-speaking Mozambique out in the cold, which is why there are so many EFL teachers posted there by Skillshare Africa and VSO.

To balance the picture, it must be said that in some countries (such as Zimbabwe, Zambia and Nigeria) the demand for English teachers has fallen off in favour of science, maths and technology teachers. And continuing unrest and hostility towards the west in the Sudan means that there are few opportunities for English teachers (in a country whose government once funded hundreds of native English speakers to teach in its schools).

Even in ex-colonies of France (Morocco, Tunisia, Senegal, etc.) and of Portugal (Mozambique), English is a sought-after commodity. For example there are two British Council Teaching Centres in Francophone Cameroon (Yaoundé the capital and Douala). The only other British Council Teaching Centre in Sub-Saharan Africa is in Nairobi. But the British Council has an English Language Officer in most African countries who may be willing to advise on local opportunities (or the lack thereof).

Political instability has beleaguered a few of the countries where English is in demand, such as Algeria (which is currently too dangerous for expat teachers to consider) and Liberia from which scores of American teachers had to be evacuated a decade ago. The situation in Zimbabwe has deteriorated alarmingly in the past year with a tragic backlash against white Zimbabweans. The situation is different in North Africa where there is relatively more stability and prosperity. Libya is more like a Middle Eastern country and indeed some oil companies employ highly qualified TEFL teachers on Saudi-style salaries.

Prospects for Teachers

Few language schools exist in most African countries and even fewer can afford to employ expatriate teachers. The British Council maintains offices in most African countries and their assessment of the prospects for teachers tallies with that sent by the Information Manager of the British Council in Mbabane, Swaziland:

English language is taught from a very early stage in Swaziland. As a result there are no institutes which specifically teach it. However you may want to consider the university and colleges as institutions which teach English, even though it is at an advanced level.

Similarly in Namibia, the Language Centre at the University of Namibia (Private Bag 13301, Windhoek) is one of the few centres in the country where English is taught.

A somewhat more promising destination is Cameroon where the ELC Managers at the British Council in Douala (Immeuble Ancien, DHL, 6 rue Drouot, Douala, Boite Postale 12801) consider unsolicited applications for five posts; CELTA minimum, Diploma preferred and a minimum of 2 years' experience are required and teachers must stay a minimum of a year, preferably two. The main office in Yaoundé can be contacted at BP 818 (e-mail british.council@camnet.com) while the address above is the Teaching Centre in Douala (the commercial capital of the country). Other teaching institutes in Douala include the American Language Center and the Linguistic Centre, while in Yaoundé, the Pilot Centre and the American Center run English courses. Government-run organisations are likely to allow only Cameroonians to teach and most schools are so small and disorganised anyway that they would not be in a position to employ a native speaker.

Because a high proportion of teaching opportunities in Africa is in secondary schools rather than private language institutes, a teaching certificate is often a prerequisite. Missionary societies have played a dominant role in Africa's modern history, so many teachers are recruited through religious organisations, asking for a Christian commitment even for secular jobs.

Apart from work with aid or missionary agencies, there are quite a few opportunities for students and people in their gap year to teach in Africa. Students and other travellers have also stumbled upon chances to teach on an informal basis.

FIXING UP A JOB

Many organisations including a range of gap year agencies send people to Africa to teach English. These postings are normally regarded as 'voluntary' since if wages are paid at all they will be on a local scale though they often come with free housing. In some cases a substantial placement fee must be paid. See the chapter *Finding a Job* for further details of the general agencies like Gap Challenge who sent Sarah Johnson from Cardiff to Zanzibar in September to teach English and geography at a rural secondary school:

The expectations which Zanzibari children have from school are worlds away from those of British school children. They expect to spend most of their lessons copying from the blackboard, so will at first be completely nonplussed if asked to think things through by themselves or to use their imagination. I found that the ongoing dilemma for me of teaching in Zanzibar was whether to teach at a low level which the majority of the class would be able to understand, or teach the syllabus to the top one or two students so that they would be able to attempt exam questions, but leaving the rest of the class behind. Teaching was a very interesting and eye-opening experience. I believe that both the Zanzibari teachers and I benefitted from a cultural exchange of ideas and ways of life.

Placement Organisations

Africa & Asia Venture, 10 Market Place, Devizes, Wilts. SN10 1HT. Tel: (01380) 729009. Fax: (01380) 720060. E-mail: av@aventure.co.ukaventure@aol.com. Places school leavers and recent graduates as assistant teachers in primary and secondary schools in Kenya, Uganda, Zimbabwe, Tanzania and Malawi, normally for one term.

Programme includes in-country orientation course, insurance, allowances paid during work attachment and organised safari at end of four months. Conservation work also available. The 2001 participation fee is about £2190 plus air fares.

Amity Volunteer Teachers Abroad (AVTA), Amity Institute, 10671 Roselle St, Suite 101, San Diego, CA 92121-1525, USA. Tel: 858-455-6364. Fax: 858-455-6597. E-mail: mail@amity.org/. Website: www.amity.org. Provides voluntary teaching opportunities in Senegal and Ghana. ATVA volunteers are given full room and board with a host family as well as pocket money amounting to about $15-$25 a week. Participants must be at least 21 and stay for one academic year from January/February or August/September. Knowledge of French is useful for Senegal but not required.

BUNAC, 16 Bowling Green Lane, London EC1R 0BD. Tel: 020-7251 2372. Fax: 020-7251 0215. Teach in Ghana programme (see section on Ghana below). Also have Work South Africa programme which allows participants to look for jobs after arrival, including as TEFL teachers.

Concern Worldwide, 248-250 Lavender Hill, London SW11 1LJ. Tel: 020-7738 1033. Fax: 020-7738 1032. Main office, which is also the recruiting office is in Ireland (52-55 Lower Camden St, Dublin 2; 1-475 4162). Recruits mostly qualified teachers over 21 for a range of development projects including education in Ethiopia, Mozambique, Tanzania, Uganda and Rwanda.

Daneford Trust, 45-47 Blythe St, London E2 0LL. Tel/fax: 020-7729 1928. E-mail: dftrust@aol.com. Small educational trust which encourages work and education exchanges between young people from inner-city London and young people from Africa (Namibia and Zimbabwe) and other parts of the world for a minimum of three months. Volunteers raise at least £2,000 towards costs with help from the Trust. Must be committed to ongoing development of overseas experience in local community in UK.

i-to-i, One Cottage Road, Headingley, Leeds LS6 4DD. Tel: 0870-333 2332. Fax: 0113 274 6923. E-mail: info@i-to-i.com. Website: www.i-to-i.com. A TEFL training and voluntary placements organisation specialising in voluntary English teaching in many countries including Ghana and Uganda.

Joint Co-operation Trust, 39 Handel Mansions, Wyatt Drive, London, SW13 8AH; tel: 020-8563 1456; fax: 020-8287 6619. E-mail: Tice@btinternet.com. JCT is a charity which recruits teachers to work in rural government primary schools in Tanzania (Morogoro region). The aim is to help Tanzanian primary school teachers become better teachers of English language (see entry under *Tanzania*).

Peace Corps, Room 803E, 1111 20th St NW, Washington DC 20526. Tel: 1-800-424-8580 (toll-free). Volunteers teach on 2-year assignments in many African countries.

Project Trust, Hebridean Centre, Ballyhough, Isle of Coll, Argyll PA78 6TE. Tel: (01879) 230444. Fax: (01879) 230357. Sends some school leavers (aged 17-19) to teach (often science rather than English) in schools in Namibia, Egypt, Uganda, Botswana, Malawi, Lesotho, South Africa, Tanzania and rural Zimbabwe. Participants must fund-raise to cover part of the cost of the placement, at present about £3,250.

St. David's (Africa) Trust, St. David's House, Rectory Road, Crickhowell, Powys NP8 1DW. Tel/fax: 01873 810665. E-mail: info@africatrust.gi. Website: www.africatrust.gi. 3-6 month placements in Ghana and Morocco for a few gap year students to work with needy children.

Students Partnership Worldwide (SPW), Westminster School, 17 Dean's Yard, London SW1P 3PB. Tel: 0171-222 0138/976 8070. Fax: 0171-233 0008/963 1006. E-mail: spwuk@gn.apc.org. Places school leavers for 6-10 months in secondary schools in Tanzania, Zimbabwe, Uganda, South Africa and Namibia.

Skillshare Africa, 126 New Walk, Leicester LE1 7JA. Tel: (0116) 254 1862. E-mail: skillshare-uk@geo2.poptel.org.uk. Website: www.skillshare.org. Registered charity has vacancies for volunteer teachers to work for two years in southern Africa (Lesotho, Botswana, Mozambique (increasing number), Swaziland, Namibia and South Africa). Pay approximately £500 per month plus flights, accommodation, insurance, etc.

Teachers for Africa, 5040 E Shea Blvd, 260, Phoenix, AZ 85254-4687, USA. Tel: (602) 443-1800 or (800) 835-3530. Fax: (602) 443-1824. E-mail: recep@ primenet.com. Website: www.ifesh.org. Under the auspices of the International Foundation for Education and Self-Help (IFESH), arranges for teachers and college/university professors to teach TOEFL/TESL (and numerous other subjects) in Ethiopia, Benin, Guinea, Malawi, Ghana, Namibia and Nigeria at colleges, universities and secondary schools. Teachers with strong French skills particularly needed. Teachers are expected to stay for an academic year (i.e. about 10 months) and must be either US citizens or permanent residents of the US. In return volunteers get a monthly stipend of US$800, health insurance, international transportation and pre-departure and settling-in allowances.

Teaching and Projects Abroad, Gerrard House, Rustington, West Sussex BN16 1AW Tel: (01903) 859911. Fax: (01903) 785779. E-mail: info@teaching-abroad. co.uk. Website: www.teaching-abroad.co.uk. Work placements in Ghanaian schools (see section below).

United Children's Fund Inc. PO Box 20341, Boulder, CO 80308-3341 (303-464-0137/888-343-3199/ www.unchildren.org). Volunteers work in rural Uganda including in primary and secondary schools teaching English and other subjects for short periods or six months. The cost starts at $820 for one week, $1,550 for three weeks up to $6,750 for six months, excluding airfares.

VSO, 317 Putney Bridge Road, London SW15 2PN. Tel: 020-8780 7500. Sends teachers to Mozambique, Tanzania, Eritrea, Ghana, Nigeria and Rwanda. Also advertising for secondary school teachers for Malawi with degree and TEFL experience.

WorldTeach Inc, Center for International Development, Harvard University, 79 John F Kennedy Street, Cambridge, MA 02138, USA. Tel: 617-5527/800-4-TEACH-O14. Fax: 617-495 1599. E-mail: info@worldteach.org. Non-profit organisation which recruits volunteers to teach English for one year in Namibia and also has a programme in South Africa. Volunteers pay about $3,500 for airfares, orientation and insurance.

Religious Organisations

The following missionary societies place English teachers in Africa; in many cases a Christian commitment is a prerequisite:

Christians Abroad, Room 233, Bon Marché Centre, 241-251 Ferndale Road, London SW9 8BJ. Tel: 020-7346 5951. Send teachers to Tanzania.

Action Partners, Bawtry Hall, Bawtry, Doncaster DN10 6JH. Tel: 01302 710570. E-mail: info@actionpartners.org.uk. Website: www.actionpartners.org.uk. Places qualified teachers in Christian schools in Africa, e.g. Egypt, Nigeria and Sudan.

Africa Inland Mission International, 2 Vorley Road, Archway, London N19 5HE. Tel: 020-7281 1184; Also: Box 178, Pearl River, NY 10965. E-mail: uk@aim-eur.org. Website: www.aim-eur.org. Offices also in France and the Netherlands. Have a few opportunities from time to time for evangelical Christians to teach English in East African nations, i.e. Kenya, Uganda, Tanzania and the Comoros Islands.

US State Department Programmes

The US State Department has English Teaching Programs at its Cultural Centers attached to American embassies in a few African countries (in addition to North Africa treated separately below). Virtually all hiring of teachers takes place locally, so speculative applications from overseas are seldom welcome. Only two American Cultural Centers in Africa made contact for this edition:

Madagascar: English Teaching Program, 4 Lalana Dr., Razafindratandra Ambohidahy, Antananarivo, Madagascar. Tel: 261-20 22 202 38. Fax: 261-20 22 213 97. E-mail: etptana@compro.mg. Website: www.usmission.mg/etp.htm. Occasionally hires native speakers of English for short-term work. Prior teaching experience is essential. Pay is on local (Malagasy) scale; i.e. US$3-6 per hour. No benefits.

Togo: Centre Culturel Américain, Rues Kouenou & Tokmake, B.Postale 852, Lomé, Togo. Tel: +228 21 21 66/21 29 91/92/93/94. Fax: 21 77 94. E-mail: usis@cafe.tge.
Other American Language Programmes in Africa might be worth trying:
Burkina Faso: American Language Center, 01 B.P. 539, Ouagadougou-01, Burkina Faso. Tel: 30 63 60. Fax: 31 52 73.
Burundi: American Cultural Center, B.P. 810, 20-22 Chee P. L. Rwagasore, Bujumbura, Burundi. Tel: 22 33 12/22 56 46. Fax: 22 45 61.
Congo: English Language Program, B.P. 2053, Brazzaville, Congo. Tel: 83 83 94. Fax: 83 46 90.
Zaire: Zaire-American Language Institute, ACC, B.P. 8622, Kinshasa 1, Zaire. Tel: 88 43604, ext. 2497/2155.

If teachers (British as well as American) are prepared to travel to an African capital for an interview, they may well get taken on, as happened to the director of one English Language Program:

> *Work in an American Cultural Center is a great way to start off. I myself did it five years ago and am now running a programme. It allows a person to work in Africa but also provides up-to-date material which teachers in the national programmes are often forced to go without. Classes are small and the hours are not too heavy but can usually be increased depending on the capabilities of the teacher. We also do outside programmes in specialised institutions and thus give teachers experience in ESP (hotels, oil companies, Ministries). People with degrees in EFL are very much in demand.*

Miscellaneous Opportunities

Commercial agencies have few clients in Africa. One exception is *Worldwide Educational Services* which recruits for English-medium colleges in Egypt, and ELS Language Centres/Middle East, PO Box 3079, Abu Dhabi, UAE (Elsme@ emirates.net.ae) which employs native speaker teachers in Cairo.

At the opposite end of the spectrum, grass roots voluntary organisations may have teaching positions. Omar Drammeh (c/o Edirssa Kujabi, Gambia Airways, Banjul International Airport, Gambia; fax +220 472277) invites volunteers to come to the Muslim village of Galoya to teach English as well as sustainable agriculture. Another possibility for teaching in the Gambia is arranged by the Marlborough Brandt Group (1A London Road, Marlborough, Wilts. SN8 1PH; tel/fax 01672 514078) which sends a few volunteers annually to teach in the Gambian village of Gunjur for 10 months. The fund-raising target is £3,000.

Eight-month attachments to village primary schools in the district of Mshiri in Tanzania are possible for about eight participants a year as part of the Village Education Project (Kilimanjaro), c/o Katy Allen, Project Leader, Mint Cottage, Prospect Road, Sevenoaks, Kent TN13 3UA; 01732 459799. Their volunteers are mainly gap year students who train in the UK for two weeks before departure. The cost to the volunteers for participating in the project is about £1,500 plus insurance.

On the Spot

The best chances of picking up language teaching work on the spot are in North Africa, in Egypt, Morocco or Tunisia (treated separately below). Language schools are thriving in South Africa staffed in large measure by English-speaking South Africans but also by foreigners (see entries for *Cape Studies* and *ih Language Lab*) or try Cape Communication Centre (66 Strand Street, Cape Town 8001). Tourists can enter South Africa on a tourist visa for three months, renewable for a further three at an office of the Department of Home Affairs.

Opportunities crop up in very obscure corners of the continent. For example EU nationals are entitled to work in Réunion, a *département* of France between Madagascar and Mauritius. Apparently there is a market for freelance teachers; consider advertising in the papers *Quotidien* and *SIR*.

PROBLEMS AND REWARDS

If teachers in Finland and Chile suffer from culture shock, teachers in rural Africa often find themselves struggling to cope at all. Whether it is the hassle experienced by women teachers in Muslim North Africa or the loneliness of life in a rural West African village, problems proliferate. Anyone who has fixed up a contract should try to gather as much up-to-date information as possible before departure, preferably by attending some kind of orientation programme or briefing. Otherwise local customs can come as a shock, for example finding yourself being bowed to (as Malawians do to anyone in a superior job). On a more basic level, you will need advice on how to cope with climatic extremes. Even Cairo can be unbearably hot in the summer (and surprisingly rainy and chilly in January/February).

One unexpected problem is being accorded too much respect, as Mary Hall describes:

> *A white person is considered to be the be-all and end-all of everyone's problems for whatever reason. It's quite difficult to live with this image...Stare and stare again, never a moment to yourself. I'd like to say the novelty wore off but it never did. Obviously adaptability has to be one of the main qualities. We had no running water, intermittent electricity and a lack of such niceties as cheese and chocolate.*

A certain amount of deprivation is almost inevitable; for example teachers, especially volunteers, can seldom afford to shop in the pricey expatriate stores and so will have to be content with the local diet, typically a staple cereal such as millet usually made into a kind of stodgy porridge, plus some cooked greens, tinned fish or meat and fruit. The cost of living in some African cities like Libreville and Douala is in fact very high, and a teaching wage does not normally permit a luxurious lifestyle.

Health is obviously a major concern to anyone headed for Africa. The fear of HIV-contaminated blood or needles in much of central Africa prompts many teachers to outfit themselves with a complete expat medical kit before leaving home (see Introduction). Malaria is rife and there is an alarming amount of mosquito resistance to the most common prophylactics, so this too must be sorted out with a tropical diseases expert before departure.

The visa situation differs from country to country of course but is often a headache. Whereas in Cameroon it is not really necessary to obtain a work permit, in Ethiopia it is much more problematic.

If all that Africa could offer was a contest with malaria and a diet of porridge, no one would consider teaching there. But anyone who has seen movies like *Out of Africa Gorillas in the Mist* or *The English Patient* can imagine how the continent holds people in thrall. A chance to see the African bush, to climb the famous peaks of Kilimanjaro or Kenya, to frequent the colourful markets, these are the pleasures of Africa which so many people who have worked there find addictive.

Egypt

Despite past attacks on tourists by Islamic fundamentalists, there is anything but hostility to the English language in Egypt. Of Egyptians who want to learn English, a large percentage is from the business community, though there is also a demand among university students and school children. Many young Egyptians who aspire to work in their country's tourist industry want to learn English. Students at tourism training centres like the one in Luxor might be looking for some private tuition from a native speaker.

At one end of the spectrum there are the two British Council Teaching Centres in Cairo and Alexandria and the International Language Institute in Cairo affiliated to International House. At the other there are plenty of dubious establishments. Whereas you will need a professional profile for the former, back street schools will be less fussy. The British Council in Cairo has a list of English medium schools in Cairo plus a short list of TEFL establishments, several of which are in the suburb of Dokki.

The British Council in Agouza, Cairo is probably the first place to check for work. The Director of TEFL will give you a form to fill out and then you may be asked to stand in for a practice lesson observed by the usual teacher. (You will have been given a lesson beforehand to prepare). If they think you are suitable they'll take you on which is more likely during the summer when the regular teachers tend to go away to escape the heat. During exam time there is also a need for paid invigilators. The British Council (as always) has a great library and is a good place to teach. There is another British Council in Heliopolis which is quite a way out of town and therefore has its own social world. The El-Alsson School (PO Box 13, Imbaba) out near the Pyramids employs a number of expat teachers.

Dan Boothby has spent time in Cairo, most recently from February 2000 and found it almost alarmingly easy to find work:

> *I taught one-to-one lessons to several people and got about 5 hours a week work and charged £10 an hour. Frankly this was much more than I was worth but if you charge less than the market rate then it is felt that you are an amateur. I taught an isolated and lonely 5 year old, son of the Georgian Consul, where I was more a babysitter than a tutor. I felt so guilty about charging E£50 an hour that I spent an hour trying to get him to learn something. I didn't feel so guilty charging E£55 to tutor the Georgian Ambassador since he probably passed the bill onto his government.*
>
> *I got a lot of students through friends that I made who were teaching at the international schools. The kids at these schools are often in need of extra tuition towards exam times when their parents realise that they've been mucking about all year and are close to failing. The problem is that the kids tend to be very uninterested and so it is difficult to make them concentrate. But I enjoyed one-to-ones. One could build up a large group of students and earn a decent wage but equally teach less hours and have more time – one of the reasons for getting out of England.*

Writing in the fortnightly newspaper *Overseas Jobs Express* in 2000, David Stanford describes his job-hunt:

> *I had had a chance conversation with a teacher in a Jerusalem youth hostel. He told me the demand for qualified and unqualified native speakers was still high in Cairo, so I put my faith in his advice and bought a cheap single from Gatwick to Cairo. On arrival I had £300 in my pocket, more than enough to support myself for the first month. Armed with Susan Griffith's excellent [sic] book from which I made a list of schools to contact, I found success on my first day. I gave my details to the receptionist at an evening classes institute in central Cairo and in the afternoon I was summoned from my hotel room to see the manager of the institute. He hired me to start on Monday.*

Cairo seems to be a city where work seeks out the casual teacher rather than the other way round. Taxi drivers and hotel staff may ask you, unprompted, if you are available to teach. Most of these are genuine offers but it is best (especially for women) to be cautious. Most job-seekers find that potential bosses are not as interested in their educational background and experience as in how much confidence they can project. It is not unknown for an interview to take place over a game of chess and plenty of glasses of tea so that your general demeanour can be assessed. Jobs seem to be available year-round, so there is no right or wrong time to arrive.

Language schools are not all located in central Cairo but also in the leafy prosperous residential areas like Heliopolis, Maadi or Zamalek. These are also the best areas to look for private clients as Ian McArthur found:

In Cairo I sought to work as a private English tutor. I made a small poster, written in English and Arabic, with the help of my hotel owner. I drew the framework of a Union Jack at the top, got 100 photocopies and then meticulously coloured in the flags. The investment cost me £3. I put the posters up around Cairo, concentrating on affluent residential and business districts. I ended up teaching several Egyptian businessmen, who were difficult to teach since they hated being told what to do.

A simpler way of advertising your availability to teach might be to place an advert in the expatriate monthly *Cairo Today* or the fortnightly *Maadi Messenger*. The American University, centrally located at the eastern end of Tahrir Square, is a good place to find work contacts. Also try the notice boards at the Community Services Administration (CSA, Road 21, Maadi, Cairo; csaegypt@intouch.com/ www.csa-egypt.com) where a range of adult education courses for expats is offered. If you do decide to advertise your services as a freelance tutor, it might be a good idea to rent a post office box from a business centre (e.g. the IBA Center in Garden City).

According to Dan Boothby, the best places to meet other expats and find out about work opportunities are Deals Bar and Aubergine Restaurant in Zamalek and Deals 2 near the American University and the BCA (British Community Association) in Mohandiseen where you can only go as the guest of a member. Sunny Supermarket in Zamalek has a good noticeboard for jobs and flat shares.

Students

Bryn Thomas describes his Egyptian pupils at the International Language Institute in the northwest suburb of Sahafeyeen (now the El-Alsson School) as 'rowdy and sometimes a little over-enthusiastic'. Having just obtained a Cambridge Certificate in London, Bryn went to visit some friends in Cairo and was immediately offered a three-month summer contract where they were desperate for a teacher. He had to adapt his lessons to please both the ebullient Egyptian youths and a group of shy and industrious Somalis. Bryn describes his predicament with such a mixed class:

Different religions, different ways of thinking and (as I learnt in my first week at the school) different modes of dress must all be taken into consideration. One of the problems that English students in this area have difficulty with is hearing the difference between B and P. The exercise for this is to hold a piece of paper in front of the mouth and repeat the letters B and P. Since more air is exhaled during the sounding of the letter P than with B, the paper should fly up when P is said, and move only a little with B. The first time I made the students do this we went round the class, first Hamid the engineer from Alexandria, then Mona who was trying to get a job at the reception in the Hilton and then we came to Magda from Mogadishu (the capital of Somalia). All the Egyptians started to laugh – her whole face apart from her eyes was covered with a yashmak. I decided that this should not impede the exercise so if the yashmak moved it was a P, and not a B!

Wages at the less prestigious schools will probably start at E£1,000 per month rising to E£3,500 (gross) at ILI Heliopolis. Living expenses are cheap in Egypt and taxes low (5-7%). This may account for the fact that the Cambridge Certificate course offered by ILI Heliopolis (an IH-affiliate) is one of the cheapest available (see entry in *Directory of Training Courses*). Anyone who obtains the CELTA in Cairo is virtually guaranteed a job locally.

Most teachers enter Egypt on a tourist visa (which can be purchased at the airport) and then ask their school to help them extend it. Work permits must be applied for from the Ministry of the Interior. (Unusually, work permits are not processed by Egyptian representatives abroad.)

The paper should flutter when you sound the letter 'p'

LIST OF SCHOOLS

AMIDEAST AMERICAN CENTER ALEXANDRIA
English Teaching Program, 3 El Pharana St, Alexandria. Tel: (3) 483 1922. Fax: (3) 487 9644. E-mail: alexandria@amideast.org. Website: www.amideast.org.
Number of teachers: 15.
Preference of nationality: North American.
Qualifications: minimum CELTA or TESOL certification.
Conditions of employment: local term-to-term hire agreements according to student numbers. 20 h.p.w. Nine 5-week sessions per year. Students are working adults and university students.
Salary: US$8.50-$15 an hour.
Facilities/Support: good teachers' resources, internet access. Operates out of two old mansions. No assistance with accommodation.
Recruitment: enquires accepted by e-mail but on-site recruitment preferred.
Contact: Virginia Carley, Academic Co-ordinator.

ELS LANGUAGE CENTERS/MIDDLE EAST
PO Box 3079, Abu Dhabi, UAE. Tel: (2) 651516. Fax: (2) 653165. E-mail: Elsme@emirates.net.ae.
Number of teachers: 2-3 full-time and some part-time for centre in Cairo.
Preference of nationality: North American, though others may be acceptable.
Qualifications: MA in TESL preferred but may accept people with BA, CELTA and 3 years' experience.
Conditions of employment: 1 or 2 year contracts. 30 contact hours p.w. Full-time teachers are permitted to give private tuition. Some summer opportunities may be available.
Facilities/Support: accommodation provided. Deductions from salary made for social security contributions and tax. Standardised orientation given to all new teachers.
Recruitment: TESOL conventions and via the internet.

Ghana

As one of the most stable countries in Africa, Ghana supports several organised schemes for volunteer teachers. BUNAC's *Teach in Ghana* is described in the entry below. BUNAC also runs a more general Work in Ghana programme for three to six months on which participants can arrange teaching placements in schools and universities. (Ghanaians all learn English at school.) *Teaching and Projects Abroad* (see chapter *Finding a Job*) sends paying volunteers mainly to village primary schools for short-term attachments. The programme offers various starting dates and durations for a fee of £1,555 excluding flights to Accra.

A grass-roots Ghanaian organisation WWOOF/FIOH Ghana (c/o Ebenezer Nortey-Mensah, PO Box TF 154, Trade Fair Centre, Accra, Ghana; tel/fax 23321-766825) runs a varied working abroad programme which includes placing foreign students and teachers in kindergartens, primary schools and a technical school to teach English and other subjects. Volunteer placements last from one to six months and accommodation is free. The application fee is US$30 plus 3 IRCs. Similarly, G-NETT the Global Youth Travel Network (PO Box M542, Kumasi-Ghana; 51-26880/goldlink@ghana.com) hosts international volunteers for three weeks to six months. Some volunteers assist with the new English syllabus in junior and senior secondary schools.

A short-term volunteer programme in Ghana is co-ordinated by Cross-Cultural Solutions (47 Potter Avenue, New Rochelle, NY 10801; 800-380-4777/ www.crossculturalsolutions.org); volunteers are placed in villages around the town of Ho in the eastern Plains of Ghana to teach English for a few weeks in village schools (among other projects). The programme fee of $1,850 covers all expenses while in Ghana but not airfares.

The British Council in Accra (PO Box 771) lists three English teaching centres:
The Language Centre, University of Ghana, Legon (21-500381)
Institute of Languages, PO Box M67, Accra (21-221052/221092)
Centre of Language and Professional Studies, PO Box 4501, Accra

TEACH IN GHANA
BUNAC, 16 Bowling Green Lane, London EC1R 0QH. Tel: 020-7251 3472. Fax: 020-7251 0215. E-mail: enquiries@bunac.org.uk. Website: www.bunac.org.
Number of teachers: limited number.
Preference of nationality: British only.
Qualifications: less than 27 years of age. Must have graduated in previous two years in English, modern languages, geography, maths, sciences, accounting or design and technology. Some classroom experience required.
Conditions of employment: 9 month positions from August.
Salary: about $50 per month. Total cost of programme is about £1,400 including 12-month return flight.
Facilities/Support: rented accommodation or homestay provided. Back up provided by sponsoring partner organisation Student & Youth Travel Organisation (SYTO) in Accra. Compulsory insurance arranged by BUNAC (included in fee quoted above).
Recruitment: applications must be accompanied by £100 programme deposit. Interviews in UK. Applications forwarded to Ministry of Education in Ghana. Balance of fees must be paid by end of June.

Kenya

Kenya is another country which has a chronic shortage of secondary school teachers. The worst shortages are in Western Province. English is the language of instruction in

Kenyan schools, so not knowing Swahili need not be an impossible barrier. However the Kenyan Ministry of Education restricts jobs in the state sector to those who have a university degree, teaching certification and at least one year of professional teaching experience. This was a major shift from the days when many teachers had no more advanced qualifications than a few 'A' levels. Obviously each case is decided on its own merits and it seems that the Kenyan government does not always enforce this stipulation rigorously, especially in the case of science teachers. The few private language institutes that there are in Nairobi (two of which are included in the Directory) are not subject to this restriction. The British Council in Nairobi which has its own teaching operation at Harry Thuku Road opposite the Norfolk Hotel (2-334855/ general.enquiries@bc-htr.bcouncil.org) may be able to offer advice.

According to the Kenyan High Commission in London (45 Portland Place,WIN 4AS), all non-Kenyan citizens who wish to work must be in possession of a work permit issued by the Principal Immigration Officer, Department of Immigration, PO Box 30191, Nairobi, before they can take up paid or unpaid work. It is not certain that immigration regulations would be strictly enforced in the case of native English speakers looking for teaching work on the spot. Certainly in the past it was possible to fix up a teaching job by asking in the villages, preferably before terms begin in September, January and April. Be prepared to produce your CV and any diplomas and references on headed paper.

Also ascertain before accepting a post whether or not the school can afford to pay a salary, especially if it is a *Harrambee* school, i.e. non-government, self-help schools in rural areas. A cement or mud hut with a thatched or tin roof will normally be provided for the teacher's accommodation plus a local salary which would be just enough to live on provided you don't want to buy too much peanut butter or cornflakes in the city. Living conditions will be primitive with no running water or electricity in the majority of cases. The Kenyan version of maize porridge is called *Ugali*. In Daisy Waugh's book *A Small Town in Africa* she describes how when she arrived at the village of Isiolo (a few miles from Nairobi) where she had arranged to teach, she was told that they didn't need any teachers and there were no pupils. She patiently waited and five weeks into term, her class arrived.

People who choose to teach in Kenya do it for love not money. In the words of Ermon O. Kamara, PhD, former Director of the *American Universities Preparation & Learning Centre:*

> *Candidates must view being in Kenya as a holiday with pay. The cost of living and corresponding local salaries sound quite low to foreigners. Consequently they must think of the opportunities to enjoy Kenya's beaches, mountains and game parks as well as experiencing a new and interesting culture. During weekends and holidays, one can travel the breadth of Kenya. Also the proximity to other countries in East and Southern Africa permits a traveller to see a good deal of our continent.*

School vacations take place in December, April and August.

Global Routes in the US offer 12-week voluntary internships to students who teach English and other subjects in village schools in Kenya. There are no specific requirements apart from an ability to afford the programme fee of $3,550 for the summer and nearly $4,000 for the spring and autumn (excluding airfares).

AMERICAN UNIVERSITIES PREPARATION & LEARNING CENTRE
PO Box 14842, (Westlands Road, Chiromo Lane), Nairobi. Tel: (2) 741764. Fax: (2) 741690. E-mail: aupi@africaonline.co.ke.
Number of teachers: 16.
Preference of nationality: American, Canadian, British, Australian.
Qualifications: BA (English)/TEFL qualification; experience preferred.
Conditions of employment: 1 year renewable contracts. Daytime only. Students aged 16-40.

Salary: stipend based on local rates.
Facilities/Support: accommodation provided and paid for by school. Training provided.
Recruitment: local interviews if possible or telephone interview.
Contact: Mrs. Martha Muchori, Director.

THE LANGUAGE CENTER LTD
PO Box 40661, (Ndemi Close, Off Ngong Road), Nairobi. Tel: (2) 569531/569532/570610/570612. Fax: (?) 569533. E-mail: tlc@africaonline.co.ke. Website: www.africaonline.co.ke/tlc.
Number of teachers: 6-8.
Preference of nationality: British, American.
Qualifications: overseas teaching experience. University education. Cambridge CELTA and other teaching certificates desirable. Preferably aged 28-36.
Conditions of employment: 1-2 year contracts. 20 hours of work, 8.25am-12.35pm plus optional afternoon/evening work. Majority of students are adults though some children's classes offered.
Salary: based on hourly rate of 430 Kenyan shillings (US$6) for the first year.
Facilities/Support: no assistance with accommodation. Medical insurance, work permit and at-work training provided.
Recruitment: through local newspaper adverts, overseas publications and word of mouth.

PEPONI SCHOOL
PO Box 236, Ruiru, Kenya. Tel: (151) 54007/54251. Fax: (151) 54479. E-mail: peponi@form-net.com.
Number of teachers: 16 (out of staff of 21) at this full-curriculum private boarding school.
Preference of nationality: must be conversant with British exam system.
Qualifications: full degree qualification plus teaching certificate and 4 years' experience.
Conditions of employment: by law, 2 year contracts (renewable). 33 40-minute lessons per week and exams and curricular help.
Salary: 92,000-109,000 Kenyan shillings per month (gross) less a third in tax and contributions.
Facilities/Support: on-site accommodation provided. School arranges work permits. Inset training meetings every term.
Recruitment: adverts and interviews in UK.
Contact: D. J. Marshall, Headmaster.

Morocco

Although Morocco is a Francophone country, English is increasingly a requirement for entrance to university or high ranking jobs, and there is increasing demand from the business communities of the main cities. Like so many African countries, Morocco has sought to improve the standards of education for its nationals so that almost all teaching jobs in schools and universities are now filled by Moroccans. But outside the state system there is a continuing demand for native speakers.

The Moroccan Ministry of Labour stipulates that the maximum number of foreign staff in any organisation cannot exceed 50%. It also insists that all foreign teachers have at least a university degree before they can be eligible for a work permit. Work permits are obtained after arrival by applying for authorisation from the Ministère de l'Emploi, Quartier des Ministères, Rabat. You will need copies of your diplomas, birth certificate and so on. Although a knowledge of French is not a formal requirement, it is a great asset for anyone planning to spend time in Morocco.

A number of commercial language schools employ native English speakers. The hourly rate of pay at most schools is between £5 and £7. American Language Centers are located in the main cities of Morocco. They are private institutes but are affiliated to and partially funded by the United States Information Agency. In addition to the three included in the Directory, American Language Centers are listed at the end of this section.

LIST OF SCHOOLS

AMERICAN LANGUAGE CENTER
Rue des Nations-Unies, Cité Suisse, Agadir. Tel: (8) 821589. Fax: (8) 848272. E-mail: alcagad@casanet-a.net.ma.
Number of teachers: 3-6.
Preference of nationality: native speakers preferred.
Qualifications: minimum BA. Teaching experience preferable, especially overseas. MA a bonus.
Conditions of employment: 10 month contracts (October-July). Hours of teaching are mostly evenings and some afternoons.
Salary: 95-100 dirhams (gross) per hour plus medical insurance and one month paid vacation leave. 24%-44% withheld for taxes.
Facilities/Support: help teachers to find apartment; small housing stipend. In-service workshops each session and annual teaching conference.
Recruitment: internet and word of mouth. Phone interviews acceptable. Interviews can sometimes be arranged in US in conjunction with TESOL Convention.
Contact: Diane J Hyra, Director.

AMERICAN LANGUAGE CENTER
1 Place de la Fraternité, Casablanca 20000. Tel: (2) 277765. Fax: (2) 2074 57. E-mail: alc.casa@casanet.net.ma.
Number of teachers: 15.
Preference of nationality: North American, but British teachers are welcome to apply.
Qualifications: BA degree (or equivalent), some TEFL Certification and a minimum of two years' practical teaching experience, preferably overseas.
Conditions of employment: a standard contract is for 12 months from 1 September to 31 August. Contact hours are from 18 to 24 hours a week.
Salary: based on qualifications and experience. For example a BA, certification and three years of TEFL experience would expect the equivalent of $12 per hour. Taxes are relatively high. Medical insurance (80% reimbursable) is provided for all full-time teachers. A ticket to New York (for North Americans) or London is provided if a teacher successfully completes two years at the Center.
Facilities/Support: one flat available to house three teachers. Help in finding accommodation is given.
Recruitment: from CVs and on spec letters of application received. All paperwork necessary for teachers to obtain work permits is done by administration staff. New teachers have to bring a copy of their birth certificate and University diplomas.
Contact: Jeffrey Bailey, Director of Studies.

AMERICAN LANGUAGE CENTER
Rue de Sebta, Complexe Mont Joli, 2nd Floor, Appt. 15, Mohammedia. Tel (3) 32 6870. Fax (3) 32 7917. E-mail: alcmoh@casanet.net.ma.
Number of teachers: 4.
Preference of nationality: none.
Qualifications: minimum BA and ESL or EFL teaching.
Conditions of employment: 1 year contracts. Most teaching is in evenings. School cannot guarantee more than 15 h.p.w. (Students sign up for 30 hour course at a time).
Salary: basic rate of 62 dirhams per hour for employee with BA. Increments of 6 dirhams an hour for an EFL/ESL qualification, 10 dirhams for an MA, and 2 dirhams for each year of teaching experience (maximum of 5 years).

Facilities/Support: no assistance given with accommodation.
Recruitment: personal application from people already resident in Morocco. Interviews in US also possible.

AMERICAN LANGUAGE CENTER
4 Zankat Tanja, Rabat 10000. Tel: (7) 761269/766121/767103. Fax: (7) 767255/767447. E-mail: alcrabat@mtds.com.
Number of teachers: 25 full-time and 20 part-time teachers.
Preference of nationality: none although mostly North American.
Qualifications: BA in arts/letters mandatory; knowledge of French or Arabic highly desirable. MA (TEFL) or TEFL qualification preferred.
Conditions of employment: 1 year renewable contracts. 20-25 h.p.w. full time. Hours of work between 8am and 10pm weekdays, 9am and 9pm Saturdays. Pupils aged from 5, mostly aged 14-35.
Salary: US$10,000-$15,000 per year (gross) for October-July school year. Possibility of paid overtime. Paid sick leave and medical insurance provided.
Facilities/Support: free housing provided for 3-4 weeks while permanent accommodation is sought. Pre- and in-service training given. Free e-mail for teachers.
Recruitment: through TESOL convention and some walk-ins. Personal interviews essential.

BRITISH CENTRE
3 rue Brahim el Amraoui, Casablanca. Tel: (2) 267019/273190. Fax: (2) 267043. E-mail: british.centre.c@casanet.ma.
Number of teachers: 27 (10 native speakers).
Preference of nationality: none.
Qualifications: CELTA or equivalent plus at least 1 year's experience.
Conditions of employment: 1 year contracts, renewable.
Salary: average 9,000 Moroccan dirhams per month (net).
Facilities/Support: help with work permits and accommodation. In-house training with regular seminars and workshops.
Recruitment: local interview preferred, but not essential.
Contact: Jeremy Morgan, Director of Studies.

EF ENGLISH FIRST
20 rue du Marché, Résidence Benomar, Maaris, Casablanca. Tel: (2) 254400/254405. Fax: (2) 25 44 43.
Number of teachers: 5.
Preference of nationality: British, Canadian, Australian, American or Irish.
Qualifications: university degree and certificate in EFL/ESL.
Conditions of employment: 10-month renewable contracts. Up to 27 contact hours p.w. School open from 9am to 9pm Monday to Friday and 9am to 1pm on Saturday.
Salary: US$720 per month plus bonus.
Facilities/Support: help with finding accommodation. Visa/Work Permit provided. Paid holidays. Flight costs reimbursed. Orientation on arrival and ongoing training. Variety of resources.
Recruitment: directly through school or through English First offices worldwide including London and Boston.
Contact: W. Benfares.

Other Schools to Try

ALC, 2 rue Ibn Mouaz, B.P. 2136, Fez (5-931608).
ALC, 2 boulevard El Kadissia, Kénitra (7-366884).
ALC, 3 Impasse du Moulin di Guéliz, Marrakesh (4-447259).
ALC, 21 rue Antsirab, 4th Floor, Meknes (5-523636).
ALC, 1 Rue Emsallah, Tangier (9-933616).
ALC, 14 Bab El Oukla, Tetouan (9-963308).

Bénédict School of English, 124 Ave Hassan II, Ben Slimane (3-290-957/fax 3-328472)
Bénédict School of English, Quartier de la Colline, rue 19 No. 79, Casablanca/Mohammedia (3-31 5084).
English Institute, 34 Avenue Lalla Yacout, Casablanca
IBA-Langues, 33 rue de Metz, Casablanca 20 100
London School of English, 10 Avenue des F.A.R., Casablanca
Ecole de Langues des F.A.R., Avenue de la Résistance, Rabat
Institute for Language and Communication Studies, 29 rue l'Oukaimeden, Agdal, Rabat
International Language Centre, 2 rue Tihama, Rabat (7-709718). One of the main centres of English but relies mainly on part-time staff, already resident in Rabat.

Tunisia

Like its neighbour in the Maghreb, Tunisia is turning away from the language of its former colonial master France. Although many of the young generation speak fluent French because they have been taught it in school, teenagers share the goal of making English their second language. People may be interested in paying you for lessons, even though you plan to be in the country for a relatively short time, as Roger Musker was in the winter a few years ago:

> *I decided to take a month off work as a kind of sabbatical and, if well planned, at no cost. I found all young people in Tunisia keen to practise and speak English whenever possible.*
>
> *I had one good contact in Sousse, who worked for the Tunisian Tourist Agency. I wrote to him from England and he replied that he could line up students on my arrival, which included himself and his ten year old daughter (who turned out to be my best student). At their house I was plied with extremely sweet tea and sticky cakes which you are obliged to eat. Altogether I had eight keen fee-paying students including a blind telephone operator, a teacher of English on a revision course and students from the Bourguiba Institute at Sousse University, which claims to be the second oldest university in the world. For the latter it was necessary to get permission from the Ministry of Education via the headmaster.*
>
> *Every day I tutored 8-10am and 5-7pm. The hourly rate was 15 Tunisian dinars (nearly £8), allowing me to just about cover basic costs and at the same time have a working holiday. Even without the contact and knowing Arabic, work is there for the asking. It just takes initiative. Go to any official institute, the tourism or municipal offices, demonstrate your availability and enthusiasm, give them your contact number and await replies.*

The University of Tunis also has a Bourguiba Institute of Modern Languages (Université de Tunis, 47 Av. de la Liberté, 1002 Tunis-Belvedere; 1-282418) though they do not enter into correspondence with prospective teachers.

Zimbabwe

When Zimbabwe became independent on 18th April 1980, it inherited an education system which was unfairly biassed towards the white population at the expense of the black. Since then the government has worked hard to redress this imbalance by building more schools and introducing 'hot seating', whereby the same building houses two schools, one from 7am to noon and an afternoon sitting from noon to 5pm. One feature which has remained the same is that English remains the principal medium of instruction. Although literacy levels and the education system generally have seen improvements, Zimbabwe still has many problems. Most recently, the presence of many white farm owners who contribute much to Zimbabwe's economy through their agricultural businesses have come up against the policy of the Mugabe government which wishes to hand these farms back to the indigenous people. In view of the violence and the threat of economic collapse, Zimbabwe is a questionable destination for any prospective TEFL teacher as, even though there is a serious shortage of teachers, particularly at secondary school level, the country seems to be in turmoil at the time of writing.

Most of the hiring that is done abroad of English teachers for schools in Zimbabwe is carried out either by the Zimbabwean government or by voluntary agencies like VSO. The Zimbabwe High Commission in London (429 Strand, London WC2R OSA; 020-7836 7755/fax 020-7379 1167) once recruited large numbers of British teachers on three-year contracts to teach English as well as the sciences, maths, geography, French and technical subjects. However now they merely refer enquirers to the Zimbabwe Ministry of Education (PO Box CY121, Causeway, Harare). The main qualification is a degree in the subject to be taught, though naturally they prefer a teaching qualification as well.

It is feasible to go to Zimbabwe on a three-month tourist visa and apply for a work permit as a teacher when you are out there. However, the red tape can be infuriating, especially if your holiday visa is rapidly running out. It is better to fix up a job beforehand if possible. British visitors do not need a visa for holidays in Zimbabwe, but in order to work they need a residence permit and a temporary work permit. These must be arranged directly through the Department of Immigration in Harare with the help of your prospective employer. Overseas candidates who apply direct to the Ministry of Education need the following documents: birth certificate, marriage certificate where applicable, proof of qualifications and previous experience, satisfactory medical certificate including a radiologist's certificate of freedom from active pulmonary tuberculosis.

LIST OF SCHOOLS

South Africa

CAPE STUDIES LANGUAGE SCHOOL
100 Main Road, Sea Point, PO Box 4425, Cape Town 8000, South Africa. Tel: (21) 439 0999. Fax: (21) 439 3130. E-mail: capestud@iafrica.com. Web-site: www.capestudies.co.za.
Number of teachers: 10.
Preference of nationality: any but preferably those with permanent residency in South Africa.
Qualifications: TEFL experience.
Conditions of employment: 3 month contracts. Hours 8.30am-2.50pm.
Salary: R20 per lesson plus R4 per student.
Facilities/Support: assistance with finding accommodation.
Recruitment: personal interview necessary.
Contact: Jens U. Bauch.

ih LANGUAGE LAB
International House, 54 De Korte Street, Braamfontein, 2001 Johannesburg. Tel: (11) 339 1051. Fax: 11 403 1759. E-mail: langlab@icon.co.za.
Number of teachers: often requires temporary teachers as student numbers fluctuate.
Qualifications: CELTA and TEFL experience.
Conditions of employment: classes in General English and ESP courses and in-company classes. Students are mainly from Africa (Mozambique, Angola and Democratic Republic of Congo).
Contact: Holly Pheby, Assistant Director of Studies.

Sudan

SUDAN VOLUNTEER PROGRAMME
34 Estelle Road, London NW3 2JY. Tel/fax: 020-7485 8619. E-mail: davidvsp@aol.com or osama@cwcom.net. Website: www.arrive.at/svp-uk.
Number of teachers: small voluntary programme.
Preference of nationality: native speakers of English resident in Britain.
Qualifications: graduates and undergraduates with experience of travelling abroad, preferably in the Middle East. TEFL certificate and knowledge of Arabic helpful but not required. Must be able to tolerate anti-malarial drugs.
Conditions of employment: 8-week summer programme and three month winter programme departing late November. Schools and colleges mostly located in Khartoum area.
Salary: modest living expenses provided and insurance covered.
Facilities/Support: volunteers must pay for their airfare (approx. £430) plus other expenses, estimated about £100. Accommodation with self-catering facilities is arranged, usually at the university where you are teaching.
Recruitment: word of mouth mainly. Application form should be accompanied by £5 administrative fee (non-returnable). Selection interviews and compulsory briefing in UK. Candidates must ask two referees to support their application.
Contact: David Wolton.

Tanzania

INTERNATIONAL LANGUAGES ORIENTATION SERVICES (ILOS)
Oysterbay, Karume Road, PO Box 6995, Dar es Salaam, Tanzania. Tel: (51) 667159/450097. Fax: (51) 112752/5. E-mail: ilos-tz@cc/udsm.ac.tz.
Number of teachers: 54 in six centres countrywide: Dar es Salaam, Arusha, Zanzibar, Mwanza, Kagera and Kilimanjaro.
Preference of nationality: British, American, Canadian, Australian.
Qualifications: bilingual graduates with EFL experience.
Conditions of employment: 2 year renewable contracts. ILOS' programmes include pre-school, primary, secondary and adults.
Salary: 150,000 Tanzanian shillings per month.
Facilities/Support: free furnished accommodation and paid residence and work permit.
Recruitment: interviews essential and are sometimes held in UK and US.

JOINT COOPERATION TRUST
39 Handel Mansions, 94 Wyatt Drive, London SW13 8AH. Tel: 020-8563 1456. E-mail: tice@btinternet.com. Also at: 1 Red Lion Lane, Nantwich, Cheshire CW5 5EP; 01270 625201. E-mail: zoe50johnson@yahoo.com.
Number of teachers: 12-20 per year.
Preference of nationality: British.
Qualifications: degree followed by a suitable attitude to developmental education.
Conditions of employment: 1-year from August to August. Normal school hours are 7.30am-3pm. Teachers help the local teachers to be better English language teachers and so teach both teachers and pupils.
Salary: local rates, i.e. the same as Tanzanian teachers.
Facilities/Support: accommodation is provided by the local community, usually in the primary school where the teachers work. Permits to work are arranged through the Tanzanian Ministry of Education.
Recruitment: adverts in *The Guardian* and university careers centres. Interviews are essential and are carried out in the UK each March/April.
Contact: Zoe Johnson.

ASIA

Although the English language is not a universal passport to employment, especially in these times of economic hardship for many individuals and companies in the Far East, it can certainly be put to good use in many Asian countries. Conditions and remuneration will differ wildly between industrialised countries like Japan, Korea and Taiwan with their western-style economies, and those of developing countries like China, Nepal and Thailand, where both wages and the standard of living are lower.

Both Princeton and Stanford Universities run voluntary programmes in various Asian countries including some TEFL teaching. Stanford's Volunteers in Asia programme has been running since 1963. Every year VIA sends about 30 volunteer English teachers to Indonesia, Laos, Vietnam and China on short (six week) and longer term (1 year) assignments. Applications are due in early February and the cost of participating starts at about $1,500. Details are available from VIA, Stanford University, PO Box 20266, Stanford, CA 94309, USA (650-723-3228/fax 650-725-1805; volasia@volasia.org/ www.volasia.org). Volunteers get living expenses and a stipend. For information about the Princeton programme, contact Princeton-in-Asia, 224 Palmer Hall, Princeton, NJ 08544 (609-258-3657/fax 609-258-08544; pia@phoenix.princeton.edu/ www.princeton.edu/~pia). They place about 65 intern teachers in China, Hong Kong, Indonesia, Japan, Korea, Laos, Singapore and Vietnam; applications must be accompanied by a $30 fee and be submitted by the beginning of December.

Recruitment organisations like *Saxoncourt & English Worldwide* and *EF English First* are active in the region. A couple of commercial recruitment agencies specialise in placing ELT-trained teachers in Asian countries. For example *APA Consultancy* (Suite 32, Nevilles Court, Dollis Hill Lane, London NW2 6HG; 020-8452 7836) fills a large number of vacancies in Thailand, Taiwan and China.

Lists of language schools in Japan, Korea, Thailand, China, Hong Kong and Singapore are sold individually by Asia Facts (PO Box 93, Kingston, Ont K7L 4V6, Canada; 613-387-2628; http://asiafacts.kingston.net). Specialist books about teaching in Asia may be of interest. The San Francisco bookstore China Books (www.chinabooks.com) at 2929 24th Street, San Francisco, CA 95110 (fax 415-282 0994/ info@chinabooks.com) carries a few titles about teaching English in Asia including *Teaching English in Asia: Finding a Job and Doing it Well* by Galen Valle (US$19.95) and *Living in China: A Guide to Teaching and Studying in China, Including Taiwan and Hong Kong* by Rebecca Weiner, Margaret Murphy and Albert Li (US$19.95).

Perhaps it is symbolic that voluntary and religious organisations are becoming more active in the provision of English in the most prosperous nations. For example at the time of writing the countries for which *Christians Abroad* was most energetically seeking teachers are Japan, Hong Kong and China.

China

Some commentators have predicted that the 21st century will belong to China. In order to fulfil this prediction, China wants to learn the language of the West. One of the first signs of China's softening towards the West in the late 1970s was the welcome it extended to English language teachers to its institutes of higher education. Two and a half decades later there are thousands of native speakers teaching not only at schools and academic institutions around the country but in companies and (what would have been unthinkable two decades ago) private language institutes. Furthermore the emerging middle class aspires to send its children for private tuition just as in the capitalist countries of Taiwan, Korea and Japan.

One estimate has been made that there are 450 million English language learners in China, due in large measure to the fact that English is compulsory for school pupils from the age of 9. Many street and shop signs in the capital and other major cities are written in English as well as Chinese, though most Beijing citizens can say very little in English apart from 'MacDonalds' A great many students and teachers are very keen to improve their English to Cambridge Proficiency standard in the hope of being chosen to study overseas. Others are simply curious. But all are eager to learn, even if the style of learning to which they have become accustomed can be difficult for foreign teachers to cope with.

The other major problem which teachers encounter and which can wear down even the most enthusiastic China buff is the bureaucracy. It is top-heavy, all-powerful and often strikingly inefficient. All teachers admit that working in China is exhausting, but most also find the experience fascinating.

Prospects for Teachers

Any educated native speaker of English should be able to find a job in China. Having a degree and any teaching experience is useful, but not so much importance is attached to TEFL qualifications.

The Chinese government classifies teachers either as Foreign Experts (FEs) or Foreign Teachers (FTs). Foreign Experts are expected to have an MA in a relevant area (English, Linguistics, TEFL/TESOL, etc.) and some teaching experience at the tertiary level. Foreign Teachers are normally under 25 and have only a university degree. The designated status FE or FT brings various privileges and conditions as described below. It is almost impossible for a non-graduate to work in a university, including students on exchange schemes likes those run by organisations like *GAP Activity Projects* and *Project Trust*. Instead these younger teachers are normally placed in middle schools (public secondary schools, often boarding schools). *i-to-i* (0870 333 23320) has also started placing volunteer teachers in China.

A large proportion of foreigners are employed in Beijing but there are many opportunities in the provinces as well, especially for FTs. The more remote the area or the more hostile the climate, the easier it will be to find a job. Many vacancies for both FEs and FTs go unfilled. Specialist recruitment organisations such as Christians Abroad in the UK or the *Colorado China Council* in the US are notified of more positions than they can find people to fill them. Demand exists in the hundreds of universities, colleges, foreign language institutes, institutes of technology, teacher training colleges (called Normal Universities) and secondary schools, especially in the provinces. Normal universities often seem to be overlooked when foreign teachers are assigned centrally, so they are a very promising bet for people applying directly or on-the-spot.

Applications can be made through the Chinese Embassy in your country, the State Bureau of Foreign Experts in Beijing (see next section), through various placement organisations and other voluntary bodies, or by applying directly to institutions. Even ordinary secondary schools employ native speakers; applications can be made through provincial education bureaux. Writing direct to the Foreign Affairs Office *(waiban)* of institutes of higher learning may lead to a job offer. Chinese institutes seem to attach more weight to the letter of application than to the curriculum vitae. Also enclose a photo, a photocopy of the first page of your passport, a copy of any education certificates and two references.

Unfortunately the mechanisms for placing teachers and communicating with them can be subject to the same tendency to bureaucratic ineptitude as plagues teachers in China. Once you have been promised a job, schools can be very remiss about keeping in touch, so keep pressing. Often this is because the person with whom you are in contact does not speak much English but doesn't want to lose face.

Any university graduate travelling in China should be able to arrange a teaching contract just by asking around at the many colleges in the towns and cities on his or her itinerary. Even when foreign travellers have not been looking for work, they have been approached and invited to teach English. It has been suggested that standing in a railway station beside a notice advertising your availability to teach English would succeed, though probably more for private tuition than an institutional job. If you fix up a job at FT level on the spot, it may not be for an entire academic year and your pay may be calculated on an hourly basis.

Opportunities are opening up in the furthest corners of China, and even beyond in the case of Mongolia and Tibet. Several private secondary schools in Mongolia have been advertising recently on the internet for EFL teachers including the Erel School in Ulaanbaatar (on whose behalf Mongol Caravan Inc, PO Box 191, Clifton, NJ 07011, USA; mc@mongolcaravan.com were recruiting) and Eagle English Language School in Erdenet 400km from the capital (rinchin@erdnet.mn). The only requirements were a college degree and a tolerance for cold temperatures and a salary of $100 a month.

Rabindra Roy has spent the past year teaching in Mongolia with VSO and reports on the situation:

Here in Mongolia there's a great demand for English teaching as people see it as a way to better jobs (though there aren't many people with enough money to pay for it). The students can be pretty good and one doesn't trip over the culture too much, but laziness, lateness and unreliability are widely recognised as national characteristics. There's a new school opening up in the building next door which is linked to inlingua via the Santis Corporation of America (fax 703 527 8693) so obviously there is potential for commercial teaching by foreigners. I think if you were a native speaker you could probably quite easily find a job with one of the few schools here if you were willing to put up with not too much money and could get them to sort out a flat for you.

FIXING UP A JOB

If you want a contract fixed up before leaving home, start the application procedure at least six months and preferably a year before your intended departure. Most recruitment is filtered through the Chinese Education Association for International Exchange (CEAIE) in the capital (Mailing address: 37 Damucang Hutong, Beijing 100816, PRC; 10-664 16582/16583/14933/18220; fax: 10-66416156; ceaieipd@public3.bta.net.cn/ www.ceaie.org) which is a non-governmental organisation with 37 local branches in every province and major cities and extensive contacts with institutes of higher education throughout China who wish to invite native speaker teachers.

CEAIE co-operates with Chinese Embassies in the West. The Education Section of the Chinese Embassy in London at 50 Portland Place, London W1N 3GD (020-7580 3533/fax 020-7580 4474) leaves the task of matching applicants with vacancies at Chinese institutions to the Central Bureau for International Education & Training and also to Council Exchanges (see entry). Details of the application procedure can be obtained from the Chinese Links Officer at the Central Bureau (10 Spring Gardens, London SW1A 2BN; 020-7389 4431/fax 020-7389 4426). The Development Officer is Dilbahar Tawakkul (e-mail dilbahar.tawakkul@ britishcouncil.org).

The Central Bureau receives information of posts in China in the new year and sends out this information to universities and interested individuals. The Bureau then screens applications and conducts interviews in March/April for positions mainly as FTs but also as FEs. The minimum requirement is a university degree, though a TEFL certificate and/or teaching experience preferably abroad improve your chances of acceptance. Dossiers of successful interviewees are then forwarded to appropriate institutes in China who then communicate directly with the applicant if they are interested in hiring them. Teachers who accept posts in China attend an orientation at the beginning of July at which they can find out exactly what will be expected of them.

Contracts are for a minimum of a year and renewable starting in September. Details of the contract are a matter of negotiation between the teacher and the hiring institution. Many applicants will have to choose among offers as Will Hawkes did:

> *During my last year at university, I obtained a list of Chinese universities and colleges looking to recruit foreign teachers, then faxed my CV and a letter to the ten which suited me most. I received several offers from around China (including a phone call at 3am) and eventually accepted an offer from Qingdao Chemical Institute on the east coast of China. The offer was quite standard: accommodation, unspectacular money... but a friend of mine had taught at this same institute and thoroughly recommended it, so I went and taught English for an academic year.*

Whereas the appointment of teachers for post-secondary institutions is carried out by the individual institution (in co-operation with a national government department), hiring teachers at the secondary level is the responsibility of the provincial education bureaux. For a list of addresses of Chinese institutes of higher education, consult the book *Living in China: A Guide to Teaching and Studying in China* mentioned above. One major institute which may be worth trying is Yunnan Institute of the Nationalities (Foreign Affairs Office, Kunming 650031, Yunnan; tel/fax: 871-515 4308), which has up to 15 foreign teachers and experts at any one time.

Limited opportunities exist for part-time teaching in Beijing through the Cultural and Education section of the British Embassy (which doubles as the British Council). Properly qualified and experienced teachers of EFL undertake a variety of teaching duties but without any guarantee of a fixed number of hours. Teachers are responsible for their own accommodation and visas.

Private Language Training

Legislation allowing privatised companies to operate in the fields of media and education has prompted a number of language schools to open. Like private schools everywhere, a certain number of these are run by unscrupulous entrepreneurs interested only in profit. A few are run by Korean businessmen, perhaps escaping the economic downturn in their own country. If considering working in the private sector, try to find out the degree of professionalism of the company you are considering. A few have recently been recruiting large numbers of untrained and inexperienced native speakers from the US who are inspired by Christian missionary zeal.

Other private companies are serious about teaching English. Joint ventures with foreign companies often mount an English training programme and advertise for English trainers in the press or on the internet. Also in the private sector, some hotels and large companies have their own language training facilities for staff, especially if they are joint ventures with Western companies. Most recruitment of teachers by business and industry takes place locally, since they do not offer accommodation. If in Beijing, check classified adverts in the English language bimonthly magazine *Beijing Scene*.

Before arriving check the internet, especially Dave's eslcafe.com. Positions as teachers of business English throughout China were recently being advertised by ALTEC, an American corporate training company with offices in Guangzhou (formerly Canton) and other cities; contact Bonita.Wang@ALTEC.com.cn.

Placement Organisations

The following organisations recruit teachers for China from the UK:

The Amity Foundation (71 Han Kou Road, Naning, Jiangsu 210008, China; tel 86-25-332 4607; fax 86-25-663-1701; in Hong Kong: 4 Jordan Road, Kowloon). Every year this voluntary organisation sends 60-80 teachers to work in Chinese tertiary institutions. Recruits are obtained through various church-related societies abroad such as the China Forum of the Council of Churches for Britain & Ireland (35-41 Lower Marsh, London SE1 7RL), the Scottish Churches' China Group (121 St. George St, Edinburgh EH2 4YN; pjohnston@ cofscotland.org.uk), Christians Abroad (projects@cabroad-u-net.com) and the National Council of Churches of Christ in the US (475 Riverside Drive, Room 668, New York, NY 10115). These organisations recruit and select teachers of English for two-year contracts beginning each August. Countries in which Amity operates through churches include Canada, Denmark, Finland, Germany, Japan, the Netherlands and the US. Enquiries welcomed from graduates and others suitably qualified (e.g. B.Ed., CELTA) with Christian commitment to live and work in simple conditions. Applications are due between October and December with final selection in February for departures in July. All travel expenses are covered (see entry).

Avalon School, 8 Denmark St, London WC2H 8LS. Tel: 020-7916 5524. Fax: 020-7916 5261. E-mail: dos@avalonschool.co.uk. 12-month contracts for teachers with a good degree and TEFL certificate. Teaching experience not essential, though candidates should have lived and worked abroad. 5000 renminbi per month plus free Western-style accommodation, health insurance and 4 weeks paid holiday. Travel costs refunded at end of contract.

Council Exchanges, – see entry.

Coventry TESOL Centre, Butts, Coventry, CV1 3GD. Tel/fax: 02476 526743. E-mail: language@covcollege.ac.uk. Can arrange for graduates to take up English teaching placements in China for 4-6 months. No teaching experience is needed as free, professional training will be provided. Free return flights. Accommodation, a salary at local rates and insurance are provided. Recruitment is done on a continuous, year-round basis.

GAP, 44 Queen's Road, Reading, Berks. RG1 4BB. Tel: (0118) 959 4914. Fax: (0118) 957 6634. E-mail: volunteer@gap.org.uk. Website: www.gap.org.uk. Offers school and college leavers six-month attachments to colleges in five provinces.

Project Trust, Hebridean Centre, Ballyhough, Isle of Coll PA78 6TE. Tel: (01879) 230444. Fax: (01879) 230357. Sends volunteers (aged 17-19) to work as teacher-aides in middle schools and teacher training colleges.

Study World Ltd., Verandah, Holywell Road, Malvern Wells, Worcestershire WR14 4ET. Tel: 01684 566347. Fax: 01684 577559. E-mail: ssearch@ compuserve.com. Recruits for a number of schools in the Beijing and Shanghai areas and has contacts all over China. The pay is about £500 per month and the contract includes accommodation, food and one return airfare. Further details are available from Laurence James.

Teaching & Projects Abroad, Gerrard House, Rustington, W. Sussex BN16 1AW. Tel: 01903 859911. Fax: 01903 785779. E-mail: info@teaching-abroad.co.uk. Website: www.teaching-abroad.co.uk. Teaching placements in Fujian Province cost of £1,695.

VSO (Voluntary Service Overseas), 317 Putney Bridge Road, London SW15 2PN. Tel: 020-8780 7500. Fax: 020-8780 7300. E-mail: enquiry@vso.org.uk. Website: www.vso.org.uk. Have quite a large contingent of teachers in China (about 150). Volunteers need a BA in English, languages or other arts subject plus some experience and a Cambridge Cert. or equivalent. Also opportunities in Mongolia (unsuitable for vegetarians).

A number of US organisations involved in teacher placements in China have entries in the listings at the end of this chapter including the *China Teaching Program* at Western Washington University, the *Colorado China Council, IEF Education Foundation* and the *New China Education Foundation*. *WorldTeach Inc.* at the Centre for International Development at Harvard University (79 John F Kennedy Street, Cambridge, MA 02138; 617-495-5527/800-4-TEACH-O/fax 617-495-1599; info@worldteach.org/ www.worldteach.org) is a non-profit organisation which sends volunteers to teach adults for six months in Yantai. Undergraduates and graduates can participate in the Shanghai Summer Teaching programme. Volunteers teach small classes of high school students at a language camp in Shanghai. Volunteers pay about $4,000 for air fares, orientation, health insurance and field support.

The *US-China Educational Exchange* based in New Jersey has a sizeable Teach-in-China (and Teach-in-Taiwan) programme. Send an e-mail message headed 'China' or 'Taiwan' to HSINTL@aol.com or telephone Dr. Yong Ho on 201-432-6861 for further details. *Global Language Villages* runs eleven language programmes worldwide including one in China since 1997. Visiting volunteer teachers work on a ratio of one per 15-20 villagers in rural China. The programme lasts 3 weeks, the latter two of which are spent working with other Americans and with Chinese teachers of English, teaching students aged 8-18. Cost is approximately US$1,795 including travel from the US and full board and lodging. An allowance of about 2000 yuan (about US$240) will be paid in China. Contact GLV at P.O. Box 163, Concordia College, Moorhead, MN 56562, USA (fax 218-863-7001; glv.@cord.edu/ www.cord.edu/dept/clv/glv and www.globallanguages.org). Another possibility is China English Language Training Services in Shanghai (2D Zhao Feng Blvd 9, Lane 396, Cheng Line Road, Shanghai 200042; fax 21-62523 5692) which recruits North Americans.

CONDITIONS OF WORK

Foreign Teachers are the poor relations of Foreign Experts. They do not have their airfares or shipping costs reimbursed and they normally earn substantially less than FEs, i.e. 1,800-2,400 yuan per month instead of 2,400-3,000 yuan. Another advantage of being an FE is that a higher percentage of your salary is converted to a hard currency, typically 50%-70% instead of 30%. While FEs are paid by central government, FTs are funded by local education authorities who do not have large budgets. All teachers have their accommodation provided by the host institution, either in on-site residences or in a foreigners' hotel.

Working and living conditions vary from one institute to the next and it is vital to negotiate as much as possible before arrival and to obtain all promises in writing. When you are first notified by your employer in China that you have a job, you should avoid the temptation to write back enthusiastically accepting it. Rather ask for more details such as your status, salary, timetable and other conditions. You could also ask for the names of any current foreign employees whom you can ask for inside information. What is agreed at this stage will set the terms of employment even though it is standard practice not to sign a contract until after two months' probation (if at all).

Will Hawkes was not dissatisfied with his monthly salary of £100:

Though my salary was twice as much as the local teachers are paid, for a foreigner it makes for quite tight living. So, like many other foreign teachers, I supplemented this with private individual tutoring which had good rates in Qingdao since it is quite a rich city with a relative lack of foreign teachers.

The Foreign Affairs Office of my institute was an important part of my life on campus. As well as being my boss, it organised my accommodation and salary, and was generally responsible for my well-being as a stranger in China. They looked after me very well, even when I had some difficulties at Christmas. State institutions generally treat their foreign teachers well, whereas private ones can have a 'fire and hire' attitude.

Better wages can be obtained in the big cities of Beijing, Guangzhou and Shanghai, and also in any of the economic zones such as Hainan Island. But Chinese cities have so many drawbacks in terms of crowds and pollution that the higher wages may not prove enough incentive to work there. For quality of life, western China is probably better than the east. Yunnan province has a particularly congenial climate. This area is also reputed to be less money-oriented than the east coast cities, which may have the drawback that it will be more difficult to find paying private students.

Most foreign teachers are expected to teach between 12 and 18 hours a week, which sounds a light load until you find that there may be 50-100 students in these classes. Often there is a heavy load of marking as well and extra duties such as staffing an 'English corner' or English club, or delivering a weekly lecture on Western culture. In fact some teachers end up working a 45-50 hour week. The administration's main ambition is often to maximise your exposure, which may have the effect of minimising your usefulness. Hours of teaching are unpredictable and the teaching days can be very long. Students get up at 6am and work at night in supervised sessions. If you want to keep your weekends free for travel and relaxation, firmly decline teaching hours on Saturday and Sunday, and be aware that it is all too easy to overcommit yourself in the first few weeks.

Terms run from early September to early July, with a three or four week (paid) holiday over Chinese New Year and the spring festival in January/February. Foreign teachers can sometimes arrange to have longer breaks depending on their exam commitments.

The Pupils

'Big noses' (foreigners) are normally treated with great respect. In the early years of Western contact with China, English teachers outside the big cities found themselves lionised, unable to complete the simplest task in public without an enormous audience. But there are not many corners of China these days into which foreigners, whether teachers or travellers, have not penetrated, and so some of the pressure has been taken off.

Slowly, newer paedagogical methods are being accepted by students and administrators alike. Attitudes differ enormously from one situation to another. Where in one place, techniques that smack of innovation are greeted with blank stares, in another, there can be lively class discussions. Adam Hartley found himself in the former situation:

> *Politics were a complete no-no in class and yet politics are so central to life that you find yourself always coming up against a brick wall of silent faces. Class participation of any kind was hard enough to achieve. I was given a class of 100 people (of vastly different standards) for listening comprehension. I was an absolute monkey, playing, rewinding and replaying a cassette with obnoxious voices and muddled questions. I'd play it twice or thrice, ask if they were ready. 'Yes.' Okay, who thinks the answer is A? No one. Who thinks B? 2 people. Who thinks C? 3 hands. And who thinks D? No one. 5 responses out of 100. I'd try it again and again, and only ever got 27 hands in the air for any one question.*
>
> *I had another class of beginners, and spent two hours reading things very very slowly for them to repeat. Immensely dull, unstimulating and tiring work. Again a tape recorder could have done just as good a job as I did.*

"A tape recorder could have done as good a job"

Will Hawkes did not find the teaching such hard going:

> *I taught 12 hours a week, each class lasting a mammoth two hours. Chinese students are more familiar with American English and thus British English is very much in demand to balance things out. The English level of my students, who were aged 17-23, was mostly fairly competent, but with extremes of good and dreadful. Getting into university in China is a great privilege, and*

most students were eager to grasp this opportunity as a route to greater things in life. I found teaching the Chinese a delight: the students were very eager to learn, ask questions, find out how life is in Britain, always looking to learn and not muck around. We discussed a wide variety of material in class and, although some political areas are best left untouched, general debate was enthusiastically devoured about, for instance, the existence of God, cloning, tradition versus modernity and aliens (a real favourite, with many believers).

In some cases the classroom is not the best place to draw out the students. Extracurricular activities can present a better opportunity for imparting the English language, as Richard Vincent found when he spent a year as a Project Trust volunteer in Southern China:

Most of the positive aspects of my year were achieved outside the classroom. The good students will always work all the hours god sends. However the less motivated can become motivated to try and learn. In my case, playing football gave lots of students who had been labelled 'dossers' the chance to speak English, and many of them became the best contributors in class. The emphasis should always be on fun and trying to get them to use the English they know.

The enthusiasm of the students goes a long way to counteracting the negative aspects. Chinese people are unfailingly polite and friendly outside official and observed situations.

Accommodation

Every university has either a purpose-built hostel or similar. Foreign teachers are generally housed in the best accommodation the university can offer, often referred to as a 'Panda House' (on the analogy that pandas are pampered in zoos). These differ enormously from place to place. In some places (such as Chengdu University of Science & Technology) the accommodation can be airy and comfortable. In other places it is decidedly spartan and in some cases downright depressing, especially if electricity and heat are rationed. Adam describes his lodgings in Linfen:

A flat containing very little was provided. A fridge and TV were provided though never used. I wanted chairs, desks, lamps, and after weeks of pushing I got them. 'Next week you shall have them.' Then next week, 'That man is away at a conference now' and so on. I got carpets put in and had a good set-up, except snow and dust managed to filter in through the windows. After a few weeks, the electricity blew, so I couldn't use the desk lamp (which I'd had to buy) or listen to music. It got depressing living under neon light, padding around on dusty carpets wrapped up in a coat to keep warm.

Many of the deprivations may sound trivial but cumulatively they can be disheartening. On the other hand local Chinese teachers consider the foreigners' accommodation (like their salaries) to be luxurious compared to their own and it may strike you as churlish to complain too vociferously.

REGULATIONS

Most institutes will issue teachers with an invitation or letter of appointment which can be taken to the Chinese Consulate or Embassy to apply for long term work visa before leaving your country. The cost of a multi-entry visa for Britons is £60 for six months, £90 for 12. One of the requirements is a notarised health certificate.

It is also possible to enter China on a tourist (L) visa and then the Foreign Affairs Office (FAO) at your institute will arrange for an Alien Residence Permit (Z visa). Make sure this happens before your visitor visa expires, which is calculated according to the date of entry to China rather than the expiry date of the visa.

Otherwise you will be liable to a fine and will have to leave the country to change status. Once outside the country you must be prepared to wait up to a fortnight for the appropriate faxes to be sent from Beijing. With the Z visa you should be eligible for a one-year multiple entry visa, though this seems to be at the discretion of the official at the Beijing Public Service office who may want to see more 'chops' (official stamps), more forms and an extra fee.

When you arrive, be sure that your host institution sorts out the various permits and teachers' cards to which you are entitled. The Foreign Affairs Office should issue you with a green card (residence permit which prevents expensive visa renewal) and an orange card (purchase document) which allows you to make purchases at the same prices as locals. Free health care of a good standard is provided, so few people bother with medical or personal insurance.

LEISURE TIME

Foreigners who teach in Beijing can lead a standard expatriate life if they want to, attending Embassy films and discos and dining in expensive restaurants. Life in the provinces will be very different. There may be no restaurants even to rival the Chinese take-away in your home town; but the locals will be far more interested in you and perhaps even teach you to cook your own Chinese food. If there are several foreigners, communal dining facilities (often segregated) will normally be provided. Glutinous rice, soy beans and cabbage are staples and fresh produce may be in short supply in winter.

Learning Chinese is the ambition of many teachers and is a great asset especially outside cosmopolitan areas. Take a good teach-yourself book and cassettes, since these are difficult to obtain outside Beijing and Shanghai. Mastering Chinese characters is a daunting business, though the grammar is straightforward. Others prefer to study Tai Chi, Wushu or other exotic martial arts.

Be prepared for noise and air pollution even in small towns, though it is usually possible to escape into the countryside by bicycle or bus. Some universities with large contingents of foreign teachers organise excursions in the same way that Israeli kibbutzim do for their volunteers after a few months. Most of the country is open to independent travellers though if you want to travel to Tibet, you will first have to get permission from the Tibet Tourist Bureau. FEs can easily afford to travel, while FTs may find that extensive travels will leave them out-of-pocket. School and college vacations take place over Spring Festival in or around February, when the trains are very crowded and the weather is cold.

Much of the time you will be responsible for your own amusement, so take plenty of reading matter, including *Wild Swans,* an astonishing account of life in the Cultural Revolution. Will Hawkes would urge anybody to do TEFL in China, concluding that the small sacrifice of a few home comforts is entirely worthwhile for the chance to live in a society rich with 5,000 years of history and culture.

LIST OF SCHOOLS

ACCESS INTERNATIONAL ACADEMY
988 Xin Da Lu, Beilun District, Ningbo City, Zhejian Province 315800. Tel: 574 687 8481. Fax: 574 687 8481. E-mail: AIA@mail.nbptt.zj.cn.
Number of teachers: 4/5.
Preference of nationality: British (to teach British syllabi).
Qualifications: experienced teachers with TEFL certificate.
Conditions of employment: one year (renewable). 20 lessons per week.
Salary: 3,500-5,500 yuan. No deductions.
Facilities/Support: free furnished lodging plus food, medical insurance and return air transportation fare provided.
Recruitment: via internet.
Contact: Dr. K. O. Li, Director of Studies.

AMITY FOUNDATION
71 Han Kou Road, Nanjing, Jiangsu 210008. Tel: 86-25-332-4607. Fax: 86-25-663 1701. E-mail: afn71@public1.ptt.js.cn. Website: wwww.amityfoundation.org.
Number of teachers: 60-80.
Preference of nationality: none, but must be native speaker or have a high level of proficiency in English and language teaching experience.
Qualifications: minimum BA degree. Teaching experience, a knowledge of Chinese or of living in Asia are useful but not essential. A Christian faith commitment is generally required, however the 'mission' expected is to serve rather than to proselytise.
Conditions of employment: initial two-year contract with possible year by year extensions. Teaching 12-16 periods per week. Teaching in tertiary educational institutions in China, mostly small teacher training colleges.
Salary: US$225 monthly plus 2,000 yuan. Expenses for travel, orientation, conferences and medical insurance are covered by the sponsoring agency.
Facilities/Support: accommodation is usually provided in the form of an apartment on the school campus.
Recruitment: teachers are recruited primarily through church sending agencies (see earlier in chapter) i.e. mission agencies of various denominations in a range of countries including, Canada, Denmark, Germany, Sweden, the UK, the US and New Zealand. Interviews in person are expected and generally take place in the applicant's own country.
Contact: Ms. Liu Ruhong, Direction, Education Division.

BEIJING NEW BRIDGE FOREIGN LANGUAGE SCHOOL
Chao Yang Qu Yong An Nan Li, Beijing 100022. Tel: (1390)117 3737. Fax: (10) 65 68 5135. E-mail: smith@public.east.cn.net. Website: www.newbrldgeschool.com.
Number of teachers: 40.
Preference of nationality: must be native-speaker.
Qualifications: BA degree. Teaching experience is an advantage but not essential.
Conditions of employment: 1 year. 26 hours per week morning and evening classes.
Salary: 3,500 yuan per month. Income tax is paid only if earning more than 4,000 yuan per month.
Facilities/Support: accommodation in dormitory rooms is provided.
Recruitment: newspapers, magazines, word-of-mouth, internet. Face to face interview not essential. E-mail questionnaire and telephone interview sufficient.
Contact: Wayne Smith, Coordinator.

CHANGCHUN FOREIGN LANGUAGES SCHOOL
No 46, Honggi Street, Changchun, Jilin. Tel: (431) 595 9261. Fax: (431) 595 7194. E-mail: edu1806@public.cc.jl.cn.
Number of teachers: 8 native speakers.
Preference of nationality: must be native speaker.
Qualifications: degree. Must be good clear speaker with good intonation and pronunciation.
Conditions of employment: usually one year minimum. 14-16 lessons a week (45 minutes a lesson).
Salary: 2,200 yuan per month.
Facilities/Support: free accommodation (but not food) is provided.
Recruitment: usually through the Jilin Provincial Educational Committee, Chinese Education Association for International Exchange. Interviews not essential.
Contact: Miss Wang Ying, Dean of Foreign Affairs Office.

CHINA AUSTRALIA COLLEGE BEIJING
P.O. Box 1010, Beijing. Tel: (10) 6078-5799. Fax: (10) 6078 5899. E-mail: cacb@public.rhnet.cn.net. Website: www.cacb.net.cn.
Number of teachers: 6-12.

Preference of nationality: none, but must be English speaker.
Qualifications: degree plus TEFL Cert.
Conditions of employment: 11 months (return air fare paid). 20-22 teaching hours per week.
Salary: 5,000 yuan per month.
Facilities/Support: full board in new 3-bedroom, 2 bathroom shared units, built especially for western teachers.
Recruitment: newspaper advertising and/or employment agencies, word-of-mouth.
Contact: Diana McGivern, Human Resources Manager.

CHINA TEACHING PROGRAM
Western Washington University, Old Main 530A, Bellingham, WA 98225-9047, USA. Tel: (360) 650-3753. Fax: (360) 650-2847. E-mail: ctp@cc.wwu.edu. Website: www.wwu.edu/~ctp.
Number of teachers: 30-45 at various institutions of higher education and secondary schools throughout China.
Preference of nationality: none, provided native speaker of English.
Qualifications: BA minimum, teaching experience helpful. Flexibility and sense of adventure needed. Opportunities also available for business and law experts.
Conditions of employment: one academic year contract starting September or February. 12-18 classroom h.p.w.
Salary: 2,400-3,300 yuan per month for Foreign Experts (with 50-70% conversion rate) and 1,800-2,400 yuan for Foreign Teachers (30% converted to foreign currency).
Facilities/Support: accommodation provided. Compulsory 5-week pre-departure summer training course in TESL, Chinese language and culture for candidates who lack TEFL training or experience, at a cost of $1,200. Recommendations for books and materials to take are given.
Recruitment: college career centres, newspaper and magazine adverts and word of mouth. Application deadline is January 31st for autumn placement. Interviews take place in Bellingham or by phone.
Contact: Todd Lundgren, Director.

COLORADO CHINA COUNCIL
4556 Apple Way, Boulder, CO 80301, USA. Tel: (303) 443-1107. E-mail: alice@asiacouncil.org. Web-site: www.asiacouncil.org.
Number of teachers: 20-35 per year placed at institutes throughout China, including Mongolia.
Preference of nationality: mostly American.
Qualifications: BA/BSc or higher degree (all majors considered, though English, TEFL, journalism, business, sciences and engineering especially welcome). Good GPA (minimum 2.5) and two strong letters of recommendation needed. Teaching background helpful but not required.
Conditions of employment: 6 months from early spring, 11 months from 30th July. August placements but not February placements are preceded by compulsory 3-week Mandarin Chinese and teacher training programme and orientation. To teach 14-16 h.p.w.
Salary: monthly stipend, free housing in foreign teachers' complex, medical benefits and one month paid vacation offered by Chinese institutions.
Facilities/Support: some schools reimburse air fare home at end of year.
Recruitment: deadline for applications for August start is 15th February. Non-refundable application processing fee of $100. Council fees for 2000/2001 are $3,2500 (including TEFL training, Chinese course and domestic travel in China), $1,350 fee (administration only) for February start.
Contact: Alice Renouf, Director.

COUNCIL EXCHANGES – TEACH IN CHINA PROGRAM
Council UK, 52 Poland St, London W1V 4JQ, UK. Tel: 020-7478 2000. Fax: 020-7734 7322. Also Council Exchanges, 633 3rd Avenue, 20th Floor, New York,

NY10017, USA. Tel: 888-268 6245. Fax: (212) 822-2689. In Australia: P O Box Q577, QVB Post Office, 1230 Sydney, NSW. Tel: (2) 9373 2730. Fax: (2) 9373 2731. E-mail: TiC@councilexchanges.org. Website: www.councilexchanges.org/work/ticfacts.htm.

Number of teachers: 200 from UK, 100 from US, 50 from Australia at tertiary institutions in China, mainly in the developed eastern provinces of Jiangsu, Zheijiang, Shandong and Hubei.

Preference of nationality: none, although non-native speakers of English must have near fluency in English.

Qualifications: university degree essential; TEFL training or experience preferred.

Conditions of employment: one semester or an academic year contracts available from February or August teaching Chinese students in colleges and schools. 11-16 hours per week classes. Extra-curricular duties may involve running an English language club.

Salary: minimum salary offered to teachers is 2,200 RMB per month (currently equivalent to £180). This is a good salary by local standards.

Facilities/Support: free accommodation, usually on-campus. One-week orientation in Beijing on arrival including basic EFL training before. Possibility of assistance with travel costs.

Recruitment: deadlines for applications are early May to depart in late August, and early November to depart in mid-February. UK programme fee, including orientation week in Beijing is £625.

Contact: Marion Clark, Programme Coordinator.

DONGYA UNIVERSITY & DONGYA SCHOOL
2 Minyi Road, Longsha District, Qiqihar, Heilongjiang Province, Northeastern China. Tel/fax: (452) 241 0042.

Number of teachers: varies.

Preference of nationality: none, but should be native speaker.

Qualifications: BA plus TEFL Certificate minimum.

Conditions of employment: to teach university students and adults and juniors conversational English.

Salary: 2,800-3,000 yuan per month with end of contract bonus.

Facilities/Support: single studio accommodation with shared utilities, outward and return airfare and medical cover are all provided free of charge. Cold winters.

Recruitment: via internet and contacts.

Contact: Li Cai, Recruitment Manager.

EF ENGLISH FIRST
No. 167 Taiyuan Road, Shanghai 200031. Tel: (21) 6466 4218 (Academic Co-ordinator ext. 107). Fax (21) 6415 0076. E-mail: lara.latcham@ef.com.

Number of teachers: 8-10.

Preference of nationality: British, Canadian, Australian, American, Irish.

Qualifications: university degree (Arts subject preferred) and certificate in EFL/ESL. Well-documented experience supported by references will be considered in lieu of certification.

Conditions of employment: 12 month contracts. Teaching between 9am and 9pm six days a week (total 24-29 contact hours).

Salary: up to 24 contact hours about US$650 (5,500 RMB), 24-29 hours attracts overtime payment. Salary paid per month plus accommodation allowance of 2,000 RMB.

Facilities/Support: accommodation provided if requested. Visa and Foreign Expert Certificate provided. 2 weeks paid holiday. Flight costs reimbursed. Health insurance. Orientation on arrival and ongoing training. Chinese lessons. Well-equipped school in pleasant and convenient area of the city.

Recruitment: lara.latcham@ef.com (in Shanghai) or siobahn.pitchfork@ef.com (in London) and amy.fenollosa@ef.com.

EF ENGLISH FIRST GUANGZHOU
East Wing Hua Xin Building (3rd Floor), 2 Shui Yin Road, Guangzhou 510075.
Tel/fax: (20) 8762 1392. E-mail: mcco12@hotmail.com (Academic Co-ordinator).
All conditions same as EF English First Shanghai (above).

HONGXIN ENGLISH LANGUAGE INSTITUTE
3rd Floor, Guantex Building, 438 Dongfengzhong Road, Guangzhou 510030. Tel:
(20) 8319 2253. Fax: (20) 8336 8867. E-mail: gzhxeli@public.guangzhou.gd.cn.
Number of teachers: 5.
Preference of nationality: American/Australian.
Qualifications: minimum BA, TEFL Cert. and two years' teaching experience.
Conditions of employment: one year. 12 hours per week.
Salary: minimum 4,500 yuan.
Facilities/Support: school provides rent-free furnished apartment. Teachers pay own utilities.
Recruitment: via internet.
Contact: Peter Tang.

IEF EDUCATION FOUNDATION
US office. Fax: (626) 965-1675. E-mail: mwurmlinger@ief-usa.org.
Number of teachers: various to teach junior high and high-school aged students in many Chinese cities.
Preference of nationality: most participants are American.
Qualifications: a degree or at least 2 years equivalent education. Must have interest in intercultural understanding. Previous ESL experience helpful but not essential.
Conditions of employment: 6-month commitment minimum; 1 year preferred.
Salary: monthly minimum 2,500 RMB.
Facilities/Support: on-campus housing and health insurance provided. Return airfare reimbursed after 2 years. 2 month paid vacation.
Recruitment: via internet (www.eslcafe.com).

JIANGXI AGRICULTURAL UNIVERSITY
Nanchang, Jiangxi 330045. Tel/fax: (791) 381 3351. Fax: (791) 381 3740. E-mail:
ieojau@public.nc.jx.cn or Dean of the English Dept (Jianghua Fu): fujianghua@
sina.com.
Number of teachers: 4.
Preference of nationality: British, American. Must be native speaker.
Qualifications: BA and TEFL Cert. Aged 21-65. Teaching experience is preferred.
Conditions of employment: to teach speaking, listening, reading, writing, business English and English Literature to students of English and Business Majors and postgraduates of various specialities. Some classes have 45 students. Some courses (speaking and writing) have 22. Total teaching hours per week is 12-16 periods (40 minutes each).
Salary: from 2,200 yuan per month. Monthly cost of food is 400 yuan. 2,000 yuan travel allowance and medical coverage, travel expenses for arrival and departure and one-way international flight when you leave China.
Facilities/Support: there is a three-bedroom apartment provided for every three teachers and utilities (except telephone) are paid by the state university.
Recruitment: via internet and exchange organisations.
Contact: Jiangxi Fu, Dean of English Department.

KAI EN ENGLISH LANGUAGE TRAINING CENTER
150 Wu Yi Road, Bldg. 1/Floor 8, Shanghai. Tel: (21) 6252 3647.
Number of teachers: varies.
Qualifications: Bachelor degree and preferably a Cambridge CELTA or equivalent and relevant experience.
Conditions of employment: one-year contract. Workloads vary from month to month but a typical workload is 18 hours contact teaching and 6 hours of other

activities (helping to produce newsletter or radio programme, designing curriculum, participating in English Club activities). Teaching is mainly in the evenings and on weekend mornings and afternoons. General and Business English.
Salary: 7,200 RMB per month.
Facilities/support: if wished, En Kai can provide accommodation in apartments (own bedroom, shared facilities) for 1,800 RMB (approximately US$220) per month. 4 weeks paid vacation and return airfares from place of origin to Shanghai or an equivalent amount. Membership of a Western clinic. Ongoing programme of teacher development and training including Chinese language classes.

NEW CHINA EDUCATION FOUNDATION
1587 Montalban Drive, San José, CA 95120, USA. Tel: (408) 268-0418.
Number of teachers: 6-10.
Preference of nationality: American, Canadian or British.
Qualifications: college grads with teaching experience preferred.
Conditions of employment: one academic year.
Salary: 1,750-2,000 Renminbi yuan per month on average.
Facilities/Support: accommodation provided. Teachers are advised to bring some teaching materials.
Recruitment: through North American colleges and direct contact. Interviews not essential.
Contact: May Hu, Chairperson Teacher Placement.

PROJECT CHINA
Tel: 01273 775000. Fax: 08700 523487. E-mail: scherto@projectchina.org.
Promotes cultural and educational exchanges between China and the UK.
Number of teachers: 30 native speakers to work at two partner schools in Beijing and one in Shenyang (Northeast China).
Preference of nationality: UK, USA, Canada and Australia preferred.
Qualifications: first degree, TEFL certificate and some experience. Interest in exploring other cultures essential.
Conditions of employment: 1-year contract. 18-22 contact hours per week. Students are 16-18 and preparing to study in the West.
Salary: RMB3,000-8,000 depending on school and qualifications.
Facilities/Support: free western-style accommodation provided. Help given with obtaining Z visa.
Recruitment: via internet, newspaper and contacts with TEFL training centres in the UK. Telephone interviews.
Contact: Scherto Lee, Project Manager.

QINGDAO E900 LANGUAGE CENTER
Zhang Shan Silu 5, Badaguan, Qingdao, Shandong Province. Tel: (532) 389 7393 (Don Lounder). Fax: (532) 389 9836/870 1007. E-mail: e900don@263.net.
Number of teachers: 5.
Preference of nationality: none.
Qualifications: degree plus TESL etc. and experience. Good qualifications and experience rated highly but applications from qualified, talented novices are also welcomed.
Conditions of employment: variable length contract. Full-time. 22 classes of 50 minutes per week using the Centre's required teaching method and materials. Classes run from Monday to Sunday morning to evenings and normally have up to 20 students.
Salary: 4,000-5,000 RMB yuan per month according to qualifications, experience and teaching term. Possession of a Foreign Expert Card allows the instructor to convert 70% of salary to US dollars.
Facilities/support: free furnished private room and shared facilities provided. Housing is on campus near the seashore of Qingdao. Classes in Chinese offered at the Center.

Recruitment: internet and Chinese network. Interviews not essential.
Contact: Don Lounder, Academic Director.

SICHUAN INTERNATIONAL STUDIES UNIVERSITY (SISU)
Lie Shi Mu, Chongqing 400031. Tel: (23) 653 45218. Fax: (23) 653 15875. E-mail: faosisu@public.cta.cq.cn.
Number of teachers: varies.
Preference of nationality: none, but should be native speaker.
Qualifications: degree plus at least two years' teaching experience.
Conditions of employment: one year.
Salary: 2,200-3,000 yuan plus holiday bonus of 2,200 after a year.
Facilities/Support: SISU will pay for the return airfare and provide free medical care. Also, free accommodation is provided.
Recruitment: via internet and international contacts.
Contact: (Mr.) Xingguo Wang.

TIMES LANGUAGE TRAINING CENTER
Hui Cheng ShangYe Zhongxin, 839 Xia He Luu, Xiamen, Fujian 361004. Tel: (592) 504 2605. Fax: (592) 504 2606. E-mail: times_xiamen@hotmail.com.
Number of teachers: 4 full-time, 4 part-time.
Preference of nationality: any native speaker with clear and standard pronunciation.
Qualifications: BA (essential for work permit) and TEFL Certificate. TEFL experience is preferred but not required.
Conditions of employment: 1 year and short-term contracts available. 17-22 h.p.w. evenings and weekends.
Salary: 3,500 Renminbi for inexperienced teachers and 4,000 Renminbi for experienced staff. (Monthly income above 4,000 RMB is subject to tax.) Salaries can be raised every 3 months based on performance (responsibility, student satisfaction, classroom observations, etc.)
Facilities/Support: full-time teachers who work only for the centre are provided with an apartment; the agent's fee, deposits and rent are paid. Utilities must be paid by teacher (100 RMB per month without and 200 RMB with air-conditioning). Help with visas given for 1-year contracts only.
Recruitment: via internet.
Contact: Julie Krolak, Academic Director.

Hong Kong

Since the former British colony became the Hong Kong Special Administrative Region (HKSAR), of the People's Republic of China on June 23rd 1997, many aspects of life and employment have changed. For example there has been a controversial switch in the state education system away from English as a medium of instruction to Cantonese. While three out of four parents want their children to be educated in English, only one in four is being given a place at schools that do this. To meet the demand, the Hong Kong authorities announced that they wanted to employ 700 native English speakers to teach in the state education system as part of the NET scheme (Native English Teacher). These foreign teachers known as 'Netters' are assigned randomly and singly to government schools across Hong Kong and working conditions can be tough especially in a Band 5 school with low-achieving pupils. On the other hand salaries and benefits are generous.

On the other hand, much in Hong Kong remains the same. For example there is still a separate currency, and the chances of the Hong Kong dollar being replaced by the Hong Kong renminbi/yuan seem remote. In fact the HK dollar has remained remarkably stable over the past few years.

The demand for English teachers continues as strong as ever. What has changed is the ease with which British nationals can sort out the red tape. Formerly they were allowed to stay for a year without many formalities. Now it is illegal to enter Hong Kong as a tourist and take up work so that all those graduates who arrive on holiday and want to change their status are out of luck. However, it is possible to visit the city, fix up a teaching job and then apply for a work permit from a neighbouring country. The authorities would like to see a university degree, five years of relevant work experience and a corporate sponsor. Teachers who satisfy these requirements should have no difficulty obtaining a work permit. Anyone who manages to find an employer before arrival can seek their sponsorship to obtain a work permit. This is a major undertaking for any employer so teachers should try to honour their commitments instead of flitting off to a better-paying school after a month or two.

FIXING UP A JOB

Recruitment rarely takes place outside Hong Kong, except by the British Council, which has a large teaching operation in Hong Kong. The government scheme to recruit English teachers is administered by the Hong Kong Education Department (Expatriate Teacher Exchange, 13F Wu Chung House, 213 Queen's Road East, Wanchai). *Christians Abroad* are actively recruiting a considerable number of English teachers (who must have a Christian commitment) to Hong Kong.

English for Asia Ltd in Kowloon (see *Directory of Trinity Courses*) is often contacted by HK institutes when they are recruiting. The internet is a useful source of jobs, e.g. www.englishexpert.com has in the past had a Hong Kong Job Board. Some notices seen recently are for the Language Learning Center (ezlearn@toplanguage.com.hk) or for Sylvan Learning Centers. The bumper Saturday edition of the *South China Morning Post* should contain some useful leads. The paper is distributed in the UK by the Powers Turner Group, 100 Rochester Row, London SW1P 1JP; 020-7952 8330; ffentiman@publicitas.com (enquiries to Fleur Fentiman).

Look for English Clubs which provide a cheaper alternative for learners than formal English classes. Joe Doughty describes them:

> *The vast majority of teaching jobs on offer at the lower end of the market are in conversation clubs where Chinese students pay a modest fee, which entitles them to attend as often as they like during opening hours for three months. What happens in practice is that there is a constant coming and going in your 'classroom,' which in my case was really just a large alcove without a door. This can be off-putting as you are not sure why students are leaving (was it something I said?) Like most things it gets better and you soon get a reasonably regular group of students. There are periodic checks by a member of the admin to see if you are keeping a reasonable number of students enthralled at any one time.*

The *Yellow Pages* are the alternative source of institute addresses. Phone calls within the city limits are free, so by phoning around you can easily get an idea of the possibilities. Although hiring is continuous, the summer months bring even more openings, while the Chinese New Year in January/February is a bad time.

Job interviews are not necessarily daunting experiences. Martyn Owens describes his initial meeting with an employer:

> *After ringing, I went to the school to have an interview with the Director. It was quite informal. She seemed to be most interested in my intended length of stay (after she realised I was 'presentable' so to speak) and asked also about my academic qualifications. She didn't expect me to have had any teaching experience and was most impressed when I presented my TEFL certificate (five-day introductory course at the Surrey Language Centre). I'm sure I would have got the job without it, merely on the basis of my willingness to work.*

Freelance teaching can prove lucrative provided you are staying in Hong Kong legally. Brett Muir describes the tactics he used to find clients:

> *My recommendation is to hire a paging device (really cheap by the month – major companies have offices in the big subway stations) and write an attractive advertisement for placing in the letter boxes of the ritzy apartment estates in Mid Levels, Jardines, Lookout and Causeway Bay suburbs. Although the gates are locked, the Filipina maids are constantly going in and out, so you just walk in with them to post your photocopied ads. In this way you are always on the phone. Generally it is housewives and businessmen who are looking for conversation practice.*

Another way to attract clients is to put notices up in busy places like Welcome Supermarkets, though you will have to keep checking that your notices have not been covered up or removed by the store manager who has a weekly clear-out.

REGULATIONS

Information about the formalities should be requested from the Chinese Embassies in London and Washington. UK nationals may stay as tourists in Hong Kong for up to six months. An application for a change of status must be lodged with the HKSAR Immigration Department (Immigration Tower, 7 Gloucester Road, Wan Chai; 2824 6111/fax 2824 1133; enquiry@imd.gcn.gov.hk/ www.info.gov.hk/immd) but the applicant must be out of the country. According to the Immigration Department, application for a change of status from within Hong Kong is only possible at the discretion of the immigration service in 'very special circumstances'. As in Taiwan, the established schools should be prepared to sponsor you for a work permit if you can persuade them that you will work for them for a reasonable length of time.

CONDITIONS OF WORK

Except for the highly qualified and privileged teachers who teach at the prestigious end of the market, low wages and long hours are the norm. HK$60 an hour is about the best an unqualified part-time teacher can expect to earn. Gavin Staples was in Hong Kong a couple of years ago and describes conditions at one school notorious for its cowboy practices:

> *One school expected its teacher to work 40 hours a week for HK$40 an hour, which is an appalling set-up. Teachers who turn up even slightly late were fined literally by the minute. One person I met teaching here was so embittered that he stood outside the door and poached students to teach privately. Like so many others, the school at which I ended up teaching on a one-to-one basis was run solely for profit. The students were never graded so you had no idea at what level they were, and the school had about eight books and one dictionary. Although I had been promised HK$50 an hour, my first pay packet was for HK$45.*

As is the case in many other places, the longer you stay, the more stable your hours become. Later Gavin was offered some hours by a reputable teaching agency which paid much better, but they could offer him only six hours a week which would rise to twelve hours after three months. Anyone prepared to sign a contract for more than six months can expect to earn more, though if you find that you can't stick it for that long, you may end up forfeiting some wages for breach of contract. One possible justification for the meagre wage is that many schools hand out detailed lesson plans to their untrained teachers which means that lesson preparation time is minimal.

Always try to collect your wages at frequent intervals since some schools have been negligent in this regard. Teachers have no health or social security protection. When Joe Doughty became ill, he was simply fired.

Erratic hours are also a problem, as Leslie Platt found out:

My institute was very vague as to what hours I would be working. I would arrive in the afternoon as instructed only to be informed that no students had turned up but that I had better hang around for a few hours just in case one did. If none did, it meant I didn't get paid.

Accommodation

Needless to say, the kind of language school described here does not offer accommodation to its teachers. Accommodation in the crowded heart of Hong Kong is astronomically expensive, so it will be a problem unless you are prepared to stay in a hostel. Teachers will probably want to avoid the infamous Travellers Hostel in Chung King Mansions. After taking a look at it, Vaughan Temby decided that the feat of maintaining a working life and dressing smartly while staying there was beyond him and he looked elsewhere. There are many other hostels in the Mansions complex. From time to time the Hong Kong authorities clamp down on hostels on the grounds of fire risk, and some of the worst ones may be closed down.

The average rent for a room in a decent shared flat is upwards of HK$5,000 a month, which is far more than most teachers can afford, and flats can easily cost £1,000 a month. Good accommodation is available more cheaply on the outlying islands such as Lamma and Lantau, which can be an attractive option in view of the cheap and plentiful public transport including ferry service, though the commute will take anything up to an hour. Here it is possible to find pleasant flats or even houses for about £400 a month.

LEISURE TIME

Not surprisingly, culture shock is kept to a minimum in Hong Kong by the Western affluence and the British bias. Hong Kong is famed as a shoppers' paradise in which the cheap food, clothing and travel help to alleviate the problem of expensive accommodation. But with inflation running fairly high, the cost of living has risen dramatically, and a teacher's wage does not go very far.

Martyn Owens describes the range of leisure activities:

Hong Kong buzzes 24 hours a day and is like a film set! Consequently there is much to do – bowling, movies, sports, restaurants, etc. all probably within walking distance. I spent most of my spare time in restaurants with friends; eating out is the most popular pastime among the locals. I also travelled around the New Territories which is a beautiful place.

LIST OF SCHOOLS

DEBORAH INTERNATIONAL PLAYSCHOOL
GF Site 9, Whampoa Garden, Kowloon. Tel: 2994 8898. Fax: 2994 8812. E-mail: maffini@pacific.net.hk.
Number of teachers: 50 for group of kindergartens.
Preference of nationality: none, but must be native speaker.
Qualifications: at least a year's experience. B.Ed preferred.
Conditions of employment: 2 year contract. School hours from 8.15am to 5.15pm Monday to Friday plus 2 Saturdays per month 9am-12pm.
Salary: HK$12000.
Facilities/Support: free shared accommodation per 3 teachers provided.
Recruitment: via the internet. Interviews not essential.
Contact: Helen Maffini, Vice-principal.

ISLAND SCHOOL
20 Borrett Road, Hong Kong. Tel: 2524 7135. Fax: 2840 1673. E-mail: school@is.esf.edu.hk.

Number of teachers: 3 ESL teachers out of staff of 85.
Preference of nationality: international.
Qualifications: graduates, PGCE and 2 years' experience.
Conditions of employment: 2 year contracts. Hours are 8am-3.30pm. Possibility of moving to another of the 15 schools run by the English Schools Foundation.
Salary: HK$29,000-$51,000 per month for a mainscale teacher. Expatriate contracts pay their own rent.
Recruitment: adverts in HK and UK in January. Interviews can be held in both countries.
Contact: David James, Principal.

READY TO LEARN
Administrative Office, 1st Floor, 4 W Ng Sing Lane, Yau Ma Tei, Kowloon, Hong Kong. Tel: 2388 1318: Fax: 2388 3081. E-mail: hr_rtl.hk. Website: www.rtl.com.hk.
Number of teachers: 30.
Preference of nationality: none, but should be native speaker.
Qualifications: degree minimum.
Conditions of employment: 1 year renewable. 30 hours per week.
Salary: HK$14,000 + $200 per month for 1st year; HK$15,000 + $200 per month for 2nd.
Facilities/Support: company accommodation provided inclusive of bills (except food) for HK$2,500. Airfares and medical insurance paid for by school.
Recruitment: via newspapers and internet. Interviews by telephone.
Contact: Paula Crowder, Human Resources.

VENTURE LANGUAGE TRAINING LTD
1A 163 Hennessey Road, Wan Chai, Hong Kong. Tel: 2507 4985. Fax: 2511 3798.
Number of teachers: 12.
Preference of nationality: British.
Qualifications: TEFL or similar/English degree. Experience more important than qualifications.
Conditions of employment: 2 year contracts. 20 h.p.w.
Salary: HK$200 per hour; $300 for Business English courses.
Facilities/Support: no assistance with accommodation. Company will sponsor teachers on 2-year contracts for a work permit.
Recruitment: word-of-mouth. Interviews absolutely essential, and can be held in the UK. Local interview essential.
Contact: Susanne Pickering, Director of Studies.

Indonesia

Indonesia is the fifth most populous nation on earth, a fact of which we are all reminded by the news media when political unrest and violence swept the country in May 1998. Many expat teachers chose that moment to leave the country leaving many schools which had had a high proportion of native speaker teachers with far fewer or none at all. The rioting erupted in the wake of the South East Asian economic crisis and when Indonesia experienced one of the most drastic currency devaluations of any country in recent history. Schools which had for years been attracting professional ELT teachers from abroad with generous salaries and benefits packages could no longer do so. As one shell-shocked teacher was overheard to say, 'I'm 32 years old and suddenly I'm working for $200 a month'.

However the crisis has been weathered, a semblance of stability has returned and the dozen or so major language training organisations have survived, despite the damaging exodus of many wealthy Chinese clients from the country. As the Director of Studies of one of the major schools wrote for this edition:

You might want to mention that despite the current 'situation' Indonesia is still a wonderful place to live and work as an EFL teacher. I've been here almost ten years now. I got my first job after writing to the schools in your publication.

The best jobs continue to crop up in the oil company cities as that industry is still stable. The so-called 'native speaker schools' with multiple branches in Jakarta and the other cities continue to deliver English courses to the millions of Indonesians who still want to learn the language. These organisations can still afford to hire trained foreign teachers and pay them about ten times the local wage. A few like *EF English First* have even expanded and others have opened like the International Language Centre in Medan (Jl. Samanhudi No 22, Medan 20151; 61-451 5766/fax 61-415 5471; ilc@mdn.centrin.net.id) whose director Stefen Wijaya opened for business in April 2000 and who claimed that they had too many students and not enough teachers.

FIXING UP A JOB

The CELTA is highly regarded in Indonesia and anyone who has acquired the Certificate has a good chance of pre-arranging a job in Jakarta, Surabaya, Bandung or Yogyakarta (arguably the most interesting city in Indonesia). While some schools clearly favour either British or North American teachers, others express no preference, and there are also quite a few Australian and New Zealand EFL teachers in Indonesia. The government's only stipulation from the point of view of awarding work permits is that the teachers must be native speakers.

In Advance

Private schools with overseas contacts advertise and recruit internationally. For example *International Language Programs* carry out interviews in London each summer for the 40 or so teaching positions they have in their branches. Advertisements in the educational press, especially *EL Prospects* appear with some regularity in the spring and summer.

Colin Boothroyd taught for a major language school in Jakarta and describes the way he arranged the job:

I answered an advertisement in the Education section of the Guardian immediately but did not get a response for a month. The response came in the form of a phone call requesting an interview with me. I was interviewed a few days later – a very relaxed affair in a South London pub – and was told on the spot that I would be recommended for a posting. Two weeks later I received a load of information welcoming me to the school. Three weeks later I was on a plane to Jakarta, having picked up a visa at the Indonesian Embassy in London.

The beauty of Colin's 18-month contract was that it included free flights, an increasingly rare perk these days. Two or three of the main schools in Indonesia do pay a one-way return fare at the end of a successful contract.

Even if you have missed an opportunity to be interviewed in your home country, it is still worth contacting the major schools by fax or e-mail. Some hire their teachers on the basis of a telephone interview and, in some cases, a taped example of your voice.

On the Spot

More and more teachers are being hired on the spot, which suits the major schools who then don't have to pay for airfares. Local recruits can negotiate shorter contracts, for example six months, unlike teachers recruited abroad who usually have to stay at least 18 months. Most teaching jobs start in July or September/October. Visit the British Council and check adverts in the English language *Jakarta Post* or *Indonesian Observer.* The Centre Supervisor of the British Council in Surabaya is sometimes asked to match up teachers already in Surabaya and schools on an unofficial basis.

With a Cambridge or Trinity Certificate and university degree your chances of being offered a job are high. Unqualified applicants would have to be extremely well presented (since dress is very important in Jakarta), able to sell themselves in terms of experience and qualifications and prepared to commit themselves for a longish spell or to start with some part-time work in the hope of building it up.

Local schools staffed by Indonesians abound, many willing to hire a native speaker at local wages. Some can even arrange a work permit. Travellers have stumbled across friendly little schools up rickety staircases throughout the islands of Indonesia, as the German round-the-world traveller Gerhard Flaig describes:

> *In Yogyakarta you can find language schools listed in the telephone book or you just walk through streets to look for them. Most of them are interested in having new teachers. I got an offering to teach German and also English since my English was better than some of the language school managers. All of them didn't bother about work permits. The wages aren't very high, about 10,000 rupiahs an hour. It is fairly easy to cover the costs of board and lodging since the cost of living is very low.*

Opportunities exist not only in the large cities but in small towns too. Tim Leffel from New Jersey noticed a large number of English schools in the Javanese city of Solo, and others have recommended Bali. At local schools unused to employing native speaker teachers, teaching materials may be in short supply. One of the problems faced by those who undertake casual work of this kind is that there is usually little chance of obtaining a work permit (see below). It is also difficult for freelance teachers to become legal unless you have a contact who knows people in power.

The problem of visas doesn't arise if you teach English on a completely informal basis as Stuart Tappin did:

> *In Asia I managed to spend a lot of time living with people in return for teaching English. The more remote the towns are from tourist routes the better, for example Bali is no good. I spent a week in Palembang Sumatra living with an English teacher and his family. You teach and they give their (very good) hospitality.*

REGULATIONS

The work permit regulations are rigidly adhered to in Indonesia and all of the established language schools will apply for a visa permit on your behalf. Some even employ a full-time visa co-ordinator. The Embassy's 'General Information for Foreigners Wishing to Work in Indonesia' starts with the warning, 'Please be informed that Indonesia has very strict and complicated immigration/visa requirements and the process can be very long.' If the job is arranged before you leave home, you should take a letter of sponsorship from your employer to the Indonesian Embassy in London and, subject to current visa requirements, they will issue you with a business visa valid for a maximum of five weeks. All other work permit arrangements will be taken care of by your school on arrival, after you have provided your CV, TEFL course certificate, photocopies of your passport and application forms. These are sent to the Indonesian Ministry of Education, the Cabinet Secretariat and the Immigration/Manpower Departments. If and when the application is approved, the work permit will be valid for one employer only and will be revoked and the offending teacher deported if work is undertaken outside the terms of the contract.

After your work permit and temporary stay permit have been granted (with a maximum validity of one year), the documentation will then be telexed to the nearest

Indonesian Embassy (normally Singapore) where the teacher can have it stamped in his or her passport. Anyone without the necessary professional qualifications is unlikely to be granted the visa.

Tourists can stay in Indonesia for two months. It is possible to renew one's tourist status by leaving the country every two months (e.g. flying to Singapore, or by ferry to Penang in Malaysia) but the authorities might become suspicious if you did this repeatedly. Anyone found working on a tourist visa will be deported and blacklisted from entering Indonesia in the future. (Also, the employer would find himself in serious trouble.)

CONDITIONS OF WORK

Despite the devaluation of the rupiah, salaries paid by the 'native speaker' schools provide for a comfortable lifestyle including travel within Indonesia during the vacations. Most schools pay about 6,000,000-8,000,000 rupiahs per month, after Indonesian tax of 10% has been subtracted. If inflation continues at the present rate, ask about mid-term salary adjustments. Since the cost of living is low, especially outside the cities, many teachers are able to enjoy a very comfortable lifestyle and travel in their free time. If you plan to complete a two-year contract, enquire about reimbursement for airfares and a possible tax rebate.

Many schools offer generous help with accommodation, ranging from an interest-free loan to cover initial rent payments or deposits, to free housing complete with free telephone, electricity and servants. It is customary in the Jakarta housing market to be asked to pay the annual rent in a lump sum at the beginning of your tenancy, and so access to a loan from your employer is often essential.

If you happen to work for a school which takes on outside contracts, you may have the occasional chance to work outside the school premises, possibly in a remote oil drilling location in Sumatra, for up to double pay. The majority of teachers, however, conduct lessons at their school through the usual peak hours of 3.30pm to 8.30pm with some early morning starts as well.

The Pupils

Outside the big cities, the standard of English is normally very low, with pupils having picked up a smattering from bad American television. Classes also tend to be large, with as many as 40 pupils, all expecting to learn grammar by the traditional rote methods. According to a VSO volunteer teaching in Western Java (as quoted in the *TES*), 'If I want to do something interesting, the students complain that it isn't in the exam'. As is the case elsewhere in the world, the average age of English learners is getting younger, so anyone with experience of teaching children or teenagers will be appreciated.

Students in Jakarta present fewer problems as Colin Boothroyd describes:

> The pupils are incredibly enthusiastic and are genuinely appreciative of the opportunity to learn from native speakers. I have never once had a discipline problem whilst I've been teaching here. My classes have varied from 2 to 20 in size. The students are generally unfamiliar with our communicative form of teaching, since kids aren't really expected to think for themselves in Indonesian schools. Students are reluctant to speak about controversial issues (the issues that should really provoke loads of communication) because they are afraid that big brother may overhear something that doesn't suit. Otherwise the students are brilliant.

LEISURE TIME

Although Jakarta is a hot, dusty, overcrowded, polluted and poverty-stricken city, there is a great deal to see and do, and many teachers enjoy living there. Indonesia is a fascinating country and most visitors, whether short-term or long, agree that the

Indonesian people are fantastic. Travel is cheap and unrestricted, and excursions are very rewarding in terms of scenery and culture. Travel by public transport can be time-consuming and limiting for weekend trips, so you might consider getting a motorcycle, although Jakarta's traffic problems make this too dangerous and unhealthy for many. Internal flights are also within the range of most teachers.

Predictably the community of expatriate teachers participates in lots of joint activities such as football and tennis matches, chess tournaments, beach excursions, diving trips and parties. Most teachers have videos but occasionally go out to see an undubbed American film. Eating out is so cheap relative to salaries that many teachers indulge themselves at restaurants most nights of the week.

The pleasant city of Bandung might prove an attractive alternative to Jakarta. It escaped the violent demonstrations which affected so much of the country in 1998 and offers a good quality lifestyle to teachers, with a good mixture of rural and city life.

Bahasa Indonesian, almost identical to Malay, was imposed on the people of Indonesia after independence in 1949 and is one of the simplest languages to learn both in structure and pronunciation. Mastering a vocabulary of about one hundred words should be enough to get by.

LIST OF SCHOOLS

BERLITZ
14th Floor, Wisma Danamon Aetna Life Bldg., Jl. Jendral Sudirman, Jakarta. Tel: 62 21 577 1519. Fax: 62 21 577 1520. E-mail: lincoln@dnet.net.id.
Number of teachers: approx. 10.
Preference of nationality: none.
Qualifications: degree minimum. TEFL Cert and or experience preferred but not essential.
Conditions of employment: open-ended. One month's notice required. School hours: 7.30am-9pm, Monday to Friday; 7.30am to 1pm Saturday. Lessons scheduled as available between these hours.
Salary: US$1,000-$1,500 depending on schedule.
Facilities/Support: no assistance with accommodation.
Recruitment: word-of-mouth, newspapers and via internet.
Contact: Lincoln Taylor.

THE BRITISH INSTITUTE
Jalan Diponegoro 23, Bandung 40124. Tel: (22) 4211556. E-mail: tbi@tbi.co.id. Website: www.tbi.co.id.
Number of teachers: 10.
Preference of nationality: none.
Qualifications: UCLES CELTA or equivalent plus minimum six months teaching experience.
Conditions of employment: 1 year. 22 contact hours per week.
Salary: 5,658,000 rupiahs per month.
Facilities/Support: an interest free loan is offered to all teachers for their accommodation. TBI organises work permits.
Recruitment: adverts in local English language newspapers, teachers passing through looking for work, teachers coming from other schools in Bandung.
Contact: Mary Collins, Director of Studies.

THE BRITISH INSTITUTE
Plaza Setiabudi 11, 2nd Floor, Jl.H.R. Rasuna Said, Jakarta 12920. E-mail: tbi@unisad.co.id. Website: www.tbi.co.id.
Number of teachers: 12.
Preference of nationality: none.
Qualifications: CELTA or equivalent minimum.
Conditions of employment: 1 year. 24 contact hours per week.

Salary: 8,200,000-8,700,000 rupiahs per month.
Facilities/Support: interest free housing loan (up to one and a half times monthly salary) repayable over 5 months. Work permits and paperwork taken care of by the school.
Recruitment: local hire through newspaper advertisements. Interviews in Indonesia only.
Contact: David Bruce, Director of Studies.

EF ENGLISH FIRST
Wisma Tamara 4th Floor, Suite 402, Jl. Jend. Sudirman Kav. 24, Jakarta 12920. Tel: (21) 520 6477. Fax: (21) 520 4719.
Number of teachers: approximately 200 for schools throughout Indonesia including 8 in Jakarta, and others in Surabaya (Plaza Surabaya, Jl. Pemuda 33-37, Surabaya 60271; 31-548 4000/fax 31-548 3000), Java (Semarang, Bogor, Bandung, Cirebon), Sumatra (Medan, Palembang, Lampung) and Sulawesi (Ujung Pandang).
Preference of nationality: British, Canadian, Australian, American or Irish only (due to work visa restrictions).
Qualifications: minimum university degree and certificate in EFL/ESL.
Conditions of employment: 12 month contracts. Teaching between 7.30am and 9pm Monday to Friday and some Saturdays.
Salary: varies according to location. End-of-contract bonus.
Facilities/Support: assistance with accommodation. Work permits provided. Flight costs reimbursed. Paid holidays. Orientation upon arrival and ongoing training. All schools well equipped with a variety of resources.
Recruitment: directly through Jakarta office or through English First offices in London and Boston (see *Finding a Job*).
Contact: Academic Support Coordinator.

EF ENGLISH FIRST – MENTENG
Jl. Timor No. 25, Menteng, Jakarta 10350. Tel: (21) 3148815. Fax: (21) 336890.
Number of teachers: varies.
Preference of nationality: native English-speaking.
Qualifications: minimum TEFL certificate. Degree and experience preferred.
Conditions of employment: One year contracts teaching a range of courses including General English, Business English, Conversation, TOEFL, one-to-one tutoring and in-house teaching.
Salary: varies according to type of work and location.
Facilities/Support: full-time teachers get round-trip airfare and medical insurance. Visa and work permit are paid for. Accommodation is provided but teachers pay rent.
Recruitment: internet or EF offices in London and Boston.
Contact: Janti.

ENGLISH EDUCATION CENTER (EEC)
Jalan Let. Jend. S. Parman 68, Slipi, Jakarta 11410. Tel: (21) 532 3176/532 0044. Fax: (21) 532 3178. E-mail: eec@vision.net.id or juspip@hotmail.com. Web-site: www.indodirect.com/eec.
Number of teachers: 30 in three schools in Jakarta.
Preference of nationality: American, British, Australian, New Zealand, Canadian.
Qualifications: BA in relevant subject, CELTA and minimum 1 year's overseas TEFL experience.
Conditions of employment: 1-year contracts. Maximum 25½ h.p.w., normally 2-9pm, but some 8.30am-12.30pm schedules. Students of all ages but many are teenagers and young adults.
Salary: 7,000,000-8,000,000 rupiahs per month (with rises expected to take account of inflation).
Facilities/Support: assistance given with finding accommodation, including initial loan. Return air fare after completion of 1-year contract.

Recruitment: teachers recruited locally.
Contact: Justin Roberts, Director of Studies.

ENGLISH LANGUAGE TRAINING INTERNATIONAL (ELTI)
Kelompok Gramedia, Jl. Sabirin 6, Kotabaru, Yogyakarta 55224. Tel: (274) 561849. Fax: (274) 561275. E-mail: eltiyk@indosat.net.id. Website: www.elti.co.id.
Number of teachers: 3.
Preference of nationality: American, Canadian, British, Australian.
Qualifications: 1-2 years teaching experience and/or TEFL Diploma/Certificate.
Courses offered: General English, English for Specific Purposes, TOEFL Preparation Program, English for Children.
Conditions of employment: one-year contracts. 18-24 h.p.w. teaching mainly adults.
Salary: from 8,500,000 rupiahs per month.
Facilities/Support: no financial assistance with accommodation.
Recruitment: adverts in the *Jakarta Post* and embassies. Interviews in Yogyakarata compulsory.
Contact: Edy Sukrisno, Director of Studies.

EXECUTIVE ENGLISH PROGRAMS (EEP) – JAKARTA
Jalan Wijaya VIII/4, Kebayoran Baru, Jakarta Selatan 12160. Tel: (21) 722 0812/720 8864. Fax: (21) 720 1896. E-mail: eepkby@pacific.net.id.
Also another branch in Jakarta and one in Bandung (see next entry).
Number of teachers: 40.
Preference of nationality: none.
Qualifications: CELTA or equivalent plus 1 year's experience preferred.
Conditions of employment: 12 month contracts. Maximum 28 h.p.w. (overtime paid when hours exceed 24). Teaching between 1pm and 9pm. Frequent opportunities for optional additional hourly-paid morning work (8.30am-12.45pm).
Salary: 5,850,000 rupiahs per month (net); higher for Diploma/MA holders or substantial full-time experience. Interest-free housing loans available for teachers hired from overseas, repayable over maximum of 5 months.
Recruitment: local newspaper advertisements, direct overseas hire.
Contact: Ted Thornton, Director of Studies.

EXECUTIVE ENGLISH PROGRAMS (EEP) – BANDUNG
Jalan Lombok No. 43, Bandung 40115. Tel/fax: (22) 708254. Tel: (22) 421 1651.
Preference of nationality: none.
Qualifications: university degree and Cambridge Cert. required; PGCE and/or 1 year's experience preferred.
Conditions of employment: 12 month contracts. 24 h.p.w. between 2pm and 9pm with some morning classes.
Salary: 3,200,000 rupiahs per month (net) with bonus of US$600 on completion.
Recruitment: local newspaper adverts. Local interviews nearly always necessary.
Contact: Mark Hallett, Director of Studies.

IALF-UNAIR LANGUAGE CENTRE
Jl. Airlangga 8, Surabaya, East Java. Tel: (31) 502 3332. Fax: (31) 502 3334. E-mail: ialfunair@ialf.edu. Website: www.ialf.edu.
Number of teachers: 7.
Preference of nationality: must be native English speaker.
Qualifications: Cambridge Cert. (minimum B), plus 2 years' experience or Dip. IELTS examiners, IELTS Prep, Academic English and Business English experience an advantage.
Conditions of employment: one year. 8 hour-day. Maximum of 22 contact hours a week.
Salary: 88,000,000-106,000,000 rupiah per annum depending on experience. There is an additional 500,000 rupiah monthly transport allowance. Teachers also get

Expacare medical insurance. US$500 (assistance for leaving fare) is given on completion of a one year, full-time employment contract or US$750 paid on signing, in good faith, a further one-year contract. No deductions for tax or social security.
Facilities/Support: loan of two months' salary to assist with payment of accommodation rental is deducted from monthly salary over six months. Assistance with work permits.
Recruitment: locally and via the internet. Interviews essential and normally take place in Indonesia.
Contact: Alex Gough, Manager of Language Programs.

INTERNATIONAL LANGUAGE PROGRAMS (ILP) - SURABAYA
Jalan Jawa 34, Surabaya 60281, Jawa Timor. Tel: (31) 502 3333. Fax: (31) 503 0106. E-mail: tjahjani@rad.net.id. Website: www.ilpsurabaya.com.
Number of teachers: 25.
Preference of nationality: none, but must be classified native speaker (to satisfy work permit requirements).
Qualifications: EFL qualification required, preferably CELTA or equivalent.
Conditions of employment: 1-year contracts. 20 h.p.w. teaching 5 days a week, between 2.30/3.45pm and 5/7/9.15pm. Pupils from age 6.
Salary: starting salary is 5,000,000 rupiahs (net) per month.
Facilities/Support: accommodation provided including utilities and servants. Regular workshops held.
Recruitment: adverts in UK or via the internet. UK recruiter can conduct interviews: Bruce McGowen, 9 Bishops Road, Bury St. Edmunds, Suffolk IP33 TTQ (01284 768957).
Contact: Peter Mudd, Director of Studies.

INTERNATIONAL LANGUAGE STUDIES (ILS)
Jl. Ambengan No. 1-S, Surabaya 60272. Tel: (31) 534 2457. Fax: (31) 532 8369. E-mail: ils2000@mitra.net.id
Also branches at Jl. Jemursari/Ruko D-18 Surabaya 60237 (31-849 7120) and Jl. Simpang Darmo Permai Utara No. 5, Surabaya 60226 (31-731 7697).
Number of teachers: 3-5.
Preference of nationality: British, American, Canadian and Australian.
Qualifications: TEFL/TESL/Diploma of Education plus minimum 1 year's teaching experience.
Conditions of employment: 1 or 2 year contracts, renewable. 100-120 hours per month. Freelance teaching is strictly prohibited.
Salary: 4,000,000-6,000,000 rupiahs per month (net).
Facilities/Support: accommodation allowance provided. Occasional training workshops and seminars held.
Recruitment: adverts in local papers. Interviews not necessary.
Contact: F. O. Dien Koeswanto, Director.

LOGO EDUCATION CENTRE (LEC)
Jl. H.Z. Arifin No. 208-A, Medan 20112. Tel: (61) 415 2823/453 4991. E-mail: lecmedan@indosat.net.id.
Number of teachers: 8.
Preference of nationality: none.
Qualifications: CELTA and/or teaching experience.
Conditions of employment: 12 month contract. Normally 85 to 100 teaching hours per month on weekdays only. Pupils from pre-school age to adult.
Salary: 4,500,000-5,000,000 rupiahs per month. Incentives in US dollars for completion of contract.
Facilities/Support: will assist in finding accommodation. Indonesian language lessons available for the first two months after arrival.
Recruitment: interviews in London or telephone interview will suffice.
Contact: Mr. Chitra Bustaf, Director.

NEW SURABAYA COLLEGE
Education, Job Training and Recruitment Center, Jl. Basuki Rakhmat 85, Surabaya. Tel: (31) 531 0331. Fax: (31) 532 3952. E-mail: era_pur@read.net.id.
Number of teachers: none at present.
Preference of nationality: USA, UK, Canada.
Qualifications: TEFL experienced and academic background.
Conditions of employment: one year renewable.
Salary: 30,000 rupiahs (US$4 approx.) per hour.
Facilities/Support: homestay accommodation provided. Help given with visa/work permit which requires six photos, photocopies of certificates and diplomas, passports and CV.
Recruitment: through newspapers.
Contact: Sukadi Senoadji, Director.

SCHOOL FOR INTERNATIONAL TRAINING (SIT)
Jalan Sunda 3, Menteng, Jakarta Pusat 10350. Tel: (21) 390 6920/337240/336238. Fax: (21) 335671. Plus two branches in Jakarta and one in Surabaya (Jl. Bengawan 10, Surabaya; 31-577141).
Number of teachers: 20.
Preference of nationality: American, Canadian, British, Australian.
Qualifications: BA/MA (TESOL or related subject) plus several years' experience preferred. Experience in Asia or developing countries desirable.
Conditions of employment: 1 year renewable contracts. 108 hours per month (8am-5pm or 1.30-9pm) 5 days work per week.
Salary: varies with qualifications. 4 weeks annual leave, 12 days sick leave, hospitalisation and accident insurance provided.
Facilities/Support: teachers are provided with housing and transport allowance in addition to base salary.
Recruitment: interviews held locally or by telephone. Local newspaper adverts, TESOL *Placement Bulletin*, foreign adverts and through graduate departments of some American universities.
Contact: Fransisca Laij, Director of Studies.

Japan

The once unassailable Japanese economy experienced a short sharp recession in the 1990s which saw the yen tumbling and unemployment a new fact of life. The impact for English teachers was that the market dipped, one or two major chains of language schools went bankrupt and the employment situation became generally much tighter with schools competing fiercely for a shrinking number of students. However, at the beginning of the 21st century, recovery looks strong and the prospects for hopeful language teachers once again rosy. The basic monthly salary of 250,000 yen for full-time EFL teachers may not have risen in ten years, but it is worth about £1,600/$2,300, considerably more than can be earned in most other countries. Wages are of course meaningless without balancing them against the local cost of living which is notoriously high. (People say that you can't expect to break even and begin to save before you've been in Japan for nearly a year.)

The demand for English continues very strong. For a start, all children must study English for at least three years in junior high school. But just as the demand is strong, so is the supply and there are still more teachers than jobs in Japan at present. University graduates throughout North America have been turning to their college development offices to find out how to organise a teaching job in the Far East. Newcomers who could once count on finding a reasonably convenient job are now having to travel up to two hours to get to work. Schools which once accepted anyone with fluency have become more selective, and it is no longer a case of prospective teachers picking and choosing among employers. Yet there is still very little emphasis on TEFL qualifications. Image is of paramount importance to the Japanese and many employers are more concerned to find people who are lively and a touch glamorous than they are to find people with a background in teaching.

Many language training organisations operate on a huge scale, with many branches and large numbers of staff. For instance Aeon has six offices outside Japan: 3 in the USA, 2 in Canada and 1 in Australia. Companies like Aeon, GEOS and Nova actively recruit in North America and Britain. These seem to be the employers most willing to consider teachers with no formal training, though all teachers in Japan must have a four-year BA degree (which is an absolute requirement for work visas). Some chains have been described as factory English schools, where teachers are handed a course book and told not to deviate from the formula. Demand for native speaker teachers is so great that they depend on a steady supply of fresh graduates who want the chance to spend a year in Japan. Often new recruits do not have much say in where they are sent and in their first year may be sent to the least desirable locations.

As long as your expectations are realistic, Japan should turn out to be an excellent choice of destination. Native speakers are hired in a surprising range of contexts: in-house language programmes in steel or electronics companies, state secondary schools, hot-house crammers, 'conversation lounges' where young people get together for an hour's guided conversation, vocational schools where English is a compulsory subject, 'ladies' classes' (quaintly so-called) where courses called 'English for Shopping' are actually offered, and also classes of children from as young as two, since it has become a status symbol in Japan to send children of all ages to English classes. In fact studying English for many Japanese is still more a social than an educational activity.

Culture shock grips most new arrivals to Japan. Incoming teachers are often so distracted by the mechanics of life in Japan and the cultural adjustments they have to make to survive that they devote too little energy to the business of teaching. On the other hand, anyone who has a genuine interest in Japan and who arrives reasonably well prepared may find that a year or two in Japan provides a highly rewarding experience.

Prospects for Teachers

Jobs teaching English in Japan can be looked for in a variety of establishments including English Conversation schools, trade schools, junior colleges, universities, high schools, junior high schools and children's schools. According to Mark Zeid of the Japanese Association for Language Teaching (JALT) which is mentioned below, there are many more teachers than positions for them which is why fixing up a job before arrival is preferable to looking for one on the spot.

Most private language schools in Japan are looking for native speakers of any nationality with a four year BA or BSc in any discipline and possibly some TEFL experience. Although only a minority are looking for professional qualifications in their teachers, there has been a noticeable increase in the number of qualified EFL teachers (especially from Australia) looking for work, and naturally schools prefer to take them over complete novices. Many schools have no set intake dates and so serious applications are welcome at any time of the year though most contracts begin in April and finish the following March (i.e. one year) which corresponds to the academic year. The Japanese government has just started issuing three-year visas, so perhaps this will lead to longer contracts in the future.

The favoured accent is certainly American and to a lesser extent Canadian. In fact, not many Japanese can distinguish a Scot from a Queenslander, or an Eastender from an Eastsider. What *can* be detected and is highly prized is clear speech. Slow precise diction together with a smart appearance and professional bearing are enough to impress some potential employers.

FIXING UP A JOB
With such a large selection of vacancies at a sub-professional level, it is often possible for university graduates to fix up a job before arrival. Most schools and companies which recruit abroad sort out visas and help with initial orientation and housing. The disadvantage is that their salary and working conditions will probably compare unfavourably with those of teachers who have negotiated their job after arrival; but most new recruits (*nama gaijin* or raw foreigners) conclude that the trade-off is a fair one. Of course the pool of foreign job-seekers already in Japan is large enough that the jobs offering good conditions tend to be snapped up quickly. Many organisations do not welcome speculative applications from outside Japan.

Before tackling the question of how to find a job after arriving in Japan, the possibilities of arranging a contract before leaving home need to be canvassed. The most prestigious programme of them all is the government-sponsored JET programme which offers what many consider to be a 'dream job' for new graduates.

The JET Programme
The Japan Exchange and Teaching (JET) Programme is an official Japanese government scheme aimed at improving foreign language teaching in schools and fostering good relations between the people of Japan and the 34 participating countries. The majority of participants are from the US (contact details below). The prospects for people who wish to become Assistant Language Teachers (ALTs) in English on the JET Programme are excellent and the requirements few. Britain annually recruits 600-700 people to the programme and any UK national who is under 35 with a bachelor's degree and an interest in Japan is eligible to apply. The programme has been in existence since 1987 and is now responsible for placing about 6,000 native speakers of English for one year in private and state junior and senior high schools throughout Japan, with an increasing emphasis on rural areas.

In the UK the scheme is administered by the Council on International Educational Exchange at 52 Poland Street, London W1V 4JQ; 020-7478 2010/fax: 020-7478 2010; e-mail: JETInfo@councilexchanges.org). Non-British applicants should contact the Japanese Embassy in their country of origin for information and application forms. US applicants can obtain details from any of the 16 Consulates in the US or from the Office of the JET Programme, Japanese Embassy, 2520 Massachusetts Avenue NW, Washington, DC 20008; 202-238-6772/3 or 1-800-INFOJET/fax 202-265-9484/e-mail: eojjet@erols.com; www.mofa.go.jp. JET USA places over 3,000 American college graduates and young professionals each year.

The timetable for applicants from the UK is as follows: application forms are available from early October; the deadline for applications is early December; interviews are held in January and February; an intensive three-day orientation for successful candidates is held in London in mid-July and departures for Japan take place in late July.

Robert Mizzi from Canada knew that the competition for the programme was intense and worked hard on his application, which paid off since he was called to an interview:

> *The interview was probably the most difficult interview I have ever had. It was only 20 minutes, but a painful 20 minutes. Besides the usual 'Why' and 'Tell us about yourself' questions, I was asked to teach a lesson on the spot using dramatic techniques I would use in class. Stunned, I managed to get out of my seat and draw some pictures of the stars and moon on the board, taught them the meaning of those words and then proceeded to ask the interview team to stand up and learn a little dance to the song 'Twinkle twinkle little star'. All I wanted to do was to create an impression and to stand out of the 300 people being interviewed. People remember you best when you are acting like a complete fool. When it is teaching English as a foreign language, the ability to act like a fool is one of the main requirements*

of the job. Getting Japanese men in suits up and dancing during a job interview with the prestigious JET programme was a half-crazed risk, but a successful one at that.

Often government-run exchanges of this kind do not offer generous remuneration packages; however pay and conditions on the JET scheme are excellent. In addition to a free return flight, JET participants receive 3,600,000 yen a year (£24,000/$33,500). From that gross salary, social and medical insurance fees of approximately 37,000 yen per month are deducted. The salary is standard for all JET participants; there is no cost-of-living bonus for people placed in Tokyo. Contracts are with individual host institutions in Japan, so there can be discrepancies in working conditions. It is the luck of the draw that determines who goes where, although stated preferences will be taken into consideration. Pension regulations mean that JET teachers can reclaim money paid into the national insurance scheme as a lump sum equivalent to about one month's salary.

ALTs are theoretically expected to work a seven-hour day, though quite often teachers are assigned only three or four classes a week. Mark Elliot feels that the JET programme is 'probably the best job in the world' and describes his situation:

I live on a wonderful island, three hours ferry ride from Nagasaki, nearer Shanghai than Tokyo. I have next to no classes, but there's lots more to the job than teaching. After all, the programme is much more about meeting people and generally having a good time/enjoying Japan than it is about teaching. If it was a teaching programme, the Ministry of Education would pay the bills rather than Jichisho, the Home Ministry.

All JET participants teach in partnership with a native Japanese teacher and so there is little scope for taking any initiative in the classroom. In fact quite a few JET teachers complain that they have too little work to keep them occupied. To a large extent it is the hours put in outside the classroom that make the difference.

As Rabindra Roy wrote from Shizuoka-ken prefecture, 'I can think of very few jobs where a freshly qualified graduate with an irrelevant degree and no experience can walk straight into such a big salary for this little work.' He also describes the programme as 'desperately well organised.' But partly because of the variety in locations and schools and partly because Japan is such a weird and wonderful place, it is impossible to predict what life will be like, no matter how many orientations you attend. About half of JET participants renew for a second year which indicates its success. Quite a few stay for a third year which is the maximum. The programme offers a tremendous amount of support and even those who are placed in remote or rural areas are usually within striking distance of other JET participants.

Theresa Bowerman enjoyed her experiences with JET so much that she joined the staff of Council in London on her return:

I was employed by the Board of Education of a small city about 45km from the centre of Tokyo, assisted in English classes at the six public junior high schools in my city, and performed various other duties as required, which included at various times joining in after-school club activities, helping out with weekly English clubs at two local elementary schools, running with students as they trained for the school ekiden (marathon), and teaching 'Emergency English' to the city's firemen. I would say that the JET Programme provided me with an invaluable opportunity to live and work in a fascinating country and experience a totally different culture and lifestyle.

In Advance

There are many other ways to fix up a job in Japan ahead of time, though these will normally require more initiative (and possibly more qualifications) than signing on with JET. Many Japanese language schools have formed links with university careers departments, particularly in the US and Canada, so anyone with a university connection should exploit it. Another possibility for Americans is to explore the Japanese-American Sister City Program which assists some native speakers to find teaching jobs in the city twinned with theirs.

As mentioned, *GEOS, Nova* and *AEON* carry out extensive recruitment campaigns in North America, Britain and Australia. *Shane English Schools* confine their recruitment to the UK through their partner, Saxoncourt & English Worldwide Recruitment. At present *Christians Abroad* are energetically recruiting TEFL teachers with a Christian commitment for two year contracts in middle and secondary schools. A steady trickle of adverts appear in newspapers, *EL Prospects, TESOL Placement Bulletin,* etc. placed by individual schools in Japan and agents. Quite often schools and groups of schools will appoint a foreign recruiter. For example the large language chain *Kent Schools of English* advertises in the *Guardian* for EFL teachers to send their CV and photo to a private address in London (see entry). Each summer Hilderstone College (St. Peters Road, Broadstairs, Kent CT10 2JW) recruits for Shumei secondary schools in the Tokyo area. The advertised pay scale is 3.4-4.4 million yen for the year plus free accommodation. A high degree of involvement in school life is expected as well as a degree and TEFL qualification, plus 2 years' full-time teaching experience, preferably already in Japan or at a UK secondary school.

Many schools have no need to advertise abroad since they receive so many speculative resumés (the American term for CV is used in Japan). The internet has evolved into a valuable job search tool. Using any of the popular household search engines such as Yahoo, type 'English Teaching in Japan' and dozens of job-related websites will appear. O-Hayo-Sensei (which means 'Good Morning Teacher') has pages of teaching positions across Japan at www.ohayosensei.com. Many of these are at the sub-professional level, but there are usually two or three university positions listed at any one time. Another internet address to try is www.eltnews.com, a website magazine for ELT teachers in Japan with news, jobs, classroom ideas, etc. For the book *Make a Mil-Yen: Teaching English in Japan* by Don Best, check the publisher's website (Stone Bridge Press – www.stonebridge.com). A two-hour *Work & Live in Japan Video* of a seminar on working in Japan, which covers social and cultural customs, travel tips and corporate work as well as teaching, can be ordered from the Japan Marketing Group, 400 Groveland Ave, Suite 312, Minneapolis, MN 55403, USA (612-871-7889).

The Prometheum School of Languages in San Francisco (415-543-2992; psl@teflpro.com/ www.teflpro.com) specialises in training teachers and placing interns in Japanese universities. Graduates with a TEFL Certificate are eligible for these paid positions that come with airfare, apartment and stipend.

A speculative job hunt from abroad has some chance of success for the well-qualified. There are various sources of language school addresses, of varying degress of usefulness. The Japan Information & Cultural Centre of the Embassy of Japan (101-104 Piccadilly, London W1V 9FN; 020-7465 6500; fax: 020-7491 9347; education@embjapan.org.uk/ www.embjapan.org.uk) will send out a fact sheet entitled *Teaching English in Japan* on request which includes visa information and a list of contact addresses which is not necessarily right up to date. The British Council in Tokyo has an outdated list with no plans to update it in the near future so recommends consulting the English language telephone directory which is on the internet (http://english.townpage.isp.ntt.co.jp). The British Council in Sapporo can send a photocopied list of language schools in the Hokkaido area, but it too is two years out of date. If you are planning to go to Japan in any event, it is a good idea to send your CV to the big schools a few weeks before arrival, make some follow-up calls and hope to arrange some interviews in your first week.

Professional teachers can make contact with JALT, the Japan Association for Language Teaching (c/o National Director of Public Relations, JALT, Hiroshima College of Foreign Languages, 1-3-12 Senda Machi, Naka Ku, Hiroshima 730-

0052; 82-241 8900; fax 82-249 2321; mzeid@ann.ne.jp). JALT is a non-profit organisation of 3,000 teachers nationwide who are dedicated to professional development and the improvement of language education in Japan. It is not an employment organisation but it does run job ads in its monthly publication *The Language Teacher*, as well as posting jobs at its annual national conference in the autumn and local monthly meetings.

An unusual opportunity to teach local people is available at a farm in Hokkaido, the most northerly island of the Japanese archipelago, known as Shin-Shizen-Juku (Tsurui, Akan-gun, Hokkaido 085-12; 0154 64-28 21), a place well known to the travelling fraternity. The owner Hiroshi Mine employs two people a year to oversee the classes and teach six hours conversational English a week. They must stay for a minimum of six months and in return will be paid a living allowance and a contribution towards their airfare. The main purpose of their visit must be to study Japanese and lessons will be provided. Australian, New Zealand and American applicants must be aged 20-29 and in possession of a working holiday visa. Others can come on a tourist visa as it is classed as voluntary work which does not require a permit. Non-teaching international travellers are welcome to help with the farm work up to six at a time. Mr. Mine organises the classes, provides transport and some teaching materials. Much depends on the personalities of the other volunteers; whereas some travellers perceive it to be a wonderful opportunity and enjoy a warm atmosphere, others find the place bleak and exploitative.

On the Spot

As has been mentioned, any native speaker with a Bachelor's degree certificate has a chance of landing a job as an English teacher on arrival in Japan. The crucial question is how long will it take. The murderous cost of living means that job-hunters spend hundreds of dollars or pounds very quickly while engaged in the time-consuming business of answering ads, sending round CVs, and going for interviews. If you're starting cold try to arrive on a weekend so you can buy the Monday edition of the English language *Japan Times* which carries many ads for English teachers. The important thing is to convince employers that you can adapt and do things the Japanese way.

Few things could be more intimidating for the EFL teacher than to arrive at Narita International Airport with no job and limited resources. The longer the job hunt takes, the faster the finances dwindle and the more nerve-racking and discouraging the situation becomes. One way to lessen the monumentality of the initial struggle would be to get out of Tokyo straightaway. Although there are more jobs in the capital, there is also more competition from other foreigners, to the point of saturation. Enterprising teachers who are willing to step off the conveyor belt which takes job-seekers from the airport to one of Tokyo's many 'gaijin houses' (hostels for foreigners) may well encounter fewer setbacks. Osaka seems a good bet since it is within commuting distance of the whole Kansai area, including Kobe which is 20 minutes away by train. In Osaka the cost of living is as much as a quarter less than it is in Tokyo. Another promising destination is Sapporo in the north, the fifth largest city in the country. Ken Foye is a reader of this book who chose to teach on Hokkaido, the northern island on which Sapporo is located:

> *I have been teaching here for a year and a half now and I would recommend Hokkaido to anyone, especially those who don't find living in a large urban metropolis very appealing. Here the people seem much friendlier than in Tokyo, the cost of living isn't as high, there's fresh air and the scenery is magnificent. And I probably would not have ended up here if not for your book.*

Tokyo

One of the most often recommended places to start a job hunt in Tokyo is the Kimi Information Center (Oscar Building, 8th Floor, 2-42-3 Ikebukuro, Toshima-ku,

Tokyo 171-0014; 3-3986 1604/fax 3-3986 3037/e-mail kimi529@gol.com; www.2dango.ne.jp/kimi). Like so many addresses in Japan, it helps to have specific directions which Deborah Cordingley has provided: take the West Exit of Ikebukuro Station, walk straight past the McDonald's for one block and turn right when you see Marui Department Store. Go three blocks past Sumitomo Bank. Kimi is on the right across from the Post Office. The Kimi Center offers a range of useful services such as photocopying, computer time and a telephone answering service as well as advising on cheap accommodation and reasonable apartments in and around Tokyo. Free Job Opportunities booklets are available. For 315 yen, they will fax your résumé to a school (more for outside Tokyo). Private rooms at nearby Kimi Ryokan (Japanese-style guest house) cost 4,500 yen (£30/$50); the address is 2-36-8 Ikebukuro, Toshima-ku (3-3971-3766).

Other gaijin houses offer dormitory accommodation for about half that price. Try to pick up a list of gaijin houses from the tourist office and look for ones which charge a monthly rather than a nightly rent since these are the ones which attract long-term residents. Among the cheapest is Mickey House (2-15-1 Nakadai Itabashi-ku; Tokyo; tel 3-3936 8889) whose room charges start at 1,700 per night for two people sharing; 10,500 for a week and 33,000 per month. For a private room the monthly rent is 45,000 yen. The manager (mobile phone no 090-4375 0851) is Masaru Kashiwabara who speaks English and Spanish. A more typical rent is from 65,000 yen. Because it is so difficult to rent flats, some teachers continue living in gaijin houses after they find work. Try to find a gaijin house favoured by teachers. Ted Travis was delighted with his when he sent a post card from Tokyo:

> *There is a wonderful guest house near Iidabashi. They have five floors, lots of facilities and it is very sociable as well as affordable. Newcomers can usually pick up work from those already employed. The majority of people tend to stay between six months and a year, but short-stay travellers are also welcome.*

The gaijin house he mentions is Orchid House which has now closed or possibly moved. Many foreigners live and work in the Roppongi district of Tokyo which might therefore be a sensible place to base yourself. A free ads paper called *Tokyo Classifieds* is distributed in this area on Fridays carrying job and accommodation ads. Once you get to know some other teachers, there is always the chance of inheriting their hours when they decide to move on. According to one report from Osaka, teachers actually 'sell' their hours when they are ready to leave. Even tourist offices such as the one at Hibuya station (exit A-3) have free notice boards where private lessons may be sought or offered, as well as accommodation.

Wherever you choose to conduct your job hunt, English language newspapers are the starting place for most. Jobs in secondary schools are advertised from September on. The Monday edition of the *Japan Times* carries fewer ads than it used to but it is still the best source. Note that ads often specify 'female' which usually indicates a job teaching young children. Male applicants for these posts may have to prove that they have prior experience of working with children.

Jobs in the Kansai region around Osaka are listed at the end of the Tokyo classifieds. The main publication in the Kansai area (Kobe, Kyoto, Osaka and Nara) is the monthly magazine *Kansai Time Out* (1-13 Ikuta Cho 1-chome, Chuo-ku, Kobeshi, Hyogo 651-0092; fax 078-232 4518; e-mail for sales and marketing: ktoedit@kto.co.jp and website www.kto.co.jp). There is also a homepage at www.japanfile.com. It carries fewer job ads than it once did, but still has pages of language school ads. Two Tokyo papers *Mainichi Daily News* (Hitotsubashi 1-1-1, Chiyoda-ku) and *Asahi Evening News* (5-3-2 Tsukiji, Chuo-ku) are also worth a look. As usual, the employers who advertise regularly tend to be the ones with the worst reputations and the highest staff turnover.

Amanda Searle describes what she found in the newspapers when she was job-hunting:

Most companies give little idea in their adverts of the hours and salary, let alone the age and number of students or the textbooks used. They are not very willing to give that information over the phone, explaining that you will get the opportunity to ask questions if you are called for interview. I sent cover letters out with my resumé, explaining that I was looking only for full-time positions which offered visa sponsorship. I sent out about 20 applications and about ten companies contacted me and I went to eight interviews. I ended up being offered two full-time positions and three part-time ones.

The initial phone call is very important and should be considered as a preliminary interview. Since you may be competing with as many as 100 people answering the same ad, you have to try to stand out over the phone. Speak slowly, clearly, and be very *genki* which means lively and fun. You may be asked to fax your CV to them; the cover letter should be short and intelligent, and the CV should be brief and interesting, emphasising any teaching experience. Always carry a supply of professional looking business cards *(meishi)*.

Demonstration lessons now form an integral part of most job interviews in Japan, regardless of one's qualifications. Try to prepare yourself as much as possible if only because travelling to an interview in Tokyo is a major undertaking which can take up to three hours and cost a lot of money; it would be a shame to blow your chances because of a simple oversight. Dress as impeccably and conservatively as possible, and carry a respectable briefcase, since books are often judged by their covers in Japan. Inside you should have any education certificates you have earned, preferably the originals since schools have long since realised that a lot of forgeries are in circulation. Your résumé should not err on the side of modesty.

REGULATIONS

The key to obtaining a work visa for Japan is to have a Japanese sponsor. This can be a private citizen but most teachers are sponsored by their employers. Not all schools by any means are willing to sponsor their teachers, unless they are persuaded that they are an ongoing proposition. Some schools rely on a stream of Canadians, Australians and New Zealanders on working holiday visas which they must obtain in their home countries through the SWAP Japan Programme. SWAP allows students aged 18-30 to work for six months in the first instance but is extendable to 18 months. To qualify you must prove that you have US$3,000 at your disposal. Further details are available in Australia from any branch of STA Travel and in Canada from any Travel CUTS office; both issue an information booklet *The Swapper's Guide to Japan*. There is no equivalent scheme for Britons or Americans. For information about obtaining a work visa in the US, log on to the Embassy's web-site on www.embjapan.org and follow the link to Visa Information.

Other nationalities will have to find a sponsor. If your visa is to be processed before arrival, you must have a definite job appointment in Japan. Your employer must apply to the Ministry of Justice in Tokyo for a Certificate of Eligibility which he or she then forwards to you. You must take this along with a photocopy of it, your passport, photograph and application form to the Embassy in your country. Normally a visa can be issued within three working days, though it can take longer. New regulations stipulate that anyone who works in Higher Education must have an MA in Education or TEFL.

Many Britons and North Americans enter with a temporary visitor's stamp (valid for three months), find a job and sponsor and then apply for a work visa. Documents which will help you to find a sponsor are the original or notarised copy of your BA or other degree and résumé. The temporary visitor's stamp can be extended for another 90 days (for example at Kushiro immigration office) for a fee. In the past, many people worked on this temporary stamp which they kept extending. Now it is unlikely that someone who has stayed in Japan for six months and then leaves the country will be granted landing permission before a reasonable amount of time has elapsed. Those found to be overstaying as tourists can be deported. Furthermore, employers who are caught employing illegal aliens as well as the foreign workers themselves are subject to huge fines, and both parties risk imprisonment.

Finding an employer to sponsor you for a work visa is very important. A number of schools advertising for teachers state in their ads that they are willing to consider only those who already have a work visa. Others are willing to act as sponsors. Sponsors obtain a Certificate of Eligibility inside Japan and then the teacher must leave the country to change their status (typically on a two or three day trip to Korea), a process which can cost as much as $500 if you fly; the processing fee is 50,000 yen. According to Alan Suter the cheapest way is to take a ferry from Kobe to Pusan, Korea.

The work visa is valid for 12 months and renewable annually. When renewing, one of the most important requirements is a tax statement showing your previous year's earnings. It is difficult to obtain a new visa unless you can show that you have earned at least 250,000 yen per month. Cash-in-hand and part-time jobs may be lucrative but they do nothing to help your visa application. If you break your contract with your employer, you will have to find another sponsor willing to act as sponsor the following year.

You are permitted to work up to 20 hours a week on a cultural or student visa. Cultural visas are granted to foreigners interested in studying some aspect of traditional Japanese culture on a full-time basis. In this case you must find a teacher willing to sponsor you. Cultural visas are often granted for shodo (calligraphy), taiko (drumming), karate, aikido, ikebana (flower arranging) and ochakai (tea ceremony). At one time these study visas were liberally handed out but nowadays you must produce concrete evidence that you actually are studying.

The tax situation is normally favourable for teachers, provided they are exempt in their home countries. Note that JET salaries are no longer tax-free. Teachers usually have the basic rate of national income tax in Japan (6-7%) withdrawn at source. A further 3% is owing for local taxes, which are the teacher's responsibility only in their second and subsequent years in Japan. The Japanese government offers nationalised health insurance which covers about three-quarters of medical and dental care bills. The cost is about 4,000 yen per month. Many employers accustomed to hiring native speaker teachers may offer more comprehensive private cover for less.

CONDITIONS OF WORK

Despite a widespread feeling that the glory days of ELT in Japan are over, all things are relative and most established teachers do not find much to complain about. After a grim stint of teaching in Korea, Tim Leffel was astonished by the contrast in atmosphere when he arrived in Japan during the worst of the economic crisis:

> The big surprise to me was the attitude of teachers in Japan. The yen had dropped to 145 but nobody seemed too bothered. As one JET teacher said, 'We earned so much for doing so little work, it's hard to get upset about the exchange rate.' Those in private language schools may disagree but it's a far cry from the universal resentment, distrust and frustration you hear from those in Korea.

Despite the high cost of living, most teachers seem to be able to save money without having to lead too frugal an existence. Some even save half their salary in their first year by avoiding eating out and going to the cinema. The longer you work in Japan the higher the salary and better working conditions you can command. Rank beginners outside Tokyo and Osaka can earn as little as 230,000 yen a month, but the steady average of 250,000 yen persists almost everywhere. Perks such as increments for higher qualifications, end-of-contract bonuses, free Japanese lessons and travel tickets, etc. are in fairly wide evidence. A tip for those who manage to save a significant sum was passed on by Ted Travis: buying an international postal money order *(yubin kawase)* from any post office is by far the cheapest way to transfer money out of the country.

Teaching schedules can be exhausting, especially if you work for a company which sends its teachers out to office premises (for which a car is sometimes made available). As usual, the timetable may be announced at the last minute, though it is more difficult to opt out in Japan than in other countries because of the dedication Japanese workers show to their firms. (At best a Japanese worker gets ten days of holiday a year and few take their full entitlement for fear of seeming lazy or disloyal to the company.) Some schools remain open all weekend and on public holidays too. Nova for example expects all its teachers to work on Sundays. But the shift system has its merits as Bridgid Seymour-East from New Zealand found out:

> *I went to Hiroshima on a six-month working holiday visa and found work at Nova. I worked their part-time shift, 10am-1pm each day and thoroughly enjoyed it. I got to know the students as the same ones came in at that time and there would only be three or four teachers on duty. Nova is good if you want to meet other teachers, and be able to swap hours or even do a few weeks in another part of the country. Smaller schools are obviously less flexible.*

One of the advantages of working in state schools (as JET teachers do) is that they close for holidays, usually three weeks at Christmas and two weeks in August between semesters. Most schools offer one-week holidays (paid or unpaid or a combination of the two) at the beginning of May (the 'Golden Week') and in the middle of August ('O-bon vacation'). Holidays for those lucky enough to work in institutes of higher education are much more generous.

Private tutoring is still lucrative, paying between 3,000 and 6,000 yen an hour. Occasionally you will meet someone who has has been paid $100 just to have dinner with a language learner and converse in English, but these plums are few and far between.

The Pupils

The stereotype of the diligent Japanese pupil has becoming somewhat outmoded. The younger generation of Japanese is not always willing to play by the rules that their elders lay down, and there is increasing tension in schools which may manifest itself in (mildly) unruly behaviour. But mostly teachers find their students eager, attentive and willing to confer great respect on their teachers and in some out-of-the-way places even celebrity status. All teachers are expected to look the part and most schools will insist on proper dress (e.g. suits and dresses). But they do not want a formal approach to teaching.

Adults will have studied English at school for at least six years, and their knowledge of grammar is usually sound. They go to conversation schools in the expection of meeting native speaker teachers able to deliver creative and entertaining lessons. Yet some are crippled by diffidence or excessive anxiety about grammatical correctness. Michael Frost is one teacher who experienced a clash of cultures when trying to encourage discussion in his classroom:

> *It is very difficult for Japanese students to come out and express an individual opinion. The best tactic is to get them in pairs, so that together they can work something out. They are more productive and open in pairs, and it takes the pressure off them. Then get the pairs into fours, to express a mini-group opinion, then work for a total group agreement. The thing to avoid at all costs is to stroll into class, saying, 'OK, today we are going to discuss environmental issues. Tetsuya, you set the ball rolling: What do you think of pollution?' It will not work.*

"Akiko, tell us your views on love and marriage"

It is a popular myth that Japanese students have good reading abilities in English and require only conversation practice. This was not the experience of Nathan Edwards, a Diploma-qualified teacher from Canada:

> *I am currently teaching at the Tokyo YMCA College of English, a pioneer in English teaching in Japan, established in 1880. The fact is that both reading and speaking in English present major challenges even to students with years of English instruction in the Japanese school system. It is highly advisable for teachers to bring a good supply of realia with them (various English brochures, used tickets, maps, coins, etc.) and old lesson plans.*

Problems can arise in team teaching situations if your Japanese colleague has not attained a high enough level of English. While teaching in the JET programme, Robert Mizzi came to admire Japanese culture, but he did find some aspects of his job frustrating:

> *A lot of times I cannot introduce a game idea because, literally, it will take 20 minutes for the teacher to understand (never mind the students).*

Among the many strange aspects of Japanese culture is one which most foreigners find particularly disturbing. A native speaker who happens to have non-Caucasian features will almost certainly be discriminated against. Bryn Thomas enjoyed many aspects of his job as a conversation facilitator at a language lounge in the middle of Tokyo but was shocked by one incident. When the publicity photos were being taken for the company brochure, a qualified teacher from Hawaii was rudely asked to step aside from the staff portrait.

Accommodation

It is not uncommon for teachers who are hired overseas to be given help with accommodation, which is a tremendously useful perk, even if the flat provided is small and over-priced, with poor insulation and a badly equipped kitchen. If you are on your own, you will be forced to use a rental agency, the majority of whom do not speak English and are not willing to rent to foreigners. Amanda Searle's advice is 'unless you have connections or are looking at 100,000 yen per month accommodation, don't break your heart trying to find a decent place.'

If you do succeed through an agency, you will have to pay a commission of one month's rent as well as a colossal deposit called 'key money' which is often six months rent in advance. Unlike rent deposits in the West you can't expect to recoup it all. Assuming the range of rents is 60,000-100,000 yen per person per month in Tokyo and perhaps 65,000 yen on average in Osaka, that means you might have to pay more than £2,700 upfront. Rents outside Tokyo and Osaka should be nearer 50,000 yen, with an additional monthly payment of at least 10,000 yen for utilities. Well-established schools may be prepared to lend you the key money or (exceptionally) pay it outright.

There are great discrepancies in the accommodation assigned to JET teachers. While some get beautiful no-rent houses, others get one-room apartments with high rent. Robert Mizzi had no complaints about the rent (just US$80 a month) but he didn't get much for his money:

I have no oven, dryer, hot water, shower or heating. A lot of things I had to buy for the apartment and a lot of things I had to give up. (The thrill of having running water certainly is a luxury where I am.)

A further problem is the near total absence of furnished apartments, so you may have to go shopping for curtains and cookers on top of all your other expenses. Again, schools which normally hire foreign teachers may keep a stock of basic furnishings which they can lend to teachers. Amanda Searle found the solution to this problem:

The 'big gomi' provides a great opportunity to get the things you need. Gomi means rubbish and it is collected from the street. The big gomi takes place in August and December when Japanese workers receive a bonus and then go out to replace many of their belongings. I have obtained a desk, heater, TV, radio (complete with instruction booklet safely stowed in the battery compartment) water pot and chair this way. Any electrical applicances considered to be dangerous or broken have their plugs cut off.

If all this sounds too much hassle, perhaps staying in a *gaijin house* long term is not such a bad idea.

Obviously it is to your advantage to live as close to your place of work as possible, but as noted above many teachers are forced to spend a sizeable chunk of their earnings and a lot of time commuting. Ask your employer to pay for your travel, preferably in the form of a monthly travel pass which can be used for your leisure travel as well. If you're in Tokyo, bear in mind that city buses charge a flat fare of 200 yen.

LEISURE TIME

According to some veteran teachers, leisure time and how to spend it will be the least of your worries. Depending on your circumstances, you may be expected to participate in extracurricular activities and social events which it would cause offence to decline – always a major concern in Japan. Although Bryn Thomas enjoyed the sushi which his school provided for teachers still at work at 9pm, he was less keen on the 'office parties when teachers were required to dress up in silly costumes and be nice to the students'. Most teachers are happy to accept occasional invitations to socialise with their Japanese colleagues or pupils, even if it does mean an evening of speaking very very slowly and drinking heavily. Many teachers find the socialising with students fun if expensive. Knowing a *gaijin* is a considerable status symbol for many Japanese, many of whom are willing to pay good money just for you to go to their houses once a week and eat their food.

But it is not like that everywhere. A glut of Westerners in Tokyo means that your welcome may be less than enthusiastic. In fact non-Japanese are refused entrance to some Tokyo bars and restaurants. Many people head straight out of Tokyo for the more appealing city of Osaka. Julie Fast describes the contrast:

> *I am still enamoured of Osaka; it is like a village after Tokyo. I am constantly amazed at the trees we see everywhere. I never realised in Tokyo how much I hated being constantly surrounded by people. I never had personal space in Tokyo. No one does – which explains the distant, sour looks on most people's faces. What a difference in Osaka. Osaka people have the roughest reputation in all of Japan. From a western point of view, they are the friendliest. I have been invited to houses for lunch, children say hello and people in shops actually talk to you. Which proves you can't judge a country by its largest city.*

All cities are expensive. Any entertainment which smacks of the West such as going out to a fashionable coffee house or a night club will be absurdly expensive. However if you are content with more modest indigenous food and pastimes, you will be able to save money. A filling bowl of noodles and broth costs less than £3, though you may never take to the standard breakfast of boiled rice and a raw egg. Staying home to listen to Japanese language tapes or to read a good book (e.g. *Pictures from the Water Trade,* a personal account of life in Japan) costs nothing. Obviously the more settled you become, the more familiar you will be with the bargains and affordable amusements.

Finding your way around is nothing if not a challenge in a country where almost all road and public transport signs are incomprehensible. What use is an A-Z if you can't read the alphabet? Many feel that it is worth making an effort to master at least something of the written language. There are three alphabets in Japanese: *kanji* (ancient pictograms), *hiragana* and *katakana* (the characters used to spell loan words from English). Amanda Searle is just one teacher who feels that *kana* can be learned through independent study so that at least you will be able to read station names and menus. Learning some of the script not only impresses students and shows that you are making an effort to absorb some of the culture, it also helps you to survive.

Japanese addresses are mind-bogglingly complicated too: the numbers refer to land subdivisions: prefecture, district, ward, then building. When in doubt (inevitable) ask a friendly informant for a *chizu* (map). It is also a good idea to get a Japanese person to write your destination in both *kanji* and transliterated into *roma-ji* (our alphabet). Japanese people will sometimes go to embarrassing lengths to help foreigners. This desire to help wedded to a reluctance to lose face means that they may offer advice and instructions based on very little information, so keep checking. Young people in jeans are the best bets. Outside the big cities the people are even more cordial. Wherever you go, you don't have to worry about crime.

Travel is expensive. For example the bullet train from Tokyo to Sendai, a couple of hundred miles north, costs about £90 one way. Yet the pace of a teacher's life in Tokyo or another big city can become so stressful that it is essential to get on a local train and see some of the countryside. Hitch-hiking in Japan is safer, easier and more enjoyable than in most countries. The risk is not of being left by the roadside or of being mugged but of being taken unbidden to the nearest railway station (which might be a major detour for the hapless driver who feels obliged to do this out of courtesy). Others will buy meals and refreshments and are genuinely interested in foreigners.

The alienness of Japanese culture is one of the main fascinations of the place. It is foolish to become bogged down worrying about transgressing against mysterious customs. The JET literature, for example, may be unnecessarily intimidating in its pointing up of possible cultural *faux pas*. But in fact Japanese people are more tolerant of foreigners than many give them credit for. Rabindra Roy taught in a state school quite happily and no comment was ever passed on his long hair and beard, earrings and bangles. Similarly Claire Wilkinson felt quite overwhelmed after reading the JET literature. One of the many prohibitions mentioned is 'never blow your nose in public', and so the heavy cold with which she arrived made her even more miserable than it would have otherwise. But she soon discovered that the Japanese allow foreigners a great deal of latitude and that she could relax and be herself without causing grave offence.

The price you pay for the tolerance extended to your alien ways is that you will always be treated as an outsider, no matter how adept you become with chopsticks or at using Japanese phrases. In Japan you will never be able to blend in or go incognito. Kristen Ghodsee sums up the potential hazards:

I have seen many foreigners leave Japan angry and full of hatred towards the Japanese because they were unable or unwilling to understand Japanese ways. Outside the metropolises, being pointed at, stared at and laughed at is commonplace. Be prepared to sacrifice all vestiges of privacy. You are fair game in Japan because you are different. You can make and save an incredible amount of money, but you must have an incredible amount of patience and self-confidence. The Japanese are wonderful, friendly people if you can get past the surface differences. If you're coming only to make the quick buck (as many do), and are not willing to be open-minded to a radically different culture, you will make yourself miserable and worsen the ever-worsening opinion the Japanese have of foreigners working in their country.

LIST OF SCHOOLS

AEON INTER-CULTURAL USA
1960 E Grand Avenue 550, El Segundo, CA 90245. Tel: (310) 414-1515. Fax: (310) 414-1616. E-mail: aeonla@aeonet.com. Website: www.aeonet.com.
One of the largest chains of English conversation schools in Japan with 270 branches.
Number of teachers: 500.
Preference of nationality: British, Australian, North American, New Zealand.
Qualifications: BA or BSc. degree in any subject.
Conditions of employment: 12 month (renewable) contracts. 5-days a week. 2 days from 12pm-9pm and 3 days from 1pm to 9pm.
Salary: 250,000 yen per month.
Facilities/Support: own furnished apartment provided with subsidised monthly rent. No sharing. 15 minutes walk from school. Teacher pays 39,000 yen per month and AEON pays the rest. Accident and sickness insurance is provided at no cost to the teacher. 4 weeks of paid vacation and paid training.
Recruitment: 6 full-time recruiting offices outside Japan including 3 in the US (Los Angeles, New York, Chicago), 2 in Canada (Toronto, Vancouver) and 1 in Sydney, Australia. Group and personal interviews held in these cities. Interviews every week in the US and twice a year in London, UK. Positions start every month. Rolling deadlines. Initial applicants should send résumé and essay entitled 'Why I want to live and work in Japan'. See website www.aeonet.com for further details.
Contact: Erik Orre, General Manager (Los Angeles).

BBA ENGLISH SCHOOL
2-14-6-6 Kita Okinosu, Tokushaima City, 770-0872. Tel: (88) 664 3767. Fax: (88) 655 0954. E-mail: brendan@stannet.ne.jp.
Number of teachers: 2.
Preference of nationality: British, Irish.
Qualifications: BA. Some teaching experience is preferred, but not absolutely essential.
Conditions of employment: 1 year renewable. Contract hours 28 per week, 5 days per week.
Salary: 250,000 yen reviewed after 3 months. Income tax is less than 10%.
Facilities/Support: accommodation in single apartments is arranged by the school.

Work permit arranged by the school.
Recruitment: *Guardian* newspaper, internet. Interviews usually over the telephone.
Contact: Ms Michiyo Baba, Manager.

CA ENGLISH ACADEMY
2nd Floor, Kotohira Building, 9-14 Kakuozan-dori, Chikusa-ku, 464-0841 Nagoya. Tel: 052-762 1135. Fax: 052-762 1137. E-mail: ca-eng-academy@mtg.biglobe.ne.jp.
Number of teachers: 2.
Preference of nationality: British, American or Canadian.
Qualifications: degree minimum. However those with teacher qualifications are preferred.
Conditions of employment: 1 year renewable. 25 teaching hours weekly and five office hours weekly.
Salary: 250,000 yen gross.
Facilities/Support: the school will act as the teacher's guarantor when arranging accommodation. Assistance with obtaining work permits.
Recruitment: overseas employment publications, newspaper adverts and word-of-mouth.
Contact: Dorothy Wang, Director.

ECC FOREIGN LANGUAGE INSTITUTE
Kanto District Head Office: 5th Floor, San Yamate Building, 7-11-10 Nishi-Shinjuku, Shinjuku-ku, Tokyo 160-0023. Tel: (3) 5330 1585. Fax: (3) 5330 7084. E-mail: eastjinj@ecc.co.jp. Website: www.ecc.co.jp.
Also Chubu District Office: Kanayama Building, 1-16-16 Kanayama, Naka-ku, Nagoya 460-0022. Tel: (52) 332 6165. Fax: (52) 332 6140. E-mail: ecchr@spice.or.jp.
Also Kinki District Office: 8th Floor, Sumisei Namba Minami Building, 3-19 Motomachi 2 chome, Naniwa-ku, Osaka 556-0016. Tel: (66) 636 0334. Fax: (66) 636 7622. E-mail: teaching@ecc.co.jp.
Number of teachers: 320 at over 120 schools throughout Japan.
Preference of nationality: none.
Qualifications: BA required.
Conditions of employment: 1 year contracts, mostly starting in April but not always. 29.5 h.p.w. mostly evenings. Sunday plus 1 other day off per week. Opportunities for paid overtime often available.
Salary: from 252,000 yen per month. Rate of tax is 6-10% per month.
Facilities/Support: assistance with accommodation. During compulsory 30-50 hour training course, wage is 1,000 yen an hour.
Recruitment: contact one of above offices upon arriving in Japan. (Applicant information is shared among districts.) Main hiring period is February/March.

ENGLISH ACADEMY
2-9-6 Ichibancho, Matsuyama 790-0001. Tel: (89) 931-8686. Fax: (89) 933-1210. E-mail: academy@interlink.or.jp. Website: www.home.interlink.or.jp/~academy.
Number of teachers: 9.
Preference of nationality: none, but most are from US/Canada.
Qualifications: BA, teaching experience preferable, and enthusiasm essential. Some computer experience desirable.
Conditions of employment: 18 month contracts. Maximum 28 contact h.p.w. between 1pm and 9pm. Pupils aged 3-70, but most are younger students.
Facilities/Support: assistance with accommodation given. Partial payment of health insurance. Training available.
Recruitment: through direct application. Interviews required but can be held over the telephone.

THE ENGLISH VILLAGE
3F Soa Building, 3-5-8 Kinshi, Sumida, Tokyo. Tel: (3) 3624 3300. Fax: (3) 3624 3700. E-mail: engvil@hpo.net. Website: www.englishvillage.gr.jp.

Number of teachers: 7.
Preference of nationality: British.
Qualifications: degree and reconised TEFL Cert.
Conditions of employment: one year renewable. 25 50-minute lessons per week and sessions supervising free conversation room.
Salary: 250,000 yen per month plus 2000 yen completion bonus.
Facilities/Support: subsidised accommodation is arranged.
Recruitment: British press adverts. Interviews in the UK.
Contact: Neil Pearson, Principal.

FOUR SEASONS
4-32-11 Sanarudai, Hamamatsa 432-8021. Tel: (53) 448 1501. Fax: (53) 448 1502. E-mail: learning@fourseasons.co.jp. Website: www.fourseasons.co.jp.
Number of teachers: 20.
Preference of nationality: UK, US, Canada.
Qualifications: MA, MAT, MA TESOL, CELTA, experience of teaching.
Conditions of employment: 2-year contract. 80 contact hours per month.
Salary: $28,000 per year. $5,600 bonus after 2 years.
Facilities/support: school pays all deposits and subsidises one third of monthly rent per month. All necessary permits and visas obtained by the school.
Recruitment: via TESOL, internet, US colleges.
Contact: William S. Anton, Director.

GEOS CORPORATION
Head Office: Shin-Osaki Kangyo Building 4F, 1-6-4 Osaki, Shinagawa-ku, Tokyo 141-0032. Tel: (3) 5434-0200. Fax: (3) 5434-0201. E-mail: gkyomu@beehive.twics. com. Website: www.geoscareer.com.
One of Japan's largest English language institutions.
Number of teachers: approximately 1,800 teachers for 450 schools throughout Japan.
Preference of nationality: Canadian, American, British, South African, Australian, New Zealand.
Qualifications: university bachelor's degree required (any discipline). CELTA or equivalent would be an asset.
Conditions of employment: 1 year renewable contracts. Long-term career commitment preferred. Full-time schedule between noon and 9pm, 5 days a week.
Salary: base salary is 250,000 yen per month less 10% tax. Extra payment available to teachers depending on student sign-up rates, student renewals, group lesson fees and overtime. Up to 100,000 yen travel benefit paid to teachers on completion of contract.
Facilities/Support: correspondence and preparatory courses and working visas provided prior to departure, and ongoing training in Japan including Japanese lessons. Single occupancy furnished apartment provided at a rental rate of about 55,000-60,000 yen per month plus 10,000 yen per month for utilities. Commuting pass provided. Health and accident insurance provided. Career positions available such as teacher trainers/curriculum development, publishing staff, hiring offices, homestay coordinators, etc. After 2 years working with GEOS in Japan, teachers are eligible to apply for positions in one of GEOS's 50 schools outside Japan.
Recruitment: all GEOS teachers are hired outside Japan. Positions commence 1-3 months after an offer of employment from GEOS Corporation in Japan is made. Contact GEOS hiring office in UK: GEOS Language Ltd., Compton Park, Compton Place Road, Eastbourne, East Sussex BN21 1EH; tel 01323-739575; fax 01323-739565; e-mail london@geos.demon.co.uk) and in North America: GEOS Language Corporation Ontario, Simpson Tower 2424, 401 Bay Street, Toronto, Ontario M5H 2Y4, Canada (416-777-0109/fax 416-777-0110/e-mail geos@istar.ca) Applicants from Australia and New Zealand should contact GEOS in Japan.

HEARTS ENGLISH SCHOOL
2146-3 Shido, Shido-cho, Okawa-gun, Kagawa 769-2101. Tel: (87) 894-3557. Fax: (87) 894-7227. E-mail: mail@e-hearts.co.jp. Website: www.e-hearts.co.jp/hearts.
Number of teachers: 2 full-time, 1 part-time.
Preference of nationality: American, Canadian, British.
Qualifications: BA with TEFL/TESL or teaching experience, preferably teaching children.
Conditions of employment: minimum 1 year contracts. Approx. 25 h.p.w. Teachers design own curriculum. Half of classes are adults, half children.
Salary: 250,000-270,000 yen per month plus bonus.
Facilities/Support: furnished apartment in quiet location at reasonable rent. Health insurance provided at reasonable cost. Weekly Japanese lessons provided.
Recruitment: adverts in *TESOL Placement Bulletin*. Send résumé, cover letter, references and photos.
Contact: Naomi Yoneda, Director.

INTERAC CO. LTD.
Fujibo Building 2F, 2-10-28 Fujimi, Chiyoda-ku, Tokyo 102. Tel: (3) 3234 7857. Fax: (3) 3234 6055. Website www.interac.co.jp/recruit.
Number of teachers: 280 in 9 branches.
Preference of nationality: none, though majority are North American, Australian and British.
Qualifications: minimum university degree plus two years business or technical experience.
Conditions of employment: 12 month contracts. Clients include top-tiered companies and some public and private schools.
Salary: guaranteed monthly minimum of 250,000 yen. 7% deducted in tax plus local taxes paid separately.
Facilities/Support: 35-hour paid training programme is compulsory. Assistance with accommodation given. One-off housing allowance paid. Company acts as sponsor for visas and guarantor for housing and telephone.
Recruitment: mostly recruit locally, though do make recruiting trips to North America and the UK in the spring and autumn. Interviews essential.

KENT SCHOOL OF ENGLISH
706 Shoppers' Plaza, 1-4-1 Irfune, Urayasu-shi, Chiba Ken 279-0012. Tel/fax: (47) 353 8708.
Number of teachers: 7.
Preference of nationality: none, but interviews in UK.
Qualifications: TEFL Cert. minimum plus 2 years' experience.
Conditions of employment: 1 year contract. 23 contact hours per week. 7 weeks paid holiday.
Salary: from 260,000 yen per month.
Facilities/Support: teachers' furnished flats available. Some shared, some single. All /deposits/key money/gratuities paid, so teachers pay only the rent and utilities charges.
Recruitment: adverts in the *Guardian* and via the internet. Interviews held in the UK in June (contact address is 7 Rutherford Court, 15 Newsholme Dr, London N21 1UE). Once contract is signed, permits are arranged and issued in mid-September.
Contact: Liz Fuse, Director of Studies.

M.I.L. THE LANGUAGE CENTER
3.F Eguchi Bldg., 1-6-2 Katsutadai, Yachiyo-shi, Chiba-ken 276. Tel: (474) 85-7555. Fax: (474) 85-7875; e-mail milmil@tky2.3web.ne.jp.
Number of teachers: 15.
Preference of nationality: Canadian, American.
Qualifications: BA in relevant subject; teaching experience and TESL qualification preferred. Must be creative, flexible and willing to teach both children and adults.

Conditions of employment: 1 year renewable contracts. Maximum 40 h.p.w. of which 25 are contact hours, between noon and 10pm weekdays. Pupils from age 4.
Salary: 252-265,000 yen per month with 5% raise for second year and bonus on completion of contract.
Facilities/Support: contribution made to initial costs of accommodation, furnishings and telephone line provided. Training given.
Recruitment: through adverts and agencies. Mainly telephone interviews. Resumés accepted throughout the year.
Contact: The Office Coordinator.

NEW DAY SCHOOL
Karakosu Sendai Building, No. 805, 13-22 Futsu Kamachi, Aoba-ku, Sendai 980-0802. Tel: (22) 265-4288. Fax: (22) 227-7421. E-mail: newday@sh.comminet.or.jp.
Number of teachers: 5.
Preference of nationality: none.
Qualifications: formal training in TEFL, e.g. MA (Applied Linguistics) or CELTA. Experience desirable. Should have interest in professional development.
Conditions of employment: 2 year contracts. 20 contact h.p.w. but 40 hours per 5-day week. Variable hours including some morning/evening shifts.
Salary: 270,000-300,000 yen per month.
Facilities/Support: assistance given with accommodation. 1 month training period. Up to 50,000 yen towards health insurance.
Recruitment: adverts in professional journals. Candidates must submit an audio tape and then have an interview by telephone.

NOVA GROUP
Carrington House, 126/130 Regent Street, London W1R 5SE. Tel: 020-7734 2727. Fax: 020-7734 3001. E-mail: tefl@novagroup.demon.co.uk. Web-site: www.nova-group.com.
Number of teachers: over 4,000 in more than 390 Nova schools located throughout Japan. An average school has 8-12 teachers and several Japanese staff.
Preference of nationality: British, American, Canadian, Australian, New Zealand, Irish. Some French, German, Italian and Spanish positions also available.
Qualifications: BA/BSc minimum. Additional TEFL qualifications or experience an advantage.
Conditions of employment: 1 year renewable contracts. Maximum class size of 4 students. Mixture of shifts (10am-5.40pm. 11.20am-7pm and 1.20pm-9pm). 35 h.p.w. including conversation room classes. Excellent opportunities for promotion to senior teacher/trainer positions and related educational departments.
Salary: salaries vary according to region. Range is from 259,000 yen in Tokyo and environs rising to an average of 284,000 yen after 2-month probationary period. Comparable salaries in Osaka are 250,000 yen and 275,000 yen; other areas vary slightly. Monthly travel expenses are reimbursed.
Facilities/Support: accommodation, health insurance and visa sponsorship arranged. Orientation given along with initial and ongoing training, regular feedback, teachers' meetings and specialised training workshops.
Recruitment: positions start at various times of the year. Interviews are essential, and are held through Nova offices in the UK, USA, Canada, Australia, France or Japan. (See accompanying advertisement for addresses of international personnel offices.)

RIDGE INTERNATIONAL
1-20-16 Teraikedai, Tondabayashi, Osaka 584-0073. Tel: (721) 299295. Fax: (721) 299202.
Number of teachers: 5.
Preference of nationality: British only.
Qualifications: university degree (any discipline), CELTA Certificate.
Conditions of employment: 1 year contracts, 4 weeks paid holiday. 100 hours per

month with overtime sometimes available. Sundays and one day off p.w.
Salary: 250,000 yen per month (plus 3000 yen per hour overtime).
Facilities/Support: shared apartment provided. Monthly rent is 45,000 yen.
Contribution to flight to Japan paid (50,000 yen). Daily travel expenses paid.
Recruitment: adverts in UK press. CV and photo sent to Japan. Interviews carried
out in the UK by appointed recruiter.
Contact: Mrs. Masako Mine, Director.

SHANE ENGLISH SCHOOL
c/o Saxoncourt & English Worldwide Recruitment, 124 New Bond St, London
W1Y 9AE, UK. Tel: 020-7491 1911. Fax: 020-7493 3657. E-mail: recruit@
saxoncourt.com. Website: www.saxoncourt.com.
Number of teachers: 180 for 100 schools in Chiba-ken (Greater Tokyo) region.
Preference of nationality: British and Irish.
Qualifications: BA, Trinity or Cambridge Cert. (preferably grade 'B') or some
teaching experience needed.
Conditions of employment: 1 year renewable contracts, usually from September or
January. Average 25 contact h.p.w. Pupils from age 3. 5-6 week paid holiday.
Salary: from 250,000 yen per month.
Facilities/Support: assistance with accommodation, health insurance and in-house
training given. Pre-service Young Learners training course available. Flights
reimbursed in some cases.
Recruitment: via Saxoncourt in London. Interviews essential.
Contact: Ian Hardman, Recruitment Manager.

YOKOHAMA YMCA
English Multimedia Systems, 1-7 Tokiwa-Cho, Naka-Ku, Yokohama 231-8458.
Tel: (45) 662 3721. Fax: (45) 664 4018. E-mail: ymjohn@yokohama-ymca.or.jp.
Number of teachers: about 200 full and part-time.
Preference of nationality: none.
Qualifications: minimum 4 year degree. TESOL training. Appropriate experience.
Conditions of employment: 1 year renewable contract. Shifts vary; maximum 22
contact h.p.w. over 5 days.
Salary: 250,000 yen.
Facilities/Support: accommodation can be arranged for some positions in a semi-
furnished apartment within commuting distance. In such cases move-in fees
(approx. 4 months rent) can be waived. The teacher pays a damage deposit, monthly
rent and utilities. In the majority of cases however, teachers arrange their own
accommodation with assistance. Teachers' visas can be arranged and renewed.
Recruitment: personal recommendation, newspaper adverts, internet. Interviews
essential; may be possible in North America.
Contacts: Mr Toshi Iwanabe, Mr Yoshihito Shiroishi.

Other Schools to Try
Note that these schools (in alphabetical order according to town) did not confirm
their teacher requirements for this edition of *Teaching English Abroad*. Upper case
entries marked with an asterisk had entries in the last edition (1999); addresses
without asterisks have been taken from various sources, such as newspaper adverts.
MATSUDO ENGLISH CENTER, Serizawa Bldg. 3F, 17-11 Honcho, Matsudo-shi,
    Chiba-ken 271 (473-660987/fax 473-660945)
Mobara *English Institute*, 618-1 Takashi, Mobara-shi, Chiba-ken 297 (475-22
    4785/fax 475-24 0194).
Fukuoka *YMCA*, 1-1-10 Nanasumi, Jyonan-ku, Fukuoka-shi, Fukuoka-ken 814-01
    (92-822 8701)
SEIHA ENGLISH NETWORK, 4F Ashu Building, Daimyo 2-chome, 114 Chuo-ku,
    Fukuoka (92-733 0205/fax 92-733 6420). 20 teachers for network of children's
    schools.

Language Education Center, 5-9, 1-chome, Kamiyacho Nakaku, Hiroshima 730-0031. Conversation school in the centre of Hiroshima

Hiroshima YMCA, 7-11 Hatchobori, Naka-ku Hiroshima 730 (fax 82-211 0366)

ABC Language Academy, 214 Nakaban-Cho Ono, Hyogo 675-1308

Tajima English Center, 2-6 Motomachi, Toyoka, Hyogo (796-24 8884/fax 796-24 6624).

CLI, Yamaha Building, 4F, Uomachi 1-1-1, Kokurakita-ku, Kitakyushu-shi 802

*NOHKAI ELS ENGLISH INSTITUTE, Kobe Harborland Center Bldg. 19F, 1-3-3, Higashi Kawasaki-cho, Chuo-ku, Kobe 650 (fax 78-371 5054). 40 teachers.

Trident School of Languages,, 1-5-31 Imaike, Chikusa-ku, Nagoya 464 (52-735 1600/fax 52-735 1788). 20 teachers.

Nagoya YMCA, 2-5-29 Kamimaezu, Naka-ku, Nagoya 460 (fax 52-331 6739)

Evergreen School, Ikku-cho, Niihama City, Ehime 792-0025 (tel/fax 81-897 34 2294; akiko@dokidoki.ne.jp). School director has studied in US and welcomes Americans as well as other nationalities.

Osaka College, 1-5-6 Tosabori, Nishi-ku, Osaka 550 (fax 6-445 0297). Affiliated to YMCA.

English Circles/EC INC., President Bldg. 3rd Floor, West 5, South 1, Chuo-ku, Sapporo 060 (11-221 0279/fax 11-221 0248). 60 teachers

*JAMES ENGLISH SCHOOL, Sendai (Main Branch), Sumitomo Bank Building, 9F, 20-2-6 Chuo, Aoba ku, Sendai 980 (22-267 4911/fax 22-267 4908; kigawa1007@aol.com). 70 for 17 branches in the Tohoku region of northern Japan.

Sendai YMCA, 9-7 Tatemachi, Aoba-ku, Sendai, Miyagi-ken 980 (fax 22-222 2952)

Cambridge School of English, 2-2-5, Hanawada, Utsunomiya-shi, Tochigi-ken 320

*ENGLISH ACADEMIC RESEARCH INSTITUTE, Maruyoshi Building 6-2-2, Higashi Ueno, Taito-ku, Tokyo 110 (3-3844 3104)

International Education Services, Rose Hikawa Building, 22-14 Higashi 2-chome, Shibuya-ku, Tokyo 150 (3-3498 7101/fax 3-3498 7113). 70 teachers.

Sakuragaoka Joshi Gakuen, 1-51-12 Takinogawa, Kita-ku, Tokyo 114

Tokyo YMCA, 7 Mitoshiro-cho, Kanda, Chiyoda-ku, Tokyo 101 (fax 3-3293 7013)

Toyama YMCA English School, 1-3-14 Tsutsumicho Dori, Toyama 930 (764-259001/fax 764-246937). 5 full-time, 15 part-time.

Kumano InterCultural Club (KICC), 1-8-13 Horai Singu, Wakayama (735-28 2234/fax 735-28 2230)

English Club, Inc., Naritaya Building, 2nd Floor, 1-3-2 Tsukagoshi, Warabi City, Saitama T335 (48-432 7444/fax 48-432 7446). 20 teachers for 7 schools in Saitama Prefecture.

Korea

Anyone who has witnessed the early morning scramble by students and businessmen to get to their English lessons before the working day begins in Seoul might be surprised to learn that the name for Korea is 'Land of the Morning Calm'. Because Korea's economy (what's left of it) is so heavily dependent on export, English is a very useful accomplishment for people in business. Korean students are often looking to export themselves, mostly to the US to acquire a college education. Both these groups have probably studied English for many years at school but need to practise conversation with native speakers. School and university vacations (July and January) often see a surge in student enrolment at private language institutes. The teaching of children is booming more than ever and there is a huge demand for English teachers to teach in schools (where English is almost universally compulsory).

The devaluation of the Korean won in 1998 and general economic slump took their toll on language schools. Some of the big chains closed and many foreign teachers who were there primarily to earn high wages to send home, fled what they perceived to be a sinking ship. This together with its less than favourable reputation among language teachers leaves major language teaching organisations perennially short of native speaker staff. (Note that in the case of Korea, 'schools' normally refer to the state sector whereas 'institutes' mean private language academies run as businesses.)

The bias is strongly in favour of North Americans, especially Canadians (who are still arriving in numbers due to their troubled economy) and there are still relatively few British TEFLers in Korea. For years advertisements around American university campuses have been luring fresh graduates to the Far East, but in the present climate, fewer are tempted.

William Naquin, a well-qualified American who taught in Kyunggi-Do, sums up the politics:

> *Korea is a divided country. We were quite nervous that war might break out here between the two Koreas. The situation in the north is universallly reported to be extremely bad, with summary executions and food riots. Experts seem to think the North Korean regime will collapse some time in the next two or three years. This could be good for English teachers in Korea, and it could also be very, very bad. The North Koreans have a lot of missiles, nerve gas and chemical weapons, and are led by the most isolated, despotic lunatic and paranoid military strongmen in the world. Prospective teachers need to know that this is one of the most likely flashpoints for war on earth, and that coming here necessarily involves some degree of risk.*

Prospects for Teachers

There are hundreds of language institutes *(hogwons)* in Seoul the capital, Pusan (Korea's second city, five hours south of Seoul) and in smaller cities. The majority of these are run as businesses, where profit is the primary or even sole *raison d'etre*. ELT training is superfluous in the majority of cases. Native-speaker status is normally sufficient to persuade the owner of an institute to hire an English-speaker, though having some letters after your name makes the job hunt easier. Education is greatly respected in Korea and degrees generally matter far more to most potential employers than specialist qualifications. An MA (no matter in which field) counts heavily in one's favour. For those trying to fix up a job ahead of time, institutes are often willing to hire a teacher without an interview, provided they have a university degree and possibly some evidence of experience as well.

In North America, brokers and agents often act on behalf of institutes or groups of institutes to recruit teachers. Typically advertisements placed by such intermediaries request only native-speaker fluency and a BA/BSc. They are being paid by the school owners so should not charge teachers a fee, though some try.

If you wait until you get to Korea, it is exceedingly easy to fix up a job without resorting to an agent, but the visa is more difficult to arrange. A typical scenario is for an American or Canadian to arrange a job through an agent and obtain the visa before leaving home, complete (or not as the case may be) a one-year contract and then move on to the more lucrative freelance market.

FIXING UP A JOB

In Advance

In 1995, the Korean government introduced an official teacher placement programme in imitation of JET in Japan. EPIK (English Program in Korea) is run by the Ministry of Education and administered through Korean embassies and consulates in the US, Canada, Australia and the UK. In its first year 150 applicants were placed; by 2000 placements were nearing 2,000 in schools and education offices throughout the country. The annual salary offered was 1.6, 1.8 or 2 million won per month (depending on qualifications) plus accommodation, round trip airfare, visa sponsorship and medical insurance. Work starting dates are staggered over the summer with application deadlines falling between January and April.

Details of the 2000/2001 programme had not been finalised at the time of writing, so current information should be obtained from the Education Director, Korean Embassy, 60 Buckingham Gate, London SW1E 6AJ (020-7227 5547/fax 020-7227 5503) or from the website epik@cc.knue.ac.kr or contact the office in Korea (82 431 233 4516/7). Americans should contact any of the dozen Korean Consulates in the US. Other nationalities can contact the EPIK office in Korea (Center for In-Service Education, Korea National University of Education, Chongwon, Chungbuk 363-791; 431-230-3943/fax 431-233 6679). Note that EPIK does not attract the praise that the JET Programme does.

Judith Night obtained her job in a provincial town in Chollanamdo Province by applying to the recruiting representative of the Korean Ministry of Education in San Francisco (415-921-2251/3). The Ministry can be contacted directly at Yong chon ri, Changsong up, Changsong gun, Chollanamdo 515-800.

Recruiters sometimes advertise in the North American ELT press. For example the Jong Ro Academy in Chonbuk Province advertised recently in TESOL's *Career Counsel* for teachers to start at any time of the year; the contact number given was in San Jose, California: 408-248-5941. Ko-Am Academy Consulting Inc. (14080-D Sullyfield Circle, Chantilly VA 20151; fax 703-815-3600/apply@koam.org) recruits year round, as does Better Resource (3700 Wilshire Blvd, Suite 955, Los Angeles, CA 90010; 213-738-100/better@wcis.com; www.eslkorea.com).

Canadians can apply to the Russell Recruiting agency (3038 West 42nd Ave. Vancouver, BC, Canada V6N 3H2; tel: 1-604-267 3648; fax 1-604-267 1539; e-mail: jimkrussell@hotmail.com), who arranges one year contracts for those with university or college diplomas. Those with additional EFL/ESL qualifications and teaching experience earn higher salaries. There is a commitment to teach 120 hours a month (more if wished). Return airfares, free accommodation, paid holidays, medical insurance and bonus on contract completion are all provided. Applicants who cannot be interviewed locally can do so by telephone or internet. Another Canadian recruiter for Korea, Taiwan and Thailand is Goal Asia (49 McCaul Street, Toronto, Ont M5T 2U7; 416-820-5042/apply@goalasia.com).

As mentioned above, it is not unusual to arrange a job without a face-to-face interview. One school suggests that would-be teachers send a cassette of their voices or, even better, a video of them teaching a lesson, which would certainly be more memorable and impressive than simply sending a CV.

William Naquin stresses the importance of arranging the details of a written contract before starting work:

> *I found my present position in Korea in the classified section of the Seattle Sunday paper. A couple of Korean-Americans in Los Angeles, calling themselves 'Better Resource,' flew to Seattle two days after receiving my faxed CV. I cannot suggest strongly enough that teachers considering a position negotiated through a US-based broker get everything in writing. My contract was written in exceedingly poor English, and what it failed to stipulate in terms of housing conditions, medical insurance, etc. was only guaranteed orally. The brokers from LA assured me that I would receive full medical and dental insurance and accommodation would be paid for, either single or double occupancy. It was a mistake on my part to take the broker at his word. Living arrangements here are substandard, with three of us sharing a two-bedroom flat.*

William's ability to save $12,000 in one year helped him to tolerate the inconvenience.

Another possibility for anyone with an MA or advanced TEFL/TESL qualifications is to work for the language department of a Korean university (of which there are nearly 100). Universities probably offer the best paid and most stable employment. Serious teachers should enquire at their local Korean Consulate for addresses.

The internet is well equipped to keep track of the volatile English language market and many Korean employers rely exclusively on it. More than one web page lists good and bad employers along with lots of horror stories. Dave's www.eslcafe.com devotes an entire section to feedback from Korea.

On the Spot

Every day there are adverts for teachers in the English language newspapers in Seoul, namely the *Korean Herald* and *Korea Times*. A personal approach to language schools in Seoul or Pusan will usually be rewarded with some early morning and evening work within a week or two. Often new arrivals stay in one of the popular yogwons (hostels) and hear on the grapevine about the English teaching scene. The Chongro area of Seoul contains a high concentration of both hostels and language schools and is a suitable area for a door-to-door job search.

Seoul has an extensive subway system which makes it possible to attend interviews at far-flung schools and (if successful) to commute to work without too much difficulty. Unlike in Japan, the subway stations are labelled and announced in English.

REGULATIONS

Anyone working without a visa risks fines and possible deportation. Similarly, the schools which hire freelance foreigners without permits can be closed down by the government. So, if at all possible, obtain a work visa which in almost all cases is available only to people with a 4 year BA or BSc.

It is much easier if this can be done before arrival. If you do find a school which wants to hire you, they should send you a contract, sponsorship documents (valid for a minimum of one year) and copy of their Business Registration Certificate. You must send these together with your CV, two photos, the original of your degree diploma and two copies (plus transcripts for Americans) and a fee to your nearest Korean diplomatic representative, who will take four to eight weeks to process the visa.

It is normally possible to reduce the time taken by requesting that documents be sent by telex (at your expense). You must collect your visa at the Consulate. Be sure to apply for a multiple-entry visa, which will allow you to leave the country for holidays without hassle. As usual the work visa (E2) is valid only for employment with the sponsoring employer and extracurricular teaching is illegal; Judith Night heard of several teachers who were deported for failing to take this regulation seriously. Apparently Koreans who inform the authorities about illegal workers are rewarded, so working illegally is more risky than ever.

Alternatively, you can enter Korea as a tourist, find a job and then go to Japan, Hong Kong or Taipei while the visa application is being dealt with. (British and American nationals don't need a tourist visa for stays of less than 90 days; Canadians get six months.) Tourist visas cannot be extended. Anyone planning to go to Korea to look for a job and a visa should dig their university diploma out of storage and bring it with them.

Teachers are liable to income tax from their first day of work. The rate of tax for most teachers seems to fluctuate according to earnings between 4% and 11%. Most teachers participate in the Korean National Medical Insurance Union; some employers cover the cost (about 3% of earnings) but most pay half.

The law permits foreigners to send up to two-thirds of their salary out of the country. This is usually effected by wire transfer, which costs money at both ends and causes delay and confusion in most Korean banks. An alternative is possible if you exploit the loophole which allows people leaving the country to buy $2,000 worth of travellers cheques'. Simply go to the airport every month, buy travellers cheques in US dollars and send them home through the mail.

CONDITIONS OF WORK

Discontentment seems to be chronic among English teachers in Korea. So many American teachers have run amok of faulty contracts, that the US Embassy in Seoul issues a handbook offering guidance called 'Teaching English in Korea: Opportunities and Pitfalls' (which can be requested from the American Citizens Services Branch, 82 Sejong Road, Chongro-ku, Seoul, or seen on the internet). The accompanying letter from the American Citizens Services office does not mince words:

> *Despite contract language promising good salaries, furnished apartments and other amenities, many teachers find they actually receive much less than they were promised; some do not even receive benefits required by Korean law, such as health insurance and severance pay. Teachers' complaints range from simple contract violations, through non-payment of salary for months at a time, to dramatic incidents of severe sexual harassment, intimidation, threats of arrest/deportation and physical assault.*

Tim Leffel is one in a long line of American EFL teachers who came to the conclusion that 'nearly 100% of the hogwon owners are crooks or unbelievably inept – sometimes both and in Korea both oral and written contracts are a joke'. He passes on the advice to carry a tape recorder to all interviews and meetings. By working for a big chain, he avoided most problems and was given a decent apartment, good wages and lots of support materials. He even got his post-contract $1,000 though he had to return to Korea six weeks afer finishing work to insist on it. (His employer was Wonderland, 1146-3 Ilsan-Dong, Goyang, 411-310 Kyungki-Do; 344-913 0533/fax 911 0544). When there are conflicts over contracts, Tim advises teachers to choose their battles carefully and to remain civilised as long as possible.

The issue of severance pay is a sore point for many teachers. By law, anyone who completes a 52-week contract is entitled to one month's salary as severance pay. (Note that the length of contract offered by EPIK varies from 44 to 50 weeks.) Employers have been known to make life quite unpleasant for their teachers near the end of their contracts, so that they're tempted to leave and forego the bonus. The opening remark in Peter McGuire's letter from Andong was 'You wouldn't believe how thrilled I am to be almost finished with a one-year contract here in Korea.' He went on to say that he made it through to the end only because he is a very determined person and the stakes were high, since he was trying to clear debts at home in Wisconsin.

The quality of *hogwon* varies enormously. Some are run by sharks who may make promises at interview which they can't fulfil, and overfill classes to maximise profits. Many schools do not use recognised course books but rely on home-made materials of dubious usefulness. Despite Korea's reputation as a centre for high tech, some schools lack basic video and computer facilities. Few schools at this level offer any training.

It must be said that not all foreign teachers are disappointed. One of them was Patrick Edgington from California who answered a recruiter's ad in a US daily paper and was soon working for *Ahil Foreign Language Institute* in Ulsan (482-138 Sebudong Dong-Ku, Ulsan 682-036). While acknowledging that contracts in Korea guarantee nothing, he was lucky enough to find an honest employer who paid him on time and provided a 'cube' apartment above the institute building (which was acceptable, though cold in winter).

The average teaching schedule in Korea is five or six hours a day, taking place in the early morning (6.30am starts are possible), five days a week. Weekend work is less commonplace than in many other countries. The teaching load in universities is often lighter. The problem seems to be that hogwons realise that teachers come to Korea for no more than a year and therefore milk them for every working minute. Kathy Panton's assessment is that the teacher is there to exploit Korea for money, so Koreans turn around and exploit teachers for labour. She topped the record quoted in a previous edition of this book by working 181 hours in a month including privates and excluding preparation.

Freelance teachers are paid handsomely. Those who go through an agent to find clients (usually on-site at company premises) earn 20,000-25,000 won an hour, whereas if they find the clients themselves they earn as much as twice that. For Tim Leffel, this was the best part of the experience:

> *For my privates, I have nothing but good things to say. Boring people to talk to sometimes, but they always paid in advance and treated me as a professional.*

The majority of Korean language learners are serious (some attend two-hour classes three or four times a week) and want to be taught systematically and energetically, though even those who have been studying for years often show precious little confidence in conversing. They also expect their teachers to direct the action and are not happy with a laid-back 'let's have a chit-chat' approach. Whereas Judith Night (a certified teacher) found her pupils in the public school system 'eager to learn and a joy to teach', Mark Vetare, with no teaching background, found things very hard going, and concluded in the end that TEFL teaching was not for him:

> *The major drawback is teaching the sullen, bored, exhausted, precocious and Mok Dong spoiled children aged 14-16 – torture. (Mok Dong means upper mid class whatever that means.) They drain me of energy. What they want is a white monkey to entertain them and make them giggle. Trouble is they provide zero material to work from. No sports, no interests. Their stated hobbies are sleeping, TV and listening to music. Their parents want their kids to move up book by book as if that's a gauge of progress. 'Oh, you're in 10B, great.' Never mind that they still can't speak English.*

Accommodation

As in Japan, a large deposit ('key money') must be paid before an apartment can be rented, but unlike in Japan this is normally refunded at the end of the tenancy. If you don't hear about available flats from your school or other foreigners, check the English language newspaper or find an English-speaking rental agent. Boarding house accommodation costs 220,000-250,000 won per month.

LEISURE TIME

Visitors are often surprised to discover the richness and complexity of Korean history and culture, partly because Japanese culture is far better known. Despite being a bustling metropolis of more than ten million, Seoul has preserved some of its cultural treasures. Assuming your teaching schedule permits, you should be able to explore the country and, if interested, study some aspect of Korean culture such as the martial art Tae Kwon Do. The country's area is small, the public transport good, though traffic congestion at weekends is a problem.

Teachers often find that their students are friendly, though relationships between Western men and Korean women are strongly disapproved of. Anyone homesick for the West will gravitate to the area of Seoul called Itaewon, where fast food restaurants and discos are concentrated, not to mention a jazz club, a decent bookstore and other expatriate forms of entertainment. Americans may find the

English language military television station a welcome recreation. Teachers in the provinces will have to become accustomed to a very quiet life as Judith Night discovered:

> *Anyone interested in coming here to have a social life will be very disappointed. In fact, they had better be ready to deal with isolation, because most likely they will be the only foreigner in the town, and the people may never even have met any foreigners before. If I stay in Korea another year, I will choose to live in Seoul, due to missing a social life.*

Although William Naquin was also working a long way from the bright lights, he fared a little better:

> *Insofar as spare time goes, many weekends are spent recovering from 40+ hours in the classroom. During periods when we aren't quite as busy we watch movies, work out at the primitive health club, go to Seoul and drink. Mountain climbing is big here and when the weather is nice our students take us along with them. Portable hobbies such as music, writing and reading are indispensable.*

LIST OF SCHOOLS

AHIL FOREIGN LANGUAGE SCHOOL FOR ADULTS & AHIL JUNIOR SCHOOL
482-138 Seobudong Dongku, Ulsan 682-030, South Korea. Tel: 52 232 2304 (adults); 82 52 252 7020 (junior pre-school). E-mail: ahil7_2000@yahoo.co.kr. Website: www.momoweb.co.kr/a/ail1/index
Number of teachers: 5 native speakers.
Qualifications: BA or BSc. degree.
Conditions of work: teaching classes conversational English in pleasant surroundings with good fresh air and pebble and sand beaches and mountains. Warm working atmosphere. Also, intensive English courses in the summer vacation (late July to late August, one month).
Contact: Ms. Eunsook Park.

BERLITZ KOREA
Sungwood Academy Building 2F, 1316-17 Seocho-Dong, Seocho-Gu, Seoul 137-074. Tel: (2) 3481 5324. Fax: (2) 3481 3921. E-mail: pamela.hughes@ berlitz.com. sg and gerald.drabick@berlitz.com.sg
Number of teachers: about 40.
Preference of nationality: native speakers.
Qualifications: 4-year degree. Personality important with ability to conduct conversation classes. Experience in business or with children is advantageous.
Conditions of employment: 1 year renewable by mutual agreement. The language centre is open daily from 6.30am to 9pm and teachers usually teach a split shift of morning and evening classes. Most students are individuals so schedules vary greatly.
Salary: 11,500 won per 40 minutes of teaching. Average salary earned is between US$2000 and $3000 per month. Taxes are about 3% and there is a social security payment after about 8 months in the form of a bill which must be paid in accordance with laws agreed between Korea and the teacher's home government.
Facilities/Support: visas are provided by the school. The visa has to be pre-approved and issued before candidates leave their own country. Two bedroom shared apartments are provided by the school.
Recruitment: mostly via internet. Interviews in person or by telephone.
Contact: Pamela Hughes/Gerald Drabick.

DING DING DANG ENGLISH SCHOOL
1275-3 Bummel-dong Soosung-gu, Taegu 706-100. Tel: (53) 782 5200. Fax: (53) 782 6434. E-mail: dings@thrunet.com.

Number of teachers: depends on the time of year.
Preference of nationality: none, but must be native speaker.
Qualifications: BA degree minimum.
Conditions of employment: one year contract. Usually 30 hours/36 classes per week. A class lasts 40 minutes.
Salary: 1.7 million won (about US$1,523) gross.
Facilities/Support: two-bedroom shared apartments are provided for teachers.
Recruitment: via internet websites and newspaper.
Contact: Janice Park.

DR. OH'S FOREIGN LANGUAGE INSTITUTE
1471-4 Sun-chon City, Chon-Nam 540-140. Tel: (61) 723 5804. Fax: (61) 723 5805. E-mail: oh9781@dream.wiz.com.
Number of teachers: 2.
Preference of nationality: North American.
Qualifications: at least a BA degree and teaching experience.
Conditions of employment: one year. 110-120 hours per month.
Salary: 1.6 to 1.8 won (approximately US$1,500 per month).
Facilities/Support: apartment provided free.
Recruitment: via internet e.g. Dave's ESL Café.
Contact: Eung-Soo Oh.

ELS INTERNATIONAL/YBM
Recruiting Office, 3rd Floor, ELS Building, 55-1 Chongno 2 ga, Chongno gu, Seoul 110-122. Tel: (2) 2264 7472. Fax: (2) 2269 0275. E-mail: teach@ybmsisa.co.kr. Website: www.ybmsisa.com or http://user.chollian.net/~teachecc.
Number of teachers: 100+ native English teachers for schools throughout Korea. YBM/ELSI schools are for adults (including possible on-site corporate training); English Conversation Centers (ECC) are for children aged 3-16, plus M-Plus for adolescents and E2 for children.
Preference of nationality: North American; others considered.
Qualifications: minimum requirement is BA/BSc in any field, CELTA and limited experience. Prefer MA TESOL plus 2 years' experience.
Conditions of employment: 12 month contracts. 6 hours teaching per day Monday to Friday. Adult schools open between 6.30am and 10pm, children's between 10am and 9pm (Monday to Saturday). Overtime may be possible.
Salary: 22.1-27.3 million won per year depending on qualifications and whether housing is included in package. Tax deductions of about 10%.
Facilities/Support: furnished shared accommodation provided by institute. Possibility of having airfares reimbursed, if hired abroad, plus relocation allowance and medical insurance. A severance bonus of one month's salary is paid on completion of a contract. Paid one-week orientation on arrival. 10 days paid vacation.
Recruitment: newspaper adverts and the internet. Recruiting office is centrally located near Chongno ga subway station (exit 15). Interviews are essential and can be conducted in US and UK. Fax in USA/Canada: 509-463-5118. The UK representative is J. Howard, c/o ELS Language Centres, Garrick House, 3 Charing Cross Road, London WC2 (0870-169 4336; jh2@mcmail.com).

ENGLISH FRIENDS
733, Bang Hak 3 Dong. Do Bong Ku, Seoul. Tel: (2) 3491 1431. Fax: (2) 3491 1264. E-mail: 2003@hotmail.com and tefa2000@hotmail.com. Website: www.tefa.net.
Number of teachers: 25-30.
Preference of nationality: none, but should be native speaker.
Qualifications: BA or BSc. minimum.
Conditions of employment: 12 months contract.
Salary: approx. US$1,500-1,700 per month.
Facilities/Support: accommodation (apartments shared by two people) provided.

Recruitment: via the internet and e-mail.
Contact: Young Kang Kim, Manager Human Resources and Franchise Dept.

LANGUAGE ARTS TESTING & TRAINING
Chung Jung-Ro, PO Box 269, Seoul 120-013. Tel: (2) 363-3291/363-1277. Fax: (2) 313-5620. E-mail: lattinst@chollian.net
Number of teachers: 6.
Preference of nationality: any native speaker.
Qualifications: BA. Experience preferred.
Conditions of employment: 1 year contract. Morning shift 7.30-10am and evening 6-9pm. All pupils are adults.
Salary: 20,000 won per hour; average above 2,000,000 won per month.
Facilities/Support: assistance with housing.
Recruitment: interviews in person or by phone. Institute moving in near future so e-mail contact preferred.
Contact: John Rowe, Vice President.

LANGUAGE TEACHING RESEARCH CENTER
60-17, 1-ka, Taepyong-Ro, Chung-gu, Seoul 100-101. Tel: (2) 737-4641. Fax: (2) 734-6036. E-mail: LTRC@unitel.co.kr
Number of teachers: 22.
Preference of nationality: none.
Qualifications: university degree. TEFL experience helpful but not essential.
Conditions of employment: 1 year renewable contracts. 5-7 hours per day in split shifts, 5 days per week. Classes for adults and children. All teachers must be willing to teach children aged 5-16.
Salary: from 13,500 won per hour. Total monthly earnings (including housing allowance) from approximately 1.7 million won (5 classes a day) to 2.3 million won (7 classes a day). Contract completion bonus.
Facilities/Support: housing allowance. One-way airfare. Training provided. Medical insurance available. Money transfer scheme (for remitting savings overseas).
Recruitment: local or telephone interviews.

OREGON LANGUAGE INSTITUTE
Beomo 4-dong 206-6, Suseoung-ku, Taegu. Tel: 82-53-741 2511. Fax: 82-53 741 2513.
Number of teachers: currently 32 employed, but there is a constant need for teachers for 5 ELIs in Korea.
Preference of nationality: none.
Qualifications: BA degree preferably language related and teaching experience preferred.
Conditions of employment: one year contract. 25 hour, 5-day week.
Salary: negotiable, but competitive.
Facilities/Support: rent-free semi-furnished apartment provided for each 2/3 teachers to share (own room). Teachers are responsible for utility fees and phone.
Recruitment: through *TESOL Bulletin*. Interviews are not essential but can be done on the telephone.
Contact: Inhee Lee, Director.

Other Schools to Try

Note that these schools were in the last edition of *Teaching English Abroad* (1999) but did not confirm teacher details for this edition.

Nelson Foreign Language Institute, c/o Mr Jay S. Wang, North American Office, Nelson FLI, 95 Hess Street South, No. 610, Hamilton, Ontario L8P 3N4, Canada (canlink@bigwave.ca). Hire 20 teachers a month for 60 branches throughout Korea.

ESS LANGUAGE INSTITUTE, 38-1, 1-ka Kwangbok-dong, Jung-ku, Pusan 600-031 (51-246-3251/fax 51-241-1988)

SOGANG LANGUAGE PROGRAM, Sogang University, 1-1 Sinsu-dong, Mapo-gu, Seoul 121-742 (tel/fax 2-705-8733/ jhong@ccs.sogang.ac.kr). 3-5 teachers per month for 15 institutes.

TOP LANGUAGE SCHOOL, 1266-14, 1-ka, Dukjin-Dong, Dukjin-Ku, Jonju-City, Jonbuk (652-254-5090/fax 652-744266/ jade72@hotmail.com). 30-50 teachers for several franchise schools in Jongu-City.

WORLD LANGUAGE INSTITUTE, 19-16 Kumnamro-1 ka, Dung-ku, Kwangju 501-021 (62-228-1723/fax 62-226-3562/ worldedu@hotmail.com)

YES ENGLISH SCHOOL, Daewon Building, 5th Floor, Daechi-dong 599, Kangnam-gu, Seoul 135-281 (2-553-8880/fax 2-553-5764; yescho@nuri.net)

South Asia

In contrast to Thailand and Indonesia with their strong demand for native-speaker English teachers, other countries between Pakistan and the Philippines (with a few exceptions) are not easy places in which to find work as an English teacher. Poverty is the main reason why there is a very small market for expatriate teachers. Outside the relatively wealthy countries of Singapore, Malaysia and Brunei, there is no significant range of opportunities to earn money while teaching English. The largest growth area has been in those countries which were cut off from the West for many years, viz. Cambodia, Vietnam and Laos, where a number of joint-venture and locally-owned language schools have been opened in the past few years employing native speaker teachers.

Elsewhere, the demand may exist but the resources do not. Very few ordinary citizens in much of South Asia can dream of affording the luxury of English conversation classes. Few Westerners could manage on the wages earned by ordinary teachers in India, Nepal, Sri Lanka, Pakistan, etc. However those foreigners prepared to finance themselves and volunteer their time can find eager students by asking around locally.

Mainstream voluntary organisations, especially *VSO*, are active in the region, especially Vietnam and Laos where they recruit teachers to work in teachers colleges and vocational colleges. *GAP Activity Projects, Project Trust* and other organisations for school-leavers send volunteers to India, Nepal, Pakistan and Malaysia. *i-to-i* send people to India, Nepal, Sri Lanka, China, Thailand and Taiwan for varying fees. Local voluntary organisations are also active, especially those concerned with improving literacy in women and children.

BRUNEI

Few people can locate Brunei on a map of the world, let alone anticipate that there is an enormous demand for English teachers there. This wealthy oil state on the north shore of Borneo, in which the Sultan famously donated a television to every household in his tiny kingdom, can afford an expensive educational system for its population of just a quarter of a million. The Ministry of Education (Bandar Seri Begawan 1170, Negara Brunei Darussalam; fax 2-240250) has been implementing a bilingual educational system which 'ensures the sovereignty of the Malay language while at the same time recognising the importance of the English language'. The British Council operates its own English Language Centre at 45 Simpang 100, Gadong BE3619, Bandar Seri Begawan 3192.

There are currently over 200 primary and secondary EFL teachers working in Brunei in state sector schools. C*f*BT (The Teaching Agency, 6 Lampton Road, Hounslow, Middlesex TW3 1JL; 020-8814 8200/fax 020-8814 8209;

teachingagency@cfbt-hq.org.uk/ www.cfbt.com) recruits suitably qualified and experienced individuals along guidelines set by the Brunei Ministry of Education. All teachers must have Qualified Teacher Status, e.g. PGCE or equivalent. Secondary teachers must also have a degree and three years' experience plus an EFL/ESL qualification or five years' experience if without an EFL/ESL qualification. Primary teachers must have either a degree, three years' experience and an EFL/ESL qualification/experience or a Cert./Dip.Ed., CELTA and five years' experience. The package currently includes tax-free salary, end-of-contract bonus, accommodation, flights, baggage allowance and other benefits. Contracts are initially for two years. A car driver's licence is essential.

INDIAN SUBCONTINENT

In former colonies of Britain, principally the Indian subcontinent, there are many private schools where English is the medium of instruction and a proportion of the educated classes speak English virtually as a first language. The small number of foreigners who do teach in this region do so in the private sector. Native English speakers have arranged to teach in the state sector, simply by entering a school and asking permission to sit in on an English class. Provided they do not expect a wage, some teaching role could probably be found for them. But it can be very challenging and discouraging. Facilities can be brutal with no teaching materials and no space. The majority of local English teachers, who have not really mastered the language, are very badly paid and can be transferred without appeal at any time; it is not too surprising to find that most are very demoralised.

One indigenous organisation which places graduates on a voluntary basis in various educational institutes in South India is *Jaffe International Education Service* (see entry). Another voluntary organisation in India which occasionally sends self-funding volunteers to projects where they teach English is JAC (Joint Assistance Centre, 6-17/3 DLF Qutab Enclave, Phase 1, District Gurgaon, Haryana 122002; fax 124-351308). The cost of participation is $230 for the first month and $130 for subsequent months.

A number of organisations in the UK send volunteers to teach English in India including the main gap placement organisations. For example *Gap Challenge* sends school leavers to teach in Goa and Manali for a fee of nearly £1,700 including flights. Teaching and Projects Abroad (Gerrard House, Rustington, West Sussex BN16 1AW; 01903 859911) arranges placements of up to six months in Kerala and Tamil Nadu, South India (£1,195 excluding travel). Postings are mainly to English medium primary schools. i-to-i International (One Cottage Road, Headingley, Leeds LS6 4DD) sends teaching assistants who have done a TEFL course to schools in Bangalore and elsewhere (fee of £1,300). Interserve (London office 020-7735 8227) can organise posts for self-funding Christian teachers in India and Pakistan.

From the US, Cross Cultural Solutions (47 Potter Ave, New Rochelle, NY 10801; 800-380-4777; www.crossculturalsolutions.org) organises volunteer vacations in India. Volunteers work alongside grassroots organisations doing a range of tasks including English teaching. The programme fee is about $2,000 excluding airfares.

Nepal

Nepal is a more promising destination than India for short-term or casual English teachers. In Nepal it is necessary to pass English exams in order to progress through the educational system in any subject, so the demand for effective tuition is strong. Richard Davies came away from Kathmandu with the impression that anyone could get a job teaching in Nepal. He had made the acquaintance of an Englishman who had simply walked into the first school and got a job teaching children and adults. He was finding the work very rewarding, but not financially, since he earned 1,000 Nepalese rupees a month (less than £10).

The British Council in Kathmandu has an English teaching operation (DTO@bc-nepal.wlink.com.np). Americans should make enquiries at the American Language Center (PO Box 58, Kathmandu; 1-419933/fax 1-416746). By British Council standards, the plethora of locally run private language schools are poorly resourced and unable to pay a living wage to teachers. However, if they are an established school, they may be able to assist in getting foreign teachers long-stay visas. Tourist visas (which can be purchased on arrival for $25 cash) are valid for 30 days, whereupon they have to be renewed which is straightforward for the first three months. A four-month visa can be applied for at the immigration office in Thamel, Kathmandu (1-470650). Note that a $4,000 fine or up to a ten-year prison sentence is imposed on foreigners found overstaying their visas.

A range of organisations makes it possible for people to teach in a voluntary capacity. No indigenous organisations can afford to bestow largesse on foreigners joining their projects, so westerners who come to teach in a school or a village must be willing to fund themselves. Of course living expenses are very low by western standards, though the fees charged by mediating agencies can increase the cost significantly. Here are a few relevant organisations:

Africa & Asia Venture Ltd., 10 Market Place, Devizes, Wilts. SN10 1HT, UK. Tel: 01380 729009. Fax: 01380 720060. E-mail: av@aventure.co.uk. Website: www.aventure.co.uk. Places school leavers as assistant teachers in primary and secondary schools in Nepal, and also India, normally for one term. Programme includes in-country orientation course and organised travel at end of four months. Fee is about £2,190 plus air fares.

Educate the Children, PO Box 414, Ithaca, NY 14851-0414, USA/e-mail: info@etc-nepal.org. Website: www.etc-nepal.org. Project operating out of Ithaca, New York and Kathmandu. ETC is non-profit and established to conduct educational and community development activities in Nepal. Volunteer positions exist in Kathmandu area schools, both for experienced teachers (especially at the primary and pre-primary levels) and those new to teaching. Experienced teachers can apply for an 'Independent Placement.' Others should apply for the three-month teaching internship programme, which runs from February to May each year. A small placement fee is charged. There are no rural volunteer opportunities. Contact the US office for more information.

Gap Challenge, Black Arrow House, 2 Chandos Road, London NW10 6NF. Tel: 020-8537 7980. Fax: 020-8961 1551. Send school leavers from Britain to teach in Nepal for a fee, as do the other gap placement organisations in Britain (see introductory chapter *Finding a Job*).

Gorkha District & Educational Development Scheme, c/o Joy Leighton, Chairwoman – 01277 840406; joy@leighton.org/ www.nepal.co.uk. Charity is always looking for volunteers to teach English to Nepalese school kids among other projects.

Grahung Kalika, Southwestern Nepal, Dol Raj Subedi, c/o Mr. Tara Prasad Subedi, P.O. Box 11272 Kathmandu (1-532674/fax 1-527317; mail@multcon. wlink.com.np). NGO established in 1996 to assist the teaching of English in Walling, a municipality in the remote Syangja District of western Nepal (260km west of Kathmandu). Volunteers are needed to improve the English of both pupils and teachers in local schools. Although qualifications and experience are not necessary, volunteers will need an enthusiastic and inventive approach as resources are basic and teaching conditions often challenging. Volunteers stay with local families for the duration of their placements and are asked to contribute Rs4,000 (US$60) to the organisation for administration and development of projects. There is also a monthly fee of Rs3000 (US$45) to the host family for food and accommodation which is payable throughout the stay. An initial registration fee of US$20 in cash is payable to cover communication expenses. Applications should be sent a month in advance of expected arrival date. Teaching posts are not available during June/July due to school holidays.

Global Action Nepal, Baldwins, Eastlands Lane, Cowfold, West Sussex. Tel: 01403-864704; Fax 01403-864088. E-mail: chrissowton@hotmail.com. GAN is a charity which works in the field of education in Nepal. One of its projects, CITE, focuses on the personal and professional development of Nepali English teachers through the use of dynmamic volunteers to support them in their work.

Himalayan Explorers Club, PO Box 3665, Boulder, CO 80307, USA. Tel: 888-420-8822/e-mail: info@hec.org. Office in Nepal (see KEEP entry below): PO Box 9178, Kathmandu. Volunteer Nepal Himalaya programme sends volunteers to a Sherpa village near Lukla (near Everest) to teach English in village schools. Volunteers stay with a Sherpa family. Departures are in September and February and programme costs are $150/month (excluding airfares). The HEC also publishes the *Nepal Volunteer Handbook* which includes a few other possibilities for aspiring English teachers.

Insight Nepal – see entry.

i-to-i, 1 Cottage Road, Headingley, Leeds LS6 4DD. Website: www.i-to-i.com New 3-month Teach in Kathmandu programme. £995 excluding travel.

Kathmandu Environmental Education Project (KEEP): P.O. Box 9178, Thamel, Jyatha, Kathmandu. Tel 977-1-259567. Fax 977-1-256615. E-mail: tour@keep. wlink.com.np. Website: www.keepnepal.org. KEEP sends volunteers to different trekking villages in Nepal to teach English Language to lodge owners, trekking guides and porters. Volunteers stay with a mountain family. Volunteers must be totally self-funding. Membership fee US$20 and pay a fee to KEEP for logistic support (US$100).

RCDP Nepal: Kathmandu Municipality, P.O. Box 14, Kathmandu (1-278305/fax 1-276530; rcdpnepal@hotmail.com or adhikmu@mail.auburn.edu; www.rcdpnepal. com). RCDP Nepal is non-profit and takes paying volunteers to work on various programmes including teaching English. Volunteers stay 2 weeks to 5 months and stay with families in villages.

Voluntary Teaching Nepal: c/o Kamal Aryal, Sangam English Boarding School, Chormara Bazar, Tamsariya V.D.C., Ward No. 7, Nawalparasi District, Lumbini Zone; e-mail: voluntary_teaching@hotmail.com. Sangam school was started in 1987 by local people and is situated in Chormara, a village in the Nawalparasi district near Chitwan and the Narayani river. The school and many others throughout Nepal need volunteer teachers to teach English (and other subjects). Qualifications are not essential but teachers must be able to create their own programme or methodology. Volunteers pay US$80 towards administration costs and US$50 per month to the host family for food and lodging. A registration fee of US$20 is payable in advance with the application form.

VWOP (Voluntary Work Opportunities in Nepal), PO Box 4263, Kathmandu (fax 1-416144; vwop2000@hotmail.com). Willing volunteers looking for a cultural experience can be placed in variety of voluntary posts including teaching English in schools, in remote areas of Nepal. No special qualifications are needed. Volunteers stay with a local family and contribute $50 a month towards their expenses. Registration fee of $20 plus placement fee of $400 must be paid.

Of course if you want to avoid the registration fee charged by the agencies you can contact schools direct. However, remember that you will be on your own, i.e. without back-up if things go wrong. One school that takes on volunteers on the spot is Shahid Dharma Bhakta School (principal Rupendra Acharya; anurup@ wlink.com.np). The school hours are 10am-4pm Monday to Friday and volunteers can stay 4, 8 or 12 months. They have to pay their own costs but will have some local hospitality extended to them.

Rachel Sedley spent six months between school and university as a volunteer teacher at the Siddartha School in Kathmandu, arranged through the UK organisation Fill the Gap (now called Gap Challenge), and conveys some of the flavour of the experience:

The sun is shining and the kids are running riot. New Baneshwar is a suburb of Kathmandu, very busy and polluted, but of course so friendly. I do get tired of being a novelty, especially when I'm swathed in my five metres of bright turquoise silk (we wear saris for teaching) but I'm really loving it here. Already after one month, the thought of leaving the kids and my simple lifestyle is terrible. I find it funny that as a Westerner I'm seen to represent infinite stores of knowledge and yet the servant girl is having to patiently teach me to wash my own clothes. And the general knowledge people have of the fundamentals of life makes me feel helpless and incapable.

The children are so gorgeous (most of the time) and the Principal's family with whom I am living are lovely. It seems to me unnecessary to come to Nepal through an organisation. Everyone here is so keen to help.

Rachel's main complaint about her situation was that she was teaching in a private school for privileged children when she had been led to believe that she would be contributing her time, labour and money to more needy children. While there, she met several people from various schools and orphanages who would love to have English volunteers.

Another gap year volunteer with GAP Activity Projects, Hannah Begbie, enjoyed her stint in a village five hours west of Kathmandu. Although she and her GAP partner would have appreciated more feedback from the headmaster of their school (they weren't sure whether or not their efforts succeeded to engage the children's interest by teaching them songs), they realised that his poor knowledge of English made this difficult. She was full of praise for the organisation and back-up offered by GAP. All volunteers in Nepal met up once a month to go on a group rafting or trekking excursion.

Insight Nepal has once again lowered its minimum age to 18 though young people might find the conditions they encounter on the programme quite a challenge, as 18-year old Giles Freeman from Australia did a few years ago:

I would advise that applicants do have some teaching practice before coming. Classes easily reach 60 or 80 in many schools, making it necessary for the patient teacher to know what they are doing. With no teaching experience, this has proved a little hard, but it's a great challenge. All in all it has been extremely rewarding.

Bangladesh and Pakistan

The need for English in Bangladesh is frequently replaced by the desperate need for more basic aid, as the country is regularly devastated by floods, water contamination and other natural disasters. But no doubt, schools will be rebuilt and the Bangladeshi people will carry on as they have had to do so many times before. Many schools are willing to take on native-speaker teachers of English, but the usual problems pertain: lack of remuneration and difficulty with visas. Most opportunities are available only to teachers willing to finance themselves and to work on a three-month tourist visa. Security clearance and visa processing can take months, and is very difficult unless you have someone to push for you. The British Council employs eight qualified teachers at its own Teaching Centre in Dhaka, who are recruited in London. The Centre also employs a number of hourly-paid teachers who are recruited locally but the demand for courses fluctuates so much that steady employment cannot be guaranteed. People who are established in Dhaka (like spouses of expat managers, etc.) manage to earn reasonable part-time wages teaching private classes.

Far fewer gap placement agencies and other educational charities send volunteers to Bangladesh than to Nepal. The Daneford Trust has added Bangladesh to the list of countries to which it sends students and school leavers resident in London. The participation fee for a minimum of three months is at least £2,000; details from the Daneford Trust, 45-47 Blythe St, London E2 0LL (tel/fax 020-7729 1928).

Few private language schools exist in Pakistan, though the British Council has four teaching centres (Islamabad, Lahore, Karachi and Peshawar) which employ highly qualified and experienced teachers. For information about employment with the British Council in Pakistan, contact the Manager of the Teaching Centre in Islamabad (PO Box 1135/e-mail: bc.islamabad@bc-islamabad.bcouncil.org). The US counterpart is the Pakistan American Cultural Center (PACC) with seven branches throughout the country; there are two Centers in Karachi; the main one is at 11 Fatima Jinnah Road (e-mail: a-mooraj@cyber.net.pk). There are two Centers in Hyderabad, one in Quetta, one in Sukkur and one in Larkana.

Sri Lanka

In Sri Lanka, attempts have been made to raise the profile of English in order to find some neutral ground between bitterly opposed Tamil and Sinhala language speakers. This has created some demand for foreign teachers, not all of whom are scared off by the threat of terrorism.

For a number of years the organisation, *i-to-i* based in Leeds (0870 333 2332) has been sending teachers to Sri Lanka. The Sri Lankan government has given permission for an increasing number of volunteers to be accepted to teach in state schools and orphanages. To become an 'i-venturer' you need a TEFL qualification (i-to-i run 20-hour courses for those with no previous training) and the ability to cover the placement fee of about £1,200 as well as insurance and travel costs.

Simon Rowland joined the scheme between school in Cambridge and university in York:

> *I am based in a private non-profit making English institute in a town called Binginya. The school, which opened 10 months ago, is run by a local school teacher of English who is very good at English. Additional classes were set up on my arrival for teachers and business people as well as children. The teaching is mostly enjoyable; classes are conducted purely in English (I know no Sinhala) except for when they occasionally communicate in Sinhala, to my disgust and telling off. They are all willing to learn and, I like to think, have mostly improved quite a lot in the three months I've been here.*
>
> *The house I'm living in next to the school is wonderful, as are the meals which are brought to us from another house. The local people are all so friendly and falling over themselves to help me. I'd recommend rural Sri Lanka to anyone and think I've had a unique experience.*

Despite a number of reservations about the level of organisational back-up provided (for example he had no idea where he would be until he arrived in Sri Lanka), Simon had to conclude that without i-to-i, he would never have been able to have the experience.

LIST OF SCHOOLS

India

JAFFE INTERNATIONAL EDUCATION SERVICE
Kunnuparambil Buildings, Kurichy, Kottayam 686549, India. Tel/fax: (481) 430470.
Placement agency for young foreign volunteers to teach in English medium high schools, hotel management colleges, teacher training centres, vocational institutes and language schools in Kerala State. Also places teachers at summer schools in various locations in India.
Preference of nationality: must be proficient in English.
Qualifications: minimum university degree in subject to be taught.
Conditions of employment: placements vary from 2 weeks to 3 months between July and March. Minimum period of 4 weeks at summer schools (between April 1st and May 31st).

Salary: none.
Facilities/Support: free homestays arranged including food. Possibility of free transport from nearest airport. Sightseeing programme arranged.
Recruitment: applications from January 1st.

MUYAL LIANG TRUST
Denjong Padme Cheoling Academy, Pemayangtse, Sikkim, Northern India (UK contact address below).
Possibility of teaching for longer periods in Darjeeling.
Preference of nationality: British, other.
Conditions of employment: maximum stay of 45 days because of Sikkim visa restrictions. School is in session between March and December. British volunteers set their own syllabus in teaching children aged 7-18 English or other subjects.
Salary: none.
Facilities/Support: Indian instructors help volunteers.
Recruitment: via members of the Trust in the UK.
Contact: Jules Stewart, 53 Blenheim Crescent, London W11 2EG, UK (tel/fax 020-7229 4772; JJulesstewart@cs.com).

ROSE (Rural Organization for Social Elevation)
Social Awareness Centre, PO Kanda, Bageshwar, Uttar Pradesh 263631, India.
Preference of nationality: none.
Qualifications: none required. Experience of teaching or living in a developing country useful. Flexibility, sense of humour and positive thinker.
Conditions of employment: grassroots development project which organises range of activities to help this rural community in the Himalayan foothills includes teaching English in the KSS/ROSE office.
Salary: none. Volunteers contribute to their living and food expenses (about £3 per day).
Facilities/Support: accommodation provided in local homes. Hindi instruction available.
Recruitment: further details in UK from Mr Bijon K Sinha and Richard Northridge, Joint Coordinators, Cwm Harry Land Trust, Lower Cwm Harry, Tregynon, Powys SY16 3ES, Wales, UK. Tel/fax: 01686 650231. E-mail: cwmharrylandtrust@hotmail.com. Website: www.cylch.org.uk. Please send an SAE or 3 international reply coupons.

Nepal

ALPHA BETA INSTITUTE
G.P.O. Box, 9026 Putali Sadak, Kathmandu. Tel: (1) 246 668/24197. Fax: (1) 241971. E-mail: alfabeta@cl.com.np.
Number of teachers: 5.
Preference of nationality: British.
Qualifications: practical experience in teaching TOEFL/IELTS and English Language.
Conditions of employment: two-year contract.
Salary: 150 Nepalese rupees per month.
Facilities/Support: school has a private hostel where teachers can be accommodated.
Recruitment: recommendation and interviews.
Contact: Dwiraj Sharma.

INSIGHT NEPAL
PO Box 489, Pokhara, Kaski, Nepal. E-mail: insight@mos.com.np. Website: www.southasia.com/insight.
Number of teachers: 15 volunteers accepted at each of three starting dates.
Preference of nationality: native speakers.
Qualifications: minimum 'A' levels for UK volunteers, high school diploma for

Americans. Age limits 18-60. Teaching or volunteering experience desirable but not necessary.

Conditions of employment: placements last 3 months starting February, August or October. Other dates can be arranged on request.

Salary: none. Programme participation fee is $800. New short-term option called Global Hands lasts 4-6 weeks and costs $400.

Facilities/Support: accommodation and two meals a day provided, usually as homestay. 3-month programme includes pre-orientation, placement in a primary or secondary school in Nepal to teach mainly English or in community development projects, a one-week village or trekking excursion and 3 days in Chitwan National Park.

Recruitment: application forms, $30 non-refundable application fee, 4 photos and introductory letter should be sent 3 months in advance of proposed starting date.

Contact: Naresh Shrestha, Director.

NEW INTERNATIONAL FRIENDSHIP CLUB (NIFC) NEPAL
Post Box 11276, Maharajgunj, Kathmandu, Nepal. Tel: (1) 427406. Fax: (1) 429176. E-mail: fcn@ccsl.com.np
Number of teachers: 40.

Preference of nationality: native speakers.

Qualifications: minimum university degree.

Conditions of employment: 3-5 hours a day teaching English in schools or colleges. Saturday is day off. In Kathmandu, Sunday is also a day off.

Salary: none. Volunteer teachers should contribute $150 per month for their keep (unless they become a project expert). Basic Nepalese standard accommodation is provided and Nepali (rice-based) meals.

Recruitment: direct application preferred by e-mail. Postal enquiries should include 2 international reply coupons.

Contact: Prakash Babu Paudel, President (1-357136).

Pakistan

CATHEDRAL EDUCATION CENTER
1 Sir Syed Road, Peshawar Cantt, Peshawar, Pakistan. Tel: (91) 270812/279734. Fax: (91) 279734. E-mail: humphrey@brain.net.pk or diredu@brain.net.pk
Number of teachers: 8-10.

Preference of nationality: none, but should be native speaker.

Qualifications: degree minimum. Able to teach English language and literature.

Conditions of employment: one to three years.

Salary: 5000-7000 rupees per month.

Facilities/Support: free accommodation and utilities.

Recruitment: through CVs and if possible, telephone interview.

Contact: Raheel Sherazer.

MALAYSIA

For the many Malaysian students who aspire to go to university in the US, Britain or Australia, intensive English language tuition is an essential part of their training. Unfortunately the South East Asian financial crisis means that fewer of their families can afford to send them abroad or even to private English classes than formerly. As proof of the decline, CfBT Education Services recruits for far fewer posts in Malaysia than a few years ago, though it was recently advertising for a project on Multimedia Education.

The government issues work permits only to highly qualified applicants, who have at least an MA. People caught working on tourist visasa can expect to be fined and deported.

The British Council has English Teaching Centres in Kuala Lumpur and Penang;

the former offers the CELTA course throughout the year. According to the British Council in Kuching, institutions in Sabah and Sarawak recruiting teachers from overseas are almost non-existent, apart from Sarawak University. If interested obtain the lists of tuition centres in Sarawak and Kota Kinabalu (Sabah) from the British Council.

Some demand may persist in the business market. Check adverts in the *Malay Mail* though the best way to learn of possible openings is to get to know Kuala Lumpur's expatriate community. The Bangsar English Language Centre in KL has employed foreign teachers to teach Business English in the past (60-1 Jalan Ma'arof Bangsar Baru, 59100 Kuala Lumpur; 3-282 3166-8/fax 3-282 5578).

One aspect of life in Malaysia which can be difficult to accept is that racial Malays are accorded special privileges over other citizens of Chinese, Indian or tribal origins. For example, places at the universities mentioned above are available exclusively to *bumiputeras* or *'bumis'*, which means literally 'sons of the soil', i.e. ethnic Malays. Otherwise teachers normally suffer less from culture shock than they do in Thailand and Indonesia. Kuala Lumpur (KL) is a model of modernity and efficiency when compared to the neighbouring capitals of Jakarta and Bangkok.

SINGAPORE

Malaysia's tiny neighbour clinging to the tip of the Malay peninsula is a wealthy and Westernised city-state in which there is a considerable demand for qualified English teachers on minimum one-year contracts. Once a teacher does get established in a school, freelance teaching is widely available paying from S$30 an hour.

The Foreign Recruitment Unit of the Ministry of Education in Singapore (Kay Siang Road, Singapore 248922; tel 470 9347/4798780; fax 470 4734807) recruits teachers of English Language/English Literature on two to three year contracts in secondary schools. Candidates must have a degree in English and relevant teaching qualifications and have at least three years teaching experience. Salaries are in the range of S$2,073-S$4,116 plus an end-of-year bonus, airfares into/out of Singapore and an end of contract gratuity. Further information is available from the Teacher Recruitment Unit, Contact Singapore, Charles House, 5-11 Regent Street, London SW1Y 4LR; tel 0207-321 5600; fax 020-7321 5601) or in the US (Contact Singapore, 929 Massachusetts Avenue, Suite 02-C, Cambridge, MA 02139; 617-492-9843/e-mail: cscboston@compuserve.com), which is part of the Ministry of Manpower and will refer those interested in teaching in Singapore to the Foreign Recruitment Unit of the Ministry of Education in Singapore.

The British Council at 30 Napier Road has a teaching operation which hires qualified teachers locally and can provide a list of 72 language schools. Many are located in the ubiquitous shopping centres, especially along Orchard Road, for example Ascada Language Centre (no. 437), Berlitz (501), Bunka Private Language School (403), Children's Language School (442), Goro (268), ILC/Syscom (545), Inoue (230), Sunnyvale (218), Thames (268) and Tien Hsia (277). Note that these are not complete postal addresses. The vast majority of these language centres are Chinese-owned with a high proportion of teachers from Australia. The Singapore branch of the main international chains and other important schools are as follows:

Advanced Training Techniques/ATT, 07-01 Tanglin Shopping Centre, 19 Tanglin Road, Singapore 247909 (65-235 5222/fax 65-738 1257; atttpr@singnet. com.sg/ www.tpl.com.sg/tplwww/tes). Several dozen teachers with degree, CELTA and two years experience.

Berlitz Language Centre, 501 Orchard Road, B1-20, Orchard MRT Station, Singapore 238878 (733 7472).

ILC Language and Business Training Centre, 545 Orchard Road 11-07, Far East Shopping Centre, Singapore 238882 (338 5415).

inlingua School of Languages, 1 Grange Road 04-01 Orchard Building, Singapore

239693 (737 6666). Other branch in the Clementi Arcade.

Singapore is not a recommended destination for the so-called 'teacher-traveller' who, without qualifications but with a smart pair of trousers, hopes to be able to impress a language school owner. Even people who have qualifications cannot count on walking into a job. However, there are exceptions, and persistent enquiries have resulted in the offer of hourly work (at about S$25 an hour).

With the necessary documents (copies of education certificates, medical certificate, etc.), getting an Employment Pass or Work Permit is fairly straightforward if you have a sponsoring employer. The Singapore High Commission (9 Wilton Crescent, London SW1X 8BR) will send a fact sheet which explains that people earning monthly income of S$2,000 or less need to apply for a Work Permit from the Work Permit Department, Ministry of Manpower, 18 Havelock Road, Singapore 059764 (65-438 5122/ www.gov.sg/mom/ftawp.htm) and those earning more than $2,000 need to apply for an Employment Pass at the Singapore Immigration & Registration Building, Ministry of Manpower, 5th level, SIR Building, 10 Kallang Road, Singapore 208718 (tel 65-438 5122 or 2975443; www.gov.sg/mom/fta/ep/ftaep.htm).

According to Lee Boon Hwee of the Singapore Immigration and Registration (at the above address) tourists are granted a 14-30 days Social Visit Pass if they meet entry requirements including a passport with at least 6 months validity and a

After 6 months of wandering around India, it may be difficult to present the right image

confirmed onward ticket/sufficient funds for the period of stay in Singapore. If they wish to remain in Singapore longer than the validity of the Social Visit Pass, they can apply for an extension of stay at the Visitor Services Centre on the fourth floor of the SIR building; this application must be supported by a local sponsor. The SIR website is www.sir.gov.sg and for e-mail: SIR_feedback@sir.gov.sg.

Bryn Thomas taught for inlingua, but broke his contract half way through the first year:

This was the only contract I broke, but then so did many of the other teachers. It wasn't just the school but the place. Singapore may be a great place for a short shopping spree but unless you like living in a shopping mall, the place isn't much fun for an extended visit and certainly not for a 1½ year contract, unless the pay is on a par with the money you can earn in the Middle East or Japan.

If shopping malls and a repressive regime (for example there are signs threatening to fine you if you fail to flush the loo or eat on the underground) leave you cold, Singapore is perhaps best avoided.

GEOS LANGUAGE CENTRE
400 Orchard Road, 14-07 Orchard Towers, Singapore 238875. Tel: (65) 734 7556. Fax: (65) 737 5856. E-mail: geosing@pacific.sg
Number of teachers: 9.
Preference of nationality: none, but should be native English speaker.
Qualifications: minimum degree in any discipline.
Conditions of employment: 6 months to a year.
Salary: negotiable depending on experience and qualifications.
Facilities/Support: no assistance given with accommodation. Work permit arranged.
Recruitment: via local newspapers. CVs welcome at any time to keep on file.
Contact: Brett Olsen or Florence Goh.

NYU LANGUAGE CENTRE
The Adelphi 04-35, 1 Coleman St, Singapore 179803. Tel: (65) 338 3533. Fax: (65) 338 4680. E-mail: nyulang@hotmail.com.
Number of teachers: 5.
Preference of nationality: American, British.
Qualifications: degree with teaching experience in English.
Conditions of employment: 1 year contracts. Hours 9.30am-5.30pm Monday to Friday.
Salary: S$2,500-S$3,000.
Facilities/Support: help given with work permits.
Recruitment: via advertisements or recommendation.
Contact: Nance Teo, Principal.

TRANSLINGUAL LANGUAGE CENTRE
3 Coleman Street, Peninsula Shopping Complex, Singapore 179804. Tel: (65) 339 7071. Fax: (65) 339 6568.
Number of teachers: average 5.
Preference of nationality: none, but should be native speaker.
Qualifications: degree in English literature or linguistics/experience in TEFL teaching.
Conditions of employment: 1 year minimum.
Salary: S$2,400+.
Facilities/Support: help not generally given with finding accommodation. Work permits arranged by the school after the teacher has produced the necessary documents for processing.
Recruitment: embassies, high commissions, newspapers. Face-to-face interview not essential.
Contact: Ms. Chan Lai Chun, Principal.

VIETNAM

The demand for English in Vietnam, Cambodia and Laos is phenomenal. In the beginning, opportunities were mainly voluntary and in refugee camps. But there is now a booming commercial market supplying English language training, particularly in Vietnam. The lifting of the US trade embargo a few years ago made it possible for foreign firms to move in to Hanoi and to a lesser extent Ho Chi Minh City, all looking for staff with some knowledge of English. The departure of the UN from Cambodia had a similar effect. Many joint ventures require varying degrees of professionalism in their native speaker teachers. In the provinces, there is very little competition to meet the demand for English.

Government agencies (both local and foreign), international aid organisations and religious groups all remain active in the region, offering extensive development and relief assistance including English language programmes. Many of the people wanting to learn English are doing so in order to be able to apply to institutes of higher learning overseas, so anyone with a background in EAP (English for Academic Purposes) will have a distinct advantage.

VSO carries out an energetic campaign to recruit TEFL teachers for the region but still can't fulfil all the requests they receive. They require a degree plus TEFL certificate and minimum six months' experience.

The demand for English has exploded in Vietnam. Volunteers and teachers are needed in the private and public sector, especially in academic institutes. Demand is strongest in the south where most of the wealth remains. The British Council in Hanoi can supply a list of 13 English teaching institutions in Hanoi and elsewhere while the Council office in Ho Chi Minh City can send a dozen addresses in HCMC. One that has been advertising extensively is the International Language Academy (part of the Nord Anglia Group – see entry in *Finding a Job*). They have many vacancies in Ho Chi Minh City; e-mail ila@hcm.vnn.vn for details. They pay their teachers US$1,200 per month for adult classes and US$850 for children's classes.

Sadly the Britain-Vietnam Friendship Society project to send English teachers to Vietnam is no longer in existence. Len Aldis, who formerly organised the project, recommends anyone interested in teaching English in Vietnam should enquire through the British Council, VSO and Christians Abroad's World Service Enquiry (www.wse.org.uk). Mr Aldis has had so many requests for teachers while travelling in Vietnam that he is considering restarting his project, so details may reappear here in future years.

Americans can contact Volunteers in Asia (650-723-3228/fax 650-725-1805; volasia@volasia.org/ www.volasia.org) which organises one year posts teaching English in Vietnam as a volunteer (expenses and stipend provided).

It may be possible to change a tourist visa into a business visa after finding an employer and leaving the country while the visa is processed. The police are reported to take an interest in the visa status and activities generally of foreigners. The daily Vietnamese paper *Nguoi Vet* publishes its Thursday edition in English, so check for adverts.

LIST OF SCHOOLS

APOLLO EDUCATION CENTRE
67 Le Van Huu, Hanoi. Tel: (4) 9432051. Fax: (4) 9432052. E-mail: Apollo@hn.vnn.vn.
Number of teachers: 16.
Preference of nationality: none (British, American, Canadian, Australian).
Qualifications: CELTA or equivalent.
Conditions of employment: 1 or 2 year contracts. 22 h.p.w.
Salary: varies according to qualifications and experience.
Facilities/Support: accommodation provided. Visa sponsorship given.

Recruitment: adverts in international press. Interviews available in UK and Thailand.
Contact: Margaret Twelves, Director of Studies.

ASIAN INSTITUTE OF TECHNOLOGY CENTER IN VIETNAM
Language and Training Unit, 21 Le Thanh Tong, GPO Box 136, Hanoi. Tel: (4) 825 3493 ext. 18. Fax: (4) 824 5490. E-mail: itu@netnam.org.vn.
Number of teachers: 3.
Preference of nationality: none.
Qualifications: at least 5 years' experience and preferably a Masters degree.
Conditions of employment: 2 months. Hours are from 8.30am-11.30am and 1.30pm-4.30pm.
Salary: US$20 per hour.
Facilities/Support: some assistance with finding accommodation. No assistance with work permit.
Recruitment: word-of-mouth. Interviews.
Contact: Michelle Noullet.

B.E.S.T. SERVICES
Better English Skills Today, 32A Cao Ba Nha, Ward Nguyen Cu Trinh, District 1, Ho Chi Minh City. Tel: (8) 837 3437. Fax: (8) 837 3438. E-mail: best.hcm@fmail.vnn.vn.
Number of teachers: several also for affiliate centres of B.E.S.T. in HCMC.
Contact: Nguyen Thi My Anh, Director.

DUONG MINH LANGUAGE SCHOOLS
424 Hai Ba Trung Street, District 1, Ho Chi Minh City.
132C Phan Nang Luu Street, Phu Nhuan District, Ho Chi Minh City.
60 Vo Thi Sau Street, District 1, Ho Chi Minh City.
Tel: 84-8 9902584, 84-8 8438099. Fax: 84-8 8447087. E-mail: nnduongminh@hcm.vnn.vn.
Number of teachers: 4-6.
Preference of nationality: American, British, Australian, Canadian or New Zealand.
Qualifications: university degrees and 1 year of teaching experience. In addition to the above, the school may need two teachers from North America, Australia or New Zealand to take over a special course of advanced and TOEFL level starting at the end of May.
Conditions of employment: 6 month contracts. Approximately 10 h.p.w. in first instance.
Salary: US$10 for 1¹/₂ hour session.
Facilities/Support: can advise teachers on finding a guest house or apartment at reasonable cost. No help given with work permits, but can assist in extending visas.
Recruitment: local interview essential.
Contact: Mr. Duong Minh, Principal.

HANOI INTERNATIONAL COLLEGE
87 Tho Nhuom Street, Hoan Kiem District, Hanoi. Tel: (4) 826 7451/826 5402. Fax: (4) 8267451. E-mail: htts@fpt.vn.
Number of teachers: one or two (volunteers only).
Preference of nationality: none, but must be native speakers. Most recently 2 Americans took the posts.
Qualifications: BA and MA, experience of teaching English, IT, Office and business managment and can teach accountancy and trade correspondence.
Conditions of employment: willing to work 6-12 months for 6-8 hours a day as volunteer.
Salary: Stipend of US$300-$600 monthly depending on the volume of teaching and qualifications.
Facilities/Support: assistance with accommodation and transportation. Live in self-

contained flat and walk or bicycle to school. Assistance given with work permits.
Recruitment: usually by word of mouth and through contacts at international universities.
Contact: Nguyen Van Minh, Director.

Other Schools to Try

Most of these addresses have been provided by the British Council in Hanoi and Ho Chi Minh City:

AIT, 21 Le Thanh Tong, Hanoi

Centre for External Professionalism & Expertise, Cooperation and Exchange, 14 Le Thanh Tong, Hanor

Hanoi University for Foreign Study, Km 8, Nguyen Trai Road, Hanoi

Language Link, 64 Nguyen Truong To Street, Hanoi (4-829 4844)

*MAY 19th FOREIGN LANGUAGES, MARKETING & INFORMATION CENTRE, 62 Hang Dau St, Hanoi (tel/fax 4-825 0282)

United Nations International School, c/o Hanoi-Amsterdam School, Giang Vo, Hanoi

*CENTRE FOR FOREIGN LANGUAGES, College of Agriculture & Forestry, Vietnam National University, Ap An Nhon, Xa Tan Phu, Thu Duc District, Ho Chi Minh City (8-896 0109/896 7808/fax 8-896 3349; dhthinh@hcm.vnn.vn)

College of Social Sciences & Humanities, Foreign Language Centre, 10-12 Dinh Tien Hoang St, District 1, Ho Chi Minh City

ELT Lotus, 8 Nguyen Cong Trang St, District 1, Ho Chi Minh City

English School 2000, 70 Dinh Tien Hoang St, District 1, Ho Chi Minh City

Ho Chi Minh University of Education, Foreign Language Centre, 280 An Duong Vuong St., District 5, Ho Chi Minh City

International English School, 101C Nguyen Van Cu St, District 5, Ho Chi Minh City

International Grammar School, HCM, 236 Nam Ky Khoi Nghia St, District 3, Ho Chi Minh City

London English School, 82 Ly Chinh Thang St, District 3, Ho Chi Minh City

SEAMEO, 35 Le Thanh Ton St, District 1, Ho Chi Minh City

TESCAN, 35 Le Thanh Ton St, District 1, Ho Chi Minh City

Vietnam America Society, 190 Pasteur St, District 3, Ho Chi Minh City (8-829 4834/fax 8-823 6002; ctavhvm@netnam2.org.vn).

CAMBODIA

The UN was virtually in charge of Cambodia until 1994 when it withdrew, leaving the market wide open to private enterprise. Although the major aid agencies like VSO still supply the majority of English teachers to Cambodia, the private sector is now flourishing. Foreign ministries and government offices are all keen to sign up for private lessons as are the diplomatic corps and their families as well as the military. The British Council does not maintain an office in Phnom Penh.

After travelling to Cambodia a few years ago, Murray Turner was impressed by the demand for English teachers:

In Cambodia they are so desperate for English teachers that I met more Dutch, Germans and Scandinavians teaching English than Brits or Yanks. Cambodia is one of the most beautiful South East Asian countries I visited and the people are among the friendliest.

Mark Vetare corroborated this on a visit to Phnom Penh:

Just rent yourself a moto for the day and have a spin around Phnom Penh. There's virtually a school on every corner. Not all schools employ native speakers (aka monkeys) since many poor Khmer can't afford them. Pay and

hours are the main problems for teachers. Time was when you could get four hours a day. Now you've got to stick around for the better times and more hours. Things are becoming more stringent in the 'real' schools. That being said, it's backpacker heaven: young men with long hair, good (but not necessarily native) English and no high level education still get jobs.

Wages for casual teachers are about $6 an hour in a country where you can live comfortably on $10 a day. Qualified EFL teachers can earn double or even treble that amount. Cambodia still operates on a dollar economy, so few wages are quoted in riels. Visa extensions are harder than they used to be since the authorities are anxious to prevent drug smuggling and sex tourism. Tourists are now being given one-month visas which are non-extendable. Tourist visas obtained in Ho Chi Minh City, have 'Employment Prohibited' stamped on them. Those who want to work should try to get a business visa at the airport, claiming (for example) to be involved in some export business.

Cambodia is still a volatile country, struggling to emerge from the shadow of its past and of its neighbours. Political instability means that it is difficult to feel safe and settled there. Incidents involving firearms are commonplace, and people are regularly robbed at gun point in Phnom Penh.

One of the longest established schools is the Australian Centre for Education or ACE (PO Box 860, Phnom Penh, Cambodia; 23-724204/fax 23-426608) which employs upwards of 30 teachers with at least the CELTA or Trinity TESOL. In addition there are many other commercial institutes like the American School for Language Arts, Piey Sianouk Raj Academy and Regent College in Phnom Penh. Opportunities can also be created in Kampong Sum, Siem Reap and Batambang.

LAOS & MYANMAR

Laos was the last country in the region to open its doors to foreigners. When English institutes began opening in the Laotian capital of Vientiane in the 1990s, most were fly-by-night operations. But there are some respectable schools now (in addition to the college whose entry appears below) such as the Lao American Language Center, 152 Sisangvone Road, Saysettha, Ban Naxay, PO Box 327, Vientiane (21-41 4321/fax 21-41 3760). These schools can help their teachers to obtain a long-stay visa since the tourist visa is valid for a maximum of two weeks. With a letter of invitation from a sponsoring organisation, you can apply for a one-month visa which can then be extended.

Matthew Williams visited Laos on one of his frequent visa trips from neighbouring Thailand and reported that the hourly rate of pay for teachers was higher than in Bangkok, yet the cost of living was far less. Vientiane is quieter and more free of hassles, not to say more boring, than other cities in Indo-China.

Surprisingly, the new regime in Myanmar (formerly Burma) has retained English as a major language and theoretically there might be scope for teaching the military rulers and businessmen (albeit for negligible wages). But as Mark Vetare says of the country, 'it is truly a place to champion the poor not cater to the murderers and thieves who run the country.' Many organisations recommend boycotting Myanmar completely to avoid bringing any wealth or comfort to the leaders. Interested teachers should find out more from Amnesty International or Tourism Concern in London (020-7753 3330; www.tourismconcern.org.uk).

The British Council has a list of about 15 English teaching centres in Yangon (formerly Burma) including Y.E.S. in the YWCA Building and the US Cultural Centre at 14 Tawwin Road (Dagon Township).

VIENTIANE UNIVERSITY COLLEGE
PO Box 4144, Vientiane, Lao PDR. Tel: (21) 414873/414052. Fax: (21) 414346. E-mail: vtcollege@laonet.net. Website: www.geocities.com/vientianecollege.

Number of teachers: 25.
Preference of nationality: none.
Qualifications: minimum bachelors degree and CELTA. ESP/EAP experience preferred.
Conditions of employment: sessional and contract.
Salary: from $1,200-$2,000 per month less 10% income tax.
Facilities/Support: assistance with finding accommodation. School arranges and pays for work permit and residence visa. In-house training programme.
Recruitment: personal interview necessary.

GARDEN INTERNATIONAL EDUCATION CENTRE
54 Pyay Road, Hlaing Tsp, Yangon, Myanmar. Tel: (1) 247682. Fax: (1) 513552. E-mail: garden@mptmail.net.mm.
Number of teachers: 5.
Preference of nationality: none, but should be native speaker.
Qualifications: degree and Cert. plus a minimum of a year's experience teaching anywhere.
Conditions of employment: two-year contract. Working hours between 8am and 2.30pm Monday to Friday.
Salary: according to hours worked, qualifications and experience.
Facilities/Support: can assist with finding accommodation or contract package may include accommodation.
Recruitment: via newspapers. Interviews not essential.
Contact: Ms. Siu Ling.

YANGON INTERNATIONAL EDUCARE
No. W-22, Mya Kan Thar Main Road, Mya Kan Thar Housing, 5th Quarter, Hlaing Township, Yangon, Myanmar. Tel: (1) 6822231/682672/724483. Fax: (1) 665904. E-mail: yiec.ygn@mptmail.net.mm.
Number of teachers: 7.
Preference of nationality: none; native speakers preferred.
Qualifications: bachelor's degree at least. Experience in primary or middle schools would be useful.
Conditions of employment: 1-2 year contracts at this international school. Hours of teaching 8.30am-3.30pm.
Salary: 1,500 kyat less 5% local tax deductions.
Facilities/Support: assistance with locating housing, maintenance and some furnishing. Assistance with complicated procedures in obtaining work permit.
Recruitment: locally, ads in Bangkok newspapers, recruitment fairs in Asia. Interviews necessary.
Contact: David A. Schaefer, Director.

Taiwan

Taiwan remains a magnet for English teachers of all backgrounds and the ELT industry is booming. It managed to escape the Asian economic crisis, and was able to absorb 'refugee' teachers from elsewhere in the region, principally Korea. The hiring policy is virtually universal in Taiwan: all they are looking for is a BA and a pulse.

Hundreds of private cramming institutes or *bushibans* continue to teach young children and high school students for university entrance examinations. The market for teaching children from about age three seems boundless at the moment, so anyone who enjoys working with primary age children, i.e. likes to sing songs, play games and comfort little ones who miss their mums, will have a good chance of finding work. Women are often considered to have an advantage in this regard, and also tend to be preferred by the mothers of female pupils. Employers in this field generally provide detailed lesson plans which means that little time needs to be spent on lesson preparation.

Many well-established legal language schools are prepared to sponsor foreign teachers for a resident visa, provided the teacher is willing to work for at least one year. Only native speaker teachers with a university degree (in any subject) are eligible. Taiwanese consumers of English have a clear preference for the American accent because of strong trading and cultural links between Taiwan and the US However many schools will hire presentable native speakers whatever their accent. Few want their staff to be able to speak Chinese; in fact one teacher reported seeing a sign in a *bushiban* window boasting 'Teachers Not Speak Chinese.' Language teachers and tutors working in Taipei are predominantly American; native speakers of other nationalities tend to gravitate to southern Taiwan. Amanda Searle from the UK felt only slightly discriminated against:

> *My employer claimed that they did not discriminate between people of different nationalities, but this is not what I have found. North Americans are the first choice when hours are allocated. I have had students complain that they wanted an American teacher because they wanted to learn 'real' English, though I have never had a student complain to me or the secretaries that my accent was difficult to understand.*

FIXING UP A JOB

A few of the major organisations hire overseas. The *Hess Educational Organisation* (see entry below), which specialises in teaching primary school aged children, has a US office whose function is primarily to send out information to enquirers. Interviews are conducted either in Taiwan or by telephone from Taiwan. The US-based franchise ELS International (see *Finding a Job, International ELT Organisations*) has 18 schools in Taiwan and is expanding. It employs more than 300 English teachers and the Academic Director there, Prentice Berge, welcomes direct applications (ELSI, 6F, No 9, Lane 90, Sung Chiang Road, Taipei, Taiwan; e-mail elsjobs@ms54.hinet.net). Alternatively you can e-mail the Head of Recruitment: elsikk@tp.silkera.net or check out the details on the website www.elstaiwan.com. The minimum starting salary for 25 hours per week is NT$50,000 (approx. US$1,600). For addresses of ELS International schools, see school listings below.

Another giant in the field is Epact Educational Services which are looking for recent graduates to join their Teach in Taiwan programme for a minimum of a year. Details are available on www.teachtaiwan.com or by e-mailing apply@teachtaiwan.com. Another website worth investigating if you would like to teach English while studying Mandarin is www.eslhouseonline.com. An agent called Jenny Lai undertakes to match teachers with schools. She charges teachers a commission of 20% of their first month's pay and can be reached by telephone on 2-2362 1695 or fax 2-2363 5424.

The YMCA in the USA runs an organised recruitment programme for Taiwan (see entry for *Overseas Service Corps*). You can also apply direct to the YMCA of Taiwan (see entry). As in Japan, the YMCA is a major provider of English language courses and is considered a good employer. There is a small British Council office in Taipei (c/o the Educational & Cultural Section, British Trade & Cultural Office, 7F-1, 99 Jen Ai Road, Section 2, Taipei 10625; e-mail: inquiries@britcoun.org.tw) but it is unlikely to be of much use to job-seekers.

Many people arrive on spec to look for work. Finding a *bushiban* willing to hire you is not as difficult as finding a *good* one willing to hire you. If possible, try to sit in on one or two classes or talk to another teacher before signing a contract. (If a school is unwilling to permit this, it doesn't bode well.)

The best time to arrive is at the beginning of summer (the end of the school year), when Chinese parents enrol their offspring in English language summer schools. Late August is another peak time for hiring, though there are openings year-round. Always check the Positions Vacant column of the English language *China Post* and the *China News* though work tends to result from personal referrals more than from advertising. Word-of-mouth is even more important in Taiwan than elsewhere because there is no association of recognised language schools. Furthermore there is no English language Yellow Pages.

If you want to meet foreigners who are clued up about the current teaching situation, try visiting well-known Taipei hostels or pubs. One of the best hostels is the Formosa on Chung Shan N Rd, Sec.2, Lane 20, No. 16 3rd Floor (2-2562 2035) which charges about $10 a night for long stays. A good notice board is located in the student lounge on the sixth floor of the Mandarin Training Center of National Taiwan Normal University at 129 Hoping East Road. You might also make useful expat contacts in Taipei at the Community Services Centre, 25 Lane 290 Chung Shan North Rd, Sec. 6, Tien Mu (2-2836 8134) or at the Gateway Community Centre, 7Fl, 248 Chung Shan North Rd, Sec. 6, Tien Mu (2-2833 7444).

Once you have decided to approach some schools for work, make contact by e-mail or telephone in the first place, possibly from the Taipei Railway Station or the Northgate GPO Telegraph Office where there are private cubicles. Next you must present yourself in person to the schools. In order to get around Taipei you should invest in the invaluable English language *Taipei Bus Guide* available from Caves Books (corner of Chung Shan Road and Minsheng E. Road) or Lucky Book Store in the university. Take along your university certificate and any other qualifications, and take the trouble to look presentable. Peter McGuire was told point blank that

Spruce up your sock collection

your appearance and how you conduct yourself at interview count for everything, and concluded that 'all your experience in life or teaching in other countries really doesn't mean a thing here.' David Hughes specifically recommends paying attention to your feet:

> *Bring plenty of socks/tights. You have to leave your shoes at the door of Chinese homes, and it's difficult to appear serious and composed with a toe poking through.*

Anyone with a high level of education (i.e. MA or PhD) might find work attached to one of the scores of universities and colleges, where working conditions are very good. Foreigners are also allowed to work in public high schools, though it is difficult to function without a knowledge of Taiwanese.

Freelance Teaching

Work visas are valid only for employment with the sponsoring employer. However many teachers teach private students, which pays about NT$600 per hour. In a country where foreigners are sometimes approached in bars or on trains and asked to give English lessons, it is not hard to set up independently as an English tutor. Peter McGuire found the dream job of tutoring a travel agent three to six hours a day, seven days a week and then was invited to accompany his client on a trip to Hawaii:

> *Some of my lessons are given at private clubs, saunas, in taxicabs and fine restaurants. Actually, it's kind of unbelievable.*

A helpful hint is to have business cards printed up, calling yourself 'English consultant'. It is even more lucrative if you can muster a small group of students and charge them, say, NT$300 per person. Women normally find this easier to set up than men. The main problem is finding appropriate premises.

Cancelled hours are a perennial problem. Freelancers will find it prudent to explain to students gently but forcefully that they will be liable to pay if they cancel without giving sufficient notice; most will not object. You can even request one month's fees in advance. Once you are established, other jobs in the English field may come your way such as correcting business faxes, transcribing lyrics from pop tapes or writing CVs and letters of application for Taiwanese students hoping to study overseas.

REGULATIONS

Working on a visitor visa is still possible but risky since the regulations are strictly enforced. Furthermore, without a resident visa/card (A.R.C.), it will be difficult to exchange any excess earnings into dollars. Information on visas should be requested from the Taiwan overseas office in your country of origin. The Taipei Representative Office in the UK is at 50 Grosvenor Gardens, London SW1W 0EB (020-7396 9152/fax 020-7396 9144). You will need the original of your university or college diploma, a medical report from an approved doctor (much more cheaply done in Taiwan) and a signed contract. The procedures are similar for US citizens. Details may be obtained from the Co-ordination Council for North American Affairs (CCNAA, 4201 Wisconsin Avenue NW, Washington, DC 20016-2137; 202-895-1800).

If you are entering Taiwan without a pre-arranged contract you should obtain a 60-day Visitor's Visa before arrival which can be single entry or multiple entry (£25 or £50). Otherwise you will be given permission to stay for just the two weeks (non-extendable) that tourists are granted. Once you find a government-approved school willing to sign a contract for at least 20 hours a week, your employer should apply for a Resident Visa. This will take four to six weeks and will require the same documents as above: your degree diploma(s) must be translated into 3 notarised Chinese copies which costs about NT$500 (approx US$15). You have to have the original (not copy) of your degree, a rigorous medical examination involving eight tests (requiring blood, urine and stool samples) at a cost of about NT$1,500. To change your status, you will have to leave the country; a round trip to Hong Kong costs at least NT$6,500 which some schools will pay. To change from a Visitor to a resident costs about NT$1,800 (approx. US$60) at the Foreign Affairs Department. The applicant then has to go to the Foreign Affairs Police to get the actual Residence Alien Certificate, which costs an additional NT$1,000. Some schools may make a contribution towards permit costs when the contract is renewed for a further year. For instance, the *Taipei Language Institute* pays for the medical and translation costs.

If your tourist visa is due to expire before you have arranged a resident visa, you will also have to leave Taiwan to renew your tourist visa, and have a plausible reason why you want to remain in the country. If you claim to need an extension because you are studying Chinese, you can expect a spot test in Mandarin. (It is not clear if the same applies if you're a student of Kung Fu.)

Tax

After the work visa has been issued, tax will be withheld from your pay. The tax rate for foreigners who stay in Taiwan for less than 183 days in one calendar year is 20%. After six months, the rate of tax drops to 6%. Once residency is established, it is possible to apply for a substantial rebate. All teachers must file their tax return before March 31st and refunds are issued by the end of August. There is a levy of NT$1,200 a month for health insurance *(Lao Bao)* though many schools pay all or a substantial part of this deduction.

CONDITIONS OF WORK

The majority of schools pay NT$500 an hour (gross) though occasionally the rate for cushy morning classes drops below and unsociable hours are rewarded (if you're lucky) with a premium rate of NT$600-$700. Rates outside Taipei (where the cost of living is lower) tend to be slightly higher due to the relative scarcity of teachers.

As usual some schools are shambolic when it comes to timetabling their teachers' hours. In a profit-driven atmosphere, classes start and finish on demand and can be cancelled at short notice if the owner decides that there are too few pupils to make it economic. When you are starting a new job, ask your employer to be specific about the actual number of hours you will be given. Although exploitation of teachers (and pupils) is not as rife as in Korea, you should be prepared for anything, as Rusty Holmes had to be:

> *The real reason there was such a high turnover rate of staff at one school was because of the supervisor's habit of barging into class at unpredictable moments and accusing the teacher (especially my Scottish colleague) of mispronouncing words, when she herself could barely speak English. The worst incidents occurred when she beat her own children in the face for getting poor grades, when she engaged a parent in a fistfight over a tuition dispute, and when she physically ran her husband out of the school, all right in front of our students.*

Rusty Holmes had gone to Taiwan with the intention of doing some serious teaching of business English to adults (on the basis of his law degree) but was disappointed to find that for most other foreign teachers, it was just a financial refuelling station for further travels:

> *I wound up teaching everyone from two year old Taiwanese babies to 60 year old Japanese businessmen. One of my jobs was in a small remote town on Taiwan's east coast. I had been lured to this God-forsaken place by an ad in the* China Post *promising 15 hours a week and a work visa. Once I got settled in, the hours dwindled to nine (just enough to break even) and the distant*

uncle in Taipei was unable to apply for the visa after all. Many teachers either burn out or become so disgruntled with the management that they are more than willing to leave when their tourist visa expires.

The usual problems which bedevil TEFL teachers occur in Taiwan, such as split shifts, often ending at 10pm, and compulsory weekend work, especially if you are teaching children. Few schools provide much creative training or incentives to do a good job. Like the educational system of China and so many other countries, Taiwanese state schools rely heavily on rote learning, making it difficult to introduce a more communicative approach, especially at the beginner level.

Whereas some schools offer no guidance whatsoever, others leave almost nothing to the teacher. What is termed a 'training programme' often consists of a paint-by-number teaching manual. Here is an extract from the Teacher's Book of one major chain of schools:

> *How to teach ABCs (e.g. the letter K): Review A-J... Using the flash cards, say 'A – apple, B – boy, C – cat... J – jacket'. The whole class repeats after the teacher. Then say, 'A-B-C-D-E-F-G-H-I-J' and have the whole class repeat. Show the letter K flashcard. Say 'K' having the whole class repeat it each time you say it. Say 'K' 4 or 5 times.*

And so on. This certainly makes the inexperienced teacher's job easier but possibly also very boring. Not everyone can be comfortable with such a regimented curriculum.

LEISURE TIME

Flats are predictably expensive in central Taipei so many teachers choose to commute from the suburbs, where living conditions are more pleasant in any case. Rents in the moderate sized town of Chiayi are NT$10,000-NT$12,000 for a three-bedroom apartment, so a flat share shouldn't cost much more than NT$5,000 plus about NT$1,500 for utilities. There are so many foreigners coming and going, and the locals are so friendly and helpful, that it is not too difficult to learn of flats becoming vacant. You will have to pay a month's rent in advance plus a further month's rent as a deposit; this bond or 'key money' usually amounts to £300-£400.

Taipei now has a rapid transit system which is far more enjoyable (and cheaper) than running a motorbike. Some teachers stay in hostels near the central station and commute to work in a satellite city where wages are higher than in Taipei (e.g. Tao Yuan and Chung Li). Dorm beds start at NT$250 a night.

Not a single visitor to Taipei, which is one of the most densely populated cities in the world, fails to complain of the pollution, second only to that of Mexico City. Not only is the air choked with the fumes and noise of a million motorised vehicles, but apparently chemicals have infiltrated the water table contaminating locally grown vegetables. It is really horrific. The weather is another serious drawback. The typhoon season lasts from July to October bringing stormy wet weather and mouldy clothes. The heat and humidity at this time also verge on the unbearable.

Taipei is not the only city to suffer from pollution; Taichung and Kaohsiung are also bad. Even Tainan with two-thirds of a million people has some pollution; 100 new cars are registered here every day adding to the problem. (This is a statistic which rather detracts from Tainan's appeal as the most historic city on the island with many old temples, etc.) Kaohsiung on the south-west coast is a large industrial city with a high crime rate but has the advantage of being near the popular resort of Kenting Beach. The geographical advantage of Taichung further north is proximity to the mountains as well as a good climate and cultural activities. The east coast is more tranquil, though some find it dull.

Taipei has a 24-hour social scene which can seriously cut into savings. Heavy drinking is commonplace. Films (which are usually in English with Chinese subtitles) cost about US$10. The serious saver will follow David Hughes' example and join the local library. For the truly homesick there are some English-style pubs with pool tables and darts boards. For Rusty Holmes, the food was a highlight:

Eating out is just as much a pastime in Taiwan as it is in Hong Kong. There are countless little mom-and-pop restaurants which offer delicious and inexpensive food. My favourite is the US$4 black pepper steak. Considering the high price of food in supermarkets, it would be cheaper to eat out than to cook at home. Taiwan is also a fruit-lover's paradise, though most are expensive by American standards. My favourite is the outstanding sugarcane Taiwan produces.

LIST OF SCHOOLS

CANADIAN-AMERICAN LANGUAGE SCHOOLS
2 Chien Hua Street, 2nd Floor, Hsinchu. Tel: (3) 562 0535. Fax: (3) 561 6905. E-mail: management@can-am.org. Website: www.can-am.org.
Number of teachers: 5-6 native English speakers.
Preference of nationality: Canadian or American.
Qualifications: BA/BSc plus one year of teaching or teaching/caring for young learners. Experience and teaching certification if possible. Interest in teaching children essential.
Conditions of employment: 1-year contract beginning August 1st or February 1st. School hours are Monday to Friday daytime and every other Saturday morning and teachers have to check the teaching schedule on the school website.
Salary: first year teachers earn New Taiwan $65,000 approximately per month (approximately US$21,000 per year). Deductions for tax are: withholding tax 20% in the first 180 days and 6% thereafter. Teachers join the school health insurance scheme.
Facilities/Support: assistance with finding accommodation near the school and close to the amenities of downtown Hsinchu. School applies for residence card (A.R.C.) and work visa on teacher's arrival.
Recruitment: by application and interview only, twice yearly. Deadline for August start is May 10; deadline for February start is November 10. Interviews essential and are conducted in Taipei, Hong Kong, Vancouver, Toronto and New York.
Contact: Alex Au Yong, Operations Manager.

CHING-SHAN LANGUAGE INSTITUTE
98 Hsin-Seng S. Rd, Sec. 3, 3F, Taipei 106. Tel: (2) 2366 1855 ext 15. Fax: (2) 2363 0650. E-mail: yehr@ms29.hinet.net. Website: www.chingshan.com.tw.
Number of teachers: 10+.
Preference of nationality: none, but must be native speaker.
Qualifications: university graduate.
Conditions of employment: 6 months. School hours are 9am-10pm.
Salary: US$20 per hour on average less 12% tax and health insurance deductions.
Facilities/support: no assistance with accommodation.
Recruitment: native speakers in Taiwan usually call in to the office and apply in person.
Contact: Ralph Yeh, Deputy Director.

ELITE LANGUAGE INSTITUTE
7F, 238, Hsing-Roung Road, Chiayi 600. Tel: (5) 223 3777. Fax: (5) 222 7661. Website: www.elite-inst.com.tw.
Number of teachers: varies.
Preference of nationality: none, but should be native speaker.
Qualifications: BA with a teacher training qualification.
Conditions of employment: one year contract. Long hours.
Salary: US$1500 to $2,000 per month (depending on hours and experience).
Facilities/Support: accommodation subsidy, health and accident insurance

provided. Local trips organised twice annually.
Recruitment: via the internet mostly.
Contact: Dr. Hsing Cheng.

ELS INTERNATIONAL
12 Kuling St, Taipei. Tel: (2) 2321 9005. Fax: (2) 2397 2304. E-mail: elsikk@tp.silkera.net. Website: www.elstaiwan.com. Also 6F, No. 9, Sung Chiang Road, Taipei. Tel: (2) 2581 8511.
Affiliated to ELS International (see introductory section *Finding a Job*).
Number of teachers: 200-300 (13 locations in Taipei plus 3 in Kaohsiung and 2 in Taichung).
Preference of nationality: passport holders of USA, Canada, UK, Australia, South Africa, Ireland or New Zealand.
Qualifications: BA/BSc minimum. Relevant qualifications preferred.
Conditions of employment: 1 year contracts. Morning and evening work. Pupils range in age from 13 to 60.
Salary: approximately NT$500 (£11) per hour or NT$50, 000 per month. Bonuses paid at end of contract, calculated according to number of hours taught.
Facilities/Support: no assistance with accommodation. Training provided.
Recruitment: direct application/walk-ins. Local interviews compulsory. Applicants may be asked to teach a sample lesson. Original of college diploma should be brought.
Contact: Luisa Sia, Academic Director.

ELS INTERNATIONAL
11 Cheng Chang Road, 3F Taichung. Tel: (4) 2233432. Fax: (4) 2204939. E-mail: elsitceg@ms41.hinet.net. Website: www.elstaiwan.com.
Number of teachers: 10-15.
Preference of nationality: none, but must be native speakers.
Qualifications: degree and TEFL Cert (preferably CELTA) and six months minimum experience.
Conditions of employment: 1 year. Minimum 18 hours per week.
Salary: 500 Taiwanese dollars per hour.
Facilities/Support: teachers are provided with studio apartments at a rent of 7-8,000 Taiwanese dollars per month.
Recruitment: locally and via the Central Office in Taipei (see above). Interviews not essential.
Contact: Ian Fletcher, Academic Director.

ELSI
No. 28, 4th Floor, Hsieh Fu Lu, Tamshui, Taipei District. Tel: 262 99706. Fax 886-2-26220995. E-mail: formoser@ficnet.net
Number of teachers: 5.
Preference of nationality: none.
Qualifications: minimum university degree.
Conditions of employment: 1 year contract. Teaching can be in the mornings or evenings.
Salary: US$16 per hour gross.
Facilities/Support: comfortable dormitory accommodation provided next to the school. Residence ID cards arranged by the school.
Recruitment: overseas agent. Newspapers.
Contact: Philip Moser.

HESS EDUCATIONAL ORGANIZATION
235 Chung Shan Road, Chung Ho City, Sec. 2, No. 419, Chung Ho City, Taipei County. Tel: (2) 3234 6188. Fax: (2) 3234 9488/3234-2200, ext 1053. E-mail: hesswork@hess.com.tw. Web-site: www.hess.com.tw.
Number of teachers: 250 or more Native Speaking Teachers (NSTs) in more than

100 language schools and 40 kindergartens throughout Taiwan; 160 new teachers hired each year.

Preference of nationality: must have passport from officially recognised English speaking country, i.e. US, Canada, UK, Ireland, Australia, New Zealand and South Africa.

Qualifications: Bachelor's degree (in any subject) plus desire to work with varied age groups and to experience Chinese culture. Knowledge of Chinese not necessary because each class has a local assistant teacher to help with translation.

Conditions of employment: 1 year renewable contracts. Three contract options. Classes at language school (for 7-15 year olds) are held in afternoons and evenings. Classes at the kindergarten (ages 3-6) are during the day; full-time kindergarten work for those interested in Early Childhood Education.

Salary: NT$500 per hour (gross), with some variation between locations. Tax rate is 20% for first six months then drops to 10%.

Facilities/Support: airport pick-up can be arranged. 6-day initial orientation with paid accommodation. Every branch assists NSTs to find housing. Actively assist NSTs to obtain resident visas and work permits. Application process should be started 3 months in advance to allow time to collect visa and work permit documents. Discounted group air travel arranged for North American recruits. Additional branch training provided following initial orientation programme. One day follow-up training at Main Office in Taipei after 1, 3 and 6 months.

Recruitment: through Hess website, universities, adverts and direct application. Telephone interviews are essential. Quarterly new teacher intakes during first weeks of September, December, March and June. Overseas hiring completed 3 months before arrival to allow time for visa applications prior to departure.

Contact: David Jackson or Christie Bray, Human Resources Department.

JORDAN'S LANGUAGE SCHOOL & BROOKLIN'S TEACHING ORGANISATION
34-7 Min-Shu Road, Hu-Wei, Yun-Lin. Tel: (5) 631 1869. Fax: (5) 631 1716. E-mail: etalan@ms45.hinet.net.
Number of teachers: 10.
Preference of nationality: British (southern English accent preferred) and Canadian.
Qualifications: first degree required. Experience of teaching desirable.
Conditions of employment: about 1 year. Basic 16 h.p.w.
Salary: NT$35,000-NT$60,000 per month less deductions (6%-20% tax depending on length of stay and NT$500 for health insurance).
Facilities/Support: help in search for affordable accommodation. Assistance with work permit application which takes about a month.
Recruitment: newspaper adverts, via TEFL training centres and word of mouth.
Contact: Alan Liao, Managing Director.

NOBLE AMERICAN CHILDREN'S SCHOOL
No 850 Ta-Ya Rd, Sec. 1, Chiayi 600. Tel: (5) 275 9951. Fax: (5) 275 9952. E-mail: shereed@telusplanet.net.
Number of teachers: minimum 20.
Preference of nationality: native speaker.
Qualifications: Bachelor degree, TESL Certificate, Early Childhood Education/teaching experience preferred.
Conditions of employment: 1 year. Teaching hours are 8am-5pm or 12pm-9pm Monday-Friday. Hours in excess of 6 per day will be paid as over-time as will Saturday work.
Salary: NT$53,000 per month. Overtime NT$400 per hour.
Facilities/Support: new arrivals are given temporary housing and will be given help in finding their own within 7-10 days. School will help those who have arrived with a 60-day Visitor's Visa to obtain Resident Visa.
Recruitment: via internet. Interviews via e-mail. (No phone calls to above number.)

Contact: Sheree Davies, Human Resources/Recruiting.

OVERSEAS SERVICE CORPS YMCA
101 North Wacker Drive, Chicago, IL 60606, USA. Tel: 800-872-9622 ext. 343. Fax: (312) 977-9036.
Number of teachers: 15-20 per year in 9 community-based YMCAs in Taiwan.
Preference of nationality: American, Canadian.
Qualifications: university degree required. Teaching (TESOL/TEFL) experience and training preferred. Must be motivated to share cultures and build international understanding.
Conditions of employment: 1 year contracts starting October 1st. 14-20 contact h.p.w. plus 10 hours in office.
Salary: NT$26,000-31,000 per month after all deductions and housing cost.
Facilities/Support: return air fare, paid vacation, accommodation and bonus after 12 months. Orientation held in the US in September and another in Taiwan.
Recruitment: application deadline is April 15th. Applicants must be in North America between then and October start date. You can also apply direct to the YMCA of Taiwan (see entry below).
Contact: Jan Sterling, Program Assistant.

RICH ENGLISH
No. 7, Alley 7, Lane 113, Min Sheng East Road, Sec. 3, Taipei 105. Tel: (2) 2712 3671. Fax: (2) 2712 3631.
Number of teachers: 6.
Preference of nationality: English, American.
Qualifications: university degree and CELTA. Experience of living abroad useful. Must be aged 30 or less and have clean-cut appearance.
Conditions of employment: 2 or 3 year contracts. Evening hours and 6 hours of work on Saturday or Sunday. Pupils are children.
Salary: £24,000 per year less 6% deductions for taxes.
Facilities/Support: housing assistance, health insurance.
Recruitment: interviews available in Taipei, London and Denver.

SHANE ENGLISH SCHOOL
5F, 41 Roosevelt Road, Section 2, Taipei. Tel: (2) 2351 7755. Fax: (2) 2397 2642. E-mail: sest@ms12.hinet.net.
Number of teachers: 50+.
Preference of nationality: British, American, New Zealand, Australian.
Qualifications: TEFL/CELTA/PGCE (dependent on position applied for).
Conditions of employment: 1 year renewable contracts. Guaranteed 80 hours per month minimum, 5 days per week.
Salary: NT$500 per hour, plus bonuses.
Facilities/Support: up-to-date facilities including interactive CD-Roms. Work permits, assistance with accommodation, and comprehensive initial and ongoing training provided.
Recruitment: applicants from outside the UK contact the Director of Studies directly. UK applicants through Claire Fryer at Saxoncourt Recruitment in London (124 New Bond Street, W1Y 9AE; tel 0207-491 1911).
Contact: David Roberts, Director of Studies.

TAIPEI LANGUAGE INSTITUTE
507 Zhong Shan 2nd Road, 2nd Floor, Kaohsiung 802. Tel: (7) 215 2965. Fax: (7) 215 2981. E-mail: tlika507@ms12.hinet.net. Website: www.tli.com.tw.
Number of teachers: 5 or more.
Preference of nationality: English native speakers.
Qualifications: BA plus teaching experience preferred.
Conditions of employment: one year contract, renewable. School hours are 8am to 9pm. Most classes are in the late afternoon and evening.

Salary: US$14 per hour for the first year for one-to-one classes. Group classes more. For the first six months there is 20% tax and deductions which may be refunded at a later date. After six months, 6% deductions.

Facilities/Support: no assistance with accommodation, but help with finding contacts.

Recruitment: rarely hire without in-person interview, but it does happen occasionally. Applicants usually apply in person.

Contact: Ms Allien Chang, Supervisor of Foreign Language Dept.

YMCA OF TAIWAN
171 Chang-an East Road, Section 2, 11F-1, Taipei 104. Fax (886-2) 2721 7475. e-mail: twn@mail.ymca.org.tw

Number of teachers: 15-20.

Conditions of employment: one year contracts.

Salary: NT$26,000-31,000 net after all deductions and including accommodation.

Recruitment: through the Overseas Service Corps of the YMCA (OSCY) in the USA (see entry for Overseas Service Corps above) or direct to the Taiwan YMCA c/o David Chang or Andrew Yeh.

Other Schools to Try

Note that these schools (in alphabetical order according to town) did not confirm their teacher requirements for this edition of *Teaching English Abroad.* Upper case entries marked with an asterisk had entries in the last edition (1999).

Broadlands English Institute (e-mail: yenjuping@hotmail.com). Need teachers to work at summer camps (offering US$1,500 for two months and free one way airfare).

Universe-American Language School, 5-231 5179/ ginnylin@hotmail.com

Dragon English Language School,- 37 Dean Road, Chaiyi (5-281 2488/terryalred@yahoo.com). Advertising on www.eslcafe.com in 2000 for teachers for pre-school and older children.

Hua Language Institute, 3F, 45 The Shin West Rd, Tien Mu, Taipei (2-2833 7851/fax 2-2831 2355). 8 branches. Good wages NT$60,000+ p.m.), maximum 20 contact hours, lots of marking, limited resources.

*KANG NING ENGLISH SCHOOL, PO Box 95, Chutung 310 (3-594 3322/595 2332/fax 3-594 3222/596 7392). Teachers for pre-school and primary aged children.

Olive Experiment English, 535 Lung An Road, Hsin Chung City 242.

*LINE UP LANGUAGE SCHOOL, 398-1 Chihsien 1st Road, 2Fl, Hsin-Hsing Area, Kaohsiung City (7-235 8015/fax 7-236 4311). 40-50 teachers preferably from North America.

Oxford Language & Computer Institute, 8 Fl, 240 Chung Shan 1st Road, Kaohsiung (7-281 2315/fax 7-211 7119.) 20 North American teachers.

Sesame Street School Tainan – e-mail: Teach@Sesame-Street.com.tw

*GRAM ENGLISH INSTITUTE, 116 Yung Ho Road, 4th Fl, Yung Ho City, Taipei (2-2927 2477/fax 2-2926 2183; gram@ms7.hinet.net). Scores of teachers for 44 branches throughout Taiwan, including 10 branches in Taipei area.

Head Start English School Taipei – e-mail: jamil@unet.net.tw

Kid Castle Language Schools, 98, 8F Min Chuan Road, Hsin Tien, Taipei (2-2218 5996 ext 341/319; fax 2-2218 9984; www.kidcastle.com/english).

*LANGUAGE TRAINING & TESTING CENTER, 170 Hsin-hai Road, Section 2, Taipei 106 (2-2362 6385/fax 2-2367 1944). 60 teachers for non-profit educational foundation with 3,400 students.

*TAIWAN ANGLO-FRENCH INSTITUTE, 2F, No. 295 Ho Ping E Road, Sec 2, Taipei (2-2755 5451/fax 2-2755 4627). 3 teachers. Generous terms.

Word of Mouth English, 4F-2, 163 Nan King East Road, Sec. 5, Taipei (2-2762 7114/fax 2-2761 8295).

Thailand

Thais have always prided themselves on being the only Asian nation never to have been under foreign domination. This may be true of their politics but not of the economy, as the Thais learned when three years ago there was a massive withdrawal of foreign investment which led to the collapse of the currency and mass unemployment. The IMF had to deliver a rescue package to the tune of US$17 billion. In fact the economic problems which at that time engulfed the whole of Southeast Asia started in Thailand, and the country has been reeling ever since.

Against expectations, the opportunities for teachers have been rising again especially in schools that teach English to children and to executives. Schools are finding it more and more difficult to attract foreign teachers because of the low wages, so there is less competition for work than in the past. Many Thais feel that in these difficult times, the best investment is in their studies, whether at university or in language instruction.

The *Bangkok Post* is as full as ever of advertisements for native speaker teachers, perhaps even fuller, since many foreign teachers left the country when the exchange rate plummeted and their wages shrank. A knowledge of English is eagerly sought by almost all urban young people and, in the context of Thailand, 'urban' is almost synonymous with 'Bangkok', which is five times larger than its nearest rival Chiang Mai.

Prospects for Teachers

The many English teaching opportunities in Thailand seldom appeal to the serious career-minded EFL teacher. Only a small percentage of recruitment takes place outside Thailand. Even the British Council has concentrated its efforts on finding staff from among the expatriate population already resident. The major schools use foreign recruitment agencies and the internet to make contact with potential teachers, but most organisations depend on finding native-speaker teachers locally, including Thai universities and teachers' colleges, as well as private business colleges which all have EFL departments. No doubt most would prefer a highly qualified and experienced EFL teacher but the fact is that they couldn't afford one before the crisis and they certainly can't now.

This means that there is a preponderance of teacher-travellers on the Thai teaching scene, earning enough money to fund a longer stay or subsequent travels. Thais are exuberant and fun-loving people and their ideas about education reflect this. They seem to value fun and games *(senuk)* above grammar, and an outgoing personality above a teaching certificate. Of course there is a nucleus of professional EFL teachers working at the most prestigious institutes in Bangkok, but the majority of teachers and tutors teach on a casual basis without formal contracts. So anyone determined to teach in Thailand is guaranteed some opportunities, provided he or she is willing to go to Thailand to seek them out and willing to work for a pittance. Most students of English want to learn the language for a purpose such as tourism or business, and a good teacher will find out their motives and tailor the lessons accordingly.

FIXING UP A JOB

In Advance

The *Anglo-Pacific (Asia) Consultancy* (Suite 32, Nevilles Court, Dollis Hill Lane, London NW2 6HG; 020-8452 7836) is an educational consultancy which concentrates on recruiting teachers for schools, colleges and universities in Thailand. Teachers are placed every month by APA who welcome graduates with a CELTA or

"They seem to value games above grammar."

Trinity Certificate but also try to place people with any TEFL background and/or appropriate personalities as long as they have a university degree. Their recruits are given briefing notes on Thailand and a follow-up visit in their schools if possible. *TEFLNet Recruitment* (tel/fax 01759-305586; teflnet@langwork.demon.co.uk) also has details of vacancies in Thailand for degree and Certificate-holders.

The agency *Search Associates* which is based in Chiang Mai (see Chiang Mai section below for address) holds recruitment fairs for experienced elementary and secondary school teachers in various countries including the UK, Dubai and Malaysia as well as Thailand. However, if you are on the spot, it is worth having a consultation with them as, according to Annette Kunigagon of the Eagle Guest House (see below), they have personally visited every school with which they deal.

Many of the large organisations like *Bell Associated Schools* with entries in the List of Schools would welcome advance applications from EFL teachers. Thai-American International (Education District Office, Bangpain District, Ayuthaya 113160; info@taiteach.com; www.taiteach.com) advertises teaching positions for anyone with a BA and a positive attitude provided they pay a placement fee of $310 (all but $25 of which will be refunded upon completion of contract). Because turnover of teaching staff at Bangkok schools tends to be so high, organisations try to make it financially worthwhile for teachers to stay for a given period.

One of the best all-round sources of information about teaching in Thailand with an emphasis on Bangkok and on inside information about the main hiring companies is the website www.ajarn.com with stories and tips as well as many job vacancies (www.ajarn.com/Jobs/jobs_offered.htm).

On the Spot in Bangkok

Any new arrival in Bangkok would be well advised to spend a week getting his or her bearings and asking foreigners living in the city for inside information about possible employers. Many people say that the teaching scene has become so exploitative and life in the city so unpleasant that it is better to leave Bangkok as quickly as you can.

For those who feel strong enough to survive in Bangkok, language schools are very easy to locate, to approach on spec. The best place to start is around Siam Square where numerous schools and the British Council are located (see map, which is courtesy of Richard Guellala). The Council has a list of private and public universities, institutes, teachers' colleges and international schools throughout the country which have English departments and therefore possible openings for a native speaker, but most people rely on the Yellow Pages, which include dozens of language school addresses.

Another excellent source of job vacancies is the English language press, viz. the *Bangkok Post* (with at least five adverts every day) and to a lesser extent the *Nation*. A favourite teachers' hangout is the Hole-in-the-Wall pub on Khao San Road. Or try the Hard Rock Café in Siam Square.

If the Siam Square schools are not short of teachers, which may be the case in the slack season, you will have to try schools further afield. Travelling around this city of six million is so time-consuming and unpleasant that it is important to plot your interview strategy on a city map before making appointments. Also be sure to pick up a map of the air-conditioned bus routes, particularly if you are contemplating a job which involves travelling to different premises. (Another handy acquisition is a smog mask which costs a few baht.)

It may not be necessary to do much research to discover the schools with vacancies. Many of the so-called back street language schools (more likely to be on a main street, above a shop or restaurant) look to the cheap hotels of Banglamphu, the favourite haunt of Western travellers in the northwest of Bangkok. There is such a high turnover of staff at many schools that there are bound to be vacancies somewhere for a new arrival who takes the trouble to present a professional image and can show a convincing CV. As usual, it may be necessary to start with part-time and occasional work with several employers, aiming to build up 20-30 hours in the same area to minimise travelling in the appalling traffic.

The teaching of children is an expanding area; if you don't want to teach the alphabet, don't accept pupils under the age of five. On the strength of her claim that she had experience of 'working with children,' Alison Eglinton was soon bringing home 6,000 baht (B6,000) per week. (She suggests that anyone teaching young children should master at least one word of Thai: *hong nam* which means toilet.)

When visiting a school, wear your posh clothes and carry CVs and passport photos to clip onto the application forms; otherwise you'll be asked to come back when you have obtained some on the Khao San Road. Don't be surprised if the application form asks some weird questions, such as asking you to give the name, age and profession of every member of your family. You won't be hired on the spot but may well be contacted within a day or two; contact is made by telephone so make sure you are staying in a guest house with a phone like the Peachy Guest House (10 Phra Athit Road, Banglamphu) or Sweety Guest House on Soi Post Office, 49 Ratchdamnoen Klang, Banglamphu.

Everyone who has ever had anything to do with teaching English in Thailand emphasises the need to dress smartly, as Bruce Lawson describes:

> *The Thais like their pet farangs (i.e. teachers) to look as much like currency dealers as possible. I bought a suit in Bangkok for £50 especially for the job hunt. Men should take out all earrings and wear a tie, thus risking asphyxiation in the heat and humidity of the hot season. Women should wear a decent skirt, not trousers.*

Ajarn (university graduates) are particularly respected in Thailand and are expected to look respectable. As well as dressing smartly for an interview, try to maintain a reserve in your manner while still projecting a relaxed and easy-going image. Too many gesticulations and guffawing are considered impolite.

The busiest season for English schools is mid-March to mid-May during the school holidays, when many secondary school and university students take extra tuition in English. This coincides with the hot season. Vacancies continue to be advertised through June, July and August. The next best time to look for teaching work in private schools is October, while the quietest time is January/February.

The noisy Khao San Road is lined with budget accommodation (where a room costs B50-80), many with notice boards offering teaching work and populated with other foreigners (known as *farangs*) well acquainted with the possibilities. They will also be able to warn you of the dubious schools which are known to exploit their teachers. It is best to be suspicious at all times, since there are stories of bogus job adverts being inserted to lure naïve new arrivals to hotels to be drugged and robbed.

On-the-Spot in Chiang Mai

According to Annette Kunigagon who has made her home in Chiang Mai and is something of a resident expert in teaching in her adopted town, far more people have been coming to Chiang Mai to look for work than was the case a few years ago, since no one wants to live in Bangkok. She co-owns the Eagle Guesthouse at 16 Chang Moi Gao Road, Soi 3 (53-874126/235387; mail@eaglehouse.com/ www.eaglehouse.com). She even organises unpaid teaching work as part of her Helping Hands Social Projects scheme (see her website).

Teaching opportunities crop up in branches of the big companies like *ECC* and *AUA* and in academic institutes. There are five international schools which employ English teachers, though most are recruited abroad (e.g. at international teachers' fairs) rather than locally. Murray Turner is one teacher who succeeded in finding work, partly with Annette's help:

> *I am working seven hours a week in Chiang Mai after arriving one week ago. I'm staying at Eagle Guest House which is run by Annette who knows everything about language schools (and everything else). I found the job by hiring a bicycle (B100 for five days' hire) and dutifully doing the rounds of the language schools, colleges and kids' schools. Although Chiang Mai is developing rapidly, it is still safe enough and small enough to cycle round, providing you don't venture out between 11am and 2pm (even in winter). I took plenty of passport photos, photocopies of my passport and of my certificate from the one-week TEFL course I'd done (at Pilgrim's in Canterbury).*

The agency Search Associates (P.O. Box 168 Chiang Mai 50 000; 53-244 322/fax 53-260118; deelman@loxinfo.co.th/ www.search-associates.com) run by Harry Deelman might be worth consulting. They do their recruiting both abroad and on-the-spot for schools whose pupils are aged 8 to 18.

The British Council in Chiang Mai can give you a list of five language institutes, six international schools and three universities. Their handout also explains that they take on part-time teachers themselves from time to time, normally with the usual British Council qualifications, but sometimes on the basis of a demonstration lesson. They run evening and weekend classes, children's summer schools, Business English courses, English for guides, etc. Contact the British Council, 198 Bumrungraj Road, Chiang Mai 50,000 (53-242103/fax 53-244781; enquiries@th.britishcouncil.org or bccm@loxinfo.co.th/. The website for vacancies in Chiang Mai is www.britcoun.or.th/english/chmvacancies.htm.

Other jobs are available in the school holidays at summer and weekend camps held at resort hotels and attended by rich children from Bangkok. Getting in to these and the summer camps run by the British Council and YMCA is by word of mouth,

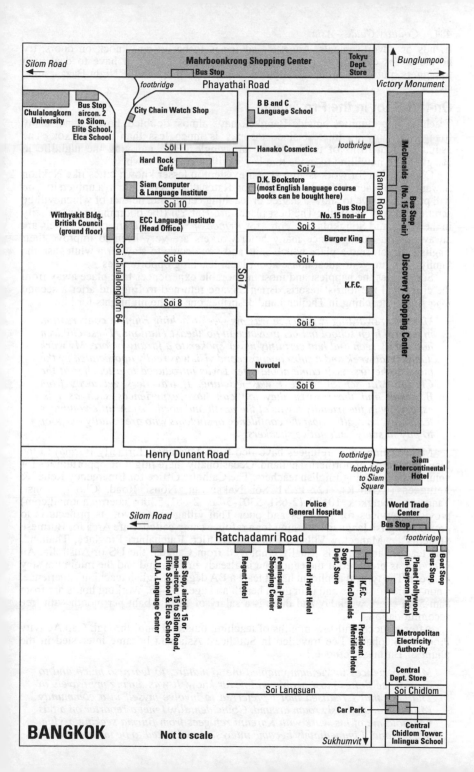

friends or advertisements. Annette's advice is to be brazen, knock on doors, try hotels, shops catering to tourists, companies which export or have to deal with foreigners, pubs, restaurants, computer shops, large shops in the Night Bazaar area, etc.

On-the-Spot in the Provinces

Teaching opportunities outside Bangkok have almost doubled, however not many foreigners show an interest since the pay is much less than in Bangkok. The estimated four-fifths of teachers who are single males enjoying the nightlife in Bangkok are unwilling to move to a less exciting country town.

Competition for work is almost non-existent in lesser known cities like Nakhon Sawan, Khon Kaen, Udon Thani and Ubon Ratchathani. For a job in a university you will probably have to show a degree or teaching certificate, neither of which will be scrutinised very carefully. The best places are Hat Yai (the booming industrial city in the south and Songkhla (see entry for *Prince of Songkhla University*). Hotels are always worth asking, since many hotel workers are very keen to improve their English. If you find a place which suits and you decide to stay for a while, ask the family who run your guest house about local teaching opportunities.

Sometimes the happiest and most memorable experiences take place away from the cities and the tourist resorts. Brian Savage returned to England after a second long stint of teaching in Thailand and describes one of the highlights for him:

> *My most rewarding experience was my week teaching English conversation in a rural high school in Loei province in northeast Thailand. These children had rarely seen and had certainly never spoken to a farang before. My work during that week and a subsequent second visit was really appreciated by the pupils. The first visit came about after I was introduced to a teacher at the Chiang Mai school where I was teaching. If travellers get away from Bangkok and the resorts, they too can have experiences such as this, especially in the friendly towns of the north and northeast. A little voluntary teaching can really boost the confidence of students who are usually too poor to pay to study with native speakers.*

Many Karen tribal refugees have fled from Myanmar (formerly Burma) to the Mae Sod region of northern Thailand. Occasionally there might be opportunities for volunteers, including English teachers. The Catholic Office for Emergency Relief & Refugees (COERR), 122-122/1 Soi Naksuwan, Nonsi Road, Chong Nonsi, Yannawa, Bangkok 10120 (2-681 5301-5/fax 2-681 5306; coerr@hotmail.com) provides services for refugees and poor Thai villagers. One of its projects is to provide English language teaching for a refugee camp called 'Safe Area for Burmese Students' in Maneeloy Village, Pak Tho District, Ratchaburi Province, Thailand. One teacher at a time is usually employed from Canada, the US or Australia. An interview is preferred if the candidate is already in Thailand and the minimum stay is a year. The typical applicant has at least a BA degree, English teaching experience, a non-political stance and is in good health and aged 25-45. Working hours are from 8am-5pm every weekday and there is a salary of 15,000 baht per month with free accommodation.

After a successful few months of teaching outside Hanoi through Gap Activity Projects, Stephanie Lee travelled in Southeast Asia and became interested in the plight of Burmese refugees:

> *My experiences in Vietnam enabled me to mature, to learn so much and to experience things most people will never know. It was during my travels in Thailand that I realised that I preferred to involve myself in a community rather than aimlessly roam around. Coincidentally, I met a reporter on a bus who told me of his work with Karenni refugees from Burma seeking asylum in Thailand. I immediately became interested and asked to be taken to one of*

the camps. I am now living and teaching in Refugee Camp No. 3 in Mae Hong Son and have adjusted to a basic life eating rice and yellow beans and showering with a bucket of brown river water. While I am working here, I am trying to raise people's awareness of the situation inside Myanmar.

REGULATIONS

The vast majority of EFL teachers in Thailand do not have a work visa, a practice to which the authorities have long been turning a blind eye. Foreigners mostly teach on a tourist visa or (preferably) a non-immigrant visa which must be regularly renewed by leaving the country.

Universities and established language schools are more willing than they were to sponsor teachers who have proved themselves successful in the classroom and help them to fill in the 50 or so documents. To be eligible for a work permit you must have a bachelor's diploma or a CELTA (which the Ministry of Education recognises) and a contract. (In the forgery capital of the world, quite a few fictitious university diplomas and even Cambridge and Trinity Certificates are in circulation.) The entire procedure should take about four months and cost around B2,000. Note that many schools which make vague promises to obtain a work permit for their staff fail to keep their promise because of the expense incurred.

Tourist visas should be applied for in your home country and are valid for an initial 60 days. These can be renewed once inside Thailand for a further month at a cost of B500. If you do not renew before the expiry date you will have to pay B100 for every day you have overstayed when you exit the country. If you make the decision to teach in Thailand before leaving home and can come up with a Thai national willing to write a letter of recommendation on your behalf, apply to the Thai embassy for a non-immigrant visa which allows you to stay 90 days. Failing that, you can apply for a non-immigrant visa at a Thai consulate in a neighbouring country such as Malaysia or Laos, provided you have the necessary papers from your employer; this will be granted in 24 hours.

A non-immigrant visa will have to be renewed every 90 days, again for B500. Most teachers and travellers choose to cross the Malaysian border to Penang (20 hours by train from Bangkok) where a new visa can quickly and easily be obtained from the Thai Consulate. Even people who have done this repeatedly report that there are no problems. The estimated cost of a visa run from Bangkok is well over B2,000; the return train fare in air-conditioned class to Butterworth near Penang is a little less. A possible alternative is to cross into Malaysia at Kota Bharu where there is a small Thai Consulate (closed Fridays). If working in northern Thailand, the obvious place to go is Vientiane in Laos (though you will have to pay for a Laos visa).

As throughout Asia, it is a good idea to look neat and respectable when entering Thailand, especially if you intend to make a habit of it. Those entering from Malaysia should keep an eye open for the sign which reads, 'The following persons will not be allowed entry: hippies, anyone wearing a headband, a waistcoat or silk shorts, anyone barechested, or anyone not wearing undergarments.' In fact Thai border formalities are usually friendly and relaxed.

So far, people teaching on a tourist or a non-immigrant visa have not been required to pay tax. Once a work permit is granted, tax will be withdrawn at a very modest rate, sometimes as low as 2%. Thailand's national health scheme applies to visitors and so not all teachers worry about private insurance.

CONDITIONS OF WORK

In a country where teaching jobs are so easy to come by, there has to be a catch. In Thailand, the wages for *farang* teachers are uniformly low. The basic hourly rate has risen only very slightly over the past six years from B150 to B180 an hour with most

*" The following persons will not be allowed
entry: hippies, anyone wearing a headband,
waistcoat or silk shorts, anyone barechested
or not wearing undergarments."*

decent schools (there are not many) paying B200. Company work pays between B250 and B450 depending on location, but as mentioned earlier the amount of in-company contract work has greatly diminished. The norm is for schools to keep their staff on as part-time freelancers while giving them full-time hours; this is primarily to avoid taxes. Most language institutes pay weekly in cash, but beware of schools which turn pay day into a moveable feast.

The best remuneration is available from international schools like the Bangkok Patana School (2/38 Soi Lasalle, Sukhumvit 105, Bangkok 10260; tel. 2-398 0200). Note that the pay at international schools in Bangkok is as much as twice that paid by international schools elsewhere in the country. University and colleges offer around B25,000 a month for a relatively light teaching load.

Few employers help with accommodation which at the present time does not matter much since vacant apartments can be found on almost every street and the rental deposit is very low. According to Helen Welch, newly returned from Thailand, many teachers in Bangkok are choosing to live in foreigners' compounds which are, increasingly, patrolled by armed guards. Things are more relaxed in Chiang Mai where a group of people can rent a house or live Thai-style in a studio room with attached bathroom for very affordable rents.

Before accepting a job, find out what teaching materials are in use, if any. A great many schools offer no more than a classroom and a few textbooks lying around, leaving the teacher to design the syllabus, etc. On the other hand there are some schools which have very rigid and unimaginative lesson plans which teachers are obliged to follow.

Thai students are friendly, responsive, eager and a delight to teach. After five years of teaching in Thailand, Richard Guellala offers his view of Thai students:

Thais are definitely fun to teach as long as you don't get too friendly with them, as then you'll find yourself in a very awkward situation having lost all credibility. It's best to keep some distance and make them aware during their first lesson that you are in control. Most Thais are false beginners and of lower intermediate levels, and you will find that very few students reach an intermediate level due to lack of motivation and commitment.

Remember never to touch a student on the head, which is difficult if you are teaching children. In class a show of anger will soon lose the students' respect since the Thais value a 'cool heart' *(jai yen)* and go to great lengths to avoid displays of negative emotion. Calm, smiling and enthusiastic personalities make all the difference.

LEISURE TIME

It has to be said that Bangkok may be an exciting and lively city but it is not beautiful. It has very few parks, bad traffic congestion and polluted air. Bruce Lawson describes the two ways of travelling between Banglamphu and Siam Square:

You can travel to work on the cesspool that they call a canal (klong). It's about a five minute walk from Banglamphu on the other side of the Democracy Monument. Get on a boat picking up on the right of the bridge. It costs a few baht and takes just over 10 minutes compared to the 45-minute ride on the non-air con bus. But you swap traffic fumes for the stench of stagnant water full of decomposing rubbish, animals and hideous eight-inch swimming millipedes. So don't fall in.

There is also a great deal of what some might consider moral pollution, and there is a certain element of the teaching fraternity in Bangkok who are there primarily for the easy availability of sex in the notorious Patpong district (despite the fact that there is a veritable AIDS crisis in Thailand). Helen Welch reports that at least one school has banned all its staff from going into Patpong, for fear of being spotted by a client or their parents. The ratio of foreign men to women teachers is at least six to one, and many women (although in great demand as teachers) do not enjoy the atmosphere in the city and leave as quickly as they can. Although there are plenty of night clubs and restaurants in Bangkok, there is a dearth of dance and film, and also of sports clubs.

Fortunately for teachers earning a low wage, the more innocent pleasures of Thailand come cheap. Try to learn a little Thai as Bruce Lawson did after getting fried battered banana when he thought he had ordered garlic chicken. He recommends organising word-swaps with students, which will also illustrate to them that they are not the only ones who have to struggle with alien sounds.

Living expenses are not high. Food bought at street stalls is very cheap and tasty, but also brings with it a risk of hepatitis. Apparently there is a national shortage of marmite, so homesick Britons will embrace any new arrival with a supply. Even part-time teachers should be able to afford to travel round the country, visiting jungle attractions like Kanchanaburi, where you can ride an elephant along the banks of the River Kwai, and islands like Koh Samet, Koh Samui and Koh Phangan where life is slow and the beaches are wonderful. Bangkok is also an important hub for travellers and cheap tickets are available to India, etc.

LIST OF SCHOOLS

AMERICAN UNIVERSITY LANGUAGE CENTER
179 Rajadamri Road, Bangkok 10330. Tel: (2) 252 8170-3/650 5040-4 ext. 2208, 2209 or 2114. Chiang Mai branch: AUA, 73 Rajadamnern Road, Amphur Muang, Chiang   Mai   50200.   Tel: 53-278407.   Fax: 53-211973.   E-mail: aualanna@loxinfo.co.th.
4 branches in Bangkok and 11 upcountry.
Number of teachers: about 200 in total: 80-90 at main branch, up to 20 at other branches.
Preference of nationality: American and Canadian accents preferred; also British, Australian and New Zealand.
Qualifications: BA in any field or CELTA and completion of high school.
Conditions of employment: 1 year commitment preferred. 4-6 hours teaching daily (no full-time positions). Teaching year consists of 7 6-week terms separated by 1 free week. Courses aimed at professionals aged 18-35.
Salary: starting rate is B189 per hour (net). B15 pay rise every 6 months.
Facilities/Support: participation in pre-service training session (20 hours) is required before teaching hours are assigned. 15,000 titles in resource library. Work permit available after 3 month probation period.
Recruitment: adverts in the *Bangkok Post*, the internet and word of mouth.

AMNUAY SILPA-BELL LANGUAGE CENTRE
304/1 Sri Ayutthya, Ratcatewi, Bangkok 10400. E-mail: gbradd@loxinfo.co.th Website: www.bkk-software.co.th/ans/index.html
Number of teachers: 60+ native speakers for this and other Bell Schools (see entry below).
Preferred nationality: majority are British, but any qualified native speaker welcome to apply.
Qualifications: degree plus UCLES/CELTA or equivalent.
Conditions of employment: 2-year contracts offered. Contract stipulates total 20 contact hours per week, but teachers are expected to be on site during the school day (8.30am-4.30pm approximately).
Salary: income tax deducted at source.
Facilities/support: assistance with finding accommodation including initial 7 days in an hotel. Work permits and visas are provided by the centre.
Recruitment: adverts on ELT related websites, *The Guardian, TES,* and *Bangkok Post.* Interviews are held in Cambridge in the UK and locally and are usually required.
Contact: Bruce Hoxton, Director of Studies.

BAAN PASA (NES)
2 Sirithon Road, T. Chang, Pueuk, Chiangmai 50300. Tel: (53) 221 764. Fax: (53) 222 361. E-mail: baanpasa@loxinfo.co.th.
Number of teachers: 12.
Preference of nationality: none, but should be native speaker. (NES stands for New Zealand Education Services).
Qualifications: should include teaching and other working experience.
Conditions of employment: 6 months renewable.
Salary: negotiable according to qualification and experience.
Facilities/Support: accommodation assistance is possible.
Recruitment: advertising.
Contact: Miss Tan Woraphant, Assistant Director.

BELL ASSOCIATE SCHOOLS
204/1 Ranong I Road, Samsen, Dusit, Bangkok 10300. Tel: (2) 6682124. Fax: (2) 6682124. E-mail: gbradd@loxinfo.co.th.
Number of teachers: 60+.
Preference of nationality: none, but must be native speaker.
Qualifications: BA and CELTA (better still PGCE and DELTA).
Conditions of employment: one or two-year contracts. 20 contact hours per week (Monday to Friday or Tuesday to Saturday between 9am and 5pm)
Salary: 34,100-48,290 Thai baht per month. Approximately 10% deductions.
Facilities/Support: hotel accommodation on arrival. Assistance in finding suitable accommodation. A loan is made available, repayable over initial three months of employment. Help with arranging work permit.
Recruitment: internet, newspapers, video application, personal interview or through the Bell Educational Trust in the UK.
Contact: Graham Braddick, Director of Operations.

BRITISH AMERICAN
Ladprao Soi 58-60, Bangkok. Tel: 2-539 4866/9. Fax: 2-538 3748. E-mail: british_american2000@hotmail.com Also 5 other British American Schools: (1) Ransit (Future Park) tel 958-0350-8; fax: 958 0359. (2) Bang Kapi (The Mall); tel 734-1791-9; fax: 734-1800. (3) Ladprao (Imperial World) tel 934-9181-8; fax: 934-9189. (4) Ramintra (Fashion Island) tel: 947-5104-5; fax: 947-5114; (5) Bang Khae (The Mall); tel: 454-8973-81; fax 454-8982.
Number of teachers: about 100.
Preference of nationality: British or American.
Qualifications: enthusiasm and positive attitude are essential.
Conditions of employment: 1 year contract. 4/6 teaching hours per day.
Salary: starts at 25,000 baht per month. Local rent for an apartment is approximately 3,000 baht monthly.
Facilities/Support: provide details of recommended apartments. All the visa paperwork is done by the school, but the teacher pays for visa.
Recruitment: advertising in national newspapers.
Contact: Jack Downes, Director of Studies.

BRITISH COUNCIL
198 Bumrungraj Road, Chiang Mai 5000. Tel: (53) 242103. Fax: (53) 244781. E-mail: enquiries@th.britishcouncil.org. Website: www.th.britishcouncil.org.
Number of teachers: 4 full-time contracted and 7/8 part-time hourly paid.
Preference of nationality: British.
Qualifications: Cert. essential. Dip. preferable.
Conditions of employment: 1 year, but less in exceptional circumstances. 18-24 hours teaching.
Salary: 300 baht per hour.
Facilities/Support: no financial assistance but help with finding, dealing with agents etc. Help with work permits.
Recruitment: full-time contracted through BC London. Hourly paid are recruited locally.
Contact: Kerry Platts.

CHIANG MAI UNIVERSITY
Department of English, 239 Huay Kaew Road, Amphur Muang, Chiang Mai 50200. Tel: (53) 211699/222177. Fax: (53) 217143.
Number of teachers: 30.
Preference of nationality: none.
Qualifications: university degree relevant to teaching English as a second language.
Conditions of employment: 1 year contracts. 12 h.p.w.
Salary: B10,000 per month.
Facilities/Support: no assistance with accommodation. Help given with work

permits.
Recruitment: direct applications. Local interview essential.
Contact: Head of English Department.

ECC (THAILAND)
430/17-24 Chula Soi 64, Siam Square, Bangkok 10330. Tel: (2) 253 3312. Fax: (2) 254 2243. E-mail: jobs@ecc.ac.th or eccthai@comnet3.ksc.net.th. Web-site: www.eccthai.com.
40 branches in Greater Bangkok, 20 elsewhere in Thailand.
Number of teachers: around 500 native speakers (normally recruit 10-15 new teachers each month).
Preference of nationality: none.
Qualifications: must have one of: Bachelor's degree, TEFL qualification, 6 months or more teaching experience, CELTA (preferred).
Conditions of employment: average of 25 h.p.w. 6 days per week between 9am and 9pm. Pupils include children and adults (general, ESP and business classes).
Salary: B19,000-B35,000 per month. Standard starting salary is B26,000 plus B12,000 bonus on completion of one-year contract.
Facilities/Support: work permit and insurance provided. Assistance given with finding accommodation. Regular workshops. Cambridge CELTA course offered five times a year; Introduction to TESOL offered monthly.
Recruitment: adverts in the *Guardian, TES, EL Gazette,* internet web site and qualified walk-ins.

E-20/CEC
Kiatphathana Language and Computer School, 29 Sirimangkalajun Road, Chiang Mai 50200. Tel: 895-202/400-201. Fax: 400 387. E-mail: cec-e20@hotmail.com
Number of teachers: 10-20.
Preference of nationality: none but must be native speaker.
Qualifications: BA degree and TEFL Cert and minimum six months experience.
Conditions of employment: minimum three months. 15-20 hours per week.
Salary: 180-250 baht per hour.
Facilities/Support: help with obtaining visa.
Recruitment: advertising in newspapers and newsletters. Personal interview necessary.
Contact: Amporn Garmolgomut.

FUN LANGUAGE INTERNATIONAL (THAILAND) LTD.
275 Lee House, 4/F, Thonglor Soi 13, Sukhumvit 55, Bangkok 10110. Tel: (2) 712 7744-7. Fax: (2) 712 7733. E-mail: engisfun@loxinfo.co.th
Number of teachers: 30.
Preference of nationality: British, American, Canadian, Australian and New Zealand.
Qualifications: Bachelor degree plus TESOL, CELTA certificate or equivalent qualification plus one year teaching experience with children aged 3-15, or experience working in foreign countries.
Conditions of employment: 1 year contract that can be renewed. Bonus upon completion of one year contract.
Facilities/support: 7 days free lodging on arrival for overseas applicants, visa and teaching permit, paid one month holiday, health insurance, training, curriculum and materials and teacher assistants provided.
Recruitment: telephone inverviews.
Contact: Mrs. Duangehai Tangsanga, Director.

KING'S COLLEGE OF ENGLISH
Central City Office Tower, Floor 5A, Central City Bangna, Bangna-Trad Road, Prakanang, Bangkok. Tel: (2) 745 6001. Fax: (2) 745 6000. E-mail:

kingth@asiaaccess.net.th
Number of teachers: 40.
Preference of nationality: British, Canadian, Australian.
Qualifications: university degree plus CELTA or equivalent and experience.
Conditions of employment: 1 year contracts. 28 contact h.p.w. 35 hours in school.
Salary: B29,000 per month plus benefits package. Less 5% for deductions.
Facilities/Support: assistance with accommodation and work permits. Training workshops.
Recruitment: local adverts and recruitment agency.
Contact: Ian Aseridge, Director of Studies.

LANNA INTERNATIONAL SCHOOL
300 Grandview Moo 1, Chiang Mai to Hang Dong Road, Chiang Mai 50100. Tel/fax: (53) 271159. E-mail lannaist@loxinfo.co.th
Number of teachers: 24.
Preference of nationality: none.
Qualifications: appropriate background and training. 2 years' experience.
Conditions of employment: 2 year contracts. Hours are 7.30am to 4pm.
Salary: according to qualifications and experience; normally starts at US$12,000-$13,000 paid in Thai baht (gross) per year.
Facilities/Support: assistance with accommodation including housing allowance. Help with entry visa before arrival and subsequent procedures.
Recruitment: from applications received, advertisements, recruitment fairs and interviews.
Contact: Robert E. (Bob) Lewis, Head of School.

MAEJO UNIVERSITY
Western Languages Section, Faculty of Agricultural Business, Chiang Mai 50290. Tel: (53) 878038-50. Fax: (53) 498862. E-mail: info@maejo.mju.ac.th.
Number of teachers: 1 or 2.
Preference of nationality: from English speaking country.
Qualifications: Bachelor's degree (any field) and experience in teaching English/TEFL/ESP.
Conditions of employment: 1 year contracts. 12 h.p.w.
Facilities/Support: assistance with accommodation, though teachers must share at first. Help given with work permits. Occasional seminars on teaching methodology.
Recruitment: word of mouth, ads in newspapers, radio, etc. Local interviews essential.
Contact: Head of Western Languages Section.

PAYAP UNIVERSITY
Muang District, Chiang Mai 50000. Tel: (53) 241255. Fax: (53) 241983. E-mail: english@payap.ac.th.
Number of teachers: about 10.
Preference of nationality: none, but must be native speaker.
Qualifications: BA or MA in English or a degree in some other discipline plus TEFL, or a CELTA/TESOL Cert.
Conditions of employment: minimum one academic year. Hours are from 8am to 5pm Monday to Friday.
Facilities/Support: allowance of 4000 baht per month for housing. Help with visa application.
Recruitment: internet, newspapers.
Contact: Oyporn Chingchayanurux.

PRINCE OF SONGKHLA UNIVERSITY
Department of Foreign Languages & Linguistics, Faculty of Liberal Arts, Hat Yai, Songkhla 90112. Tel: (74) 446-494. Fax: (74) 446-679. E-mail tsukanya@ratree. psu.ac.th. Website www.psu.ac.th

Number of teachers: 3.
Preference of nationality: native speakers of English.
Qualifications: BA in English or any other fields with TESOL/TEFL diploma and some teaching experience preferable or MA in English, TEFL/TESL, or Applied Linguistics.
Conditions of employment: 1 year contracts. 14+ h.p.w.
Salary: B17,580-B21,600 per month. Annual bonus of one month's pay on completion of one-year assignment.
Facilities/Support: free accommodation (a newly-built apartment on the foothill) on campus. Administrative details concerning visa/work permit taken care of by the department. Transportation to the immigration office and labour office in Songkhla offered. Textbooks, teachers' manuals, cassettes and worksheets provided.
Recruitment: apply in person or via e-mail to tsukanya@ratree.psu.ac.th
Contact: for more information contact: Sukanya Tanewong, Deputy Head for Academic Affairs.

SIAM COMPUTER & LANGUAGE INSTITUTE
471/19 Ratchawithi Road, Bangkok 10400. Tel: (2) 247 2345 ext. 370-373. Fax: (2) 644 6974. E-mail michael@siamcom.co.th Website www.siamcom.co.th
Number of teachers: 37 at 35 school locations in the greater Bangkok area and 49 at 38 external Thai school locations in the greater Bangkok area.
Preference of nationality: none.
Qualifications: college degree; CELTA or equivalent and experience preferred.
Conditions of employment: 1 year contracts. Full-time internal teachers 6 days per week in air-conditioned facilities; 15 or fewer students per class. All ages. Full-time external teachers five days per week in Thai classrooms. 50 students per class from kindergarten to high school level.
Salary: Baht 25,000 and up per month based on experience. Baht 150 daily travel allowance for external teachers. Hourly rates for part-time internal and external teachers.
Facilities/Support: assistance with finding local accommodation. 15 paid Thai vacation days per year, assistance in obtaining a teacher's licence, work permit and one year visa. Complete teacher orientation and teacher training before entering the classroom, bi-monthly teachers' meetings, sound lab and computer labs.
Recruitment: adverts in the *Bangkok Post* and on the worldwide web, and contacts with schools in Australia and the US. Interviews in Bangkok required.
Contact: Mr. Chalermchai or Mr. Michael.

TATE LEARNING CENTRE
1792/5-6 Chan Road, Sapan 3, Sathorn, Bangkok 10120. Tel: 662 674-9488. Fax 662 6749482. E-mail: nvongpad@loxinfo.co.th
Number of teachers: 5.
Preference of nationality: school is a franchise of Le Club Francais UK, so prefer British.
Qualifications: BA degree, TEFL Cert. under 30 preferred. Must enjoy teaching young learners.
Conditions of employment: 1-year contracts. Teaching hours are 25 per week.
Salary: package is around 30,000 baht per month plus health insurance. Tax is about 5%.
Facilities/Support: help with finding accommodation within walking distance and negotiating the best price is always offered. Work permit processed by the school.
Recruitment: adverts in UK press and related internet sites. Interview essential, often by telephone.
Contact: Ms Nisa Vongpadungkiat.

TRAINING, CREATIVITY, DEVELOPMENT (T.C.D.) CO. LTD.
399/7 Soi Thongloh 21, Sukhumvit Soi 55, Bangkok 10110. Tel/fax: (2) 391 5670. Tel: (2) 712 8503. E-mail: johnstcd@hotmail.com

Number of teachers: 45.
Preference of nationality: North American, British or Commonwealth.
Qualifications: TEFL/TESL training preferred, plus as much experience as possible. Preferably aged less than 38.
Conditions of employment: 6 month-1 year commitment preferred. Newcomers start with a few hours a week and build up to 25-35 per week, mostly one-to-one teaching. Prime hours of work between 3.30pm and 8pm. Pupils aged 6-60, most of them Japanese. Academic tutoring for children in international schools.
Salary: B300-600 per hour.
Facilities/Support: school provides list of cheap housing. Some training given. Large ESL etc. resource library.
Recruitment: word of mouth. Local interviews essential. Speculative applications cannot all be answered.
Contact: John F. Moriarty, Owner.

Other Schools to Try

Note that these schools (in alphabetical order according to town) did not confirm their teacher requirements for this edition of *Teaching English Abroad*. Upper case entries marked with an asterisk had entries in the last edition (1999); addresses without asterisks have been taken from various sources, such as British Council lists.

Chulalongkorn University Language Institute, Prem Purachatra Building, Phaya Thai Road, Bangkok 10330 (2-218 6031/fax 2-252 5978). 15 teachers.

ELCA (English Language Centre of Australia), 313 CP Tower, 26th Floor, Silom Road, Bangkok 10500 (e-mail elcas@loxinfo.co.th)

ELITE TRAINING INSTITUTE, 2nd Floor, Kongboonma Building, 699 Silom Rd., 10500 Bangkok (2-233 6620/fax 2-237 1997; elite_training@hotmail.com). 60-70 teachers placed in private and government primary and secondary schools.

English for Busy People, 268 Siam Square, Soi 3m, Rama I Road, Patumwan, Bangkok

inlingua School of Languages, Head Office: 7th Floor, Central Chidlom Tower, 22 Ploenchit Road, Pathumwan, Bangkok 10330 (2-254 7029/fax 2-254 7098; ctd.bkk@inlingua.com). Many full-time teachers at several branches in Bangkok and also Phuket.

NAVA Language Schools, 34 Paholyothin 7, Phayathai, Bangkok 10400 (2-617 1391; navaoperations@nls.ac.th/). Experience and TESOL certificate not required. Pay of 26,000-29,000 baht per month plus other benefits. Associated with TEFL International certificate programme (see entry in *Directory of Training Courses Abroad*).

NORTH AMERICAN LANGUAGE SCHOOL, 36/1 Ngam Wongwan Road, Bangkok 10900 (2-953 0416/fax 2-953 0417; northam2000@yahoo.com). 15-18 teachers.

Ake Panya International School, 158/1 Moo 3, Hangdong-Samerng Road, Bangpong, Amphur Muang, Chiang Mai 50230

Australia Centre, 75/1 Moo 4, Tambon Suthep, Amphur Muang, Chiang Mai 50200

CEC Chiang Mai Education Centre, Nimanhaemin Road, Chiang Mai 50200 (see entry for E-20/CEC Language School above).

Chiang Mai International School, 13 Chetupon Road, Tambon Watkate, Amphur Muang, Chiang Mai 50000

Nakorn Payap International School, 114 Moo 1, Tambon Nong Pa Krung, Amphur Muang, Chiang Mai 50000

Nava Language Centre, Nimahnaemin Road, Chiang Mai 50200 (53-400388/9)

Prestige, 3rd Floor, CM Education Centre, 108 Chiang Mai (53-410618; pelt@loxinfo.co.th). British English only.

Tridhos Three Generation School, PO Box 1, Amphur Mae Rim, Chiang Mai 50180

YMCA, 11 Mengrai Rassamee Road, Amphur Muang, Chiang Mai 50200 (53-221819). Also run summer language camps.

*ANANDA SHYAMA, 45 Mu 2 Parksong, Patho, Chumpon 86180. 2-3 volunteers to teach in remote village areas

Patong Language School, 95/23 Mu 4 Soi Bangla, Patong Beach, Kathu, Phuket 83150 (76-340373/fax 76-340873).

*SIAM COMPUTER & LANGUAGE SCHOOL PHUKET, 2 Soi, 7 Phung-nga Road, Muang, Phuket 83000 (76-219914/fax 76-218720; narisara@phuket.a-net.net.th). Teachers of young children needed.

*STAMFORD COLLEGE, Soi Ju-teeuthit 3, HatYai, Songkhla 90110 (74-347203/fax 74-347201; chain@hatyai.inet.co.th)

LATIN AMERICA

Spanning 75 degrees of latitude, the mammoth continent of South America together with the Caribbean islands and the eight countries of Central America, offer a surprising range of teaching opportunities. With the important exception of Brazil where Portuguese is spoken, most South American countries have a majority of Spanish speakers and, as in Spain itself, there is a great demand for English teaching, from dusty Mexican towns near the American border to Punta Arenas at the southern extremity of the continent, south of the Falkland Islands.

The countries of most interest to the travelling teacher are Chile, Argentina, Colombia, Ecuador, Venezuela, Brazil and Mexico. Certain patterns emerged during the research for this book, though sweeping generalisations are of limited value and will not apply to all countries and all situations. Inflation is still a problem for many of the nations of Latin America, especially Ecuador, which means that salaries quickly lose their value unless there are frequent adjustments. Although pay scales are often quoted in US dollars, wages are almost always paid in the local currency which in many cases is worth little outside the country.

The economies of Latin American nations are much less volatile than they were at the beginning of the decade. Urban life in the big cities of Argentina or Chile is more like that of Europe than of developing countries. In such cities, the greatest demand for English comes from big business, and because of the strong commercial links between the two American continents, the demand tends to be for American English, though an increasing number of British and Australian teachers are finding work in these countries.

Among the most important providers of the English language are Bi-National Centers and Cultural Centers, the American counterpart of the British Council. There are scores of these centres in Latin America, including over 60 in Brazil and about 15 in Argentina and ten in Mexico. A complete list (under the rather worrying heading 'American Republics' instead of 'Latin America') is available from the United States Department of State, Cultural and Binational Centers, English Teaching Fellow Program. Contact information for the individual binational centres can be obtained from the website http://e.usia.gov/education/engteaching/eal.elp1.htm. These centres are all engaged in the teaching of English, some on such a large scale that they employ more than 20 teachers. While some want a commitment to stay for two years, others are happy to take someone on for two or three months. While some require only a good command of English (whatever the accent), others want teachers with a BA/MA in TESL from a US university.

Britain also has cultural representatives in nine Latin American nations. The longest established *Culturas Inglesas* are in Argentina, Brazil, Chile, Mexico, Peru and Uruguay, with Costa Rica, Paraguay and Guatemala having joined the list more recently. These Cultural Associations aim to teach English within the framework of British culture and work closely with the British Council and represent the elite end of the market. Normally they require their teachers to have specialised ELT training and experience. Only a few recruit abroad so it is worth making local enquiries on arrival.

Several South American nations have a number of British or American-style bilingual schools and *colegios*. Although this book is not centrally concerned with English-medium schools, which are normally looking for teachers with a PGCE or full teacher accreditation, international schools in South America are mainly for local nationals (rather than expatriates) who want a bilingual Spanish-English education and have a very strong emphasis on English language teaching. Despite the prestige of these schools, some are willing to consider EFL teachers who have not done teacher training. For example many of them accept school leavers participating in gap year projects.

Finally there are private and commercial language institutes from International House (in Brazil and Argentina) through Berlitz (which is strongly represented in Latin America) to the cowboy operations where standards and wages will be extremely low. David Hewitt, a computer programmer from Yorkshire with no TEFL training or experience, was surprised not only to walk into a teaching job in Brazil but also to find himself giving lessons to the director of the school.

In whatever kind of school you teach, or if you just give occasional private lessons to contacts, you will probably find the local people extremely friendly and eager to help. The ethnic diversity and Latin warmth encountered by foreign teachers and travellers throughout the continent usually more than compensate for low wages and (in the big cities) a high crime rate.

Prospects for Teachers

In a land where baseball is a passion and US television enormously popular, American (and also Canadian) job-seekers have an advantage. The whole continent is culturally and economically oriented towards the States. There is a decided preference among language learners for the American accent and for American teaching materials and course books, which explains why so many language institutes are called Lincoln and Jefferson. Business English is gaining ground throughout the region, particularly in Argentina, Chile, Venezuela, Colombia, Brazil and Mexico, and anyone with a business background will have an edge over the competition.

The academic year begins in February or early March and lasts until November/December. In the southernmost nations of Chile and Argentina, January and February are very slack months for language schools; while further north in Bolivia, for example, the summer holiday consists of December/January. The best time to arrive to look for work is a few weeks before the end of the summer holidays. But many institutes run eight to twelve week courses year round and will be eager for the services of a native speaker whatever the time of year.

Very seldom will you find the glut of teachers you find elsewhere in the world, as Nick Branch found:

> *English teachers are still much in demand in South America, probably because fewer native speakers visit this region than other parts of the world, due to the perception by many that it is the world's most dangerous/corrupt continent – partly true, but hugely exaggerated in the minds of many. I had no problems at all in South America. One just has to be a little more vigilant than usual.*

FIXING UP A JOB

Speculative enquiries from EFL teachers are much less likely to work if sent before arrival than after, although sending a 'warm-up' CV may help your job search. What the principal of a girls' school in Lima wrote to us is echoed by many other institutes. 'Anyone interested in a job is welcome to write to me at any time. If they happen to be in Lima they are equally welcome to come into school.' Unless you are very well qualified or have met your prospective employer before, you are unlikely to be offered a contract while out of the country. This is unfortunate since work visas are best applied for in the country of origin of the teacher (see below).

In Advance

Very few Latin American language schools advertise in the UK press. Even the most prestigious schools complain of the difficulties they encounter recruiting teachers abroad, mainly due to the low salaries they can offer and the very bureaucratic procedures for obtaining a work permit. Some British Council offices in South America keep lists of schools, as do some embassies and consulates in London and Washington. When 20 year old James Gratton was making plans for his first trip to South America, he wrote to all the embassies in London and received quite a lot of literature, including a number of lists of language schools, for Paraguay, Uruguay, Peru, etc. He claims that the Argentinian Embassy was particularly helpful and friendly. Serious candidates might ask the Cultural Attaché for advice.

LAURELS (the Latin American Union of Registered English Language Schools) currently has more than 70 members in Uruguay (all in Montevideo) and Brazil in most of the important cities. The schools are noted for the high quality of tuition they provide, and are active in cooperating with the British Council in the field of teacher development, particularly in improving services to young and teenage learners. The LAURELS prospectus is updated annually and circulated to institutes considering applying to become members (rather than to prospective teachers). LAURELS may be contacted at International House Goiania, Rua 4, 80 Setor Oeste, Goiania 74110-140, GO, Brazil (62-224 0478/fax 62-223 1846; www.laurels.org).

Language school chains and organisations which might be of assistance to qualified British TEFL teachers are *International House, Berlitz* and *Wall Street Institute. Saxoncourt Recruitment & English Worldwide* are active in several countries of South America (see chapter *Finding a Job*) and sometimes recruit on behalf of *Culturas Inglesas* and international schools.

School leavers should contact the *Project Trust* (which has links with schools in Brazil, Chile, Guatemala and Cuba), *GAP Activity Projects* (which make TEFL placements in Mexico, Argentina, Paraguay, Ecuador, Chile and Brazil) and *Gap Challenge* (Belize and Peru). *i-to-i* (0870 333 2332) send people to teach in Costa Rica and Bolivia. Amerispan Unlimited in the US (PO Box 40007, Philadelphia, PA 19106; tel/fax 215-751-1100; info@amerispan.com/www.amerispan.com) is a Spanish language travel organisation that offers unpaid volunteer placements – some as teachers – in Argentina, Bolivia, Costa Rica, Ecuador, Guatemala, Mexico and Peru. Internships lasting one to six months follow on from a language course. The placement fee of $350 includes travel insurance.

TEFL training colleges in the US often have close ties with Latin American language schools. The training centres in California like *Transworld Teachers* and *New World Teachers* send large numbers of their graduates to posts in South America.

ELS International has affiliated language schools in Santiago, Buenos Aires, Rio, São Paulo and Curitiba. Bénédict Schools are well represented in Ecuador. *EF English First* has been expanding on the continent with schools in Colombia, Ecuador, Mexico, etc.

The *Central Bureau for International Education & Training* arranges for language assistants to work in a number of Latin American countries for an academic year. Applicants must be aged 20-30 with at least A Level Portuguese or Spanish. The level of placements and the nature of the duties are more suited to graduates than undergraduates. Application forms are available from October; the deadline is 1 December of the year preceding placement.

Certified teachers interested in EFL posts might like to contact *Gabbitas Educational Consultants* which send teachers to schools in South America on two or three year contracts, such as Cambridge College in Lima which was recently advertising posts.

PGCE-holders who are committed Christians will be interested to hear that SAMS, the South American Mission Society (Overseas Personnel, Unit 11, Prospect Business Park, Langston Road, Loughton, Essex IG10 3TR; 020-8502 3504) recruit teachers of English for three schools in South America with an Anglican foundation, Colegio San Andres (Asuncion, Paraguay), St. Paul's School (Viña del Mar, Chile) and a new school in Peru. In addition to these formal settings, the Church in some areas is establishing high quality English language institutes to provide a service to university students and as a means of forming a bridge into the community.

The Association of American Schools in South America (AASSA, 14750 NW 77 Court, Suite 210, Miami Lakes, FL 33016; 305-821-0345/fax 305-821-4244) coordinates teacher recruitment for its 32 members, all American-international schools in 11 South American countries. Candidates who attend a recruiting fair in December must be state-certified teachers. The placement fee is $300, payable only on being hired, and often reimbursed by the employer.

The *TESOL Placement Bulletin* carries occasional notices of vacancies in South American schools. A few schools, including some of the biggest Bi-National Centers, attend TESOL Conventions.

South American Explorers (formerly the South American Explorers' Club) keeps lists of schools which employ English teachers. At the time of writing they were compiling an extensive volunteer database in order to make information about volunteering opportunities throughout South America available to members. Many of the organisations listed will take on English teachers without a TEFL certification. Membership costs US$40 per year and residents outside the USA pay an additional US$10 for postage. Membership in the UK is administered by Bradt Publications, 41 Nortoft Road, Chalfont St. Peter, Bucks SL9 OLA and in the USA at 126 Indian Creek Road, Ithaca, NY 14850 (tel 607-277 0488; fax 607-277 6122; e-mail explorer@samexplo.org Website: www.samexplo.org).

Amity Volunteer Teachers Abroad are increasingly active in Latin America. Having successfully recruited volunteer teachers to teach in Argentina, they have recently expanded to other countries - Peru (Lima), Mexico (Guadalajara), Costa Rica and the Dominican Republic. The nine-month teaching placements start in late February in Argentina and Peru, and in January/February for the others. Details are available from AVTA at the Amity Institute, 10671 Roselle St, Suite 101, San Diego, CA 92121-1525 (858-455-6364/fax 858-455-6597; mail@amity.org/ www.amity.org). Applicants for these positions must be at least 21 and must demonstrate that they have a working knowledge of Spanish by writing a letter of intent in Spanish and being interviewed over the phone in Spanish. ATVA volunteers pay their own travel expenses and insurance but are given full room and board with a host family as well as pocket money amounting to $15-$25 a week. (See section below on Argentina for a first-hand account of an Amity placement.)

Other voluntary and international exchange organisations involved in arranging for young people to do some English tutoring include *WorldTeach* with programmes in Costa Rica and Ecuador and *Alliances Abroad* which arranges for fee-paying volunteers to teach in various Latin American countries.

On the Spot

The concept of 'job vacancy' is very fluid in many Latin American language institutes and, provided you are willing to work for local teaching wages, you should be able to create your own job almost anywhere. As throughout the world, local applicants often break into the world of language teaching gradually by teaching a few classes a week. Non-contractual work is almost always offered on an unofficial part-time basis. So if you are trying to earn a living you will have to patch together enough hours from various sources. Finding the work is simply a matter of asking around and knocking on enough doors. For those who speak no Spanish, the first hurdle is to communicate your request to the secretaries at language schools since they invariably speak no English. Try to memorise a polite request in Spanish to pass your CV (*hoja de vida*) and letter (in Spanish if possible) to the school director who will know at least some English. Try to charm the receptionist, librarian or English language officer at the British Council, Bi-National Center or any other institute (like the South American Explorers in Peru and Ecuador) which might have relevant contacts or a useful notice board. Check adverts in the English language press such as *The News* in Mexico City or the *Buenos Aires Herald*. English language bookshops are another possible source of teaching leads.

Ask in expatriate bars and restaurants, check out any building claiming to be an 'English School' however dubious-looking, and in larger cities try deciphering the telephone directory for schools or agencies which might be able to use your services. There is more competition as well as more opportunities in the major cities (for example it is said that up to half a million Americans live in Mexico City), so if you are having difficulties rounding up work, you could try smaller towns and cities off the beaten track.

The crucial factor in becoming accepted as an English teacher at a locally-run language school may not be your qualifications or your accent as much as your appearance. You must look as neat and well-dressed as teachers are expected to look, at least when you're job-hunting. Later your standards might slip a little; Nick Wilson who taught for two years in Mexico says that it is easy to spot the English teachers in banks and office buildings; they're the ones wearing jeans, T-shirts and carrying cassettes.

Freelance Teaching

In most Latin American cities, there is a thriving market in private English lessons, which usually pay at least half as much again as working for an institute. It is not uncommon for teachers to consider the language school which hires them as a stepping stone to setting up as a private tutor. After they have familiarised themselves with some teaching materials and made enough contacts among local language learners, they strike out on their own, though this is far from easy unless you can get by in the local language and also have a telephone and suitable premises. Clients can be found by advertising in the quality press, by placing notices on strategic notice boards or by handing out business cards. If the latter, use the local method of address and omit confusing initials like BA after your name: teachers often call themselves 'Profesor' or 'Profesora.'

REGULATIONS

Of course requirements vary from country to country but the prospects are dismal for teachers who insist on doing everything by the book. It is standard for work visas to be available only to fully qualified and experienced teachers on long-term contracts. Often you will have to present an array of documents, from university certificates and transcripts to FBI clearance, which have been authenticated by your Consulate abroad or by the Consulate of the host country. Although many schools will not offer a contract before interview and then will make it contingent on a work permit, the procedures should be started in the teacher's country of origin, which makes the whole business very difficult. All of this can take as long as six months or even a year and involve a great deal of hassle and expense, not least for the employer.

The upshot is that a high percentage of teachers work unofficially throughout Latin America. It is hardly an issue in some countries, for example virtually no one gets a work permit in Costa Rica, not even the long-resident directors of language schools and no one seems to worry about it. Teaching on a tourist visa is a widespread practice in Mexico and Peru. Brazil is much stricter: all exchanges of money are supposed to be accompanied by receipts, which is likely to make life more difficult for casual teachers. There are ways round the regulations, for example to work on a student/trainee/cultural exchange visa (as in Ecuador or Venezuela).

CONDITIONS OF WORK

The problem of low wages has already been emphasised, and is even worse when inflation is rising. It is customary to be quoted a wage in American dollars (often in the range US$2-4 per hour) and to be paid the equivalent in the local currency. Assuming you are able to save any of your earnings, you will be unable to convert it into a hard currency except on the black market.

Some schools offer perks such as 14-month salaries or return flights to teachers who stay for a two-year contract. Contracts are fairly hard to come by and almost always require a minimum commitment of a year. The advantages are that you are guaranteed a certain income and you have a chance of applying for a work permit.

Teachers without the CELTA or Trinity Certificate are not greatly disadvantaged, partly because this qualification is not as widely known in Latin America as it is in Europe. One exception might be in Uruguay where two institutes offer the Trinity Certificate in TESOL: Dickens Institute (21 de Setiembre 2744, Montevideo) and *English Lighthouse Institute* (see entry at end of Latin America chapter). Many institutes offer their own compulsory pre-job training (to be taken at the teacher's own expense) which provides a useful orientation for new arrivals.

One of the seldom-mentioned perks of teaching in Latin America is the liveliness and enthusiasm of the pupils. Brazilian students have been described as the 'world's most communicative students' and classrooms around the continent often take on the atmosphere of a party. You may also be dazzled by the level of knowledge of Western pop culture, and should be prepared to have your ignorance shown up. Also be prepared to lose their attention if a lesson coincides with a major sporting event.

LEISURE TIME

Whether you are a serious student of Spanish or a frivolous seeker after the excitement generated by Latin carnivals, South America is a wonderful place to live in and travel. Women teachers may find the *machismo* a little hard to take, but will soon learn how to put it in its place. If you want to travel around, the annually revised *South American Handbook* definitely justifies the initial outlay of £22.

Argentina

Argentina has always had a substantial English-speaking population and therefore teaching jobs for unqualified foreigners are relatively scarce. Buenos Aires is a sophisticated city with a high standard of education and a thriving market for business English. Most jobs begin in March/April and last through until Christmas. As in other South American capitals like Santiago, in-company teaching to middle managers and executives in big corporations is booming.

As mentioned earlier, the *Buenos Aires Herald* regularly carries job adverts for English teachers. The newsletter for teachers of English in Argentina and southern South America is called *ELT News & Views* (e-mail me@interlink.com.ar). There is also a useful notice board in El Ateneo, the bookshop at 340 Calle Florida (the main shopping street). Another good contact point is the Instituto de Lengua Espanola para Extranjeros or ILEE where many foreign residents take Spanish classes.

The network of *Culturas Inglesas* which operate under the auspices of the British Council hire only teachers at the British Council standard. Contact names for the following institutes can be obtained from the British Council Argentina website www.britishcouncil.org/argentina/spanish/english/culturas.htm.

Asociacion Bahiense de Cultura Inglesa, Zelarrayan 245, 8000 Bahia Blanca.

Instituto Chaqueno de Cultura Inglesa, Saenz Pena, 25 de Mayo 480, 3700 Chaco.

Asociacion Argentino de Cultura Britanica, Av. Hipolito Yrigoyen 496, Cordoba.

Instituto Cultural Argentino de la Plata, Calle 12 No 869, 1900 La Plata, Buenos Aires.

Instituto Cultural de Mendoza, Necochea 552/56, 5500 Mendoza.

Cultura Inglesa de Neuquen, Carlos H Rodriguez 439, 8324 Neuquen.

Asociacion Pergamino de Cultura Inglesa, 25 de Mayo 746, 2700 Pergamino, Buenos Aires.

Asociacion Puntaltense de Cultura Inglesa, Paso 364, 8109 Punta Alta, Buenos Aires.

Instituto Argentino de Cultural Britanico, Alsina 296, 1878 Quilmes, Buenos Aires.
Instituto Chaqueno de Cultura Inglesa, Don Bosco 256, 3500 Resistencia, Chaco.
Asociacion Rosarina de Cultura Inglesa, Buenos Aires 1174, 2000 Rosario, Santa Fe
St. John's Language College, Avenida Cordoba 261 Este, 5400 San Juan.
Instituto Cultural Argentina, 25 de Mayo 347, 4000 San Miguel de Tucuman.
Instituto Cultural Anglo Argentino de San Rafael, Avellaneda 250, 5600 San Rafael-Mendoza.
Instituto Cultural Anglo Argentino, Tucuman 367, 4200 Santiago del Estero.
Asociacion Venudense de Cultura Inglesa, Marconi 631, 2600 Venado Tuerto-Santa Fe.
Asociacion Victoriense de Cultura Inglesa, Abasolo 28, 3153 Victoria.
Instituto Ocampense de Cultural Inglesa, 25 de Mayo 1530, 3580 Villa Ocampo, Santa Fe.

The Amity Foundation (contact details at beginning of this chapter) has a strong Volunteer Teachers Abroad programme in Argentina in which Americans over the age of 21 with a grasp of conversational Spanish live with a family and teach at a language institute for eight or nine months. Board and lodging are free plus pocket money is paid. Elizabeth Tenney joined the programme and was sent to the small city of Rafaela in the Argentinian Pampas:

That city became my second home. I was lucky to find home life so rich and open, ameliorating my fears of being so far from my real family. As much as family life was comforting, my work life was challenging and rewarding. I taught at a small private language institute and spent a lot of time visiting classes and planning English lessons from the kindergarten level to adult classes. My favourite experience was heading my own free-conversation classes for adults in which I was able to get to know my students on a deeper level. The programme ensures enough free time so that you can travel, take classes (I took French, computing and Latin dance) and get involved in community activities.

Bi-national centers (Instituto de Intercambio Cultural Argentino-Americano) also offer English courses, as do the three International House schools in the capital (located in Recoleta, Belgrano and San Isidro). To work at one of these, you normally have to have worked for IH before. A large number of full-curriculum private schools prepare students for Cambridge and other exams, such as the Belgrano Day School (Juranmento 3035, 1428 Capital Federal) which has pupils from kindergarten to school leaving age.

Private institutes in Buenos Aires to try are American English (Esmeralda 853, P.B.9), Wall Street Institute (Av. Santa Fe 2429, 1123 Capital Federal) and Centum, Servicios de Idiomas, (Bartlomé Mitre, 4th floor, 1036 Buenos Aires; fax 1-1432 82385) which offers the Trinity College Certificate in TESOL part-time and therefore has a ready supply of qualified teachers. You might also try Links English Language Centre in the centre of Buenos Aires (fax 1-825 5735).

Red Tape

Working papers can be obtained from the National Direction of Migrations by employers, though a school will be willing only for long-term propositions. It will be necessary for the applicant to provide a contract of employment for a minimum of a year, certificate of good conduct from the police authorities in his or her country or countries of residence in the five years prior to applying, birth certificate, all authenticated by the Argentine Foreign Ministry. Teachers generally work on a visitor's visa, leaving the country every three months to renew their tourist visas when they recross the border back into Argentina.

Most teachers are paid hourly by the language institute/s employing them. Self-employed people are obliged to register with the DGI (tax office) and pay approximately 15% of their full-time earnings in tax.

LIST OF SCHOOLS
A.C.R.I.C.A.N.A.
Escalada 1567, Comodoro Riuadavia, 9000 Chubut, Argentina. Tel: 54 297 4466311. Fax: 54 297 4472483.
Number of teachers: varies.
Preference of nationality: none, but should be native speaker.
Qualifications: must be graduate with at least 5 years' teaching experience.
Conditions of employment: 6-month contract. Four to eight hours per week.
Salary: depends on number of teaching hours.
Facilities/Support: no assistance with finding accommodation.
Recruitment: varies.
Contact: Rosana Elatigny.

ASOCIACION ARGENTINA DE CULTURA BRITANICA
Av. HipólitoYrigoyen 496, 5000 Córdoba, Argentina. Tel/fax: (351) 469 1000. E-mail: aacb-cba@satlink.com
Number of teachers: 2.
Qualifications: qualified teachers with at least 3 years' ELT experience.
Conditions of employment: 1 year contract.
Salary: US$15 per hour.
Facilities/Support: teachers normally resident in Córdoba already. In-house training and assistance with work permits given.
Recruitment: CVs and personal interviews.
Contact: Raquel Z. de Garber, Director.

CAIT (Capacitacion, Interpretación y Traducciones)
Maipú 863, 3rd Floor 'C', 1006 Buenos Aires, Argentina. Tel: (11) 4311 8544/4314 2583. E-mail: cait@ciudad.com.ar.
Number of teachers: 30 freelancers for in-company language training.
Preference of nationality: American or British.
Qualifications: TEFL qualification CELTA or equivalent plus experience in teaching Business English.
Conditions of employment: minimum 1 year (March to December). Teachers are required to have their own tape recorder and to register with the local IRS. School does not demand exclusivity but expects a firm commitment. Priority given to teachers who are available early mornings and evenings.
Salary: US$15 per hour.
Facilities: sizeable library. Teachers are supplied with materials plus coaching on business English methodology. No assistance with accommodation.
Recruitment: local interviews necessary (can be pre-arranged by e-mail).
Contact: Alejandra Mercedes Jorge, Director.

Bolivia

Even the poorest of Latin American nations offers reasonable possibilities to EFL teachers, provided you are prepared to accept a low wage. In contrast to the standard hourly wage of $15-$20 per hour in Buenos Aires, the wages paid by language schools in Bolivia are about 12 bolivianos ($2 at the time of writing). But many teachers touring South America prefer it for cultural reasons. La Paz is a city with a low cost of living and a colourful social mix. The class structure is immediately apparent with the upper class consisting of people of Spanish descent, the middle class or *mestizos* of mixed Spanish/Bolivian ancestry and the underclass of Indians still wearing their traditional costume.

Only a handful of language schools and a couple of colegios (private schools) are listed in the La Paz Yellow Pages and they are unlikely to commit themselves to hiring a teacher without meeting them first. The biggest language school in the country is the Centro Boliviano Americano or CBA (Parque Iturralde Zenon 121, Casilla 12024, La Paz; 2-431779; cbalp@datacom.bo.net) with three other locations in La Paz plus schools in other cities like Sucre and Santa Cruz. Despite its name it has been trying to increase the number of British native speakers on its staff and has also employed Irish nationals. Diana Maisel turned down a job offer here because she didn't feel comfortable with the unrelaxed atmosphere, for example police were posted at the door of the school to prevent late entry by tardy students. Instead she accepted work with the Pan American English Centre (Edificio Avenida, Avenida 16 de Julio 1490, 7° piso, Casilla 5244, La Paz; tel/fax 2-340796) where she found the atmosphere much friendlier and more relaxed. Classes rotate teachers every two or three months so that students are exposed to a variety of English accents. It also has a branch in Cochabamba.

After finishing university and working briefly for a multinational, Ben Yeomans decided that the corporate environment was not for him and that instead he wanted to teach English in Latin America. He chose Bolivia after meeting the director of i-to-i (an agency which makes placements in that country):

> *I arrived in La Paz in February of this year and worked at the Pan American English Center, teaching all levels of English. The director is an Englishwoman who receives teachers from i-to-i as well as from individual applications. (She acts as the i-to-i representative and is very helpful.) My working hours varied, but were on average about four hours a day. I also worked as a volunteer for a children's interactive museum using my computer skills. I spoke no Spanish when I went, but now can hold a reasonably intelligent conversation.*
>
> *Bolivia is a great country to be in. It has a huge amount of natural beauty, a very varied geography, interesting and colourful customs and friendly people. I am now in a serious relationship with a Bolivian girl and am planning to stay. My experience of teaching English has shown me that I don't want to continue with this as a career (as I considered once, in a rush of enthusiasm during my TEFL course), so I am quite happy to return to my real profession in computing but in a different environment.*

Colegios employ native speakers for their English departments and tend to pay as much as twice as much as the private language schools. Also, the hours of 8.30am-1.30pm are more convenient. Three *colegios* in La Paz are:
Colegio Ingles Saint Andrews, Av. Las Relamas, La Florida, La Paz (2-792484/794041).
Colegio San Ignacio, Av. Hugo Ernest 7050, Següencoma, La Paz (2-783720/784680).
Colegio San Calixto, C/ Jenaro Sanjinés 701, La Paz (2-355278).
Private classes are even more lucrative. The standard rate for beginners is 20 bolivianos, rising to 30 or even 40 bolivianos an hour, but private pupils are even more unreliable than elsewhere in the world. The best place to advertise private English lessons is the Sunday edition of the newspaper *El Diario.*

Jobs can be found outside the capital as well. Judith Twycross received three job offers within a week of arriving in Bolivia's growing city Cochabamba. After Judith's pre-arranged job in Bolivia fell through at the last moment (not an uncommon occurrence), she decided to go in any case. She arrived in January so as to be there a couple of weeks before the beginning of the term. Terms normally last from early February to early September, resuming at the end of September to the beginning of December. With the advantage of a year's teaching experience in Spain and France and a good knowledge of Spanish, she soon found employment:

> *I took with me a letter of introduction and a CV both in Spanish plus a photocopy of my degree certificate. These I photocopied and delivered by*

hand to the directors of schools and institutes in Cochabamba. I got a list of schools from the Yellow Pages (which you could borrow at a hotel, photocopying kiosk, tourist information office, etc.). I told everyone I met what I was trying to do and received help and advice from hotel managers, taxi drivers and people I stopped on the street to ask for directions.

Most teachers arrive on a tourist visa and with the help of their employer get a one-year visa (at a cost of $180). Long stay visas are generally not available unless you commit yourself to staying for a minimum of one year. If you do sign a contract and pay a sizeable fee, you should be able to obtain at least a student visa which means you don't have to leave the country at regular intervals to renew your visa.

The British company *i to i* goes to Bolivia; the 'i venture' scheme will cost participants £1,300 for an English teaching job to be set up for them.

Brazil

The stabilisation of Brazil's currency over the past two years has encouraged the market for English teaching, which is not confined to the major cities of São Paulo and Rio de Janeiro. There are more than 39 SBCIs *(Sociedades Brasileiras de Cultura Inglesa)* and 60 bi-national centers scattered all over the fifth largest country in the world. Schools in smaller places often notify cooperating institutes in the big cities of any job vacancies for native speakers. But speculative visits to towns of any size would probably be successful eventually. Any of the five British Council offices in Brazil (Brasilia, Recife, Rio, Curitiba and São Paulo) should be able to send a list of Cultura Inglesas and LAURELS member schools. Alternatively, the *Culturas Inglesas* with e-mail addresses are listed on the Brazilian British Council website www.britishcouncil.org/brazil/english/english/braenci.htm. Here you can also see a page called 'Teaching English in Brazil for Native Speakers'.

The distinguishing feature of Brazilian EFL is the high proportion of well qualified Brazilian English teachers. Recruiting teachers from overseas is seen to be unjustifiably costly and also very difficult from the visa point of view. Only individuals with very specialised expertise are invited to work in very senior posts.

The Administrative Director of one of Rio de Janeiro's upmarket schools describes the difficulties:

> Unfortunately, teaching English is not an area the government considers a priority in issuing visas. There are only two situations in which foreigners can teach in Brazil. Illegally, since there are numerous small schools who can afford to run the risk of hiring illegal foreigners. As a result, pay is usually bad and employment unstable. The alternative is available only to specialists, and is extremely rare. Because we have a web page, I get requests from foreigners all the time. I basically tell them that it is an adventure here, only for the strong of stomach, and you have to be willing to subject yourself to the unsavoury experiences that go along with working without proper papers. I have come across dozens of foreigners who have been promised work-related visas. In 27 years of living in Brazil, I have never, not once, seen this happen. The only cases I know of where a person has taught legally, it has been when they enter the country with visas issued at the Brazilian consulate in their country of residence.

At the prestigious end of the market, schools like the Culturas Inglesas, bi-national cultural centres and International House schools (the five Britanic Schools in Recife are affiliated to IH, plus there is an IH school in Goiania), do recruit outside Brazil and enable their contracted teachers to obtain permits, though it can take up to six months.

Otherwise it will be a case of looking around after you arrive, by using the

Yellow Pages and expatriate networks. If you want to study Portuguese, you can apply for a student visa which would make it easier to stay on. For example, many foreigners register at the Pontificia Universidade Católica in Rio de Janeiro (Extension Department, Casa 15, Rua Marques Sao Vincente 225, Gávea, 22453-900 Rio; 21-529 9212). This is an excellent place to link up with students and advertise classes if you want to offer private lessons (which pay much better than working for an institute). You can also advertise in local papers like *O Globo, O Dia* or *Jornal do Brasil*. People on tourist visas can renew them by taking a trip to neighbouring Paraguay.)

The best time to start work is following *Carnaval* which takes place during the week over Ash Wednesday every February. Bear in mind that the cost of living in the big cities is very high, probably on a par with US cities, so that it is difficult to live on earnings of $8-$10 an hour. Foreigners who do stay usually bring a financial cushion with them or are lucky enough to get private students straightaway.

Difficulties over obtaining visas have caused the organisation Teaching and Projects Abroad (Gerrard House, Rustington, West Sussex BN16 1AW, UK) to cancel their teaching project to send English speakers to Brazil for between one and three months. The programme has been replaced by a similar one in Peru.

LIST OF SCHOOLS

BRITANNIA IPANEMA
Rua Garcia d'Avila 58, Ipanema, Rio de Janeiro. Tel: +55 21 511 0143. Fax +55 21 511 0893. E-mail: sdmale@britannia.com.br
Number of teachers: 12-15.
Preference of nationality: North American and British.
Qualifications: degree plus recognised TEFL Cert.
Conditions of employment: 1 year renewable.
Salary: US$20,000 per year approximately (very good for Brazil).
Facilities/Support: accommodation subsidised.
Recruitment: advertising and via contacts in the UK.
Contact: Susan Mace, DOS.

BRITANNIA SCHOOLS
Central Department, Av. Borges de Medeiros 67, Leblon, Rio de Janeiro (RJ). Tel/fax: (21) 511 0143. E-mail: sdmace@britannia.com.br. Web-site: www.britannia.com.br Website www.britannia.com.br
Number of teachers: 70 teachers of which 20 native speaker teachers for schools in Rio de Janeiro and Porto Alegre.
Preference of nationality: British, American, Canadian.
Qualifications: Cambridge Cert. (Grade 'B') essential, BA and experience.
Conditions of employment: 1-2 year renewable contracts. 25 h.p.w. Students grouped according to age starting at 14-15 up to adults.
Salary: varies according to teacher's scale.
Facilities: subsidised assistance with accommodation provided. Orientation and teacher development provided.

CULTURA INGLESA – BLUMENAU/FLORIANOPOLIS
Rua Marechal Floriano Peixoto 433, Centro, Blumenau 89010-000, SC. Tel/fax: (47) 326 7272; also (48) 224 2696. E-mail: mike@bnu.nutecnet.com.br
Number of teachers: 3.
Preference of nationality: British.
Qualifications: minimum Cambridge Certificate and 2 years' experience.
Conditions of employment: 1 year contracts. Maximum 24 contact h.p.w. Hours of teaching between 7.15am and 9.40pm and Saturday mornings. Some off-site business teaching.
Salary: US$800-$1000 per month.
Facilities/Support: shared accommodation in a four-bedroomed flat provided free.

Flight reimbursement of US$500. Training provided.
Recruitment: through TEFL journals. Interviews and references essential and are occasionally held in Britain.
Contact: Mike Delaney, Cultura Manager.

CULTURA INGLESA
Rua Ana Bilhar 171, Aldeota, Fortaleza, CE. Tel/fax: +55 85 244 3784. E-mail: cultura@roadnet.com.br Website: www.culturainglesa.ce.com.br
Number of teachers: 7.
Preference of nationality: none.
Qualifications: TEFL plus one year's experience.
Conditions of employment: 12 months minimum. 30 hours per week (80% contact hours).
Salary: depends on qualifications and experience. Deductions for tax and social security about 12%.
Facilities/Support: assistance with finding accommodation. No assistance given with work permits.
Recruitment: mainly personal recommendation.
Contact: N Irving.

CULTURA INGLESA DE GOIANIA
Rua 86 No. 07, Setor Sul, Goiania, GO. Tel: (62) 241 4516. Fax: (62) 241 2582. E-mail: cult.ing.sul@persogo.com.br
Number of teachers: 7.
Preference of nationality: British and Irish.
Qualifications: CELTA plus 3 years' experience.
Conditions of employment: 2 year contracts with option to renew for 2 years.
Salary: 1,500 reals (US$800 a month) less deductions of approximately 18%.
Facilities/Support: no assistance with accommodation. Help given with work permit (teachers must pick up visas at embassy in London.)
Recruitment: direct application or via agency. Detailed questionnaire sent to candidates' past employers.
Contact: Noel Downer, School Principal.

FOREVER ENGLISH AND SPANISH
Rua Rio Grande do Sul 356, Pituba Salvador, Bahia 41830-140. Tel: (71) 240 2255. Fax: (71) 248 8706. E-mail: forever@forever.com.br Website www.forever.com.br
Number of teachers: 5.
Preference of nationality: British, American, Australian, Canadian.
Qualifications: minimum two years EFL experience.
Conditions of employment: minimum 5 month contract. Around 30 h.p.w. Pupils from 8 years to adults. General and Business English.
Salary: $700 per month (the minimum salary in Brazil is US$90 for a 44-hour week).
Facilities/Support: no assistance with visas. One week in-service training before start of school year and 4 hours training monthly. (School is a member of LAURELS).
Recruitment: via AIESEC (International Association for Students of Economics and Management, 2nd Floor, 29-31 Cowper St, London EC2A 4AP). Interviews not essential, but contact made by phone.
Contact: Dinara Cavalcanti, Director or Juliana Cavalcanti, Academic Director.

IBI-INDEPENDENT BRITISH INSTITUTE
SHCGN 703, Area Especial 70730-700 Brasilia, DF. Tel: (61) 322 8373/322 0976. Fax: (61) 323 5524. E-mail: ibi@nutecnet.com.br
Number of teachers: 12-15.
Preference of nationality: British.
Qualifications: CELTA (grade A or B), BA, 2 years' experience.

Conditions of employment: 2 year contracts. 22-24 h.p.w. Students of all ages.
Salary: varies according to experience.
Facilities/Support: training/supervision provided.
Recruitment: through contact with former UK teachers. Interviews essential and held in UK.
Contact: Sara Walker, Principal.

M&M CONSULTARIA LINGUISTICA – INTERLANGUAGES
Av. Presidente Vargas 446, grupo 1407 Centro, Rio de Janeiro (RJ). Tel/fax: (21) 224 9413. E-mail intlang@domain.com.br Website: www.domain.com.br/clientes/inlang
Number of teachers: 18.
Preference of nationality: British, American.
Qualifications: TEFL, experience of working with executives.
Conditions of employment: freelance only.
Salary: varies according to qualifications.
Facilities/Support: no assistance with accommodation or work permits.
Recruitment: direct application. Local interviews.
Contact: Marisa Domingues, Principal.

NEW START COMUNICACOES Ltda.
Av. Rio Branco 181/702, Centro, 20040-007 Rio de Janeiro, RJ. Tel: (21) 240 5807. Fax: (21) 524 6579. E-mail: newstart@prolink.com.br. Web-site: www.newstart. com.br.
Number of teachers: variable, between 4 and 15.
Preference of nationality: must be a native speaker of English.
Qualifications: CELTA or TEFLA certificate and preferably professional experience in a non-teaching area.
Conditions of employment: minimum 5 months work.
Salary: R$17 (£6) per hour.
Facilities/Support: assistance with accommodation. Training in business English.
Recruitment: direct application by CV via e-mail and telephone. Possibility of interviews in UK.
Contact: Stephanie Crockett, Director of Studies.

Other Schools to Try

The following did not confirm their teacher requirements for this edition. Upper case letters and asterisks indicate that an institue had an entry in the last edition (1999). Other addresses have been gleaned from British Council lists, etc.

ACE American Center of English, Avenida Beira Mar 406, gr. 207, Castelo, 20025-900 Rio de Janeiro (RJ). Tel: 21-220 3345.

Beeline, Avenida 13 de Maio 23, Gr. 429, Centro, 21031-000 Rio de Janeiro (RJ). Tel 21-222 7238/532 5792.

BRASAS English Courses, Brasil América Sociedade de Ingles, Rua Voluntários de Pátria 190/325, Botafogo, 22270-010 Rio de Janeiro (RJ). Tel: 21-527 8399/fax 21-286 8996/www.brasas.com. Lots of branches.

Britannia Special English Studies, Av. Borges de Medeiors 67, 22430 040 Rio de Janeiro (RJ)

CCAA Centro de Cultura Anglo Americano, Rua 14 de Maio, 347, Riachuelo, 20950 090 Rio de Janeiro (RJ) (21-501 5000; www.ccaa.com.br). Employs more than 4,000 teachers at hundreds of branches.

Centro Cultural Brasil Estados Unidos, Avenida T 5, no. 441, Setor Bueno, 74230-040 Goiânia, GO (62-833 1313/fax 62-833 1308). E-mail: ccbeu@international.com.br.

Context Cursos, Rua Marques de Olinda 75, Botafogo, 22251 040 Rio de Janeiro (RJ)

Curso Oxford, Rua Duvivier 28/SL, (Sobreloja), 22020 020 Rio de Janeiro (RJ). 10 teachers.

ELS International, Rua Antonio Viera 24a, Leme, Rio de Janeiro (RJ). Tel: 21-293 4962.

English Center, Rua Toneleiro 219, Copacabana, 22030-000 Rio de Janeiro (RJ). Tel: 21-255 0014.

Feedback, Rua da Quitanda 74, 1 andar, 20011 030 Rio de Janeiro (RJ)

FISK English School, Avenida 13 de Maio 33, SI 306, Centro, 21031-000 Rio de Janeiro (RJ). Tel: 21-220 4110.

IBEU (Instituto Brasil-Estados Unidos), Av. N.S. de Copacabana 690, 5 andar, 22050 000 Rio de Janeiro (RJ) (Caixa Postal 12154). Tel: 21-255 8332/fax 21-255 9355.

Phoenix – Ingles Empresarial, Rua Gal. San Martin 974/102 Leblon, 22631 390 Rio de Janeiro (RJ)

Wizard, Rua Marechal Henrique Lott 120/107, Barra da Tijuca, 22631 390 Rio de Janeiro (RJ) www.wizard.com.br. Dozens of branches listed on website.

Britanic International House, Recife, Rua Hermógenes de Morais 178, Madalena Recife, PE (81-445 5564/fax 81-445 5481). 7 teachers.

Lex English Language Services Ltda, Rua Humberto I, No. 318, Vila Mariana, Sao Paulo 04018-030 SP (tel/fax 11-5084 4613; www.lexenglish.com.br). Want lawyers and law students to teach legal English.

Oxford Street School of English, Avenida Juriti 441, Moema, Sao Paulo (tel/fax 11-5051 4747; oxfordstreet@wac.com.br). 6 or 12 month contracts.

Chile

Chile's economy is flourishing, attracting a great deal of foreign (mainly American) investment. At the turn of the 21st century, Chile has achieved a remarkable ten percent rate of growth and unemployment is less than 5%. As commercial, touristic and cultural contacts with the outside world have increased in the new democratic Chile, so has the demand for the English language. The most booming market is for business English, though there is also a growing demand for teachers of children.

Of course most of the opportunities are in the capital Santiago where there are more than 30 major language schools, though there are some relevant institutes in the Valparaiso-Viña del Mar area. There will be less competition for teaching vacancies in smaller places like the aptly named La Serena in the dry north of the country.

The prestigious Instituto Chileno-Britanico de Cultura at Santa Lucia 124 in Santiago recruits only highly qualified teachers, and has a good library which incorporates the British Council's resource library for teachers; anyone who pays the modest membership fee can borrow materials, though many schools in Santiago have good libraries themselves. Native speaker teachers are also hired by the Institutos Chileno-Britanico de Cultura in Concepcion, Arica and Viña del Mar (listed below). A further possibility is to teach at English-medium *colegios,* where a longer commitment will be necessary and a reasonable salary paid. Although they employ mainly certified teachers, often hired at recruitment fairs and through international advertising, they do need some native speakers for their English departments.

The commercial institutes in Santiago vary greatly in size, reliability in their treatment of employees and teaching methods. Newcomers to the city quickly learn which are the better schools and gradually acquire more hours with them. Some of the smallest companies do not teach on their own premises at all, but send their teachers out to teach classes in the offices and occasionally the homes of their clients. Most offer a combination of on-site and off-site teaching. In-company teaching usually takes place early in the morning; middle-ranking staff tend to be taught before the official working day begins while directors and higher-ranking executives take their classes at a more civilised mid-morning hour. Most teachers enjoy the variety of off-site teaching rather than classroom teaching which tends to be more textbook-based. Diana Maisel greatly enjoyed teaching small groups of executives from IBM and Ernst & Young when she was in Santiago.

The academic year runs from March to December with a two-week winter holiday in July and one week recess in mid-September. The British Council's Information Office can send a list of 11 private language schools, seven British-Chilean Institutes and 13 British curriculum schools. The Santiago *Yellow Pages* are also a useful source; look up *Instituti de Idiomas*.

The following schools are among the best known language schools in Santiago. Typically these schools offer a newcomer a few hours and will offer them a full timetable only after a probationary three months.

Berlitz, Av Pedro de Valdivia 2005, Providencia, Santiago. Tel: 2-204 8076. Berlitz has a substantial establishment in Santiago but prefer to interview only candidates who already have a work permit.

British English Centre, Av. Providencia 1308, p.2. Oficina D, Providencia, Santiago. Tel: 2-496165. Prefer teachers who are fluent in Spanish.

Burford, Avda. Pedro de Valdivia 511, Providencia, Santiago. Tel: 223 9357/274 4603. Fax: 2-223 5944. A small 'agency-type' institute which favours British English.

ELADI Instituto Professional, José M. Infante 927, Providencia, Santiago. Tel: 2-251 0365. Fax: 2-225 0958.

Fischer English Institute, Cirujano Guzman 49, Providencia, Santiago. Tel: 2-235 9812/235 6667. Fax: 2-235 9810. Contact Adriana Otero Renau. Teaches both on and off-site. Offers plenty of structure in planning lessons.

Impact English, Rosa O'Higgins 259, Las Condes, Santiago. Tel: 2-211 1925/212 5609. Fax 2-211 6165. Contact Señora Pepa. Reputed to offer high rates of pay.

Linguatec, Av. Los Leones 439, Providencia, Santiago. Tel: 2-233 4356 ext.15: www.linguatec.cl. Linguatec's head office is in Denver: 915 South Colorado Blvd, Denver, CO 7783; esl@bridgeschool.com. Compulsory one week training course for all accepted teachers which is unpaid but it guarantees the offer of some hours of work on completion. Teaching schedule of 80-100 hours a month earns $580-$730.

Sam Marsalli, Av. Los Leones 1095, Providencia, Santiago. Tel. 2-231 0652. Hires only North Americans on 1-year contracts. 250,000 pesos per month (£300).

Non-contractual work is usually paid by the hour, starting at less than 3,000 pesos per hour. Most good schools pay more than 4,000 pesos per hour and up to 5,000 pesos to those who have a recognised qualification. The cost of living is higher than in many other places on the continent but not high enough to absorb all of a teacher's earnings. Normally 10% of earnings must be paid in tax, which in some cases can be reclaimed the following year. Diana Maisel started gradually with a few hours from several of the above companies, but after two months was teaching 30-35 hours per week and saving a lot of money (helped by the low rent of 50,000 pesos a month she was paying to lodge with a language school owner). She had sent her CV from England to about 20 schools in Santiago before arrival but got a very discouraging response. Undaunted, she landed in Santiago on her own in early October and easily found work, helped no doubt by her Cambridge Certificate. Several of the schools she approached recalled that they had already read her CV which she felt worked to her advantage. (A friend from the US with no TEFL training failed to persuade any language institute to hire her and so turned to waitressing instead.)

Red Tape

If you are offered a job before arrival, there are two ways to obtain the appropriate visa permit. Either your employer submits the application at the Ministry of Foreign Affairs in Chile (Direccion de Asuntos Consulares y de Imigracion, Bandera 46, Santiago) or you apply at the Chilean Consulate in your country of origin. You will need a signed and notarised work contract and a full medical report. If granted, the visa will be valid for one or two years. After that you may be eligible for a *visacion de residencia* which allows an unlimited stay.

If you arrive to look for work, you will not be able to get a working visa without leaving the country. If you are able to commit yourself for a year, your employer may be willing to help. Most teachers who stay for shorter periods do not bother trying to change their visa status knowing that the immigration authorities are much less likely to raid language institutes than they are hotels and restaurants where migrant Peruvians work.

Advertising for Private Clients

There are many ways to meet the expatriate community from playing cricket at the Prince of Wales Club to frequenting the English language bookshop Books and Bits (Av. Apoquindo 6856, Las Condes-Santiago; 2-229 9026; fax 2-211 8717; booksbit@entelchile.net/www.booksandbits.co.cl).

You can advertise for private clients in *El Mercurio*, the leading quality daily. Other newspapers such as *La Epoca* and *La Tercera* have classified ads sections which will cost slightly less than *El Mercurio*. There is a magazine called *El Rastro* consisting of nothing but advertisements into which you can phone in a small ad free of charge (though the response may be less than spectacular). If you need to be written to rather than telephoned or e-mailed it might be useful to take out a Post Box number with the Chilean Correo, particularly if your address is not stable.

A useful option is to find a supermarket which has a noticeboard for small advertisements in their entrance halls. For example the Almac and Jumbo chains of stores have such noticeboards. Almac is located on the corner of Avenida Pedro de Valdivia and Bilbao, while Jumbo is on the corner of Portugal and Diagonal Paraguay. If you can translate between English and Spanish, it will be worth advertising yourself as a translator as well.

LIST OF SCHOOLS

ACPEN ACADEMY
949 Alameda Ave (Lib. B. O'Higgins Ave.), Of. 2103 Edificio Santiago Centro. Tel/fax: (2) 6724460. E-mail Acpen-Academy@ceprivet.cl
Number of teachers: varies.
Preference of nationality: none.
Qualifications: as many as possible.
Conditions of employment: only teachers with a work visa are offered contracts. 20-25 hours per week. Mainly teaching adults and English for specific purposes.
Salary: around $6 per hour.
Facilities/Support: no assistance with accommodation. Work permits are generally obtained by the teacher.
Recruitment: interview necessary.

THE BRITISH SCHOOL
Casilla 379, Punta Arenas. Tel: (61) 223381/223233. Fax: (61) 220120/248447. E-mail: vracadem@ctcreauna.cl
Number of teachers: employs overseas contract staff from time to time.
Qualifications: university degree and appropriate teaching diploma. English mother tongue and a working knowledge of Spanish is essential. The institute is an official Centre for the University of Cambridge Examinations.
Conditions of employment: 2 year renewable contracts for work in the language institute and the School. Students aged 4-18.
Salary: negotiable.
Facilities/Support: assistance with accommodation.
Recruitment: directly with school.
Contact: John Poppleton, Headmaster.

INSTITUTO CHILENO-BRITANICO DE CULTURA
Santa Lucia 124, Santiago. Tel: (2) 638216. Fax: (2) 6326637. E-mail: direccion@britanico.cl Website: www.britanico.cl
Number of teachers: 10.
Preference of nationality: none, but should be native speaker.
Qualifications: a degree in English or Modern Languages, plus a TEFL qualification. However, experience is valued more than TEFL qualification.
Conditions of employment: one year, March to February. 30 teaching hours per week mostly evenings.
Salary: £600/US$1000 monthly.
Facilities/Support: help with finding accommodation is provided. Teachers are provided with a settling in grant towards their accommodation.
Recruitment: usually on the spot.
Contact: Anthony Adams, Director General.

INSTITUTO CHILENO-NORTEAMERICANO DE CULTURA
Moneda No. 1467, Santiago. Tel: (2) 696 3215. Fax: (2) 698 1175. E-mail: academic@hood.ichn.cl or info@norteamericano.cl. Website: www.ichn.cl.
Number of teachers: 15-20.
Preference of nationality: American, Canadian.
Qualifications: BA in Education or TESL/TEFL and 6 months' teaching experience, or BA in related field with Certificate in TESL/TEFL and 2 years' teaching experience.
Conditions of employment: 1 year contracts starting in March. 30 h.p.w. Peak hours of work early morning and early evening, and some Saturdays. Classes for adults, children, teens, business and academic English.
Salary: equivalent of US$1,100 per month in Chilean pesos.
Facilities/Support: assistance given in obtaining visas. Training provided. Teacher's room with computers, e-mail access and cafeteria privileges.
Recruitment: direct application by mail, e-mail, phone or fax. Applicants should send cover letter, resumé, recent photo, copy of diplomas/certificates and letters of reference from recent employers.
Contact: Jacqueline Abt, Educational Services Director.

POLYGLOT
Villavicencio 361 Of. 102, Santiago. Tel: (2) 639 8078. Fax: (2) 632 2485. E-mail: application@polyglot.cl Website www.polyglot.cl
Number of teachers: 40-50 a year.
Preference of nationality: none.
Qualifications: TEFL or Cambridge Certificate; university degree; business experience.
Conditions of employment: at least 6 months for freelancers. Teaching hours: 8-10am, 12-3pm and 6-9pm.
Salary: US$8-$12 per hour, depending on location.
Facilities/Support: assistance with accommodation and work visas for permanent staff.
Recruitment: adverts. Local interview essential.
Contact: José Sepúlveda, Academic Director.

REDLAND SCHOOL
Camino El Alba 11357, Las Condes, Santiago. Tel: 2-214 1265. Fax: 2-214 1020.
Number of teachers: 16.
Preference of nationality: British.
Qualifications: university degree and teaching qualification. In some cases a short TEFL course is sufficient.
Conditions of employment: 1-3 year contract. Classes run 8am-3.30/5pm.
Salary: starting salary about US$9,500 per year. Pupils aged 4-18.
Facilities: free accommodation and utilities provided.

Recruitment: direct contact with British universities and recruiting agencies. Interviews normally take place in the UK.

TRONWELL S.A.
Apoquindo 4499, Piso 3, Las Condes, Santiago. Tel +56-2 2461040. Fax: +56-2 2289739. E-mail: tron.dnd@ctcreuna.cl. Website: www.tronwell.com.
Number of teachers: 40-50.
Preference of nationality: none.
Qualifications: native speakers. Preferably with degree in English or CELTA or equivalent.
Conditions of employment: minimum one year. Hours for full-time staff include 7.35am-4.45pm or 1.15-8.15. Part-time positions also available.
Salary: full-time 325,000 pesos gross. Approximately 20% deductions for tax and social security.
Facilities/Support: no assistance with accommodation. Advice on work permit procedure.
Recruitment: Interview followed by a five-day training programme to learn the Tronwell methodology and instructional system. After the training period teachers are asked to prepare and teach a demonstration class on which depends the job offer.
Contact: Claudia Bunce, Academic Director.

Other Schools to Try

INSTITUTO CHILENO BRITANICO DE CULTURA, San Martin 531, Concepción (41-242300/fax 41-234044)
Academy of English Studies, Esmeralda 1095, La Serena
Instituto de Ingles Icen SAE, Eduardo de la Borno 222, Paisage Santo Domingo, La Serena (51-224523)
Welcome to English Institute, Paisage Francisco Araya 631, La Serena

American Language Center, Av. Libertador, B. O'Higgins 1941, Santiago.
American Language Institute, San Ignacio 277, Santiago
BEA, Salvador 95, 505-515 Providencia, Santiago
Centro Chileno Canadiense, Av. Luis Thayer Ojeda 0191, Of. 601, Tobalaba
English Express, Del Metro Los Leones, Providencia 2133 Of. 703, Santiago
IBC, Av. Presidente Errázuriz 3328, Las Condes, Santiago (2-242 9292/fax 2-233 8143; ibc@reuna.cl). 5-10 teachers for this business consultancy.
Inbusiness, Fidel Oteiza 1971, Ps. 5° Y 7°, Metro P. de Valdivia, Santiago
Lorbeth, Cabo Arestey 2468, Republica, Santiago
SANTIAGO COLLEGE, Los Leones 584, Casilla 130-D, Santiago (2-232 1813/fax 2-232 0755). 13 certified teachers.
Wall Street Institute Chile, Av. Apoquindo 3502, Las Condes, Santiago (2-335 6256/fax 2-335 6258; wsichile@netline.cl Master franchise for country.
INSTITUTO CHILENO – BRITANICO DE CULTURA, 3 Norte 824, Casilla 929, Viña del Mar (32-971061/fax 32-686656). 6 Certificate-holders.
English Alive, Av. Vitacura 7125, Vitacura

Colombia

Since most people's only associations with Colombia are with crime and violence, it is not surprising to learn that teaching institutes in that country sometimes have trouble attracting qualified foreign teachers. Foreign teachers are extremely unlikely to become involved in any drug-inspired tensions but are guaranteed to be welcomed by the locals. Memories will be of a local carnival rather than of a neighbourhood shoot-out. With the opening up of trade (called *Apertura*), interest in English has increased, as evidenced by the popularity of English language media like newspapers and radio stations.

Colombia is even more strongly oriented towards the US than elsewhere in South America with an extensive network of Colombian-American Cultural Centers around the country. However Charles Seville from Oxford, who spent a year as an English language assistant at the University de Los Llanos in Villavicencio, was struck by how keen Colombians were to learn British English. There are British Council Teaching Centres in Bogotá and Medellin, catering mainly for the executive market. One ELT organisation which is expanding in the country is EF English First; the main school in Bogotá is at Calle 76, No. 9-66, Santafé de Bogota (1-347-8055; Diana.Pinilla@ef.com).

It is possible to access the Colombian *Yellow Pages* on the internet (www.quehubo.com) which might provide a starting place for finding school addresses. Anyone considering Medellin as a destination (despite associations with the drug trade) should look at the website www.ontonet.be/~karel7/cworklistschools.htm. It carries some personal notes on the job hunt and an annotated list of language schools. The main newspaper *El Tiempo* carries numerous adverts for language schools in the capital. There are plenty of local language schools where untrained native speakers can find work, but there are two main disadvantages. Wages and conditions are very poor; many schools offer just a few thousand pesos an hour (possibly about US$2.50), though the schools listed below offer more attractive dollar salaries than that. The second problem is the red tape. As usual, temporary working visas must be applied for in your country of residence. The Colombian Consulate in London sends out clear information about the requirements which include an undertaking by the employer to bear the cost of repatriation if the visa is cancelled and a letter from the Ministry of Work & Social Security testifying that the Colombian employer is not exceeding the legal limit on foreign employees. The visa fee is £128 plus £16 for notarisation charges. If a teacher intends to stay in Colombia longer than six months, he or she must register in person at DAS, the Colombian equivalent of the FBI, within 30 days of arrival. Approval will mean that you are entitled to acquire a *Cédula de Extranjería* (foreigners' ID).

LIST OF SCHOOLS

CENTRO CULTURAL COLOMBO AMERICANO – BARRANQUILLA
Carrera 43, No. 51-95, Apartado Aereo 2097, Barranquilla. Tel: (5) 340 8084. Fax: (5) 340 8549. E-mail: colombo@b-quilla.cetcol.net.co Website: http://b-quilla.cetcol.net.co/~colombo
Number of teachers: up to 10.
Preference of nationality: none, but must be native speakers.
Qualifications: BA (English or Education) with 1 year's teaching experience or MA (TEFL/TESL) and some teaching experience.
Conditions of employment: 1 year renewable contracts. 6 hours of work a day between 7am and 8.30pm, Monday-Friday. Students aged 5-58 but mostly 18-25.
Salary: from 12,300 pesos per hour plus 2 months' pay and 15 days paid holiday after 1 year.
Facilities/Support: will reimburse one-way airfare from Miami after 4 months and return portion after 1 year. Assistance given with finding accommodation. Some training provided.
Recruitment: interviews not essential. Send résumé.
Contact: Khaitoon M. de Osorio, Academic Director.

CENTRO COLOMBO-AMERICANO – BOGOTA
Avenida 19, No 3-05, Santafé de Bogota. Tel: 571-334 7640. Fax 571 282 3372. E-mail: biblioteca@unete.com
Number of teachers: 2-3 a year.
Preference of nationality: American or Canadian because of the cost of bringing them to Colombia.

Qualifications: a teaching certificate or a degree in TESL or TEFL and/or extensive experience preferred.
Conditions of employment: one academic year. Six hours a day during the school hours from 6am to 9pm.
Salary: varies from year to year. 7% deductions for social security.
Facilities/Support: help with finding somewhere to live and give them US$300 towards settling in expenses. Work contract and all other documents for obtaining a work permit sent to candidate. School reimburses cost of obtaining permit.
Recruitment: through school web page, word of mouth.
Contact: Josephine Taylor.

CENTRO COLOMBO AMERICANO – MEDELLIN
Cra. 45 No. 53-24, Medellin. Tel: (4) 513 4444. Fax: (4) 513 2666. E-mail: lshem @colomboworld.com (Re: Academic Director) Website: www.colomboworld.com
Number of teachers: 140 in programme with 6 US/UK teachers.
Preference of nationality: American, Canadian, British. Other countries welcome.
Qualifications: BA or MA (Education, Language Teaching, TESOL).
Conditions of employment: 1 year contract (renewable). 6 contact hours per day. English for children and adults.
Salary: 900,000-1,500,000 pesos per month (about £200).
Facilities/Support: round trip ticket and visa expenses paid. Housing assistance. Pre-service and in-service training. Medical benefits and Spanish lessons provided.
Recruitment: direct application with CV and 3 letters of recommendation. Selection made through references and phone interview. The best time to apply is November to start February.
Contact: Lai Yin Shem, Academic Director or Steve Ingham, Academic Coordinator.

CENTRO CULTURAL COLOMBO AMERICANO – CALI
Calle 13 Norte 8-45, A.A. 4525 Cali. Tel: (2) 668 5960/661 4303. Fax: (2) 668 4695. E-mail: cencolam@colnet.com.co Website: www.colombocali.edu.co
Number of teachers: 5-10 foreign teachers out of 50-60 for several locations in Cali.
Preference of nationality: American, Canadian.
Qualifications: at least a BA in an English teaching related field and a minimum of 6 months' teaching experience.
Conditions of employment: 1 year renewable contracts. 33 h.p.w. including evening and Saturday work. Students aged 6-60.
Salary: average 800,000 pesos per month.
Facilities/Support: assistance given with finding accommodation. Training provided.
Recruitment: through advertising in newsletters and at conventions. Interviews by phone if necessary.

OXFORD CENTRE
AA 102420, Bogotá. Tel: (1) 345 1059. Fax: (1) 255 8758. E-mail: javiersanchez90@hotmail.com
Number of teachers: at least 10.
Preference of nationality: British, Australian.
Qualifications: BA or MA (languages, English, literature).
Conditions of employment: 5 month contracts, starting February or July. 25 class hours a week.
Salary: US$600 per month.
Facilities/Support: bed and breakfast accommodation provided with host families.
Recruitment: through phone interviews and references.
Contact: Javier Sanchez, Principal.

Other School to Try

CENTRO DE INGLES LINCOLN, Calle 49, No. 9-37, Bogotá (1-288 0360/fax 1-287 3806). 25 teachers.

FIRST CLASS ENGLISH LTDA., Carrera 12 No. 93-78 Piso 4°m Santafé de Bogotá, D.C. (1-623 2374/fax 1-623 2379). 5 teachers.

*COLEGIO BRITANICO DE CARTAGENA, Anillo Vial Km. 16, A.A. 20156, Cartagena (tel/fax 5-668 6280). Handful of ESL positions at full curriculum school

International Language Institute, Cra. 13 No. 5 - 79, Castillo Grande, Cartagena (5-66 51 672). 6 teachers.

American English Academy, Cr 50, No. 48 – 45 Of. 311 Rio Negro (4-561 79 30). 1 hour from Medellin.

AVC Audiovisual Center, Cr 45 (El Palo), No. 52 –59, Medellin (4-513 18 40)

Berlitz, C7, No. 39 – 215, Edf. Granhorrar, Medellin (4-381 70 04)

El Centro Ingles, C11, No. 43D – 11, Medellin (4-311 48 88). Start by giving applicants a few hours a week. Pay US$4-5 an hour. Must have working visa.

Inlingua, Cr 77B, No. 47 – 70, Medellin (4-250 97 46)

Lexicom, C 17A Sur – 44 – 276, Medellin (4-313 36 04). Part-time only.

Lubigon English Academy, Cr 68, No. 48D – 5, Medellin (4-260 54 13)

Meyer School, Cl 34B No 65D –7, Medellin (4-265 9733; www.meyerinstitute.com). Provide training in their own method.

Natural Learning, C49, No. 79 – 29, Medellin (4-234 65 66). Business English.

Praxis, C 79, No. 39 – 30, Medellin (4-411 51 52/250 05 15/fax 4-250 82 39. 2 schools in Medellin. Offer 3-month contracts. US$300 for full-time timetable, 6 days a week.

Winston – Salem, Cr 43, No. 17 Sur – 63, Medellin (4-313 76 39). Full-time work.

Ecuador

Compared to its neighbours, Peru and Colombia, Ecuador represents an oasis of political stability. But in the past two years, the country has been experiencing an economic crisis resulting in a radical devaluation of its currency. One possible solution would be to adopt the US dollar as the national currency. Teaching wages worth $5 or $6 a couple of years ago are now worth only $2 or $3 or even less. But obviously EFL teachers do not go to Ecuador to save money and it is still possible to live on the wages paid. For example a night in a budget hotel costs less than $3 and a three-course meal costs 50 cents.

Despite the crisis, the demand for English still thrives, particularly for American English in the capital Quito, the second city Guayaquil and in the picturesque city and cultural centre of Cuenca in the southern Sierra. The majority of teaching is of university students and the business community whose classes are normally scheduled early in the morning (starting at 7am) to avoid the equatorial heat of the day and again in the late afternoon and evening. Many schools are owned and run by expatriates since there are few legal restrictions on foreigners running businesses.

Damaris Carlisle had no trouble finding work when she arrived in Quito because she had a Cambridge Certificate and also a friend who was one of the bosses at Lingua Franca. After 18 months she switched employers and worked for the Experiment in International Living, turning down the offer of a contract so that she could take three months off to climb, cycle and explore the region. Although she was content with the wages paid, she says that there is no point in trying to save money since the currency is worth little outside Ecuador. She found Ecuadorian students to be polite and enthusiastic, though a little over-optimistic about what they could achieve.

Wages are not as high as in Chile but higher than in Colombia, and normally allow teachers to enjoy a comfortable lifestyle since the cost of living is low. Accommodation is harder to find in Quito than in Cuenca. Qualified TEFLers should not accept less than 25,000 sucres an hour though the private institutes which accept unqualified teachers pay accordingly less. All teachers (both contract and freelance) have taxes withdrawn at source of between 3% and 8%, with the majority deducting a flat rate of 7%.

Quito is not as large and daunting a city as some other South American capitals and it should be easy to meet longer term expats who can help with advice on teaching. The helpful British Council will give you a list of ELT schools throughout the country and will (unofficially) indicate which offer the best teacher support and modern teaching methods and resources. One possible source of information is the South American Explorers clubhouse (membership costs $40). In Quito the Club is at Jorge Washington 311 y Leonidas Plaza (Apartado 17-21-431; tel/fax 2-225228). They include language schools in Ecuador on their database and have a useful notice board.

As throughout the continent, charitable schools for disadvantaged children can always use voluntary help. Nick Branch worked in Quito at Guarderia Maria-Ausiliadora (Don Bosco y Paraiso; 2-51034), a pre-school for disadvantaged children where he did some teaching from the front as well as painting, PE activities and games with the children.

Red Tape

Technically you shouldn't work on a tourist visa but there is little control. Britons are entitled to a stay of six months on a tourist visa whereas Americans can stay 90 days. If possible, teachers should get a 12-IX document in their country of origin, which can be extended by visiting a neighbouring country (usually Colombia). Most employers will help teachers who commit themselves for a reasonable stay to obtain a cultural exchange visa, normally valid for a year. The requirements are as follows: two letters attesting to good character, a notarised copy of a police report, health certificate (including HIV test) and birth certificate, letter of invitation from an Ecuadorian employer, letter of financial support from a backer and a return airline ticket.

LIST OF SCHOOLS

BENEDICT SCHOOLS OF LANGUAGES
PO Box 09-01-8916, Guayaquil. Tel: 4-444418. Fax: 4-441642. E-mail: benecent@telconet.net.
Number of teachers: 15 in several branches in Guayaquil (Urdesa, Centro, Garzota, Centenario, Entrerios).
Preference of nationality: British, American, Canadian, Irish.
Qualifications: proficiency in English and teaching certificate or college degree required.
Conditions of employment: minimum of two courses (4 months). Exclusive contract.
Salary: US$2-3 an hour.
Facilities/Support: assistance with accommodation. Pre-service training provided.
Recruitment: local hire.
Contact: Mercedes de Elizalde, General Director.

BENEDICT SCHOOLS OF LANGUAGES
Edmundo Chiriboga N47-133 y Jorge Paez, Quito. Tel/fax: 2-432729. Tel: 2-462972/ 269542. E-mail: benedict@accessinter.net. Web-site: http://www.virtualsystems. com.ec/benedictq
Number of teachers: 8-10.
Preference of nationality: British, American, Canadian.
Qualifications: good knowledge of grammar. Responsible and hard working.

Experience desirable but not a requirement. Young teachers (aged 18-19) can be hired if sufficiently mature.
Conditions of employment: freelance only.
Salary: US$2 per hour plus free Spanish lessons.
Facilities/Support: assistance with finding accommodation. In-house training provided.
Recruitment: via the internet. Interviews not essential.
Contact: Mrs. Jesús de Jaramillo, Director.

CENTRO DE ESTUDIOS INTERAMERICANOS/CEDEI
Casilla 579, Cuenca. Tel: 7-839003. Fax: 7-833593. E-mail: English@cedei.org
Number of teachers: 18.
Preference of nationality: native English speakers.
Qualifications: minimum university degree in related field and TEFL Certificate or university degree in TESL/TEFL. Experience in teaching EFL/ESL.
Conditions of employment: minimum 6-month stay, preference given to year-long commitments. Courses run from January to mid-March, early April to early June, mid-June to mid-August and early October to mid-December. Teachers teach on average 15 hours per week. Most classes meet Monday to Thursday only.
Salary: $2.25 per teaching hour (which is high for Cuenca).
Facilities: apartments are very reasonably priced. Cost of living is low. Free Spanish classes for teachers. Beautiful school building. Very charming city in an Andean setting.
Recruitment: via http://tefl.com, or TESL-L list serve. Use the website www.cedei.org
Contact: Holly Holder Sanchez, English Director or Cathy Molina, Assistant Director.

INLINGUA
Arroyo del Rio y Manuel Maria Sanchez 320, Quito. Tel: 593-2 243 788. Fax: 593 378455. Website: www.inlingua.com
Number of teachers: 30.
Preference of nationality: none.
Qualifications: 2 years' experience; preference given to teachers with Inlingua experience.
Conditions of employment: 1 year. Hours vary.
Salary: US$500.
Facilities/Support: school can find accommodation with families. School pays for visa.
Recruitment: internet and local recruitment.
Contact: Jonathan Turner, Academic Director.

KEY LANGUAGE SERVICES
Alpallana 581 y /Whymper, Quito (Casilla 17-079770). Fax: (2) 220956. E-mail: kls@hoy.net
Number of teachers: 10-15.
Preference of nationality: any native speaker welcome.
Qualifications: TEFL qualification. Experience preferred. Tidy appearance and professional manner essential.
Conditions of employment: 3 months absolute minimum, 6 months or longer preferred. Mainly off-site business classes offered 7-9am, 12-2pm and 4-8pm.
Salary: 75,000 sucres per hour which works out at a good salary in local terms.
Facilities/Support: notice board in office carries details of rental accommodation. Advice given on visas. Monthly professional development sessions. Teachers are allocated a paedagogical mentor.
Recruitment: local interview and observation. Longer-term preferred. Any time of year.
Contact: Ida Dolci and Clare St. Lawrence, Directors of Studies.

SOUTH AMERICAN LANGUAGE CENTRE
Amazonas 1549 y Santa Maria, Quito. Tel: (2) 544715. Fax: (2) 226348. E-mail: sudameri@impsat.net.ec
Number of teachers: 15 (depending on number of clients).
Preference of nationality: all native speakers of English.
Qualifications: teacher's degree and experience preferable but not mandatory.
Conditions of employment: minimum 3 months. Full-time hours are 8.30am-5.30pm Monday to Friday. Part-time schedules between 8am and 5pm. Some Saturdays.
Salary: hourly rate from 30,000 sucres (if working less than 19 hours) to 33,000 sucres for Saturday work or if working more than 35 h.p.w. (US$1.20-US$1.30).
Facilities/Support: advice may be given on accommodation. Help given with cultural exchange visa.
Recruitment: via e-mail, ads in magazines or through universities. Interviews not necessary.
Contact: Mario Cabrera, Staff Manager.

TOP PROFESSIONAL
Tamayo N22-14 and Carrion, Quito-Ecuador. Tel/fax: 593-2-226871. E-mail: topprofessional@hotmail.com Website: www.topprofessional.cjb.net
Number of teachers: 5.
Preference of nationality: British or North American.
Qualifications: the school has its own methodology, so the usual TEFL Cert or experience are not essential.
Conditions of employment: one month up to a year. The teacher chooses hours to suit from 7am to 7pm.
Salary: US$2 per hour.
Facilities/Support: assistance given to find inexpensive, safe accommodation.
Recruitment: adverts and word-of-mouth.
Contact: Fausto, Maria Elena or Ricardo Jácome.

Other Schools to Try
Note that these schools did not confirm their teacher requirements for this edition. Upper case letters and asterisks means that the institute was listed in the last edition. Other addresses have been gleaned from the British Council list and other sources:

NEXUS LENGUAS Y CULTURAS, Jose Peralta 1-19 y 12 de Abril, Cuenca (7-888220/fax 7-888221; nexus@cue.satnet.net). 10 teachers.

JEFFERSON BILINGUAL SCHOOLS, PO Box 09-01-4180, Guayaquil (4-853752/fax 4-854274; admissions@jefferson.ed.ec). Some native speakers for international college, high school and primary school.

UNILIT *(Unidad Informatica del Litoral),* Avenida 2 Calle 11, Manta, Manabi 192 (5-623353; unilit@porta.net). Advertising for a teacher on www.eflweb.com (Sept 2000). $200 per month.

ALPHA ENGLISH PROGRAMS, Salazar 427 y Coruna, Casilla 17-16-18, Quito (tel/fax 2-235068; alpha@hoy.net). 6-10 teachers.

COLEGIO LOS PINOS, Pedro Dionisio 702, Quito (2-240601/241200/fax 2-434021; pinos@pin.k12.ec). 3 teachers, Americans preferred.

Experimento de Convivencia Internacional del Ecuador, Hernando de la Cruz 218 y Mariana de Jesús, Quito (2-551937/550179/fax 2-550228). 10-15 teachers.

FULBRIGHT COMMISSION, Almagro 961 y Colón (PO Box 17-07-9081), Quito (2-562999/563095/fax 2-508149; fulbright@uio.satnet.net). 15-20 teachers. MA TESL preferred.

Harvard Institute, 10 de Agosto y Riofrío, Edif. Benalcázar 1000, Piso No. 17, Quito

Instituto Winfield, Orellana 1171 y La Rabida, Quito

Lingua Franca, Casilla 17-12-68, Edificio Jericó, 12 de Octubre 2449 y Orellana, Quito (2-546075/fax 2-500734/568664).
Princeton International Language Institute, 1133 Colon y Amazonas, Quito~

Mexico

The lure of the United States of America and its language is very strong in Mexico. The frenzy of American investment in Mexico after the North American Free Trade Agreement (NAFTA) saw a huge upswing in both the demand for English by businesses and the resources to pay for it. That boom is now over, but the market for English is still enormous in universities, in business, almost everywhere. Proximity to the US and a tendency towards what Australians call the cultural cringe (in Mexico called *Malinchism* after the lover of Cortès who betrayed her people) means that there will always be an unquenchable thirst for English taught by native speakers in Mexico. Foreign teachers are automatically respected and are often promoted almost immediately.

Companies of all descriptions provide language classes for their employees especially in the early mornings and evenings (but seldom on weekends or even Fridays). Roberta Wedge even managed to persuade a 'sleek head honcho in the state ferry service' that he needed private tuition during the sacred siesta and that busy executives and other interested employees of a local company needed English lessons at the same time of day.

It is not surprising that enrolment in English courses is booming when some employees have been threatened with dismissal unless they master some English. A vet going to Dubai, a stockbroker doing deals with the New York Stock Exchange, housewives who have to go to parties with their executive husbands, teenagers with exam worries, all are keen to improve their English. After each six-year presidential term of office, the top layers of management in companies (especially oil and banking) are replaced by new staff who need new training, especially English. Elections always boost the demand for English not only in Mexico City and the border cities to which US industries looking for cheap labour have relocated, but throughout the country, including the Yucatan Peninsula and other unlikely places, at least one of which must remain nameless in order to preserve Roberta Wedge's dreams:

After doing a 'taster' ESL course in Vancouver, I set out for Nicaragua with a bus ticket to San Diego and $500 – no guide book, no travelling companion, no Spanish. On the way I fell in love with a town in Mexico (not for worlds would I reveal its name – I want to keep it in a pristine timewarp so I can hope to return) and decided to stay. I found a job by looking up all the language schools in the phonebook and walking around the city to find them. The problem was that many small businesses were not on the phone. So I kept my eye out for English school signs. I had semi-memorised a little speech in Spanish, 'I am a Canadian teacher of English. I love your town very much and want to work here. This is my CV...' Within two days I had a job at a one-man school.

The British Council in Mexico City can provide the addresses of the 25 or so language centres attached to state universities and also keeps the Yellow Pages which has a few pages of language schools. Also check the website of the Unión Nacional de Escuelas de Idiomas A.C. www.unei.org. The Council does not have an English teaching centre itself but works closely with the Cultura (Instituto Anglo-Mexicano du Cultura) which has 12 branches in four cities. Some of their foreign recruitment is the responsibility of *Saxoncourt & English Worldwide Recruitment*.

Mexican-American bi-national centres employ scores of native speakers, mostly on a local basis. Typically the *Instituto Mexicano Norteamericano de Relaciones Culturales de Saltillo (IMARC)* in northern Mexico takes on 7-10 enthusiastic graduates in TEFL or a related field, to teach young children aged 5 to 8 for 6 hours per day. The school year starts in early August and lasts for 11 months (see entry). Other US cultural institutes include:

Centro Mexicano-Americano de Relaciones Culturales (CEMARC); Xola 416, Colonia del Valle, 03100 Mexico City 12, DF. Tel: (5) 536 5520. E-mail: cemarc@sisisa.podernet.com.mx.

Instituto Cultural Mexicano-Norteamericano de Jalisco, Enrique Díaz de León 300, CP 44100, Guadalajara, Jalisco. Tel: (36) 825 58 38. Fax: 825 16 71. E-mail: cultural@acnet.net. Employ up to 25 teachers on minimum 6 month contracts.

Instituto Mexicano-Norteamericano de Relaciones Culturales, Blvd. Navarrete y Monteverde, Hermosillo, Sonora. Tel: (621) 40781.

Instituto Cultural Mexicano-Norteamericano de Michoacan, A.C., Guillermo Prieto 86, 58000 Morelia, Michoacan. Tel: (43) 124112.

Instituto Mexicano-Norteamericano de Relaciones Culturales de Nuevo Leon, Hidalgo 768 Pte, Apdo. Postal 2602, Monterrey, 64000 Nuevo Leon. Tel: (83) 340 1583. E-mail: bibbfranc@intercable.net.

Instituto Franklin de Yucatan, Calle 57, No. 474-A, 9700 Merida, Yucatan. Tel: (99) 215996. E-mail: franklin@pibil.finred.com.mx.

A further possibility is to work at English medium schools modelled either on the American or British system. Many of these advertise internationally for certified teachers or recruit through recruiting fairs but, as in Chile, Peru and elsewhere, some are willing to interview native speakers locally to work in the EFL department. Without a TEFL background or at least a solid university education you are unlikely to break into any of these more upmarket institutes.

Gap year students and other inexperienced travellers might want to have a job and accommodation fixed up before arrival. If so, try *Teaching Abroad* in Sussex which runs a teaching programme in Mexico. The fee is £1,395, so teachers cannot break even.

The Private Sector

A host of private institutes supplies language training to business either on their own premises or in-company. The norm is for teachers to freelance and work for a combination of companies. There are also full-time school-based jobs with teaching companies like Harmon Hall and Interlingua which have a national network of branches. Wages are higher (as much as four times higher) at the former, but hours are fewer and less predictable and a lot of time is taken up travelling from office to office. Getting three hours of work a day (early morning and early evening) is easy. Anything above that is much trickier. Freelance teachers must be prepared for frequent holidays cutting into earnings. No institute pays for public holidays, sickness or annual leave. For example attendance goes into a sharp decline after Independence Day on November 20th in the month leading up to Christmas and there are no classes over Easter. Most courses run for three months and there may be a lapse of one or two weeks before another starts. Usually freelancers are paid cash-in-hand with no deductions for tax. Few have working papers (see *Red Tape* below.)

The spectrum of institutes varies enormously. At one extreme there is the employer who pays the equivalent of $3.50 an hour, never pays on time, and who employs only Mexicans with poor English or native speakers who have just arrived with their backpacks and no interest in or knowledge of teaching. The top of the range pays $10 an hour, offers free training and gives contracts that aren't cancelled. These institutes are of course a lot more choosy about their teachers. Whereas a few companies want to control their teachers completely and send inspectors into classes, most leave teachers alone as long as the clients are happy. The typical institute consists only of four people: the owner who gets the contracts, a teacher co-ordinator, a secretary and an office boy. According to Nick Wilson from Cumbria, who spent several years teaching freelance in Mexico City, there is a lot of jealousy between the training institutes with mutual accusations of spying, so discretion is advised. He was working for the wife of his director in her own school along with three other teachers she had poached from her unwitting husband. Some institutes try to poach teachers from rival institutes by offering more money.

On arrival in Mexico City, a good place to meet foreigners is the famed Casa de los Amigos, the Quaker-run guest house at Ignacio Mariscal 132 (5-705 0521/705 0646; o mail friends@avantel.net website www.avantel.net/~friends), centrally located near Metro Revolucíon. This guesthouse is firm about who it will receive as guests and does not regard itself as a casual guest house. They are, however, always happy to put people in touch with volunteer organisations. Check adverts in the major Spanish-language daily *El Universal* as well as the English language newspaper *The News*. Rupert Baker answered an advert in *The News* and was invited to attend a disconcertingly informal interview at a restaurant (to which he still wore his tie). He ended up working for six months.

Obviously a TEFL qualification is an advantage though few employers are concerned about whether it is from a 130 hour or a 30 hour course. Business and financial experience is also beneficial, possibly more than a university degree. An ability to make a class interesting and patience are the two key qualities that many employers are looking for. As one of Nick Wilson's bosses said, 'The most important thing is that the students enjoy their classes and *think* that they are learning English; don't just teach or we'll lose customers.' Word-of-mouth recommendations are very important in Mexican culture, and jobs are seldom filled by postal applications.

Michael Tunison contacted half a dozen major teaching organisations from the Yellow Pages and was interviewed by Berlitz and Harmon Hall. Both offered tentative positions based more on his native speaking than his American university degree and journalism background. The starting wage at both schools was the peso equivalent of US$400 per month which seemed typical of the large chains. One problem here is that these organisations do not pay cash-in-hand and therefore they want to hire only teachers with working papers. Another international chain of language schools represented in Mexico is Wall Street Institutes with 21 schools (addresses on website www.wallstreetinstitute.com/locator/center_HTML/mexico.html).

Guadalajara and resorts such as Puerto Vallarta, Cancun, Acapulco and Mazatlan are places where a great many locals need to master English before they can be employed in the booming tourist industry, though wages tend to be lower than in the capital. Several independent US training organisations have set up TEFL training centres in Guadalajara (see *Training* chapter).

Leaving England for the first time, Linda Harrison travelled on a one-way ticket straight from the picturesque Yorkshire town of Kirkbymoorside to the picturesque state of Michoacàn, and suffered severe culture shock at first (despite a professed love for Mexican food developed the year before when she was a student at the University of Central Lancashire). She and a Spanish-speaking friend had pre-arranged jobs at the Culturlingua Language Center (Plaza Jardinadas, Local 24 y 25, Zamora, Michoacàn) which has the distinct advantage of offering its half dozen native speaker teachers accommodation. However it does not offer any pre-service training as Linda found out:

> *The director told me that I might as well start teaching the day after I arrived. I stumbled into my first class with no experience, qualifications or books. Twelve expectant faces watched while I nervously talked about England. Twelve faces went blank when I mentioned soap operas.*

Zamora is an unpretentious off-the-beaten-track agricultural centre. Culturlingua is always looking for teachers and will consider hiring anyone who is a fluent English speaker and is not painfully shy. The school pays its teachers enough for them to live comfortably and to tour the state of Michoacàn, one of the most beautiful in Mexico. In fact if you get talking to anyone in an out-of-the-way place, sooner or later you will be introduced to the director of the local English institute, as happened to Robert Abblett when he went to work on a remote organic farm near Coatepec, Veracruz. After doing a stint of weeding and planting, the farmer's wife whisked him off to her English language school where a class of Mexican teenagers fired dozens of questions at him to practise their English and improve their knowledge of British culture.

Stuart Britton spent a couple of years in Mexico living on his teaching, often in a hand-to-mouth fashion. His initial job hunt took place in Ensenada, a tourist town in Baja California:

> *What a strange sensation it was to be in Mexico after the States, but the people I met were so warm and friendly and helpful as soon as I crossed the border, that I felt more at home. I felt that with these warm people around me, I couldn't starve or be eaten up. As far as work, I found a school from a fisherman who had befriended me at the bus station who knew someone etc. etc. and then I finally found a commercial institute, a sort of training school for adults where they teach typing, tourism, English, etc.; there are many of these institutes in Mexico. Mostly the pay is very poor and conditions are basic.*

Working for Yourself

Private lessons are in great demand, and may be given informally in exchange for board and lodging. But it is also possible to teach on a more business-like footing. With so many clients seeking one-to-one tuition through institutes, it is worth considering setting up as an independent tutor and offering private lessons at a rate which undercuts the institutes. Teachers who are tempted to poach students from the organisation they work for should bear in mind that employers who find out have been known to set the immigration department on errant teachers. However it is legitimate to advertise yourself in the press and distribute printed business cards. Elizabeth Reid based some of the material in her book *Native Speaker: Teach English & See the World* on her experiences of teaching in a small Mexican city. She started by developing her own private classes in borrowed premises (a disused shop). She recommends approaching the local community centre *(casa de cultura)*, chamber of commerce or public library and offering one free sample class before signing up paying students. To increase goodwill she offered 'scholarships' to a limited number of students who really couldn't afford to pay.

Teaching in companies sometimes produces lucrative spin-offs in the field of translation and editing documents in English. Clients may offer other kinds of work too; for example Nick Wilson was asked to set up a Mexican-British arts foundation through a bank trust by someone he tutored in English.

Regulations

The red tape situation in Mexico is a difficult one. Visitors are not allowed to work or engage in any remunerative activity during a temporary visit. The Free Trade Agreement makes it somewhat easier for Americans and Canadians but still not straightforward. As has been mentioned, established schools are not normally willing to contract people with only a tourist visa, unlike private institutes who often employ teachers on tourist visas for a short period. The most respectable schools may be willing to help full-time contracted teachers with the paperwork but won't pay the cost (estimates vary between $100 and $700). Among the required documents are a CV in Spanish, notarised TEFL and university certificates which have been certified by a Mexican consulate and, if you are already in Mexico, a valid tourist visa. Tourist visas must be renewed every 90 days either by proving at a local government office that you have enough funds to support yourself or (more inconveniently) by leaving the country and recrossing the border to get a further 90 days. Check the website www.mexicanconsulate.org.uk 'Visitors on a Profitable Trip'.

ABC ENGLISH
1616 Suite 6 Blvd. Ruiz Cortines Fracc. Palmas, Poza Rica 93300 Veracruz. Tel/fax: 782 23981.
Number of teachers: varies.
Preference of nationality: none.
Qualifications: TEFL Cert. and teaching experience. Should also have experience of living, and preferably working in a third world country.
Conditions of employment: 3 months (renewable).
Salary: from US$5 per hour plus 15 peso per hour bonus for out of institute classes. Classes are mornings and evenings, Monday to Thurday with the occasional Friday class. Also Saturday intensive courses 8am-12.30pm. All ages.
Facilities/Support: shared apartment or board with a host family can be arranged.
Recruitment: via internet.
Contact: Alanna May.

ARIZONA SCHOOL OF ENGLISH
Blvd. 1 Rosales y Ortega, Deco Plaza, Loc. 7, Col. Centro, Los Mochis, Sinaloa 81200. Tel: (68) 18 56 71. Fax: (68) 15 65 65. E-mail: azschool@bigfoot.com.
Number of teachers: 6-8.
Preference of nationality: American, Canadian, British, Australian.
Qualifications: any combination of BA, Cambridge CELTA or other TEFL qualification, and 1 year teaching experience (preferably abroad).
Conditions of employment: 6 month contracts. 25-30 h.p.w., split shift.
Salary: 6,000-8,000 pesos per month.
Facilities/Support: school owns 2 houses which can be rented by teachers but not compulsory. Help with visas if necessary.
Recruitment: internet ads, correspondence by e-mail, personal recommendation and direct application.
Contact: Larry Klaudi, Director.

ENGLISH FIRST – MEXICO
Londres 188, Col.Juarez, 06600, D.F. Mexico; tel +52 5514 3333; fax +52 5514 1362. E-mail: sharon.reed@ef.com Website: www.ef.com and www.englishtown.com
Number of teachers: 12 for 4 schools (3 EFL schools, 1 business English School).
Preference of nationality: British, North American, Australian, New Zealand.
Qualifications: EFL/ESL Certificate plus university degree.
Conditions of employment: 9-12 month contract (renewable). Schools open from 7am to 9pm Monday to Friday, 9am-6pm Saturdays. 26 real contact hours per week, visa, return flight, paid holiday, bonus, ongoing teacher training, medical insurance.
Salary: 7000-9,500 Mexican pesos depending on experience and qualifications, plus bonus scheme, automatic review on renewal.
Recruitment: telephone, fax or e-mail directly to Mexico head office.
Contact: Sharon Reed, Academic Director.

HARMON HALL PACHUCA
Blvd. Valle de San Javier 225, Fracc. Valle de San Javier, Pachuca Hidalgo, CP 42086. Tel/fax: (7) 71-80900/81910. E-mail: harmonpa@mail.giga.com.
Number of teachers: 8+.
Preference of nationality: British, Canadian.
Qualifications: must be responsible, interested in Mexican culture, energetic and have a desire to teach.
Conditions of employment: standard length of stay is 1 year. Usual hours are 7am-11am and 5pm-8.30pm.

Salary: from 40 pesos per hour.
Facilities/Support: school has teachers' house. If full, help is given in finding alternative accommodation. Help given with work permits provided teacher has brought university certificate or diploma and ESL certificate stamped by the Mexican Consulate.
Recruitment: telephone and internet interviews acceptable.
Contact: Wenceslao Torres.

INSTITUTO MEXICANO NORTEAMERICANO DE RELACIONES CULTURALES (IMARC)
Pres. Cardenas 840, Saltillo, Coahuila 25000. Tel 52 84 14 84 22. Fax: 52 84 12 06 53. E-mail: academ@imarc.edu.mx Website: www.imarc.edu.mx
Number of teachers: 7-10.
Preference of nationality: none.
Qualifications: BA or higher degree in TEFL or related field. TEFL certificates accepted, minimum one year experience.
Conditions of employment: one year renewable contract. 6 contact hours per day.
Salary: from 4,000 to 12,000 pesos gross monthly, depending on experience.
Facilities/Support: shared accommodation in a partially furnished apartment is provided. Own room but share bathroom. IMARC pays half the cost of a work permit.
Recruitment: via internet requesting CV and references. Interview essential. May be carried out at TESOL conferences in the US.
Contact: Lisa C Carter, Academic Co-ordinator.

Other Schools to Try

COLEGIO INTERNACIONAL DE CUERNAVACA, Apartado Postal 1334, Cuernavaca, Morelos, C.P. 62130 (73-132905/116260/138496/fax 73-117451; cintc@infosel.net.mx). 15 teachers to teach primary aged children at this bilingual kindergarten and primary school.

Anglo Mexican Cultural Institute, Rio Nazas 116, Colonia Cuauhtémoc, 06500 Mexico (5-208 5547/fax 208 5460; iamc@fsmail.net). 40 teachers (preferably Britons) for branches in Mexico City, Guadalajara, Puebla and Toluca. Advertised in *Guardian* summer 2000 for teachers to be interviewed in London.

Universidad Autonoma de Chiapas, Departamento de Lenguas Tuxtla, Blvd. Belisario Dominguez Km. 1081, 29000 Tuxtla Gutierrez, Chiapas (961-50650/fax 961-52392)

Universidad Autonoma de Chihuahua, Facultad de Filosofia y Letras, Lengua Inglesa, Apartado Postal 744, Chihuahua (14-13 54 50/fax 14-14 49 32).

Berlitz Mexico, Ejercito Nacional 530 2° Piso, Col. Polanco, 11550 Mexico D.F. (507120)

Glen Internacional Instituto Superior de Idiomas, Viena No 71-301 Col. Del Carmen, Coyoacan, 04100 Mexico D.F. (56-59 37 74; www.solucion.com/glen)

Hamar Sharp, 112 Internacional S.A., Rio Danubio 69-101, Col. Cuahtemoc 06500, Mexico D.F. (55-11 22 08; 112inter@conecta.com.mx)

Harmon Hall, Puebla No 319, Col Roma, 06700 Mexico (11 60 60/fax 11 81 88; informes@harmonhall.com/ www.harmonhall.com.mx)

Wall Street Institutes, Presidente Masaryk No. 49, Mezzanine, 11570 Mexico D.F. (5-45 23 53; wsimarcillac@infosel.net.mx). Master franchise in Mexico; 21 other WSI schools.

Centro Mexicano Internacional, CMI Institute, Calz. Fray Antonio de San Miguel 173, Morelia 58000 (http://208.137.153.15/spanish/intern/edu/cmi.htm). Volunteer teachers for adults and children needed year round.

Universidad Autonoma del Edo de Mexico, Centro de Ensañanza de Lenguas, Cerro de Coatepec, a un costado de la Facultad de Geografia, Ciudad Universidad, C.P. 52100, Toluca, Edo. de Mexico (72-15 18 60/fax 12 07 03).

English Unlimited, Valentin Gama No. 800, esq. SCOP, San Luis Potosi, SLP, Mexico 78270 (tel/fax 48-33 12 77; teaching@englishunlimited.com/ www.englishunlimited.com).

Language Connect Institute, e-mail: jobs@syrlang.com

Universidad del Mar, Centro de Idiomas, Carretera a Zipolite km 1.5, Puerto Angel, Oaxaca, C.P. 70902, Oaxaca (958-43049/fax 958-43078). Take-home salary is US$750/£570.

Global English, San Juan del Rio, Queretaro (geone@prodigy.net.mx)

Mexican Cross-Cultural Institute, 121 Centro Historico, Queretaro (42-12 34 35; e-mail mcciqro@infosel.net.mx).

American School of Veracruz, Progreso 52, Jardines de Mocambo, Boca del Rio, Veracruz (29-21 97 78).

Peru

Lima has in the past been considered one of the most stressful and dangerous South American cities in which to live, however threats from guerilla groups have largely passed and Peru is returning to the mainstream of destinations for English language teachers. Continuing low wages and the difficulty of obtaining working papers mean that few professional teachers can be attracted to the private EFL sector. For those who are, it is worth sending a CV to the English Language Officer at the British Council. He will send a list of British schools and language teaching institutes to anyone sufficiently well qualified or alternatively pass the CV to potentially interested institutions such as the five branches of the British-Peruvian Cultural Association (known familiarly as Britanica).

Yet the range of opportunities in Lima is enormous. The stampede to learn English is unstoppable. Many company employees have been told by their bosses to learn English within three months or risk demotion. Some employers organise a course at their place of work, but most expect their staff to fix up private lessons making the freelance market very promising at the moment. In-company training courses in all industries are often offered in English, so knowledge of the language is becoming essential for all ambitious Peruvians. The Peruvian economy is not in dire straits at present, as evidenced by the remarkable stability of its currency, the new sol.

Many temporary visitors to Peru who lack a TEFL background end up doing some English teaching once they have established a base in the capital, usually earning about $5 an hour at an institute. Some employers offer a free or subsidised training course to new potential recruits, at which native speakers usually excel over the locals whose knowledge of English is often very weak.

James Gratton arrived in Lima to take up what had sounded like a dream job. He had contacted the institutes included on the list sent by the Peruvian Embassy in London and was contacted enthusiastically by one (on the strength of a certificate earned from a one-week intensive TEFL training course in London and nine months of living and teaching in Venezuela the year before.) High wages and many perks were offered, including a promise to meet him at the airport. His new employers' non-appearance at the airport was just the first promise they broke, and the lesson he learned over the next few months was that in Peru (and probably more widely in the continent), you must confirm and reconfirm any arrangements. He lasted only six weeks with this company (and was told that this was a record stay for an expat teacher) but concluded that such bad employers can be used as stepping stones to better opportunities.

For those who prefer to organise in advance, a safer bet might be to join the scheme organised by Teaching and Projects Abroad (tel 01903-859911) which has a programme in Peru for volunteer teachers with proper supervision from back-up staff. Good food and lodging are provided. The minimum stay is a month and the cost for up to three months is about £1,400. Longer stays can be arranged.

A list of bilingual and English medium schools plus a few private schools and universities is available from the Cultural Office of the Peruvian Embassy in London. The list (a couple of years out of date now) is reproduced here:

Freelancing

Setting up as a freelance tutor is potentially very lucrative. A standard fee is $10 a lesson, though this can be reduced for clients who want to book a whole course. With wages like that and assuming you have found enough clients, it is not difficult to earn over $1,000 a month (in a country where the minimum wage is $70). James Gratton put a cheap advertisement (written in English) in the main daily *El Commercio* and signed up two clients. This was possible in his case since he was staying at his girlfriend's house where he had free access to a telephone. His new students were both employees of Petro-Peru, and soon other clients contacted James for lessons. He admits that freelancers do lose out to cancellations, though some of his students willingly paid for missed lessons. Freelancing is a continual process of advertising and getting new students to replace the ones that fall by the wayside. James continued giving private lessons for six months and now wonders about the possibility of returning from Northampton to Lima to set up his own small institute.

Regulations

Peruvian work visas are very rare and most people teach on a tourist visa. As in most other countries, a tourist visa cannot be switched to a work visa inside Peru. The immigration authorities on arrival grant either two or three months; one month renewals are granted by the immigration office in Lima up to a total of five months without leaving the country. After that it is necessary to cross the Peruvian border and have your passport stamped for another two or three months, which can be renewed locally as before. One reason which many people use to extend their stay is that they have formed a romantic attachment to a local woman/man. James Gratton felt that the authorities were not interested in rooting out illegal workers. When he approached the immigration office about the requirements for a work visa, they knew he was working but took no steps to stop him.

In his quest for a work visa, James gathered together all the necessary documents, including contract (the duration does not matter particularly), notarised certificates and documents translated into Spanish. All of this cost him a lot of money and time, and he still didn't succeed. He concluded that it would be possible only if you knew someone in the Immigration Department who could give your application a safe passage without having to pay fines (bribes) at every stage. Making key contacts is more important than gathering documentation.

The Peruvian Consul in London will send an information sheet entitled 'Non-Immigrant Working Resident Visas' which explains that after the visa has been obtained outside the country it is necessary to present it within a month of arrival at the *Dirección General de Migraciones* at Av. España 700 in Lima. Care must be taken to keep on the right side of the tax office (SUNAT) to which about 15% of earnings are supposed to be paid. James Gratton obtained a tax number even though his passport clearly indicated his status as tourist, but ended up paying virtually no tax.

Schools to Try

No Peruvian schools replied to a request for information for this edition. It might be worth pursuing schools that have appeared in previous editions:

Berlitz, Av. Santa Cruz 236, San Isidro, Lima 00 (1-440 8077).

EFL Institute, Av. Aviacion 2747, Piso 4, San Borja, Lima 41 (1-225 1331)

Foster & Foster Private Institute for English, Miguel dasso 139-301 San Isidro, Lima (1-949 1902/fax 1-442 7520).

Instituto Cultural Peruano-Norteamericano de Arequipa, Melgar 109, Apartado 555,

Arequipa (54-24 38 41).
Pontificia Universidad Catolica del Peru, Centro de Idiomas, Jr. Camaná 956, Lima 1 (tel/fax 1-431 0052).
William Shakespeare Instituto de Ingles, Avenida Dos de Mayo 1105, San Isidro, Lima (tel/fax 1-440 1004/422 1313).

Venezuela

Proximity to the US and the volume of business which is done with *El Norte* mean a strong preference for American accents and teaching materials in Venezuela. Oil wealth abounds in the business community and many corporations hire in-company language trainers through Caracas-based agencies.

But work is not exclusively for Americans, as Nick Branch from St. Albans discovered, nor is it confined to the capital:

> *Merida is very beautiful and a considerably more pleasant place to be than Caracas. The atmosphere and organisation of the institute where I worked were very good. But alas, as with all the English teaching institutes in Merida, the pay is very low. Merida is three times cheaper to live in than Caracas, but the salaries are 5-6 times lower.*

Nick Branch investigated most of the schools and agencies in Venezuela and worked for several of them including one based in the Oriente coastal resort of Puerto la Cruz. Once again the pay was less than in Caracas but advantages like easy access to the Mochima National Marine Park compensated. Opportunities for English teachers even exist on the popular resort island of Margarita.

Check adverts in Caracas' main English language organ, the *Daily Journal.* Most give only a phone number. A typical advert might read:

> *We need English teachers and offer remuneration according to the market, stable incomes, paid training, organization in the work, more earnings according to commissions. Excellent working condition. Work with best team. Punctual payment.*

The last item is worth noting, since many institutes do not pay as much or as often as they promise at the outset. In fact Caracas has more than its fair share of shady characters running language schools, so that newcomers should take their time about signing any contracts. Nick Branch describes what happened after he was hired by a well known institute:

> *The director is a seriously dodgy character. He pays his teachers $100 a month for a 40-hour week (not stated in the offer of employment I received in England). The materials were appalling, written by the school and very outdated and riddled with mistakes. The teacher training was a farce, consisting of a one-day stint run by a relation of the director. Another trainee (a Venezuelan) got up and started his practice class with 'My teacher is a metaphysicist'. Alas, in reality this guy would have had difficulty ordering a bag of King Edwards from his local greengrocer.*

There are plenty of professional and efficient companies as well, though competition from the expat community will be greater to be hired by them. In fact there is less competition for teaching posts than might have been expected, apart from some teachers from neighbouring Guyana (formerly British Guyana). Tensions between these teachers and North American and European teachers have been reported.

Almost no potential employers require a TEFL certificate, although some require teachers to have a degree or at least be on an intellectual par with a university graduate. Almost all schools will tell you that they want you to stay for six months to a year. In reality, few make you sign a contract.

Regulations

Most people work on a tourist visa which is valid for two months but extendable to six. A combined work/study contract (internship in American parlance) is the solution which the *Centro Venezolano Americano* and *Venusa* have come up with (see entries) but this is available only to US citizens.

Most long-stay foreigners take brief trips to Curacao or Trinidad and Tobago and get an extension of their tourist visa when returning to Venezuela. Work permits are available only if the employer has obtained approval from the Ministry of Internal Affairs (DEX) and sent the necessary papers to a Venezuelan consulate in the teacher's country of residence. Even with a backer as well established as the British Council, the visa problem looms large. Nick Branch describes the process of getting a work permit in Caracas as a nightmare:

> *On no account attempt to get one on your own, since this involves dealing with the DEX, a truly horrific organisation housed in what resembles a prison and with appalling disorganisation. Two years ago they lost 3,000 passports of people who were applying for work permits. It was later discovered that they had been sold on the black market.*

The Venezuelan Consulate in London (020-7387 6727; embvenuk-seccons@dial.pipex.com) can describe what to do if you have an employer willing to apply to DEX. The current fee is £42. James Gratton obtained a definite job offer from a university extension department on Margarita Island (address below) and presented the letter to the Venezuelan Embassy in London. His application was turned down. His main complaint was that you hear a different story from every official. Even renewing his tourist visa at the Immigration Office took a week and involved his having to present a typed letter in Spanish (and why would a bone fide tourist be expected to do that?) Yet he managed to stay legally in Venezuela for nine months, leaving the country when necessary and returning without once being asked to show a ticket home as proof of his intention to leave the country. His most serious problem occurred when one of his employers threatened to report his tourist status to the police if he quit to look for a better job (James did quit and the police were not called.)

CENTRO VENEZOLANO AMERICANO DEL CARACAS
Av. José Marti, Edf. CVA, Urbanización Las Mercedes, Caracas 1060-A. Also:
Apartado 61715 Del Este, Caracas 1060-A. Tel: (2) 993 7911. Fax: (2) 993 6812. E-mail: becarios@sa.omnes.net. Website: www.cva.org.ve
Number of teachers: 33 interns out of 110 locally hired teachers for approx. 6,000 students. Other branches include Merida (61-911436).
Preference of nationality: American, Canadian, Venezuelan.
Qualifications: BA or teachers with EFL/ESL experience. A written and oral test is given to all non-native English speaking applicants.
Conditions of employment: minimum 6 months with renewals up to 2 years. Choice of children's courses (for ages 9-11), teens (12-15) and regular and Saturday courses for adults. Minimum 6 academic hours per day.
Salary: 5,200 Bolivars per 90 minute class. Approx. Bs327,600 per month plus a 100,000 bolivar housing bonus.
Facilities/Support: assistance with obtaining accommodation, health insurance and visas. $3^{1}/_{2}$ week pre-service training course for interns is paid. Free Spanish course. Computer lab and access to cultural centre activities.
Recruitment: mail, fax, e-mail. Telephone interviews.

CENTRO VENEZOLANO AMERICANO DEL ZULIA (CEVAZ)
Calle 63, No. 3E-60, Apartado 419, Maracaibo. Tel: +58 61 911436/911880; Fax: +58 61 921098. E-mail: cevaz@cantv.net Website: www.cevaz.com

Number of teachers: varies, but currently 8.
Preference of nationality: none, but should be native speaker.
Qualifications: degree minimum. Experience an advantage.
Conditions of employment: no set contract. The school hours are 7am to 9pm, Monday to Friday and 8am to midday on Saturday.
Salary: depends on educational background and hours. Generally the salary will cover living costs but will not allow savings.
Facilities/Support: pre-service training provided as well as in-service workshops. Accommodation assistance in the form of a contact list and 25% housing allowance.
Recruitment: many applications are unsolicited and the school advertises on an institutional webpage. Interviews are not required but complete information by e-mail or some other correspondence is essential.
Contact: Ann Kubler, Academic Director.

IOWA INSTITUTE
Avenida Cuatro con Calle 18, Mérida Edo. Mérida. Tel (58) 74 526404. Fax: (58) 74 449064. E-mail: iowainst@ing.ula.ve Website: www.ing.ula.ve/~iowainst
Number of teachers: 7 native speakers.
Preference of nationality: American, British.
Qualifications: degree in education, linguistics, modern languages or some related field. If degree not in TEFL related field then a TEFL Cert. is essential. All teachers must attend a two-week seminar on school teaching methods held during September. Jobs for less qualified (i.e. native speakers who have not yet completed their degree) also possible. Those with camp counselling experience for example have been ideal for helping with children's classes.
Conditions of employment: one year minimum. Full-time posts 6-8 hours a day. Part-time can be as few as 2 hours a day.
Salary: by the hour, always a bit above the standard rate.
Facilities/Support: no accommodation assistance. Help with obtaining work permit is given. Spanish lessons at cost price.
Contact: Cathy Jensen.

VENUSA
Instituto de Estudios Internacionales, Merida. US contact: 6542 Hypoluxo Road, PMB 324, Lake Worth, FL 33415, USA. Tel: (561) 357-8802. Fax: (561) 357-9199. E-mail: venusa@flinet.com. Website: www.flinet.com/~venusa/main.html.
Number of teachers: work-study positions.
Preference of nationality: none, but mostly American.
Qualifications: programme open to new graduates, current English/Spanish majors and EFL teachers.
Conditions of employment: minimum stay 3 months. Choice of full-time or part-time (combined with course in Spanish and Latin American studies)
Salary: full-time ESL teachers receive wage but no accommodation. Part-time participants receive free lodging and courses but no wage.
Recruitment: via Florida address above or Office of International Programs, Box 2000, SUNY Cortland, Cortland, NY 13045 (607-753-2209; www.studyabroad.com/suny/cortland).

Schools to Try

Eduform, Av. Venezuela, Caracas (2-763 1621). Specialises in teaching business people.

Instituto Venezolano Britanico, Av. Humboldt Mari Carmen, Urb. Bello Monte, Sabana Grande, Caracas/PO Box 51867 (95-25443). On-site and in-company work.

Inversiones English & Spanish for Jobs (ESJ), Av. Libertador, Res. Florida, Apto 5, La Florida (2-712069). Relatively new Caracas company undertaking in-company work.

Loscher Ebbinghaus, La Campina, Centro Comercial, Avenida Libertador, Torre Oeste, 2nd Floor, Off. 2/5, Caracas (2-766 5101/2-713680). Other branches e.g. La Trinidad, Calle San José, Quinta Kateriñe, Sorocaima (tel 945 2459) and in Valencia west of the capital (41-236052). Long hours of preparation at institute are compulsory.

Wall Street Institute, Avda. Francisco de Miranda, Torre Lido piso 11 torre C Ofic., 113C El Rosal, Caracas (2-953 71 02; wsiven@cantv.net). 6 other WSI centres in Venezuela.

Anglo American Centre, San Cristobel (433116/444410).

Centro de Idiomas Modernas, Valera (314313).

FISA, Puerto la Cruz (81-815734).

Instituto Educativo de Idiomas, C.C. Real, Piso 1, Oficina 17, Porlamar, Isla de Margarita.

Fundacion para la Promotion Desarrollo de la Universidad Oriente, Fundaudo NVA Esparta, Calle Guevara, Quinte Palguarima, Al Frente del Colegio, Las Monjas, Porlamar, Isla de Margarita.

Central America & the Caribbean

If you keep your ears open as you travel through this enormous isthmus squeezed between two great oceans, you may come across opportunities to teach English, especially if you are prepared to do so as a volunteer. Salaries on offer may be pitiful but if you find a congenial spot on the 'gringo trail' (for example the lovely old colonial town of Antigua in Guatemala), you may decide to prolong your stay by helping the people you will inevitably meet who want to learn English.

As the wealthiest country in Central America, Costa Rica is sometimes referred to as the Switzerland of the region and there are plenty of private language academies in the capital San José. It is government policy to teach English in primary schools which has greatly increased the demand for English teachers. Although state schools can't afford to import expat teachers, they are often willing to accept an offer of voluntary assistance. The school year runs from March 1st to December 1st. Temporary six-month renewable working visas are now issued to teachers working for established employers like the *Instituto Britanico*.

A few voluntary organisations are active in the region including *WorldTeach* and *i-to-i*; the latter charges a placement fee of £1,195/$1,900 for three months.

Unfortunately the student exchanges organisation BUNAC has cancelled its Teach in Jamaica programme. It might be worth approaching the relevant government department independently: Permanent Secretary, Ministry of Education, Youth and Culture, 2 National Heroes Circle, Kingston, Jamaica (809-922-1400).

LIST OF SCHOOLS

Costa Rica
INSTITUTO BRITANICO
PO Box 8184, San José 1000, Costa Rica. Tel: 225 0256/234 9054. Fax: 253 1894.
E-mail: instbrit@sol.racsa.co.cr
Number of teachers: 15 (variable).
Preference of nationality: British, American, Canadian.
Qualifications: CELTA or equivalent and one year of teaching experience.
Conditions of employment: minimum commitment of 12 months. Classes morning and evening; Monday to Saturday am. Average working week is 28 contact hours. Children and adults.
Salary: average $450 a month.

Facilities/support: airport pick-up and first month accommodation provided free. Introductory training and in-service workshops provided. End of contract bonus.
Recruitment: via e-mail, print advertisements. Only local interviews.
Contact: Maria Puro, Co-ordinator of Teacher Training.

El Salvador
MELIDA ANAYA MONTES (MAM) LANGUAGE SCHOOL
Boulevard Universitario, Casa No. 4, Colonia El Roble, San Salvador, El Calvador. Tel/fax. (503) 220-2623. E-mail: cis@netcomsa.com. Website: www.cis-elsalvador.org.
Number of teachers: 2-8 volunteer teachers at any one time.
Preference of nationality: none.
Qualifications: no experience needed. Interest in issues of social justice since CIS-MAM works with members of the Salvadorean opposition.
Conditions of employment: minimum stay 2 months. To teach 3 days a week 5.15pm-7pm.
Salary: none.
Facilities/Support: help given in finding but not paying for accommodation. Training provided. Tourist visa ($10 at border) is sufficient.
Recruitment: word of mouth, internet, travel publications.
Contact: Jennie Busch, Volunteer Co-ordinator.

Paraguay
CENTRO CULTURAL PARGUAYO AMERICANO
Avenida Espana 352, Asuncion, Paraguay. Tel: (21) 224831/224772. Fax: (21) 226133. E-mail: ccpa@sce.cnc.una.py.
Number of teachers: 4.
Preference of nationality: American.
Qualifications: EFL/ESL training and experience of living outside the US.
Conditions of employment: 1 year contracts. Hours of work between 7am and 9pm. Choice of 4 programmes: teaching children (7-11), adolescents (12-15), adults and in-company courses.
Salary: US$5 an hour.
Facilities: no assistance with accommodation. Training provided.
Recruitment: direct application, best times are February and May. Local interviews necessary.

Uruguay
ENGLISH LIGHTHOUSE INSTITUTE
Sarandi y V. Alegre, Torre Maldonado Shopping, Maldonado, Uruguay. Tel: (42) 233893. Fax: (42) 5222.
Number of teachers: 3-4.
Preference of nationality: Canadian, American, Australian, British.
Qualifications: Bachelor of Education or PGCE in primary education plus a TEFL/TESL Certificate.
Conditions of employment: 9 month contracts (10th March to 10th December). 40 h.p.w. Courses for children, juniors and adults.
Salary: US$1,200 per month less deductions of 10%.
Facilities/Support: accommodation provided; rent of $150 per month plus water, electricity and phone bill deducted from salary.
Recruitment: direct application by fax. Interviews not essential. Couples are welcome.

Other Schools to Try (countries in alphabetical order)
Ingles Empresarial, Apdo. 12 471-1000, San José, Cost Rica (506-272-2000/272-8686/fax 506-272-3772; englishcostarica@hotmail.com). Business English. $6-

$8 per hour. Contact David Dubeau.

INSTITUTO CULTURAL DOMINICO-AMERICANO (ICDA), Av. Abraham Lincoln 21, Santo Domingo, Dominican Republic (533 4191/fax 533 8809). Many part-time freelance native speakers. Director: Elizabeth de Windt.

American School of Guatemala, Apartado Postal No. 83, 01901 Guatemala

MODERN AMERICAN ENGLISH SCHOOL, Calle de los Nazarenos 16, Antigua, Guatemala (932-3306/fax 932-0217). 6 North American or British teachers for minimum of 1 year. 25-50 quetzales per hour. Telephone interview required.

Centro Linguistico 'La Union', Avenida Sur 21, Antigua, Guatemala (tel/fax 502-832-7327). Volunteers to teach, etc.

Deliciosa, S.A., 3a Calle Poniente 2, Antigua, Guatemala (502-832-0713). To teach local school children.

Universidad del Valle de Guatemala, Apartado Postal No. 82, 01901 Guatemala

HAITIAN-AMERICAN INSTITUTE, Angle Rue Capois et Rue St. Cyr, Port-au-Prince, Haiti (22 2947/22 3715). Bi-national center employing quite a few teachers.

Discovery School, TGU 00015, PO Box 025387, Miami, FL 33102-5387 (504-236-7006). Bilingual school in Tegucigalpa, Honduras.

Centro PanUsa, Apartado 4581, Panama City 5, Panama (507-315-1184/fax 507-315-1183; pan_usa@cwpanama.net). 15 teachers.

NORTH AMERICA

Countless programmes in English as a Second Language (ESL) in the US are subsumed under several distinct programme types, in contrast to the heavy emphasis on 'academy' type EFL or 'workplace' ESP in Europe. Just about every university and college in the major cities has an ESL programme, as do a range of government and charitable organisations. Commercial schools offer a wide variety of classes but tend to focus on survival ESL and EAP (English for Academic Purposes) with writing as a major component. Berlitz and inlingua are represented throughout the USA and are a completely different type of commercial school, concentrating on conversational skills and foreign languages for business people.

Bilingual/bicultural classes are run in thousands of high schools across the country. Many require staff who are not only state-certified teachers but also bilingual in exotic languages like Hmong or Gujarati. Most larger cities have at least one free or low-cost workplace literacy/vocational ESL programme which caters for immigrants needing assistance with the basics of English. Some of these programmes operate in outposts (e.g. churches, libraries) and many depend on local volunteers as tutors. Volunteer positions can conceivably lead to better things. Another way of getting your foot in the door is to make yourself available as a substitute (for which you will need a telephone and preferably an answering machine).

Although the demand for ESL teachers is enormous, it is very difficult for foreigners who do not have a 'green card' to obtain the necessary working visa. The J-1 visa is available to university students participating in an approved Exchange Visitor Programme (which are only for the summer) and to researchers and teachers whose applications are supported by their employing institution in the US. Similarly it is extremely difficult to obtain the H-1B 'Temporary Worker' visa which is available for prearranged professional or highly skilled jobs for which there are no suitably qualified Americans, an increasingly unlikely circumstance as more and more Americans are becoming qualified to teach ESL/EFL. Although more US organisations now recognise the Cambridge Certificate than before, the MA in TESOL still dominates the American EFL scene. *EL Prospects,* the monthly job supplement to the *EL Gazette,* carries some ads for openings in the US, though most of those are academic posts in universities where it might be possible for the employer to overcome the visa problem in the case of highly qualified candidates.

Even for qualified American teachers, part-time work is the norm, often referred to as being hired as an 'adjunct'. Many contracts are not renewed creating a transient English teaching population. Pay is hourly and varies according to region, e.g $20-$30 in Chicago, $25-$40 in San Francisco. Part-timers almost never get benefits which means no health insurance or vacation pay. Even full-time teaching openings may be for just nine months with pay as little as $20,000 in the Midwest.

One possibility might be to teach at summer courses or work on summer camps attended by young people from overseas. For example the Council on International Educational Exchange (205 42nd St, New York, NY 10017) recruits ESL instructors for language camps on the east and west coasts, responsible for teaching English language classes to high school age international students in July and August. Even for such short appointments they look for an MA in TESOL or at least a strong background in ESL.

The situation is not dissimilar in Canada, including the difficulty of getting a visa. People with experience might have expected to be able to do some casual one-to-one tutoring of new immigrants, but stiff competition makes this difficult. When David Hughes arrived in Vancouver after a lengthy stint of teaching English in Taiwan, he felt fairly confident that with his experience he would be able to acquire a few fee-paying students from among the huge Chinese population in the area. But he didn't get a single reply to his advert.

AUSTRALASIA

While Europeans tend to have a somewhat Eurocentric view of the world, the Antipodean English language industry has built itself into a giant. However the loss of financial confidence in Southeast Asia has seen a decline in the number of fee-paying students going to Australia resulting in a loss of job opportunities for Australian teachers, never mind foreign ones.

Teaching English as a Foreign Language has a very high profile in both Australia and New Zealand. There are no less than 15 Cambridge Cert. training centres in Australia and five in New Zealand, most of them attached to flourishing English language colleges. There are a further five Trinity TESOL centres in New Zealand, despite its tiny population of about three million. With the decline in students from the Pacific Rim, more and more Australians and New Zealanders are recognising the value of an EFL qualification for the purposes of working abroad.

For many years there have been very active ESL programmes in all the major Australian cities to cater for the thousands of migrants who have come to Australia since the war. In recent years, the proportion of immigrants coming from Southeast Asia (especially Hong Kong and Vietnam) has nearly overtaken the number accepted from Europe. In addition, Australian universities attract foreign students from China and Southeast Asia, many of whom want English language training before or during their courses. Government-run language teaching programmes operate in universities, colleges of further edition and TAFE (Technical and Further Education) centres.

The ELICOS Association is the national association of institutions, both private and public, accredited to teach English Language Intensive Courses to Overseas Students in Australia. The EA can be contacted at Level 3, 162-4 Goulburn Street, Sydney, NSW 2000 (2-9264 4700/fax 2-9264 4313; www.elicos.edu.au). The Association is particularly strong in Perth where there are ten ELICOS centres. They have developed rigorous national guidelines on the qualifications expected of full-time teachers at ELICOS centres. Teachers must have either a three-year teaching qualification with a TESOL option or a three-year degree plus 800 hours of classroom teaching experience plus an approved TESOL qualification. However these are not enforced for casual contract teachers and ELICOS can point enquirers towards its member schools.

The profession is strictly regulated in Australia and standards are high in both the private and public sector. There is a nationally agreed pay scale ('award') for EFL teachers which falls in the range of A$18,000-$30,000 a year. Even highly trained Australian nationals cannot always find jobs. As in the US, a large proportion of local ESL teaching is done by volunteers. Ben Hockley did a four-week training course in Adelaide (now ELLS, English Language & Literacy Services) and gathered that it would be very difficult to find full-time work in Australia. This did not matter to him since he had chosen to do a course which was geared to working abroad, to fulfil his ambition to return to Spain with his Spanish girlfriend to teach.

Unless you are an Australian or New Zealand resident, you must either obtain residency (very difficult unless you have such specialist qualifications that an employer will undertake to support your application) or work on a working holiday visa. In Australia this non-renewable 12-month visa is available to Britons, Irish and Canadians less than 30 years of age who must not work at any one job for more than three months.

This is ideal for the traveller with a TEFL certificate who can take advantage of the seasonal demand for English tuition created by 'study tours,' popular among Japanese, Indonesian and other Asian students during their autumn and winter holidays. Demand for these holiday English courses increased dramatically as soon as the Australian immigration authorities relaxed the restrictions on visas, allowing foreign students to undertake short courses on a tourist visa. With a working holiday visa and a dash of luck, Simon Brooks fixed up several short contracts for February/March and July/August with no difficulty at all:

> *It's just a question of timing really and getting an interview two or three weeks before a new course starts. It took me two weeks to get work in Sydney but only five days in Perth where I had five offers on the same day. Even if you don't get a three-month contract straightaway, get yourself on the relief list and get a mobile phone (or at least stay in a backpackers' hostel with a reliable receptionist) and persist. Talking to one Director of Studies in Sydney whom I met by chance socially, there's no doubt that effort counts a lot with them and tells them something about you.*

In Sydney Simon worked for Universal English College (Level 12, 222 Pitt St, Sydney 2000; 2-9283 1088/ www.uec.edu.au) and Sydney English Language Centre (Level 2, 19-23 Hollywood Avenue, Bondi Junction, NSW 2022; 2-9383 3300/ www.ics.com.au/selc) while in Perth he happily worked for *Milner International College* (see entry).

For example *International House Queensland* (130 McLeod St, Cairns, Queensland 4870) sometimes offers short-term opportunities to people on working holiday visas, provided they have the CELTA. The Waratah Education Centre in downtown Sydney affiliated to International House in 1996. Both employ teachers on a casual basis as well as on contracts. The *Milner International College of English* (see entry) has occasional temporary positions for CELTA-holders on a working holiday visa. In New Zealand, try the Auckland Language Centre (PO Box 105035, Auckland; 9-303 1962/fax 9-307 9219).

ACCESS LANGUAGE CENTRE
Level 7, 28-36 Foveaux Street, Surry Hills, Sydney, NSW 2010. Tel: (2) 9281-6455. Fax: (2) 9281 7455. E-mail: english@access.nsw.edu.au Website: www. access.nsw.edu.au
Number of teachers: 9.
Preference of nationality: none.

Qualifications: BA or Bsc plus TESOL Cert. Experience not essential.
Conditions of employment: 4 weeks renewable.
Salary: depends on qualifications and experience.
Facilities/Support: no assistance with accommodation.
Recruitment: advertising and respond to general enquiries about work.
Contact: Salah Sawson; Director of Studies.

EAST COAST COLLEGE OF ENGLISH
295 Ann Street, Brisbane, Queensland 4001 Tel: (7) 3229 0350. Fax: (7) 3229 0850. E-mail: ecce@bit.net.au
Number of teachers: approx. 30.
Preference of nationality: none, but should be native speaker.
Qualifications: degree plus TEFL teaching certificate.
Conditions of employment: no set contract. 5 hours per day about 15 hours per week.
Salary: from AU$25 per hour.
Facilities/Support: no help with accommodation.
Recruitment: local newspaper adverts.
Contact: Linda Towler.

EMBASSY CES LANGUAGE CENTRE
Taylors House, 399 Lonsdale Street, Melbourne, Victoria. Tel: (3) 9670 3788. Fax: (3) 9670 9356.
Number of teachers: 50.
Preference of nationality: none.
Qualifications: NEAS minimum qualifications: pre-service teaching, appropriate TESOL Cert.
Conditions of employment: sessional: up to 12 months. Casual. School hours are from 8.30am-5pm (sessional teaching). Casual teaching (one-to-one) up to 15 hours per week.
Salary: A$29-43 (sessional) or A$25-38 per hour casual.
Recruitment: CV then interview.

EMBASSY CES
55 Oxford Street, Sydney, N.S.W. 2101. Tel: (2) 9291 9342. Fax: (2) 9283 3302. E-mail: a.wright@edu.au Website: www.sgintl.edu.com
Number of teachers: 35.
Preference of nationality: none.
Qualifications: degree and TESOL/CELTA Cert. minimum.
Conditions of employment: 4-12 weeks. 5 hours per day between 8am and 5pm.
Salary: from $25 per hour.
Facilities/Support: students may apply for homestay or lodge accommodation.
Recruitment: local advertising.
Contact: Ann Wright, Director of Studies.

GRIFFITH UNIVERSITY
English Language Institute, Nathan Campus, Brisbane, Qld. 4111. Tel: +61 7 3875 7089. Fax: +61 7 3875 7090. E-mail: p.steinhausen@mailbrox.gu.edu.au Website: www.gu.edu.au/centre/call
Number of teachers: 30-50 approx (seasonal).
Preference of nationality: none.
Qualifications: NEAS approved teaching and TESOL qualification.
Conditions of employment: casual only. 10 weeks (i.e. one course) minimum. Up to 18 hours teaching per week.
Salary: A$ 40.60 per contact hour.
Facilities/Support: no accommodation assistance.
Recruitment: casual recruitment from CV and interview.
Contact: Paul Steinhausen, Director of Studies.

INTERNATIONAL HOUSE QUEENSLAND
P.O. Box 7368, Cairns, Queensland 4870, Australia. Tel: +61 74031 3466. Fax: +61 7 4031 3464. E-mail: admin@ihqld.com Website: www.ihqld.com
Number of teachers: approx. 20.
Preference of nationality: none.
Qualifications: CELTA or equivalent and minimum 1 year experience.
Conditions of employment: 2 year contract. 25 hours per week.
Salary: Australian award rates.
Facilities/Support: accommodation department provides assistance.
Recruitment: CV and interview. Interviews occasionally conducted overseas.
Contact: Simon Bradley, Director of Education.

MILNER INTERNATIONAL COLLEGE OF ENGLISH
379 Hay Street, Perth, Western Australia 6009. Tel (8) 9325 5444. Fax (8) 9221 2392. E-mail: milner@wantree.com.au Website: www.milner.wa.edu.au
Number of teachers: 25-35.
Preference of nationality: none. Teachers from the UK can come on a Working Holiday visa if they are under 26/30.
Qualifications: Degree plus CELTA (or equivalent).
Conditions of employment: no contracts for casual teachers. School hours are from 9am-3pm.
Salary: there is an award scale for EL teachers so the salary depends on the level of the teacher.
Facilities/Support: teachers find their own accommodation.
Recruitment: CV and interview.
Contact: Deborah Pinder, Director of Studies.

THE UNIVERSITY OF QUEENSLAND
Institute of Continuing & TESOL Education, St. Lucia, Qld. 4072. Tel: (7) 3365 6565. Fax: (7) 3365 6599. E-mail: tesol.enrol@mailbox.uq.edu.au Website: www.icte.uq.edu.au/tesol/tesol.htm
Number of teachers: 25-30 depending on time of year.
Preference of nationality: none.
Qualifications: minimum degree + a TESOL qualification.
Conditions of employment: 10 weeks but could be 3-4 weeks for study tours.
Salary: approx. A$39 per hour.
Facilities/Support: no assistance with accommodation.
Recruitment: CV submission then interview.
Contact: Stephen Heap, D.O.S.

PART III

Appendices

Currency Conversion Chart
Embassies/Consulates in London and Washington
British Council Offices Around the World

Currency Conversion Chart

COUNTRY	£1	US$1
Argentina	1.44 peso	1.0 peso
Australia	A$2.70	A$1.86
Austria	22.8 schilling	15.8 schilling
Belgium/Luxembourg	67 franc	46 franc
Bolivia	9.1 boliviano	6.2 boliviano
Brazil	2.67 real	1.85 real
Brunei	2.5 Brunei dollar	1.7 Brunei dollar
Bulgaria	3.2 lev	2.2 lev
Canada	C$2.17	C$1.50
Chile	811 peso	560 peso
China	12 renminbi	8.3 renminbi
Colombia	3,170 peso	2,200 peso
Czech Republic	59 koruna	40 koruna
Denmark	12.1 kroner	8.5 kroner
Ecuador	36,163 sucre	25,000 sucre
Egypt	5.3 Egyptian pound	3.6 Egyptian pound
Finland	9.9 markka	6.8 markka
France	10.9 franc	7.5 franc
Germany	3.2 DM	2.2 DM
Greece	565 drachma	390 drachma
Hong Kong	11.2 HK dollar	7.8 HK dollar
Hungary	436 forint	300 forint
Indonesia	12,750 rupiah	8,800 rupiah
Italy	3,220 lira	2,225 lira
Japan	157 yen	108 yen
Kenya	114 shilling	79 shilling
Korea	1,616 won	1,117 won
Malaysia	5.5 ringgit	3.8 ringgit
Malta	0.66 Maltese lira	0.45 Maltese lira
Mexico	13.7 peso	9.5 peso
Morocco	15.9 dirham	11 dirham
Nepal	106 rupee	74 rupee
Netherlands	3.6 guilder	2.5 guilder
New Zealand	NZ$3.60	NZ$2.48
Norway	12.6 krone	9.2 krone
Peru	5 new sol	3.5 new sol
Poland	6.6 zloty	4.5 zloty
Portugal	335 escudo	230 escudo
Russia (market rate)	40.4 rouble	28 rouble
Saudi Arabia	5.4 riyal	3.75 riyal
Singapore	2.5 Singapore dollar	1.75 Singapore dollar
Slovakia	73 koruna	50 koruna
Slovenia	348 tolar	241 tolar
Spain	276 peseta	191 peseta
Sweden	14.2 krona	9.8 krona
Switzerland	2.5 franc	1.75 franc
Taiwan	45 Taiwan dollar	31 Taiwan dollar
Thailand	61 baht	42 baht
Turkey	970,000 lira	675,000 lira
USA	1.44 dollar	
Venezuela	999 bolivar	6911 bolivar

*Current exchange rates are available on the internet, for example the Universal Currency Converter can be found at www.xe.net/ucc. Also the Monday edition of the *Financial Times* carries a full list of world currencies.

Embassies/Consulates in London and Washington

AUSTRIA: 18 Belgrave Mews West, London SW1X 8HU. Tel: 020-7235 3731; www.bmaa.gv.at/embassy/uk/.
3524 International Court NW, Washington DC 20008-3035. Tel: (202) 895-6700.
BELGIUM: 103 Eaton Square, London SW1W 9AB. Tel: 020-7470 3700/0891-660255; www.belgium-embassy.co.uk.
3330 Garfield St NW, Washington DC 20008. Tel: (202) 333-6900; www.diplobel.org.
BRAZIL: Consular Section, 6 St. Alban's St, London SW1Y 4SG. Tel: 020-7930 9055; www.brazil.org.uk.
3006 Massachusetts Ave NW, Washington, DC 20008. Tel: (202) 238-2700; www.brasilemb.org.
BULGARIA: 186-188 Queen's Gate, London SW7 5HL (020-7584 9400/0891 171208).
1621 22nd St NW, Washington, DC 20008. Tel: (202) 387-7969; www.bulgaria-embassy.org.
CHILE: 12 Devonshire St, London W1N 2DS. Tel: 020-7580 1023; e-mail: cglonguk@congechileuk.demon.co.uk.
1732 Massachusetts Ave NW, Washington DC 20036. Tel: (202) 785-1746.
CHINA: Visa Section, 31 Portland Place, London W1N 3AG. Tel: 020-7631 1430; www.chinese-embassy.org.uk.
2300 Connecticut Ave NW, Washington DC 200078. Tel: (202) 328-2500; www.china-embassy.org.
COLOMBIA: Suite 14, 140 Park Lane, London W1Y 3DF. Tel: 020-495 4233.
1875 Connecticut Avenue NW, Suite 524, Washington, DC 20008. Tel: (202) 332-7476; www.colombiaemb.org.
CROATIA: 21 Conway Street, London W1P 5HL. Tel: 020-7387 0022.
2343 Massachusetts Ave NW, Washington DC 20008. Tel: (202) 588-5889; www.croatiaemb.org.
CZECH REPUBLIC: 26-30 Kensington Palace Gardens, London W8 4QY. Tel: 020-7243 1115.
3900 Spring of Freedom St NW, Washington DC 20008. Tel: (202) 274-9100; www.czech.cz/washington.
ECUADOR: Flat 3b, 3 Hans Crescent, Knightsbridge, London SW1X 0LS. Tel: 020-7584 8084.
2535 15th St NW, Washington, DC 20009. Tel: (202) 234-7200; www.ecuador.org.
EGYPT: 2 Lowndes St, London SW1X 9ET. Tel: 020-7235 9777; www.egypt-embassy.org.uk.
3521 International Court NW, Washington DC 20008. Tel: (202) 966-6342.
FINLAND: 38 Chesham Place, London SW1X 8HW. Tel: 020-7838 6200; www.finemb.org.
3301 Massachusetts Ave NW, Washington DC 20008. Tel: (202) 298-5800; www.finland.org.
FRANCE: 21 Cromwell Road, London SW7 2EN. Tel: 020-7838 2000; www.ambafrance.org.uk.
4101 Reservoir Road NW, Washington DC 20007. Tel: (202) 944-6200/6215; www.info-france-usa.org.
GERMANY: 23 Belgrave Square, London SW1X 8PZ. Tel: 020-7824 1300/0906-833 1166; www.german-embassy.org.uk.
4645 Reservoir Road NW, Washington DC 20007-1998. Tel: (202) 298-4000; www.germany-info.org.
GREECE: 1A Holland Park, London W11 3TP. Tel: 020-7221 6467.
2221 Massachusetts Ave NW, Washington DC 20008. Tel: (202) 939-5818; www.greekembassy.org.
HUNGARY: 35b Eaton Place, London SW1X 8BY. Tel: 020-7235 2664/09001-171 204; http://dspacc.dial.pipex.com/huemblon.
3910 Shoemaker St NW, Washington DC 20008. Tel: (202) 362-6730; www.hungaryemb.org.
INDIA: India House, Aldwych, London WC2B 4NA. Tel: 020-7836 8484; www.hcilondon.org.
2107 Massachusetts Avenue NW, Washington, DC 20008. Tel: (202) 939-7000; www.indianembassy.org.
INDONESIA: 38 Grosvenor Square, London W1X 9AD. Tel: 020-7499 7661; www.indonesia.org.uk.
2020 Massachusetts Ave NW, Washington DC 20036. Tel: (202) 775-5200; http://kbri.org.
ITALY: 38 Eaton Place, London SW1X 8AN. Tel: 020-7235 9371; www.ambitalia.org.uk.
1601 Fuller St NW, Washington DC 20009. Tel: (202) 328-5500; www.italyemb.org.
JAPAN: 101-104 Piccadilly, London W1V 9FN. Tel: 020-7465 6500; www.embjapan.org.uk.
2520 Massachusetts Ave NW, Washington DC 20008. Tel: (202) 939-6700; www.embjapan.org.
KOREA: 60 Buckingham Gate, London SW1E 6AJ. Tel: 020-7227 5505.
2450 Massachusetts Ave NW, Washington, DC 20008. Tel: (202) 939-5600; www.koreaemb.org.
LAOS: 74 Avenue Raymond Poincare, 75116 Paris, France. Tel: 1-45 53 02 98.
2222 S St NW, Washington, DC 20008. Tel: (202) 332-6416/7.
LATVIA: 45 Nottingham Place, London W1M 3FE. Tel: 020-7312 0040.
4325 17th St NW, Washington, DC 20011. Tel: (202) 726-8213; www.latvia-usa.org.
LITHUANIA: 84 Gloucester Place, London W1H 3HN. Tel: 020-7486 6404; www.users.globalnet.co.uk/lralon/.
2622 16th St NW, Washington, DC 20009-4202. Tel: (202) 234-5860; www.ltembassyus.org.
MALAYSIA: 45 Belgrave Square, London SW1X 8QT. Tel: 020-7235 8033.
2401 Massachusetts Ave NW, Washington DC 20008. Tel: (202) 328-2700.
MALTA: Malta House, 36-38 Piccadilly, London W1V 0PQ. Tel: 020-7292 4800.
2017 Connecticut Ave NW, Washington, DC 20008. Tel: (202) 462-3611.
MEXICO: 8 Halkin St, London SW1X 7DW. Tel: 020-7235 6393; www.mexicanconsulate.org.uk.

1911 Pennsylvania Ave NW, Washington, DC 20006. Tel: (202) 728-1600; www.embassyofmexico.org.
MOROCCO: 49 Queen's Gate Gardens, London SW7 5NE. Tel: 020-7581 5001.
1601 21st St NW, Washington DC 20009. Tel: (202) 462-7979.
NETHERLANDS: 38 Hyde Park Gate, London SW7 5DP. Tel: 020-7590 3200/09001-171 217; www.netherlands-embassy.org.uk.
4200 Linnean Ave NW, Washington DC 20008. Tel: (202) 244-5300; www.netherlands-embassy.org.
OMAN: 167 Queen's Gate, London SW7 5HE. Tel: 020-7225 0001.
2535 Belmont Road NW, Washington DC 20008. Tel: (202) 387-1980-2.
PERU: 52 Sloane St, London SW1X 9SP. Tel: 020-7838 9223; http://homepages.which.net/peru-embassy-uk/.
1700 Massachusetts Ave NW, Washington DC 20036. Tel: (202) 833-9860; www.peruemb.org.
POLAND: 73 New Cavendish St, London W1N 4HQ. Tel: 020-7580 0476; www.poland-embassy.org.uk.
2640 16th St NW, Washington, DC 20009. Tel: (202) 234-3800; www.polishworld.com/polemb.
PORTUGAL: Silver City House, 62 Brompton Road, London SW3 1BJ. Tel: 020-7581 8722; www.portembassy.gla.ac.uk.
2125 Kalorama Road NW, Washington DC 20008. Tel: (202) 328-8610; www.portugalemb.org.
ROMANIA: Arundel House, 4 Palace Green, London W8 4QD. Tel: 020-7937 8125.
1607 23rd St NW, Washington, DC 20008. Tel: (202) 328-8610; www.roembus.org.
RUSSIAN FEDERATION: 5 Kensington Palace Gardens, London W8 4QS. Tel: 020-7229 8027; www.russialink.couk.com.
2650 Wisconsin Ave NW, Washington, DC 20007. Tel: (202) 298-5700; www.russianembassy.org.
SAUDI ARABIA: 30 Charles St, London W1X 7PM. Tel: 020-7917 3000; www.saudiembassy.org.uk.
601 New Hampshire Ave NW, Washington DC 20037. Tel: (202) 337-4076; www.saudiembassy.net.
SINGAPORE: 5 Chesham St, London SW1X 8ND. Tel: 020-7245 0273.
3501 International Place NW, Washington, DC 20008. Tel: (202) 537-3100; www.gov.sg/mfa/washington.
SLOVAK REPUBLIC: 25 Kensington Palace Gardens, London W8 4QY. Tel: 020-7243 0803; www.slovakembassy.co.uk
2201 Wisconsin Ave NW, Suite 250, Washington, DC 20007. Tel: (202) 965-5160; www.slovakemb.com.
SLOVENIA: Cavendish Court, 11-15 Wigmore St, London W1H 9LA. Tel: 020-7495 7775; www.embassy-slovenia.org.uk.
1525 New Hampshire Ave NW, Washington, DC 20036. Tel: (202) 667-5363; www.embassy.org/slovenia.
SPAIN: 20 Draycott Place, London SW3 2RZ. Tel: 020-7589 8989.
2375 Pennsylvania Ave NW, Washington, DC 20037. Tel: (202) 452-0100; www.spainemb.org/information.
SUDAN: 3 Cleveland Row, St. James's, London SW1A 1DD. Tel: 020-7839 8080.
2210 Massachusetts Ave NW, Washington DC 20008. Tel: (202) 338-8565
SWEDEN: 11 Montagu Place, London W1H 2AL. Tel: 020-7724 2101; www.swednet.org.uk/sweden/.
1501 M St NW, Washington, DC 20005. Tel: (202) 467-2600; www.swedemb.org.
SWITZERLAND: 16/18 Montagu Place, London W1H 2BQ. Tel: 020-7616 6000/0891-331 313; www.swissembassy.org.uk.
2900 Cathedral Ave NW, Washington DC 20008. Tel: (202) 745-7900; www.swissemb.org.
TAIWAN: Taipei Representative Office, 50 Grosvenor Gardens, London SW1W 0EB. Tel: 020-7396 9152/0891-300 615; www.tro.taiwan.roc.org.uk.
CCNAA/Co-ordination Council for North American Affairs, 4201 Wisconsin Ave NW, Washington DC 20016. Tel: (202) 895-1800.
THAILAND: 29/30 Queen's Gate, London SW7 5JB. Tel: 020-7589 2944.
1024 Wisconsin Ave NW, Suite 401, Washington DC 20007. Tel: (202) 944-3600; www.thaiembdc.org.
TURKEY: Rutland Lodge, Rutland Gardens, London SW7 1BW. Tel: 020-7589 0949/0891-347 348; www.turkconsulate-london.com.
2525 Massachusetts Ave NW, Washington DC 20036. Tel: (202) 659-8200; www.turkey.org/turkey.
UKRAINE: 78 Kensington Park Road, London W11 2PL. Tel: 020-7243 8923/09001 887 749.
3350 M St NW, Washington, DC 20007. Tel: (202) 333-7507; www.ukremb.com.
VENEZUELA: 56 Grafton Way, London W1P 5LB. Tel: 020-7387 6727; www.venezlon.demon.co.uk.
1099 30th St NW, Washington, DC 20007. Tel: (202) 342-2214; www.embavenez-us.org.
VIETNAM: 12-14 Victoria Road, London W8. Tel: 020-7937 1912.
1233 20th St NW, Suite 400, Washington, DC 20037. Tel: (202) 861-0737; www.vietnamembassy-usa.org.
ZIMBABWE: 429 Strand, London WC2R 0SA. Tel: 020-7836 7755.
1608 New Hampshire Ave NW, Washington DC 20009. Tel: (202) 332-7100; www.zimweb.com/Embassy/Zimbabwe.

For the names of the relevant personnel in the UK, e.g. the Education Attaché, see *The London Diplomatic List* published frequently by the Foreign & Commonwealth Office and held in most libraries. Check the internet on www.embassyworld.com and www.embassy.org.

British Council Offices

ARGENTINA: Marcelo T de Alvear 590 4th Floor, 1058 Buenos Aires. Tel: (11) 4 311 9814/7519. Fax: (11) 4 311 7747. E-mail: britcoun@britcoun.int.ar

AUSTRIA: Schenkenstrasse 4, A-1010 Vienna. Tel: (1) 533 2616. Fax: (1) 533 261685. E-mail: bc.vienna@bc-vienna.at

AZERBAIJAN: 1 Vali Mammadov Street, Baku 370004. Tel: (12) 971593/972013. Fax: (12) 989236. E-mail: staff@britcoun1.baku.az

BAHRAIN: AMA Centre, (PO Box 452), Manama 356. Tel: 261555. Fax: 241272. E-mail: bc.manama@bc-bahrain.bccouncil.org*

BALTIC STATES: 5a Blaumana iela, Riga LV-1011, Latvia. Tel: 732 0468/1165. Fax: 783 0031. E-mail: bc.riga@british-council.sprint.com

Vilnaius 39/6, 2001 Vilnius, Lithuania. Tel: (2) 616607/222615. Fax: (2) 221602. E-mail: egle@bc-vilnius.ot.it

BANGLADESH: 5 Fuller Road, (PO Box 161), Dhaka 1000. Tel: (2) 868 905-7/868867-8. Fax: (2) 863375/870483. E-mail: britcoun@TheBritishCouncil.net

BELGIUM/LUXEMBOURG: Rue de la Charité 15, 1210 Brussels. Tel: (2) 227 0840. Fax: (2) 227 0849. E-mail: bc.brussels@be.britcoun.org

BOLIVIA: Avenida Arce 2708 (esq. Campos), Casilla 15047, La Paz. Tel: (2) 431 240. Fax: (2) 431 377. E-mail: firstname.surname@britishcouncil.org.bo

BOSNIA-HERZEGOVINA: Obala Kulina Bana 4, 2nd Floor, 71000 Sarajevo. Tel: (71) 207836/200895. Fax: (71) 200890. E-mail: British.Council@ba.britcoun.org

BRAZIL: SCS, Quadra 1, BLOCO H, Edificio Morro Vermelho, 8 Andar, 70399-900 Brasília DF. Tel: (61) 323 6080. Fax: (61) 323 7440. E-mail: brasilia@britishcouncil.org.br

Rua Presidente Faria, 51, Conjunto 705, 80020-290 Curitiba PR. Tel/Fax: (41) 232 2912. E-mail: curitiba@britcoun.org.br

Av. Domingos Ferreira 4150, Boa Viagem, 51021-040 Recife PE. Tel: (81) 465 7744. Fax: (81) 465 7271. E-mail: recife@britishcouncil.org.br

Rua Elmano Cardim 10, Urca, 22291-040 Rio de Janeiro RJ. Tel: (21) 543 1253. Fax: (21) 543 1060. E-mail: riodejaneiro@britishcouncil.org.br

Avenida Brigadeiro Faria Lima 1485, 10 Andar, 01451-000 São Paulo SP. Tel: (11) 3039 0500. Fax: (11) 813 6217. E-mail: saopaolo@britishcouncil.org.br

BRUNEI: No 45 Simpang 100, Gadong BE3619, Bandar Seri Begawan 3192, Brunei Darussalam. Tel: (2) 453 220/216/218/219. Fax: (2) 453 221. E-mail: bcbrunei@brunet.bn*

BULGARIA: 7 Tulovo St, 1504 Sofia. Tel: (2) 946 0098/946 0099/463 346/943 4425. Fax: (2) 946 0102/462 065. E-mail: bc.sofia@britcoun.ttm.bg*

BURMA (MYANMAR): 78 Kanna Road (PO Box 638), Rangoon (Yangon), Union of Myanmar. Tel: (1) 254 658/256 290/256 291. Fax: (1) 245 345. E-mail: admin@bc-burma.bcouncil.org

CAMEROON: Avenue Charles de Gaulle, (B.P. 818), Yaoundé. Tel: 211696/203172. Fax: 215691. E-mail: bc.yaounde@bc-yaounde.iccnet.cm*

CHILE: Eliodoro Yáñez 832, Providencia, Santiago. Tel: (2) 236 1199/236 0193. Fax: 235 7375/235 9690. E-mail: info@britcoun.cl

CHINA: British Embassy, Landmark Building, 8 North Dongsanhuan Road, Chaoyang District, Beijing 100004. Tel: (10) 6590 6903. Fax: (10) 6590 0977. E-mail: enquiry@bc-beijing.sprint.com

British Consulate, Dong Yi Plaza, 77 Chang Shu Lu, Shanghai 200040. Tel: (21) 6249 3412/3/4. Fax: (21) 6249 3410. E-mail: bc.shanghai@bc-shanghai. bcouncil.org

British Consulate General, GITIC Plaza Hotel, 339 Huanshi Dong Lu, Guangzhou 510098. Tel: (20) 8335 1316/1354. Fax: (20) 8335 1321. E-mail: guangzhou@bc-guangzhou.bcouncil.org

China-British Trade Group, Rm 1410, Shaocheng Building, 225 Shaocheng Rd, Chengdu 610015. Tel: (28) 624 7870. Fax: (28) 625 0424. E-mail: bcchengdu@public.cd.sc.cn

COLOMBIA: Calle 87, 12-79, (Apartado Aéreo 089231), Santa Fe de Bogotá. Tel: (1) 618 0118. Fax: (1) 218 7754. E-mail: brit.council@bc-bogota.bcouncil.org*

Calle 22 N Number 8N-52, Cali. Tel: (2) 661 3612/667 8147/668 5195. Fax: (2) 660 1502. E-mail@bc-cali@colomsat.net.co

Carrera 42, No 16A Sur-41, Medellin. Tel: (4) 313 1867/313 6543/313 6544. Fax: (4) 313 7516. E-mail: cbritani@epm.net.co

CROATIA: Illica 12/1, (PO Box 55), 10000 Zagreb. Tel: (1) 481 3700/424 888 (EFL Unit). Fax: (1) 421 725. E-mail: bc.zagreb@bc.tel.hr

CYPRUS: 3 Museum St, (PO Box 5654), CY 1387 Nicosia. Tel: (2) 44 21 52. Fax: (2) 67 7257. E-mail: enquiries@britishcouncil.org.cy

CZECH REPUBLIC: Narodni 10, 12501 Prague 1. Tel: (2) 2199 1111. Fax: (2) 2491 3839. E-mail: info@britcoun.cz

DENMARK: Gammel Mønt 12.3, 1117 Copenhagen K. Tel: 33 369 400. Fax: 33 369 406. E-mail: british.council@britcoun.dk

EAST JERUSALEM, WEST BANK & GAZA: Al-Nuzha Building, 4 Abu Obeida Street, (PO Box 19136), Jerusalem. Tel: (2) 6282545/6271131/6264392. Fax: (2) 6283021. E-mail: bc.ejerusalem@bc-ejerusalem.bcouncil.org*

14-706 Al-Nasra Street, Al Rimal (PO Box 355), Gaza City. Tel: (7) 2825574/2825394. Fax: (7)

2820512. E-mail: Gaza@bc-gaza.bcouncil.org*
Ein Sarah Street, (PO Box 277), Hebron. Tel/Fax: (2) 2226353.
Harwash Building, Rafidia Main Street, (PO Box 497), Nablus. Tel: (9) 2385951/2375950. Fax: (2) 2375953.
ECUADOR: Av. da Amazonas 1646 y la Niña, (Casilla 17-07-8829), Quito. Tel: (2) 540225/225421/508282/4. Fax: (2) 508283. E-mail: erey@britcoun.org.ec*
Costanera 504 entre Ebanos y Las Monjas, (Casilla 09-01-06547), Guayaquil. Tel: (4) 885100/885047. Fax: (4) 884932. E-mail: bcouncil@srvl.telconet.net*
EGYPT: 192 Sharia el Nil, Agouza, Cairo. Tel: (2) 3031514. Fax: (2) 3443076. E-mail: britcoun@eg.britishcouncil.org*
9 Batalsa St, Bab Sharki, Alexandria. Tel: (3) 482 0199/482 0047. Fax: (3) 484 6630. E-mail: bc.alexandria@eg.britcoun.org*/
ESTONIA: Resource Centre, Vana Posti 7, Tallinn EEOOOO1. Tel: (6) 441550/314010/418288. Fax: (6) 313111. E-mail: british.council@bctallinn.ee
ETHIOPIA: (PO Box 1043), Artistic Building, Adwa Avenue, Addis Ababa. Tel: (1) 550 022. Fax: (1) 552 544. E-mail: bc.addisababa@bc-addis.bcouncil.org
FINLAND: Hakaniemenkatu 2, 00530 Helsinki. Tel: (9) 701 8731. Fax: (9) 701 8725. E-mail: infocentre@britishcouncil.fi. Website: www.britishcouncil.fi
FRANCE: 9-11 rue de Constantine, 75340 Paris Cedex 07. Tel: (1) 45 55 73 00. Fax: (1) 47 05 77 02. E-mail: information@bc-paris.bcouncil.org
Université Victor-Segalen, 3 Place de la Victoire, 33076 Bordeaux Cedex. Tel: (5) 57 57 19 52. Fax: (5) 57 57 19 50. E-mail: Bordeaux.enquiries@bc-paris.bcouncil.org
GERMANY: Hardenbergstrasse 20, 10623 Berlin. Tel: (30) 31 10 990. Fax: (30) 311 09920. E-mail: bc.berlin@britcoun.de*
Hahnenstrasse 6, 50667 Cologne. Tel: (221) 206 440. Fax: (221) 206 4455. E-mail: bc.cologne@britcoun.de
Rothenbaumchaussee 34, 20148 Hamburg. Tel: (40) 446 057. Fax: (40) 447 114. E-mail: bc.hamburg@britcoun.de
Katharinenstrasse 1-3, (Alte Waage), 01409 Leipzig. Tel: (341) 140 641-0. Fax: (341) 140 641-41. E-mail: bc-leipzig@britcoun.de
Rumfordstrasse 7, 80469 Munich. Tel: (89) 290 0860. Fax: (89) 290 08688. E-mail: bc.munich@britcoun.de*
GHANA: 11 Liberia Road, (PO Box GP 771), Accra. Tel: (21) 223415. Fax: (21) 240330. E-mail: bcaccra@bcgha.africaonline.com.gh
Bank Road, (PO Box 1996), Kumasi. Tel: (51) 23462. Fax: (51) 26725. E-mail: bckumasi@bcghk.africaonline.com.gh
GREECE: 17 Kolonaki Square, 10673 Athens. Tel: (1) 369 2333/363 3211-5. Fax (1) 363 4769. E-mail: British.Council@britcoun.gr*
Ethnikis Amynis 9, (PO Box 50007), 54013 Thessaloniki. Tel: (31) 23 52 36/7. Fax: (31) 28 24 98. E-mail: bc.thess@britcoun.gr*
HONG KONG: 3 Supreme Court Road, Admiralty, Hong Kong. Tel: 291 35100. Fax: 291 35102. E-mail: bc.hongkong@britcoun.org.hk*
HUNGARY: Benczúr Utca 26, H-1068 Budapest. Tel: (1) 321 4039. Fax: (1) 342 5728/352 8779. E-mail: hungary@britcoun.hu*
INDONESIA: S Widjojo Centre, Jalan Jenderal Sudirman 71, Jakarta 12190. Tel: (21) 252 4115/4122/4126. Fax: (21) 252 4129. E-mail: bc.jakarta@britcoun.or.id*
ISRAEL: 140 Hayarkon St, (PO Box 3302), Tel Aviv 61032. Tel: (3) 522 2194/524 2558/524 1350. Fax: (3) 522 1229. E-mail: bc.telaviv@britcoun.org.il*
3 Shimshon St, (PO Box 10304), West Jerusalem 911021. Tel: (2) 6736733. Fax: (2) 6736737. E-mail: caron.sethill@britcoun.org.il*
PO Box 2545, Nazareth 16121. Tel: (3) 6579570. Fax: (3) 6550436.*
ITALY: Palazzo del Drago, Via delle Quattro Fontane 20, 00184 Rome. Tel: (06) 478141. Fax: (06) 4814296. E-mail: Enquiry.BCRome@britcoun.it*
Corte Isolani 8, Strada Maggiore 19, 40125 Bologna. Tel: (051) 225142. Fax: (051) 224238. E-mail: Enquiry.BCBologna@britcoun.it*
Via Manzoni 38, 20121 Milan. Tel: (02) 772221. Fax: (02) 781119. E-mail: Enquiry.BCMilan@britcoun.it*
Via Morghen 31, 80129 Naples. Tel: (081) 5788247. Fax: (081) 5562585. E-mail: Enquiry.BCNaples@britcoun.it*
Via Saluzzo 60, 10125 Turin. Tel: (011) 6699575. Fax: (011)657157. E-mail: Enquiry.bcturin@britcoun.it
JAMAICA: c/o The British High Commission, Trafalgar Road, (PO Box 235), Kingston 5. Tel: 9296915/9297049. Fax: 9297090. E-mail: bcjamaica@bc-caribbean.org
JAPAN: 2-Kagurazaka 1-chome, Shinjuku-ku, Tokyo 162-0825. Tel: (3) 3235 8031. Fax: (3) 32358040. E-mail: bc.tokyo@britishcouncil.or.jp*
77 Kitashirakawa, Nishi-Machi, Sakyo-ku, Kyoto 606-8267. Tel: (75) 791 7151. Fax: (75) 791 7154. E-mail: bc-kyoto@bc-kyoto.sprint.com*
Sapporo International Communication Plaza, Main Building 3F, North 1, West 3, Chuo-ku, Sapporo 060-0001. Tel: (11) 211 3672. Fax: (11) 219 1317. E-mail: bc.sapporo@bc-tokyo.bcouncil.org
Nagoya Daiya Building, II 5F, 3-15-1, Meieki, Nakamura-ku, Nagoya 450-0002. Tel: (52)

5812016. Fax: (52) 5812017. E-mail: bc.nagoya@bc-tokyo.sprint.com
Seiko Osaka Building 19 Floor, 3-5-1 Bakuromachi, Cho-ku, Osaka 541-0059. Tel: (06) 6314 5271. Fax: (06) 6314 5274.*
JORDAN: Rainbow St (off First Circle), Jabal Amman, (PO Box 634), Amman 11118. Tel: (6) 4636147. Fax: (6) 4613389/4656413. E-mail: bc.amman.bcouncil.org*
KAZAKHSTAN: Panfilova 158-1 (corner Abaya), Almaty 480091. Tel: (3272) 637743/633339. Fax: (3272) 633443. E-mail: bc@britcoun.almaty.kz
KENYA: ICEA Building, Kenyatta Ave., (PO Box 40751), Nairobi. Tel: (2) 334811/334885/6/7. Fax: (2) 339854/334875. E-mail: bc.nairobi@bc-nairobi.bcouncil.org.*
KOREA: Joongwhoo Building, 61-21 Taepyungro 1ka, Choong-ku, 100-101 Seoul. Tel: (2) 3702 0610. Fax. (2) 3702 0660. E-mail. info@britcoun.or.kr '
KUWAIT: 2 Al Arabi St, Block 2 (PO Box 345), 13004 Safat, Mansouriya, Kuwait City. Tel: 252 0067/8. Fax: 2520069. E-mail: britcoun@kuwait.net*
LEBANON: Sidani Street, Fawzi Azar Building, Ras Beirut. Tel: (1) 739459/60, 740123/4/5. Fax: (1) 739461. E-mail: general.enquiries@bc-beirut.sprint.com*
MALAWI: PO Box 30222, Lilongwe 3. Tel: 783244/419. Fax: 782945. E-mail: bc.lilongwe@bc-lilongwe.sprint.com
MALAYSIA: Jalan Bukit Aman, (PO Box 10539), 50916 Kuala Lumpur. Tel: (3) 298 7555. Fax: (3) 293 7214/293 0807. E-mail: kualalumpur@ britishcouncil.org.my*
No 3 Weld Quay, 10300 Penang. Tel: (4) 263 0330. Fax: (4) 263 3589. E-mail: penang.info@britishcouncil.org.my*
MALTA: Education Information Centre, c/o British High Commission, 7 Saint Anne Street, Floriana VLT 15. Tel: 226227. Fax: 226207. E-mail: britcoun@waldonet.net.mt
MEXICO: Lope de Vega 316, Col. Chapultepec Morales, 11570 Mexico City DF. Tel: (5) 2631900. Fax: (5) 263 1910. E-mail: bc.mexico@mx.britcoun.org
MOROCCO: 36 rue de Tanger, (B.P. 427), Rabat. Tel: (7) 760836. Fax: (7) 760850. E-mail: britcoun.morocco@britishcouncil.org.ma*
MOZAMBIQUE: Rua John Issa 226, (PO Box 4178), Maputyo. Tel: (1) 421574/5. Fax: (1) 421577. E-mail: root@bcmaputo.uem.mz
NEPAL: Kantipath, (PO Box 640), Kathmandu. Tel: (1) 221305. Fax: (1) 224706. E-mail: bcnepal@bc-nepal.wlink.com.np*
NETHERLANDS: Keizersgracht 269, 1016 ED Amsterdam. Tel: (20) 550 6060. Fax: (20) 620 7389. E-mail: bc.amsterdam@britcoun.nl
NORWAY: Fridtjof Nansens Plass 5, 0160 Oslo 1. Tel:(22) 426 848. Fax: (22) 424 039. E-mail: british.council@britcoun.no
OMAN: Road 1, Medinat Qaboos West, (PO Box 73), 115 Medinat al Sultan Qaboos, Muscat. Tel: 600548. Fax: 699163/698018. E-mail: bc.muscat@om.britishcouncil.org*
Al Haib-Seeb, (PO Box 63), 121 Seeb. Tel: 542737/76. Fax: 542276.*
PAKISTAN: Block 14, Civic Centre G 6,(PO Box 1135), Islamabad. Tel: (51) 111424424/829041. Fax: (51) 276 683. E-mail: bc-islamabad@bc-islamabad.bcouncil.org
20 Bleak House Road, (PO Box 10410), Karachi 75530. tel: (21) 111424424. Fax: 5683694. E-mail@bc-karachi@bc-karachi.bcouncil.org*
PERU: Calle Alberto Lynch 110, San Isidro, Lima 27. Tel: (1) 2217552. Fax: (1) 4215215. E-mail: bc.lima@bc-lima.org.pc
POLAND: Al Jerozolimskie 59, 00-697 Warsaw. Tel: (22) 695 5900. Fax: (22) 621 9955. E-mail: bc.warsaw@britcoun.org.pl
PORTUGAL: Rua de São Marçal, 1294 Lisbon Codex. Tel: (1) 347 6141-7. Fax: (1) 347 6152. E-mail: lisbon.enquiries@britcounpt.org*
Casa da Inglaterra, Rua de Tomar 4, 3000 Coimbra. Tel: (39) 823549. Fax: (39) 836705. E-mail: coimbra.enquiries@britcounpt.org*
Rua do Breiner 155, 4050 Oporto. Tel: (2) 207 3060. Fax: (2) 207 3068; email: oporto.enquiries@britcounpt.org*
Rua Dr. Camilo Dionisio Alvares, Lote 6, 2775 Parede. Tel: (1) 458 7370/9. Fax:: (1) 457 9918. E-mail: parede.inquiries@britcounpt.org*
QATAR: 93 Al Sadd Street, (PO Box 2992), Doha. Tel: 426193/4. Fax: 423315. E-mail: firstname.lastname@bc-doha.bcouncil.org*
ROMANIA: Calea Dorobantilor 14 71132 Bucharest. Tel: (1) 3104140. Fax: (1) 2100310. E-mail: bc.romania@bc-bucharest.bcouncil.org*
RUSSIA/CIS: Ulitsa Nikoloyamskaya 1, Moscow 109189. Tel: (095) 234 0201. Fax: 234 0205. E-mail: bc.moscow@bc-moscow.bcouncil.org*
Naberezhnayareki Fontanki 46, St Petersburg 191025. Tel: (812) 325 6074. Fax: (812) 325 6073. E-mail: bc.stpetersburg@britcoun.spb.ru*
SAUDI ARABIA: Tower B, 2nd Floor, Al Mousa Centre, Olaya Street, (PO Box 58012), Riyadh 11594. Tel: (1) 462 1818/464 4928. Fax: (1) 462 0663. E-mail: enquiries@bc-riyadh.bcouncil.org*
Fourth Floor, Middle East Centre, Palastine St (PO Box 3424), Jeddah 21471. Tel: (2) 672 3336/670 1420. Fax: (2) 672 6341. E-mail: enquiries@bc-jeddah.bcouncil.org*
2nd Floor, Al-Waha Mall, First Street, (PO Box 8387), Dammam 31482. Tel: (3) 826 9036/9831. Fax: (3) 826 8753. E-mail: enquiries@bc-dammam.bcouncil.org*
SENEGAL: 34-36 Bd de la République, BP6232, Dakar. Tel: 822 2015/822 2048. Fax: 826 8753. E-

mail: Information@bc-dakar.enda.sn*
SIERRA LEONE: Tower Hill, (PO Box 124) Freetown. Tel: (22) 222223/7, 224683/4. Fax: (22) 224123. E-mail: bcouncil@sierratel.sl
SINGAPORE: 30 Napier Road, Singapore 258509. Tel: 473 1111. Fax: 472 1010. E-mail: britcoun@britcoun.org.sg*
SLOVAK REPUBLIC: Panská 17, (PO Box 68), 81499 Bratislava. Tel: (7) 54431074/54431185. Fax: (7) 54434705/54430371. E-mail: bc.bratislava@britishcouncil.sk*
SLOVENIA: Cankarjevo nabrezje 27, Ljubljana 1000. (61) 125 9292/9032. Fax: (61) 126 4446. E-mail: info@britishcouncil.si*
SPAIN: Paseo del General Martínez, Campos 31, 28010 Madrid. Tel: (91) 337 3500. Fax: (91) 337 3573. E-mail: General.Enquiries@es.britcoun.org*
Calle Amigo 83, 08021 Barcelona. Tel: (93) 241 9700. Fax: (93) 202 3168. E-mail: info@bc-barcelona.sprint.com*
Avenida Lehendakari Aguirre 29-2o, Deusto, 48014 Bilbao. Tel: (94) 476 3650. Fax: (94) 476 2016. E-mail: 100536.3066@compuserve.com*
Antiguo Edificio de Ciencias, Económicas y Empresaiales, Campus Universitario de Tafira, c/ Saulo Torón, 4 (Urb. Zurbarán), 35017 Las Palmas de Gran Canaria. Tel/Fax: (928) 355 256. E-mail: 102467.3374@compuserve.com
Universidad de Murcia, Edificio C Campus de Espinardo, 30100 Murcia. Tel: (968) 364 273. E-mail: joy@fcu.um.es*
Edifici Árxiduc Lluis Salvador, Universitat de Illes Balears, Ctra. de Valldemossa Km 7.5, 07071 Palma de Mallorca. Tel: (971) 172550. Fax: (971) 172552. E-mail: 102467.3373@compuserve.com*
Instituto Británico en Segovia, Centro de Enseñanza de Inglés, Avda. Padre Claret 3, 40003 Segovia. Tel: (92) 1434813. Fax: (92) 1443283.*
c/o British Consulate, Plaza Nueva 8 bis, 41001 Seville. Tel: (954) 228 873. Fax: (954) 210 323. E-mail: 104472.1776@compuserve.com
General San Martín 7, 46003 Valencia. Tel: (96) 352 9874; (96) 352 8688. E-mail: valencia.enquiries@bcvalencia.bcouncil.org*
SRI LANKA: 49 Alfred House Gardens, (PO Box 753), Colombo 3. Tel: (1) 587078/580301/581171/2. Fax: (1) 587079. E-mail: enquiries@britcoun.lk*
SUDAN: 14 Abu Sin Street, (PO Box 1253), Central Khartoum. Tel: (11) 780817/770760. Fax: (11) 774935. E-mail: bc.khartoum@bc-khartoum.bcouncil.org
SWEDEN: c/o British Embassy, (PO Box 27819), S- 11527 Stockholm. Tel: (8) 663 6004. Fax: (8) 663 7271. E-mail: british.council@britcoun.se
SWITZERLAND: Sennweg 2, (PO Box 532), CH 3000 Berne 9. Tel: (31) 301 1473/1426. Fax: (31) 301 1459; e-mail: britishcouncil@britishcouncil.ch
SYRIA: Al Jala'a, Abu Rumaneh, (PO Box 33105), Damascus. Tel: (11) 3310631/2. Fax: (11) 3310630. E-mail: Britcoun@bc-damascus.bcouncil.org*
THAILAND: 254 – chulalongkorn Soi 64, Siam Square,Phayathai Road, Pathumwan, Bangkok 10330. Tel: (2) 252 6136/7/8. Fax: (2) 2535312. E-mail: bc.bangkok@britcoun.or.th*
198 Bumrungraj Road, Chiang Mai 50000. Tel: (53) 242103. Fax: (53) 244781*
TUNISIA: c/o British Embassy, 5 Place de la Victoire, (B.P.229), Tunis 1015 RP. Tel: (1) 259053/351754. Fax: (1) 353411. E-mail: general.enquiries@bc-tunis.bcouncil.org*
TURKEY: Istaklal Caddesi 251/253, Kat 2-6, Beyoglu, 80060 Istanbul. Tel: (212) 252 7474. Fax: (212) 2528682. E-mail: bc.istanbul@britcoun.org.tr
Esat Caddesi No 41, Kucukesat, Ankara 06660. Tel: (312) 4686192. Fax: (312) 4276182. E-mail: bc.ankara@britcoun.org.tr
1374 Sokak No. 18, Selvili Is Merkesi, Kat3, Daire 301-306, Cankaya 35210 Izmir. Tel: (232) 4460131/2. Fax: (232) 4460130. E-mail: bc.izmir@britcoun.org.tr
UKRAINE: 9/1 Besarabska Ploshcha, Flat 9, 252004 Kiev. Tel: (44) 247 7235. Fax: (44) 247 7280. E-mail: bc.ukraine@be.kiev.ua
UNITED ARAB EMIRATES: Villa no 7, Al Nasr Street, Khalidiya, (PO Box 46523), Abu Dhabi. Tel: (2) 659300. Fax: (2) 664340. E-mail: information@bc-abudhabi.bcouncil.org*
Tariq bin Zaid St, Nr. Rashid Hospital, (PO Box 1636), Dubai. Tel: (4) 370109. Fax: (4) 370703. E-mail: information@ae.britcoun.org*
VENEZUELA: Torre Creditcard, Piso 3, Av. Principal El Bosque, Av. Sta Isabel/ Sta Lucia, El Bosque, Caracas. Tel: (2) 952 9965/9757. Fax: (2) 952 9691. E-mail: bc-venezuela@ve.britcoun.org*
VIETNAM: 18b Cao Ba Quat, Ba Dinh District, Hanoi. Tel: (4) 8436780/1/2. Fax: (4)8434962. E-mail: bc.hanoi@bc-hanoi.sprint.com*
25 Le Duan Street, District 1, Ho Chi Minh City. Tel: (8) 8432862. Fax: (8) 8232861. E-mail: bchcmc@britcoun.org.vn*
YEMEN: As-Babain Street 7, (PO Box 2157), Sana'a. Tel: (1) 244121/2. Fax: (1) 244120. E-mail: bc.sanaa@bc-sanaa.bcouncil.org*
ZIMBABWE: 23 Jason Moyo Avenue, (PO Box 664), Harare. Tel: (4) 790627. Fax: (4) 737877. E-mail: general.enquiries@bc-harare.sprint.com
75 George Silundika Street, (PO Box 557), Bulawayo. Tel/Fax: (9) 75815. E-mail: general.enquiries@bc-byo.sprint.com

*Offices marked with an asterisk have their own English Teaching Centres.